The Market Revolution and its Limits

Privatise, liberalise, deregulate, downsize the state. . . . Have economists got what they want? The collapse of East European central planning and East Asian 'relational' capitalism has sparked much debate today as to whether the free market approach to economics has finally run its course; *The Market Revolution and its Limits* is a timely consideration of the arguments. Non-polemical and accessible in its approach, this book provides a comprehensive appraisal of the market and its alternatives, backed up with empirical international illustrations.

The Market Revolution and its Limits explains why many economists think that markets are best, explores how it can be claimed that even 'market failures' can be given market solutions, and investigates why market ideas have taken such a firm political hold. It is argued that the static and dynamic cases for market superiority rest on two very different views of the information processing and co-ordinating capacities of markets. By identifying the wide transaction area between market and plan, the author concludes that the 'revolution' to date lies less in recreating market outcomes than in redefining the market process, with large businesses playing a crucial organising role. Whereas central planning replaces markets, corporate planning may be needed to create and complete them.

Clarifying a complex and often confusing subject, *The Market Revolution and its Limits* will be of interest to students and researchers in Economics, Business Studies, Sociology and Politics.

Alan Shipman is an economist currently researching at the Judge Institute of Management Studies, Cambridge.

The Market Revolution and its Limits

A price for everything

Alan Shipman

London and New York

First published 1999
by Routledge
11 New Fetter Lane, London EC4P 4EE

Simultaneously published in the USA and Canada
by Routledge
29 West 35th Street, New York, NY 10001

Typeset in Baskerville by
M Rules
49, Southwark Street, London, SE1 1RU
Printed and bound in Great Britain by MPG Books Ltd, Bodmin

British Library Cataloguing in Publication Data
A catalogue record for this book is available from the British Library

Library of Congress Cataloguing in Publication Data
Shipman, Alan, 1966–
    The market revolution and its limits: a price for everything/
    Alan Shipman
    p. cm.
    Includes bibliographical references and index.
    1. Free enterprise.   2. Markets.   3. Privatization.
    4. Deregulation.   I. Title.
    HB95.S53   1999
    338.9–dc21   98-35365
                                                   CIP

ISBN 0 415 15736 6 (hbk)
ISBN 0 415 15735 8 (pbk)

Contents

Figures and tables

Figures

Tables

Acknowledgements

Few knew this book was on its way until I started borrowing their photocopiers and stopped returning their phone calls. But while they could never eradicate all the misinterpretations, most of those with whom I worked as student or understudy can claim credit for anything original in what follows. Pamela Palmer and Valerie Lynch provided an effective introduction to market economics, and tolerated some early swerves into possible alternatives. Dr Geoffrey Harcourt and Dr Peter Nolan helped me follow the mainstream back to its source, and showed how rival systems also flow from it. Terence Gorman and Dr David Hendry put up with my increasing confusion between the textbook market's American, Austrian and East Anglian accents. Dr Dieter Helm and two anonymous referees grappled with an MPhil thesis whose few serviceable ideas take a more useful role here. Professor Peter Hart and Professor David Mayes found some useful applications for research skills misleadingly claimed on this basis. Michael Ridge, then and after, was a much-valued source of ideas on economic life and the life of the economist.

The book took shape after I'd left market economics to test the market for economics. Barbara Beck provided a chance to meet some of those who made and moved markets, in the guise of a business journalist. Keith Craggs and Catherine Mayer dragged my prose style from working-paperese back to something approaching English. William Kemble-Diaz, whose *Emerging Markets Monitor* is always first to chart the market's advance (and retreat) in untraded terrain, put up with the increasing intrusion of half-formed theory into practical financial reporting. Dr Kevin Grice, Jonathan Feroze, Richard Londesborough, Mike Wright, Mike Russell, Bernard Kennedy, Rose Deverell, Kelly Beaconsfield and Robert Baptiste were among others at Business Monitor International who put up with erratic performance on the day-job as bigger ideas were being devised and discarded at night.

Final revisions to the text were made on a similarly nocturnal schedule during a regrettably brief tenure at the Economist Intelligence Unit. Particular thanks for sharing ideas and workloads there are owed to Laza Kekic, Simon Tilford, Kitty Ussher, Merli Baroudi, Joan Hoey, Peter Palmer, Fiona Mullen, Emily Morris, Adrienne Pratt, Annette Drepaul and Mary Curran. At Routledge, Alison Kirk obligingly accepted the case for a 'missing market' under this title and, with Andreja Zivkovic and Sally Carter, battled through various missed deadlines and breached guidelines to get the project into print. Christine Firth worked wonders on the final, wordprocessor-tormented typescript. Two more anonymous referees helped allay fears that this was one product differentiation too many.

Outside the job market, a number of others unknowingly provided ideas and encouragement that avoided various wrong turnings in the argument. Dr Patrick Baert has been a source of inspiration, hospitality and multilingual humour for many years, as a constant reminder that economics is not the only socially useful 'science'. Gyorgy Martin Hajdu and Radu Gavrila helped break down many linguistic and logical barriers to an understanding of 'transition' economies, and the survival of a tourist therein. Kavita Sehbai supplied cross-Channel escape from the excess demands of the keyboard. Intellectual refuge closer to home was provided by Dr Sonia Bhalotra and Ganesh in Bristol, and Professor Ben Fine and Naomi Collett in London. With Cavelle Creightney and Dr Will Cavendish, theirs proved among the more persuasive advertisements for keeping economic life out of the market. Helvia Bierhoff pleasantly corrected some of my wilder ideas about the German economy. Saira Shah confirmed there can be life after deadlines, and still something worth watching on TV.

So often left to the end, Alex Parr has suffered longer than anyone with the insanity that is (this) authorship and, true to form, brought the resources of Prague's oldest bank to the rescue when information's newest technologies tried to swallow the text. Among other formative and informative influences, Gary Numan taught me that complicated philosophy can be condensed into tuneful two-liners, and Russell Feaver that when all else fails, you can always go for a ten-mile run.

Gratitude is inevitably undersupplied to my parents, who shielded me from the market long enough to let me study it, and didn't try to persuade me I'd be better off reading history. Finally, backhanded compliments must go to Bill Emmott, Martin Wolf and Peter Jay: three distinguished economist-editors, without whose refusal of work this would probably never have been written.

Alan Shipman
London, June 1998

Introduction

The market revolution

Soon after the Mexico World Cup, bright lights began appearing in the sky. Sometimes as a continuous, relentless red or white beam. Sometimes as a rhythmic flash or dancing on-off sequence. They belonged not to stray fireflies or unidentified flying objects, but to light-emitting diode lamps that ran forever on two small batteries. Cyclists and joggers used them to stay visible at night. Rural dog-walkers (who exemplified the separation of ownership from control long before economists identified it) tied them round collars to keep track of their canine charges in the undergrowth. Yuletide celebrants found in them a cordless alternative to fairylights. Another small invention had altered the landscape, giving suburbia something it never dreamt of and now could not live without.

A still more dazzling revelation, at least to viewers of the cold-war generation, was that much of this new enlightenment came from the People's Republic of China. Not Hong Kong, the legendary free-market enclave that had moved from cheap toys to sophisticated electronics in two generations, but from its stolidly communist neighbour, which now seemed set on achieving a similar progression in one. Where Mao's Great Leap Forward had stumbled beneath the weight of bureaucracy and brutality, the market's million small steps were adding up to something revolutionary. It was an unexpected message from the model to which many non-market hopes had turned when eastern Europe's 'democratic central-ism' waned and 'African socialism' wilted before worldwide supply and demand. But by this time, the former Soviet Union was in full flight from central planning, its one-time satellites were staging the world's biggest privatisation, and even the 'mixed economies' of North America and western Europe were finding their public sectors ripe for scaling down.

Governments everywhere seemed to be finishing the century scrapping their price controls, shedding their trade barriers, shrinking their tax-and-spend ambitions and archiving their five-year plans. Soldiers, scholars and surgeons were being told to make their operations pay, and those without work to price themselves back into it. State spending to relieve deprivation and depression was being accused of keeping them alive, while the market could make good if only given the right incentives. The revolutionaries no longer had a price on their heads, but prices in their heads. Even redistribution's protective arm was pushed aside in the rush to unshackle the invisible hand.

Soon after this book was started, the free market's global march appeared to have gone off track. Most of the 'dynamic' East Asian economies, recently praised as an example of how free trade and minimum government could sustain fast and fairly distributed growth, had been plunged into depression as exports stagnated, currencies crashed and foreign capital took flight. Japan and China were threatening to be brought down with them, dragging Latin America and eastern Europe into competitive devaluation which could dislodge the 'developed' world from its already modest growth path. The immediate effect of emerging-market capital flight was to swell the already bloated financial centres of New York and London, arousing fears of a speculative bubble in which expenditure fuelled by rising asset prices raised those prices still further, until another wave of panic selling struck. Against this background, South Asia's trading of nuclear bomb blasts in defiance of sanctions threats was a reminder of the power of politics to override economic interests, even with democratic approval; Russia's desperate search for cash to pay off state wage arrears and save the rouble proved that private ownership and price stability were less than half the recipe for a functioning market economy; and the US government's anti-trust case against Microsoft showed that even a successful market can be undermined from within. With second thoughts setting in about capital mobility – even if no one dared step back from full convertibility or contemplate a 'Tobin' transaction tax – attempts to secure a Multilateral Agreement on Investment were quietly shelved, its protagonists' consoling promises of another free trade round failing to calm the fear that more competitive devaluation and defensive protectionism were on the way.

Yet if economists could draw any lesson from the 'crash of 98', it was that free markets were more inescapable than ever, with any alternatives shown to be unviable. 'Relational' transaction had degenerated into Indonesian and Korean 'crony capitalism'. Bureaucratically informed and administered transaction had gone down – with the growth rate – in France and Japan. The market had beaten off the plan, and those who submitted to the market now looked down on those who tried to make it their servant, preparing to acquire what they had once been told to admire. Anglo-American financial markets might not have backed winners any more reliably than government, but their more ruthless rejection of mistakes had allowed them to gain through innovation more than they lost through underinvestment, or to cut their costs to match their productivity. Within the free-enterprise realm, continuous-trading discipline was ousting strategy, private ownership outperforming mutuality, and unadulterated markets outgrowing the mixed economy. The rising sun's rude awakening showed a powerful downside to free trade and capital movement, but the remedy carried a market price. With problems ascribed to the shortage or short-circuiting of price signals, the solution was more of the same.

This book is an investigation of why economists find the market so theoretically appealing, and why politicians and businesspeople – whom economists had long expected to pursue private gain by dodging market forces – appear to have resigned themselves to it or even actively embraced it. At times, it will appear to be dealing with a stylised model of the economy, rather than the economy itself. The distinction is often overlooked in recent economic writing, and one which has the extenuating merit of showing the very different assumptions on which components of the same argument are sometimes based.

After a definition of markets and assessment of their institutional context in Chapter 1, the main arguments for and against market transaction arrangements are summarised under three headings. Chapter 2 examines the claim that a system of free markets leads to optimum static allocation, identifying the conditions for existence of general equilibrium as a source of arguments for microeconomic market failure, and the way in which refinement of the mainstream theory has fought back against these arguments. Chapter 3 explores the compatibility between free markets and full employment, observing how the difficulty of getting into general equilibrium, establishing its uniqueness and staying in it has given strength to arguments for macroeconomic market failure. Chapter 4 charts the market's return as a promoter of growth, and the switch from an outcome to a process view of competition that underlies this.

Having identified perfect information, rather than perfect competition, as the foundation of 'neoclassical' market views (and of their 'classical' alternative), Chapter 5 outlines the 'rational choice' origin of individual maximising choice, and its dual challenge to the neoclassical market process (where ignorance and interdependence may deprive agents of a solution that is both complete and computable) and to its centrally co-ordinated alternative (individual choices being impossible to aggregate consistently). This leads on to the discussion, in Chapters 6 and 7, of alternative transaction types – 'relational', 'administered' and 'informed' – which might allow individual agents to fill the information gaps that stop the best actions being identified under market transaction, and overcome the co-ordination problems that prevent them being implemented. With business organisation emerging as a forum for administered and informed transaction and as a common source of relational transaction, Chapter 8 seeks a new characterisation of the firm: less as a replacement for the market, as earlier 'transaction cost' approaches argued, as an attempt to restore the effectiveness of market transaction where the missing information and co-ordination can be supplied, and protect other types of transaction from destructive market pressures where these gaps cannot be filled.

Thus characterised, the firm offers the possibility of restoring the market's allocative virtues and linking these to its full-employment and growth advantages, but also threatens to outgrow and subordinate the market so that incentives to fulfil that potential fade before the temptations of monopoly. Although some safeguards against such monopoly can be imposed within a national economy, the main defence is to put the giant fishes into a bigger pond; Chapter 9 examines the drive to extend markets for products, capital and labour to the global level, and the equally ambitious defence of free trade against the political pressures and occasional economic arguments for protectionism. Chapter 10 examines another fightback by free market principles against early interventionist arguments, over the income distribution that results from market exchange. Chapter 11 considers the full range of charges now laid against the state, the traditional alternative to market arrangements; and reaches some tentative conclusions as to why, given interventionism's aparent ability to sustain itself regardless of efficiency or equity arguments, an enthusiasm for the market long held by economists should suddenly have captured the political agenda. Chapter 12 concludes with a discussion of whether the market revolution will continue, or whether limits are being reached and counterarguments already beginning to win through.

This is the product of a synthesiser, not the full orchestral work. The many whose arguments and models are featured in what follows may object that they have been selectively quoted or paraphrased. Any treatment of a subject which is virtually coterminous with mainstream economics is necessarily selective; any less so, and the printers of this one would have caused an imbalance in the market for pulp. As far as possible, representatives of the main viewpoints in the market debate have been presented in their own words, with market arguments assessed from within before the more critical external judgements are considered. This is one of many possible assessments of market economics' appeal and application, but one which does its best to engage mainstream arguments on their own terms.

The 'market revolution' is neither comprehensive nor complete. Its failures leave it open to much justifiable criticism, and its successes may carry the seeds of its own reversal. There remain large areas of the economy – within government, business enterprise, voluntary organisations, armies, families, gangs – in which transactions are administered and resources go unpriced. As will be argued in what follows, even those areas which pass as market-mediated contain many exchanges in which command or compromise rule and competition is pushed into the background. But markets as a way of thinking, and of organising people with little in common except their diverse aims and scarce means, have made a decisive return, in economies still looking for a life beyond subsistence as much as in those wondering what to do with it.

Markets can also create wasteful rivalry and artificial scarcity, distribute resources unfairly and squander those which are in naturally limited supply. There is a fragility in social peace whose only shared value is market value, and a sterility in social relations which ascribe purpose only to that which carries price. But the organisational alternatives to market transaction have, over time, been found wanting in still more unattractive ways. The wave of a banknote at the kiosk may seem no more powerful than the wave of a ballot paper at the polling booth, but buyers at least come away with what they paid for, and can return to re-trade if the deal was not what they thought.

Until recently, prices and policy appeared to be complements in search of an ideal combination. Public authority could, it was believed, constructively extend to the many areas of supply whose provision through the market seemed inadequate or unjust, and to the management of demand to stabilise a market system which would otherwise swing between irrational boom and intractable slump. Some economies appeared to have gone too far in their replacement of the market, and were expected to backtrack. But persistent poverty, inequality, unemployment and inflation suggested others had not gone far enough. The two were expected to meet

in the middle, neither as centrally planned and pen-pushed as old-style communism, nor as haphazard and pursestring-pulled as old-style capitalism.

Even when the synthesis turned sour, the immediate response was a renewed
attempt to mix and manage the market. Restoring its unadulterated version seemed
a blast from the romantic, pre-enlightenment past. Like rare-gas compounds, regulation and commerce were hard to mix, but inseparable once brought together.
Once such political economy relapsed into politicised economy, in the mafia-driven
market squares of Russia and the bureaucratically carved bazaars of Indonesia, the
inseparability took on a far more negative meaning. Breaking mandarin and marketmaker apart is now a priority for many marooned on the 'middle way', even if
the centrifugal force required will also split many more essential social ties.

Markets had never gone away. Even at the height of imperative and indicative
planning, mixed-economy theorists needed them as the case to be redeemed by
selective intervention. Planned-economy practitioners relied on them as safety-
valves when intervention stumbled with its sums. When disillusionment with other
transaction types set in, there was therefore a ready-made store of free-trading
wisdom on which to draw. Ever since they had seized the subject from historians
and philosophers, economists had been working to dispense with the political.
Their premise, that unrestricted deals between competing buyers and sellers would
best develop and distribute an economy's resources, had drawn much strength
from the commercial and mathematical logics of the time.

At first, the economists who advanced the market message most boldly were generally resigned to its falling on blocked bureaucratic ears. And many others found
their enthusiasm tempered as the theory and practice diverged. Even before consultancy and city salaries started to draw them out of the redbrick towers,
economists were aware of a real world very different from the one that moved their
models. Just as natural science had found that parallel lines might meet and waves
behave like particles, social science was unearthing ways in which markets seemed
systematically to fail, or rely on intervention to resolve their differences. There was
even a suggestion that unfettered transaction would refine itself to death, and that
perfect markets couldn't work at all.

Like the physicists who pronounced against split atoms delivering energy, or
metal aircraft taking flight, the market's theorists had to change their views when its
practitioners successfully took the concept further. Politicians and business leaders
may have begun by borrowing pages from unfashionable textbooks, but they went
on to write the new sections, with economic commentators editing the copy some
way behind. Where market arrangements had seemed to fail, the diagnosis was now
that they had not been allowed to work. The cure lay in removing obstructions to
free enterprise taking its full effect. As well as explaining why markets as now understood have such an appeal to those who observe the economy, this book seeks some
answers as to how they won back the loyalty of those who oversee it. The revolution
was consumer-led, with many producers still struggling to keep up with its demands.

Most natural science popularisation sets out to celebrate the discovery of something new. This attempt at social science popularisation frets about the rediscovery

of something very old. Consideration of whether the first market bubbled up from the primordial soup or had to wait for a more solid foundation will be postponed until the final chapter. But few can doubt that economists' earliest big idea remains their newest and liveliest contribution to current debate.

That debate still centres on the oldest problem: how to feed, clothe and furnish an unprecedentedly crowded planet in which aspirations spread faster than the resources to fulfil them, and actions have effects beyond the individuals who take them. The solution, a revolutionary break with past theory and much of past practice, is to leave people to do what they instinctively do: obtain what matters to them most by exchanging it for what matters to them least.

Surrounded by the material accomplishments of the market and the billboard blandishments of marketing, the shock value of this development is sometimes hard to grasp. But few predicted the revival of the market. Its supporters entered the tail end of the twentieth century as convinced as its critics that this transformer of technologies and subverter of societies was destined to be ditched by its own success. As the world recovered from a war that seemed to establish competition as the enemy of co-operation, co-ordination of activity seemed a rational step forward from its chaotic individual pursuit.

At best, *The Market Revolution and its Limits* only half succeeds. It has much to say on how the market was rescued, in theory and practice, from its earlier failures. It is more hardpressed to explain why a conceptual vehicle mothballed for so long should suddenly be polished and put back on the road. Enthusiasts had lovingly retuned and re-engineered it during the long, enforced hibernation. When the garage door they pushed at was eventually flung open, they seemed as shocked as those who had mocked them that anyone should wish to drive it again. The engine of growth roared magnificently and the suspension absorbed the more obvious bumps, but the variable transmission speed had unseated previous chauffeurs, and versions without exotic styling but with steering wheels always seemed likely to be preferred.

Once on the road, however, there may be no turning back. Like a one-way street, one market leads to another. Deregulation becomes contagious. With rebuilding a market system, as with painting a wall, the suggested cure for a fault is often a further application. Only later can we judge whether we have painted ourselves into a corner, whether serial transaction was the start of a glorious ascent or of a slippery slope.

Despite its confidence in having established a unique method that can even account for events beyond the economic realm, the market perspective is seen to reach outside the subject for resolution of some of its graver operational problems. Difficulty with the applicability of its traditional models, and the accuracy of its statistical inferences, has not caused economics to retreat from its traditionally imperialistic stance. But it has allowed other social disciplines to strike back against the invader, offering insights which explain why a purely economic approach interprets and predicts wrongly. Or, equally damagingly, why its conclusions are tautologous, or right for the wrong reasons. Forced to turn to business studies, organisation theory, sociology and politics for additional insights, economists' professional boundary has started to soften. It is hoped that this book, although imperfectly screened for economic jargon, will be of interest – and accessible – to students of the market in other social disciplines, and none.

At all times, the account tries to be sympathetic to the market and to criticise constructively. Attacks carry weight only when they come from those who have proved their understanding of the market, of which the market test is how much money they have made from it. As the first draft of this book was taking shape, George Soros (1997) expressed many of the same concerns about the market in a widely circulated essay. Soros, one of the world's most successful players of financial markets, had also committed much of his personal fortune since the late 1980s to promoting the civic conditions for market regeneration in formerly state-socialist eastern Europe. Now he was wondering out loud whether the price-driven pursuit of private gain, which he had identified as the foundation for an open society, might now be undermining it through the subjugation of all values to market values, recalling Hegel's 'crack and fall of civilisations owing to a morbid intensification of their own first principles.'

Deep pockets and deep thought are rarely believed to coexist, and few were impressed that one who had profited so much from the market system should now become its prophet of doom. 'Hopelessly muddled . . . woefully ignorant . . . a rodomontade of sloppy thinking', *Fortune* magazine reassured corporate America, charging the billionaire with attacking yesterday's brand of *laissez-faire*. 'He seems to think economists generally believe that there is perfect competition in real-world markets and that markets invariably move toward equilibrium. In fact, only a very few extremist academic economists endorse these views' (Norton 1997). Certainly, this would have been weak ground for a mover of markets to bite the invisible hand that fed it. Economists have documented in great detail the decline of perfect competition into oligopoly, monopoly and cartelisation, theorised extensively over what firms do with the power over markets that this gives them, and argued extensively over how wages, output, employment and inflation are affected, and what can be done to restore the free market to health.

The master manager of the Quantum hedge funds could afford to shrug off such criticism, and within a year could claim vindication from the unfolding 'East Asian crisis'. Redistributive international capital flows had became a retributive, self-compounding battle to feel falling stock-markets, turning international trade into a battlefield of competitive devaluation. The prophet of doom continued to profit from it, with presidents replacing the business-press critics, Malaysia's Mahathir Mohamad famously calling on currency speculation to be made an arrestable offence. But Soros's main attack was not on the ancient punchbag of perfect competition, but on a much more recently recognised ailment of free market theory: its assumption of perfect information, allowing actions to be chosen according to accurate anticipation and consistent valuation of their effects. If full information were available, choice was 'rational', but such rationality became a remorseless restraint on the freedom to choose. If information were missing or inaccurate, irrational expectations could become self-fulfilling or rational expectations self-denying. Markets would succumb to dangerous trends, wild swings or awkward seizing-up of activity, providing profit opportunities to shrewd individuals such as Soros but inflicting losses on the system as a whole. Value was destroyed if the market turned out to hang and swing by its own bootstraps. Equally, values were destroyed if, in the more traditional account, rational calculation put only one price on an asset and prescribed just one best way to trade it.

More than a few (and by no means extremist) economists have expressed similar fears about the market, as both admirers and detractors. They have questioned its stability when it leaves out knowledge of interdependent expectations and state-contingent actions, and its desirability when it leaves out the wider impact of individual maximising actions. For a century, pro-market economists and philosophers had railed against Marxism for falsely claiming scientific status for a theory which saw history as the unfolding of impersonal forces which made individual choices ineffectual or trivial. Yet in its moment of triumph, with the Berlin Wall demolished and tariff walls crumbling, the market looked like filling exactly that role, poisoning those economies that have rushed to re-embrace it.

> The supposedly scientific theory that has been used to articulate it turns out to be an axiomatic structure whose conclusions are contained in its assumptions and are not necessarily supported by the empirical evidence . . . The combination of *laissez-faire* ideas, social Darwinism and geopolitical realism that prevailed in the US and UK stood in the way of any hope for an open society in Russia.
>
> (Soros 1997)

Having ranged over the same marketmaking ground, the present analysis can claim to share neither Soros's skill in playing the markets nor his pessimism in assessing them. If there is not a higher logic to which markets might lead, there is at least a more constructive way in which they might devour themselves. In getting to grips with its information and co-ordination problems, the market develops forms of social relation and commercial organisation which potentially release it from the rampant materialism and social fragmentation of which its unnerved unleashers complain. Conventions, institutions, corporations and long-term associations form shelters within the turmoil of transaction, within which market pressures are eased and wider-range or longer-term concerns can be addressed. Above them stands government, neither as powerful nor as benign in its use of power as 'social market' visionaries once hoped, but still able to build on these relational developments and prevent the market from reclaiming them. The open society is a framework within which beliefs compete, actions combine, and the knowledge and capabilities of a people move slowly forward. So is the market; but only when confined to a subsection of products which are infinitely reproducible and individually tradable under sustainable distributional conditions. It is a framework within a framework, and both can be undermined if this too-persuasive part is allowed to take over the whole.

*

Those who, through scepticism or impecunity, scan the text carefully before forming their preferences, will see that this is not a conventional economic presentation. Algebraic models and geometric illustrations have been kept to a minimum, and other authors are quoted on their conclusions rather than their equations. Not only is this due to a belief that their main message can be put across in words, and a concern not to give undue space to particular model specifications, but also it reflects an intention, inadequately fulfilled, to find common elements in the often disparate ways that different groups have tackled the subject. My brief experience as an economist suggested that models and frameworks come naturally to the subject's theoreticians and practitioners, perhaps because, like a landscape in bright sunlight, the reality is at once too beautiful and too mysterious to look upon directly. Many contributions leap straight into the simplifying assumptions and specifications, with only a cursory attempt to relate the findings to the world behind the model. My experience in exile is that non-economists often find this approach hard to understand: in part because of the grammatical and mathematical shield that builds up around the conclusions, and in part because so rigorously narrowed a field of vision gives few clues as to how widely those conclusions can be applied.

Increasingly, professional economists are invading journalistic ground in an effort to rescue their ideas from non-specialist users who have seized on the results they want and ignored the special conditions that give rise to them. This is one journalist's attempt to reverse the invasion, trying to identify what is now generally agreed among economists about the market, and what is still in contention. The concept of agreement among economists, so long renowned for holding opinions in excess of their numbers, is perhaps a telling comment on the way the world has changed.

Like all journalism, this account draws heavily on ideas advanced by others, trying to give them credit where it is due and to keep the more telling statements in their own words. Unlike journalism, it steps back from the top layer of the publications in-tray, and tries to trace the market's inspiration and implementation back to its sources. Returning to the contributions of Hobbes and Smith, Marx and Keynes, Hayek and Kaldor is not just an escape from the greater density and expense of newer literature. It reflects a rediscovered respect for these pioneers. They often got it wrong. But equally often they not only grasped much of the message of later, more formal models, but also sensed their wider implications in ways more model-bound thought is liable to miss.

This search for the shared origins of increasingly compartmentalised economic ideas has, it is hoped, broken through some of the traditional divisions between micro and macro, neoclassical and alternative, short-run and long-run economic analysis. The design of the book stems, in part, from my own frustration as a student at not finding a single treatment that could summarise the market's complementary claims relating to efficiency, full employment and growth, distinguish its 'neoclassical' and 'Austrian' interpretations, and chart its progression from an end-state view based on the mathematics of general equilibrium theory to an information-processing view with its roots in rational choice.

*

Despite the aspiration to eclecticism, some restrictions are inescapable. Coming from a monolingual economist of Anglo-American extraction, the analysis takes the competitive general equilibrium and neoclassical growth models as its reference points. It is hoped that the thought of other traditions and the experience of other economies have been given due attention; and that those on all sides whose views are criticised will not find their analysis too badly misrepresented. Some standard illustrations, such as the 'well-behaved' supply and demand diagram and the prisoners' dilemma payoff table, are included because they seem to have passed into the collective economic consciousness. There is no space, however, for the Keynesian crucifix of IS-LM (see p. 111).

Much more could and should have been said: about the multinational firm which has become so important an arena for transaction between 'plan' and 'market'; the brave 'transitions' to the market now under way in eastern Europe and China; non-linearity, chaos, complexity, game theory and other techniques for assessing information flows and expectation formation within decentralised free markets; different individuals', groups' and nations' contrasting experiences of the market; recent steps towards world trade liberalisation, and the regional market integrations now taking shape within the context of growing global free trade, and the ongoing debate over whether East Asia's 'miracle' was one of free markets or inspired state action. Readers will also have to look elsewhere for the missing mathematics behind the main models discussed in the text.

Of the areas covered, little of what is said here is entirely new. But there is a good reason why old economic ideas tend to come round a second time. For most of the twentieth century the subject has been retranslating its central conclusions, from the verbal and diagrammatic intuitions of its (often amateur) pioneers to the seemingly more rigorous algebraic and statistical models of today's highly professional research specialists. Since there is little time to read what went before, especially when written in a strange dialect, new practitioners often do not know that they are reaching conclusions already arrived at. Economic literature boasted many titles but little heredity, even before the computerisation of library catalogues put a layer of dust on anything published before the age of the personal computer. The problem is especially acute when, as with economics' prodigal return from the long excursion into rational control and rational choice, the newest ideas also tend to be the oldest, separated from today's leading edge by several geological layers which seem to go against the grain.

From what survives, however, it is hoped that some practical conclusions can be drawn. That market forces may arise naturally but are heavily dependent on institutional conditions for their operation and informational conditions for their effectiveness. That 'market or plan' is too simple a distinction, with many of the most important transactions sharing elements of both. That the firm's ability to mix market transaction with other transaction types, within and beyond its boundaries, gives it an allocative role which varies across national economies but is important in all of them. And that the market process's ability to win out over other transaction types, when released from organisational or regulatory constraint, does not necessarily mean that the market outcome is the best a society can expect.

Market transaction is, like the language used to discuss it, a process that comes naturally, but only once a set of terms has been agreed for its operation. We are bound by the terms, but, individually or collectively, we still have opportunities to change them. The market can endogenise much, but not the setting of its own rules. Some come from mother nature, some from human nature, but some can still be influenced by voice and vote. Therein lies the hope of our remaining free to choose within constraints that we ourselves have freely chosen.

1 What markets are

The market is a means of social organisation – one way people can coexist while choosing varied routes to different personal goals. Other such means have been tried, most being regarded (at least for a time) as more legitimate organisational means with worthier ends. When social organising principles are allowed to compete, however, few have proved able to conquer or even hold their own against the market. Even those not persuaded by the elegant theories promoting the market's efficiency properties have been forced to concede its resilience, sustained by individuals' willingness to trade in it, with socialism resigning to market forces, and once-mighty governments and corporations submitting to market discipline.

Economists' two-centuries-old claim that a free interplay of markets is the best way to allocate and expand a society's material wealth is increasingly accepted as a simple truth, even as the theoretical explanations for its success grow more mathematically complicated. Interdependent groups of people can let their members choose and pursue their own objectives without exhausting the natural resources of the group, overloading (and corrupting) its political institutions or destroying its cohesion in a storm of incompatible demands.

Before examining the basis of these claims for the market and its progress in practice against other transaction types, some definitions are needed. The next section summarises the conventional microeconomic representation of a market. How such markets interact across space and develop across time are the subject of the next three chapters, after which an alternative characterisation of the market in information-processing terms is given in Chapter 5. This sets the scene for assessing alternative ways of conducting transactions, which are most easily characterised as more case-hardened versions of the market 'ideal type'.

1.1 The logic of individual transaction

The claim that markets play an unavoidable, and increasingly universal, role in social organisation has three main foundations: that market dealing is more natural, more non-discriminatory, and more capable of optimising scarce resources than any other means of allocation. This threefold contention of evolutionary fit, social justice and economic efficiency underlies the increasing depth and geographical extent to which market principles are now being applied.

Belief in the special properties of markets has also led to their adoption, both concretely and conceptually, far beyond the physical marketplace in which their workings were first observed and explained. The idea of markets for political programmes and social provisions, for natural landscapes and charitable contributions, for birth and marriage, even for ideas (and markets) themselves, has come to shape the way people think and act, in areas once regarded as well sheltered from dry cost-benefit calculation. Much of the world now finds it surprising that, only a short while ago, even the idea of labour, land and capital trading through markets was viewed with scepticism and suspicion. Markets' rise to primacy in social organisation has two powerful components: a theory depicting it as the best means of harnessing and fairly sharing natural and human resources, and experience which seems to show that no alternative can do the job so well.

Market theory suggests that the unrestricted right to trade, at prices agreed between trading partners and accompanied by a free flow of information about the resources being traded, outperforms other allocation methods in terms maximising the quantity and choice of articles available and getting them to the people who value them most. These collectively beneficial results are shown as arising from individuals' pursuit of their own self-interest, and so being achievable without any intervention to regulate or modify individual behaviour. Although they operate at the level of the microeconomy (deploying resources efficiently in the most socially valued tasks), markets are therefore also argued to lead to desirable outcomes for the macroeconomy in terms of output growth, full employment, productivity growth (hence rising incomes) and technical progress which, as well as promoting efficiency, introduces new products, which widens the range of markets on offer to accommodate unmet needs.

Many advocates go on to identify unrestricted ('free') markets as a necessary (if not sufficient) condition for social freedom and democratic politics. Leaving individual choices to determine the allocation of human effort and its products not only makes them richer, more leisured and more educated – all extensions of choice and useful preparations for political participation – but also establishes a 'consumer sovereignty' under which governments and bureaucracies, as well as businesses, are constrained by their own self-interest to serve the public good. Other methods of allocation are, in this conventional economic analysis, not only less able to maximise the quantity and efficiency of a society's resources, but also less compatible with unrestricted choice in other areas of life, and more vulnerable to the imposition of choice by strong governments and special interests. Non-market methods of transaction are, in comparison, held either to sacrifice individual interests to the collective good (failing to maximise either), or to benefit some at the expense of others, with a loss of efficiency (and justice) for the system overall.

1.1.1 The market: a definition

A market exists where many differentiated, uncoordinated agents engage in voluntary exchange of a reproducible product or productive service at openly advertised prices. Prices adjust through time to keep the product's demand and supply in balance. At any one time, in any one place, the same price is available to all agents trading a homogeneous product.

An *agent* is an individual or cohesive group which takes and implements decisions to buy or sell, these being the two sides of any exchange.

Differentiation, of what agents currently have and of what they currently want, creates the conditions for mutually beneficial exchange between them. Agents will exchange units of one product for units of another if they believe this will come closer to satisfying their wants. The existence of *many* buying and selling agents ensures that each has a wide choice of agents with which to exchange. The differentiation among buyers and sellers, and their number, ensures that transactions are *uncoordinated*. Exchange can then take place without any elements of monopoly (co-ordinated selling) or monopsony (co-ordinated buying).

By *product* is meant any raw material, manufactured good or consumable service which one agent can supply in return for specified products from another agent. It is here defined to include two sub-categories often used as synonyms: good (a manufactured product) and commodity (a raw material which has undergone little or no processing).

Productive services arise from a special type of product which enters into the process of creating other products, but is not itself contained in them. The two most usually examined in economics are labour (the working-hours produced by employees who trade in the labour market) and capital (which trades in the financial markets as loans and share subscriptions, or in the capital-goods market as plant and machinery). Following convention, these will subsequently be referred to as 'factors', and the services they perform as 'factor services'.

The term *resources* will be used to denote all products and factor services – all items which, because they have value to someone, command a positive price on the open market. Resources whose value arises from a stream of future income or utility, rather than a one-off burst of either, will also be referred to as *assets* in what follows.

A product is *reproducible* when its production process can continue indefinitely without permanently exhausting any of the resources that go into making it, and hence without its price trending inexorably upwards as supply is irreversibly run down. This makes production and transaction into endlessly repeatable 'flow' processes. A product's supply may run out between one production run and the next but always being replenishable if demand still exists. Transactors need this assurance in order to form stable expectations of future prices, and avoid destabilising price movements due to panic buying or speculation.

Units of a product or productive service are *homogeneous* when they are sufficiently similar to be treated as interchangeable with other units of the product. Homogeneity ensures that buyers and sellers can decide whether (and how much) to exchange solely on the basis of the price being offered. Resources which are not fully interchangeable will trade in different markets at different market-clearing prices.

Exchange involves the voluntary transfer of resources from one agent to another, in return for other resources or for the legal entitlement to them. (In what follows, the terms exchange, transaction and trade will be used interchangeably.) Legal entitlement can include *money*, a product with little or no intrinsic value which is recognised as a medium of exchange, allowing flows of one product in exchange for another to be displaced in time or space. The special properties of money, which has replaced direct exchange (barter) in almost all market-based societies, are considered further in section 1.5. In general, the sale of a good involves its permanent physical transfer from buyer to seller, while the sale of a service (including productive services) involves the temporary transfer from buyer to seller of the product or factor that provides the service, for a specified time or until a specified amount of the service has been received. All forms of exchange entail the permanent or temporary transfer of mutually recognised *property rights*, which are defined and examined in more detail in section 1.4.

Price denotes the rate at which one product or productive service is exchanged for another. It is expressed as a sum of money or, where barter still occurs, as a ratio of physical amounts of the resources being exchanged. An agent's *demand* is the amount of any product or productive service they wish to buy at a particular price, and *supply* is the amount they wish to sell at a particular price. These individual schedules come together to determine the market demand and supply, which set the equilibrium (market-clearing) price at which agents actually trade.

1.2   The market: a representation

The concept of demand and supply gives rise to possibly the most familiar picture in economics, reproduced with some embarrassment as Figure 1.1. Market demand for a resource is shown as a declining function of its price, and market supply as an increasing function of its price. Both functions apply within a *market period*, the time it takes for all resources brought to the market to be exchanged and consumed, and for the supply of products – and the consumer wants that they satisfy – to be regenerated by another production run.

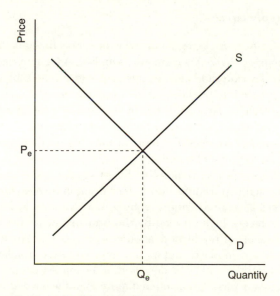

Figure 1.1 Demand and supply for a typical market

1.2.1   The demand curve

Market demand is shown as declining as the price increases. Since price has been placed on the vertical axis, it would conventionally be interpreted as a function of quantity, the price that agents are willing to pay to the quantity of the product they already have. By the principle of *diminishing marginal returns*, agents value each extra unit slightly lower than the previous one. The price they are willing to pay – the *opportunity cost* of other resources they will have to give up – therefore declines as purchased quantity rises.

The market demand function is also commonly interpreted as relating the quantity that buyers wish to purchase to the price they are asked to pay. As each agent has only limited funds (or resources that can be sold to raise funds), a rise in price reduces the total amount they can buy. It also induces them to switch, where possible, all or part of their previous expenditure to a substitute product which has now become relatively cheaper. (The substitute product is traded on another market, and its price is assumed to remain unchanged.) Market demand, the total of agents' demands at each price posted, carries over (and probably accentuates) the downward slope of the individual demand functions.

In practice, therefore, the demand function can be taken as representing either quantity as a function of price or price as a function of quantity. Economists maintain a tactical ambivalence over which is the dependent and which the independent variable. Although price is placed on the vertical axis when demand is represented diagrammatically (as in Figure 1.1), quantity is made a function of price when demand is expressed as an equation.

1.2.2   The supply curve

Similarly, there are two ways of reasoning why the supply function shows a positive relation between price charged and quantity supplied. A higher price induces each selling agent to offer more, and more agents to join in as sellers, because they now expect the sale proceeds to be sufficient to buy something else that is worth more to them. And to obtain a larger quantity, buying agents must be willing to offer a higher price at the margin, because for selling agents the principle of diminishing marginal utility works in reverse. The more of the resource that is parted with, the more valuable the remainder becomes.

If the selling agent is also responsible for producing the resource, a further reason for rising supply price arises from their need, in turn, to buy more inputs and factor services. Increased quantity requires more labour, which will make itself available only if paid a higher wage. By the principle of diminishing marginal returns to fixed factors of production, another worker will not match the productivity of those already in place until more capital has been installed for them to work with, which cannot usually be done within the market period. If there is full employment, new workers must be offered more than the current wage to induce them to move from other employers. And if it is not possible to recruit more labour in the market period either, existing workers must be paid more to induce them to do the extra work themselves.

1.2.3 Equilibrium price

The equilibrium price for this market is Pe, where demand and supply functions intersect. This is the price all buyers can expect to pay for the product, and all sellers can expect to receive. If a buyer offers, or a seller demands, any other price, 'market forces' will push them back towards transacting at Pe. With too high an initial price, the excess of supply over demand forces sellers to clear their stock by cutting prices. With too low an initial price, the excess of demand over supply pulls price upwards, as buyers try to outbid one another for the remaining stock. Only at Pe can the market 'clear' within the market period.

The whole marketable stock of the product is assumed to change hands during this period, either because it is perishable so that suppliers must sell it to recover any value, or because buyers cannot delay receiving it without relinquishing some of that value. If the product is non-perishable, sellers are free to withhold part of their stock if they believe stronger demand or thinner supply will lead to a higher equilibrium price in subsequent periods. If the product is not essential to survival, buyers are free to delay their purchase if they believe greater supply or weaker demand will lead to a lower equilibrium price. However, although these speculative shifts in the supply and demand schedules will tend to be self-fulfilling – an outward shift in the supply curve reducing equilibrium price and an outward shift in the demand curve raising it – such movements will be stabilised by profit-seeking 'speculators' who, anticipating future price movements, will buy up non-perishable products whose equilibrium price is depressed by temporary oversupply or withheld demand, so as to re-sell at a higher price when this lapse below equilibrium causes demand to be stepped up or supply withheld. Under this stabilising characterisation, professional speculation concentrates trade temporally within the market period, since buyers and sellers cannot expect any windfall gains from delaying their transaction into future periods.

Just as speculation stabilises prices of non-perishable products across time by keeping supply and demand curves close to their fundamental levels (shown in Figure 1.1), 'arbitrage' equalises prices across space. If the same product trades at several different physical locations, professional 'arbitrageurs' will respond to any divergence in equilibrium prices among those markets by buying from those where it is lower and re-selling in those where it is higher. Transport costs between the two locations may prevent profitable arbitrage below a certain absolute magnitude of price divergence, but this remaining divergence is attributable to transport being a separate item, trading on a separate market but jointly consumed with the physical product by buyers who want it in a different place from that where it is sold. Under this stabilising characterisation, arbitrage concentrates trade spatially within one market (or a network of identically priced markets), since buyers and sellers cannot expect any windfall gains from moving their transaction from one market to another.

Beyond the market period, consumers' diminishing returns are overcome because their appetites have time to recover, and producers' diminishing returns are overcome because the quantities of all factors can be adjusted. The same exchanges may then be repeated. Or, because they now hold different amounts of each resource and may have discovered different preferences, a new pattern of exchanges may unfold.

1.3   The market economy: a definition

A market economy is one in which most or all resources are exchanged through markets. Exchange relations are upheld by the right of agents to own, exploit and transfer private property rights, to enter into legally enforceable contracts, and to trade using money, being a legally recognised medium of exchange.

In essence, a market economy is one in which all reproducible resources trade through markets. Individual (and legal) persons sell their factor services to obtain income with which to buy products, which flow from ther application of these factor services to raw materials. Firms make profits provided they offer products whose market price exceeds the cost of inputs and factor services used up in their production. Individuals maximise their satisfaction (welfare) provided the costs of time and effort in supplying their factor services (principally labour) remain below the value of products they can consume with the income from that supply.

Each resource's price is set by the interaction of demand and supply for it, as outlined in section 1.2, but under a market system these demand and supply functions are affected by concurrent developments in other markets. Demand for a product will shift upwards (and, *ceteris paribus*, its equilibrium price will go higher) if the price of a complementary product falls (encouraging higher consumption of it, hence of its complements); or if the price of a substitute product rises (encouraging lower consumption of it, through a switch to substitutes). Demand for products in general will rise if there is an increase in the price of the factor services whose sale finances that demand. The theoretical ability of an economy of markets to inform and simultaneously adjust to these interactions, combining microeconomic efficiency with macroeconomic stability without any central co-ordination, is central to the case for the superiority of markets, and is examined in more detail in the next three chapters.

1.4   Property rights

To sell a product or productive service through the market, its present owner has a generally recognised entitlement to hold it, and to receive the benefits that arise from its possession or use. This *property right* allows the agent to charge the market price when selling a product, or the products and services that flow from a productive service. Transaction involves a transfer of property rights between individuals, at a price set by the balance of demand and supply within the market for this resource (and for its complements and closest substitutes). The terms of transfer, including the purchase price, are agreed on the buyer-beware (*caveat emptor*) principle. They can be annulled or revised if the buyer were illegally misinformed over the nature or provenance of the product, but not if the buyer paid too much (or, indeed, too little) through miscalculating its worth on the basis of legitimately provided information.

1.4.1 The division between ownership rights and user rights

In most market-based societies, a distinction is drawn between rights of ownership and rights of use. Ownership is a legal entitlement to store, use or re-sell a resource, and to receive the benefits from doing so (in cash or in kind, although sometimes with a tax imposed, especially if the benefits are in cash). With most resources, however, as well as selling the full *ownership right*, an owner has the option of selling *user rights*. These allow the buyer to use the resource and to keep any proceeds (in cash or kind) from this use, but leave the owner the right to reclaim the resource (after a specified term of use, or sometimes at will) and to receive a share of the income it generates while under someone else's use.

Whereas ownership rights are generally vested in a single, clearly identifiable natural or legal person, user rights to a particular resource can be divided among several users. Division can be simultaneous, as when the owner of a building rents out different floors to different tenants, or sequential, as when the owner of a carpet-cleaning machine hires it out to different premises each week.

Ownership rights generally confer user rights, which the owner may choose to sell (in a series of one-off transactions, or through a rental/franchise contract giving one buyer a longer-term right to use the asset). Where initial ownership is unclear, user rights may sometimes confer ownership rights (though squatters who take over their land, and firms whose premises were once expropriated by the state from previous owners, will generally claim to have made investments and improvements which strengthen their title to the asset).

User rights may include the right to their own subsequent re-trading (e.g. a leaseholder may be able to re-sell the lease without reference to the freeholder who owns the asset), but more usually the owner reserves the right to re-purchase user rights or exercise choice over who subsequently buys them. Sometimes user rights must be exercised periodically to retain ownership rights, an obligation imposed to avoid potential users leaving plant and real estate idle when its ownership is unclear because of the threat of a residual claimant. Under some legal systems, one way to settle ownership uncertainties and reduce the threat of residual claims is to confer ownership rights on those who have long exercised user rights.

In principle, the division of ownership and user rights is possible for any resource which does not disappear during use, but still exists (in marketable, if possibly altered, form) when the user has completed the task or time for which user rights were purchased. The distinction between ownership and use means that, for most resources, there is a separate market for each. By selling user rights, an owner substitutes a fixed income (paid as a lump sum or a periodic rental) for the more uncertain income derived from consuming or trading the output of the asset. Only by selling ownership rights does the transfer turn from one of 'hiring' into 'buying', and the buyer acquire full power to dispose of the resource as well as trade with it under owner-specified rules.

1.4.2 *Residual claims and capital gains*

Acquisition of the full ownership rights to a resource is usually termed purchasing or buying. Acquisition of user rights is termed renting, hiring or licensing. Where user rights and ownership rights to a resource are divided, so (with rare exceptions) is the income generated by its use. Usually, the holder of user rights will agree to pay a fixed fee (royalty or rent) to the owner, proportional to the time for which rights are held. The user then becomes a *residual claimant*, entitled to keep all the benefits (in cash and kind) from the resource and its products over and above the owner's fee. (By the same token, the residual claimant must bear any losses if the proceeds from use come to less than the owner's fee.) In conventional terms (which Anglo-American theorists, as always when nearing the philosophical edges of the subject, borrow from the French), the holder of ownership rights who sells user rights with residual claims attached becomes a rentier. The acquirer of those user rights becomes an entrepreneur.

Occasionally the owner will split the residual claim, demanding a set proportion of the benefits, and so sharing in any success the user has in raising the resource's productivity or value in use (along with any losses or liabilities arising from the way they deploy it). In general, however, the sale of user rights by an owner is closely identified with the transfer of the residual claim to them. If an owner merely entrusts the resource to a specialist manager, but retains the power to acquire and dispose of the products of its use (and the income they generate), then no transfer of property rights has taken place. User rights, and the residual claim on proceeds from use, stay with the owner, who pays the manager (or agent) a fee fixed in advance, and keeps any benefits (or bears any losses) that remain once this fee has been paid.

The residual claim allows the holder of user rights to enjoy any additional income arising from improved application or exploitation of the resource, which the owner (having not been capable of making, or not foreseen) may not have included in the price at which the user rights were sold. User rights with residual claims attached thus command a market price, which the buyer hopes will be exceeded by the income the rights will generate, in contrast to user rights without residual claims which are merely exercised for a fee on behalf of the property owner. The transfer of residual claims is at the basis of mutually profitable trade in property rights: a business rents offices and hires equipment in the expectation that the income they can generate will more than offset the rent paid for them. The residual claim does not usually extend to changes in the value of the resource itself. This protects the user of resources that tend to depreciate in value as a result of normal use, against compensation claims from the owner when user rights revert to them. Hired machines, premises and vehicles are subject to 'normal wear and tear' which will be defrayed in the rental fee agreed with the owner.

However, the restriction of residual claims to exclude changes in resale price can cause problems for users of resources which appreciate in value as a result of use. When user rights revert to the owner at the end of a contract, renters of land and buildings cannot usually ask the landlord for compensation for improvements they have made to them, and hirers of labour cannot usually ask the worker to pay for any knowledge and skills they have acquired on the job. This can be an obstacle to the agreement of some otherwise mutually beneficial transactions, and may lead to the transactors agreeing to extend the residual claim so that the trade can go ahead. Appreciation during use is especially characteristic of factors of production (land, labour, capital), which are also the resources in which ownership rights and user rights are most commonly detached. (With labour, ownership rights cease to be legally tradable once slavery is abolished.) Land and physical capital can rise in price, even when nothing is done to improve them, if the discovery of new uses or destruction of substitute products raises the price of what they produce (and hence the profit they are expected to yield in use). Labour – human capital – can likewise rise in price if demand for its services increases relative to supply, or if it gets better at the job through having done it. The owner of a resource who chooses to sell user rights must therefore decide not only how to price them, but also how to price in – or otherwise arrange the allocation of – any 'capital gain' that arises while user rights are being applied.

Determining the equilibrium price of user rights is a hazardous process, involving information problems due to uncertain future values as well as possible market-power and monopoly problems (explored further in Chapter 2). In separating ownership and user rights, therefore, both parties run a financial risk. Too low a price deprives rentiers of income they could have received by maintaining ownership rights, and too high a price prevents entrepreneurs from recovering their expenditure on acquiring user rights. One characteristic feature of a market system is that these risks are accepted on both sides when a transaction takes place. The loser does not expect to renegotiate, or receive a share of the profit, if the winner from the gainer from a poorly priced trade makes substantial profits at their expense, provided no misleading product information was on offer at the time of the trade.

1.4.3 *Owner–user separation in different transaction types*

No separation of ownership and user rights is possible if a resource disappears (or is rendered valueless) during normal use. Thus trade in 'consumable' products (such as food and fuel) involves the simultaneous transfer of all property rights. Ownership and user rights are normally also kept together, even where separation is possible, for material products which are durable but cannot be used to add resale value to other resources. Purchasers of such a product thus take it over for as long as they wish to hold it, and may store, use or re-trade it without further reference to the original seller. There may still be obligations to specific third parties, or to society in general, in the form of legal restrictions on what the owner can (or legal requirements for what the owner must) do with the product. For example, vehicle owners must observe the speed limit and other road rules, obtain registration documents and pay certain taxes.

For physical resources which can be used to process or otherwise add value to other resources – principally land, property and capital equipment – transaction may involve ownership- and/or user-rights transfer, depending on the owner's preference. Ownership rights will be sold, or user rights transferred with residual claims attached, if the owner believes that the (one-off or recurrent) payment raised will be more than would be earned by continuing to exercise the residual claim, or that the loss of future income is justified by its greater immediacy and security.

For the other main factor of production, labour, transfer of ownership rights is not usually an option. (Slavery is formally outlawed in most countries, and even those who 'sell' their bodies do so only for a pre-set period of time.) Workers can sell user rights in their labour by agreeing contracts enabling an employer to assign them to certain tasks during a working day of maximum length. The contract can specify a fixed wage, in which case the worker has transferred the residual claim to the employer buying the user rights. Or remuneration may include an element of residual claim, through an employee shareholding in the company or a direct entitlement to a portion of the product.

Whereas productive factors (with the exception of labour) may be either rented or sold outright, the factor services that flow from them are – like other tradable services – open only to user-rights transfer. Just as the hirer of a worker or machine enjoys the use of it for a specified time or until a specified task is completed, and then returns it to the owner, the buyer of a theatre ticket enjoys the use of the seat for the duration of the performance, and the client of a launderette can use the machine until its cycle is complete.

Like firms, individuals can opt to buy the resource yielding the productive service (car, house, washing machine, etc.) rather than renting the service. By adding ownership rights to user rights, through purchase, they in most cases also acquire the residual claim. Where individuals prefer to rent rather than buy, it is usually because they do not wish to bear the additional financial risk that goes with the residual claim (e.g. having to pay for repairs in the case of breakdown); because they do regard price the premium for outright ownership as excessive (e.g. if they want to watch a video only once, owning the tape is no better than hiring it); or if they cannot afford the up-front purchase of ownership rights (although if outright ownership works out cheaper than repeated rental in the long run, a 'perfect' capital market would allow them to buy the ownership rights on credit).

Products cost more to buy than rent (or hire) because the equilibrium price of ownership rights is assumed to capture all the future income that would have been expected from a sequential sale of user rights (maintaining ownership of the asset and continuing to rent it out). Although this implies that ownership rights will sell for a multiple of user rights, the price gap is often relatively narrow, for two reasons. First, user rights may be acquired indefinitely, or for a large proportion of the asset's productive life. Second, the holder of ownership rights 'discounts' future earnings, placing a higher present value on rental income received now than on that expected at various moments in the future. For capital goods, the rate of discount (in a market system) is set in the capital market as the interest rate. As interest rates rise, the price of acquiring user rights tends to move closer to that of acquiring ownership rights.

1.4.4 Intellectual property rights

To exercise user rights profitably, and so obtain benefits (in cash or kind) in excess of the costs of buying and hiring, agents must know how to use what they have bought. For the individual who buys a video recorder, this may involve following a complicated set of programming instructions. For the firm which assembles diverse labour and capital equipment in several locations, it means co-ordinating the flow of material within and between the various workplaces so as to turn out goods and services of the right design, quantity and quality at an acceptably low cost.

Unlike the productive services of labour, intellectual property can be separated from the person who initially owns it, so that ownership rights as well as user rights are in principle tradable. A consultant can hire herself out for a presentation, or put it on video and sell it. Unlike a consumer service, the act of consuming it does not destroy it – conversely, its supply is expanded, to the extent that the audience carries away a correct recollection of the information put across. This means that, unlike a physical product, its trade – even if in ownership rights as well as user rights – does not involve the physical transfer of the property from one agent to another. The intellectual property not only transfers to the buyer, but also stays with the seller, who may be able to destroy her notes but cannot wipe her mind clean. By the same token, the seller cannot offer it for pre-sale inspection, claiming it back if the prospective buyer refuses to pay for it, because the buyer will be able to retain the information without having paid.

The usual defence of intellectual property has been to assign legal rights to it, in the form of patent, copyright or design right. The intellectual property rights (IPRs) give the originator (or the first to file) exclusive authority to exploit the new knowledge for a specified period. The intellectual property-owner can then sell ownership rights (transferring the legal title) or user rights (licensing it out), as might be done with more tangible forms of capital. Unauthorised use of the knowledge covered by patent or copyright then becomes equivalent to unauthorised use of physical property (e.g. through trespass or theft), and punishment or compensation can be demanded accordingly. But applicants for patents must make their bright ideas public, and holders of patents may be required to license them out. Societies encounter a trade-off between the *ex-ante* incentive to do something new by being allowed to keep it to oneself, and the *ex-post* diffusion of best practice by letting others adopt it. Commoditising inspiration, and creating a market in ideas, has been one of the principal challenges of a trading economy when capital turns from physical to human and products flow from minds as well as from machines.

1.5 The private possession of ownership rights

The distinction between ownership rights and user rights helps to avoid the identification – often made both by its supporters and detractors – of a market system of exchange with a capitalist system of property ownership. The private possession and exchange of user rights is a necessary condition for a market system to operate.

The private possession and exchange of ownership rights is not a necessary condition, and is characteristic only of the subset of market systems defined as 'capitalist'. Market transaction usually takes place under such arrangements, but can also occur when the majority of resources are owned by a government (as with most product markets in contemporary China), an organisation representing communal interests (as with the housing market in a number of European economies), or by one immensely wealthy individual. Indeed, markets can even operate where ownership rights are unassigned or undefined, provided user rights are legally constituted and freely traded.

Capitalism is the particular property-holding arrangement under which ownership rights are held by private (legal or natural) persons. These owners (capitalists) may choose whether to hire in agents to exercise their user rights (keeping the residual claim and paying the agents a fixed fee), or to sell user rights to others (transferring the residual claim to them). Because user rights revert to the owner when the contracted task or term are finished, and can then either be kept or re-sold, capitalists can use the periodic adjustment of user-rights prices to capture any unexpectedly large residual claims or capital gains.

1.5.1   *Capitalism as one variety of market system*

The distinction between user rights and ownership rights means that private property is not essential to market transaction. It would be possible for all resources to be owned in common (or by one individual, or by the state), but still traded on open markets through the transfer of user rights. Such systems have been observed, for example, in the operation of collective farms in the former Soviet Union (where capital goods formally belonged to the state but were frequently traded among users); and among Latin American street traders, who have no legal rights to their 'pitches' but still manage to charge other traders who take them over (de Soto 1989). In mixed economies, broadcasting franchises and fishing quotas are examples of user rights which are tradable between private agents, but apply to property whose ultimate ownership lies with the state. Property leases are user rights whose ultimate ownership lies with another private agent.

However, the fact that user rights can be reclaimed by their ultimate owner reduces their value and increases their risk relative to equivalent exchanges involving full ownership rights. A successful market economy is generally assumed to require private property rights to apply to most resources where they are applicable, and to be sufficiently well spread so that all or most agents have some.

The case for superiority of capitalist market transaction over other forms of market transaction rests on the belief that user rights are more effectively deployed when ownership rights rest with a private person (natural or legal) than when divided among a community of such persons or held by the state. The principal argument is one of incentives, arising from the equilibrium price at which the user rights trade. A private owner will offer user rights at a price which captures the present value of the future income they believe they would otherwise receive if they kept those user rights for themselves. Since another agent will buy the rights at this price only if they believe they can generate a bigger income stream, the transaction ensures (unless one or both sides have miscalculated) an improvement in the allocation and application of the resource, as evaluated by the two transacting parties. This incentive to set the best attainable price and so maximise the efficiency of use of an allocation is held to be blunted (by diffusion) when ownership rights are communally held, and often completely absent when they are held by government or by (other) monopoly owners of a resource.

A second superior incentive effect for private ownership arises from the changes in the value of a resource while its user rights are being exercised. If the holder of user rights is not permitted to benefit from improvements made to the resource, they will not be inclined to make such improvements. Similarly, if they are not penalised for damage done to the resource, they will not be inclined to avoid such damage. Private owners can avoid these problems by exercising user rights themselves, or selling them on terms which include capital gains and losses as part of the residual claim. Although government or communal owners could also do this in principle, they may be less able or willing to do so in practice. So the occupants of houses rented from government may lack the incentive to improve them, and the users of a government-owned scarce resource may have nothing to lose from over-exploiting it.

Just as a market system can exist without the private ownership of property, private property ownership can exist without a market system. But there is enough of a historical overlap to allow the increasingly confident assertion that private ownership leads to the spread of markets, and markets to the creation of an 'open' society through greater material provision and choice. Whether the coincidence is as great as is claimed, and whether it implies a causal link, is a question to be revisited as market transaction and its main alternatives are examined in more depth.

1.5.2 *The capitalist firm*

'Firms' have so far been slipped in to the discussion of supply and demand, as collections of agents acting with a common economic purpose. The treatment of the firm as a single agent, buying or hiring resources and productive factors so as to sell (or hire out) goods and services at profit, creates a convenient symmetry with the treatment of consumers as single agents. As a co-ordinator of agents, the firm may also be seen as solving certain information problems arising from market transaction, a possibility explored further in Chapter 8. Of more immediate relevance is the ability of firm formation to solve another set of problems arising from application of private property rights to production.

As depicted above, the issue of shares in a firm is initially a means by which owners may transfer user rights in their physical capital while retaining certain ownership rights, including (in principle) the residual claim and any capital gain. Once issued, however, shares in publicly quoted companies may be openly re-traded. The market value of the shares will, in aggregate, represent the present value of profit its owners expect to receive through their residual claim, once all input and factor costs have been paid (and once future profit flows have been discounted by the owners' rate of time preference). Shares, as entitlements to the profit of the whole operation, thus enable a firm composed of diverse physical and human resources to be valued by a single market price.

By exchanging their ownership of particular items of capital equipment into ownership of shares, owners can spread their risks from one specific asset into a portfolio of assets, acquiring a tradable entitlement (which can be sold in the secondary share market) in place of an entitlement to equipment whose cost is largely unrecoverable ('sunk') once installed. Owners' risk is further spread by according the company limited liability, restricting a shareholder's maximum loss to the amount of the investment should the firm go out of business.

The exchange of titles to fixed assets for titles to company shares forestalls any disputes among owners of machines, whose contributions to production are hard to separate, over entitlement to revenues and liability to costs; it also prevents a dissatisfied equipment owner from stopping production by wihdrawing their contribution revenues owed to them for their contribution to production (Leijonhufvud 1982: 218). Once the share market is sufficiently transparent and liquid, issue of shares may allow the firm to raise new capital at lower cost (and with less residual liability) than by borrowing from a bank. By placing a value on its existing capital, share issue allows owners to incentivise employees, by giving them a direct stake in the rewards (and risks) of the firm's investment. 'It's no accident that employee stock ownership is widespread in knowledge-intensive businesses . . . The knowledge worker is as much an investor as the shareholder' (Stewart 1997: 68). Share issue also enables cross-ownership links to reinforce trading relations with other firms, through a similar alignment of incentives.

Over time, most market systems have seen their production-related private property structured into firms, owned by their shareholders (limited companies), workers who have financed their own equipment (producer co-operatives), or their customers (consumer co-operatives and mutual societies). By regarding firms as 'legal persons', symmetrical with the 'natural persons' with whom they trade products and labour services, economic analysis of markets can continue to represent both sides of a transaction as single agents. However, firms' plurality of owners and inclusion of members who are not owners can lead to divergence of objectives, whose consequences for corporate behaviour are assessed further in Chapter 8.

1.5.3 *Changing forms of capitalist property?*

In its earliest form, capitalism was closely identified with the ownership of physical property. Later, through the invention of shares, bonds and other tradable debt as instruments for financing private enterprise, a second substantial group of capitalists arose whose ownership was of titles to the financial return on physical capital. Economic opinion on the significance of this shift is sharply divided between Marxists, who have generally viewed it simply as a change in the form of ownership from 'physical' to 'financial' capitalism, and managerialists, who depict it as the effective disappearance of capitalism as management seizes user rights, turning itself from hired agent into effective residual claimant.

In principle, debt (bonds) and equity (shares) are two forms of payment (from users to owners) for two very different forms of capital transaction: an owner of shares retains the residual claim on the firm's physical and human capital stock, receiving as dividend whatever is left over when wages, managerial salaries, costs and agreed investment outlays have been paid out; whereas an owner of bonds has transferred the residual claim and merely receives interest at the pre-agreed (or capital-market-determined) rate. In practice, many large-company managements have been able to detach the rate of dividend from the rate of profit, turning equity into a fixed cost that closely resembles debt, and so effectively capturing the residual claim from the company's owners.

To many managerial theorists, the general transfer of user rights and residual claims from owners to meritocratically appointed managers – the separation of ownership from control – marks the end of capitalism as a property system worth penning manifestos and waging class wars against. Provided employees can bargain effectively with management over wage-setting, they can begin to share out the residual claim that previously flowed to the external owners. And if they can then go out and spend the extra income buying up publicly quoted equity, workers may even be able to supplant capitalists by becoming major owners of shares and bonds – thus insuring themselves against any attempt by the remaining non-working capitalists to use their more concentrated residual owner-power to push up the rate of dividend.

An equally forceful (Marxist) counterargument is that capitalists still own the institutions that manage workers' mutual- and pension-fund shareholdings, and have allowed employees to become part-owners simply to spread the risks of the residual claim (which, unlike wages, can vanish when losses strike), thus defusing labour protest as workers start to worry about the rate of profit.

The substitution of titles to the income from physical capital for ownership of the capital itself has a further important implication if, as has recently been argued both by Marxists and managerialists, capital is changing its form again, from the financial capital that funds the deployment of physical capital to the 'intellectual capital' that co-ordinates that deployment. In this view, 'lean' production and distribution techniques are creating an ever more continuous flow of resources from extraction through processing to consumption, along with feedback from consumer to producer over precise present and future design. Formerly separate workplaces and companies are thus becoming interconnected into 'production chains', the residual claimant will in future be whichever agent co-ordinates transactions along the chain (and so sets the prices at which transactions take place along it). Exercising power based on knowledge, the chain co-ordinator can acquire user rights which are entirely detached from either physical or financial capital ownership:

> Virtual companies are being established without an office and in some cases without even a staff. Others have no easily definable property . . . even the idea of property becomes suspect, since where information is concerned no clear divide can be made between what is owned and what is not.
>
> (Mulgan 1997: 246)

If this hypothesis is correct, it implies a further managerial erosion of traditional capitalist ownership rights, but it also suggests a method of price-setting and trans-action co-ordination very different from that of the market system outlined in this chapter. The possibility of production-chain 'hierarchy' as a distinct alternative to the market is examined further in Chapter 8. The role of information flows in cre-ating – and destroying – administered alternatives to the market is probed further in Chapter 7.

1.5.4 *Property distribution*

To establish private property rights, there must be an agreed legal system to define, ascribe and enforce them. Most of the resources in a modern economy have been processed using capital and labour, and the usual condition for entitlement to a resource is that the agent who owns it should have had responsibility for producing it. But produced resources arise ultimately from natural resources, which at the outset were unowned or communally owned. Those who now own them, or capi-tal equipment made from them, may have acquired their ownership rights through transaction, but at some stage in these property rights have been 'privatised' by an act of appropriation or assignment not arising from any exchange. It is in this sense that some philosophers regard all property as theft. At the opposite extreme is property that is inherently private, residing in natural skill or talent which an agent obtains through heredity rather than exchange. User rights to the skill may be traded, but ownership rights stay with them.

The initial distribution of private property rights may thus raise questions about the social justice of market exchange conducted through them, even if the terms of subsequent exchanges are regarded as fair. Excessive concentration of private property rights may, additionally, threaten the justice of later transactions, by empowering one agent to coerce another into accepting inferior terms, or depriv-ing an agent of the information necessary to agree on fair terms.

Two arguments have been advanced for accepting private property as the basis for market exchange, even if the distribution of private property is unequal and of doubtful historical legitimacy. One, developed philosophically and owed mainly to Nozick, concerns the process of property acquisition, and effectively takes the current distribution as innocent unless proved guilty. Previously unowned property is justly acquired as long as it leaves no one worse off (compared with a state-of-nature without private property rights), and previously owned property is justly acquired provided it has been voluntarily and fairly traded (Nozick 1974: 151).

The second argument, developed mainly by economists, justifies the current property distribution by the efficiency of its results. The process of acquisition may have been arbitrary, or even obviously unjust, but it is redeemed if it produces a better economic outcome for society as a whole than would have pertained if property had remained unowned, or more equally owned. A society's resources are argued to be better used and faster developed when privately owned, generating economic advantages for the whole society. Individuals have a greater incentive to conserve and improve natural resources and create new artificial resources when allowed to own them and pass them on; a greater incentive to reach the best allocation of resources when they can personally profit from trading them; and a greater incentive to invent new products, and new ways of producing, when given (intellectual) property rights over them, guaranteeing profitable trade. Unequal distribution also preserves aggregations of property which yield economies of scale (e.g. clusters of capital equipment). Ownership rights to such aggregations could be shared among individuals but, given unequal natural distribution of the ability to manage, and the efficiency of unified management, it may be economically more efficient to concentrate ownership among a small number.

Even if private property rights are arbitrarily assigned, they may produce social benefits if the property is a scarce natural resource, vulnerable to competitive depletion in its previous unowned state. Assigning ownership rights gives the recipient an incentive to conserve the resource, by restricting consumption to sustainable rates, and possibly to invest in expanding the resource so it is no longer depletable (see section 2.5).

The economic argument, linking unequal distribution to efficiency gains via incentives, has tended to displace the appeal to legitimacy as a reason for respecting the present holding of private property. Nozick, recognising the difficulty of proving that property has been justly acquired and transferred all through its history, also argues that relative inequality can produce absolute advantage by enabling economic activities that lift everyone above the state-of-nature baseline. This helps in particular to avoid a problem over property inheritance, which can now be an incentive to efficiency even if hard to defend as a just entitlement. Even Rawls (1971), in devising rules for a property distribution for a society whose members are unaware of where they will stand in it, presumes in favour of differences which produce an 'inequality surplus'. Natural resource rights may have been arbitrarily assigned or seized, natural abilities may be inherited by chance and new discoveries made by accident, but society tolerates the unequal starting-point because everyone benefits from what it gives rise to.

1.6 Money

Money is a (usually physical) product which becomes accepted as a medium of exchange because of convenient characteristics (durability, portability, homogeneity, identifiability), and because there is confidence that it will hold its value (and retain recognition) over time. Value stability requires that its circulating volume varies in line with that of other products, making it a common denominator in which their prices can be expressed. Retention of value, at least its relatively slow and predictable decline, allows money to function as a store of wealth and as a unit of account.

The development of money, as generalised purchasing power, releases agents from the need to find a mutual coincidence of wants when bartering physical products. It allows the receipt of products to be separated from the payment for those products, in space or through time. An agent can pay into an account in one location for delivery at another location, put down a deposit for later delivery, or receive products on credit which is paid off later. Money also allows agents to save or store the rewards of their productive efforts, an option not open through storage of the products themselves if these are perishable or liable to lose their value.

Over time, products adopted as money tend to give way to tokens which have exclusively these characteristics, and no intrinsic value. Those market systems blessed with sufficient electronics are now taking portability, durability and homogeneity to their logical conclusion, by replacing physical money with computer memory entries which are in principle instantly transmissible and infinitely storable.

1.7 Credit

By facilitating the separation of purchase and sale, money promotes the introduction of credit. Income can be obtained in advance of the sales that generate it, and products obtained in advance of the payment required for them. Credit, in turn, enables entrepreneurs to adopt more sophisticated processes whose costs of labour, plant and materials are incurred some time before their sale proceeds become available. Under these circumstances, unless there is previous stored income to draw on, 'profits can only become available as cash income to entrepreneurs if their working capital is financed by borrowing' (Godley and Cripps 1983: 66).

While credit arrangements are not exclusive to money-using market systems, these appear most adapted to creating credit at low cost and channelling it to the most efficient uses. As in any other market, competitive forces assign credit a price – the rate of interest – which adjusts to ensure that supply and demand are in equilibrium. The supply and demand functions are themselves optimally established by society, through the incentives provided to borrowers and lenders by prices in other markets. The centrality of credit, allowing agents to separate purchase and sale in space and time and to preserve an optimal course of action through time, will recur as the efficiency and growth claims made for market exchange are examined in more detail.

1.8 Contracts

Only the simplest transactions are agreed and completed at one point in time. Most product transactions involve intervals of time between agreement and enactment, and between enactment and payment. The delay in enactment often results from the need to process or transport the product as part of the agreed transaction. The delay in payment often reflects the buyer's need to check that the specified product has been delivered, or to raise money through a separate sale in another market. One reason for the use of money and credit is to allow for this temporal separation of product delivery and payment. In most service transactions, delivery itself requires an interval of time, during which the seller must enter into a certain configuration with the buyer (in the case of a personal service) or with resources controlled by the buyer. The inclusion of services along with a product (e.g. a guarantee or repair obligation with an item of equipment) locks buyer and seller into a relationship running for a specified length of time, or until a specified task has been completed.

Market systems are characterised by the use of legally enforceable *contracts* to specify the responsibilities of the transacting parties. These contracts may be verbal for simple, discrete transactions (such as buying an item in a grocery store). For transactions which are spread out across time, and/or whose payment or delivery takes time to enact, contracts are more usually stated in writing. By specifying the products and services that a buyer will receive at future times or under certain contingencies during the lifetime of the contract, these formal agreements effectively telescope a recurrent or continuous trading relationship into a set of rights and obligations defined at one point in time. The contract becomes a product in its own right, which can be instantly valued and traded even if the transaction it specifies has not yet taken place, or will take time to complete. In this way, money and credit can be viewed as general forms of contract: paper money was originally a contractual entitlement to the precious metal that backed it (and is now an entitlement to the products that circulate in exchange for it), and a loan is a contractual entitlement to a certain stream of future income (or to the security backing the loan, if this income is not received).

The use of contracts is one of the principal distinctions between market transaction and the other types of transaction to be examined in Chapters 6 and 7. 'Relational' transaction involves setting and enforcing transaction terms through intangible ties of reciprocal obligation, trust or sanction; formal contracts are not needed, and their introduction may even harm the intrapersonal goodwill that sustains the transaction. Significantly, this informal, socially embedded form of trading is generally regarded as belonging to an earlier age in which transactions were easier to monitor through being simpler and less spatially and temporally dispersed. The move from 'status' to 'contract' in the assignment of property rights and obligations has been identified as one of the defining steps from pre-industrial to industrial society.

'Administered' transaction, in which an employer–employee relationship replaces the buyer–seller relationship and resources are transferred between them by administered order, is assumed to arise when information and co-ordination problems make a normal contract impossible to write. The precise nature, timing and pricing of the transaction depends on future states of the world whose possibilities are too numerous, or effects too uncertain, for a 'contingent contract' to be workable or acceptable to the other party. Instead, it is necessary for buyer and seller to enter an ongoing relationship, allowing the precise terms of their transaction to be specified and modified as new information becomes available. A contract may be signed, but it is open-ended, the gaps to be filled in either by one of the transacting partners (who becomes 'residual controller' in the transaction) or by both under a negotiation process which may itself be set down in the contract.

All methods of transaction can on occasions give rise to 'implicit' contracts, under which one party infers a contractual obligation on the part of another even if nothing is formally agreed or written down. Under relational transaction this generally occurs through tradition or custom: a repeated pattern of behaviour becomes interpreted as an exchange, or an informally agreed exchange becomes sufficiently regular for one party reasonably to expect that it will not be unilaterally terminated (at least without due notice and/or compensation). Under market transaction, a contract may remain implicit because there is no market in which the product it refers to can be traded. The case that has drawn most attention is that of employees unable to hedge or insure themselves against future income variation, who may instead enter an 'implicit contract' with their employer to maintain a steady wage. (Economists' interest is aroused because this may explain the failure of real wages to adjust to changing conditions in the labour market, which may in turn explain involuntary unemployment.) Whether the contract has not been or cannot be written down, both cases involve an information problem of the type likely to lead to administered transaction. Indeed, the employment relationship is one of those most frequently cited as having moved from 'market' to 'administration', with the implicit contract becoming one of the open-ended, contingent elements too complicated to fit into the complete, discrete, easily enforceable contract that underlies market transaction.

1.9   What markets do: five types of efficiency

Five important claims have been made for the advantages of markets as a social organising principle. These will be examined in detail in the next five chapters. They may be summarised as follows.

First, market transaction ensures that production is accomplished with a minimum of priced resources (productive efficiency) and, relatedly, that the society's resources are always put to the best uses (allocative efficiency). 'Allocative efficiency will automatically be violated in the absence of productive efficiency . . . the latter is a necessary condition for the former, though the converse is not the case' (Domberger and Piggott 1994: 36). In what follows, these will together be termed 'static efficiency'.

Second, market transaction ensures that all resources are in use at all times (full capacity working and full employment). Clearly, productive and allocative efficiency are violated if a price is paid for labour, or any other resource, without putting it to use.

Third, market transaction ensures that the availability and productivity of resources grows at the fastest sustainable rate permitted by natural resource availability (optimum growth). In what follows, this will be termed 'dynamic efficiency'.

Fourth, market transaction extended across national economies allows each to achieve efficient allocation, full employment and growth, beyond what would be available in a closed economy, without having to submit to culturally and politically destabilising cross-border migration.

Fifth, market transaction gives rise to a distribution of income whose inequalities are no greater than is needed to incentivise the first four sources of social gain.

These five factors underlie markets' rise to prominence in economies. The success in giving them a theoretical foundation explains their matching rise to prominence in economics. Chapters 2, 3, 4, 9 and 10 examine in more detail the ways in which markets are argued to achieve these five types of efficiency.

1.10   How markets arise: rules and roles

If markets possess all, or even some, of the desirable properties outlined in section 1.8, and if markets can turn self-interested action to the collective good, then a market system can be expected to arise from the interaction of a society's members in pursuit of their economic needs. This is, indeed, what some market philosophers and historians have suggested. Markets will arise spontaneously, and maintain themselves as a 'natural' order, unless subverted from within by monopoly or without by the malign interventions of governments, bandits or invading foreign powers.

In this minimal-government view, central political authority is needed for only two purposes: to defend the market against these internal and external threats, and to allocate any resources which a majority in society believe should not be traded through the market. The government thus protects the market system, once established, against possible 'market failures', examined in more detail in Chapters 2 and 3. In addition, some market analyses, by detaching the aggregate efficiency results from the initial distribution of property, concede government a possible role in redistributing income before trading starts, as reviewed in section 1.5.4. Any other political action, at least in the economic sphere, is likely adversely to affect the workings of the market.

However, the spontaneous generation of markets through voluntary human interaction is in danger of confusing cause and effect. Once a market system exists, self-interested transactions may have collectively beneficial results, thus keeping the market system viable. But the market system must come into existence before such mutually beneficial interaction can take place, and there is no obvious voluntary mechanism by which this can take place.

1.10.1   Establishing and maintaining market rules

The market system is a form of network, in which those who want to buy and have things to sell can connect with others with the reciprocal need. Like other networks, its advantages to any one agent rise with the number of other agents who are linked into it. The more potential buyers can be connected to a seller, and the more potential sellers to a buyer, the less risk is run of falling victim to monopoly or monopsony (or being caught in their indeterminate confrontation, bilateral monopoly). Increasing the number of regular buyers and sellers in one market also improves the chance of being able to buy or sell at any time, at a predictable price (the market's 'liquidity' rising with transaction volume). Increasing the number of markets improves the chance of matching a sale opportunity in one market to a buying opportunity in another.

Money, as the mediator of market transaction, has even more powerful network properties. Its usefulness as a medium of exchange and store of value rises in proportion to the number of other agents willing to trade through it (the proportion being to the square of the number of users, according to 'Metcalfe's Law' of communication networks). As well as motivating decisions (e.g. sale of labour services in anticipation of having goods to purchase with the wages) that may prove misguided if the relevant markets are absent or distorted, market trade entails a number of transaction-specific investments – ranging from informative advertising and display space to research into customer preferences and appropriate pricing – which will prove useless and unrecoverable if the market is supplanted by another means of allocation.

The 'external benefits' of network membership – the advantages it confers on those who are already members or become members later – mean that no entirely self-interested agent will be the first to join the network. Like an important subset of the resources traded through it, to be examined in Chapter 2, the market system is a 'public good' to which rational agents will contribute only if assured that other agents will also do so. Since networks require continued maintenance, and extension into new areas, members must also be assured that others will continue to abide by the rules and share the costs of upkeep. Even though the benefits of membership make joining worthwhile, self-interested agents could gain even more by staying outside the network and taking a 'free ride' on the existing members. Just as the watcher of an unlicensed television receives programmes financed by those who paid up, the agent who trades in stolen property, or takes advance payment for goods but then fails to deliver them, makes additional profit – but through an action which, if it is copied by others or deters them from staging further trade, could quickly lead to the disintegration of the network.

Two important additional roles for central political authority are therefore opened up, as the agency which gets the market network established and which polices trading activity to ensure that it is maintained. The minimal-government view always acknowledged that government needed to intervene to establish and uphold property rights, so that agents could hold and trade resources without the risk that ownership or user rights would be taken from them without realistic recompense. Some concession was usually also given to the need for government to stop wealth becoming concentrated to a degree that could create monopolies within the system, if not to redistribute wealth for fairness in advance of market trade. Viewed as a public good, however, the market needs a wider range of government actions to set it and keep it in motion. The government needs to set and enforce rules for market trade, define any limits to the coverage of markets, and guarantee the acceptance and stability of money as a means to link purchase and sale transfers which are separated across time or space.

1.10.2 *Preventive rules and curative rules*

Rules are costly to enforce and abide by, and even where members of a society agree on their necessity they will be keen to minimise their number and costs of implementation. Within market systems, two alternative approaches to rule-setting can be identified. One seeks to maximise the transparency and perceived fairness of a transaction before it takes place, so as to minimise the rejection of, or reneging on, the contract after one agent has moved to enact it. The other aims for maximum efficiency and fairness in the resolution of disputes after the transaction, so that any unjustified breach of a contract can be quickly sorted out, in a way which prevents further breaches from occurring.

Any systematic difference in cost between the 'pre-sale consensus' and 'buy now, sue later' approaches to rule-setting might be expected to allow one system to prevail over another, trading companies – and countries – that adopt the cheaper method growing at the expense of others until these are forced to change. The continued coexistence of the two systems suggests that in practice there is no systematic cost difference between preventive and curative approaches – or that the balance of cost advantages changes with the number of adopters, post-trade litigation losing its edge the more the courts get clogged by people using it. At one extreme, business analysts identify a Japanese-style 'consensual' system in which transactors try not to set formal rules, relying on mutual understanding to ensure that both sides get what they expected. At the other extreme stands the US-style legalistic approach, in which sellers routinely buy insurance against post-sale lawsuits, even from parties they trust and expect to do business with again. Pre-sale consensus shades into 'relational' transaction, explored further in Chapter 6. Post-sale courtroom confrontations, arising from missing or misleading information, are one motivation for the 'informed' transaction structures explored in Chapter 7, and their encapsulation in company structures examined in Chapter 8.

1.11 Conclusion: what are the alternatives?

Having offered a detailed definition of the market in this chapter, Chapters 2–5 examine the way that markets are conventionally shown to work, and the problems that arise from their use in social organisation. Chapters 6 and 7 discuss the main alternatives to market organisation. Chapters 8–12 examine the ways in which they have recently come to be challenged both in theory and practice. Rather than concluding the present chapter with a summary statement of what a market system is, it is useful to set the scene for these later chapters by suggesting what a market system is not. Markets cease to exist, or lose their optimising characteristics, when one or more of the following 'market failures' arise:

- There are only a few buyers and/or sellers.
- Buyers and/or sellers discriminate among themselves by refusing to trade with certain other agents, or setting them varying prices for a homogeneous product.
- Procedural rules for transaction, and for resolving disputes arising from transaction, are the subject of informal agreement between pairs or sets of traders rather than being formalised in rules applying to all traders.
- Parties to a transaction can appeal to have it modified or reversed, even if no formal rules have been broken.
- Certain economically valuable products are unpriced or mispriced, so that trade in one or more markets does not take place at equilibrium prices.
- Certain means of production are not in clearly defined private ownership, their ownership and user rights not clearly distinguished and/or not competitively priced.

The next four chapters examine how the violation of these conditions can negatively affect the outcome of market transaction. Chapters 6 and 7 assess three other approaches to transaction which try to turn some of the violations into virtues. The remainder of the book attempts to explain why, against initial odds, policy and social practice came to favour the market approach.

2 Markets as efficient allocators

Many markets are at work at any one time, and the income raised from selling on one market will be used to buy in another. Agents' views of the value of consumption goods will depend on judgements of how supply and demand add up across space, and their evaluation of investment goods also requires an anticipation of how supply and demand will develop across time. Market theorists' most remarkable claim is that spatially and temporally interdependent markets do not require central co-ordination for their individual balances to sum to something harmonious. Instead, the best outcome for all is ensured by letting individuals seek the best outcome for themselves. Prices provide all the necessary information and co-ordination – provided there are prices for everything, adjusted to clear all markets at all times.

The market was introduced in section 1.2 as applying to a single product. One supply function and one demand function show the quantities offered and requested at different prices. The two 'curves' arise from different considerations (firms' costs and technologies, consumers' preferences and budgets), so they are influenced independently by changes in conditions surrounding the market. A rise in consumers' disposable income will shift the demand curve outwards, and a rise in the price of a complementary product will shift it inwards. A cost-reducing innovation will shift the supply curve downwards, and a new excise tax on the product will shift it upwards. Once they have occurred, however, these extraneous 'shocks' are absorbed entirely within the market, as transactors' interactions lead them back to the new intersection point. Resultant changes in income and relative prices will cause functions to shift in other markets, but these too will adjust, the price system providing all the feedback required to get all markets back to equilibrium.

2.1 All clear: the general equilibrium vision

The one-market, partial equilibrium view of Figure 1.1 is immensely useful for studying the economics of particular companies and industries, and forms the basis of most market microeconomics. But proving that the simultaneous adjustment of interdependent markets leads to a general equilibrium, in which one set of relative prices clears all markets (including labour and capital markets), now and in the future, has not been an easy task. An intuitive grasp of the power of prices to align individuals' transaction plans, without recourse to a central one, was reached at least two centuries ago. Its mathematical refinement is still in progress, and has revealed shortcomings as well as strengths in the intuitive view. Markets' move from micro- to macroeconomics is, like rockets' move from exploding the earth to exploring the moon, one small step for economic man and one giant leap for salesman-kind.

This chapter summarises the efficiency claims made for price-based general equilibrium, the conditions required for these claims to hold, and the debate on whether decentralised trade should be reinforced or renounced when such conditions do not obtain. It is the longest of the chapters, despite skating round the mathematical detail of how the competitive general equilibrium (CGE) models' conclusions are reached. This reflects the heat generated in the process of proving CGE's possibility and desirability, as well as the light thrown on economic policy requirements for a CGE and the consequences of those requirements not being met.

2.1.1 *Dividing input and multiplying output*

Reliable markets make way for the division of labour, the central means by which relations of production can be reorganised to make societies richer. Once they are sure that products of which they have too much can be exchanged for products they lack, people once condemned to do everything themselves can now concentrate on what they do best. 'It is the great multiplication of the productions of all the different arts, in consequence of the division of labour, which occasions, in a well-governed society, that universal opulence which extends itself to the lowest ranks of the people' (Smith 1776/1979: 115). Specialisation raises labour productivity within each industry by simplifying and standardising tasks so that labour becomes ever more practised at them, and so that machines can be designed to assist or replace them. Productivity is raised further by reallocating resources between industries. Product prices guide agents towards their most rewarding specialisation. Relative wages show workers which occupations are most in demand. Relative profits show firms which lines it is best to invest in, and draw attention to any cost-reducing or sales-raising methods they might adopt.

Under any other arrangements, competition between agents for material gain had seemed a formula for civil war and anarchy. Market signals appear to ditch the martial arts and marshall individual, self-interested action towards a collectively beneficial outcome. 'Give me that which I want, and you shall have this which you want . . . it is in this manner that we obtain from one another the far greater part of those good offices which we stand in need of' (Smith 1776/1979: 118–19). Adam Smith's empirical observation, that unregulated market trade can allow all agents to maximise their material advantages simultaneously, began the division of 'political economy' into the separate disciplines of politics and economics. The first pursues a long-held view that central rules must be set to prevent uncoordinated, competitive action producing recurrent social conflict. The second develops the more recent insight that markets provide the necessary rules, without central intervention. Much of the subsequent study of society has involved a battle between these two views, with sociology caught in the shifting middle ground.

Smith's intuition about the essential harmony of markets as a system was gradually refined and recast in mathematical form, to which Walras (1874/1954), Wald (1936/1951) and Hicks (1939) were among the most influential contributors. While they were working to knit the workings of separate markets into a coherent whole, supporting breakthroughs were made in partial equilibrium analysis: notably the use of differential calculus to derive maximising conditions for firms, consumers and workers in the 'marginal analysis' of Jevons (1871) and Marshall (1961), and the related welfare economics of Edgeworth (1881) and Pareto (1909/1971). From the marginal analysis came the general concept of individual optimisation, through which an agent maximises its objectives by taking actions whose benefits exceed their costs. Firms' objective is to maximise profits (the excess of revenue over cost within a market period), and consumers' objective is to maximise utility (a subjective measure of satisfaction which relates positively to the amount they consume). From welfare economics came the general concept of the best collective outcome from these optimising individual actions: a Pareto optimum, occurring on the core of product distributions among agents, to which no change can raise one agent's utility (or profit) without reducing that of at least one other agent.

The search for a rigorous proof that decentralised market trade could result in a welfare-maximising general equilibrium culminated in the Arrow-Debreu (AD) existence proof (Arrow and Debreu 1954) and the similar, simultaneous presentation by McKenzie (1954). An accessible account of these, and of CGE theory's subsequent lines of development, can be found in Madden (1989) and more technical accounts in the collection in Eatwell *et al.* (1989a). Although since much refined, by its originators and others, the AD model remains a reference point for CGE theory. It grounds all macroeconomic aggregates (output, consumption, income, employment) in the optimising choices of individual agents, and derives the unique set of relative prices at which all agents can optimise through trades that make their respective markets clear.

2.1.2 *General equilibrium through trade and production*

In a pure exchange economy, with all products already in existence, CGE arises once people have made all the trades that enhance their utility. This is maximised through the exchange of products, of which their initial endowment sets a limit on the consumption from which utility is derived. Mutual gains from trade arise because of individual differences, complementarities or substitutabilities between products, and diminishing marginal utility in consumption. Two consumers with the same initial quantities of a product but different (average or marginal) utilities can gain if the consumer with lower utility sells units to the consumer with higher utility. This is possible as long as the higher-utility consumer has something to offer in exchange – units of a product from which the other consumer derives higher utility at the margin, or enough money to buy another product that brings them higher utility. Two consumers with identical preferences but different initial quantities of a product can likewise make mutual utility gains if the consumer with more sells units to the consumer with less, until they hold the same amounts. In both cases the gains from trade are exhausted when marginal utility per monetary unit is equalised across all consumers. A consumer's marginal utility from different products will still differ, but by a ratio matched by that of their respective prices.

Because preferences vary between individuals and between situations, consumers differ in the utility they derive from an identical bundle of products. (Bacon and eggs appeal more to the carnivore than the vegan.) Because its use-value depends in part on those of the products already held, equal amounts of a new product yield different utility to different consumers. (Among carnivores, the bacon may be worth more to someone who already has the eggs.) Because the next unit of a product is never quite as satisfying as those that went before, within a market period, an extra unit of a product will be worth more to a consumer the less they already have. (Bacon and eggs are worth more to someone who has fasted for a week than one who has just had a four-course meal; they may even have some appeal to starving vegans.)

In the (more recognisable) production economy, where products consumed must first be produced, consuming agents have two sets of decisions to make. As well as trading their existing products to get the maximum utility, they have the option of getting extra income with which to buy additional products. This can be done by setting up in production as a firm or, more usually, by selling labour services to an existing firm. The provision of labour services is assumed to be (at least for the hours usually demanded) a disutility. So consumers' utility now relates positively to the amounts of product they consume and negatively to the amount of labour they supply. Consumers' income, which continues to put a restraint on their utility maximisation, is now derived from their initial endowment of products, the income from labour services performed, and any share of profits distributed to them by firms.

Firms aim to maximise profit by expanding their output of each product until the revenue from selling the last unit exactly matches the cost of producing it. Previous units are made profitable by the assumption that unit costs are rising over the relevant output range, because extra quantities of labour and materials are having to be put to work with a fixed stock of capital equipment, or are being drawn from a pool in descending order of quality. The product's marginal revenue is constant under conditions of perfect competition, being the equilibrium price set for it in a market with many competing buyers and sellers. If competition is less than perfect, so that the firm can depress market price by raising output, marginal revenue is falling and profit is maximised at a lower level of output.

Perfect competition is assumed in the simplest CGE models because it ensures that even maximum profit is only just sufficient to cover the costs of the most effective firm in any industry. Firms are thus compelled to keep their cost schedules to a minimum, ensuring efficiency not only in allocation (production where marginal costs and benefits balance) but also in production (average costs are at their lowest attainable level). With no 'supernormal' profit or loss, firms also have neither means nor incentive to invest in increased production or disinvest from existing production, so that the equilibrium is not undermined by changing supplies and relative prices over time.

2.1.3 *Equilibrium efficiency outcomes*

By maximising utilities and profits in this way, firms and consumers bring the economy into an equilibrium with three distinct welfare-maximising attributes.

Allocative efficiency in consumption is reached because consumers continue to exchange products until each yields the same marginal utility (MU). The ratio of products' marginal utilities, their marginal rate of substitution (MRS), is thus equalised between all products. The MRS expresses, for each pair of products, the amount of one that would have to be received in return for giving up one unit of the other. Trade can equalise this across consumers because of the diminishing marginal utility each obtains from a particular product. If one consumer's MRS between two products (x and y) is above that of another, both can gain utility by exchanging x and y until their two substitution rates are brought into line.

Since consumers continue to acquire a product until the extra benefits (marginal utility) are offset by the extra cost (price), the ratio of marginal utilities between any two products will also be equal to the ratio of their prices. When prices are expressed in money terms, this can also be viewed as an efficient allocation of the consumer's holding of money – since a unit of this now yields the same marginal utility from each of the products it is spent on. Allocative efficiency in consumption, for products x and y and consumers A and B, can thus be summarised as

$$\text{MRS}x,y\ (A) = \text{MRS}x,y\ (B) = Px/Py = MUx/MUy\ (A) = MUx/MUy\ (B)$$

Allocative efficiency in production is reached because firms adjust their output until the marginal rate of transformation (MRT) between each pair of products is everywhere equalised. The MRT is the number of units of one product that must be given up if resources are to go instead to producing one extra unit of another product. Since firms expand output of each product until its marginal production cost (MC) equals its marginal revenue (MR), the 'equilibrium' MRT is the ratio of marginal costs for each product. With perfect competition keeping marginal cost equal to average revenue (price), the products' MRT is also the ratio of their prices.

Market exchange between firms and households thus reaches equilibrium when

$$\text{MRT}x,y = \text{MRS}x,y\ (A) = \text{MRS}x,y\ (B) = Px/Py = MUx/MUy$$
$$(A) = MUx/MUy\ (B)$$

Productive efficiency (sometimes also termed X-efficiency) is reached because firms, as 'consumers' of factors of production, will also arrange these to yield marginal utility in proportion to their market prices. Assuming that each product requires labour (L) and capital (K), and that these can be deployed in any proportions, firms will combine the two factors to equalise their marginal rate of technical substitution (MRTS), the amount of one factor that must be substituted for another to obtain the same physical output. Households must sell labour to gain additional income for expenditure, and they do so up to the point that the marginal disutility of extra work rises to match the marginal utility to be gained from extra consumption. Each firm recruits factors until their marginal utility (in this case marginal product, MP) equals their marginal cost. Under perfect competition this is also the average cost: wage W for labour and interest rate R for capital. So firms P and Q reach productive efficiency when

$$MRTSk,l\ (P) = MRTSk,l\ (Q) = MPl/MPk = W/R$$

2.1.4   Optimum properties: the 'fundamental welfare theorems'

These general-equilibrium efficiency outcomes, beginning with the two-product, two-agent case (which can be represented geometrically for consumers and for firms), give rise to the two 'fundamental theorems' of welfare economics:

1   Every competitive market process will, under the assumed conditions, lead to a Pareto optimal allocation.
2   Every Pareto optimal allocation can be the result of a competitive market process, given appropriate starting conditions (in terms of preferences, technologies and initial endowments).

The second statement concedes the very limited power of Pareto optimality to identify social preference among different market outcomes, arising from its assessment of utility only at the margin. No attention is paid to absolute levels of utility (individual or aggregate), or to the distribution of income and initial endowments that underlie them. Because utility, and its relation to a person's income or consumption, is regarded as wholly subjective, interpersonal comparisons of utility cannot be made. Robbing the ultra-rich to save the poor from starving is not a Pareto improvement, however much the recipients might argue that the extra money is worth more to them than to one already rolling in it.

The welfare theorems thus demonstrate that there are any number of possible Pareto optimal outcomes, each resulting from a different initial distribution. Once set up, the market system produces a uniquely optimal outcome; but there may be many equally good ways to set it up. In the two-consumer (A and B), two-product (X and Y) representation, each initial allocation of X and Y between A and B leads to their trade producing a different Pareto optimal allocation.

2.1.5   Collective utility's futility: the impossibility theorems

Welfare theorists working with partial equilibrium had tried to break through this indeterminacy by constructing a 'utility possibility frontier' (U in Figure 2.1),

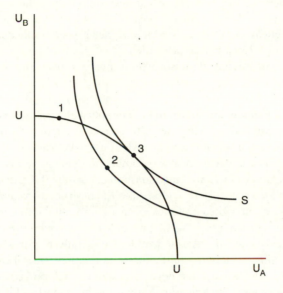

Figure 2.1 Equal utility combinations and utility possibilities

representing all the combinations of A's and B's maximum utility resulting from particular initial distributions. Although not necessarily regular, this frontier is continually downward sloping, the positive relation between consumption level and utility (a product's marginal utility declines but never becomes negative) ensuring that a rise in one agent's utility, caused by an initial redistribution in their favour, always means a fall in the other agent's utility. This frontier was then superimposed on the society's 'social welfare function' (S in Figure 2.1), representing combinations of A's and B's utility which have equal social value. This frontier is assumed to be concave to origin, society having a presumption in favour of equal enjoyment of utility and thus reqiring an ever larger rise in one agent's utility to compensate for a fall in another agent's. The fact that a point on the utility frontier (like 1) can be on a lower social welfare function than a point below the frontier (like 2) confirms that, where this presumption prevails, some distributions can be Pareto preferred but socially rejected.

In principle, a unique socially optimum distribution can now be identified, where the highest attainable welfare function is tangential to the utility possibility frontier (point 3). But unless agents can openly express their utilities in commensurable units – an option ruled out by the subjective measure used in this form of welfare analysis – calibrating the social welfare function is no easy task. Arrow (1951) demonstrates the impossibility of constructing a social ranking of individual preference orderings (of distributions) that satisfies four apparently innocuous conditions:

• that any individual can rank the states in any order

- that the social ranking of any two states depends only on how each individual ranks them
- that one state is socially preferred to another if every individual prefers it to that other (the 'weak Pareto principle')
- that the social ranking does not wholly coincide with any one individual's ranking.

The first three conditions are shown to be met only if the fourth is violated, and so on with other combinations. More needs to be known about individuals' utility, its absolute size or comparability, if a social ordering is to be reached which satisfies all four conditions. 'If utility functions are ordinal and noncomparable, then the only possible consistent social welfare function is a dictatorship' (Johansen 1991: 31).

Sen (1982) shows that it is also impossible to construct a social ranking which allows any order of individual preferences, carries over unanimous individual preferences, and allows each individual to have at least one preference reflected in the social ordering. Solving the Arrow problem generally requires restricting the number of possible preferences individuals can express, specifically to 'single-peaked' rankings under which a moderate option is never ranked in between two extremes. Sen's impossibility theorem is advanced in support of his argument that social preference must treat individuals' welfare using something more than just their preferred ranking of end-states. There is 'a need to relax the Pareto principle if rights are to be substantially incorporated in moral or political systems' (Sen 1982: 28).

These impossibility theorems, put forward at a time when the role of the state in raising and redistributing national income (and welfare) was not widely questioned, provided a foretaste of the 'government failure' arguments whose development will be charted much more fully in Chapter 11. Initially, however, they appeared to deliver an equally negative judgement against a decentralised market system: that it can yield any number of final distributions for which optimising properties can be claimed. To move beyond this, a CGE must find ways of establishing preference either among the initial distributions from which trading starts, or among the different Pareto optimal results arising from different starting-points.

2.1.6 *What general equilibrium represents*

CGE characterises the market economy as a collection of demands (for factor services and inputs by firms and products by consumers) and supplies (of factor services by consumers and products by firms), yielding a set of simultaneous equations whose solution shows the (non-negative) equilibrium prices and associated quantities which optimising individuals must trade. Since there are initially as many equations as unknowns, the system is made soluble by expressing prices as ratios to one of the products. Assigning unit value to this numeraire removes it from the list of unknowns.

The challenge for CGE theorists has been to prove that the solution consists entirely of positive prices, one for each market. Negative price in any market would suggest that it cannot clear, so that a CGE does not exist. More than one positive price in any market would suggest that the CGE is not unique, and therefore cannot be shown to have optimising properties. Having established that all prices are positive and unique, it is also necessary to show that they are stable, returning to equilibrium if displaced from it. This requires that supply exceeds demand when price is above equilibrium, and demand exceeds supply when price is below equilibrium – as in the 'well-behaved' S and D functions shown in Figure 1.1.

Arrow and Debreu (1954) identify conditions for the existence of a unique equilibrium price vector, confirm that it is locally stable, and demonstrate its consistency with the fundamental welfare theorems. For CGE to be achieved, every product (including the factors of production) must have a unique price at which demand matches supply. The expression of prices as ratios to a numeraire requires that output of any product can be scaled up or down by the same proportion as each of its inputs, implying first-degree homogeneity of the production function. Consumers must always prefer more to less, even though marginal utility diminishes (technically, utility is a monotonically increasing function of consumption). Diminishing marginal utility means that consumers' 'indifference curves', representing equally valued bundles of products, are assumed to be convex: ever larger amounts of one product are needed to compensate the sacrifice of units of another product (all products assumed to be gross substitutes). This also results in the utility function being quasi-concave (utility would always rise if the consumer were allowed to take a weighted average of the bundles at two points on an indifference curve). The utility function must also be continuous – consumption goods being infinitely divisible – so that the consumption level with maximum utility can be found by differentiation. The production function, relating volume of output to volume of inputs, must also be continuous to ensure that there are no indivisibilities, which would lead to increasing returns to scale (section 2.7).

Markets must extend into the future, so that consumers (who know their future preferences) and firms (who know their future technological possibilities) can plan the whole sequence of their transactions, including those that are contingent on future states of the world. For the CGE to be locally stable, agents' responses when a market fails to clear must cause price to adjust back towards this equilibrium. For the CGE to have Pareto optimal welfare properties, prices must capture the full social opportunity cost of acquiring an additional unit of a product. Social opportunity cost is the maximum utility that could be derived from spending the same amount on the best alternative product.

Since its publication, the basic Arrow-Debreu model and its variants have served two purposes of equal and opposite importance. For supporters of decentralised, competitive markets, it confirms what Adam Smith's intuition had said all along, that unregulated trade by free agents can lead to an optimum allocation of resources. It also provides a testing-ground for the necessity of the conditions, and the model's ability to retain its optimum properties when these are relaxed. For the market's detractors, the number and restrictiveness of conditions needed for existence, uniqueness and stability suggests denies that general equilibrium has any use in the analysis of actual economies, and the presence of initial endowments' among their number shows that the essential arbitrariness of Pareto-optimal outcomes has not been laid to rest.

2.1.7   The spectre of second best

For a unique equilibrium to exist:

1   All sources of utility must be available as separate products.
2   All products must be provided and priced for individual consumption.
3   Price must be set in a competitive market, so that private marginal utility (to the household) equals private marginal cost (to the firm). To ensure a competitive market for each product, buyers must
  (a)   reach their decisions independently from sellers
  (b)   reach their decisions independently from other buyers
  (c)   have as much information about the product as its sellers, and other buyers.
4   To ensure that individual agents' optimisation adds up to optimisation for the whole society, the market price must capture all the costs and benefits of a transaction, so that private marginal utilities equal those of society.

Violation of any of the general equilibrium conditions leads to one or more products going unpriced or incorrectly priced, preventing agents from converging to a unique set of trades at which their own, and total, utility are maximised. Displacement of the price in one market from the perfectly competitive equilibrium level (equal to marginal cost) does not merely cause a slight deviation from CGE. It may displace prices in many other markets from equilibrium, causing a general breakdown. If the equilibrium price vector cannot be attained, the 'second-best' vector may involve systematic deviation from normal welfare-maximising properties (Lipsey and Lancaster 1957).

A standard example is of monopoly in one product market (X), which causes its price to be set above marginal cost. X's marginal rate of substitution with product Y (given by Px/Py) now permanently exceeds consumers' marginal rate of substitution between the two (given by MCx/MCy), so that it may no longer be optimal to set MC=P (and so ensure that MRS=MRT) in any other market. The first-best solution is to get rid of the monopoly. But if this is impossible, the second-best entails a wholesale departure from first-best efficiency conditions. With just one monopoly, this is achieved by replicating its displacement of price above marginal cost in all other markets. 'Where at least two industries in the deviant sector have different marginal cost price ratios, the exact second-best rule is difficult to calculate' (Mishan 1982: 111).

The rest of this chapter is concerned with the 'market failures' that can arise when one or more of the conditions for CGE is not met. Its length indicates the number of violations with which those refining the AD model have had to deal. Their scale was initially large enough to put the market paradigm on the defensive, conceding a broad range of transactions which were best conducted outside the market, or regulated within it. Subsequently, reviving confidence in the market mechanism and disappointment with the alternatives has encouraged the view that perfecting the market is preferable to replacing it. After introducing each violation and outlining the traditional (interventionist) solution, attention is given to the newer, pro-market responses. The counterattack has three components – minimising the scale of the problem, showing how it might be solved within the market, and revealing how the non-market 'cure' may be worse than the disease.

2.2 Public goods

All products in the basic CGE model are private. Those who sell them are sole recipients of the revenue they bring and those who buy them are the sole recipients of the utility they provide. A *public good* goes unproduced or underproduced by competing private agents because it cannot command a price that would induce any of them to produce it – even though there is an optimal output for the economy as a whole. The conflict arises because public-good benefits are *non-excludable*. Any agent who buys it incurs the full cost but enjoys only a fraction of the benefits, since these are also received by agents who have not paid. Payment from these other recipients is impossible to extract because it is unclear that they are consuming it, or want to consume it, and frequently because the costs of assessment and collection of the payment outweigh the benefits.

Free-riding by agents who receive its benefits without paying is hard to detect because the public good is *non-depletable*, its availability and utility extending to any number of users once initially produced. In the AD model, non-excludability is ruled out by assuming that each product is allotted exclusively to one agent, and non-depletability by the assumption that each agent's utility derives solely from the products they possess or consume.

Non-excludability often arises when a product is indivisible, not capable of being broken into individual portions without seriously reducing its effectiveness or raising its cost. Agents who want a small quantity of the product may then have to pay an extremely high price and/or buy much more than they would like, making available surplus capacity on which others can free-ride. *Indivisibility* means that below a certain level of total willingness-to-pay, there is insufficient funding available to provide any of the public good. Once this level is reached, a unit of the good comes into existence, but further contributions will not bring any increased provision until the next step-change is reached.

Standard examples of public goods are national defence, policing, roads, street lighting, radio broadcasting, public libraries and parks. If these are provided at all under a pure market system they are likely to be underprovided, since it is rational for agents who realise the publicness of the product to free-ride on those who actually try to pay their share. The marginal social benefit of the public good is the sum of its marginal utilities to each agent, whereas the marginal social cost is the marginal private cost of anyone who chooses to pay for it. They end up paying for all. Free-riding is likely to increase with the extent of non-depletability and indivisibility, the difficulty or cost of enforcing excludability, and the number of agents among whom the product's benefits are spread.

A popular representation of the public goods problem, and of collective action problems more generally, is the two-person prisoners' dilemma (PD) game. In this, the usual starting-point for non-cooperative game theory, two suspected criminals are being separately questioned about their latest felony. Each has the option of co-operating (C) by confessing to the crime, or non-cooperating (N) by blaming the other. The payoffs under each combination of these strategies are given in Figure 2.2.

		Sentences in years (A,B)	
		Agent A	
		C	N
Agent B	C	1,1	0,10
	N	10,0	5,5

Figure 2.2 The prisoners' dilemma

The Pareto optimal outcome (for the two prisoners) is for both to confess (C,C) and receive a light sentence. But without the option of communicating, and knowing that an unreciprocated confession would earn a heavy sentence while letting the accomplice walk free, both prisoners are driven to blame the other (N,N). They thus end up with longer sentences than would have been given if both had been able to get together and agree the optimal, co-operative strategy.

Applying the logic to public goods, the socially optimal strategy (C) is for agents to reveal their true preference for the level of provision, and incur whatever shared cost is needed to attain this level of provision. The suboptimal strategy (N) is to conceal their true preference and refuse to subscribe to the good, resulting in its underprovision. State intervention is needed to enforce the (C,C) optimum, however, since an agent will lose heavily if it chooses C and then finds other agents free-riding on it by choosing N. With simultaneous decision and no co-operation – the characteristic features of decision in a free-market economy – the game results in suboptimal non-cooperation (N,N).

2.2.1 *Interventionist solutions*

As the name implies, the traditional response to this situation has been to force all (or most) benefiting agents to finance public goods through a tax. Non-excludability then ceases to matter because everyone has paid their share of the costs. Under a progressive tax system those with high incomes will pay more than those with low, but this is often consistent with their receiving proportionally more benefits. For example, the private utility from defence and policing relates at least in part to the property damage they prevent. Once financed, the public good is usually provided free to reflect its non-depletability, which allows its output (i.e. number of users) to expand at zero marginal cost. (Free provision may also be judged on grounds of merit – see section 2.6.)

Establishing the 'socially optimal' output of a public good, and hence the taxation needed to provide it, requires some measure of the public's actual utility and willingness to pay. The tendency to free-ride means that this information is not available directly in the market. For less divisible products, indirect measures of private demand may be derived from agents' behaviour towards the public goods that currently exist. Thus demand for a public park may be gauged by the costs that visitors incur in travelling to it, or the variation in price of otherwise identical properties located at varying distances from it. Mechanisms have been suggested which give agents an incentive to reveal their true preference, each being asked their willingness to pay for the public good and then charged the absolute difference between the total with and without their own expressed willingness. But the cost and complexity of such exercises weighs against their implementation.

More usually the level of provision is left to political judgement, with voters being allowed periodically to choose between different programmes for public expenditure and associated taxation. In this case indivisibility can be advantageous in narrowing down the range of possible options. You either install the new bypass/library/anti-missile system or you don't.

2.2.2   *Market counterattack: are public goods a problem?*

Indivisibility is ruled out of the AD model through the assumption of convexity in each firm's production function, as is the closely associated violation of increasing returns to scale (section 2.7). Convexity means that as more of one factor is added to the process, ever diminishing amounts of the other can be withdrawn if output is to stay at the same level. However, the empirical evidence for increasing returns to scale makes this assumption hard to maintain, and indivisibilities would undermine it by introducing sudden jumps into the production function. A later development of the AD model by Arrow and Hahn (1971) shows that the existence proof can hold in some cases of increasing returns, but still does not survive indivisibilities.

Non-depletability is inherent in most public goods but non-excludability can be tackled, as can the provider's inability to extract charges from those it cannot exclude. Although their possibility was recognised early on, the true extent of public goods' occurrence (or more correctly lack of occurrence) has always been disputed. Private armies, police forces and fire services have existed in the past, sometimes sustained by forcible extraction of fees from beneficiaries but at other times by voluntary subscription. One of the anti-interventionists' favourite cases concerns lighthouses, seemingly an obvious public good because lights cannot be turned off for ships that pass in the night without paying their fees. In practice, some lighthouses were built at private expense, usually financed from a levy on ports or main shipping companies. These may well end up subsidising free-riders (free floaters?) who see the light without paying the fee, but if they are the main beneficiaries, and most others also pay up, this may be a spillover that it is still cost-effective to accept. Similarly, police and defence services can be financed by those whose wealth or insecurity lead to their being valued especially highly (though in the days when large landowners ran private armies, they could usually pass much of the cost on to the peasantry through rents or compulsory service).

Other 'public' goods have become more private over time as providers find more cost-effective ways to make them excludable and/or to charge those who use them. Thus private motorways appear if the builders are allowed to recover their costs through charging tolls. Private broadcasting becomes possible once signals can be scrambled, forcing viewers to buy a decoder. Commercial broadcasters have also shown how non-excludability can be turned to commercial advantage, recovering their costs through advertising attracted by the large 'free-riding' audience. Even branches of government short of funds for 'public' projects have discovered the advantages of planning gain, under which (in return for planning permission) a supermarket might fund road improvements which it knows will bring in more customers, or a new factory pay for water supply that will also go to the rest of the neighbourhood.

The resultant preservation of 'public' goods even in highly privatised economies has led some market theorists to argue that the category is of trivial importance. 'Exclusion devices abound in practice and the evidence that there is a wide range of goods characterised by "non-congestibility" or "non-rivalness" is slim indeed' (Peacock 1979: 205). Seldon (1990) estimates all 'unavoidably collective' goods at no more than 15 per cent of an industrial country's GDP, which is less than half what most actually spend on public-sector provision. The category essentially comes down to a small number of institutional services, mainly related to law and contract enforcement, which provide the framework for private, competitive market transactions. Provision of all other goods can be left to the market, being rendered 'public' only through the artificial imposition of non-excludability or non-depletability. For example, 'public' parks could be privately provided if admission charges were imposed, 'public' broadcasting could be turned over to advertisers, and 'public' forests could be self-financing if allowed a certain (sustainable) rate of commercial exploitation.

2.2.3 *Private provision of public goods 1: consumption clubs*

Agents aware of a co-ordination problem such as public good provision may not need to wait for government to enforce the collectively optimum solution. Where the product's benefits are mainly confined to a cohesive subsection of the population (by geography or some other identifiable characteristic), it may be possible for a consumption club to arrange collective provision without state help. These clubs, in such forms as hospital and educational trusts, newspaper and magazine subscriber-bases, motoring organisations and credit unions, form a voluntaristic 'middle way' between privatised individual consumption and nationalised collective consumption.

Provided that members of the club have a sufficiently strong interest in adequate provision of the public good, they will truthfully represent their preferences. Provided they receive sufficient assurances against free-riding, they will accept the levy needed to finance the agreed output. Members may agree to receive the product free at point of use, in which case part of their levy will probably have to go towards maintaining a mechanism for excluding non-members. Alternatively they may agree to pay a standing charge for the fixed costs of provision plus an incremental charge for use, this second charge serving (along with proof of membership) as the exclusion mechanism. Thus riverside villages build their own bridges, discotheques hire their own security guards, network television users pay a licence fee, and some industries operate a levy system for financing transferable training.

These are cases where excludability, and the monitoring of users to ensure that they have paid their dues, can be arranged at fairly low cost. The costs of monitoring club members to assess their utility from the public good, of computing and collecting their subscription and of excluding non-members will generally rise as the club expands, mainly because free-riding becomes harder to detect. While the assessment can be simplified by assuming equal benefits to each member, and hence charging them equal fees (perhaps with a very simple range of concessions), this leads the club towards voting problems which can unbalance the public provision of public goods. To take a simple example, a club of five which can assess its own preferences, and charge accordingly, will build a new shared facility for itself if members' willingnesses to pay are respectively $5, $10, $15, $30 and $40 and the construction cost is only $100. But if it simply charges each the average cost ($20) and puts the proposal to a vote, three out of the five will vote against. This is an example of the voting paradox attributed originally to Condorcet, which is an important element in the Arrow impossibility theorem on social welfare fuctions (section 2.1.4).

In general, public goods with the widest non-excludability are unlikely to be amenable to club provision, unless individuals are able to express the intensity of their preference (in this case, the amount they are willing to pay) as well as its direction. Problems of preference misrepresentation and free-riding persist. Club provision also relies on members' ability to express their willingness-to-pay financially, and so could still lead to underproduction of public goods which are more appropriately allocated on 'merit' than on ability-to-pay (see section 2.6). Another consequence of public goods also being merit goods is that a club may have the wrong charging structure, for example demanding flat fees when there is a social case for asking the better-off to cross-subsidise the worse-off. Conversely, club provision could lead to overproduction of the public good if there are large economies of scale in its production. For example, while each town might be able to set up its own heart transplant unit or missile early-warning system, the extent of duplication and/or undercapacity working would mean significant savings from a move to national provision.

2.2.4 *Private provision of public goods 2: co-operation in repeated games*

Although the prisoners' dilemma is a persuasive two-person simplification of the public goods situation, it is not the only non-cooperative game that may characterise a collective action problem. Since agents' difficulty is essentially one of co-ordination – they would pay their share of the production cost if they could be sure that all other agents would pay their share – the payoff structure could equally well be that of an assurance game (AG – Figure 2.3). Here mutual co-operation

(C,C) is still the collectively best choice, but mutual non-cooperation (N,N) is not as bad for either player as the situation where one co-operates and one does not. Since the incentive to trick the opponent (by playing N when they play C) is removed, this could make it easier to move to the best outcome (C,C), if agents have any way of signalling their willingness to co-operate. 'A contract of mutual non-confession does not need any enforcement in the Assurance game, whereas it is the crux of the matter in the Prisoners' Dilemma' (Sen 1982: 78).

		Agent A	
		C	N
Agent B	C	1,1	6,10
	N	10,6	5,5

Figure 2.3 The assurance game

A third possibility is the chicken game (CG – Figure 2.4), in which the consequences of mutual non-cooperation are even worse than those of co-operating when the other agent does not. (The name has been traced to a contest, apparently popular among US teenagers in the 1960s, of driving two cars towards each other at maximum speed, the chicken being the first to swerve to avoid a head-on collision.) One player can thus be relied on to co-operate, whether or not the opponent does so. It is noticeable that few countries lack military defences, a police force, roads, broadcast television and immunisation programmes, even if there is eternal complaint about the numbers who allegedly dodge paying for them.

		Agent A	
		C	N
Agent B	C	1,1	0,4
	N	4,0	5,5

Figure 2.4 The chicken game

A fourth possibility is the reciprocation game (RG – Figure 2.5), in which mutual co-operation is better for both agents than mutual non-cooperation, but an agreed alternation of co-operative and non-cooperative behaviour would work out even better in repeated plays of the game.

		Agent A	
		C	N
Agent B	C	2,2	0,3
	N	3,0	5,5

Figure 2.5 The reciprocation game

By playing (C,C) every time, the agents reduce their losses to two in each round, compared with the five that would be lost by playing (N,N). But if each could agree to make an opportunistic deviation from co-operation on alternate rounds, and allow their co-operation to be similarly exploited on the intervening rounds, the succession of low and high penalties from continuous (N,C) and (C,N) alternation is a better result than the constant medium penalty from continuous mutual co-operation. Although it requires strong trust or strict monitoring to avoid sliding into the mutually ruinous (N,N) outcome, this strategy may be sustainable by small groups who know they are destined to play repeatedly.

A common example is the 'collusive tender' in which construction companies, which incur a large sunk cost when drawing up plans which are not commissioned, take it in turns to bid for big government tenders, the winner on one round agreeing to stand aside for another on the next. Top athletes have been observed to adopt a similar tactic, avoiding one another in major races to prevent the mutual burn-up which can lead to a lesser contender stealing through to take the tape.

Even if the PD is accepted as representing most public goods situations, there are reasons for believing that mutual co-operation (C,C) will be achieved if the same agents are required to play the game repeatedly. In this long-run 'supergame', provided future payoffs are not too heavily discounted, the loss from experimentally playing C and being rebuffed with N is small compared with the potential gain from playing C and being rewarded thereafter with reciprocal plays of C. The rewards of a conditional co-operation tit-for-tat strategy – playing C on the first round and sticking with it if the opponent plays C, defecting otherwise – identified by M. Taylor (1976), were subsequently confirmed in experimental work by Axelrod (1984). This confirmed that in a two-person PD supergame, mutual payoffs are highest if each agent opts for conditional co-operation, unless a very high value is placed on first-round outcomes (where any loss will be incurred) in comparison with future outcomes.

These two-person results could be misleading, given that the scope for successful free-riding (playing N while others play C) is likely to expand with the number of players (here being less chance of large losses either through detection and punishment, or through everyone else opting for the mutually damaging N). M. Taylor (1987: 85) shows that a larger group can reach and sustain the mutually co-operative outcome provided they follow a strict conditional co-operation strategy, in which C is played on the first round and played again in succeeding rounds provided all other agents play C on the first round (i.e. share the conditional-co-operation strategy). In this situation each agent knows that selecting N on the first round will cause everyone else to select N thereafter. There is a credible threat of long-lasting mutual damage which constrains everyone to continue co-operation. An equally credible threat prevents any agent from trying to get an initial advantage by playing N on the first round, deferring conditional co-operation until subsequent rounds. Because others play C on the first round, the renegade will switch to C on the second round – when, because others have switched to N because of their experience in the first round, this unreciprocated co-operation will get the disastrous (C,N) payoff, followed by mutually ruinous (N,N) on every subsequent round.

Co-operation is more fragile, however, if conditional co-operators become more tolerant, sticking with the C strategy even if a certain number of agents fails to co-operate on a particular round. Since some players of N can now get away with it (perhaps because their free-riding is not detected), and secure the higher payoff of playing N when others hold to C, other agents will be tempted to switch to non-cooperation on subsequent rounds. Co-operation could still be sustainable if enough agents condition their co-operation on the co-operation of all others, and if discount rates are low enough to make future (N,N) losses outweigh present (N,C) gains, but co-operation is – perhaps paradoxically – doomed if too few players of C make a credible threat to withdraw co-operation when one player switches to N. It is possible that an immediate but once-for-all partial collapse of co-operation would ensue, or that there would be a progressive collapse, perhaps with an additional player or a small number of players dropping out of co-operation on successive games (M. Taylor 1987: 87).

The survival of mutual co-operation in a PD supergame also depends on its being played indefinitely, or having no known end-date. Any agents who know that they are entering the final round have an incentive to withdraw co-operation, in the hope of one last maximum (N,C) payoff. But as other agents know that N will be played again in the last round, they lose the incentive to play C on any previous round, 'backward induction' returning the players to mutual non-cooperation starting in the current round.

If public goods provision does present a case of the PD, then repeated playing of the game among a large number of agents can guarantee provision only under strict conditions of conditional-co-operation commitment and non-cooperation detection.

Self-interest, in obtaining the benefits without paying the full costs, will otherwise undermine the collectively optimum solution and leave everyone worse off. 'This problem is one of the chief reasons why we need more than *laissez-faire* economics – why we need both politics and morality' (Parfit 1987: 62). To the extent that a private exchange economy achieves adequate provision of public goods it does so, ironically, because agents move away from the PD payoff structure by looking beyond their narrow economic interests, moving the game towards a one-off AG or CG. 'Some simple variations of the preference pattern in the Prisoners' Dilemma make morality and rational behaviour perfectly consistent' (Sen 1982: 83).

For some neoclassical observers, however, collectively rational behaviour can be sustained in the presence of public goods problems and other market failures without appeal to politics or morality. Sufficient co-ordination can be accomplished by a system of law which permits agents to achieve the required co-ordination contractually, fixing the payoffs so that everyone gains something from co-operation (as in the co-operative solution to a PD game), and using penalties to deter opportunistic reneging on that solution (as in non-cooperation when the PD opponent co-operates).

The best interpretation of current legal institutions, especially the private law of property, contract and tort, understands them as designed either to facilitate market exchange or to rectify market failure . . . rational individuals will not engage in cooperative endeavors unless they can rely on the compliance of others . . . The solution is to develop bodies of law that provide resources capable of reducing uncertainty and fostering market cooperation.

(Coleman 1992: 3, 30, 69)

An initial 'pre-market' act of co-operation, to establish and obey the law, creates a framework for market competition which, by implication, minimises the need thereafter for moral codes which might limit market choice, or political intervention which could invite coercive restriction of subsequent market interaction.

2.2.5 Public bads

The likely breakdown of private provision of 'unavoidably collective' products suggests some need for state provision, even if the range of products affected is relatively small. Even where some public goods are still seen as needing public provision, through being unprovided, underprovided or unevenly distributed in a fully private economy, it need not follow that public provision will lead to net efficiency or social welfare gains. The interventionist solution assumes that governments can identify the optimal level of public goods provision, provide it at the lowest attainable cost, and fund its provision without adverse effects on other parts of the economy. Studies of state provision in practice have often identified 'government failure' in all these areas, sometimes causing at least as bad an allocative efficiency breakdown as the market failure it (ostensibly) aims to resolve.

Tax-financed provision introduces a new free-rider problem which can cause private-sector underprovision to turn into public-sector overprovision. Where provision is to be financed through taxation that affects only a subsection of the population, there is a possibility of overproduction as non-taxed voters vote for generous provision knowing they can free-ride on those who pay tax. Taxation itself can pull the economy away from allocative efficiency. An indirect tax, adding to the price of privately traded products, raises their price above their marginal cost and so distorts private consumption and production decisions. A direct tax, on labour incomes, reduces the opportunity cost of leisure and so distorts private labour-supply decisions.

Even if the government manages to provide the optimum level of public provision through a non-distorting system of taxation, so restoring allocative efficiency, public production of the good can fall short of private standards for productive efficiency. Nationalised industries have been accused of systematic inefficiency, based on the inadequate financial discipline and distorted incentives and price signals given to management. Being monopoly providers of the public good, they are under no competitive pressure to minimise its production costs. Being government-owned, they also lack the clear profit-maximising pressures of private shareholders. The state's desire to keep costs down (to lighten the tax burden) is offset by the usefulness of public goods provision as an indirect means of redistribution, employment creation and macroeconomic control.

More generally, state-enterprise managers are under the command of politicians who, in the increasingly powerful 'public choice' perspective, are not so much public-spirited guardians of collective wefare as self-interested maximisers of their own political and bureaucratic privilege. Though not adopted by every pro-market economist, public choice has destroyed any automatic link between market failure and public provision. Even if public goods can be shown to exist, a further step is now required to show that there are net social gains if the state provides them. Imperfect markets may be second best, but governments can sometimes rank as third.

2.3   External costs and benefits

Public goods can be seen as an extreme case of positive consumption externality, under which one agent's purchase of a product delivers utility gains to one or more other agents. Non-excludability condemns the purchaser to supply the product's utility free to the rest of the community. Social benefit is above private benefit because the market price paid by one agent fails to capture the utility that spills over to other agents. The same spillovers can occur in production, but here the more usual concern is that producers' private costs are below the social cost because they are dumping by-products on the wider community, or extracting inputs from it, without being charged. Privately incurred costs and benefits are often above or below those for the society as a whole, giving rise to four main types of externality.

First, positive consumption externality. A homeowner's tree-planting improves the appearance of the neighbourhood; a train traveller relieves congestion on the roads; an advertiser's purchase of space keeps down a magazine's cover price. One case that has drawn special attention is that of network goods, which are capable of a bandwagon effect in which one agent's purchase of a product increases its utility for other past and future purchasers. For example, a new telephone subscriber or internet user expands the network (and spreads the fixed costs) for later subscribers. It could even be argued that the dominant picture of the market economy, from Adam Smith to Arrow-Debreu, is of one giant consumption externality, the pursuit of private self-interest meshing to promote the best outcome for all. However, in Chapter 3, which looks in more detail at the market macroeconomy, another concept will be counterposed – that of external benefits from expenditure on capital goods which can lead to investment being undersupplied, and the economy lapsing from full employment.

Second, negative consumption externality. A city motorist adds to pollution and congestion for residents and other road-users; a patient's use of antibiotics accelerates the arrival of resistant bacterial strains which invalidate the medicine for later users; wealthy buyers of second homes inflate house prices beyond the reach of low-income buyers; a takeaway-food eater drops litter which must be picked up at public expense. One case that has drawn special attention is that of positional goods, the converse of network goods, whose purchase by one agent reduces their utility for past and future purchasers (Hirsch 1976). The disutility may be a practical one (roads and beaches get crowded, qualifications and gold watches become more common and so less highly valued), or a psychological one, if utility is derived from exclusivity and relative consumption levels. CGE theory, and conventional models of aggregate demand, require that an agent's utility arises solely from their own consumption and is unaffected by what others consume. 'The evidence that social comparisons are important to consumers is now overwhelming, and the conventional neoclassical theory of the consumer will remain unconvincing so long as it refuses to recognise this fact' (Baxter 1988: 179).

Third, positive production externality. A firm's *art deco* office block becomes a local tourist attraction; a water company's reservoir becomes a free boating lake for nearby residents; employees enrich themselves through undetected theft from their employer. Many of these externalities, such as that arising when a firm trains employees in skills which they can take to other firms, can provide their host location with external economies of scale (see section 9.3.3).

Fourth, negative production externality. A manufacturer discharges pollutants into local air and groundwater; a firm pays such low wages that employees need to claim relief from charities or state agencies; a railway line keeps residents awake at night.

The AD model rules out exernalities by assuming that firms pay for all their inputs and are paid for all their outputs, and that consumers receive all the utility from the products they pay for. Even externalities, since they impose costs or yield utility, must have their price. But as soon as one of the inputs or outputs in a transaction goes unpriced, it will become over- or underprovided in relation to the efficiency conditions. External costs imply that the individual's marginal costs understate the total (social) cost, so that the MC=AR equilibrium will occur at a higher output than is socially optimal. External benefits imply that price understates the (social) utility generated by the purchase, so that the MC=AR equilibrium occurs at a lower output than is socially optimal.

2.3.1 *Interventionist solutions*

Since externalities are social costs and benefits that market-clearing prices fail to capture, intervention may play a useful role through adding them back in. External production costs must be added to the producer's private costs incurred and external consumption costs to the private price paid by the consumer. Similarly, producers and consumers should be enabled to keep their external benefits for themselves, or recover equivalent compensation from those they spill over onto.

The Cambridge economist Pigou, an early loser in the unemployment debate with Keynes (see Chapter 3), gains some consolation from being credited with the idea of using taxes and subsidies to align private and social costs and benefits. Originally these were aimed simply at correcting departures from optimum resource allocation, and it was hoped that the taxes (set equal to, and imposed on the producers of, external costs) would roughly match the subsidies (equal to, and received by the producers of, the external benefit). Interest in Pigouvian taxes has been heightened recently by the possibility that they could become significant revenue raisers, especially if external benefits are judged too subjective to merit much concern. Pollution and congestion are especially likely targets, since taxing them is likely both to win public support and to generate large revenues, given the insensitivity of demand for most pollutive and congestive activities (e.g. city motoring) to changes in price.

This 'price inelasticity' of demand is a serious drawback for taxes aimed at deterring the external-cost activity, since it means that most of the tax will be met by higher prices (and passed on to consumers), with little reduction in the oversupply. Pigouvian taxes may also be costly to calculate on a case-by-case basis. For environmental externalities, a more uniform 'green' tax on specific polluting products (e.g. fossil fuels, landfill waste, heavy goods vehicles) would achieve lower implementation costs at the expense of less accurate internalisation, and promote the search for substitutes. But again this is not guaranteed (and may not be intended) to bring about a significant fall in the external-cost activity, and at best may merely offset (implicit) subsidies given to the polluter by other means. Governments have also been cautious over green taxes because of their regressiveness (many polluting products, such as fuel, loom large in lower-income earners' budgets), their possible impact on industrial competitiveness (unless trading partners impose similar taxes), and the danger that consumption will be displaced onto substitutes which turn out to have equally serious external costs (such as some early replacements for refrigeration CFCs, which turned out to attack the ozone layer even more powerfully).

Where the main concern is to curb the externality rather than generate public revenue from it, governments have generally sought to restrict harmful activities directly. External-cost processes may be banned or, more usually, quantitatively restricted. External-benefit processes may be made compulsory in the private sector, or taken into the public sector so that pricing can be decided with the externalities added in. To simplify enforcement, however, regulation usually applies to an environmental end-state rather than a specific process. Factories are given a purity target for the air or water they discharge into, construction firms and fairground operators an accident reduction target for their sites, and the producers of the external cost are left to decide how to keep within this limit. Where processes are regulated, it is usually with a general directive (to eliminate certain practices or install certain equipment) rather than anything specific to the firm.

2.3.2 Cost-benefit analysis

The most comprehensive approach to internalising external costs and benefits is cost-benefit analysis (CBA), usually applied to large projects before they are undertaken in either the public or the private sector. CBA aims for a comprehensive inclusion of present and future externalities in the project assessment, usually to determine whether it should go ahead, sometimes to decide which of several options is socially preferable. For a proposed private-sector project, CBA must determine whether what is (expected to be) privately profitable will also be socially profitable. For a public-sector project, there is the further requirement to show that the excess of benefits over costs exceeds that of any available alternative project.

In higher-income countries, CBA's main use has been planning large state-sector energy and transport initiatives, where it is expected that these will have to run with an ongoing subsidy, and the government wishes to know whether this can be justified by social benefits to firms and consumers. As well as considering unpriced costs and benefits, CBA often calculates the present value of future costs and benefits at a lower discount rate than that set in the private market (the long rate of interest), on the judgement that present users are placing too little value on future users' benefits from the project. In this, and in the determination of social (shadow) prices, CBA tries to evaluate externalities through implicit market signals: the social cost of an airport by depression of property prices observed near it, the social benefit of a park by costs incurred in travelling to it, the value of time saved by the average wage if someone spent that time at work, the price of a life saved by private expenditures on life insurance.

CBA has tended to be more widely applied in lower-income countries, partly because more of their large projects are funded by governments or multilateral agencies which must be seen to be accountable to the wider society (and future generations), partly because market imperfections are believed to displace private from social costs and benefits on a much larger scale. High inflation may be causing relative price distortions because of differential adjustment speeds in different sectors, or the capping of certain prices; trade barriers and an over- or undervalued exchange rate may be distorting the price of imported inputs; underemployment may mean that (rural) labour is being payed more than its marginal product, so that the 'shadow price' of labour (the opportunity cost of employing it on the project) is below its market price; imperfect capital markets may have pushed long-term interest rates a long way above the appropriate social discount rate; a project's 'linkages' may raise profits in other sectors, as well as generating its own; and the project may cause income-distribution changes (e.g. creating a small group of high-wage workers) which have social welfare implications. 'A rather strong case has now been presented for saying that a project's anticipated receipts and expenditures cannot be relied upon to measure social costs and benefits in most developing countries' (Little and Mirrlees 1968: 37).

2.3.3 *Market counterattack: are externalities serious?*

Virtually every act of production and consumption inflicts some external costs and benefits. How serious these must be before action is taken to enforce their internalisation is a matter of judgement, which must in turn take account of the costs and benefits of such action. Few market economists deny the widespread occurrence of external costs whose incidence should be curtailed, and external benefits whose incidence should be increased. Few deny that government must play some role in this curtailment and promotion. But there is a strong 'positive' case that government's role should go no further than simple rule-setting, enabling internalisation and a return to optimum allocation through private transaction within a modified market setting. There is an even stronger 'negative' case that any more detailed intervention by government generally does more harm than good.

2.3.4 *Private internalisation of externalities*

External costs and benefits are effectively products to which no price has been attached, because the recipients of the benefit (and the imposers of the cost) are able to get away without paying it. 'The notion of externalities is linked with the non-existence of markets, and indeed, one could define an externality to occur whenever a decentralised economy has insufficient incentives to create a potential market in some commodity and where, as a result, the market equilibrium is Pareto inefficient' (Dasgupta and Heal 1979: 45). A market system can deal with the problem if agents who suffer from incurring external costs, or giving out external benefits, are empowered to charge the extra cost or claim the extra benefit. Pigouvian transfers can then effectively take place within the private sector, avoiding the distortions that arise from imposing subsidies and tax.

Social costs turn back into private costs if they can be made to enter directly into another agent's cost or utility function. Similarly, social benefits can be turned back into private benefits if the agent who gives them away perceives that it is worthwhile reacquiring them or charging for their loss. Thus the owner of a holiday resort has a private interest in extracting compensation from the chemical plant which opens next to it and sulphurises the atmosphere, or even bribing it to relocate. If the plant were replaced by a film studio that drew celebrities and allowed sneak previews through the holiday-camp fence, it might be the studio that demands a fee from the resort owners.

Coase (1960) established the proposition that every social cost (and, by implication, social benefit) could be priced back into the market system through a clear and universal assignment of private property rights, provided there are no serious transaction costs in reaching a transfer-payment deal between the owners. The classic social-cost problems are, in Coase's view, simply the result of certain resources being unowned or in dispersed and uncoordinated (or non-profit-maximising) ownership. A railway company may get away with spark discharges which incinerate adjoining woods, if these are on common or uncultivated waste land. A private owner of the woods would have no hesitation in demanding compensation for the fires, or forcing the company to keep its sparks to itself.

The Coase 'theorem' demonstrates that any assignment of property rights will internalise social costs, on the assumption that transaction costs are small enough to be ignored. The assignment of property rights is, however, an action which may generate social costs of its own. It may have adverse income-distribution implications, allowing the new owner to reclaim external benefits which had a vital role in supplementing low incomes (as with the enclosure of common farmland, which may have sparked an agricultural revolution but also enriched large landlords while poorer peasants were driven off the land). It may allow potential entrepreneurs to generate income simply by threatening to start external-cost activities and getting those who would be affected to pay to keep them away. Sometimes there are strong objections to letting anyone claim property rights to an item which was previously common property, or not considered tradable. North American biotechnology companies have recently obtained patents over several natural products, including new high-yield seed varieties (royalty payments for which may put them out of reach of subsistence farmers), and even the disease-resisting genes of a south American tribe. Research and development (R&D) costs are thereby recovered and incentives for medicinal breakthroughs maximised, but with economic and social side-effects that may themselves now need to be priced.

Even without these objections, privately generated solutions will often stall over transaction costs – of negotiating the agreement, monitoring adherence to it and getting courts to try violations of it. As soon as the cost of reaching and enforcing the cost-internalising transaction structure approaches the costs themselves, assignment of private ownership rights ceases on its own to ensure that social costs will be eliminated or social benefits maximised. Effort has therefore concentrated on finding ways to reduce the transaction costs involved in putting a price on externalities. With external costs, probably the most successful approach has been to 'privatise' the quantity restrictions used in regulation. An outside agency still sets limits on the process or outcome of an external-cost activity, but leaves the market to put a price on the right to act within those limits, and to distribute the activity according to that price.

Pollution licences are among the best developed of these schemes, having already been applied (e.g. for sulphur dioxide emissions under the US 1990 Clean Air Act). Government intervenes to the extent of deciding how much pollution (e.g. tonnes of poisonous discharge) is socially/environmentally acceptable in a given period, and issuing discharge entitlements which sum to this amount. Firms must now buy their 'licence to pollute' or, if issued with licences worth less than their current discharge, must pay either to reduce the discharge or to acquire additional licences. Over time, the government may reduce the annual amounts of pollution it licences, forcing a gradual clean-up of the industry. Committed environmentalists who feel this rate of progress is too slow may put their money where their belief is by buying licences and keeping them off the market. In principle, licences combine the main advantage of regulation – achieving a definite reduction in output of products with external costs – with the main advantage of taxation, that it leaves competing private agents free to choose how resources should be allocated once the necessary change to their supply conditions has been made.

In practice, tradable licences have also carried over one of regulations' main problems, the cost of monitoring and enforcing quantitative limits. They have also come under attack for seeming to legitimise an antisocial activity, with only the very distant promise of its elimination – even though the economic infeasibility of such elimination has long been recognised in regulators' tendency to limit rather than ban. 'Permit trading schemes have an intellectual elegance that academic economists love, but they are even less common than green taxes' (Cairncross 1995: 68). The strength of the argument for leaving externalities to the private sector, with only framework-setting public intervention, lies once again in the even worse consequences that can arise if government gets more heavily involved.

2.3.5   *Interventionism's negative externalities*

The state is not entirely absent from the private-sector solutions to externality discussed above. Lawcourts are a backstop in the enforcement of compensation agreements. Governments or conservation agencies quantify and issue licences and quotas. A role for government seems to persist, if not as an imposer of taxes to align private and social costs and benefits, then as an owner which can set the internalising price while correcting any adverse distributional implications.

However, the concept of the state as an efficient externality-reducer is idealistic in at least two ways. First, it assumes superior knowledge. The government must be able to calculate the socially optimal rate of tax and subsidy, or the precise output that would be privately produced if all prices reflected social opportunity costs. Second, it assumes that public officials equipped with this knowledge will use it entirely to serve the public interest. The record of governments engaged in central planning, which in principle had unparalleled knowledge about the structure of transactions in their economy and an ideological interest in maximising social welfare for both present and future generations, is a stern lesson that neither of these assumptions is necessarily valid. Many regulations against externally costly activities were strongly worded but weakly enforced. Others were missing or misdirected because the externality was wrongly measured. State-owned firms often became the worst polluters and social dumpers as they struggled to stay in profit, even ignoring their external costs, and externalities arose artificially because administered prices bore no relation either to private or social marginal costs.

Mixed economy governments' record is equally chequered, with regulatory agencies being 'captured' by the firms they are intended to discipline, and taxes often exchanging one externality for another. Other demands on government may leave them subsidising external-cost activities (e.g. mining, intensive farming) or taxing external-benefit activities (e.g. saving and the income from it). Attention has also been drawn to the very different valuations placed on apparently similar externalities, often by the same regulatory agency.

> The Office of Management and the Budget, looking at the cost-effectiveness of a number of rules devised by the Environmental Protection Agency, has calculated that the answers range from $200,000 a life saved (for a drinking-water standard) to $5.7 trillion (roughly equal to America's GDP) for a rule on wood preservatives.
>
> (Cairncross 1995: 23)

Such findings are, in principle, a success for the comprehensive probing of cost-benefit analysis, but government-sponsored CBA has drawn economic fire from both sides. Market sceptics reject the attempt to put a price on everything, arguing that such items as human life or the survival of a rainforest, if not infinitely valuable, are at least worth more than the upper limits CBA tends to place on them (without which many projects would never gain approval). Market enthusiasts, even if they accept such quantification, tend to question government's ability to set socially optimal prices and discount rates, arguing that private agents would do the job better if it intervened less.

Many of the 'market failures' listed in support of CBA could be ascribed to state intervention – imposing tariffs, setting minimum wages or restricting capital mobility, regulating the capital market. Such measures were especially prevalent under import-substituting industrialisation strategies, widespread at the time when CBA was being developed for use in development planning, but subsequently downgraded in favour of 'outward-looking' strategies which place great emphasis on exposing the economy to world prices as a solution to domestic misallocation. CBA's attempts to anticipate future project results also expose it to the same information incompleteness problems as private decision, since it may fail to take account of other large projects also now being planned which will affect the results of this one. These projects may well be under way by other governments which keep quiet about their plans. Even if they are taking shape within the same public sector, lack of intra-government co-ordination can lead to separate CBAs which fail to take their interactions into account.

2.4　Joint products

The by-products of an industrial process are not necessarily dumped on the environment as external costs. Some take the form of other marketable products, which can be sold for additional private profit if the price more than covers the extra separation and distribution cost. Thus oil producers who once flared off their gas began to collect it for separate sale; some power plants pipe their waste heat to nearby houses; broken biscuits can be swept up and packaged as an additional line to the round and square ones from whence they came; and bus companies rent out the sides of their vehicles as advertising space.

Joint production arises whenever one production process yields two or more products in a proportion which (because set by technology) cannot be varied. A firm which selects the equilibrium output of one product (setting MRTS=MRT=MRS) will be unable (except by coincidence) to set its output of the others according to the same equilibrium conditions. Their relative market-clearing relative price ($Mx/My=MRSx,y$) will not be the technically efficient price (setting MRS=MRT).

Getting two or more outputs from one process may seem a further step towards productive efficiency and optimum resource use, but it presents two sorts of difficulty for the attainment of general equilibrium. If the proportions in which the products emerge are fixed, their ratio will only by chance coincide with that required for efficient allocation. Usually, the optimal output of one product will entail too high or too low an output of the others. Even if the proportion of by-products to core product can be varied, their emergence from the same process may make it impossible to separate their respective marginal costs, so that none can be reliably priced at marginal cost.

2.4.1   *Market counterattack: everything has its price*

The non-interventionist reassessment of external costs and benefits suggests joint production to be a non-problem. If the market can be made to internalise by-products that are harmful and initially go unpriced, it has an even stronger incentive to internalise by-products which are useful and command a market price. Joint products that emerge from the profitable production of another product (natural gas from oil, gelatine from beef) are a bonus shared between producer and consumer. Joint products that bring the main product into profitability open up (or keep alive) new sources of utility. Thus some small farms survive by turning one field into a pick-your-own operation, and affordable commercial broadcasting is made available by turning some of it into advertising space.

Since profits and utility are maximised when all products are separable, so that marginal conditions can be satisfied for each, the market offers strong incentives for breaking apart joint products. Bonds and other debt instruments offer a combination of income and capital gain, but not always in the proportions or with the relative risks that buyers want. Financial engineering has now been able to separate the two, making instruments which pay only interest or no interest at all. Yeast extract, once a brewing by-product sought mainly for medicinal purposes, now sits on supermarket shelves under brandnames that have never been near a beercan. Down on the farm, dairy cattle and beef cattle have been bred differently for excellence in their own fields, so that optimal allocation can be restored.

Joint production has generally attracted state intervention only where one of the by-products has other problematic characteristics, such as those of a public good (section 2.1) or merit good (section 2.6), which present a social case for stopping private firms putting a price on it. The state intervenes to prevent the internalisation of a social benefit, the obverse case of intervention to internalise a social cost. In other cases, even if joint production leads to allocation problems in some markets, intervention has no obvious role, since public provision seems unlikely to be any better.

Indeed, joint production appears far more of a problem in the public than the private sector. Governments tend to be chosen according to manifestos containing a wide range of promises, only a few of which may be wholly endorsed by any of their voters. State-owned industries tend to be asked to help fight inflation, create employment and generate some useful non-tax revenue, as well as filling in the missing market for which they were set up.

The bundling of products, in ways which fail to match consumers' specifications and so deny them the chance of all-round maximisation, is inherent in the political and social 'markets', where – in contrast to the economic market – it may be impossible to fulfil all agents' wishes simultaneously. But the absence of a market incentive to separate the products and separately charge for them probably worsens the problem. Even the growing trend towards marriage breakdown has been ascribed to the multiple 'service obligations' imposed by a marriage contract, whose separation (through contracts with outside cleaning and maintenance staff, childminders, lovers and even surrogate parents) may be the market society's way of keeping it intact.

2.5   Common-pool resources

A common-pool resource (CPR) goes unpriced because it came into existence naturally, and is open to all who have an economic use for it. A CPR shares the public-goods characteristic of non-excludability, but this is initially of no consequence because no one has to be rewarded in order to make it available. A problem arises when, either inherently or above certain rates of use, the CPR lacks the public-good characteristic of non-depletability. Agents then need to act collectively to hold down consumption to the sustainable rate, but their self-interest leads them to consume it as fast as possible.

CPRs comprise exhaustible resources (such as oilfields and coal seams) whose life is finite however slowly they are depleted, and renewable resources (such as forests, grazing lands, fish stocks and endangered species), whose life is finite if depletion goes above a maximum sustainable rate. Technical progress has moved CPRs beyond natural resources into such product areas as broadcasting frequencies and roadspace, where excessive depletion takes the form of congestion as too many users try to gain access at one time.

From a social viewpoint, the optimal price for a renewable resource is that which conserves the stock by restricting consumption to its increment – e.g. the amount of wood that can be chopped without shrinking the forest, or the annual catch that keeps the fish population stable. The optimal price for an exhaustible resource is initially set by the rate of depletion, but subsequently rises with the social discount rate, which equals the market interest rate provided the capital market accurately expresses the social rate of time preference. The social discount rate, in turn, captures society's assessment of the degree to which present capital accumulation out of the income from the resource, and future technical progress adding prospects for substituting it when exhausted, justify valuing its consumption today above the forgone later consumption.

The competitive market, designed to match supply and demand for flows of products which are consumed to be continuously producible, will tend to under-price CPR products, which form a fixed stock (for all time, or during their regeneration period). A CPR's scarcity, far from pushing prices upwards to ensure sustainability or optimum depletion, is likely to drive them downwards as agents compete to consume while they can. A 'tragedy of the commons' ensues which, as in the case of public goods, leaves agents in a prisoners' dilemma type situation (Figure 2.1). Society is better off if everyone restricts their consumption (co-operates) to preserve the CPR. But since any one agent who co-operates simply leaves more of the resource to be captured by those who do not co-operate, the competitive equilibrium leads to non-cooperation (unrestricted consumption) by all. A renewable CPR is thus destroyed, and an exhaustible CPR depleted too quickly.

General equilibrium models abstract from CPR problems through the treatment of all products as flows and assuming-away of externalities, in this case the negative consumption externality which leads to overconsumption and over-rapid depletion (Hardin 1968). Once the sustainable or optimal rate of depletion is reached, additional private users gain utility for themselves only by taking it away from other present and future users, imposing a social cost in terms of the long-term destruction of the resource. The rush to buy 'while stocks last' becomes a closing-down sale.

In contrast to other externalities, the problem is not necessarily solved by assigning one agent exclusive property rights to the CPR. The externality this time is an intertemporal one, so that 'internalisation' must take place through time rather than across space. Only an agent with an infinite life, or whose utility function extends to the consumption possibilities of future generations, is likely to set prices high enough to restrict access to optimal levels. Thus private watercourses can still be overfished, oil reserves run down and rainforests razed for a short-lived cash crop, if their owners strongly prefer present over future consumption, having no regard for posterity or believing it will be better served by maximising short-term extraction and investing the proceeds elsewhere.

Even if private owners could (as in the property-rights approach to externality) be trusted to price a CPR optimally for society, there may be distributional objections to letting them do so. Many CPRs (watercourses, grazing land, road space, radio frequencies) have 'merit good' characteristics (section 2.6), suggesting that access should be rationed according to criteria other than willingness or ability to pay. Many also require little or no upkeep, so that the 'scarcity premium' added to price to prevent excessive depletion is effectively a rent, whose benefit should more appropriately be shared by society than kept by one private agent who happens to have taken on the ownership role.

The need to restrict user rights while not unfairly benefiting the holder of ownership rights points to economic and social advantages in common ownership of common pools. 'Communal [land tenure] systems are characterised by a set of features which makes them attractive to those concerned with combining sustained growth of output, the alleviation of poverty, the provision of basic needs and the creation of an egalitarian society' (Griffin 1987: 80). But sharing the scarcity premium also means sharing the benefits of any private investment in improving the resource, so disincentivising such investment. Agents gain immediate advantages from working the land privately and, despite is long-term advantages for development, 'the communal sector is starved of resources, denied credit and technical assistance, and confined to inhospitable terrain' (Griffin 1987: 86).

2.5.1 Interventionist solutions

Since a free-for-all can develop if private agents compete for use of a CPR, and even a monopoly private owner cannot be relied on to price it for optimal depletion, many CPRs – especially natural resources – have come under ownership or heavy regulation by the state. Where a tragedy of the commons is already under way, the government's task is to impose consumption restraint all round so that sustainability or optimal depletion resume. Where exploitation has yet to begin, the government has an optimal control task involving the rates of resource depletion and investment; its judgement must include an evaluation of the relative merits of present and future consumption claims, via the social discount rate (Dasgupta and Heal 1979: ch. 10).

Governments also tend to step in where there is a social case for rationing CPR access on a non-price basis, as with such assets as grazing land or road space which tend to be held 'in common' until sustainable capacity limits are reached. The CPR can then be collectively financed and made available on the basis of need, in a similar way to public goods (section 2.2) or merit goods (section 2.6). This has been the main justification for state provision of manufactured CPRs such as urban roads and broadcasting wavebands, as well as state takeover of many natural resource CPRs.

2.5.2   Market counterattack: greedy government

As with their record in internalising externalities, governments' history of managing exhaustible resources is rarely an impressive one. Like private owners, politicians tend to value present income significantly higher than future income, since it enriches the current electorate and improves the revenue stream so that tax rates can be held down. The most significant case of CPR depletion being slowed by government action was probably the 1973 Organisation of Petroleum Exporting Countries (OPEC) oil price rise, when the adoption of a cartel by the world's main exporters brought the objective of revenue-maximisation into line with that of consumption-reduction. But maintaining a cartel also has the character of a prisoners' dilemma, and OPEC's price-fixing power has since declined as non-members' exports expand and members return to extracting at full capacity to maximise current revenue. In general, the depletion behaviour of state-owned resource extraction companies does not seem to have differed systematically from those in the private sector. Indeed, it was under some of the twentieth century's most all-controlling and supposedly long-lasting governments that the Aral Sea dried, Lake Baikal took poison and northern Russian farmland turned to dust.

2.5.3   Private-sector preservation

Against the public sector's patchy conservation record can be set many instances in which private agents have successfully co-operated to avert a commons tragedy and preserve their CPRs. Herders agree to leave hillsides ungrazed for part of the year, crop growers draw water from the shared irrigation system at set times (Ostrom 1982), and street traders set rules to avoid invading one another's pitches (de Soto 1989). In some cases, as in a consumption club (section 2.2.3), users pay a fee to obtain access rights and support the means for exclusion of non-members; the fee buys a certain amount of access, across space or time, and compliance is monitored by other members. In other cases a profit-seeking owner takes control of the CPR but, having an interest in its continuation, prices access sufficiently highly to ensure sustainable depletion. Thus landowners enclose commons and watercourses so that grazing and fishing can be charged for; urban developers enclose car-parking space and impose charges in a similar fashion; writers establish copyright over previously handed-down stories, and can charge subsequent users for retelling them.

Private ownership of a CPR conserves it by turning natural scarcity into an equivalent 'social' scarcity. Whereas the privatisation of a public good reduces collective welfare, because benefits once shared by all at no extra cost are now confined to one owner, the privatisation of a CPR recognises and resolves the threat of depletion. The encloser of land can (claim to) stop excess ramblers eroding it, and the private owner of paintings to save them from too much exposure to gallery heat and light. Private-ownership solutions to the natural scarcity of CPRs may, like private solutions to the social scarcity of positional goods (section 2.3), determine access by ability to pay when merit allocation might be preferable. But if merit would lead to depletion, then society may be better off if only the rich can access the grazing land, just as only the rich can afford lakeside holiday homes – relying on allocative efficiency or mobility to justify the resultant inequality (section 10.3).

Other attempts to solve CPR problems by assigning private property rights appear to have failed not because the concept is flawed, but because the allocation of rights was inappropriate. An absentee private owner, with the opportunity to reinvest income from the CPR elsewhere, may indeed encourage its accelerated depletion knowing that other profit sources can later be found. Those who use the CPR tend, in contrast, to have their long-term financial fortunes closely tied to it, and so have a strong interest in its continuation – the more so if they expect their descendants to continue in the same business. A consumer-co-operative or mutual ownership structure can then produce efficient alignment of utility-maximising and resource-conservation incentives within the private sector.

Wholly private CPR preservation tends to occur where numbers are agents in small and stable communities, where compliance is easy to monitor and dispute-settlement procedures have evolved that are recognised on all sides. Where numbers are larger or change more frequently, so that agents are less familiar with the constraining rules or less motivated (because of lower detection) to obey them, external enforcement may still be needed to restrain private-sector depletion. But here, as with the use of pollution licences to resolve external costs, the most effective method may well be to set broad limits and let the market decide the rest. Licences to drill a certain oil block, fish certain waters to a specified quantity and catch type, broadcast on a certain frequency or deliver within a pedestrian zone at certain times keep depletion to what is believed to be sustainable, are backed by enforcement and impact assessment by the issuing authority. Within these parameters, however, the re-trading and pricing of licences directs the CPR into its highest-value uses and signals to marginal users when it is time to find a substitute resource.

CPR licence trading remains an inexact science. Quotas may be set too high, through miscalculation or under pressure from an industry with excess capacity from its previous free-for-all extraction; future generations have no lobby group. Quota trading may, like assignment of private property rights to resolve externalities, cause adverse income distribution trends as wealthy buyers build up a monopoly hold over the CPR. Enforcement may prove difficult and its costs, if not charged to the CPR depleters, represent a distortive tax on the rest of the economy. But the licence approach can, as ever, be defended on the grounds that deeper state involvement might only make things worse. Allocating the right to impose external costs according to price may apear inegalitarian and defeatist, but it rarely performs worse than allocation according to success in lobbying or bribing politicians; and rarely does as much damage, at least economically, as government attempts to ban outright an activity whose complete cessation involves expenditures which might otherwise have substantially reduced or remedied a range of other environmental abuses.

2.6   Merit goods

A merit good is one which, for economic or social reasons, a society chooses to allocate on grounds other than ability or willingness to pay. Rationing on merit replaces rationing by the purse. Economically, a demand-side reason arises from positive consumption externalities. Where other agents benefit from one agent's consumption of a product, the product may be underconsumed unless provision is subsidised. Compared with merely supplementing their income, provision 'in kind' ensures that the subsidy does actually go towards achieving socially optimal consumption. (This reveals the paternalistic side to merit-goods designation – the aim is to correct for perceived unwillingness to pay, as well as inability to pay.) Where the product takes the form of an investment generating future (private or social) returns, rationing on merit grounds promises to maximise the return on the investment. Thus in health care, expensive treatments are given first to those whose survival chances are greatest, and treatments with external benefits (vaccinations, Aids tests) may be given out free or even made compulsory. Merit goods are excluded from the basic CGE model by the assumption that private consumption is shaped by private preferences alone, and limited by private budget constraints.

There is also a supply-side rationale for non-price allocation, resting on the belief that quality will suffer if producers of the merit good compete to drive down prices. This danger usually arises where product quality is difficult to judge, so that lower price due to greater production efficiency is indistinguishable (without detailed inspection) from lower price due to lower quality of provision. It is compounded when time horizons are short, so that extra sales in the short term compensate for loss of quality consumer trust and market share in the long term, a form of 'commons tragedy' applied to scarce reputation. Thus in education there is concern not to let teaching standards drop in pursuit of cost savings, and not to let examination standards drop in order to boost results to attract new students from a demographically declining pool.

The social reasons for non-price allocation reflect other assessments of need or desert which do not correlate with an agent's private income or spending patterns. Such items as health care, shelter, literacy and mobility may be regarded as basic human rights which should not be confined to those who are able to afford their market price.

Prominent examples of merit goods include the following:

1   *Basic education*, which is judged to have a positive social return (in terms of mass literacy, numeracy, etc.) even if its private returns are in some cases judged negative, given the opportunity costs of leisure or paid work forgone. Making it compulsory, as well as free, reflects a social judgement that some individuals' discount rates (rates of time-preference) are 'too high', so that they undervalue the future gains from being educated compared with the present gains from being paid (and other present opportunity costs of going to school).

2   *Higher education*, social returns (in terms of future labour productivity, knowledge, discovery, etc.) will generally be maximised if allocated to those with the highest proven academic ability, rather than those who can afford the market fees. The private returns may also be higher, but merit provision is still justified economically because the capital market may not provide private financing secured against the future income gains from being educated, and socially because it is unfair for the wealthy to buy privilege through better education.

3   *Preventive health care*, which brings external benefits in the form of infectious-disease prevention and higher labour productivity.

4   *Curative health care*, whose private and social returns relate to a range of quality-of-life factors (age, medical history, recovery prospects) largely unrelated to an individual's ability to pay.

5   *Basic nutrition*, hunger's impact on social harmony and productivity making its prevention a similar social investment.

6   *Social insurance and pensions*. Payment of welfare benefits and retirement pensions from a central government fund was mainly intended as an act of social justice. By averaging out the premium for such insurances (such as a tax payment), those at low risk of needing a payout subsidise those at high risk. The very rich will even pay more for cover which they use less if the tax system is progressive, while the very poor can have contributions made up by the state, until the tax burden becomes too heavy: the current push towards part-privatising pension provision is examined in section 11.5.3.

7   *Transport*. Subsidised public transport may reflect a social belief in the right to personal mobility, but more usually relates to the economic benefits of ensuring that people can travel to work and to consume. (To the extent that it relieves private-vehicle congestion, the subsidy may also have a common-pool resource element – section 2.5.)

8   *Housing*. The right to basic accommodation again reflects a social principle strongly reinforced by the perception of social benefits from preventing homelessness (better public health, reduced crime, better application of entrepreneurial talent). As with basic nutrition, a quality gulf between social and private provision preserves dwellers' incentives to 'trade up' from the first to the second if they can, and so prevents merit-goods intervention from destroying private incentives and private markets.

9   *Information*. The belief that certain information, although privately tradable, should be made freely available 'in the public interest' underlies the

provision of public libraries, open-access to government records, public broadcasting services, and (arguably) state subsidies to the arts.

10   *Criminal justice.* Equality before the law demands that the right to legal redress rests on the strength of the case, rather than the ability to pay legal fees. These thus tend to be defrayed, through legal aid or subsidies to lawyers.

11   *Rural post and telephone connections.* Charges for connection to and use of a network are usually averaged across all users, those cheap to connect and service (e.g. clustered city-dwellers) cross-subsidising those at distant outposts. The motive is mainly one of social justice, though it also recognises the external benefit of rural dwellers connecting themselves to the network. The need for cross-subsidy has been one of the main deterrents to privatising postal and phone services, and to breaking up their fixed-network monopolies when they are privatised; if users did not absorb the cost, governments would have to step in with a direct subsidy, or abandon the principle of universal access on equal terms.

Merit goods provision can also be part of a strategy for income redistribution, since it delivers at public expense certain benefits 'in kind' similar to state-provided benefits in cash. Rather than seeking to narrow income inequalities directly, the approach is to narrow the differences in consumption possibility that would otherwise arise from income inequality. In conventional economic terms, cash benefits are preferable because they leave the recipient some choice over how the extra income is spent; however, the external benefits from merit goods may make provision in kind socially preferable. (The paternalistic argument resurfaces here: in-kind provision may be individually preferable, where cash would be 'unwisely' spent because of incorrect perception of utility, or too high a time-preference rate.)

A further opportunity for redistribution arises when taxes are levied to pay for the subsidies or free provision of merit goods. Where existing income inequalities are judged to have gone beyond what is needed to promote economic efficiency (perhaps because differential income from 'unearned' wealth is adding to differential income due to 'earned' labour skills), merit goods provision can thus become an element in a wider 'strategy of equality' (Le Grand 1982).

2.6.1 Market counterattack: do merit goods exist?

The basic CGE model achieves its result only if all products are valued and traded by price. There is no room for non-price allocation on either social or economic grounds. Agents' preferences are judged as the best indication of what is best for them, and agents' budget constraints result from an income distribution based on optimum factor supply and property allocation. Merit goods are recognised neither in their own right, nor as a second-best solution when market-based income distribution leaves some agents without the purchasing power to meet basic needs. If they occur at all, it is as a transitory phenomenon in the very early stages of development, before growth has raised incomes all round sufficiently to let everyone buy what they need as well as what they want.

The only 'pure' merit goods that fit happily with the market system are those which form part of its framework: a policing system for trade, an open-access judiciary to resolve contract disputes, one vote each for the government that will set the provision of essential public goods. Other instances can be reclassified as cases of positive externality, common-pool resources or unavoidably collective consumption, solutions to all of which have, as seen, been proposed within the market. The economic gains from providing such products to those who cannot (or will not) pay for them can incentivise agents to find a market solution, with any state intervention confined to setting the framework and then leaving allocation to private trade.

2.6.2   *Market provision of merit goods: empowering private demand*

Where it is conceded that some consumers really are too badly off to afford products they 'ought' to consume on social justice grounds, the first-best market solution is to supplement their incomes with cash. This rolls back the budget constraint while leaving free choice over how income is allocated. If people are believed to be the best judges of their own welfare, they will spend the extra income on rectifying deficiencies in their previous consumption, in descending order of utility. This may include a larger helping of merit goods, but if consumers choose to spend the extra on ordinary consumption goods, the market perspective gives no grounds for trying to alter what they do.

If the 'merit goods' designation is made on external-benefit or paternalistic grounds, however, there may be a case for giving the income-supplement in kind rather than in cash. The interventionist solution is to provide the product free to those consumers judged to merit it, often taking production into public ownership to cope with the fact that it needs to be subsidised. The market solution is to empower consumers to demand the product regardless of their income. A clear separation of demand and supply is established, leading to competitive prices and an optimum allocation, even if the resources to express demand and supply still have to be provided at public expense.

One way of empowering merit-good demand already widely used is the issue of legal entitlements (vouchers), which (public or private) producers must accept in exchange for a specified amount of the merited product. The voucher sets the direction and total volume of demand, while leaving both sides of the transaction as much as possible to individual choice. Consumers may exercise choice over which supplier they exchange the voucher with, re-sell the voucher if they value it less highly than another product, top up the voucher with their own money if they wish to consume more than the specified amount, and save the voucher if they wish to consume the product at some future time. Producers may still be able to collect a subsidy on presentation of the vouchers they receive, but it is now profitable for supply capacity to be built up in the private sector, and its product may exceed that of (monopoly) public provision because different providers must now compete (on quality) for consumers' vouchers.

The voucher is a demand-side equivalent to pollution licences and common-pool extraction quotas: a public authority (or private consumption club) decides the minimum amount that should be consumed (by each agent, or by society overall), but then parcels out this entitlement to private consumers, who can decide the best final allocation of the merit product. Recent applications of the voucher principle include the following:

- The sharing-out of public property in eastern Europe, where most adult citizens were made eligible but special allocations were made to such subgroups as expropriated owners, war veterans, and workers whose state pensions are to be part-privatised because of budgetary pressures.
- The allocation of pre-school nursery education, the subject of a short-lived UK experiment in 1996–7, where the aim was to create demand by letting parents claim a year's provision for their offspring from any recognised provider, and so encourage increased quantity and quality of supply.
- 'Training bank' proposals, under which new workers receive a basic allowance for vocational training which they can exchange for externally accredited training from their employer or an outside provider, saving the allowance if they need it and topping it up if they want more than the minimum (merited) training.
- The introduction of a purchaser–provider split into health service provision, under which funds are made available to patients on an assessment of their medical need, and used to buy services from hospitals or clinics which compete on a combination of quality and price. (The motives for and design of such health 'quasi-markets', and related applications to school education, are considered further in section 11.6.)
- The European Union has decided that televised coverage of major sporting events has merit-good characteristics. Various member governments, and the European Commission, are preparing legislation that would keep live relays on public channels rather than costlier private pay-for-view or subscription channels. France has long considered domestically produced films to be a merit good, their consumption to be spread both through subsidy and restrictions on the import of foreign (English-language) films.

Few of these schemes have gone the full way towards the 'market' model of merit goods provision. Re-trading of vouchers may be prevented (e.g. by name-stamping) to prevent the holders re-trading them, on the paternalistic grounds that exchanging them is in their best interests. Topping-up of vouchers may be banned on the grounds that it reintroduces consumption differences based on ability to pay, which provision in kind was supposed to replace. Vouchers may be given a use-by date to assist suppliers in forecasting future demand, even though this reduces the holder's ability to time consumption optimally. The government may try to reduce the costs of the scheme by means-testing voucher issuance, to ensure that those who would have paid for the product anyway will not receive it free.

Perhaps most problematically, demand reinforced by vouchers has not automatically brought forth the required quantity and quality of supply, without additional intervention. Because demand was previously absent, or significantly below the level now introduced, government is put under the often contradictory pressures of expanding capacity to ensure sufficient capacity and competition on the supply side, and of ensuring that new and existing suppliers meet acceptable quality standards. Even where consumers enjoy strong competition for their vouchers and are well informed on where is best to exchange them, there may be adverse distributional complications. A UK experiment with pre-school learning vouchers in 1996–7 encouraged nurseries with links to primary schools to offer guaranteed access to these as a way of attracting vouchers. Some stand-alone nurseries warned they might be put out of business by this discrimination, a form of 'vertical foreclosure' which is heavily policed in private industry but in which private non-profit services had not been expected to indulge, before competition was introduced. Similar problems have arisen where doctors are turned into purchasers of health care on behalf of their patients; having been turned into profit-making operations, some practices develop commercial interests in certain health providers which may come to cloud their judgement of medical interest. Despite the quest for choice, mobility or variety limitations can lead to empowerment without enlightenment on the consumer's part, and leave government with a large regulatory task still to do.

2.6.3   *Problems of public provision: the meritorious turns meretricious*

Before methods of empowering private demand received serious study, most merit goods were treated as public goods, whose characteristics many of them (including basic health and education) share. Demand and supply were absorbed into the public sector and, usually, combined in the same state agency, which both financed supply (through state-owned hospitals, schools, etc.) and determined demand (by deciding who should get the service, or giving entitlement to everyone but making the queue).

The criticisms are also the same as those levelled at public provision of public goods. Products become allocated according to administrators' needs as much as those of customers; they are provided at inefficiently high cost because of lack of competition on the supply side, and the 'capture' of consumers by producers; many receive at public expense what they would willingly have bought at private expense; and people's tendency to undervalue what they have not paid for may depress the return on merit goods intended as (social) investments. The state as combined buyer and supplier is in permanent tension between minimising costs and maximising provision, a tension which may have contributed to the long-term tendency for public-sector deficits to grow even when the actual size of the sector has levelled off. The tension can lead to governments undersupplying the public good (as seen in the growth of health-care waiting lists) or oversupplying it (letting quality fall by expanding supply to meet demand with insufficient resourcing or adjustment time). Attempts at separating the two sides of the market within the public sector can lead to an inappropriate choice of method for funding merit-goods provision, compounding the allocation problems it is seeking to solve. For example, there is much concern (at least within them) that linking universities' funding to the standard of their examination results will, far from raising their teaching standards, drive them down by forcing faculties to drop their standards so as to hand out more degrees.

These failures usually result from inadequate information on product quality. Better-informed consumers could enforce higher standards, by complaining or shopping around, and where the product is truly important to them they have an incentive to do so regardless of who is paying. But the necessary information often remains a private product, access to which is still determined by income. The ability of higher-income households, which pay more towards producing merit goods, also to consume more of them than those on lower incomes, has limited state provision's effectiveness even as a crude redistribution device (Le Grand 1982).

2.7   Increasing returns to scale

To ensure that all equilibrium prices are positive, the basic CGE model requires that firms make at least 'normal' profit (revenue sufficient to cover costs) at the equilibrium production point where marginal revenue equals marginal costs. This is achieved by requiring that firms' average costs, as a function of output, are constant or rising in the relevant production range. In the usual 'representative firm' illustration (Figure 2.6), diminishing returns to scale cause average costs (AC) to turn upwards after an initial decline, so that marginal cost (MC) moves from below average cost to above it. Perfect competition adjusts the firm's demand function (D), horizontal to show that any amount can be sold at the market price, into tangency with the minimum average cost point, so that allocative efficiency (optimum output) and productive efficiency (lowest attainable cost) are achieved simultaneously. The firm can make 'supernormal' profit if it manages to force average costs down further, but these will be competed away as others are forced to adopt the same efficiencies.

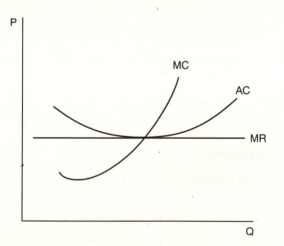

Figure 2.6 The perfectly competitive firm

Constant returns to scale, under which average and marginal costs coincide as a horizontal line, pose problems for the diagrammatic representation but can still be accommodated within CGE. Indeed, constant returns are implied by the assumption of first-degree homogeneity in the production function required to move from absolute to numeraire-relative prices (section 2.1.5), to express the marginal products of labour and capital entirely as functions of the capital–labour ratio, and to ensure that no 'excess' profit is left over when output is distributed among factors according to their quantity multipied by marginal productivity. If this third condition (Euler's theorem) were violated, CGE theory would have to explain how the excess profit is distributed without destabling the demand and supply patterns that underlie the equilibrium. Arrow and Hahn (1971) adapt the AD model to diminishing returns (and positive profits) by assuming non-marketed inputs to production which fall outside the homogeneity condition.

> But whether or not an input is marketed or held for reservation uses will depend on the equilibrium configuration of prices . . . if some factors were hidden from exposure to scarcity-reflecting market prices, then there could [be] no assurance that an equilibrium would be allocatively efficient.
>
> (Ellerman 1992: 190)

The picture worsens when increasing returns to scale (IRS) cause average costs to keep falling over the relevant output range. IRS are excluded from the basic CGE model, which must assume convexity in the production function (output rising less rapidly than factor supplies) to ensure the existence and optimality of an equilibrium proce vector. Yet economies of scale appear increasingly relevant in a world whose technologies are software-based on the production side and networked on the consumption side.

> Software has a special property: the first copy may cost millions or even billions, but the second copy is prarctically free to produce. This is the strongest possible form of increasing returns to scale . . . right-wing theorists pushing for privatisation and deregulation have seized on every case where technology has eroded IRS – but the overall trend is in the opposite direction.
>
> (Costello *et al.* 1989: 99)

Difficulties of fully accommodating IRS in later versions, even under highly restrictive conditions, has become one of the CGE model's most enduring vulnerabilities.

2.7.1   *Natural monopoly*

A firm whose plant-level scale economies deliver continuously falling costs becomes a natural monopoly, able to supply the whole market demand more cheaply than any number of competing firms producing at a smaller scale. Its demand is now the market demand curve (AR in Figure 2.7), showing that it can directly alter price by varying its output. Higher output drags down the price for the latest and all previous units, so that marginal revenue (MR) lies below the declining average revenue.

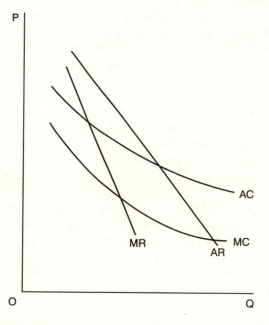

Figure 2.7 Natural monopoly

Because declining average cost means that marginal cost is below the average, pricing according to the MC=AR rule means that the natural monopolist cannot achieve the socially optimal allocation and operate at a profit. To survive, it must either set price at least equal to average cost (AC=AR), resulting in lower output and higher prices than would maximise welfare, or collect an ongoing subsidy to cover the losses through setting marginal cost equal to average revenue. If allowed to exercise its monopoly, the still lower output and higher price at MC=MR results in supernormal profit, and an even greater welfare loss than that for break-even MC=AR pricing.

Natural monopolies mainly involve 'network' products with very high fixed costs but low variable costs (and hence low marginal costs of adding extra consumers) once the network has been installed. This means some overlap with the category of public goods, even though the monopoly is here traced to cost rather than demand characteristics. Traditionally recognised cases include postal services, telecommunications, roads, railways, electricity generation and distribution, water and gas supply. A few non-network industries with significant economies of scale, such as automobiles and microchips, have also been recognised at certain times by certain governments as 'natural' near-monopolies, and encouraged to amalgamate in pursuit of efficiency savings. In markets for more sophisticated products, monopoly can arise not just from sole possession of the product, but also from sole possession of relevant facts about the product. 'The separation of purchaser and provider means that the purchaser has less information about the technology and conditions of production than the provider. The provider can exploit this to extract rent from the purchaser and/or engage in inefficient production' (Propper 1993: 35–6).

To get established, a network requires standardisation of the channels down which its traffic travels and the gateways by which that traffic enters and leaves. The pioneers of network and other increasing-returns technology assumed that the quest for efficiency would automatically impose the best standard.

> The standardisation which it was believed mass production demanded was welcomed by modernists. Not only did it imply system, order and rational-ist . . . The anonymity of these chosen designs was to be celebrated; the designs were the result of impersonal, almost 'natural' forces.
>
> (Batchelor 1994: 95–6)

But the large sunk costs involved in connecting to a network or equipping for mass production means that the first standard to be widely adopted tends to be the one that persists, even if better standards were around at the time or become available later. VHS video cassettes, Qwerty keyboards, Windows operating systems and petrol-driven cars maintain market dominance because they are the systems round which supporting infrastructure, skills and add-on products have been shaped, not because they are necessarily the best basis for standardisation. 'Even if every player makes completely rational decisions, the end result may be the choice of an infe-rior technology' (Pool 1997: 173). Just as the 'prisoners' in section 2.2 found it less damaging to co-operate than compete, but needed external help to standardise on the co-operative solution, an industry is likely to do better from adopting even an inferior standard than from failing to agree on a standard. 'The proliferation of standards has created serious technical problems where different systems need to be connected. This apparently minor technical detail has done much to retard the development of integrated information networks' (Monk 1989: 67).

2.7.2 *Interventionist solutions*

One possible approach to natural monopoly arising from IRS is to leave the prod-uct in private hands but insist on an AC=AR pricing rule. This constrains the monopolist to earning only normal profits, but still means undersupply and over-pricing from a social viewpoint because AC>MC. The government can try to restrict these monopoly profits by limiting the firm's rate of return, but can be dif-ficult to measure (especially with multi-product operations). Return regulation also raises the danger that firms will drag their feet on cost-reducing innovations, or overinvest (Averch and Johnson 1962), so as to keep their profits below the speci-fied ceiling.

In general the favoured alternative has been to stick to MC=AR pricing and subsidise the monopolist for the loss incurred. With networks, this can usually be justified on the grounds that the charge on competitive firms to finance the subsidy is outweighed by the cost savings they achieve from optimal provision of network services. Natural monopolies have thus tended to be left in the hands of heavily regulated private suppliers or, where their products are also public goods, taken into public ownership.

For network products, regulation includes the setting of a standard for the network's channels and interconnections so that agents supplying and using it experience no barriers to entry or discriminatory costs. The Global System for Mobile (GSM) cellular phone protocol, air traffic control, and the European 4ft 8.5in railway gauge are among centrally imposed standards that have helped networks expand, refocusing competition on the services carried rather than the carrier.

> Each of us ends up placing bets on which technology or software will be the most popular and used the most often . . . given the inter-connection of decisions that must occur for a standard to be set and equilibrium to be reached, it is safe to assume that technological progress will be truly realised only half as fast as technology permits.
>
> (Chakravorti 1998)

Auctioning of licences for use of the standard also allows public authorities to capture some of the monopoly rents which might otherwise accrue to the private provider of a network monopoly; although the possibility of competition for provision via a standardised network generally allows more than one licence to be issued, the risk to consumers being one of oligopoly rather than pure monopoly.

2.7.3 *Market counterattack: is natural monopoly a problem?*

Competitive market models rely on firms' costs turning upwards in an output range well below that demanded by the market, so that many profit maximisers can compete for custom, their 'given' prices being driven down to match minimum (and minimised) average costs. Natural monopoly ceases to exist, even in form, if the point of minimum average cost is reached at a fraction of total market demand, or if demand expands to bring maximising output into the increasing-cost range. Even where it exists in form, natural monopoly may have no adverse effects if there are potential entrants or substitute products waiting to move in on any departure from competitive pricing.

Some temporary monopolies are desirable for internalising external benefits and so restoring private production incentives previously destroyed by the free-rider problem. Some may even be deliberately created, as with the granting of patent protection to inventors, and of exclusive franchises to companies which promise to invest and operate infrastructure. R&D may also be likened to a natural monopoly to the extent that its rising costs lead to a net private and social loss if more than one firm pursues a particular new product or process. This is one reason for the growing tendency to promote technological collaboration between firms (Dodgson 1993), especially in high-tech industries where firm sizes are generally small.

The success of private co-operation in 'pre-competitive' research and standard-setting has been cited against the need for central co-ordination of network technologies. The disk operating system, internal combustion engine, video cassette and internet file-transfer protocol were all established privately, through the success of early providers in expanding their share of – and imposing their standard on – the market. (In the case of telephones and railway gauges, public authorities generally legislated for conformity with the dominant private standard rather than devising a superior one of their own, sunk investments in the existing one already being substantial.) Although the privately generalised standard may not be the best one, and may put its provider into a monopoly position, the monopoly can be defended on the grounds that its holders created the market they now dominate, and could still be displaced by rival networks. The 1998 US Justice Department prosecution of Microsoft was not intended to reverse their 80–90 per cent share of the market for computer operating systems, only to prevent them using this 'earned' network monopoly to establish another – over the already-established internet access and service markets.

2.7.4 *Private conquest of natural monopoly: contestability*

Even when not held in check by regulation, a supplier who appears to enjoy a natural monopoly may be forced to behave as if in perfect competition, for a number of reasons.

Competitive entry threats

Costs must still be kept as low as possible, and prices set only to cover costs, if rival producers can costlessly enter and exit the industry. Any attempt to price above the break-even level, or to let costs rise unnecessarily, will bring in entrants who can capture the monopolist's profit by undercutting it on price. The monopolist is forced either to drop costs and prices back to the competitive level (in which case the entrant costlessly leaves) or to leave the industry itself (in which case the entrant takes over but is under similar constraints from other potential entrants).

By the time of its formalisation by Baumol *et al.* (1982), this contestability model had gained credibility from recent economic developments. On the demand side, the ongoing move towards free trade (especially in manufactures) and reduction in transport costs has given many industries a new supply of potential entrants in the form of foreign counterparts, previously confined to their own national markets. Rather than regulating or nationalising a company because it dominates the domestic market, governments may now have the option of integrating with the regional or world market, so that the company can now meet only a fraction of total market demand and faces a range of ready-made competitors.

On the supply side, improvements in capital markets have improved the possibilities for financing new entry, even where a large starting scale is required because of the incumbent firm's cost advantages. The cost of exit has also been brought down, with increased opportunities to recover capital outlays by re-selling equipment (on larger, more liquid secondary markets) or by switching it to other uses (economies of scope, improved by the growing flexibility of equipment design).

Potential entrants' power to discipline a monopolist depends on even a short 'hit and run' competitive foray being profitable, by winning temporary profits through a lower price which the incumbent cannot immediately match, and preserving some of that profit even if subsequent matching price cuts force them to give up the fight.

Technological change

There are several ways in which new technology can break a natural monopoly, allowing several firms to compete for demand which previously only one (or none) could service profitably. Innovation can make alternative networks economically viable (e.g. cellphones and cable phones competing with the traditional copper-cable network). It can allow efficient production on a smaller scale (e.g. reprogrammable machine tools allowing small runs of vehicles, and 'mini-mills' small runs of specialised steel, at the same costs as the mass producers). It can remove the scarcity that creates congestion and common-pool resource problems (e.g. high-capacity digital broadcasting superseding the strictly limited analogue bandwidths). It can also bring formerly differentiated industries into competition, by making their products more closely substitutable. Thus the heavy truck (with an improved motorway system) can challenge the railways for freight business, the fax machine rivals postal delivery, and networked computers may soon challenge the services currently provided by telephones and television.

'Natural' market expansion

Even where actual and potential competitors cannot easily be introduced, either through technical change reducing efficient scale or trade-barrier reduction making way for foreign competitors, the expansion of demand over time may be enough to create space for several providers. Natural monopoly may turn out to have been a transitory, infant-industry or closed-economy phenomenon, market growth soon leaving room for several firms to produce under increasing-marginal-cost conditions.

Corresponding diseconomies

Increasing returns usually arise from a mixture of technical scale economies at plant level and organisational scale economies at firm level. While often significant from a technical viewpoint, many managers argue that they are vitiated in practice by organisational diseconomies, particularly the loss of middle-management autonomy, flexibility and initiative under a top-down, technologically driven production plan. 'Either you can adopt sophisticated, complex systems to try to manage the complication, or you can simplify everything . . . [at Semco] it's every micro-processor for itself and to hell with the economies of scale' (Semler 1992: 93). The economic problem of ever-decreasing costs may be eliminated by the managerial problem of running large enterprises effectively. Further, more dynamic reasons for ignoring technical scale economies (adopting alternative technologies or not expanding them to the 'efficient scale') are considered at the start of Chapter 4.

Where these features are not present, it may still be possible to replace old-style regulation of the natural monopoly, involving specification of the product and capping of prices and/or rates of return, by a newer form of 'market-enhancing' regulation.

Competition from within

Monopolies with no 'horizontal' competitors can still be subjected to market discipline 'vertically', if some parts can be made to compete against others. A favoured tactic with network-based monopolies is to separate the management of the network from that of the services run through it (train services, phone connections, etc.), whose monopsony position will often allow them to force competitive internal pricing terms. At the very least, such a purchaser–provider split forces more detailed internal accounting, which brings any inefficiencies to light and helps minimise costs even in the absence of outside competition.

Best practices and benchmarking

If discipline has to come from public regulation, there may be ways of letting the market decide how this should be designed. Even where geographically spaced natural monopolies cannot be made to compete directly with each other (e.g. by allowing them access to one another's networks), their performances can be compared so as to detect and eliminate any inefficiency. 'Yardstick competition' provides a market guideline for the generalisation of best-practice, helping turn the public regulator from an imposer of administratively generated commands into a transmitter of competitive signals drawn from rival markets.

From natural to sequential monopoly

Where natural monopoly cannot be eliminated, it may be possible periodically to let rival companies compete for the right to exercise it. The monopolist has to keep costs at a minimum and prices at a socially desirable level for fear of being ousted when the franchise comes up for renewal.

Dismembering into competitive parts

If all else fails and one firm must be left providing for the whole market with a public subsidy, the government can at least ensure value-for-money by submitting sub-parts of the operation to competition. There may be only one viable electricity grid or railway network, but here are plenty of places it can buy its steel supplies, vehicle fleets, catering services, etc. At its limit, such contracting-out would still leave production and delivery in the private sector, the public role being simply to finance and co-ordinate the supply chain.

2.7.5   The state's mistakes: natural monopoly becomes national monopoly

The difficulty of steering private natural monopolies problems between the unsustainable loss-making of MC(<AC)=AR and the unacceptable profit-making of MC=MR(<AR) has traditionally made public ownership a preferred alternative to public regulation of private monopoly. This was especially the case where the private firm was seen to have 'captured' the regulator, or deceived it as to true costs and revenues, and was reinforced by such systematic inefficiency dangers as Averch-Johnson overinvestment. But the difficulty of separating government's interests as natural monopoly manager from those as employment generator, inflation controller and ultimately vote-winner has tended to reverse this presumption. Especially with more market-based methods of regulation, keeping natural monopolies private may be preferred because state ownership leads to the following:

- Underinvestment, as governments pursue current spending programmes with short-term (political) benefits at the expense of capital programmes with (longer-term) economic benefits.
- Slowness to innovate, based on unwillingness to invest in innovation, inability to notice its desirability, and reluctance to allow the labour-shedding it is likely to lead to.
- Underprovision and overpricing of the product, no different from when private monopoly sets MC=MR, as the state reverts to exploiting its production monopolies as a disguised form of taxation (which was historically one of the original reasons for taking major industries into public ownership).
- An upward drift of average costs (identifiable through comparison with similar private-sector providers) as a result of the slow innovation and general inefficiency engendered by competitively sheltered, politically directed management.

While the private market may handle IRS badly, state intervention once again risks doing the job even worse. Economic analysis increasingly veers towards enlarging the market as the first-best solution to natural monopoly, regulating private monopolies as a transitional second-best until technology, improved capital markets or foreign competition come to the rescue, and direct public provision as, at best, third-best, to be mixed with market ingredients whenever subcontracting allows.

2.8   Non-natural monopoly, imperfect competition and oligopoly

Natural monopolies' profit gains from matching marginal costs to marginal rather than average revenue are at least offset by the fact of marginal costs being less than average costs. The full-fledged monopoly situation (Figure 2.8) occurs where the perfect competitor's upward-sloping cost functions meet the monopolist's downward-sloping demand. Profit-maximising output, where MC=MR, falls a long way below the minimum-cost level, and the elevated price Pm allows the monopolist significant supernormal profits. The profit-maximising monopolist undersupplies the market and, as well as capturing surplus from consumers, causes a net reduction in total surplus. There is exploitation of consumers, as well as any exploitation of workers that arises from being a monopsony buyer in the labour market.

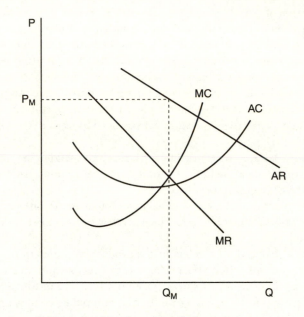

Figure 2.8 The imperfectly competitive firm: on arrival

Introducing a small number of competitors may compound the problem rather than solving it. Most theories and observations of oligopoly point towards price-setting which is not only above the socially optimal (MC=AR) level, but also insensitive to changes in demand and supply conditions. Firms are unwilling to raise prices unilaterally because they will lose customers to rivals who keep their prices down; cost increases can be absorbed out of supernormal profit, and increased demand will tend to be met at an unchanged price. Price-cutting might, on the same basis, win a large amount of new business, but firms avoid it on suspicion that rivals would follow, driving down profits throughout the industry. Indeed, oligopoly is closely associated with collusion in which, tacitly and sometimes overtly, firms conspire to keep to a price which yields supernormal profits for all.

Oligopolists' small numbers, close monitoring of rivals and knowledge of the cost and demand conditions they are likely to face are favourable conditions for a co-operative solution to a prisoners' dilemma-type joint profit-maximising problem – though this time, unlike the case of public goods provision (section 2.2), one which is likely to work against the public interest. The price established by such collusion is likely to be the maximum that deters entry by firms that can sustainably undercut the incumbents, or (where such entry is relatively easy because of low sunk costs and supportive capital markets) at least slows the entry rate to achieve optimal profits over time (Masson and Shaanan 1982).

Collusion can harden into cartel if oligopolists are able to pool cost and demand information and set price as if the industry were a monopoly, using quotas to enforce the associated output restriction. Cartels invite entry by lower-priced competitors, but these may be brought into the cartel if the resultant profit and security are favourable enough, or may lack the scale to make a serious dent in the cartel's profits. Although cartel arrangements are usually illegal, and prosecuted if discovered by competition authorities, they have sometimes been encouraged in industries (or economies) where demand is seriously depressed, because of their potential to restore prices and profits by cutting industry capacity.

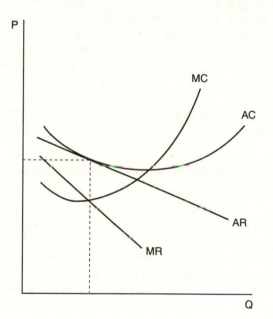

Figure 2.9 The imperfectly competitive firm: after competitive entry

Even introducing a large number of competitors may not restore the virtues of perfect competition, if each manages to retain some price-altering power by differentiating their product. This introduces some price-sensitivity into their demand function (AR in Figure 2.9), which with the displacement of marginal cost below average cost allows some supernormal profit in the short run, but with free entry may eventually push demand down into tangency with average costs (as shown), fulfilling the optimum conditions of MC=MR with only normal profit, but still doing so at a lower output and higher costs and prices than would have prevailed under the perfect competition of Figure 2.6.

2.8.1 Interventionist solutions

Monopolies without 'natural' foundations are even less welcome in a CGE framework. Anti-competitive action, inferred from high industry concentration, persistently high profits, invariant prices or explicit price-fixing arrangements, is assumed to be against the public interest, unless the firms involved can prove otherwise. Monopoly profit may be permitted for a time if it is judged necessary to finance research into future innovation, or repay the costs of past innovation; this is generally recognised in the granting of patents giving those who design a new product or process the exclusive right to use it for a number of years, or to license it to other agents of their choosing. Cartel arrangements may be allowed for a time in the cause of downsizing declining industries. One 'national champion' may be promoted for a time to ensure the stability and internal investment finance needed to build up an infant industry, especially where it is up against a global oligopoly.

Aside from these cases, governments usually work to stop non-natural monopolies forming, via cartels or over-concentrating mergers, and to break up those that have formed by organic growth. Action is also taken against practices that appear designed to eliminate competitors or deter entry in pursuit of future monopoly power, such as below-cost 'predatory pricing' (cross-subsidised by a diversified incumbent to stop one-product entrants from making a profit), or vertical restraints (threatening to withdraw custom from an upstream supplier if they agree to supply a price-cutting downstream entrant).

2.8.2 Market counterattack: are monopolies a problem?

Although aware of producers' inclination to collude, few early economists – with the notable exception of Marx – took the development of monopolies as a serious threat to efficient market outcomes. Firms were generally expected to rise and fall rather than grow inexorably; the growth and decay of plant species was a favoured analogy, reinforced by the observation that enterprises that grew dynamically under their founder-owners tended to lose momentum when passed down to the second generation. Even when certain firms carried on growing, it was assumed that markets would grow at least as fast, keeping market shares beneath a limit that could still be judged competitive. Cartels were adjudged to have a short lifespan because of their difficulty in monitoring adherence to quotas (members being able to boost short-run profits if they overproduce while others exercise restraint, the non-cooperation incentive in the prisoners' dilemma); and their difficulty in signing up new entrants, or the gradual loss of control as their membership grows.

Large firms and highly concentrated industries are now a reality, but this still does not prove that monopoly or oligopoly behaviour will occur as in the theories described, or that it will necessarily be economically damaging. Potential entry and 'contestability' have already been cited as reasons why a 'monopolist' may be constrained to produce and price competitively. Tariff removal can, in industries with low transport costs and high cross-country product standardisation, turn a large player in a national market into a very small player on the world stage; and the threat of such exposure may again force competitive behaviour on a structurally concentrated industry. Disciplined monopoly and oligopoly may, in fact, bring the best of both efficiency worlds, combining the scale economies that are absent or missed under perfect and imperfect competition with the cost discipline and lowest possible price and profit which they seem to promise.

2.8.3 Government failure: mishandling monopolies

The potential-entry discipline and natural decay of non-competitive structures may well be enough to prevent any lasting threat to the level or distribution of social welfare, temporary monopoly profits giving more through incentive effects than they take away in supernormal profits. Even if net losses do arise, outside agencies' efforts to rectify the 'market failure' may be no more successful than in their regulation of natural monopoly. Competition policy, aimed at the static welfare gains from having more competing producers, has frequently run counter to (another department's) more forward-looking industrial policy, where the emphasis is often on cartelising sunset industries, shielding sunrise-industry pioneers from too much domestic competition, and assembling midlife industries into larger units to achieve economies of scale.

The launch of a state-owned competitor, through state-sponsored start-up (justified by capital market imperfection) or nationalisation, has rarely subjected oligopolies to significant new competition, and the more sceptical observers view this as little more than bureaucrats' incapacity to run efficient commercial operations. Some of the earliest monopolies were sanctioned by government as an undeclared source of revenue, the motivations for which have grown as taxation becomes ever harder to enforce on critical electorates. State-owned monopolies and oligopoly participants may easily drift from protecting the public to profiting from it, and the prospects for raising tax from private monopolies may supplant the original mission to force them to compete.

2.9 'Well-behaved' demand and gross substitutability

To ensure that general equilibrium prices are positive, unique and re-established after any small disturbance, each market's demand and supply functions must be derived independently from each other, and subject to a number of restrictions regarding possible shape. On the demand side, each individual's utility must be determined solely by the quantity of a product they consume, utility always rising with consumption even if its increments diminish at the margin (the requirement of *monotonicity*). Diminishing marginal utility for any one product means that ever increasing amounts of it must be received if utility is to stay constant while units of another product are taken away (the condition of *quasi-concavity* in the utility function, which ensures that the equilibrium consumption bundle contains positive amounts of each product). Utility must also be a continuous function of the amount consumed, products being infinitely divisible, so that their marginal utilities and rates of substitution can always be calculated by differentiation.

Market demand for a product is usually drawn as inversely proportional to price, as in Figure 1.1, ensuring that it intersects with upward-sloping market supply to give a positive market-clearing volume and price, which 'market forces' will re-establish after any disturbance. In partial equilibrium, equilibrating price adjustment is still possible when both supply and demand are decreasing functions of price, provided the price-elasticity of demand is greater than that of supply at the point of intersection. Existence and stability of partial equilibrium are also ensured if both supply and demand are increasing functions of price, provided the price-elasticity of demand is less than that of supply. In both cases, adjustment to market-clearing is still assured because demand exceeds supply at prices below the equilibrium and falls short of supply at prices above it.

Uniqueness under general equilibrium sets a more stringent requirement of weak gross substitutability on the demand side: demand for a product must be decreasing (and that for all other products non-decreasing or increasing) whenever its price is raised. Market demand must therefore be literally downward-sloping, as in Figure 1.1. Three violations of this 'well-behaved' demand requirement have caused particular problems for this assumption.

2.9.1 Product market misconduct: Giffen goods

Individual consumers' demand for a product can be a positive function of its price over a certain range if its substitution effect, which is always positive, is outweighed by its income effect, which can sometimes be negative. While lower price would normally lead the agent to consume more, in preference to substitutes whose relative price has now increased, its effect in raising the agent's real income may lead them to a general reassignment of income under which less of the product is consumed.

Such 'Giffen' products are not easy to identify. The Victorian economist after which they are named is credited with identifying potatoes, for which a sufficiently large price drop led to reduced consumption because households could now afford to eat bread. More modern examples might include bicycles and monochrome televisions, whose demand has fallen even though relative price (including licensing costs) has fallen relative to close substitutes. Even in these cases, 'Giffen' demand for some individuals need not undermine well-behaved demand for the market as a whole, provided not too many individuals exhibit it and they do so over different price ranges. But to some critics, the mere possibility of one or more Giffen products is enough to undermine CGE, which must assume their non-existence.

> In the interests of professional stability and security, the tradition has been to accept almost any ad hoc argument which would do the job of eliminating the logical possibility of upward sloping demand curves . . . If we are free to ignore Giffen goods, then we are free to ignore the remainder of neoclassical demand theory as well. Stated another way, Giffen goods and market-determined prices do not go together.
>
> (Boland 1992: 197)

2.9.2   *Labour market misconduct: efficiency wages*

Well-behaved demand depends on agents making their utility calculations on the basis of product utility knowledge acquired outside the marketplace. Individuals' demands may become an increasing function of price if they try to use this as an indication of quality. Employers, who usually know nothing of job applicants and must expend time and cost to find out more, are especially likely to use labour's wage demands (offer price) as a quality signal. Higher wages may then become associated with higher demand if they are believed to signal higher quality, as ascertained by a previous employer or professed by applicants themselves.

The association is reinforced if a higher wage induces higher productivity, by making employees work harder or more productively, either through the positive incentive of feeling rewarded for their efforts (Akerlof 1982) or through the higher opportunity cost of losing the job or having pay docked (Bowles 1985). Raising the wage can improve employees' scope for self-improvement (e.g. by making better diet, health or training more affordable), but it may also be a compensation for the way firm-specific training or cultural adaptation reduces employees' chances of re-entering the external labour market and finding work with another employer (Marsden 1995). Wage reduction, as well as damaging internal workforce relations and the firm's external image as a recruiter, may reduce overall labour quality because the most productive workers will leave first (an example of 'adverse selection', revisited in section 6.4.4). The converse can also apply, with a rise in wages attracting applicants who are more concerned to earn money than to do a good job, but this inversion of the economist's usual incentive view is generally used only in public services which are unable to keep pace with private-sector pay. Clearly, efforts by all employers in one occupational or regional labour market to pay above the average will cause a self-fuelling wage inflation, making wage restraint a 'public good' which may require rival employers to form one recruitment 'consumption club' (section 2.2.3) or reach a co-operative game solution (section 2.2.4). In the present context, the main implication of these efficiency wage arguments – effectively an economic formalisation of the well-known pay bargaining adage 'You pay peanuts, you get monkeys' – is that generalisation of recruitment behaviour of the wage-buys-productivity type can produce upward-sloping market demand for certain types of labour over the relevant wage range.

2.9.3   *Capital market misconduct: circular valuation*

Although the 'neoclassical' downward-sloping investment demand function makes a firm-level reappearance as Keynes's 'marginal efficiency of capital', the concept of fixed capital demand varying inversely with the rate of interest has come under sustained attack from one branch of post-Keynesian theory. Traditionally a fall in the interest rate (being the cost of capital) makes it profitable to deploy additional capital stock, and so leads to a rise in the volume and monetary value of the capital stock. The adjustment is achieved through investment, so investment demand varies inversely with the interest rate.

However, the present monetary value of the capital stock is calculated by using the interest rate to discount expected future profit flows. The approach fails to distinguish between physical additions to the capital stock and upward revaluation of the existing stock when the interest rate falls.

> When we combine the two kinds of value changes that we have just considered separately, it seems that little or nothing of general validity can be said concerning the form of the relationship between the value of physical capital and the rate of interest. If we represent the relationship on a diagram with the rate of interest on the vertical axis, the curve may as well slope up to the right as down to the right, and it may alternate such slopes any number of times.
>
> (Garegnani 1983: 41)

Once the link between lower interest rates and larger physical capital stock is broken, it is also necessary to abandon the assumption that a fall in the real wage will expand the demand for labour to work with the 'given' capital stock. Real wage changes, which affect the prospective rate of return on capital, can similarly alter the monetary valuation of capital even if its physical quantity is unaltered. The possibly perverse behaviour of demand in the capital market can undermine general-equilibrium conditions, even if product demand behaves normally. 'It is not possible to prove, without resort to additional assumptions devoid of economic content (like weak gross-substitutability between all commodities), that demand and supply functions will yield stable equilibria' (Eatwell and Milgate 1983b: 2n).

2.10 Conclusion: everything needs its price

The possibilities for market failure seem numerous, and any instance could invalidate the uniqueness, stability or desirability of a competitive general equilibrium. There has been only limited progress in relaxing the conditions for the basic CGE proof without losing the main properties of the model. In a favourite analogy of its critics, it is difficult to remove the axiomatic scaffolding of competitive general equilibrium theory without the whole grand structure starting to fall down.

A three-pronged counterattack has been offered by the market perspective: denying the seriousness of the problem, showing how modifications or natural developments of the market can contain it, or demonstrating how intervention can cause damage at least as serious through government failure. The conclusion, that most of the market failure cases result from unpriced or underpriced resources – missing or misfiring markets – shows market theory choosing attack as the best form of defence. The market 'project' has underperformed, according to its sympathisers, because markets have not attained adequate coverage, or have been interfered with and prevented from adjusting. If CGE is all-or-nothing, the mission is to let markets have the all.

3 Markets as the route to full employment

Putting everything to its best use implies that everything finds a use. Full employment of labour, capital and other 'factors of production' emerges from the formal competitive general equilibrium (CGE) model through the same market-clearing mechanism that efficiently allocates their output. Factor-owners decide how much they should rationally offer at different prices; factor-users decide how much they should rationally employ; and market adjustment simultaneously decides the equilibrium factor prices (wages and interest rates), the factor quantities employed at these prices, the output arising from this employment, and the product prices that will clear the markets for these products given the incomes paid out to factor-owners and the way they choose to spend them.

Without full employment, the price of a product or factor would lie above its social opportunity cost (the loss of utility or product value in one use when it is redeployed to another), implying that its production or employment is too low for social welfare to be maximised. Without full employment, too, owners of factors and products surplus to their requirements would be unable to realise the income needed for their equilibrium expenditure plans. In any situation where factors are unemployed or products unsold at their market-clearing prices, a Pareto-improving trade is possible, from which buyer and seller would both gain.

According to CGE theory, the market system drives an economy towards full employment by constantly reducing the prices of products in oversupply and raising the prices of products in undersupply, until the vector of prices is established which allows all markets (including labour markets) to clear. Throughout, the adjustment process conforms to Walras's Law. Any excess demands in some markets are matched by excess supplies in others, so that the appropriate price adjustment will eliminate both. Since this establishes continuous full employment, the CGE also conforms to Say's Law. Any firm which sets out to raise its production will, through the equilibrium wages, interest and input costs it pays, inject into the economy exactly enough new demand to absorb the new production. Some of the income paid will be saved rather than spent, but since the interest rate adjusts to match this saving with investment, markets still clear, an overall rise in rates of saving simply shifting the production structure from consumption towards investment goods.

3.1   A tactical redefinition: 'natural rate' unemployment

In the short run, some labour may be unemployable in the sense of its subsistence needs exceeding its marginal product in any use. Some labour may be 'voluntarily' unemployed, not immediately willing to take a job at its market-clearing wage rate, perhaps because it does not regard this as matching the disutility of the work, or expects better-paid jobs to become available. Some unemployment will be frictional, involving people moving between jobs, or seasonal, where jobs provide work for only part of the year. There will also be some unemployment due to mismatches between labour demand and supply which slow down the matching of excess demands and excess supplies. This is mostly structural, with workers having the wrong skills until they retrain, and/or regional, with workers being in the wrong place until they move.

So the CGE's full employment means, in practice, a 'natural' rate of unemployment, being the residue of labour which does not want to work, is not socially worthwhile employing given its current productivity, or is undergoing reallocation as part of the system's adjustment towards better allocation. The natural rate leads on to the concept of a non-accelerating rate of unemployment (Nairu), being the rate of unemployment at which prices are stable. Workers who are 'naturally' unemployed can be brought back into employment only by deceiving them (and their employers) about real wages, through an inflation which they temporarily interpret as relative price change. Under standard CGE conditions inflation caused by money-supply growth will raise all absolute prices equally, leaving relative prices unchanged, and once they realise this agents who were voluntarily unemployed will return to being so. The Nairu also includes a component of people who would like to work at the current real wage, but whose unemployment is socially efficient because its disciplining effect on the productivity and wage bargaining of those in work outweighs the sacrifice of output.

Acceptance of a 'natural' unemployment rate may also avoid a possible objection to neoclassical marginal-productivity income distribution theory when all resources are fully employed. To measure a factor's marginal physical product by withdrawing one unit of it from its current production task would require, if full employment is to be preserved, redeploying that unit in another production task. The marginal physical product is then not the amount of production lost by withdrawal, but the difference between that amount and the additional product resulting from redeployment in an alternative use. Establishing the value of the marginal product requires multiplication by a relative price which will itself have been changed by the alteration to the composition of production. If marginal productivity is to be anything more than a thought-experiment, then under completely full employment, 'The value of the marginal product has no unambiguous meaning, since the pattern of prices, of factors and commodities, is altered by the change in productive capacity' (Robinson 1971: 56).

The natural rate of unemployment and Nairu represent market imperfections. The natural rate could be brought down if faster response to price signals accelerated workers' move to the right place with the right skills and reduced the length of their 'search' for a better wage. The Nairu could be brought down if greater competition in the labour market (especially through better information to strengthen unemployed workers' 'potential entry' threat) prevented upward pressure on nominal wages as the economy moves close to literal full employment. Both approaches regard unemployment, whether voluntary or involuntary, as a result of slow or stalled price adjustment in the CGE system.

3.2 Involuntary unemployment as imperfection 1: in labour markets

A competitive factor market should allow labour and capital providers to sell as much as they wish, driving income up to the point where work's disutility (exhaustion, depreciation, etc.) starts to outweigh it. One of economists' oldest challenges has been to explain why most market-based societies, most of the time, have some labour unemployed and some capacity idle even though their owners could expect a positive return if they were put back to work.

Once trading in the labour and capital markets has been identified as a complement to profit- and utility-maximising trade in product markets, an obvious explanation for unemployment is that factor prices have failed to find their market-clearing levels. Labour is unemployed because the wage it seeks is above what employers will pay, given its quality (marginal productivity) and their derived demand. Capital stock is idle because the interest rate on funds needed to work it is above the profit rate it is expected to deliver. Too high an interest rate can also prevent saving from being converted to investment, and so give rise to unemployment and spare capacity though a downturn on the demand side.

This price rigidity explanation of unemployment predates the formal CGE model, arising from a partial-equilibrium perspective which treats the market for labour as functionally equivalent to that for apples or ice cream. Unemployed workers can always find jobs if they are willing to offer their services for less. Their plight arises from an unwillingness to lower their wage offer, or some factor which prevents them from doing so. Prime suspects are union-negotiated pay agreements, statutory minimum wages, inappropriate skills or location, high food or housing costs which make it impossible to survive on the market wage, or an over-generous social security system (perhaps reinforced by the 'poverty trap' of tapering benefits and income-graded taxes) which give a more comfortable existence out of work than in.

The downward rigidity of real wages, and their tendency to move upwards at a faster rate than is 'justified' by labour productivity, both appear to gain strength as aggregate demand rises and labour markets tighten. Strong product demand also makes it easier for employers to finance a nominal wage rise through a rise in prices, especially when they know that rivals are under the same labour-cost pressure, and when their industry's annual wage rounds are temporally clustered. The cost of lost product demand through a higher price must be weighed against the cost of lost product supply through a strike, which also rises as the firm runs down its inventories and moves closer to full capacity working. 'Wage-push' from a buoyant labour market is the standard explanation for the remarkably durable empirical finding of a 'Phillips curve' trade-off between price inflation and unemployment, with wages and prices spiralling upwards once unemployment falls below its 'natural rate'.

Reasons why falling unemployment should add to real wage pressures are less clear. While Anglo-American theorists have tended to blame over-powerful unions for restricting labour supply, the limited change in cyclical pay patterns after extensive curtailment of bargaining rights suggests that employers' battle to recruit and retain increasingly scarce skilled labour may produce the same effect from the demand side. Union resistance to productivity-enhancing technology also tends to be anecdotal, and often provoked by lack of consultation over (and training for) its introduction rather than inherent Luddite inclinations. The relatively benign inflationary experience of some industry- or economy-centralised bargaining systems, notably in western Europe, suggests that labour unions with enough coverage for the general price implications of their demands to become visible alongside the specific wage implications, enough disciplinary power to force a 'socially responsible' settlement onto sectionally militant members, and enough bargaining power to trade non-wage benefits against wage moderation, may be more conducive to real-wage moderation (and the occasional downward adjustment) than weaker and more dispersed union systems.

Whatever its causes, however, the persistence of an inverse relation between wage inflation and unemployment reinforces the neoclassical message that the successes of aggregate demand management are likely to be transitory. A fall in unemployment, at least once the 'natural rate' is undercut, creates labour-market conditions which will subsequently reverse it. Generous welfare provision appears to compound the trade-off by weakening employees' incentive to avoid inflationary wage settlements which may price some of them out of work.

3.3   Involuntary unemployment as imperfection 2: in capital and product markets

A general equilibrium perspective alters this picture only by widening the range of markets whose imperfection might lead to unemployment. The prices firms pay for factors are also the incomes from which factor-owners buy the products of the firms, so that optimum allocation also determines income distribution. Recalling the 'second fundamental theorem' of welfare economics (section 2.1.3), any change in initial distribution means a different pattern of Pareto-efficient trades. Cutting the wage to labour or the interest rate on financial capital to its 'market-clearing rate' may therefore cause that rate to change. Adjustment to full-employment equilibrium now becomes more of an iterative process, spread across all product and factor markets as well as the one that is initially in disequilibrium.

Imperfection in the capital market may cause real interest rates to stick above the level that allows investment (an addition to aggregate demand) to match savings (a withdrawal from it). Unemployment follows as a result of deficient demand.

Keynes (1936: ch. 15) traces this rigidity to the money market, where interest – the compensation for parting with liquidity – should adjust to bring private demand for money into balance with an exogenous money supply. Since money demand takes the normal form, varying inversely with the opportunity cost of not investing, a rise in real money supply must thus cause interest rates to fall (and hence bond prices to rise) to induce investors to hold their wealth as money rather than bonds. However, a floor is placed under the interest rate by slow-changing perceptions of the long-term rate. If short (money-market) rates fall much below this investors believe that the next move will be upwards, and so are persuaded to hold any amount of additional money, for a 'speculative' move into bonds once their price had fallen. If this lower limit to the interest rate is above that needed for full-employment investment, the 'equilibrium' is one of constrained output and unemployment.

Keynes's closest followers have, however, downplayed this 'liquidity trap' as a component of his equilibrium-unemployment theory. On one interpretation, investment volatility is due less to changes in the interest rate than to changes in the volume of fixed investment undertaken at any particular rate, as long-term expectations shift. On another, there is no reliable connection between investment undertakings and interest rates because the concept of a well-behaved demand for fixed capital is logically flawed (this 'neo-Ricardian' interpretation is considered further in sections 2.9.3 and 3.16).

Meanwhile, economists more concerned to square Keynes's results with CGE have shown that capital-market influence can be as much benign as malign, adjusting to compensate for rigidities in other markets. If the real wage cannot be reduced, because nominal wage cuts are matched by (cost-based) price cuts, full employment is restored by automatic monetary expansion. The price cut means a higher real money supply and (assuming no liquidity trap) a fall in interest rates which (assuming a well-behaved capital demand function) boosts investment. Even if the real interest rate does not fall (because price cuts are assumed to be ongoing, or because of the liquidity trap), aggregate demand is restored by the rise in the real value of 'outside' money holdings (Patinkin 1965).

Real monetary expansion is, however, a second-best solution, with real wage flexibility restoring full employment at less economic cost. The danger with manipulating money supply is that governments may start to use this to drive unemployment below the 'natural' rate for short-term political purposes, by introducing inflation which fools private agents into offering more factor services and products until they recognise that relative prices have not changed. This is made worse if marginal workers have their wage expectations raised while they are temporarily in employment, so that their next spell out of work is voluntarily prolonged as they search for work at a wage above what the market can offer given their productivity.

Product-market imperfection has also been held responsible for unemployment, since monopolies reduce output compared with the same industry under perfect competition, and oligopolies tend to respond to a downturn by reducing output rather than adjusting prices (section 2.8). A shift from perfect competition to monopoly and oligopoly may therefore, *ceteris paribus*, cause a fall in output and employment and a tendency for future demand changes to impact directly on output and employment. Some oligopoly models predict a tantalising coexistence of unemployed labour and unused capital stock. From a simple welfare viewpoint there would clearly be a Pareto gain in bringing the two together to raise production. But if the unemployment is intended as a device for disciplining the effort and wage demands of those in work, and the excess capacity is intended as a credible retaliation threat should new entrants make a grab for the oligopolist's profits, firms' own economic interests are served by keeping the two apart.

Keynesian theory has sometimes veered towards an imperfect-competition explanation for unemployment, although the General Theory assumption that real wages equal labour's marginal product (the 'first classical postulate', Keynes 1936: 5) implies that firms are setting price equal to marginal cost, thus facing perfect competition at least in the product market. Even if firms are allowed a monopolistic mark-up of prices over costs, the resultant labour-market situation – with lower real wage and lower employment – still represents full employment in the 'natural rate' sense, marginal workers having voluntarily withdrawn because they are paid less. Imperfect competition may even assist the return to full employment after a labour market disturbance, since releasing firms from the obligation to cut prices in line with costs makes it more likely that workers can convert a money wage cut into a lower real wage.

The general equilibrium perspective thus widens the range of disturbances that could result in unemployment, while also increasing the number of ways in which unemployed agents can be 'priced back into work'. Unemployment may be a result of personal work-leisure choice, unemployability, or an institutional (labour-union) blockage to wage adjustment, but money wage rigidity is no longer the only mechanism. Interdependence between markets redirects attention from the theoretical existence of general equilibrium to the ways in which a competitive economy can actually achieve it.

3.4   The market system exonerated

Ascribing involuntary unemployment to price or wage rigidity essentially denies the main assertion of Keynesian theory, which is that the economy can reach a situation in which no amount of price or wage adjustment will clear the labour market – essentially an unemployment equilibrium. Keynes (1936) had argued that equilibrium merely meant stability in the circular flow of income. For a closed and fully privatised economy this required that savings, households' withdrawal from the circulation, equalled investment, firms' injection into it. Whereas households' saving was a fixed proportion of their income, firms' investment was based on their perception of likely future investment returns, based on a view of the long-term future which rested heavily on experience of the recent past. This made investment the active component in the flow, too low a rate causing a matching shrinkage in savings by reducing aggregate income. As income fell, unemployment and spare capacity would appear which, far from restoring full employment by price adjustment, was likely to dampen investment expectations and so compound the downturn. Previous theory had argued that savings automatically concerted to investment, so that only the composition of aggregate demand could change and not its level.

To market theorists, even if the reversed investment-savings relation is accepted, Keynes's argument is still underlain by price rigidity. People could get back to work if they reduced their real wages. If they cannot, because prices fall as fast as wages, the rising value of real assets will restore aggregate demand. To the 'Keynesian' prescription that government spending above its income can restore the imbalance caused by private agents spending below theirs is counterposed the view that what government adds to demand through its deficit will be offset by an equivalent private-sector surplus, households saving or the tax they know they must eventually pay to service and repay the government's debt (Barro 1974). State intervention would impede rather than assist the adjustment of markets, and the 'automatic' return to full employment.

The defeat of Keynesian policy was more a result of its own difficulty in correcting the market's deficiencies than of the market rediscovering self-correction. After two decades during which aggregate demand management appeared to keep the economy at full employment, a firm link between unemployment and wage growth explaining the accompanying rate of inflation, interventions began to draw only the inflation. Defenders of the 'neoclassical' theory, of which Keynes had tried to dispose, saw vindication for the view that past interventions had been tricking agents into abandoning (temporarily) their voluntary unemployment rather than curing involuntary unempoyment. However, the price rigidity arguments drawn from partial equilibrium analysis to support this view do not convert easily to the general equilibrium context in which neoclassical macroeconomic arguments proceed. Keynes's intuition, that unemployment can still occur when all prices are flexible, will return, in two distinct guises, once the problems of moving from existence to attainment of general equilibrium have been addressed.

3.5 Getting into equilibrium: the too-invisible hand

Price adjustment in one market involves separate decisions by each of the producers and consumers there, co-ordinated by what the market tells them about other agents' behaviour. Agents take market prices as given when forming their utility or profit expectations, but the actions they take as a result alters industry output and raises price. Provided demand and supply are well behaved, excess supply pulls prices down and excess demand lifts them up. Using Boland's (1992) terminology, excess supply can be given a Walrasian interpretation (supply exceeds demand at the non-equilibrium price initially offered in the market) or a Marshallian interpretation (supply price exceeds demand price at the non-equilibrium quantity initially brought to the market). Under Walrasian adjustment, competing suppliers will battle to undercut one another until market price has fallen to the equilibrium, with some supply withdrawn and some additional demand attracted until quantity is consistent with this price. Under Marshallian adjustment, marginal suppliers unwilling to sell their output at the market price will start to withdraw, others start reducing their supply price, while demand price rises in response to the falling supply until quantity has adjusted to the equilibrium price.

These conclusions are drawn on the assumption that conditions in other markets stay the same. This implies a sequential determination of equilibrium prices, however, whereas under CGE these are determined simultaneously. The step from proving the existence of an equilibrium price vector to showing how the economy attains it has not proved an easy one to take.

Even if full employment does not depend on it, perfect competition enters the CGE's optimum allocation properties by ensuring that the 'representative' firm's price just covers marginal costs at the point of minimum average cost (Figure 2.6). The firm must accept whatever price results from industry supply and demand. All agents under CGE are 'price takers', too small to influence market price through a unilateral change in output.

> In the models of the theorists such as Arrow, Debreu and Hahn, which are the focal influences in general equilibrium theory, not just households but firms are assumed to act as price taker. These models are exactly applicable only to agriculture, forestry, fishing and part of the mining sector, industries whose outputs account at the very most for 20% of GDP in most modern economies.
>
> (Morishima 1992: 70)

The partial-equilibrium intuition is that any price disequilibrium will cause all firms and consumers to adjust supply and demand in a consistent direction, re-establishing equilibrium through continuous feedback between prices and quantities, achieving an adjustment for which all are responsible though not consciously planned. Any agent who could affect market price through their own quantity adjustment would possess monopoly power, and could not be expected to follow optimal pricing rules.

In general equilibrium the feedback gets more complicated because of spillovers into other markets. Increased output of one product necessarily raises that of its joint products. A change in one product's price affects demand for any complementary or substitute products. Changes in product-market conditions affect factor markets, whose adjustments cause generalised change to the composition (and possibly level) of aggregate demand. Changes in factor-market income distribution would also alter the composition of aggregate demand, if neoclassical theory did not adopt abstract from consumption externalities (section 2.3) and adopt wholly autonomous perspective on consumption.

> It is assumed that utility is acquired in a very specific manner, which does not allow for any influences arising from consumption of others in society . . . a view of the consumer which is no more than a special case . . . Yet the special case is presented as a general case.
>
> (Baxter 1988: 123–4)

With all decision-makers waiting for an aggregate outcome which is not established until they decide, an indeterminacy sets in, and arrival at the equilibrium price vector is usually ascribed to a mechanism outside the system. For Adam Smith this was the 'invisible hand', which metaphorically steered agents' self-interested actions towards the socially beneficial outcome. For early CGE formalisers it was an 'auctioneer' (named after, but not invented by, Walras), who assesses agents' trading plans and announces the set of equilibrium prices before any trading takes place. The Walrasian auctioneer is, in effect, charged with solving the simultaneous equations which comprise the CGE system, having first obtained a reliable record of the production functions, utility functions and initial endowments that underlie it. No trading is permitted until the auctioneer has announced the equilibrium prices.

The Walrasian auction involves a *tatonnement* process, the successive announcement of an (initially arbitrary) set of prices to which agents state their demand and supply responses, allowing the price vector to be revised and reannounced. The process continues until 'convergence', where the prices announced are the same as those that result when agents design their transactions using these prices. This process is similar to that now used to solve large econometric equation systems, though these can generally rely on cheap computing power not available to the classical auctioneer. CGE theory guarantees that prices will eventually converge to equilibrium by this method, from any starting-point, provided its conditions are met in full – and provided an auctioneer, or its invisible-hand equivalent, is present at the start.

3.6 Staying in equilibrium: the intertemporal dimension

Although tatonnement has remained a dominant metaphor for equlibrium price-setting, it sets stringent demands on the auctioneer, who must set prices to structure trades that keep supply and demand in balance not just across space but also through time for as long as the competitive economy lasts. This would be straightforward if agents' preferences and technologies were set for all time, and if their trades exactly reproduced the initial equilibrium prices, resource allocation and income distribution. But preferences change over time as people incur new needs or discover new pains and pleasures, technologies change as a result of innovation, and income distribution changes as a result of trading, modifying the choices made out of consumption and technology sets.

The basic (Arrow-Debreu) general equilibrium model does its best to minimise such changes, principally by keeping firms' profits down to 'normal' levels or, if they do more than break even, distributing any supernormal profit to consumers. This rules out investment, so ensuring that there is no change in the capital–labour ratio (or consequent change in market-clearing relative factor prices), no installation of new process technologies or introduction of new products (which would change relative product prices), and no growth in income that could alter existing consumer preferences or reveal new ones. The assumption of no investment impact on capacity makes basic CGE a short-run model, a status confirmed by the equilibrium price vector's failure to equalise profit rates across firms in different sectors.

In the long run, competition causes migration of firms and their fixed capital from lower-profit to higher-profit sectors, until sectoral profit rates are equalised. (Since wage rates also differ across sectors, labour might also migrate to those with higher wages if mobility and training were allowed.) Investment is the process by which firms alter their capital stock and introduce new technology, so a long-run CGE model must allow for change in the capital stock, relative prices and incomes. Unless the auctioneer is to stay on the scene and re-run the tatonnement process every time any determinant of the equilibrium price vector changes, it must offer agents a means of incorporating new price information through time to retain a Pareto optimal allocation, without departing from market-clearing and full employment. This involves supplementing the existing product and factor markets with a complete set of forward markets, allowing agents to set up their supply and demand plans (and hence know their incomes) at every future period. For intertemporal general equilibrium, the set of equilibrium prices with which trade begins must include forward prices for all resources to be traded now or in the future.

The absence of public goods – or an assumption that the private sector will eventually find ways to supply them – avoids a steady rise in unemployment and allocative distortion as demand grows for products which only government can offer. Rising income is entirely spent on products which satisfy the basic CGE requirements (section 2.1.5), sidelining government as producer or employer.

On these heroic assumptions, the auctioneer gets to the general market-clearing result more quickly than price adjustment in individual markets, since it can adopt price adjustment rules which take account of imbalances all across the economy, not just in one particular market (Arrow and Hahn 1971). As a device to establish the viability of competitive markets this must remain a metaphor, since the auctioneer taken literally resembles nothing so much as an omniscient central planner. Indeed, Lange (1936) turns the CGE model into a blueprint for the socialist economy. Reclaiming CGE for the market system requires a more decentralised adjustment process, with each market price responding to its own demand–supply balance. Yet without the device of the auctioneer, agents' powerlessness to affect market price unilaterally makes it hard to see how such unassisted adjustment can take place, unless some departure from perfect competition is allowed (Arrow 1959).

3.7   Unemployment as a consequence of disequilibrium trading

Simply launching into trade, and relying on price adjustments in individual markets to sort out the initial disequilibria, does not ensure that decentralised agents will duplicate the auctioneer's price-adjusting work. False trading, the exchange of products at non-equilibrium prices, pushes agents away from their equilibrium incomes. So, by displacing demand and supply schedules, it may cause prices to converge to an 'equilibrium' lacking optimum allocation and full-employment properties, or perhaps even fail to converge at all.

Disequilibrium trading can cause a downward spiral in output and employment if current income is a binding constraint on current expenditure. If an agent sells products or labour services for less than their general equilibrium price, or is unable to sell all they want to at that price, their income is less than would have been received in general equilibrium. Unless the agent can draw on savings, or a capital market willing to lend on the security of higher future income (an unlikely move given that equilibrium prices and incomes are not yet known) it must cut down on current spending plans to keep within the tighter budget constraint. Other agents who had planned to sell to them will now also receive less than they expected, and so reduce own spending. A downward multiplier sets in, forcing the economy into an equilibrium with less than full employment.

> Orthodox analysis does not provide a general theory of disequilibrium states: first, because it yields no direct information about the magnitude of realised as distinct from planned transactions under disequilibrium conditions; second, because it tacitly assumes that the forces tending at any instant to change prevailing market prices are independent of realised transactions at the same moment.
>
> (Clower 1965: 108)

Walras's Law is violated, because an actual excess supply of labour coincides with an excess demand for products which is only notional, given that consumers cannot match it with ability to pay. Say's Law holds, but is stood on its head: firms cut back production because demand is falling, and this cuts income and expenditure to match the lower level of output.

Clower's analysis confirms Keynes's (1936) intuition that with aggregate expenditure a fixed fraction of aggregate income (the consumption function), the circular flow of income is likely to be brought into balance by changes in aggregate output rather than changes in relative prices. A fall in expenditure, caused either by lower income (due to false trading) or a rise in the savings rate, leads to a fall in aggregate output, and workers become unemployed without any necessity for their wage to be above their marginal productivity. Subsequent analyses of trading at non-equilibrium prices have confirmed that constraints on the quantities that agents can sell may lead to a settled pattern of trading activity in which aggregate demand falls short of aggregate supply. 'Disequilibrium analysis . . . generalises the traditional theories of demand, supply and price formation to cases where, in the absence of an auctioneer, markets do not automatically clear' (Benassy 1989: 127).

Such aggregate demand failure can be prevented by detaching current consumption from current income and linking it instead to 'permanent' income (Friedman 1957), the agent's assessment of its long-run budget constraint which is assumed to be that which emerges from continuously maintained general equilibrium. Any short-run demand constraint is recognised as temporary, and prevented from transmitting through the system because agents maintain their previous level of consumption, even if this temporarily moves above their current income. The tendency for outputs to adjust instead of relative prices now looks once again like price rigidity, resulting from labour or capital market imperfection. But this again presupposes that agents' perception of permanent income is consistent with the income they receive in intertemporal equilibrium, and that they have the resources to override a current income constraint.

> The whole of traditional price theory rests on the tacit assumption that market excess demands are independent of current market transactions . . . the Keynesian consumption function and other market relations involving income as an independent variable cannot be derived explicitly from any existing theory of general equilibrium.
>
> (Clower 1965: 111–12)

3.8   Equilibrium without intention 1: evolutionary selection

If the equilibrium price vector can be neither announced beforehand by an auctioneer nor arrived at by trade among competing agents, it might still arise through some form of evolutionary selection process. Those who fail to alight on an optimum trading pattern might be squeezed out of business (the Darwinian mechanism), or induced to adopt a better pattern by imitating those who are observed to be getting better results (the Lamarckian mechanism, rejected by biologists but more appropriate to social science in which agents are assumed able to learn and adapt). One or both mechanisms could lead agents to an optimising result without their consciously optimising, hence without their being inhibited with lack of the price information needed to optimise. Non-optimising agents must adapt or die, so that optimum behaviour spreads even if initially based on ill-informed conjecture. 'Conjectures may be such that if an agent acts on any conjecture other than the perfectly competitive one, his profits will be lower' (Hahn 1989: 102).

The evolutionary explanation has obvious affinities to a model founded on competition, but strong conditions are needed if selection is to guarantee convergence to a general equilibrium.

> This may be true in a static world with perfect foresight, in which profits can be made only through the relentless pursuit of the principle of substitution. But in a world of imperfect foresight and changing technology, the Darwinian process may favour the successful innovator who operates on hunches rather than the homo oeconomicus of the more pedestrian type, the careful equator of marginal substitution ratios.
>
> (Kaldor 1978: 83)

Optimisers will prevail in the selection process only if the action that is optimal under general equilibrium is also optimal when some or all other agents are trading at disequilibrium prices. But such 'exogeneity' of the selection rule is rare in interdependent situations. If a person is selling something too cheaply because he doesn't know the true value of the product, it often pays to buy from him; even if the buyer has no use for the product, she can gain from re-selling it at a more realistic price. If everyone else is running for the exit, it may be less injurious to run with them, even if the building is not on fire. Optimising agents must be able to condition their action on correct anticipation of what actions others are taking, a computational requirement which defeats the 'as if optimal' outcome which evolution was meant to achieve.

Since agents generate their own competition, which intensifies as the weaker ones leave the scene, selection rules are likely to get tougher over time. This makes it unclear whether evolution will lead to more optimal performance, even if the optimisers survive the earlier rounds. Intensified competition might actually eliminate the best performances as well as the worst, narrowing the dispersion of performances but leaving the average unchanged. 'As play improves and bell curves march towards the right wall, variation must shrink at the right tail' (Gould 1996: 116). Even worse for the assumption of evolutionary progress, intensified competition might eliminate 'strategic' actions which sacrifice immediate optimisation so as to make more lucrative actions available later. If selection requires efficiency at all times, strategic optimisers might be eliminated before the merits of their choice become apparent. (Problems of strategy and its protection are considered in more detail in Chapter 4.)

3.9 Equilibrium without intention 2: game theory solutions

With just two competing agents, equilibrium can be reached even if one agent incorrectly guesses the other's price or quantity setting behaviour. In duopoly, for example, the Cournot model shows both firms adjusting to equilibrium output (from which neither has an incentive to depart) even though each had assumed that the other would keep output fixed. Whereas in small-numbers games of this type the resultant (Nash) equilibrium may differ substantially from the optimising (Pareto-efficient) equilibrium, increasing the number of agents can bring the two closer (Shapley and Shubik 1977). 'When there are a large number of agents of each type, the Nash equilibria of the Shapley-Shubik game give nearly identical allocations to the the the competitive allocations of Arrow-Debreu' (Geanakoplos 1989: 59).

However, agents still require full information on other agents' demand and supply plans for the relevant product before knowing the payoffs from such a game. Even then, there is no guarantee that the equilibrium reached will be the one that could be attained if agents had perfect information. In general, game-theory treatments of CGE weaken the traditional definition of equilibrium, retaining the property that agents in equilibrium no longer wish to change their plans, but losing the property that transactions at these self-fulfilling price expectations are necessarily those that ensure utility/profit optimisation for the agent and Pareto optimisation for the system as a whole.

3.10 Disequilibrium as a consequence of uncertainty

Agents forced, in the absence of an auctioneer, to trade without knowing equilibrium (current and forward) prices, do so under conditions of uncertainty. Across space, they do not know what other agents plan to demand or supply this period, and thus cannot be sure whether their own current sale and purchase plans are based on correct expectations of this period's market-clearing prices. Across time, they do not know how aggregate supply and demand for products and factors will develop, and so are equally unsure whether their own forward purchase and sale plans are based on correct expectations of future market-clearing prices.

Current-period uncertainty is a problem of communication. In the case of involuntary unemployment resulting from the current income constraints observed by Clower (1965), unemployed workers cannot persuade firms to recruit them – even at the current market wage – because they cannot persuade employers that the extra wage-bill they incur will be justified by market-clearing sales of the extra product. Workers in excess supply cannot express its excess demand until firms actually re-employ them, which they will not do unless the excess demand is signalled in advance. Communicating a credible commitment to spend the extra income would still not be enough, since firms could not be sure that the spending would go on their particular product.

Decentralised agents are held back by the interdependence of their decisions. In the current period, interdependence means that an agent's information is incomplete, relying on beliefs about the plans of other agents which are in turn conditioned on the plans of other agents, including the first. Tracking the dependence of each agent's expectations on all others' may well produce an infinite regress. Even if it does not, it is likely to produce a calculation so complicated as to run up against computational limits. Bounded rationality then replaces the normal optimising process, as agents are forced to simplify their decision so as to arrive at an answer within the time available.

Even if agents do manage to arrive at conjectures of one another's intentions that are mutually consistent, the resultant conjectural equilibrium need not have the efficiency properties of a full-information CGE (Hahn 1989). Under some conditions of less-than-perfect competition it may not even exist. A weak definition of equilibrium conjecture, as one motivating an action which the agent has no reason to change when its results are observed, can result in an equilibrium in both perfect and imperfect competitive conditions, and may even induce 'as if' perfectly competitive actions in an economy whose structure is imperfectly competitive. But such arbitrary conjectures still give no guarantee that an equilibrium exists or is unique.

An intermediate definition, under which a 'reasonable' conjecture maximises profit given other agents' conjectures, also fails to overcome these problems, because those other conjectures may not be rational. Investors in Russia's stock-market in

1996–7 profited greatly from their shared conjecture that post-privatisation prices were grossly undervalued. Those who stayed in the market as it crashed in 1998 discovered their conjectures, though temporarily consistent, were built on expectational sand. A stronger definition, requiring the conjecture to be 'correct' (i.e. fulfilled in practice), leads to general equilibrium only in perfectly competitive conditions. Once more, the price-adjustment problem means that mere existence of a unique equilibrium does not ensure that decentralised trading can bring agents to it.

Future-period uncertainty begins with the consequences of current decisions taken under incomplete information, but takes on another dimension in the absence of a complete set of forward markets. In forming future price expectations, agents must also grapple with imperfect information – about their own and others' future preferences and technologies, and the supply and demand conditions for products and factors that result. Changes to these can arise endogenously from the collective results of agents' actions (e.g. capital accumulation changing factor prices and causing preferences to change as income grows) or exogenously (e.g. preferences changing spontaneously, new inventions being made, new material sources suddenly being unearthed).

Without an auctioneer or a forward transaction structure to dispel these spatial and temporal uncertainties, the demands on agents' information-processing or markets' information-transmitting power become even steeper if optimum allocation and full employment are to be preserved through time. Instead of setting out a definite purchase and sale plan for all future periods at the start of trading, each agent must now devise a trading strategy which 'determines inputs and outputs at each date as a function of incoming information' (Radner 1968: 31).

Waiting for information to become available before taking firm decisions in later periods gets round the problems of computing endogenous changes and anticipating exogenous changes. But it adds another dimension to the CGE price vector. 'Commodities are to be distinguished, not only by their physical characteristis and by the locations and dates of their availability, but also by the environmental event in which they are made available and/or used' (Radner 1989: 306). Unless blessed with a complete set of forward markets, or the power to think through any number of decisions based on incomplete and endogenously imperfect information (and correctly anticipate any exogenously imperfect information), agents must literally set out a separate set of transaction plans for each future period under each possible 'state of nature', delaying the choice of plan until the prevailing state can be observed. The state of nature reflects the combined result of all transaction plans chosen by other agents in previous periods, plus the impact of any exogenous changes.

3.11 Price rigidity as a consequence of uncertainty

Even if complete forward markets were to eliminate future-period uncertainty, by assuring agents of the prices and quantities they could expect to buy and sell at later dates, present-period uncertainty would still arise through competing agents' problems of communication. Traders are left with imperfect information about the quality of the products on offer, and incomplete information about the intentions of those who are offering them. This raises the possibility of price rigidity which has nothing to do with any institutional barriers or perverse expectations, but merely reflects agents' caution when trading in products of which they lack full knowledge. Failing to trade can do as much damage to the CGE's optimum allocation and full employment properties as trading at disequilibrium prices. But without full information about the resources they are dealing with, consumers and firms may fail miss out on transactions which it would have been mutually beneficial (and Pareto optimal) to conduct.

In an influential example of information asymmetries in the product market, Akerlof (1970) shows that certain welfare-enhancing transactions (in this case of second-hand cars) may not take place in the market, because the seller cannot persuade the buyer that the vehicle has no hidden defects making it worth less than the advertised price. The price that would permit a transaction under perfect information is too high for the buyer who, knowing less about it than the seller, assumes that a vehicle for sale is more likely to be a substandard than a well-performing one. While the quality of 'identical' items will always vary, that of new cars can be expected to be symmetrically distributed around the average for that model, whereas that of used cars (whose owners have got to know them and are more likely to sell those they do not like) is expected to be skewed in the below-average direction. Transaction is likely to go ahead only if the seller accepts a discounted price to take account of the missing information, or if one or both parties incurs extra costs to fill the information gap (e.g. getting the vehicle independently checked and certified), or if the two agree to an extended relationship allowing redress if new information shows one party to have been misled.

In the labour market, employers' special problems in judging the quality of labour before hiring it give rise to several cases of likely disequilibrium trade or missed equilibrium trade. In the efficiency wage case (section 2.9.2), employment demand becomes an increasing (or at least non-declining) function of employees' wage demands, because employers see a positive link between the wage they pay and the productiviy they receive. This may arise from *ex-ante* signalling (higher-quality employees demand higher wages), or *ex-post* incentive effects (higher-paid employees work harder and are more concerned to be flexible to retain their jobs). It means that unemployed workers may not be able to price themselves into work, even if they offer their services below the market wage, because it is assumed that their productivity will be lower by at least the same proportion. Indeed, some employers may deliberately pay above the market wage, to make quitting a less tempting option and dismissal a more damaging threat.

'Insider' workers may also command a wage premium because employers know more about them, and have invested them with skills which make for a higher unrecoverable cost if they quit. Employing 'outsiders' will entail extra costs of pre-recruitment selection, post-recruitment probation and productivity loss before unsuccessful recruits can be discharged. So outsiders' offers to do the job for less may well be rejected, even if there were no labour-law restricting their doing so (Lindbeck and Snower 1985). Wage flexibility is unimpeded but, as with efficiency wages, it cannot clear the labour market because of the adverse signals that it gives. Price adjustment works only if quality information is fed into the demand function from other sources; it breaks down if price and price movement become a proxy for quality.

In the capital market, lenders encounter two well-known problems when they contemplate setting a high interest rate to compensate for lack of information about a prospective borrower. Before the loan is given, there is an *adverse selection* danger that the expectation of high interest rates will restrict applications to those borrowers who are highest on risk (chasing high but volatile returns) or lowest on honesty (with little or no intention of paying back). After the loan is given, there is a *moral hazard* danger that the borrower will take avoidable or excessive risks in the hope of getting a higher return. There is anecdotal and experimental evidence to suggest that, if the probabilities are not too adverse, agents will prefer gambling for a gain with the risk of a large loss rather than settle for a certain small loss.

Since few lenders can exhaustively establish their clients' credentials before lending, and since this still does not insulate them from moral hazard dangers after it, lenders may deliberately keep their interest rates below the market level, and deal with the excess demand by rationing credit via queuing (as a test of applicants' commitment) or merit assessment (Weiss and Stiglitz 1981). (In these days of banking-sector fragility, partly based on their difficulty in selecting reliable clients, it should perhaps be noted that long-term borrowers may have the same informational difficulties about the quality of their banks.) Once more, prices are rigid and the market fails to clear because of one agent's attempts to infer quality from the price demanded by the other.

3.12 A market for uncertainty?

The absence of a complete set of forward markets, and of full information about present product characteristics and intentions, does not automatically condemn agents to live with uncertainty or computation-straining contingent trading plans. Markets exist through which agents can reduce or transfer their uncertainty, swapping a variable prospect for a fixed one of lower mean but lower variance, or paying a fixed price to limit the consequences of an adverse future event. Thus an agent can hedge against unpredictable movements in relative prices, insure against future loss of earnings through unemployment or the collapse of planned trades, or purchase options to buy or sell a product conditional on certain future conditions prevailing.

Such trade in uncertainty is made possible by agents who find it profitable to purchase risk from others, or (equivalently) to sell them insurance cover for a predetermined fee. Specialist risktakers aim to profit from the transaction by assembling risks into a balanced portfolio, whose pooled variance is less than that of the outcomes taken separately. Risk-spreading may work because of complementarity (one risk's negative outcome being another risk's positive outcome), or lack of correlation under given future states of the world (the same low-covariance outcome that investors use to reduce portfolio variance). Alternatively, specialist risktakers may simply believe that they know more about the likely outcomes than the risk-seller, or may derive utility from taking risks.

Whatever their motive, the existence of these 'marketmakers' allows others to sell risks (or buy relief from risks) that they do not wish to run. Although the trade in 'exotic' risks (disasters, currency movements, buyer bankruptcy) tends to get attention, any act of production 'for stock', without a specific buyer lined up at an agreed price, entails a risk which the producer will try to pass on. 'Competitive markets are inconceivable without intermediaries – merchants or "dealers" – who are both buyers and sellers at the same time (at different prices) and who carry stocks so as to make "a market" that enables producers to sell and consumers to buy' (Kaldor 1978: 190).

There is, however, an uneasy coexistence between those marketmakers who target income from stockholding, by charging a fixed mark-up of selling over buying price (as the charge for production-smoothing, storage, presentation, buyer–supplier matchmaking, etc.) regardless of which way the buying price moves, and those who seek capital gain from stockholding by taking a definite view on whether buying price will move up or down. Both activities have the potential to stabilise prices and reduce risk for other agents, since they generally involve the marketmaker buying when others are keenest to sell (with prices below the equilibrium) and selling when others are keenest to buy (with prices above). But both can also introduce inefficiencies. The income-oriented stockholder, whose income is proportional to the frequency of trades, has an incentive to 'churn' the market with regular upward and downward price movements which allow stocks to be accumulated and decumulated, generating charges whenever they change. The gain-oriented, 'speculative' stockholder, whose income is proportional to the magnitude of correctly anticipated market price movements, has an incentive to exaggerate these swings. Where speculators outnumber underlying traders and reach the same view about future price movements, their activity becomes destabilising, as they cluster on either the buying or selling sides of the market and destroy the profitability of trades planned to run the other way.

Further limits to this 'market' solution to future uncertainty are revealed by the tactical substitution of the term 'risk'. This implies that future transaction outcomes and states of the world, although not knowable, can be subjected to some kind of probability analysis, so that actuarial valuations can be made on the basis of expected values and risk preference. Probabilities, or related quantitative measures of relative likelihood, are essential for risk-absorption to be a reliable trade. But many future contingencies have no past precedents from which to derive probability/utility valuations and frequency-based probabilities, and give no firm foundation for forecasting outcomes or their probabilities by any other method. As with forward markets, insurance markets are likely to exist for only a small subset of the future contingencies and timescales with which agents have to deal. There is a market for risk, but not for the uncertainty of which it is only a small component.

Like the labour and capital markets, insurance markets also suffer a pricing difficulty arising from uncertainty about client characteristics. If premiums are raised too far to provide cover for large risks, the insurer risks adverse selection (of clients who are more than likely to suffer the contingency insured against) and moral hazard (as insured clients are drawn towards behaviour which makes the contingency more likely). So even where it is available, insurance may be underpriced and subject to quantity rationing. The market economy's limited ability to compensate for risks (already a second-best solution, given that many of those risks arise within the market from inadequate communication and co-ordination) and the transaction costs of transferring risks, still leaves open many cases of disequilibrium trading and of failure to conduct equilibrium trades.

3.13   Money as a defence against uncertainty

The basic CGE model establishes equilibrium prices relative to a numeraire, one of the products within the system against which other products' value can be valued. There is no obvious role in the model for money, a medium of exchange with no intrinsic value which earns no interest. The numeraire makes money unnecessary as a unit of account. Agents' success at structuring market-clearing deals, across space and through time (assuming full forward markets), makes money unnecessary as a store of value, since the mutual coincidence of wants is predetermined and there is no need to bridge the gap between purchase and sale.

Money does make an appearance in overlapping generations models of intertemporal CGE, which imagine that agents live for two market periods, supplying labour to earn income in the first and then spending it after retirement in the second (P. Samuelson 1958). Agents now need money as a store of value to transfer consumption from the first period to the second. But it is still not required as a medium of exchange unless there are appreciable transaction costs in exchanging spatially separated physical products, or a requirement on consumers to balance their budget at the end of each period so that they have a precautionary motive for holding money balances. 'Incorporation of monetary exchange tests the limits of general equilibrium theory, exposing its implicitly centralised conception of trade and calling for more decentralised models of exchange' (Ostroy 1989: 187).

Demand for money as a store of value arises in the overlapping generations model if there is uncertainty – over ability to liquidate capital assets in retirement, or being able to stay within the budget constraint at each period in a lifetime consumption plan. It arises in CGE models more generally once the assumption of complete forward markets is dropped, and agents must form trading plans on the basis of uncertain future prices. Money acquires utility as a form of postponed decision, the medium in which income is stored until information arrives showing which state-contingent trades will prove profitable in this particular market period. But while the appearance of a role for money may add realism to the CGE perspective, it does further damage to the prospects for getting into equilibrium.

3.13.1   *Money and inflation: 'neoclassical' disturbances*

The basic general equilibrium model maintains a strict separation between the 'real' and 'money' economies. Relative (real) prices reflect only tastes, technologies, initial endowments and the pattern of trades which follow from them. Absolute (monetary) prices depend on the amount of money in circulation, and monetary changes have purely monetary effects. In the traditional 'quantity equation', MV=PQ, the supply of money (M) multiplied by its velocity of circulation (V) equals the physical output (Q) multiplied by its absolute price level (P). That is, the volume of expenditure equals the monetary value of output in each market period. Output Q is assumed fixed by full employment, and velocity V by banks' and businesses' institutional payment systems. Therefore changes in the money stock M are automatically and directly matched by changes in absolute prices P.

Although monetary disturbances have no effect on the real economy in the long run, they can distort it in the short run, because of dispersed, competing agents' difficulty in distinguishing relative price changes, caused by altered supply and demand conditions in a particular market, and absolute price changes caused by a change in money supply. Confronted with an unexpected drop in money supply (or its failure to grow in line with real output), firms may mistakenly believe that the fall in their product price is unique, and so reduce their output, consequently raising unemployment. Not until they realise that wages have fallen by the same proportion will they re-employ the sacked workers and return to equilibrium output. Likewise, unanticipated inflation caused by a monetary expansion can induce unemployed workers to take jobs believing that their real wage has risen (and employers to take them on because they believe real product price has risen), causing unemployment to dip below its 'natural' rate until agents realise their mistake and reverse the transaction (Sargent and Wallace 1975).

To stop money, introduced to help agents cope with uncertainty and so stay on their full-employment equilibrium path, dislodging them from it, holders of this 'monetarist' view advocate transparent and fixed rules for monetary management. Monetary authorities are advised to set a growth target for money supply, preferably in line with, or just above, the real output growth rate, so that aggregate prices stay stable or grow at a regular low rate. At too low a monetary growth rate, unless the velocity of circulation can speed up, prices must fall to accommodate the rising real output, unemployment resulting if wages or any other price are downwardly inflexible. If money grows too fast there is inflation which, if it gets out of hand, can have equally serious real impacts. Unindexed savings are wiped out, fixed-rate borrowers gain at the expense of lenders, idle workers are tricked back into employment, and investment decisions become more error-prone as future profits and real interest rates become still more difficult to forecast.

3.13.2   *Money and inflation: 'Keynesian' disturbances*

Against this monetarist account, which regards unemployment and misallocation as short-run consequences of abnormal (unpredictable) money supply changes, there is an alternative (again attributed to Keynes, especially by the 'post-Keynesians') which sees money demand changes as a much more intrinsic source of real disturbance. Unemployment is traced to the effect of money in breaking the automatic link between saving and investment. In the pre-Keynesian model of circular income flow, saving converts to investment automatically, either because the same agents (firms) are responsible for both, or because the interest rate adjusts to keep the two in balance. A rise in the rate of saving shifts the structure of aggregate demand (and hence the long-run structure of production) from consumer goods to investment goods, but does not reduce the level of aggregate demand because investment always rises to fill the gap.

Keynes (1936) identifies a circularity in the concept of a 'market for loanable funds'. The demand for saving (to use in investment) is set by the marginal productivity of capital, which depends on a monetary measure of the present value of capital. This requires its expected future profits to be discounted, using the market rate of interest – the same rate that savings demand is supposed to help determine. Keynes's suggested alternative traces the interest rate to the money market, where it equates money demand (liquidity preference) with an exogenous money supply. This externally determined interest rate then sets the level of investment via the 'marginal efficiency of capital', the schedule of rates of return on successive increments in investment, down which a fixed investor moves until the next project promises to yield no more than could be gained by putting the money into banks or bonds instead.

The Keynesian derivation is equally circular, since money demand depends in part on the level of income, of which interest rates (via their effect on investment) are one main determinant. This pitfall in the move to general equilibrium was resolved by the General Theory restatement by Hicks (1937) in which interest rate and output/income are determined simultaneously where the loci of money-market (LM) and capital-market equilibria (IS) cross.

Having identified consumption and investment as the components of aggregate demand in a closed economy, and observed consumption to be a stable proportion of income, Keynes (on this interpretation) traces unemployment to the effect of uncertainty on the marginal efficiency of capital. This depends on entrepreneurs' perceptions of long-term profit rates, which are highly unstable because of changes in expectation of future market conditions and in the 'animal spirits' that accompany new investment ideas. It may thus be only by chance that, on occasions, the volume of investment chosen at market interest rates matches the volume of saving chosen by households at full-employment income. If investment falls below this, there is a multiplied fall in income, which restores the savings–investment equality at the lower rate of investment. Although this 'equilibrium' is below full employment, the fact that the money and capital markets still clear prevents any tendency for a fall in the interest rate to rebuild the level of investment, even if the investment demand schedule has the necessary interest-sensitivity.

Money compounds the destabilising effects of the uncertainty already observed in barter-based intertemporal equilibrium, by giving agents the option of holding their income as cash – 'generalised purchasing power' – instead of committing it immediately to current or forward purchases. 'In the Keynesian view, the organisation of a private enterprise economy incorporates a tension between the public good secured by accumulation of capital and the reason private individuals hold their wealth in liquid form' (Caporaso and Levine 1992: 53). Money is an instrument for postponing decision until further information becomes available. With it, sales can be made without equivalent purchases, violating Say's Law, and savings can be made which do not immediately convert into investment, violating Walras's Law. A rise in liquidity preference caused by increased uncertainty is one possible catalyst for the downward multiplier already identifed, in which falling aggregate demand shrinks income and saving to the level consistent with lower investment. Lapse from full employment is made possible without any monetary disturbance, and, since the expenditure constraint is now psychological, it cannot be prevented by appeal to the permanent income hypothesis.

3.14 Optimal imperfection

Whereas partial equilibrium analysis showed the importance of perfect competition to optimum allocation and full employment, general equilibrium analysis has shifted the focus to perfect information. Without full knowledge of others' intents and future events, and the necessary computing power to process it, agents are left guessing about their future income and frustrated in their efforts to sell to finance new purchases. The resultant preference for money-holding and constraint on consumption out of current income can both push the system away from equilibrium output and full employment.

There is a tendency, especially when assessing pure exchange economies in the current period only, to assume that the two problems can be solved together: full information leading automatically to perfect competition.

> The information highway will extend the electronic marketplace and make it the ultimate go-between . . . this will carry us into a new world of low-friction, low-overhead capitalism, in which market information will be plentiful and transaction costs low. It will be a shopper's heaven.
>
> (Gates 1995: 158)

Markets simultaneously maximise the speed at which relevant information reaches decentralised agents and, by summarising it in relative prices, minimise the amount of information they must process to reach optimising decisions.

But while perfect competition may produce perfect information about existing price and purchase decisions, it only adds to the problem of incomplete information when it comes to repeating or revising those decisions. If the perfectly competitive firm really faces a perfectly price-elastic demand curve that is tangential to its average costs, any fall in price will bankrupt it because costs are no longer covered and any rise in price will bankrupt it because all customers will switch to rival (identical) firms. Any rise in price will also bankrupt it because all consumers will immediately switch to a lower-cost supplier. Even if they survive an initial disturbance in market demand or supply, perfectly competitive firms can make no rational response to a change in price or the announcement of a new discovery, because they cannot know how fast and how far other firms will respond with investment in new capacity, products or processes (Richardson 1960).

The vision of a globally wired, instantly updated network supplying perfect information to consumers highlights the information-incompleteness problem for firms, and for consumers planning future purposes. In enhancing the ability of agents on the demand side to act on current prices, it compounds the inability of price-taking agents on the supply side to initiate the price changes that would lead the system into competitive general equilibrium. The interdependence of competitive decision-making means that information may never be complete across space, and this inherent lack of certainty over what other agents are doing makes it equally unlikely to become perfect across time. Alerted to the possibility of better networking and information-sharing among customers, and unification of segregated markets, driving down their profit margins by generalising the lowest price (or best price-quality combination), suppliers are also finding ways to keep the picture confusing. Where products and product qualities cannot be differentiated (e.g. through proliferation of brands, leaving buyers to guess which are generically identical), prices themselves can be differentiated. Two-part rental/user charges, different weight and volume units, different levels of follow-up service and various discount and loyalty bonuses are among techniques of 'confusion' or 'chaos' pricing now identifiable in markets where products have become too homogeneous and customers too well-informed to preserve past margins.

Information incompleteness can be reduced if agents cease to compete and start communicating information by means other than price, and because such co-operation becomes easier the smaller the number of agents. Imperfect competition, far from causing unemployment and suboptimal allocation, may now become a solution to the adjustment problem, allowing firms with limited price-setting power to substitute for the Walrasian auctioneer. 'They adjust price to eliminate any excess demand and they do not trade out of equilibrium' (Sawyer 1992: 84). As noted in the discussion of prisoners' dilemmas and related games (section 2.2), smaller groups of agents generally find it easier to attain and sustain mutually beneficial strategies, to identify any opportunistic defection from them, and to punish such opportunism (or make a credible threat to do so). As the number of competing agents falls, or co-operation and collusion among them increases, the system moves away from perfect competition but improves its flow of strategy and payoff information. The possibility of 'market power' enabling firms to become vehicles for better-informed decision is examined in more detail in Chapter 8.

3.14.1 A financial test

The limitations of perfect competition are perhaps best illustrated by those markets which at the present time are widely regarded as our closest approaches to it: the large, liquid stock and bond markets of financial centres such as London and New York. These enable continuous trade among many competing buyers and sellers, each able to buy or sell as much as they want without individually affecting prices (perfect competition), each well informed about the (homogeneous) instruments traded, the quality of the assets (companies and credit risks) that underlie them, and the economic conditions affecting those assets' performance. Agents are instantly informed of new developments through movements in market price (per-fect information), and can execute trades cheaply and near-instantaneously (minimal transaction cost). Markets clear continuously, or after very short order-matching intervals. There is an expanding range of forward markets to structure transactions through time, and derivatives markets to offset some of the risk of future trades.

Empirical proof of these markets' perfection is offered by the apparently unsys-tematic movement of their prices. This implies that agents have already, through their transaction behaviour, priced in all the relevant information already known, so that prices change only in response to randomly arriving bits of new informa-tion. A stock's 'spot' price measures the market's current assessment of its present value (total discounted future profit), while movements in the price result from the arrival of new information, or changes in traders' assessment of existing informa-tion, which alter the aggregate balance between buying, holding and selling. Although some 'rules of thumb' based on past regularities (the 'January effect', 'Sell in May and go away') seem to persist, the normally random movement of indi-vidual prices should mean that no investor can hope to make money simply by projecting from past price trends. They will have to seek new information ahead of other profit-maximising agents, or be faster or more ingenious in the way they interpret it. But if it were literally true that an instrument's current price conveys all relevant information about it, and that 'news' is immediately incorporated into it, such research activity would cease to be worthwhile. Market prices would always be the best available valuation of an instrument's discounted lifetime earnings, and those who merely act on these prices could free-ride on those who incurred the research and transaction costs which discounted the information into them. Trade on a perfectly competitive market brings external benefits, implying an undersup-ply which will undermine the perfect competitiveness.

The enduring success of 'chartists', who forecast future stock price movements through extrapolating past patterns, could be seen as a case of free-riding on those who do more systematic (e.g. econometric) calculations about fundamental values. But it also casts doubt on the hypothesis that there is nothing to learn from past price movements, as do the more recent successes of chaos theoreticians in fore-casting short-run stock index movements. Program trading, under which computers are instructed to buy or sell certain stocks solely on the basis of their price levels, is a clearer instance of free-riding on the information human traders have brought to the price.

A free-riding strategy might be imitative or contrarian; there are often short-run gains from following the crowd, even without questioning its choice of direction, but longer-term rewards from going against the market. Observed success for either strategy will tend to turn more traders into imitators rather than calculators, and the change in price patterns resulting from this rise in free-riding may well be part of the reason why such techniques as chartism – focused on the way markets respond to information flow rather than the actual information and decision that shape those responses – predict at least as well as more 'fundamental' analysis, and enjoy endur-ing success. The possibility of simplified decision being rational, the savings on 'fundamental' calculation outweighing any losses from not using it, are reinforced by the relative measures usually adopted to assess investors who choose to calculate. Professional fund managers tend to be judged by whether they beat a market index whose movement is itself heavily influenced by their decisions. If performance is normally distributed, half the class can be expected to fall below an average standard even if all perform well against some fixed external standard. None the less, the regular failure of experts in the market to 'beat the market' gives an enduring appeal to lower-cost methods of stock selection, of which the (by now very rich) monkey throwing darts at the *Wall Street Journal* is a much celebrated example.

Even the willingness to trade can, in certain circumstances, cause an information spillover which may prevent the transaction going ahead. Normally, investors with apparently identical preference functions can still be expected to reach mutually beneficial trades because stocks still have different values to them, either because they assess its future earnings prospects differently or because it has different covariances with the stocks already in their portfolios. But with a non-portfolio investment, such as ownership of a single firm, an outside agent's willingness to bid for more than the market price will suggest to the existing owner that their stock is undervalued. The bid is likely to be turned down; or, because (few hostile bids staying secret) the stock has now been identified as a takeover target, its owner may wait for a takeover battle to bring higher offers.

With information transmitted so quickly, and with agents so tempted to imitate others rather than do their own calculations, financial markets have the potential to become highly unstable. Agents can become clustered on the 'buy' or 'sell' sides of a transaction, leaving those who wish to trade against the run of play confronting an improbably high or low price, or at the limit having no one to trade with. The number of contrarians, willing to bargain-hunt on the basis of rosier growth and yield predictions or merely a sense of undervaluation, can be critical in arresting sudden slides in the price of an asset, which in a highly imitative market can otherwise snowball from one attitude-changing event or report.

The possibility that market prices are incorrect (i.e. not an accurate measure of net present value of future returns), as a result of agents concentrating on information about other agents' action to the exclusion of information relevant to actual valuation of the stock, is the main motive for refraining from free-riding and continuing to process information other than current prices and the behaviour that has led to them. Often praised for summarising all transaction-relevant information in the market price, markets actually risk undermining themselves if they do so. Some scope must be left for further profit-enhancing information gathering or processing by each agent, if they are to continue to behave in ways which steer the price towards its equilibrium level. The paradox is that it can never reach that level, or be known to have reached it, if rational action is to continue to push it towards that level.

The interdependence of decision calculation means that full information about future supplies, demands and prices may be impossible to achieve, however good the dissemination of those already announced. One or more agents are left with an information set which includes details of other agents' present or future actions, which cannot be known or even accorded a probability distribution. By preventing mutually beneficial trades, and permitting trades from which one or both parties lose, such interdependence can block the path to optimum market adjustment. General equilibrium prices can remain elusive even if they exist.

3.15   The market for information: golden goose or Trojan horse?

Information, like money, occupies an uneasy ground between being 'subject' and 'object', enabler and participant, in the market process. As a prerequisite for optimising decision by competing private agents, it belongs with other public and merit goods (defence, law and order, judiciary) among the framework elements that must be kept outside the market system if this is to work. But as a tradable resource, for whose production agents incur costs which they expect to recoup through intellectual property rights, it must be admitted within the framework like any other private product. Costless transmission of information through the price mechanism is appropriate to its role as a public good, but inimical to its role as a private product, where the inability to keep it secret or charge for its revelation threatens underinvestment in its generation and dissemination.

As with the 'market failures' discussed in Chapter 2, information's dual role led first to an interventionist response, then – when the counterproductive and second-best aspects of this became clear – to the search for a self-generated cure. In the early stages of market development, governments were heavily involved in generating and disseminating transaction-relevant information – through state-funded research facilities, libraries and communication networks, regulation to standardise quality (and sometimes prices) across markets, patent and copyright systems which made innovations freely available once the private monopoly phase ended, and the public-good provision of products requiring specially informed decision (e.g. through state-run health and education purchasing operations).

More recently, through deregulation propelled by technical changes in the form and transmission of information, production and dissemination of information has moved predominantly into the private sector. Some producers of information have learnt to internalise its benefits and so charge for it directly: consultants bill for their time, academics find industrial sponsors (with first-refusal rights) for their research, documentaries decamp to subscription-only television. Some have managed to link it to a physical product with portability, durability and excludability characteristics, as when newsagencies make their coverage available only to those who have installed the appropriate electronic equipment, and musicians and database compilers put their performances on disk. Sometimes information is provided free as a 'loss leader' designed to generate follow-up purchases, as with advisory services offered by financial product or household equipment suppliers. And sometimes the spread of information has been assisted by non-market motivations on the part of its producers, with scientists putting the acclaim of being first-to-publish above the financial rewards of being first-to-patent, and new celebrities preferring to tell the world than sell their story for a fraction of the coverage.

While this 'marketisation' of information has swollen and quickened its flow, there is room to doubt the information technologists' promise that this will lead the economy out of its information problems. As already seen, the conquest of imperfect information (about present and future 'exogenous' states of the world) does not necessarily solve the problem of incomplete information (about other agents' knowledge and motives and the 'endogenous' consequences of their action). By increasing the amount of second-guessing that agents can bring to their interdependent calculation processes, the speed with which they can react to new information and the amount of new information they react to, greater perfection may even lead to less completeness as old expectation-stabilising behavioural conventions break down. Much of the recent growth in information technology has consisted of new messages being swollen and stretched to fill new media: there is much repetition, mild differentiation, over-elaborate presentation and sheer invention in the escalating flow, as well as genuinely authentic and authenticated ideas. And there is room to doubt whether agents' ability to process information will ever grow as rapidly as the amount they receive, even though microelectronics offers stimulus to both. The ratio between information, the stream of detail that washes around us, and knowledge, the part of that flow that we have actually processed and assimilated, seems set to rise inexorably for as long as random access memory-power keeps to its exponential curve.

Just as perfect competition is a condition for the existence of a general equilibrium price vector which may ultimately stand in the way of its attainment, perfect information provides a means of attaining general equilibrium which may in the process destroy the conditions for its existence. This possibility is perhaps best seen in a trend already under way, towards the assembly by manufacturers and retailers of ever more detailed information about present and potential clients. At stake are two major steps towards further maximisation of profit: the presentation of the product to all those whose income or preferences might dispose them to buy it, and the determination of a price that more closely reflects their willingness to pay. The (competitive) seller's desired outcome is something akin to generalised monopoly price discrimination, buyers' demand functions being separately identified so that each can be treated as a separate market, and consumers' 'surplus' being captured by the producer as they lose the chance to buy at a generalised market price below what they would willingly have settled for.

Individualising transaction terms in this way is a significant departure from the market as defined in Chapter 1, where products are homogeneous and charged at a common, advertised price despite the diversity of buyers. While it may appear a completion of the market process, information-based 'consumer differentiation' may in practice be as much a recipe for imperfect competition as is product differentiation. Personalised dealing has the potential to destroy or greatly downsize markets which depend on cross-subsidy of some buyers by others, like insurance, and to stifle investment and innovation-related transactions by allowing the provider (of capital or R&D support) to capture all the potential proceeds from the buyer. By eroding the anonymity of the marketplace, data-based 'relational marketing' in fact gives rise to a new form of transaction with very different characteristics, considered further when consideration of non-market forms of exchange begins in Chapter 6.

One other aspect of new information systems whose 'perfection' of the market may be counterproductive is the much-discussed 'disintermediation', as consumers bypass wholesalers, retailers, advisers and financiers and go straight to producers to conclude and enact their exchanges. Where intermediaries simply act as match-makers trading on consumers' and producers' lack of communication and information, there is a clear transaction-cost saving in bringing them together by cheaper electronic means. But where the intermediary is a marketmaker, actually buying and re-selling the product, disintermediation also forgoes the bulk dis-counts they might have won by aggregating purchases, and the market price stabilisation that can be achieved by intermediate stocking and destocking in oppo-sition to the final demand cycle. The new world of dealing direct may be one in which high streets regain their non-commercialised glory, but it could also bring higher and more volatile prices or items where continuous production meets dis-continuous consumption.

3.16 Too much to adjust: overloaded prices and unemployment

Were an electronic Walrasian auctioneer finally to happen on the scene, the full-employment properties of general equilibrium might still not be assured. So far in this presentation, and in the basic CGE model, prices have been given the sole function of clearing particular markets. But factor prices in general equilibrium have two distinct roles. As well as clearing the market for factors, they generate the income which furnishes market-clearing demand for all other products. The intro-duction of uncertainty, across space or through time, gives factor prices a third function: signalling the quality of the services offered and the expectations shaping other agents' present and future plans to trade them. Product prices, similarly, now take on two functions in the presence of uncertainty: equating the present demand and supply brought about by past decisions, and conveying information relevant to the present decisions that will shape future demand and supply. In Chapter 4 a further function for product prices will be considered, that of funding the investment needed to provide the capacity for future supply plans.

The public/private nature of information has already been shown to give prices ambiguities or incentive effects which can impede or prevent trading in the markets they are intended to clear. If these arguments are correct, prices may be adjustable to their 'equilibrium' levels only through violation of the very conditions of perfect information and perfect competition that is supposed to characterise that equilibrium.

A sympathetic criticism, but one that does not depend on any information problems, argues that economic co-ordination can break down because price takes two distinct forms which are falsely run together in the orthodox (CGE) analysis. Reverting to the previous ('classical') tradition, associated with Adam Smith among others, it is argued that CGE is inherently unstable because it deals only in short-run prices, those that adjust in each market period to match demand and supply. The system's centres of gravity are actually long-run prices of production, derived from income distribution and the technical conditions of supply. These indicate where market prices would settle down if released from the temporary disturbances of day-to-day trading, and it is these that the 'classical' theory of value sets out to explain.

3.16.1 An alternative 'general equilibrium' model

The derivation of prices of production begins in a similar way to that of neoclassical general equilibrium prices, with consideration of n sectors, each of which delivers a final product using inputs of itself and all other products. (Some of these inputs can be zero.) Inverting this input–output matrix solves the system for the vector of gross outputs, and the vector of prices is derived by constraining profits to be uniform, at a rate linked to the subsistence wage of labour. By using uniform profit and wage rates to close the equation system, no reference is made to market demand, whose movement simply causes period-by-period fluctuations around these 'centre of gravitation' prices. 'Prices capable of reproducing the economy exist, so long as the technological and subsistence data render the augmented technology capable of producing a surplus' (Roemer 1988: 45, of whose succinct algebraic statement of this is a necessarily inadequate verbalisation).

Prices of production represent a long-run equilibrium, but on a very different definition from the equilibrium market prices whose existence CGE theory atempts to prove. This 'neoclassical' equilibrium price vector clears all markets, but leaves profit rates to vary across sectors. The 'classical' equilibrium price vector equalises profit rates, with no particular implications for the balance of supply and demand in particular markets (Garegnani 1983). Neoclassical equilibrium prices are set period-by-period, changing whenever agents find their last-period actions inconsistent or their preferences or technologies changing. Classical equilibrium prices are set for the long period, changing only as a result of changed technical production coefficients or a shift in income distribution between wages and profits. Since prices are determined separately from quantities, on the basis of the wage-profit distribution and with no reference to demand conditions, the economy on this interpretation has no natural tendency to full-employment output even under conditions of perfect competition and perfect information.

The price-of-production concept was refined by Ricardo, redesigned by Marx and finally rescued from its labour-theory-of-value confusions by Sraffa (1960), who showed how a composite numeraire could be constructed whose valuations of other products is invariant to the wage–profit distribution. Whereas the CGE model shares the price-setting task between supply and demand, with demand tending to be interpreted as the active component ('consumer sovereignty'), the classical model (long-run) traces prices to technical conditions on the supply side, demand being little more than a validating flow set in motion by investment in fixed and working capital. The CGE is a short-run model which, as noted above, has considerable difficulty moving into the long run. In contrast, 'classical' equilibrium is a perspective on the long run, far more adapted to the analysis of growth and capital accumulation (the subject of Chapter 4) than of present-period allocation (the subject of Chapter 2).

The classical approach's implications for full employment follow from its rejection of the basis for a 'well-behaved' factor demand function, introduced in section 2.9. The tendency of any distributional change (between wages and profits) to alter the equilibrium price vector makes it impossible to show capital demand as a smoothly declining function of interest rates, so that the capital market (and by implication the labour market) cannot be expected to clear as a result of price adjustment. To its proponents, this view raises the possibility of unemployment persisting at equilibrium, even in the absence of any price rigidity and any uncertainty. 'The level of employment is determined by the level of effective demand; a magnitude which is not susceptible to systematic variation in the face of changes in relative prices, the wage rate or the rate of profit' (Eatwell and Milgate 1983b: 16–17).

In the Marxian development of Smith's and Ricardo's work, persistent involuntary unemployment is a deliberate device in the hands of capitalists to keep the remaining workforce disciplined and prevent wages moving above subsistence. In its neo-Ricardian development it is the accidental consequence of the flaw in neo-classical CGE, which Keynes proposed solving through the variation of government spending or the socialisation of investment. Price rigidity, uncertainty and liquidity traps are seen as conceptual detours used to sideline the General Theory as an imperfection in the CGE framework, when it actually points to a fundamental flaw in the belief that a stable and unique short-run market clearing price vector can even exist. If the argument over 'logical priority' of distribution over allocation is accepted, classical theory shows that unemployment can appear at equilibrium with no 'disequilibrium' trading due either to price inflexibility or informational imperfection.

3.17 Conclusion: overworked prices, underworked labour

Adjusting prices to clear all markets presents an additional set of problems for the decentralised economy, on top of those encountered in establishing a unique set of equilibrium prices to adjust to. Lack of information and co-ordination can cause aggregate demand to lapse from the rate needed to validate agents' supply choices, with the introduction of money as an uncertainty-reducing device only compounding the problem as spending and saving decisions are postponed. Even in the absence of uncertainty, and of any wage or price rigidity, unemployment can arise because of the unclear link between lower wages and higher employment demand. The dependence of equilibrium relative prices on the initial distribution of income reverses the normally perceived link between distribution and employment levels.

However, any unemployment that results will still tend to appear to follow from the real wage being stuck above its equilibrium level. With prices acting to determine income and signal quality as well as to balance demand and supply, adjustment to equilibrium across a set of interdependent markets may be delayed or prevented indefinitely. Getting into equilibrium may require an imposed price-setting mechanism not available under perfect competition, and a consistency of expectations not attainable with less than perfect information. Expanding the number of markets to ensure the general equilibrium's existence may even add to the problems of attaining and retaining it. Destabilisation seems inherent in a market system which allows for changes in capacity through investment and tastes and technology through innovation. The need is revealed for a more dynamic perspective on adjustment, in which the market's ability to improve allocational possibilities with a minimum of information for decision eclipses its ability to optimise current allocation when provided with the maximum.

4 Markets as engines of growth

Superior ways of sharing count for little if there is not enough to go round. Squandering matters less as scarcity recedes. Any difficulty the market system experiences in achieving optimum allocation and short-run full employment would be easily redeemed if it could be shown to generate faster growth. Potential for 'static' efficiency may be the competitive market model's most mathematically elegant feature, but it is on 'dynamic' performance that the system's practical virtues are judged.

Calculations of welfare losses due to monopolistic or otherwise non-optimal pricing have generally put the results at a few percentage points of national income at most. Losses from unemployment generally emerge as more substantial, especially if social costs are added to those of support costs paid out and output forgone. But the gains to be had raising resources' volume and productivity growth rate overshadow any that arise from improving their current allocation. Starting from parity, an economy growing annually at 3 per cent will take only 71 years to reach twice the national income level of one that grows at only 2 per cent – the time taken falling to 36 years if it accelerates to 4 per cent and 24 years if it attains 5 per cent, at which rate its own GDP will be set to double in just over 14 years. Official calculations of the likely income gains from European Union market integration (Cecchini 1988) relied mainly on the levelling-down of costs and prices and the attainment of scale economies. Considerably larger long-run gains have been forecast from the dynamic impact on investment, innovation and reorganisation incentives (Baldwin 1989).

The processes leading to growth – reallocation of labour, accumulation of capital and new ways of technically combining them – can be viewed as a continuation of the quest for allocative and productive efficiency, taking in firms' efforts to modify their technology sets, consumers' efforts to roll back their budget constraints, and the efforts of both to adapt to new preferences revealed as income grows and innovation proceeds. This, essentially, is the 'Austrian' view of market processes, which sees a natural progression from the static to the dynamic advantages of decentralised competition, and which is examined in the second half of this chapter.

However, attempts to introduce this progression into the mainstream 'neoclassical' market model encounter difficulties related to inadequately informed or shifting expectations about future market conditions, as Chapter 3 has tried to relate. The general equilibrium that exhausts beneficial trades and optimises current allocation is not necessarily consistent with arrangements to maximise the growth of resources. A simplified range of 'neoclassical' growth models attempts to bridge the gap between making the most now and making more later. But the mechanical fashion in which they do so runs up against history, in the form of production arrangements shaped by mistaken or modified expectations but not immediately replaceable, which eventually forces a switch back to the more organic 'Austrian' view of markets as agents of growth.

4.1 Short-run v long-run optimisation

Dynamic efficiency, the continual reallocation of resources to higher-productivity uses, might seem to follow automatically from the incentives that guide static allocative and productive efficiency. The price system encourages profit-maximising firms to begin or expand production in product areas where returns are currently high (because demand is outpacing supply), contract or close producion in low-profit areas (where demand is disappearing), find cheaper substitutes for inputs wherever possible, drive production costs down (through process innovation, scale economies and improved organisation), and launch new products in the hope of enjoying temporary monopoly until rival maximisers imitate or trump the innovation.

In practice, the translation of static into dynamic efficiency is far from automatic. Chapter 3 identified spatial inconsistencies in the transition from one-market to all-market equilibrium at a point in time. A similar temporal inconsistency can arise in the transition from short-run to long-run efficiency, again caused by information and co-ordination difficulties (now across time rather than space). The competitive pressures that enforce the best choice at one time may impede strategic actions designed to enable a better choice later.

> A system – any system, economic or other – that at every point of time fully utilises its possibilities to the best advantage may yet in the long run be inferior to a system that does so at no given point of time, because the latter's failure to do so may be a condition for the level or speed of long-run performance.
>
> (Schumpeter 1942: 83)

Some examples of this trade-off between 'continuous' and 'final' optimisation will help to identify the possible contradiction.

4.1.1 Strategic action

When undertaking something big, it is rare to go straight there. It may be necessary to move to a better starting-point, wait for more information to become available, or assemble a wider range of possible actions before choosing between them.

Sometimes these processes are in themselves a source of utility, so that each step towards the final goal can itself be a maximising action. But sometimes future gain requires present pain. Typical strategic actions are displayed by an army falling back to prepare the next advance, a driver heading south to join the northbound motorway, a courtier going hungry today to heighten the enjoyment of tomorrow's twelve-course banquet, and a partygoer using chat-up lines in pursuit of a date. More narrowly economic examples might include living on a student's (negative?) income in pursuit of qualifications commanding higher pay, incurring R&D costs in the hope of a cost-saving innovation, and pricing a product below cost so as to build up market share and drive out competitors so that monopoly profits can be captured later on.

The more significant the target, the more intermediate steps people tend to be prepared to take before making their final advance on it. Deferring gratification wins more respect over living as if there were no tomorrow and, if the strategy works, it eventually also brings more fun. Technically, the present discounted value of the results achieved by strategy is judged to exceed the value of any single action taken to the same end. The current sacrifice is measured as the utility or profit loss compared with the maximising action in the current period. The future gain is the excess of lifetime (discounted) utility or profit over the lifetime of the strategy over that from a one-off action, or a strategy with shorter horizons.

Considered in isolation, early actions in a strategy are suboptimal. But they make a wider and more rewarding range of actions available later, and/or a larger stock of knowledge with which to select the best action. Maximising choice at the early stages closes off subsequent options which, if made available, would improve the agent's long-run results. Enforced maximisation at every period need not therefore lead a system to its best results, individually or collectively, even if the selection rule does not itself alter with the changing conduct and composition of agents in the system.

Strategy may be regarded as a form of positive consumption or production externality (section 2.3), but with the external costs and benefits being inappropriable by the decision-maker by their displacement across time rather than space. To be worthwhile, a strategic act must leave open at least the possibility of reaping the later rewards it brings into prospect. Strategy protection is a way of bringing those gains forward, usually in discounted form in recognition of the uncertainty being passed to the protector, so that an agent has the means and the incentive to position for long-term gain.

4.1.2   *Cost minimisation versus adaptability*

Equipment which is purpose-built for one task will generally do that task more efficiently than other less specialised equipment. Extensive practice on this equipment, with workforce deployment shaped around it and training targeted at it, will move the firm even closer to best-practice in this particular line of production. But the sunk costs of the investment, and the costs of teaching old cogs new tricks, can make it expensive to move to new best-practices when the product or the process equipment change. US car makers which drove down production costs close to

Japanese levels in the early 1980s, through relentless pursuit of scale economies and automation, found that the disadvantage reappeared when it came to updating the products and switching to a more modular method of production (Klein 1988). The Japanese had invested in relatively unspecialised systems (multiskilled labour, reprogrammable machine tools, small-batch subcontractors) which probably never attained the lowest-cost production on any one model, but could produce a wide range of variant models at one time and switch to the next model generation at low cost. The non-maximising strategists had won out over those whose selection of the optimum action at one time confined them to a highly sub-optimum set of choices in subsequent periods.

4.1.3 Competitive pricing versus internal investment funding

The 'normal' profits of a perfectly competitive firm are assumed to cover an element of new and replacement investment as well as current costs of production. Since perfect competition is an extreme case, most firms can also expect some residual 'supernormal' profit to distribute among shareholders or spend on further investment. But strong product-market competition, or heavy calls from other elements of cost, may still leave supernormal profits below the level needed to finance the firm's strategic plans, especially if strong ownership-market competition requires a significant proportion to be distributed to shareholders.

Although not a binding constraint on investment, internal profit sets limits on the amount of external finance that can be raised by borrowing (which lenders must collateralise against future profits) or new share issue (for which existing shareholders must be compensated, possibly through higher payouts). Strategies at risk from the internal finance constraint if competition proves too strong include investment in capacity expansion, new product and process development, training, and administrative reorganisation, all of which might eventually yield more profit than is sacrificed to attain them, but only if that initial sacrifice is allowed.

4.1.4 Competitive diffusion versus innovation

Although sometimes still the result of sudden, costless inspiration, new product and process development is increasingly the result of costly R&D expenditures. These are intended to be paid back during a subsequent phase of exclusive rights to profit from the new product or new cost-reducing process. A small number of commercially successful innovations may have to pay not only for themselves, but for many related lines of research that came to nothing.

The innovator's temporary monopoly is usually defended by keeping the new technique concealed from rivals, or taking out patent protection which forces imitators to take out a licence beforehand (or pay even more heavily afterwards). But even where patent laws are strong, competitors will try to circumvent them by innovating around the patent, or striking back against it with one of their own. The consequent threat of too fast an erosion of monopoly profits may undermine

R&D-based innovation incentives. The observation that second-move refiners of an innovation frequently wrest the initiative from first-mover inventors (e.g. Tellis and Golder 1996) reinforces the danger that pressure for continuous maximisation will suppress R&D, as firms switch to free-riding on one another's efforts.

4.1.5 *Optimal standardisation versus path dependence*

'Network' products seem to offer an exception to R&D free-riding, since their characteristic for consumers – that utility rises with the number of existing users – offers a significant first-mover advantage to producers who get theirs adopted first. If the original supplier of a network or hub, or of any network-linked product, can lock early users into it, later customers have an added incentive to join it. The product acquires a self-reinforcing advantage over those that are launched later on. Locking-in can take the form of investments made in the network product itself, or in arrangements to make it operational (training, maintenance capability, leasing arrangements, hardware and software support, etc.).

To attain the private benefits of first-mover advantage, it often pays the innovator to 'seed' a network's user-base by giving subsidised or free access or terminal equipment, another strategic balancing of present loss against future gain. But this is similar to the 'predatory pricing' with which aspiring monopolists sometimes try to keep out or drive out rival suppliers of an existing product, and can have equally damaging social effects if the sole supplier cannot be constrained to be the best. The network provider is likely to become a natural monopolist (section 2.7.1), its supernormal profits persisting after initial costs have been repaid because even dissatisfied users have no alternative network to turn to (or would find its benefits outweighed by the switching costs).

Since the pioneer network's advantage lies in the size of its user-base, as well as its intrinsic qualities, it may be able to resist replacement by better, later-arriving technologists. Loyal users of Macintosh computers, Betamax video recorders and non-mountain bicycles will all attest that theirs was the better product, squeezed out by inferior products which through chance or clever marketing reached the mass market first. US cable companies which rushed to wire up homes as soon as the technology became available now find themselves stuck with a network which has proved difficult to adapt to new high-growth demands, such as heavy data traffic and two-way transmission. Adoption of a network standard is a collective choice which an economy cannot approach strategically if network creation is left to competing firms under continuous profit-maximising constraints. The difficulty of getting an innovation right first time increases the chance that agents forced to choose competitively will lock in to an inferior standard, whereas those allowed to wait, forgoing the early advantages, could have tied themselves in to a superior product.

4.1.6 *Discretion versus rule-following*

Competition regulators must play along with agents' strategies if investment and innovation are to proceed. Such outlays are incentivised by the prospect of future profits, which must be left intact if expectations are to be fulfilled – as they must if their related spending plans are to be maintained, and if other agents are to be encouraged to such outlays of their own. But if regulators were to maximise at every moment they would change the rules once agents had made their move – exposing the investor to immediate competition and subjecting the innovator to immediate imitation, so that their supernormal-profit paybacks never arise. This opportunism would maximise social welfare for the moment, but is avoided because of the damage it does to the growth of that welfare if agents are subsequently deterred from following strategies.

The regulator's interests, reflecting those of the economy, are time-inconsistent. While the promise of patent protection may be a necessary spur to the generation of inventions, the economy benefits from rapid diffusion of inventions that have proved successful, putting the authorities under pressure to force compulsory licensing of the new technique, or let the patent be infringed. Banks encounter the problem when they attract money into a term account with the promise of high interest (why not cut the rate once customers have signed over their money?), and businesses when they take payment in advance for a service whose delivery the consumer cannot accurately monitor. In general, time inconsistency arises whenever continuous optimisation is forced on an agent (or agency) whose actions set the parameters for those of agents who are considering strategic optimisation.

A noted macroeconomic example concerns monetary authorities, whose stated policies shape investment behaviour through real interest rate expectations, and price-setting behaviour through inflation expectations. Continuously maximising authorities would be tempted to announce a restrictive (low-inflation) policy so that private agents agree moderate wage and price increases, then switch to an expansive (high-inflation) policy to bring down unemployment once these agreements are in place (Kydland and Prescott 1977). It is assumed that keeping inflation low would have been the long-run preferred alternative (especially if, as monetarists suggest, the fall in unemployment is a purely temporary achievement based on tricking private agents). The interdependence between regulator and agent marks another appearance of the prisoners' dilemma, in which mutual co-operation would benefit both parties but does not happen because it involves one agent in time-inconsistent actions which the agent is likely to defect from. Price-setters and investors may expect the monetary authorities to relax from their announced tough targets, even if this is not their intention.

As in the repeated prisoners' dilemma game, the authorities must usually prove their sincerity several times, keeping policy tight when they could make short-term gains from loosening it, before announcement of a time-inconsistent rule will be widely believed. Similarly, strategists committed to big early sacrifices in pursuit of long-term rewards may have needed dramatic measures to enforce (or convince others of) their resistance to the expedient option, as with central bank governors fixing their salary in nominal terms to prove their anti-inflation commitment, or Ulysses being tied to the mast to avoid the Sirens' serenade (Elster 1980). With a strategy's final objectives under constant threat of abandonment, through a rise in uncertainty and in current time preference, success may depend on altering the short-term payoffs so as to align the intermediate and final goals.

4.1.7 Costly calculation versus gratis guesswork

A case closely related to time-inconsistency arises if optimising choices are difficult or time-consuming to make, and computing power or time have costs attached. Rule-followers may now outperform continuous maximisers in the long term not because of any strategy, but because the gains they sacrifice by making simple, rule-of-thumb decisions are outweighed by the costs they avoid by not 'rationally' running and revising the full calculation. The first agents to escape a burning building are rarely those who stop to measure which exit route is the shortest. Simplified decision is especially likely to win through if the optimising version involves much thinking-through of mutually dependent expectations, or if a wide range of possible outcomes is equally rewarding to the agent. Although it can be depicted within the subjective expected utility (SEU) framework as a rational decision to be less than rational, this seems difficult in practice without the full-rational decision being worked through (see section 5.6.2).

The antagonism is the same as that between static maximisation and adaptability, but arises this time from the costs of information processing rather than the costs of switching. The two cases are often mixed, as with firms in an industry whose product characteristics change only slowly but market demand is prone to fluctuation. A firm experiences this as upward or downward shifts of its own demand curve. Continuous optimisation would mean responding to every change in demand by adopting the technology whose average costs are lowest at the output where marginal costs equal marginal revenue. Under perfect competition, where revenue only just covers costs even at the lowest-cost production level, this is the only viable option; choice of an alternative strategy opens up if there is some sensitivity of price to output and some scope for 'supernormal' profit. If the changeover costs between technologies outweigh the benefits, the next closest approach to optimality would be to install the process which minimises costs at the median level of demand. But where this process's average-cost curve is steeply U-shaped, and where demand fluctuations are large, better profitability over time may well be achieved with a process whose average costs are higher at minimum but more gently rising either side of it. Again, the investor in 'generalist' labour and capital capacity will at most times be producing less efficiently than they could if there were no recalculation or adjustment costs, but will still on average be closer to best practice than a firm which keeps revising its technology choice, and so be seen to outperform.

The long-run superiority of strategic over continuous maximisation is especially likely in situations where re-running the decision process is expensive, or where the costs of deviating from an optimising action are expected to be small. In this case, even if they do not contribute to any long-run maxmising strategy, decision-simplifying rules may produce higher (present discounted) rewards over time than a continuous maximisation process. Rule-setting is common for choices taken repeatedly by people in organisations, within parameters which have been narrowed to ensure consistency with other departments' actions and minimise principal–agent conflicts (Simon 1947). A requirement to maximise continuously might, in this situation, lose more on the time- and organisational-impact costs of getting things right than it could otherwise lose by getting them only slightly wrong.

4.2 Capital markets as strategy protection

Private investment delivers to an economy two forms of external benefit. Across space, it contributes to a multiplier effect which raises the level of income and current capacity use, delivering derived demand to many who played no part in the investment. Through time, it opens the prospect of a stream of future profits, whose later arrival means that it may not be the investor who receives them. Markets 'solve' these externality problems – which would otherwise cause investment to be underprovided – by creating tradable entitlements to capital whose present value captures their discounted future value. 'While the social purpose is best served by the accumulation of means of production (plant and equipment), the private interests of individuals are best solved by holding wealth in a liquid form' (Caporaso and Levine 1992: 110).

Capital markets perform a unique role in supporting investment decisions, because of the way they help investors overcome these externalities. Across space, they allow those who will benefit from the project to contribute to its cost. Across space, they replace the uncertain future gains with present gains which the investor is sure of making. The strategist's cost of capital is the fee paid for this process of internalisation. The 'market' approach of creating transferable entitlements to the income from capital, actively traded in large and liquid bond and stock markets, stands in contrast to the 'relational' approach of creating non-tradable commitments between financial and physical investors, characterised by long-term bank loans and inactively traded institutional shareholdings.

Present pain for future gain can be sustained under competitive conditions, provided the right palliatives are available. An agent must either have the resources to survive the initial loss-making (or profit-sacrificing) phase, or be able to obtain them from the capital market. (Or, if the capital market's patience has already been exhausted, to escape pressure for short-run performance improvement by restoring solvency under protection from creditors, as permitted by procedures such as the US 'Chapter 11'.) Capital-market support requires that creditors and shareholders share the strategist's long-run objective, agree with its evaluation of future outcomes under the strategy, and set a discount rate which allows those long-run results to compare favourably with those of continuous maximisation. Foresight need not be perfect but must be shared, if capital providers are to offer strategy protection.

Once they have chosen to support a strategy, capital providers must ensure that it is implemented – that the strategist's initial, non-optimal actions really are those designed to bring long-term gain, and not just the result of laziness or incompetence brought on by the 'moral hazard' of being freed from continuous profit-maximising constraints. Strategic behaviour must be monitored – but neither so closely that it reimposes the continuous maximising requirement, nor so loosely that it allows the strategist to cheat and start making losses which do nothing to raise later rewards. The performance target chosen for monitoring must be neither too crude so that it loses key aspects of the strategy and so impedes its implementation, nor so detailed that it pushes monitoring costs high enough to vitiate the long-run strategy gains.

Even if the operational difficulties of a perfect capital market (section 3.13) are ignored, strategists' quest for financial support is likely to be a frustrating one, especially where the final-goal horizon is long and intermediate losses (or forgone gains) substantial. Creditors and shareholders, lacking detailed knowledge of the strategist's business, personal characteristics and motivations, are likely to be more uncertain than the strategist about the future outcomes predicted in the long-term plan. Being under short-term profit pressures themselves (shareholders wanting maximum portfolio value, creditors having to satisfy their own shareholders), they are also likely to discount long-term gains more heavily in relation to shorter-term losses. This tendency is enhanced if they regard moral hazard, and the chances of the strategist cheating, as increasing with the length of the plan.

The longer the strategy and the larger its early-stage sacrifices, the less likely it is to receive capital market support. Just as the capital market cannot necessarily be relied on to rescue agents from an income-constrained downward multiplier in short-run general equilibrium (section 3.5), it cannot necessarily be relied on to rescue strategists from continuous maximisation pressures in an intertemporal general equilibrium, once the assumption of shared (perfect) foresight is relaxed.

4.3   Temporary monopoly as strategy protection

Strategy is especially vulnerable when its intermediate steps bring external benefits, one agent incurring costs to open up new action possibilities which others can access free of charge. Necessity may be the mother of invention, but innovation – its commercial application – requires additional incentives. Once on the market, a new product or service can be studied by rivals (by sampling or reverse-engineering), as can the size and nature of its market and the price it can command there. First-movers may still win out – if they keep a hold on the secret process, or if the new product is a network good whose adoption beomes contagious, or if it opens up a new 'technological paradigm' whose follow-up refinements the originator can expect to profit from even if the initial breakthrough diffuses quickly. Some suppliers of network and paradigm-shifting products (personal computers, internet browsers, Grateful Dead concert recordings) have even acquiesced in unauthorised imitation of their initial innovation, because of its role in expanding the market for incremental versions. But in other cases, which appear empirically at least as common, imitators can steal a march on innovators by coming in later with an improved product or process, capturing a technology and a market developed at someone else's expense. Like investment, innovation brings external benefits which point towards its competitive undersupply.

Recognising that innovation investment is also one of the types least likely to obtain capital-market support – because product, process, producer and market potential are all to a great extent unknown – most market economies have legislated to protect creative behaviour through 'intellectual' property rights (IPRs). Patents, copyrights and design rights assign originators an exclusive period during which they have sole authority over the innovation, selling it for monopoly profits or charging others to produce it under licence, with the right of compensatory damages against unauthorised imitators.

From a conventional market perspective, government is a second-best strategy protector. It is too remote from markets to arrive at a detailed assessment of the optimal IPR life, resorting to standard timespans with no adjustment for development costs, profit rates or the costs of IPR enforcement, and falling prey to zero-sum lobbying battles between those wanting reward for a discovery and those wanting its rapid diffusion. IPRs may be allowed to run on too long if the innovator is a 'national champion' firm (from whose monopoly profits the government can expect a revenue boost), or if the likely imitators are foreign. However, IPRs will be foreshortened, or not extended sufficiently to compensate for rising development costs, if faster diffusion of the innovation promises more in enhanced economy-wide efficiency and consumer surplus gains than it loses in the innovator's producer surplus losses. Time inconsistency arises because rapid diffusion maximises current productive and allocative efficiency, but will slow the growth of that efficiency if firms are now deterred from making further innovations.

4.4 Telescoping the long run: intertemporal equilibrium

The simplest form of competitive general equilibrium (CGE) model avoids the strategy problem by allowing all agents to plan their lifetime transactions before trading begins. The Walrasian auctioneer dispels spatial uncertainty by announcing equilibrium prices for all spot markets, and temporal uncertainty by extending these prices into the future through a complete set of forward markets. Agents' subsequent lives consist of carrying out the series of transactions they have already agreed.

> Economists hit upon the idea of regarding the same 'good' (such as a loaf of bread) as a different commodity depending on the date or place at which it exists. In this way proofs of atemporal general equilibrium could be reinterpreted to be proofs of intertemporal general equilibrium.
>
> (Hausman 1992: 99)

Consumers in intertemporal CGE aim to maximise their lifetime utility, by distributing consumption across time until the marginal rate of substitution for each product is equal at each time period. (Equalisation is at unity if the consumer is indifferent to when the utility is received, or at $U_0(1+r)^t$ if there is a marginal time preference rate r for consumption at the present time 0 over some future time t.)

The consumer's budget constraint is the present value of wages, profit shares and endowments received through time (discounted at the same rate of time preference). Similarly, firms now aim to maximise the present discounted value of their future profits. If there is a stock-market, the firm's share price will adjust to represent the present discounted value of future profits.

Through forward markets, the same product at any future date is treated as a different product, though its characteristics and price can be known at the present time. 'This natural extension of the notion of commodities (i.e. time dated commodities) allows one to incorporate time into the theory of competitive equilibrium of a private ownership economy' (Dasgupta and Heal 1979: 100). With consumption and production plans mapped out at the start of trading there is no scope for disruption due to changing preferences, new technologies or inconsistent decisions over time: production and consumption in future periods is simply the enactment of a plan set down at the start. All the characteristics of static CGE – existence, stability and Pareto efficiency – are carried over into the intertemporal version.

As observed in the examination of CGE's full-employment claims (Chapter 3), this is an intertemporal model without competition's usual long-run properties. Capacity growth is ruled out by the distribution of all profits. The absence of expansion investment prevents the system from destabilising itself through factor reallocation and preference change, but also prevents the equalisation of profit rates across sectors. Where reinvestment of profit is permitted, it is usually on the assumption that capital and labour productivities are affected equally, avoiding disturbance to the ratios of capital to output, labour to output and hence capital to labour (Samuelson and Modigliani 1966) so that relative factor prices are not affected.

These dynamic properties can be incorporated if, instead of being mapped out at the beginning, prices are permitted to adjust at each period to accommodate any exogenous or internally generated changes that alter the market-clearing vector. The long run is now constructed from a succession of short-run equilibria, as if the Walrasian auctioneer is continuously recalled to rework its original calculation. Problems arising from the absence of full information, a consequence of missing or incomplete forward markets, can be removed by two further assumptions. Agents are allowed to form price expectations which, if not 'correct' according to any external standard, are at least mutually consistent. This leads them to take actions whose outcomes fulfil the expectation, simulating the effects of perfect and complete information, and so preventing misallocations which might lead the economy away from full employment. And real money balances are added to agents' budget constraints, so that any deferment of spending and saving decisions at times of uncertainty through precautionary money holding is offset by the rise in real balances when prices fall as a result of the drop in demand. This 'real balance effect' cures unemployment from the demand side even if the price fall matches nominal wage cuts and prevents lower real wages from curing it on the supply side.

From consistent expectations it is a short step to rational expectations, formed through an understanding of the actual model in which the agents are embedded. This ensures that agents' actions continue to reproduce the conditions whose prospect gave rise to them and so turns a sequence of temporary equilibria into a stable intertemporal arrangement. Rational expectations substitute for missing forward markets to carry the Arrow-Debreu (AD) result into the long run.

> The implicit assumption that every agent 'knows' all the prices is highly non-trivial. It means that at each date each agent is capable of forecasting perfectly all the future prices until the end of time. It is in this sense that the AD model depends on 'rational expectations'.
>
> (Geanakoplos 1989: 51)

Agents' task in arriving at correct price expectations, quickly enough to avoid disequilibrium trading, can be simplified if the equilibrium price vector is usually assumed to be stationary. Market-clearing prices are stable through time, so that agents can learn the appropriate transaction pattern even if they cannot compute it. However, this assumption limits the scope for incorporating technology and preference change, investment and scarce resources, and is in conflict with the short-run AD requirement that agents detach their expectations from current prices (to enable these to adjust to market-clearing). More sophisticated models allow prices to vary through time, but only according to a regular cycle which the agent can observe and learn to predict from (Grandmont 1985). The overlapping generations model (introduced in section 3.13) simplifies agents' prediction problem to just one future period, but still leaves a variety of ways in which expectations might be formed.

4.4.1 Intertemporal destabilisation through uncertainty

Even more than its static version, intertemporal CGE makes demanding calculation requirements on the agents within it, and is liable to break down when these cannot be met. Without a complete set of forward markets, the computation of a complete transaction plan for each commodity would probably overwhelm agents' information-processing power (Radner 1968). Incorporating this uncertainty into transaction plans required a set of state-contingent strategies which seem likely to exceed computational limits, and the markets in which risk-averse agents can buy protection against this uncertainty are no more complete than the forward markets whose absence caused the original problem. Under these conditions, a route – though not the only route – to unemployment and misallocation of resources at 'equilibrium' appears to open up.

If the move to trading through time occurs with anything less than rational expectations, problems of imperfect and incomplete information reappear. Uncertainty about other agents' actions and their collective results clouds agents' vision of the equilibrium price vector, now and in the future. They must now judge the future utility of current savings plans and future profitability of current investment plans with no guarantee that prices will evolve in the manner expected.

'In the absence of forward markets, stock markets clear on the basis of expectations about future prices that may be incompatible' (Dasgupta and Heal 1979: 108). Dealing with this uncertainty (as through buying insurance or holding money) involves further expectations which may turn out to be mistaken, and incurs dead-weight costs – even if the relevant risk-trading market is available, which requires a certain number of risk-attached agents to wish to buy what the risk-averse wish to sell (section 3.11).

The work of forward markets can, to a certain extent, be substituted by stock- and bond-markets, which most economies now possess in an increasingly comprehensive and liquid form. In principle an efficient stock-market, by valuing firms according to market expectations of their future profitability, can help achieve consistency among investors' plans, time preferences and assumptions about future states of the world. An efficient bond-market allows consumers to distribute their expenditure across time, compensating for deferral of expenditure with the appropriate interest rate. But even if these fully substitute for missing forward markets, only a small proportion of agents' uncertainty has been eliminated. There is still no room for technologies and preferences to change over time, or for the preferences of future generations to be taken directly into account. Meanwhile, the logical difficulty of maintaining a perfect capital market (section 3.14) leads on to some further disequilibrating consequences for the expenditures it affects.

Consistent expectation formation is made especially difficult when public policy parameters are among those to be guessed, and a rational-expectations equilibrium once achieved can still break down whenever a change is externally imposed rather than generated by agents' own actions. Conventionally, the main 'exogenous' shocks of this kind are assumed to be monetary disturbances, which cause aggregate price level changes which agents can mistake for changes in relative prices. As observed in section 4.1.6, such shocks can be avoided if monetary authorities stick to known and predictable rules. Long-run intertemporal models of this type can not only incorporate the long-run impact of investment, but also acknowledge its sunk (unrecoverable) nature by taking the last period's sector capital–labour ratios as given, the resultant constraints on wage and profit rates (whose ratio is that of their marginal products) being accommodated by variations in product prices.

Even a 'conjectural' equilibrium, weakly defined as a situation where no agent expects more profit or utility from another action given the conjectures taken by others, may not retain the collectively optimal or stability properties of static CGE. 'If equilibria exist they may be "bootstrap equilibria", that is they will depend on beliefs about the actions of others, which beliefs may be incorrect. There is certainly no ground for believing that they will be efficient' (Hahn 1989: 101). The move to rational expectations, under which conjectures are not only consistent but also formed from a correct understanding of the model in which the agents exist, makes even stronger requirements about agents' ability to correct their initial mis-understandings of the model and so correct systematic expectational errors that arise from them. The process of discovering an action to be suboptimal is not straightforward (Cohen and Axelrod 1982), and the costs of moving to the optimising action may not always justify the benefits (Akerlof and Yellen 1985), even if the move can occur quickly enough to avoid false trading at non-rational-expectations-equilibrium prices.

4.4.2 *Intertemporal destabilisation through investment*

The shift from 'static' general equilibrium to a fully dynamic intertemporal version requires that the long-run effects of investment be introduced. For aggregate supply to expand in step with demand (in individual markets and for the macroeconomy), the income- and capacity-generating effects of investment must be balanced. Allowance must also be made for the use of investment to shift capital from lower- to higher-profit sectors, with resultant impact on the relative price of factors, and of products which use them in different proportions. 'The time paths of output, input, and prices are interpreted as paths generated by maximising firms in a moving equilibrium driven by changes in product demand, factor supply, and technological conditions' (Nelson and Winter 1974: 887).

For the time paths to represent the fastest attainable growth rate, the investment demand schedule and the interest rate it confronts must adjust through time to stay at levels compatible with full-employment income. Such adjustment may be possible on a period-by-period basis if investment is confined mainly to financial capital (stocks, bonds, securitised loans) or working capital (raw materials, unskilled labour), which can be bought at short notice when conditions improve and sold with little or no loss of value if they deteriorate again. However, fixed investment outlays (specialist machinery, buildings and skills) cannot respond to product and factor current market conditions in the same way, since such assets generally carry a large sunk-cost element. Fixed capital may have only limited value when transferred to another use or location, and the small number of agents willing to take it over in the current cost and location gives any buyer the chance to bargain its price right down. This compels fixed investors to base their decision on the long-run profit potential of the asset, evaluated by long-run expectations of future revenues, costs and interest rates.

At certain times, this relative independence of fixed investment decisions from short-run demand conditions has helped to keep the economy on a stable growth path, immunising entrepreneurs from loss of confidence due to temporary over-supply in product markets or bottlenecks in factor and input markets. Once early expectations have been fulfilled and early investments repaid, a conventional belief develops that recent experience will be broadly replicated in future, and the stock-market can indeed take the place of forward markets by letting financial investors simulate the work of more far-sighted fixed investors.

> Investment becomes reasonably 'safe' for the individual investor over short periods, and hence over a succession of short periods however many, if [the stock or bond investor] can fairly rely on there being no breakdown in the convention and on his therefore having an opportunity to revise his judgment and

> change his investment . . . Investments which are 'fixed' for the community are
> thus made 'liquid' for the individual.
>
> (Keynes 1936: 153)

Without such expectational conventions, however, the markets' continuous revaluation of financial instruments becomes a destabilising influence on fixed
investment.

> Day-to-day fluctuations in the profits of existing investments, which are obvi-
> ously of an ephemeral and non-significant character, tend to have an
> altogether excessive, and even an absurd, influence on the market.
>
> (Keynes 1936: 153–4)

The reasons Keynes cites for this excessive sensitivity arise directly from the near-
perfection of the financial capital market, compared wih the 'extreme
precariousness' of prospects for fixed capital performance. Financial investors
need not bother making detailed assessments of the earnings prospects of fixed
assets (the 'fundamentals' of the capital market) when they can immediately gauge
from current market values how other agents are assessing them. Even if they do
so, the assessment may no longer shape their decision. The ability to re-trade
stocks and bonds refocuses investors' attention from their lifetime income, if held
to maturity, to shorter-run capital gains if bought low and sold high. Calculation
therefore switches from objective valuation of the underlying asset to subjective
estimation of how other investors' opinion about it is likely to change.

The possible unemployment impact of this situation, when a general downturn
in expectation deflects investment from financial instruments into cash, has already
been identified in section 3.12. Once the capacity-expansion effect of fixed investment is added to its income-generation effect, a potential for constraining growth
can also be identified. The multiplier effects of fixed investment mean that those
who undertake it risk failing to capture its full economic benefits, and so give it a
public-good aspect which could cause competitive markets to undersupply it.
Although in the aggregate investment generates the demand needed to take up the
new capacity, no one firm has any certainty that the demand-side spillovers from
its own investment outlays will be matched by its share of those from others. 'If
some capitalists spend money, their money passes to other capitalists in the form of
profits. Investment or consumption of some capitalists creates profits for others'
(Kalecki 1966: 14).

To the extent that their outlays are sunk, those who borrow to finance fixed
investment risk ending up with an enterprise which is profitable (revenues exceeding costs) but insolvent (liabilities exceeding assets), and so effectively given away for
a less indebted owner to extract the profits. Investors who forsake the relative security of financial investment for the irreversible commitment to fixed investment will
seek compensation in a higher rate of return, depressing demand for capital projects in general, and especially those whose heaviest costs fall early and whose
largest projected revenues arrive late on.

4.4.3 Intertemporal destabilisation through innovation

Process innovation can enter the intertemporal model as a discrete change in supply, demand and price for the inputs affected, as complements or substitutes. Product innovation enters as new markets which appear at certain moments in the future, prices effectively having been infinite (and so trade zero) until then. Limited 'technological foresight' may be possible if firms can plot a probability distribution for their R&D results, but these are not usually shared with other agents; in the absence of forward markets, innovation effectively arises outside the system as an exogenous change to firms' production or consumers' utility functions.

This problem would be reduced (by slowing technological progress) if innovation is undersupplied in a competitive market economy, because inventors cannot successfully sell their good ideas to firms or to the capital market (section 3.15), or because the first to innovate tend to lose out to later arrivals who escape the development costs and capture the market with small improvements (section 4.1.4). However, this not only seems to eliminate the disequilibrating effect of growth by removing one of its principal causes, but also is challenged by evidence on the wider link between innovation and corporate performance. Innovating UK firms recorded significantly faster profit margins and sales growth compared with a matched sample of non-innovators in the period 1972–83, not least because they weathered recessions better and were less likely to shrink or go out of business. The effect persisted long after the main innovation had been made, leading the authors to conclude that the process surrounding the innovation contributed more to long-term performance than the innovation itself: 'Innovative activity may transform the internal capabilities of firms in a way which affects how they generate profit and growth . . . innovators are more flexible and better able to adapt to changes in the market environment' (Geroski and Machin 1992: 87–8). While causation might work the other way, the implication is that firms still have an incentive to seek innovation even if it is snatched away by imitators when they find it.

Internal benefits to the innovation process may overcome the external benefits of the innovation outcome, and so eliminate the time-inconsistency problem created if innovators must be incentivised with temporary monopolies, but only by setting up endogenous forces for innovation which further complicate the attainment of intertemporal equilibrium. If new products' or processes' arrival were pre-announced by inclusion in forward markets beyond a certain date, there would also be little to stop agents bringing them forward from that date. Introducing innovations as changes in a transaction sequence mapped out in advance effectively makes them public goods, removing the uncertainty surrounding feasibility, timing, costing, customer acceptance, etc., but in the process removing the delay in diffusion which incentivises agents to make them. To the extent that agents innovate to capture monopoly profit or wrench customers away from their current consumption patterns, technical change is inherently destabilising to the process of keeping agents on an intertemporal equilibrium path.

4.4.4 *Intertemporal destabilisation through exhaustible resources*

Competitive equilibrium's problem with fixed investment highlights its more general difficulty in incorporating stocks, which exist as a finite quantity through successive market periods rather than being consumed and reproduced in each market period. Because the starting-point and rate of change of their equilibrium price path is determined on the supply side, stocks' price and quantity may not be as responsive to demand conditions as is required to keep the rest of the system in equilibrium – unless they are to be underpriced from a long-run welfare viewpoint, and suddenly disappear. Natural resource stocks typify the problem. The dependence of their current value on long-run expectations of supply, demand and discount rates makes for volatility in the spot market, which – like capital markets – tends to see speculative trade rise to match or even overtake 'underlying' trade. Owners of scarce resources, uncertain of their future price, will tend to bring them to the market as quickly as possible. The private discount rate for future valuation is thereby pushed above the social rate, which takes account of scarcity. A competitive economy thus tends to deplete its renewable resources above the sustainable and its exhaustible resources above the optimal rate, causing markets to disappear when they would still have been a source of Pareto-improving transactions.

The tendency of competing agents in free markets to deplete scarce resources faster than is consistent with long-run optimisation was noted in section 2.5. For renewable resources, common-pool problems can push the rate of extraction above the rate of regeneration, or let stocks get too small before it brings the two into balance, unless the cost of entry and extraction is sufficiently large compared with the initial revenue. For exhaustible resources, price must exceed marginal cost (of extraction) by a royalty rate which grows at a compound interest rate accurately capturing social time preferences, and the royalty rate must begin at a level that avoids excessive depletion (if too high) or excessive conservatism (if too low) (Dasgupta and Heal 1979: 125, 190).

Neither of these requirements is easily satisfied, in the absence of regulation to restrict access to the stock of the renewable or exhaustible resource, and to align market interest rates with social time-preference rates. Even if optimal depletion is attained, the rising price (and eventual disappearance) of exhaustible resources adds a further complication to agents' efforts to forecast prices in the absence of forward markets, especially as most exhaustible resources are inputs to a wide variety of industrial processes in which their substitutability depends on future technical change.

4.5 Escape by aggregation: the neoclassical growth model

While attempts to develop a more fully dynamic general-equilibrium model continue, simpler ways have been sought to bring the dynamic effects of investment and innovation into models of the market system. Rather than a multiplicity of separate product and factor markets, the economy is pictured as producing one homogeneous output (Y) with two factors (labour L and capital K), preserving the more certain adjustment properties of partial equilibrium by scaling up the markets for these three resources to comprise the whole economy.

The simplest of the resultant growth models, originating with Solow (1956) and Swan (1956), is labelled 'neoclassical' because it shows how growth can be kept on its equilibrium path through price adjustments, especially those of interest, profit and wage rates ensuring that savings track investment and factors' relative prices move to keep them fully employed. The response of labour and capital costs to changes in their relative supplies ensures that the ratio of their use in production adjusts to keep factors fully employed as the economy grows.

Starting with the accounting identity that national income breaks down into consumption and investment

$$Y = C + I \tag{1}$$

the 'intensive' production function is obtained by dividing both sides by quantity of labour L so that $y = Y/L$, $c = C/L$, $i = I/L$ and

$$y = c + i \tag{2}$$

National income equates to national output, Y, which is produced by labour L and capital K under the neoclassical production function

$$Y = f(L,K) \tag{3}$$

Growth can thus occur through an expansion of K or L (a movement along the production function), or through technical change which raises the productivity of K or L (an upward movement of the production function).

By the same process of dividing through by L,

$$y = f(k) \tag{4}$$

The move to relating growth to the capital–labour ratio (k) rather than the supplies of both factors reflects the assumption (conventional in higher-income economies) that labour supply is essentially static, so that growth depends 'intensively' on adding to the capital that labour works with rather than 'extensively' on bringing more (rural) surplus labour into employment. Early econometric tests of the neoclassical theory were conducted on US and higher-income European economies, where average annual labour force growth was already well below average GDP growth, and there was very little underemployed rural labour still available to redeploy into industry. The move also allows changes in the capital–labour ratio ($k = K/L$) to be analytically (and econometrically) separated from changes in technology, which are assumed to change Y by a different route that raises total factor productivity.

From these emerges (via intermediate steps given in the appendix to this chapter) the basic neoclassical growth equation:

$$dk/dt = sy - nk \tag{5}$$

The capital–labour ratio adjusts to close any gap between savings per worker and the investment needed to equip new workers at the existing capital–labour ratio; k converges to a constant level determined by n. The NGM thus establishes an automatic identity between savings per worker and investment per worker, confining Keynesian unemployment-equilibrium to the short run and showing that, through appropriate factor-price adjustment, the economy's growth rate is limited only on the supply side by the labour force growth rate and the rate at which income recipients choose to save.

4.5.1   Rescue from 'Keynesian' instability

Solow's model was an early riposte to those put forward by Harrod (1939) and Domar (1947) as dynamic extensions of Keynes's (1936) anti-neoclassical account of output and employment determination. Keynes had abstracted from the capacity-building effects of investment in order to examine its potentially destabilising demand-side effects. Harrod offered a simple dynamic version of the theory using Keynes's static equilibrium condition S=I (aggregate savings equal aggregate investment), the familiar savings function S=sY, and the aggregate identity of national income, expenditure and output. Firms which were in equilibrium at time (receiving just enough demand to absorb their current output, the 'circular flow' remaining constant) will invest to expand capacity in period t if aggregate expenditure moved above its previous level in the previous period t–1:

$$I_t = v(Y_t - Y_{t-1}) \tag{6}$$

The response coefficient v is the ratio of capital stock change (investment) to income change (= output change), and so is also termed the marginal capital–output ratio. Its inverse $1/v$ can be taken as a measure of average fixed-capital productivity. Equation 6 is a simple form of 'accelerator' through which forms raise output if there is pressure on current capacity from rising demand. (Accepting the then general interpretation of Keynes's as a short-run theory, Harrod assumes that demand deficiency is overcome in the long run so that firms are working at full employment and full capacity.)

Putting investment equal to savings in equation 6, restating savings as a fraction s of income and eliminating I from the equation produces the fundamental Harrod-Domar (HD) growth equation

$$g = (Y_t - Y_{t-1})/Y_t = s/v \tag{7}$$

where g is the warranted growth rate, at which the economy is capable of growing for so long as its savings rate remains s and its average (hence marginal) capital productivity remains 1/v.

The warranted growth rate is the one that maintains the S=I identity through time, by ensuring that the extra income generated by investment in each period is exactly enough to absorb the output from the new capacity installed by that investment. But although the result is a dynamic equilibrium of sorts, and assumes that short-run Keynesian unemployment has been overcome, it identifies two ways in which steady-state unemployment can arise. First, there is no mechanism to match g (the warranted growth rate) with the natural rate arising from growth in the labour force, which once more is assumed to be exogenous. An economy on its warranted growth path may experience continued growth in unemployment as it fails to absorb all new labour, or hit an inflationary ceiling as it absorbs new labour faster than it reaches the labour market.

Second, even if natural and warranted growth coincide, there is no assurance that the rate of investment required for warranted growth will actually be undertaken. For actual growth $a = (Y_t - Y_{t-1})/Y_{t-1}$ to be equal to warranted growth $g = s/v$ would require that

$$v(Y_t - Y_{t-1}) = sY_{t-1} \tag{8}$$

so that this period's investment (given by the accelerator, equation 6) matches the previous period's saving. The model does not specify this, and so lacks any mechanism to ensure that the extra demand generated by new investment will exactly match the new capacity it creates. Investment decisions at time t are based on an expectation of the change in aggregate income and expenditure already taking place at time t. If this is underestimated, investment will fall below that consistent with the warranted growth rate.

> [The] warranted rate of growth is not the rate of accumulation that firms want to carry out at that rate of profit, but the rate they have to carry out if that rate of profit is to be realised . . . greater thriftiness requires a higher rate of growth, but does not provide any motive for it.
>
> (Robinson 1962: 100n)

The dynamic investment–savings mismatch in the HD model is potentially explosive. To sustain the warranted growth path, the warranted investment rate as a share of national income must equal the ratio of the savings rate to the capital–output ratio. If actual investment falls below this, income must fall proportionately, a potentially explosive development since the accelerator determining investment will (if expectations are purely adaptive) cause it to be cut again. Conversely, overinvestment will cause a self-reinforcing rise in income until the ceiling imposed by the natural (labour force) growth rate is reached, whereafter continued acceleration of output will presumably give way to a burst of inflation. Given the cyclical behaviour of actual economies, Keynesian growth models have tended to be subsequently modified to allow for cyclicity by introducing a multiplier effect (of investment on income) to discipline the accelerator effect of income on investment (e.g. Britton 1986: 27).

Keynes had argued that in the short run, too low an investment rate will cause unemployment of labour (capital stick assumed fixed) by dragging down the savings rate through a downward multiplier on income. The basic HD extension suggests that in the long run, too low an investment rate can cause the unemployment of both labour and capital by installing more new capacity than it generates income to absorb it, thus not only confirming but actually intensifying the underinvestment. The case for Keynesian demand management to avoid extended bouts of mass unemployment is extended into the long run. Although demand-management will choke off phases of over-fast growth as well as avoiding phases of over-slow (or negative) growth, it is also generally assumed that a demand-managed economy with stable investment expectations will grow faster through time than an unregulated economy. This role for government comes on top of any relating to the 'public good' spillovers from industrial investment, which might lead private agents to undersupply it, and of public infrastructures whose capacity must grow in line with private sector needs.

The neoclassical model overcomes this problem by letting the savings rate s and the capital–output ratio vary according to price signals, so that actual, warranted and natural growth rates are brought into line. If the warranted rate falls below the natural rate so that unemployment starts rising, excess labour supply will drive down the price of labour and induce the substitution of labour for capital, reducing the capital–output ratio v. At the same time, the growing relative scarcity of capital will drive up the rate of interest and increase the savings rate s. Factor-price adjustment thus aligns the warranted rate with the natural rate, while product price adjustment prevents any divergence between the warranted rate and the actual rate. If investment ever adds more capacity than it can furnish demand for, the capital–output ratio automatically increases and the excess capital stock drives down interest rates, so reducing savings until all the extra output is being absorbed. If investment introduces more demand than it has installed capacity for, the savings rate rises to bring demand and supply back into line.

> If refashioned in this way, Harrod's 'warranted rate' would have a long-run tendency (at least) to converge upon his 'natural rate', or ceiling rate; and for the system to grow thereafter at the maximum possible rate consistent with population-growth and technical progress.
>
> (Dobb 1975: 230)

Neoclassical theory reduces the dynamic Keynesian instability results, like the static equilibrium-unemployment result, to an essentially short-run price rigidity in the factor market. In doing so, it finds an unexpected ally in the 'Keynesian' growth model introduced and successively refined by Kaldor, which explicitly eliminates the HD conflict between warranted and actual growth rates by assuming a rate of investment which, through time, generates sufficient saving to keep the economy at full employment.

It postulates an economy in which the mechanism of profit and income generation will create sufficient savings (at any rate within certain limits or 'boundaries' to balance the investment which entrepreneurs decide to undertake . . . investment is primarily induced by the growth in production itself, and the underlying conditions are such that growth-equilibrium necessarily carries with it a state of continuous full employment.

(Kaldor 1978: 55–6)

The economy's investment rate is thus constrained only by the 'natural' growth rate of the labour force and the growth in the capital–labour ratio.

Kaldor's emphasis on technical progress and alternative views of distribution leave his approach sharply opposed to the neoclassical in most other respects (see section 4.8), but they added to the earlier 'Keynesian' theories' isolation. Indeed, later models in the Keynesian tradition such as those by Kaldor (1962) and Pasinetti (1962) detach the growth rate from the rate of saving, which becomes passively determined by the rate of investment and technical progress. Under this combined neoclassical and neo-Keynesian onslaught, the HD model is relegated to a special case where the capital–output ratio is fixed through time (a condition which subsequently came to be known as Harrod-neutrality). Instability disappears in the long run and, while demand management may play a part in maintaining full employment, the government's main task – if it has one – shifts to the supply side, promoting the invention and adoption of new techniques.

4.5.2 *Rescue from path dependence and 'unbalanced growth'*

Once the assumption of complete forward markets is relaxed, intertemporal general equilibrium involves agents in transaction decisions they may come to regret if price expectations prove unreliable. Even if they can quickly learn from mistakes, gauge the structure of the model and arrive at rational (or at least consistent) expectations, agents will be left with the consequences of any past mistakes which involved them in transactions whose costs they cannot fully recover. Such 'sunk' costs are most prevalent with regard to capital equipment, and the 'history' represented by past fixed investments thus becomes a central obstacle to the constant adjustment of period-by-period equilibrium and the timelessness of one-off intertemporal equilibrium achieved through forward markets.

The basic NGM effectively sidesteps history by assuming that fixed capital is malleable, not only in the present period (being applicable to any use, including consumption at the margin if the savings rate falls), but also between periods (being convertible from one established use into any other). However, a step back towards general equilibrium, extending of the NGM to two sectors, removes the requirement for cross-period malleability. The economy can now live with its inherited capital stock (and associated capital–labour ratio) at each period and still follow an optimum growth path. In the two-sector model, capital and labour are both divided between a capital-goods and consumption-goods sector, each with a separate production function whose derivative (marginal product) with respect to the two factors gives their rewards, the wage and profit rates. These adjust to ensure full employment of both factors, with any rise in the savings and investment ratios merely transferring capital and labour from consumption- to capital-goods production. With the assumption (appropriate in low-income countries, and arguably still true elsewhere due to the growth of consumer credit) that all wages are spent and only profits are saved, the wage-bill matches the value of consumer-goods production and profits match the value of capital-goods production, ensuring the full-employment equality of savings and investment (Jones 1975: 105 provides a formal exposition).

Without technical change or depreciation of capital, the economy's natural growth rate is again determined by the growth rate of the labour force. Balanced growth is achieved when this exactly matches the marginal productivity of capital in the capital-goods sector, so that the economy's capital–labour ratio stays constant through time. The economy converges to balanced growth, regardless of the initial capital–labour ratio, provided consumption-goods production is more capital-intensive than capital-goods production (Jones 1975: 106, 110). Market-led adjustments to wages and profits (assumed equal across the two sectors) are thus sufficient to put the economy onto a unique long-term growth path, regardless of its previous history.

Just as the one-sector NGM disposes of instability models such as those of Harrod and Domar, the two-sector version allows a rejection of 'unbalanced growth' models such as those associated with Mahalanobis (1953) and Feldman (1964). These adopt the same two-sector division and, in their simplest form, the same assumption that saving occurs only out of profits. But by assuming fixed capital–output ratios in both sectors, profits in the capital-goods sector now determine wages and expenditure in the consumptuon-goods sector, and the rate of investment (i.e. rate of saving) in the capital-goods sector sets the 'natural' rate of growth. The labour force may be growing faster than this, but income and consumption in the consumption-goods sector can rise only as a result of higher investment in capital goods. The result clearly parallels Harrod's, with 'warranted' growth determined by an investment growth rate which equals the rate of saving (out of profits on capital goods) divided by the capital–output ratio in the capital-goods sector.

These 'unbalanced' two-sector growth models supported an argument by early development economists that prioritising investment in capital goods would raise the growth rate and so lead to a faster rise in welfare over time, even if the same investment would currently earn a higher return (or maximise static welfare) if invested in consumption goods. 'The resulting "strategy of unbalanced growth" values investment decisions not only because of their immediate contributions to output, but because of the larger or smaller impulse such decisions are likely to impart to further investment' (Hirschman 1989: 210). Although the two-sector 'unbalanced growth' models had roots in Marxian theory, an analogy could also be drawn with the 'Keynesian' argument that heavy investment in capital projects could accelerate the growth rate through multiplied income generation, even if the projects themselves were of low (perhaps even zero) productivity.

Heavy emphasis on capital-goods investment (sometimes to the point of short-term hunger and material deprivation) was evident in the early Russian and Indian five-year plans, among others. The two-sector unbalanced growth model also reinforces unequal exchange theories (section 9.3.5) in arguing that technologies 'appropriate' to present lower-income country conditions (abundant labour, scarce capital) might be detrimental to their longer-term development.

However the two-sector NGM reveals these results, like that of Harrod instability, to be heavily dependent on the assumption of fixed capital–output ratios in the two sectors, as well as the fixed rate of investment out of capital-goods-sector income. Capital and labour are being treated as necessary complements, when in practice they may be used as substitutes, a rise in the reward to one factor leading to increased redeployment of the other. By letting the ratios vary, and allowing malleablity of capital between the two sectors in the present period, the NGM restores a natural growth rate set by labour (even in a 'labour surplus' economy) and allows price adjustments to guide the warranted rate towards it. Demand and supply grow together to preserve full employment, sectors expand and contract in response to demand, and price signals reallocate resources whenever technical change alters sectors' relative factor or input proportions. As before, the NGM introduces an alternative constancy, that of the whole-economy capital–labour ratio, kept level by the present-period malleability of capital. But this is now only a long-run requirement, since capital can be reassigned only incrementally as time moves forward, and the adjustment of marginal products in response to wage and profit signals provides a clear explanation of why the long-term constant ratio is restored.

4.5.3 Rescue from 'capitalist' class relations

The neoclassical growth equation (5) shows how investment changes the capital–labour ratio to keep growth on its maximum path, given the (exogenous) labour-force growth rate and the (socially determined) savings rate. It makes no assumptions about how the investment is funded, or who makes it. This is in contrast to the non-neoclassical models that followed those of Harrod-Domar, which ground the savings rate in the distribution of income. These derive a direct link between distribution and growth by assuming differential savings rates between capitalists and workers (Pasinetti 1962), or between work income and investment income (Kaldor 1966). Here 'capitalists' are those who own the capital stock and receive its residual income, after contractual payments have been made to the 'workers' who are hired to keep it running, work the capital stock and, at best, are paid the value of their marginal product.

When two classes of income-earner are admitted to the model, the equilibrium growth path is independent of income distribution only if workers' savings rate out of wages is the same as that out of any capital income that is passed on to them (e.g. through shareholdings or profit shares), or if workers' (higher) savings out of capital income are matched by the issue of new shares in constant proportion to companies' investment. In this second case, capitalists who are investing in excess of their retained profits must, to prevent a gradual transfer of their property-income claims to labour, ensure that their own portfolios produce consistently larger capital gains than those of workers, perhaps by keeping the entitlements to new capital and issuing claims to older, less productive capital.

> It is reasonable to assume that the value of the shares of the newly formed and growing companies grows at a higher rate than the average, whilst those of older companies (which decline in relative importance) grow at a lower rate. This means that the rate of capital appreciation of the shares in the hands of the capitalist group as a whole . . . is greater than the rate of appreciation of the assets in the hands of pension funds . . . I think it can be shown that there will be, for any given constellation of the value of the parameters, a long-run equilibrium distribution of the assets between capitalists and pension funds which will remain constant.
>
> (Kaldor 1978: 99)

Neoclassical general-equilibrium theory abstracts from these distributional considerations by assuming that there are no residual profits (because of constant returns to scale), or that (under diminishing returns) workers receive as a profit-share any income left over when labour and capital have been paid according to their marginal productivity. 'In the Arrow-Debreu model each consumer-resource-holder is endowed prior to any market exchanges with a certain set of resources and with shares in corporations' (Ellerman 1992: 194). This generalisation of (indirect) capital ownership absolves the neoclassical growth model of any class considerations, by giving workers an interest in the generation of profit (for accumulation), and making corporations their specialist vehicle for accumulation.

> Capitalists . . . represent future universal interests while interests of all other groups appear as particularistic and hence inimical to future developments . . . Increased output requires investment, investment is financed by savings, savings are financed by profit. Hence profits are the condition for growth.
>
> (Przeworski 1985: 139, 212)

Ellerman and Przeworski use their mathematical Marxism to identify the sleight of hand involved in 'classless' neoclassicism. The CGE still allows workers to be exploited because they must still sell their labour to a firm which seizes the profits from any decreasing-returns production technology, even if some of those profits are later passed back to shareholders. The NGM claims for capitalists a falsely unique role in the growth process by identifying growth with private profit, when in fact the identification is with investment of which private profit is only one possible source. Equally strong and sustainable growth might be possible if governments taxed private profit severely in order to fund public investment (a model pursued, within very different frameworks, by communist Russia and social-democratic Sweden), or if workers held user rights (as well as property rights) over the capital stock through mutual and co-operative ownership. But these considerations of who determines, and profits from, the rate and direction of investment are buried in the basic neoclassical growth presentation, which is inter-preted as applying to any society, regardless of its institutional arrangements for property ownership and property-income distribution.

4.6   Neoclassical growth limitations: the spectre of sunk investment

Through its disposal of the Harrod-Domar instability result and its espousal of a period-by-period optimal resource allocation, the neoclassical growth model (NGM) appears to bring competitive markets into dynamic stability without the information and uncertainty problems that affect intertemporal CGE. Sustained full employment and optimal growth appear possible without any demand-managing or invesment-promoting intervention, once price rigidities are overcome. Investment's previously destabilising forces appear tamed. Its addi-tions to capacity, like nature's additions to the workforce, are accommodated through relative factor prices changes allowing capital to complement or substitute labour. Similar price adjustments, in product markets, accommodate its effect in lowering production costs and changing spending patterns through income and substitution effects.

This tranquil picture depends, however, on three very strong conditions: the flu-idity of capital between flow of investment and stock of machinery; the stable inverse relation between investment demand and the rate of interest; and the unproblematic expectations that position the schedule of investment demand. Once these are relaxed, adjustment problems return to haunt the neoclassical theory, and the co-ordination and information problems of long production chains begin to rattle again.

4.6.1   Sunk costs and specificities: the ghost of capital's past

The NGM sidesteps rather than surmounts the general-equilibrium problems of uncertainty and disequilibrium price adjustment. Economy-wide price changes through aggregated factor and product markets rule out any difficulty in eliminat-ing imbalances in individual product markets, or in changing relative factor rewards to ensure full employment. However, the return to an 'aggregate produc-tion function' is not without problems. In using interest-rate and wage adjustments to clear the aggregate capital and labour markets, the NGM must still assume 'well-behaved' demand functions (inversely related to the rate of return) for both the flow of new fixed investment and the stock of existing fixed capital. For the flow of new investment, this reintroduces the circularity through which equilibrium inter-est rates are part-determined by a marginal investment productivity schedule into whose calculation they have already entered (section 2.9.3).

A simultaneous adjustment to investment-market and money-market equilib-rium might overcome this problem, as it does in the popular IS-LM interpretation of Keynes's General Theory (originating with Hicks 1937). However, the NGM also shares with intertemporal general equilibrium a practical problem of maintaining efficient allocation of the stock of existing fixed capital. As before, the destabilising effect of future expectation on present investment behaviour can be defused only if those who sink their capital into plant and equipment can be assured that their costs are recoverable should expectation change or be frustrated. Although the requirement for malleability of capital is reduced in two-sector presentations, instantaneous flexibility (and period-by-period equilibrium) still requires either that past capital stock can be costlessly transformed to what is currently appropriate, or at least that the appropriate capital–labour ratios can be restored by marginal adjustments in the current period.

In arguing that the growth in capital and labour supplies will automatically cause price changes that ensure their full employment, neoclassical theory must abstract from any unrecoverable (sunk) costs of investing in particular types of equipment or occupational skills. Stock and flow distinctions are blurred to render capital completely 'malleable'. The reallocations that occur when wage or interest rates change are assumed to take place not only for factors newly arriving on the scene, but also for factors already in place, regardless of how specialised are the machine tools in their current tasks and how happy the workers in their current jobs.

When investment growth exceeds the resultant demand growth so that interest rates fall, there is not only a substitution of capital for labour at the margin, but a reallocation of existing production towards more capital-intensive techniques. As the return on capital falls, firms employing more capital-intensive techniques will find their profit rates falling compared with those with more labour-intensive techniques, implying that competition will shift capital towards the labour-intensive sectors until profit rates are once more equalised. If investment growth failed to generate matching demand, causing an excess labour supply that drove down wages in more labour-intensive sectors, workers would presumably bring about a similar re-equalisation by migrating to more capital-intensive sectors.

The costless reallocation of labour between uses according to price (wage) changes is relatively easy to conceptualise, at least in conditions where work is relatively unskilled (thus easy to learn), or where workers are sufficiently well endowed with general skills that they can adapt quickly to new technology or a new occupation. Costless reallocation of capital is harder to envisage, since industrial capital generally takes the form of relatively specialised physical equipment, which cannot be turned to radically different uses or turned back into financial capital without a substantial depreciation loss. In general, capital turned into physical plant is a sunk cost, with a narrow range of uses and little more than scrap value outside those uses.

Since it deals with the long run, the neoclassical growth model cannot (as in basic general-equilibrium theory) avoid this problem by assuming that differential profit and wage rates are allowed to persist. But the only way to ensure that growth takes place without differential changes in firms' profit rates is to assume constancy in the capital–labour ratio – a condition (known as Hicks-neutrality) no less restrictive in theory and arguably less consonant with experience than the constant capital–output ratio (Harrod-neutrality) which allowed the Harrod-Domar and

Mahalanobis-Feldman models to be cast aside. Kaldor (1958) contends that the 'stylised facts' point towards a 'continued increase in the amount of capital per worker . . . [and] steady capital–output ratios over long periods' (in Kaldor 1978: 2), Harrod neutrality being preserved by the tendency of fixed investment, while expanding the capital stock, also embodying innovation that raises its productivity. This forms the basis of a series of models in which, while the warranted growth rate converges to the natural rate, it does so through investment decisions which owe little to calculations of the marginal productivity of investment, and nothing at all to wage and profit adjustments to clear the capital and labour markets (Kaldor 1962/1978: 75).

4.6.2 Reswitching and reversal: the ghost of capital's present

The neoclassical aggregate production function, an economy-wide relation between aggregate output and aggregate factor input (or between output per worker and capital per worker), requires summation of the factors in each sector. At least when skill requirements are low, labour might be regarded as homogeneous, so that aggregate labour could conceivably be a physical number. Capital goods, however, are physically diverse, so that aggregation almost inevitably involves summing their present monetary values, being the discounted sum of expected future profits. The fundamental ('Cambridge') criticism of this procedure is that the appropriate discount rate is the equilibrium rate of profit on the capital; yet this rate is determined in neoclassical theory as the marginal product of capital, which can only be computed when its monetary valuation is already known. The Cambridge critics provide an alternative derivation of the rate of profit, independent of marginal productivity, through the Sraffa price-of-production system (section 3.16.1). But this requires wage and profit rates to be fixed outside the neoclassical model.

Any change in wage and profit rates alters the valuation of aggregate capital. The neoclassical argument that a rise in wages causes capital to be substituted for labour, and so raises the capital–labour ratio, thus becomes difficult to sustain outside the very simple NGM. With just one sector, the aggregate production function can if necessary be calibrated in physical terms. With more than one sector, where monetary aggregation becomes necessary, the dependence of capital valuation on the rate of profit makes it impossible to generalise that lower profit (and higher wages) will be associated with higher capital-intensity. The aggregate production function need not be 'well behaved', in the sense that a rise in the capital–labour ratio always causes a rise in labour productivity. As the profit-rate descends, it is quite possible for a firm which switched from one ('labour-intensive') to another ('capital-intensive') technique at an earlier stage to revert to the same technique, its factors having been revalued to make it even more 'labour-intensive'.

Samuelson (1962) shows that some of the properties of the one-sector model might carry over to more general specifications if the wage-profit frontier is itself 'well behaved', so that its gradient yields the aggregate capital–labour ratio. But for the other neoclassical conclusions to hold, this ratio must be constant across the relevant range of wage and profit rates. Rescuing the one-sector 'parable' entails a constant capital–labour ratio across space, rather as the NGM requires a (Hicks-neutral) constant capital–labour ratio through time. Somewhat to Cambridge UK's delight, Samuelson was shown to have resurrected an assumption originally credited to Marx of the same capital–labour ratio in all sectors. Different techniques would make different wage–profit frontiers available in a particular sector. If some of these are non-linear, a maximising firm – looking for the highest profit rate attainable at any given wage rate – may still end up, as the wage rate increases, 'reswitching' from one technique back to another which was abandoned earlier. (For a much fuller discussion of this and other Cambridge controversies, see Harcourt 1972.)

4.6.3 Expectational instability: the ghost of capital's future

Because of their conditioning on future demand, supply and prices, investment decisions are also the ones most exposed to the information failures noted in Chapter 3. For intertemporal equilibrium, today's product prices must not only establish equality between today's demand and supply, but also provide sufficient cashflow to pay off (and so validate) yesterday's investment, and provide the internal finance (or collateral) for tomorrow's investment.

> Prices cannot be treated as though their only function is to allocate resources and distribute income. Prices also must be related to the need for cash flows to validate the capital assets, financial structure, and business style of the economy. The cash flows that prices carry enable debts to be paid, induce and partially finance investment, and enable new financial obligations to be accepted.
>
> (Minsky 1986: 142)

Maintaining a consistency between these three functions of price should be possible if there are sufficient forward or insurance markets to allow investors to eliminate or transfer future capital-cost and payback risk. Failing this, however, it may require a departure from perfect competition sufficient to give investing firms the power to set prices above marginal cost, with a view to recovering past investment costs or financing future outlays. Even then, capital goods' introduction of 'history' in the form of past debts and future expectations makes the neoclassical CGE inherently unstable. In probably the most empirically grounded development of this financial-instability interpretation of Keynes, Minsky (1986) argues that mistaken expectations of future profit can repeatedly cause investment outlays to over- or undershoot those needed for full employment given current savings propensities. An especially serious situation arises when present market-clearing requires a fall in the absolute price level, since negative inflation cannot be offset by a negative interest rate and thus imposes potentially catastrophic repayment demands on those who borrowed for past investment.

In the 'Patinkin resolution' of Keynes's criticism of real-wage flexibility (Patinkin 1965), falling prices boost the real money supply and so return the economy to full employment. But this real-balance effect requires a stock of 'outside' money, independent of that held by creditors (which will be offset by that owed by debtors).

> In a thorough deflation, all private debts are eventually repudiated . . . While this process of debt repudiation is taking place, things are made worse by the effects of decreased profits, wages and investment upon the validation of debts and the paralyzing effects of corporate reorganizations upon investment. Only after the financial structure is radically simplified, which may take many years, may falling prices be expansionary. In a world with complicated financial usages, if there is a road to full employment by way of the Patinkin real balance effect, it may well go by way of hell.
>
> (Minsky 1986: 176–7)

4.6.4 Profit-driven investment: the dual role of pricing

In models derived from partial-equilibrium treatment of markets, both of intertemporal general equilibrium and neoclassical growth, the primary function of prices is to clear product and factor markets. Price adjustments can affect the growth rate by altering relative wage and profit rates (and hence the division of expenditure between consumption and investment if capitalists' and workers' savings rates differ), and cause changes in related markets by transmitting new information. But consistency between the prices' allocative effect in product markets and distributional effect in factor markets is always maintained, under CGE by simultaneous clearing of all markets, and under the NGM by the determination of real wages after product-market adjustment has determined the aggregate price level. 'In the Neoclassical closure, growth and consumption are "prior" to distribution – not in a temporal sense, but in the sense that distribution adjusts to an exogenously given [natural] growth rate' (Marglin 1984: 117).

This result depends on the NGM's assumption of Hicks-neutrality (a constant capital–labour ratio), and the resultant adjustment of growth to its maximum attainable (natural) rate. Where these assumptions are dispensed with, automatic consistency between the allocative and distributional role of price adjustment is lost. There must now be a causal priority between allocation (the determination of relative product and factor prices) and distribution (the division of aggregate income between factors, namely relative wage and profit shares), with the underlying price change for one driving that for the other, even if adjustments still take place simultaneously. Most non-neoclassical models, making the further assumption of imperfect competition giving firms some price-setting power, resolve the priority in favour of distribution. Prices adjust to clear the product markets and set one of the real factor prices, after the other factor price has been set by the stronger factor-owning party.

During the comparatively brief time of legislatively backed union power under near-full employment, iterative or bargaining processes tended to be depicted in which organised labour with a target real wage confronted employers with a target mark-up of price over (predominantly wage) cost (e.g. Blanchard 1985, Layard and Nickell 1985). Steady output and productivity growth may have enabled labour to meet its target for long periods without upsetting employers' profit targets, but when productivity growth slowed for exogenous reasons (e.g. in oil-importing nations after the 1973 oil shock), the demands became incompatible – resulting in industrial relations breakdown as old co-operative bargains broke down (Schott 1982), a stagflationary wage–price spiral (Rowthorn 1980), and additional wage pressure as the resulting recessions deflected government from its full-employment and welfare pledges (Goldthorpe and Hirsch 1978).

The subsequent decline in union power, under pressures of higher unemployment often reinforced by legal curbs, has tipped the balance back towards an earlier set of models in which employers hold the upper hand. Firms again set prices as a mark-up over costs to raise the profits needed for targeted investment, which they prefer to finance internally, because they are unable to communicate a project's profit potential to them or unwilling to submit to outside monitoring and control. However, price has the additional function of clearing the firm's output market given the current position of the demand schedule. These two price calculations – one based on capacity needs at the end of the next market period and the other on demand conditions at the beginning – need not be consistent, and there is little except the gradual alignment of expectations to make them so.

> When firms are successful in setting mark-ups which yield sufficient retained profits with which to expand capacity in the desired manner in step with the growth in market demand, a stable situation is possible where investment keeps capacity growing in step with market demand in a tranquil world of stable market shares . . . as soon as investment plans are formulated in the next period on the basis of demand conditions in the period following, the price so set in the next period may be inconsistent with demand conditions and with the marginal capacity of that period.
>
> (Harcourt and Kenyon 1976: 453, 462)

In the macroeconomy, prices adjust after the output arrives to clear the product markets and set the real wage, but with no guarantee that this will give rise to full employment. By giving the investment-finance motive priority in imperfectly competitive firms' price-setting, these 'neo-Keynesian' models show that growth can be unstable over the long run even if prices adjust to eliminate short-run unemployment. The attempt to derive balanced growth from a general-equilibrium perspective is returned to square one, showing the possibility of optimum allocation and full employment in the short run but with no clear mechanism for adjusting towards it or maintaining it as agents' activities push the economy into growth.

4.7 Rescue by the residual: technical progress

Both main attempts to extend the macroeconomic market model through time – the pre-planned maximising trades of intertemporal CGE and the continuous aggregate price adjustment of the NGM – run into trouble over the volatility of expectations due to imperfect and incomplete information, and its impact on current demand for fixed capital and other stocks. The market's limitations as a generaliser of decision-relevant information and co-ordinator of action, already identified in short-run static CGE (Chapter 2), are no less acute when the capacity effects of investment, and changing consumer preferences due to learning or product innovation, are admitted to the picture. Although some forecasters project a high-growth, full-employment 'golden age' from the conditions of the mid-1990s, there have been few precedents, with the main high-income economies' growth experience between the early 1950s and late 1960s perhaps being the longest near-coincidence of actual and natural rates.

However, other aspects of the growth record do much to redeem the NGM, less by supporting its conclusions than by showing that the most important causes of growth may lie in mechanisms outside it. Econometric tests of the NGM, from Solow (1957) onwards, have consistently shown that the residual in the equation – 'technical progress' raising the productivity of capital and labour – contributes far more to growth than increases in the labour and capital stock. The role of technical progress may have been overstated in early tests, because of its assumed separability from increases in the capital–labour ratio; in practice, process change often needs embodiment in new investment, since improved techniques and skills can be added only at the margin. But even when this is corrected in more recent estimates, the residual continues to take most of the credit (e.g. Mankiw 1995). Growth in factor inputs account for only half of Japan's 8.8 per cent average real growth between 1953 and 1971, and 52 per cent of the US's 4.0 per cent growth between 1948 and 1969, leaving the rest to technical progress, when disaggregated by the neoclassical method (Denison and Chung 1976).

Technical progress can be incorporated into the fundamental neoclassical growth equation (5) as an addition to the investment rate needed to keep the growing economy at full employment through time:

$$dk/dt = sy - (n+p)k \tag{5'}$$

The capital–labour ratio (k) now grows whenever savings per worker (sy) exceed the investment needed to stabilise it at the given labour-force growth rate (n) and the labour productivity growth due to technical progress (p). Instead of settling at an equilibrium level determined by n, the capital–labour ratio can now grow steadily at the rate determined by p: Hicks-neutrality need no longer be assumed. This specification requires, instead, that the capital–output ratio remains constant. This Harrod-neutrality ensures that the marginal product of capital (and hence distribution of national income between profits and wages) is unaffected by growth, an empirically more supportable assumption. Constant returns to scale ensure that the rise in labour productivity can be analytically separated from the rise in stocks of capital and labour. In its 'dynamic' specification (equation 5'), the NGM continues to keep savings and investment (per worker) in equality at full employment. With technical progress taken as exogenous, all the determinants of long-run growth remain on the supply side, as in the previous 'static' specification (equation 5).

Whereas the NGM concentrates on movements along an aggregate production function, as additions to capital and labour raise total output while also adjusting marginal productivities to match full-employment wage and profit rates, it seems that far greater additions to output result from upward shifts in the production function. Indeed, since the investment rate adjusts to keep capital stock growing at the same rate as the labour force, keeping the system at its balanced-growth capital–labour ratio, only technical change can explain the 'stylised fact' that capital–labour ratios (capital intensity of production) rise over time. Alternative one-sector growth models which take account of the sunk nature of the existing capital stock, allowing new techniques of different capital-intensities to be introduced only at the margin through new investment, are even clearer on the importance of technical progress to growth.

> The model shows technical progress – in the specific form of the rate of improvement of the design, etc, of newly produced capital equipment – as the main engine of economic growth, determining not only the rate of growth of productivity but – together with other parameters – also the rate of obsolescence, the average lifetime of equipment, the share of investment in income, the share of profits, and the relationship between investment and potential output (i.e. the 'capital–output ratio' on new capital.
>
> (Kaldor 1962/1978: 74)

4.7.1 Poaching the 'Post-Neoclassical' Theory

Although a large technical progress (TP) residual helped deflect the 'Cambridge' attack on the theoretical meaning of the aggregate production function, it invited a more mainstream attack on empirical applications of the neoclassical growth model. By ascribing the same (linear) production function to each economy, the static NGM implies that countries will converge to a constant per-capita income, conforming to the equilibrium capital–labour ratio (at which gross investment just offsets depreciation of capital and growth in the labour force). The dynamic NGM implies convergence to the constant growth rate made possible by TP, assuming this is evened out by international diffusion of new technology. In practice, nations that have attained steady growth have done so at disparate rates that show few signs of converging, and nations which fail to attain growth have stopped at very different per-capita incomes and capital–labour ratios. 'Production functions may differ by country and by sector, and disaggregation of the economy is needed to estimate the development process correctly. The data needed for such sectoral estimates are not available' (Ito 1997: 187).

By assuming such convergence, the NGM plays down the importance of higher national savings rates for generating faster growth. These merely speed up convergence to the common long-run growth rate, rather than raising that rate (which remains constrained by the number and productivity of workers). Empirically, a rise in national savings rates was one of the first developments to be associated with a 'take-off' into faster growth, and its importance is confirmed once the assumption of convergent growth rates is abandoned.

Moreover, TP in neoclassical growth equations lumps together all developments which might raise the productivity of labour, while excluding (through Harrod-neutrality) any developments that change the productivity of capital. Separately identifying and quantifying the different determinants of rising labour productivity, and introducing variables which might promote growth by raising capital productivity (or the productivity of factors in combination) has become a priority both for economic historians dissatisfied with the 'black box' of a large TP residual, and for economic policy advisers wanting practical guidance on how to generate faster growth.

The 'new' post-neoclassical growth analysis relaxes the NGM assumptions of constant returns to scale and constant capital productivity, by relating (per-capita) output growth to the growth rates of factors' availability supplemented by a range of variables that might improve their efficiency, or 'total factor productivity'. Estimations based on 'new' growth theory, sometimes called 'endogenous' theory because of its search for the underlying causes of TP, avoid imposing the convergence assumption: kost employ cross-sectional data (average growth of variables across the same period for several national economies) or panel data (the cross-section tracked across individual years) in place of the one-country time-series favoured by earlier NGM studies. Explanations can thus be offered for the tendency for some economies to outgrow others over long periods, and for economies to stabilise at different per-capita incomes.

The explanatory variables assigned significance by post-neoclassical studies extend to the demand side, and to aspects of the supply side which can be altered by policy intervention. They thus open the way for a substantial break with the *laissez-faire* conclusions of the NGM, which discounts the importance either of short-run intervention to keep investment matched to the full-employment savings level or long-run intervention to raise the rate of saving. While the dynamic NGM leaves room for state intervention to promote technical progress (e.g. through sponsorship of basic research and vocational training), neoclassical theorists tend to regard these too as best left to the market, for reasons outlined in section 4.8. In contrast, 'new' growth studies have identified significant contributions from such government-manipulable variables as the quality of human capital and physical infrastructure, and the presence of industries with significant scale economies or horizontal linkages. One recent study reconsiders 'big push' ideas, previously marginalised by the NGM (section 4.5.2), in the light of new econometric evidence on increasing returns within key sectors and linkages between them (Murphy *et al.* 1989). Another finds that industrial policy to direct investment into such high-growth sectors, previously shown as effective (if at all) only in lower-income economies with a ready-made technological trajectory to follow, may in fact make significant growth contributions only to economies already close to the technological frontier (Kekic 1998).

The move from neoclassical to post-neoclassical growth models is not without

cost. In abandoning the imposed production function and its convergence implications, the new specifications also muddy the direction of causation, so that such
'significant' variables as better education and infrastructure quality could be the
consequences of faster growth rather than their cause. The choice of single indicators for complex variables (such as inflation-rate variation for 'macroeconomic
stability', education spending for 'human capital', trade share in GDP for 'economic openness') and the quantification of subjective indices (such as economic
freedom, social cohesion and institutional quality) can always be criticised, as can
the instrumental proxies chosen to substitute those explanatory variables between
which collinearity is suspected. Different measures, and different data sets and
time periods chosen for these measures, lead to very different conclusions on the
impacts of different variables on growth, and the statistical significance of that
impact.

Far from displacing the NGM, 'new' models have often reinforced its conserva-
tive conclusions. Foremost among the variables they tend to associate with faster
growth are low and stable inflation, low rates of government spending and taxation
(especially welfare-supporting payroll taxation), cautious monetary policy (promoting positive real interest rates and underpinned by low public borrowing),
flexible exchange rates, openness to international trade, and openness to flows of
foreign direct and portfolio investment. 'Getting macroeconomic fundamentals
right – that is, low inflation, low budget deficits, and few distortionary taxes – is crucial' (Ito 1997: 195). The initial level of income per head emerges as a strong
negative influence on growth, redeeming the long-run convergence of growth
rates implied by the NGM, with its implication that background supply factors
dominate any demand or behavioural changes imposed by government. 'It is
surely an irony that one of the lasting contributions of endogenous growth theory
is that it stimulated empirical work that demonstrated the explanatory power of the
old neoclassical model' (Barro 1996: 2).

The uncertain benefits of state intervention to stabilise aggregate demand, capture and nurture increasing-returns industries, build up physical infrastructure
and promote human capital accumulation (and the frequent side-effects of public
sector vote-buying and rent-seeking) must therefore, in post-neoclassical light, be set
against the certain costs of high government spending, distortive taxation, and
crowded-out private investment and saving. Damage done by strategic trade and
industrial policy in obscuring relative price signals and obstructing competition
may outweigh any gains from promoting infant industries with scale, scope and
learning economies. Evidence of 'policy complementarity' – several beneficial
interventions needing to be present at once for the effect on growth to be significantly positive – stacks the odds against government doing more harm than good.
And the areas in which post-neoclassical analysis suggests threshold levels may need
to be reached before growth is sustainable – physical infrastructure, education and
training, increasing-returns industries, basic food and energy supply – tend to be
those that neoclassical analysis now seeks to return to the market, after the 'failure'
of government to provide them more effectively (sections 2.2 to 2.8).

Above all, the 'new' approach to growth, even in its most detailed specifications, has not resolved the mystery of the large residual. It still produces significant 'total factor productivity' residuals, with inter-regional differences especially difficult to explain. Technical progress, whether through lower-income economies' rapid uptake of existing technologies or higher-income economies' invention of new ones, remains central to the attainment of growth and the alleviation of its environmental and social side-effects. This being the case, competitive markets' ability to generate faster technical change could far outweigh any shortcomings in its assignment of existing factor stocks, whether caused by the sunk nature of fixed capital or the instability of investment demand based on uncertain expectations. From co-ordinating agents' responses to existing information, a process equally frustrated by the absence of price-setting power and by its introduction, the market's task shifts to the introduction of new information into the system, which it can more easily achieve at the level of the agent even if subsequent diffusion proves problematic.

4.8 Markets as discovery: the Austrian perspective

Although its pace may be increasing, as more inventions are produced and their rates of adoption and diffusion quicken, technical progress is hardly new to economics. Indeed, it could be argued to have formed the centrepiece of employment and growth theories, before the neoclassical partial-equilibrium and CGE model refocused attention on prices, factor rewards and static allocation. For Adam Smith, the vast productivity increase made possible by division of labour began with extensive practice at one task and the time saved in not switching to others, but continued with 'the invention of a great number of machines which facilitate and abridge labour, and enable one man to do the work of many' (Smith 1776/1979: 112). For Marx, innovation raising the rate of exploitation (relative surplus value) or bringing temporary monopoly power was one of the few devices by which capitalists could slow the inexorable fall in profit rates as they raised the organic composition of capital (the neoclassical capital–labour ratio) and pushed absolute surplus value to its limits (Habermas 1976: 55). And in the more contemporary 'Austrian' approach, markets' ability to cause disruption by changing expectations and revealing new preferences is transformed from a weakness of the system into its fundamental strength.

Austrian theory overthrows the distinction between optimum allocation and growth by fusing the two together. Market transaction becomes a process of continuous improvement in the use of resources, but moving not to a definite end-point (as in CGE theory) so much as towards an ever-extending horizon. 'Development depends not so much on finding optimal combinations for given resources and factors of production as on calling forth and enlisting for development purposes resources and abilities that are hidden, scattered or badly utilised' (Hirschman 1958: 5). Exchange, investment and innovation are means by which individual agents try to improve their material situation – full employment and growth being unintended results which none the less prevail, provided prices are openly advertised and freely adjustable. Firms continue to chase profit and consumers utility, but they achieve it through the early discovery of new technologies and preferences, or trades made lucrative by privately held information not yet captured in prices. These are precisely the imperfections which neoclassical theory glosses over so as to concentrate on optimal end-states.

> Economic theory went astray . . . when the theory of value took the centre of the stage – which meant focusing attention on their allocative functions of markets to the exclusion of their creative functions – as an instrument for transmitting impulses to economic change.
>
> (Kaldor 1972/1978: 181)

4.8.1 *Creative destruction*

Technical change does not fit easily into the general equilibrium framework. By punishing strategic action with immediate losses, which the instant competing-away of monopoly profits makes irredeemable, the constraints of continuous maximisation and perfect competition challenge agents' means and incentive to innovate. But if innovations arise exogenously at certain moments in the future, further constraints may have to be put on the evolution of product and factor prices to explain why agents do not use knowledge gained from forward markets or perfect foresight to bring their discovery forward. Whereas innovators break through their constraints, creating new resources or finding new ways to apply them, agents in the CGE remain content to optimise subject to existing constraints, merely seeking a better arrangement for existing resources according to the technologies and preferences already revealed.

The neoclassical growth model gives a similarly offstage role to technical change, with process innovation showing up as an unexplained shift in the aggregate production function, while product innovation falls outside the one-sector characterisation altogether. The information required for current resources to be allocated and known techniques to be adopted efficiently leaves agents knowing too much for innovation, which essentially results from techniques unknown at the start of the transaction process being discovered by the agents conducting it. If new products or processes arise from within, the question arises as to why agents did not know of them at the beginning, and what happens to their transaction plans now that a new preference is revealed or a new production technique made available. But if innovation is exogenous its origin is unclear, and its arrival likely to be equally disruptive of the transaction processes already in motion.

The Austrian perspective turns this problem neatly on its head, turning attention from the existence of equilibrium – with its demanding requirements for full information and co-ordination – to the process of acquiring knowledge in the pursuit of higher utility and profit. This is essentially a disequilibrating process, leading agents to regret their earlier actions and change their plans, but it leads the system over time towards a higher level and more efficient allocation of production. Whereas the neoclassical growth model treats the economy at a high level of aggregation in order to produce a model that can be tested against actual data, and is pushed towards assuming perfect foresight on the part of agents as a condition for steady-state growth, Austrian theory treats individuals as grappling with highly imperfect information flows, and accepts that growth cycles and bubbles may develop in the macroeconomy as a result of their behaviour.

Technical change – defined broadly as any change in capital equipment, labour skill or the organisation of factors – now fits more easily into the perspective. Competition induces process as firms battle to reduce their costs, and product innovation as they seek temporary shelter in an uncontested market terrain. Relative price changes guide the search for new ideas and the direction of technical change, with the relative cheapening of capital encouraging its substitution for labour, and bottlenecks in a particular process focusing attention on the need to raise efficiency there (Moss 1982). 'The influence of demand side factors on successful innovations can be very great. Indeed constant attention to user needs on the part of the innovator is often emphasised as a necessary feature of success' (Coombes *et al.* 1987: 104).

In probably its most influential presentation, Schumpeter (1942) characterises capitalism as a process of 'creative destruction' in which agents battle against their constraints and look for more profitable ways of acting, in a manner which constantly destabilises the system but thereby moves it to higher levels of productivity. His intuition that 'non-optimal' actions can produce better long-run results than relentless optimisation has subsequently gained much empirical and theoretical support, as has his argument that the market's strength lies in the speed and informational economy with which it alerts agents to challenges and opportunities in their environment.

> In the Schumpeterian scheme, the limits of what can be done are never fixed and never clearly in view. Discovering what can be done is part of the problem for the problem for the individual actor . . . Information imperfections, and informational differences among the actors, are not complications of the basic structure, but are central.
>
> (Nelson and Winter 1977: 271)

Aside from Schumpeter, 'Austrian' economic analysis is most closely associated with Rosenstein-Rodan (1934), Hayek (1944, 1949), von Mises (1949), Schmookler (1966), Kirzner (1979) and a number of non-Austrians including Shackle (1972) and Rosenberg (1976). It also has close philosophical links with views on the growth of knowledge and the foundations of open society associated with Popper (1962). Since it eschews any concept of general equilibrium allocation or steady-state growth, the Austrian approach has no problem allowing mistaken expectations, inappropriately sunk investments, and a resultant path-dependence in which different or differently timed discoveries and choices could have sent the economy in different directions.

Whereas the neoclassical approach assumes a regular structure to the economy, and a path for its progress through time, which theory and investigation may eventually discover, the Austrian concern is with the way individuals act and systems evolve, with no claim to be able to discern the 'big picture' or to chart the movement of aggregates independently of the agents who collectively produce them. It is sympathetic with Popper's philosophical contention that all present knowledge is provisional, capable of being overthrown by new discovery, and that it is by seeking to criticise and improve on existing knowledge that science moves forward.

Despite its decentralised and competitive starting-point, neoclassical theory is deterministic in the sense of identifying one best arrangement for economic activity, at a point in time or through time. It carries much the same conviction, about the discovery of an underlying economic rationality and its ability to guide individuals and societies towards their one 'best' outcome, that underlies the Marxian perspective which neoclassical theory claims to have displaced. Correspondingly, the general-equilibrium model, and its extension through time by neoclassical growth models, attracted considerable interest from the students of central planning. Austrian theorists, many of whom were forced to flee fascist and socialist planning experiments, celebrate the unpredictability of the growth of knowledge, and vehemently resist any idea that there is one 'best way' into which planners (however enlightened) can try to guide the system. One of Schumpeter's greatest fears was that capitalism, in trying to rationalise the discovery process and and stabilise its results through corporate and bureacratic co-ordination, would smother the creativity that had set it in motion.

4.8.2   *Testing the Austrian perspective: behavioural models and evolution*

Whereas conventional economic theory aims for an abstract characterisation of the system as a whole, the Austrian concern is to view things more subjectively from the viewpoint of the individual agent. The market's strength lies, in fact, in allowing individuals to work out what is best for them with a minimum of knowledge about what is happening around them.

> If it were the result of deliberate human design, and if the people guided by the price changes understood that their decisions have significance far beyond their immediate aim, this mechanism would have been acclaimed as one of the greatest triumphs of the human mind . . . It is not necessary, for the working of the system, that anybody should understand it.
>
> (Hayek 1949: 87, 124)

The external benefits of private transaction, a threat to the existence of equilibrium under the neoclassical system, are now a vital element in the continual improvement on that equilibrium, individual action unavoidably feeding back onto the prices that guide it. The Austrian perspective is thus insulated, even before they arrived, against postmodern critiques of top-down theorising which question how one individual (the social scientist) can step outside the system they are in to establish superior knowledge about it. It is consistent, again well ahead of its time, with the recent synthesis of structural and phenomenological social theories into 'structuration' theory, which sees individual action as both influenced by and impacting on the institutions and information flows around it.

> It is only in so far as knowledge and reason guide action that people are free to discern alternative responses and frame purposes. The available knowledge . . . however . . . is, in part, acquired through the individuals partaking in society and the social practices which continually reproduce it.
>
> (Lawson 1985: 909)

Philosophically, the Austrians' account is existential (depicting thought and experience from the individual's perspective) and ontological (being concerned with immediate reality), compared with the neoclassical perspective's rationalism (the belief that objective external assessment can identify a deeper and more consistent reality than subjective experience, thus helping individuals transcend this) and teleology (the belief that rational investigation will reveal the ultimate and optimal state towards which present actions will lead). Hayek also anticipates, again before it had been introduced into economics, the temptation to assume rational expectations in building macroeconomic models, and the problems it introduces of how agents come to know the precise structure of the economy they are in, and how they can compute the impact of their actions on the rest of the system.

Concentration on the process of improving and rearranging resources rather than their end result, and its optimality properties, renders the Austrian approach more descriptive and less analytical than its neoclassical counterpart. 'Constructive theories must describe a process of groping experiment and gambling for knowledge, of being wrong many times in order to be right, while analytic theories describe what things will be like when, if ever, they have attained rightness' (Shackle 1972: 53). Emphasis is placed on the conditions of imperfect knowledge and disequilibrium from which neoclassical theory tries to abstract, through its appeal to Walrasian (tatonnement) price-setting and to highly aggregated, smoothly adjusting growth processes. Whereas neoclassical theory lends itself to formal models, which can then be econometrically tested by introducing runs of data for the components of growth and testing the predictions for output, Austrian theory in the Schumpeterian tradition lends itself to historical analysis, whose closest approach to numerical test is the creation and analysis of simulation models.

Nelson and Winter (1982) present a series of simulation models in which firms are constrained in their information gathering and processing capacities, and so follow satisficing rules for the choice of technology and setting of investment. In one of the earliest studies, firms begin with an inherited capital stock, and technical conditions which determine how output relates to labour and capital input. Wages adjust to equate the supply and demand for labour, but capital costs are taken as given. Firms continue producing with their current technique unless profit falls below a minimum satisfactory level. This can occur either because of 'endogenous' changes in the capital stock (augmented by investment out of profit but eroded by depreciation), or because of 'exogenous' changes in product prices caused by the trend in aggregate output. When a firm wishes to change technique, it runs through a list of alternatives and adopts the first one that satisfies the minimum profit target.

In an early test of this framework, using a computer to simulate firms' evolution and aggregate the resultant output, Nelson and Winter (1974) were able to provide a direct comparison with the econometric results of Solow's original (1957) test of the NGM. Despite the path-dependency produced by firms' fixed starting-point and rule-governed adaptation, 'the historically observed trends in the output–labour ratio, capital–labour ratio and the wage rate are all visible in the simulated data' (Nelson and Winter 1974: 898). Just as econometric 'fit' could be improved by dropping insignificant variables from initial estimations, the simulations' accuracy could be improved by altering the behavioural assumptions (such as a labour-saving bias in the new techniques from which firms select, and an assumed 2 per cent payout ratio as the cost of capital).

4.9   The market as a process

For neoclassical critics, the Austrian approach – based on a 'behavioural' depiction of consumers and firms – shares the drawbacks of behaviourism as it was originally developed in psychology. Agents are treated as acting mechanically according to oversimplistic rules, leaving their conduct to be shaped by the environment when in fact, over time, they can learn about this and adopt more deliberative conduct in response. The possibility of investment plans being frustrated and profit targets missed, which may lead to slumps and cycles in the aggregate, can be avoided if, instead of reacting 'adaptively' to past changes in demand, firms are able 'rationally' to anticipate the consequences of their own and rival firms' actions. The economy might then arrive at its steady-state growth path, without initial lapses from it as firms respond to price swings caused by decisions taken in expectational error, and without those lapses permanently altering the path taken by the economy.

If, instead of basing investment decisions on past changes in aggregate demand, firms can learn (perhaps by their forecasting mistakes) to anticipate future demand trends, they will be able to adjust aggregate investment to a level that can be absorbed by the demand it generates, given current capital productivity and savings behaviour.

> At any time firms are viewed as facing a set of alternatives regarding the inputs and outputs they will procure and produce. Firms choose so as to maximise profit or present value, given external conditions facing the firm. The sector is assumed to be in equilibrium in the sense that demand and supply are balanced in all relevant markets and no firm can improve its position given what other firms are doing.
>
> (Nelson and Winter 1974: 887)

However, this requires firms to anticipate future technological opportunities, the demand and factor-price trends that will govern their uptake, and future preference revelation in response to new products, in addition to the firm's already challenging task of anticipating the current market-clearing price vector. Later neoclassical models have allowed some information imperfection by requiring firms to search for new technologies rather than being costlessly informed of them, but they are still assumed to know the costs of search and to arive at an expected benefit through knowledge of the probability distribution of innovation outcomes. Risk of being wrong can be introduced into the neoclassical model, but not the unquantifiable uncertainty over whether innovation is worthwhile. The model thus appears to add a requirement for consistent expectations over time to the swift price-adjustments needed to achieve optimal allocation at a point in time.

Studies of the way firms actually operate have tended to cast doubt on whether their information availabilities and processing capacity can ever support this type of accurate expectation formation. Empirical evidence goes the way of the 'evolutionary' model, and there is notably more sympathy for Schumpeter than for rational maximisation in most practical observations of how firms operate. Decisions on the future scale and composition of output must generally be taken in ignorance of the contemporaneous production and investment decisions of other firms, which will shape the future relative prices that determine payback on the investment. Even if the firm knew the price expectations and objective functions of all other firms, these are likely to be conditioned partly on expectations of its own (and other rival firms') price expectations and objective functions, setting up a second-guessing process which will severely test the firm's computational power and may well result in infinite regress. This bounded rationality at the firm level is one reason why it may settle for 'satisficing' pricing and investment decisions aimed at a target level of profit, rather than trying to maximise profit (March and Simon 1958). A reinforcing reason is that the firm, condensed by neoclassical theory to a single production function with a single profit-maximising objective, may actually be a coalition of agents with inconsistent subgoals (sales maximisation, stock minimisation, etc.) whose joint satisfaction is incompatible with profit maximisation (Cyert and March 1963).

As in static general-equilibrium analysis, appeal could be made to 'evolutionary selection' as a means by which firms can end up maximising profit even if they do not intend it or cannot formally calculate how to do it. Perfect competition, under which even the best-performing firms make only normal profits, implies that any firm which fails to maximise profit will go out of business, its production share being filled by those that do. Even if imperfect competition allows some non-profit-maximisers to survive, the differentially faster growth of higher-profit firms, and less successful rivals' attempts to imitate them, could lead to a generalisation of maximising behaviour.

Some of the obstacles to evolutionary selection producing maximising results were reviewed in section 3.8. Selection imposes a minimum survival constraint which changes over time because of modifications imposed from outside (such as changes in labour costs or product prices) and actions taken by firms themselves (changing technique when profit becomes inadequate). Because the selection rules change over time, it is not the case that profit-maximisers will come to dominate the economy by outgrowing (or being imitated by) non-maximisers. Since profit-maximising is more a result of coincidence than calculation, behaviour which is maximising now will cease to be so as relative prices change, so the changing rules will pick a different set of winners each time. The direction of causation within the evolutionary process is correspondingly non-neoclassical. Firms' rule-based output and input decisions determine prevailing market prices rather than being determined by them, with rule-based investment driving the capacity change which alters the outcome of output and input decisions next time round. Changes in firms' rules provide a ready characterisation of innovation, in contrast to the neoclassical perspective under which one (maximising) procedure is always followed (Nelson and Winter 1974: 894).

4.10   Conclusion: from achievement award to progress prize

The dynamic and destabilising impact of investment, innovation and preference change, and the external effects of private production and consumption, peripheral and troubling aspects to the 'neoclassical' end-state perspective on markets, find a central and constructive place in the more process-oriented 'Austrian' perspective. Philosophical and stylistic differences mean that there has been little interaction between the two approaches. The concentration on process renders Austrian presentations much more verbal and empirically based than their neoclassical counterparts, with less scope for formal building and testing of models. But a common enemy in the Marxian and 'Cambridge' alternatives has brought the two together.

Despite their lack of methodological common ground, Austrian and neoclassical schools are in agreement on the virtues of the market. Central European subjectivism complements North American rationalism in showing how the market guides agents towards a better economic situation, even when they lack the information to see it coming. It is to the Austrian treatment of markets, as efficient means of information processing, that the neoclassical system appeals for reconciliation of its static efficiency claims with those of growth and dynamic efficiency, and for a clarification of the link between free markets and free society. Chapter 5 tries to formalise this by recasting market transaction – and its alternatives – within the framework of individual decision.

Appendix: deriving the neoclassical growth equation

Section 4.5 presented the 'intensive' national income identity

$$y = c + i \tag{2}$$

where Y is the output–labour ratio (average labour productivity), c is consumption per worker and i is investment per worker.

National income equates with national output, which results from the 'intensive' production function

$$y = f(k) \tag{4}$$

where k is the capital–labour ratio or average capital stock.
   Combining equations (2) and (4),

$$c + i = f(k) \tag{A5}$$

Investment per worker i represents the period's change in capital stock per worker, dK/L. The growth rate of the capital–labour ratio is approximated by the difference between the growth rates of the capital stock and the labour force:

$$1/k.dk/dt = 1/K.dK/dt - 1/L.dL/dt \tag{A6}$$

Multiplying through by $k=K/L$ and fixing labour force growth at the exogenous rate n,

$$dk/dt = (dK/dt)/L - nk \tag{A7}$$

from which the per-worker investment rate $i = (dK/dt)/L$ emerges as

$$i = dk/dt + nk \tag{A8}$$

Investment per worker serves to expand the capital–labour ratio, after first maintaining it against the natural expansion of the workforce.
   Combining equations (4), (5) and (8) produces

$$y = c + dk/dt + nk \tag{A9}$$

Restating the difference between per-worker income and consumption, $y - c$, as the growth in per-worker saving, S/L, and assuming saving to be a fixed proportion of income, $S=sY$, allows (9) to be rearranged into the basic NGM equation

$$dk/dt = sy - nk \tag{A10}$$

(Equation (5) in the text.)

5 Markets as information processors

The challenge for any social organising principle is to promote independent thought alongside interdependent action. People must be permitted to pursue their self-interest without infringing the self-interest of others. The advantages of co-ordination and collective action must be harnessed without destroying individual motivation or distorting individual reward. An ideal market actor must be both a self-starter and a team player. Such a combination rarely occurs naturally outside the pages of high-flying job applications, and the market's unique claim is to bring out the best of both contrasting worlds.

To motivate the best use of knowledge and resources, and to respect personal freedom, agents must be allowed wherever possible to act individually in their own self-interest. But to prevent some agents disadvantaging others through concentration of selling or purchasing power, or disadvantaging themselves through continuing to compete where co-operation would bring better results all round, agents need a facility for the sharing of information and the co-ordination of activity. Division of labour, allowing agents to do what they like best but making them reliant on others to do the rest, is the ultimate expression of this mutual expansion of the solo and the shared. The proposition that markets promote division of labour, and so turn interdependence from a source of conflict into one of cohesion ('organic solidarity'), is one of the oldest in economics. Equally venerable, but only recently rediscovered, is the proposition that markets tell agents what they need to know to co-ordinate their actions over space and time, without overloading them with detail or confronting them with clusters of power which give political authorities the excuse to intervene.

Markets' special appeal lies in their ability to reconcile growing freedom of action with growing interaction, conjuring a harmonious whole out of the self-interested sums of the parts. Whereas earlier social theorists had argued that a complex society needed co-ordination from the centre, with resource allocation imposed by a dictator or negotiated by a democratic government, economists suggested – and eventually found an axiomatic way to prove – that free decentralised trade could successfully harness private greed to the social good. Strict conditions are needed to achieve this happy balance, as observed in Chapters 2 and 3. There are many circumstances that can deflect the outcome of market transaction away from its optimum-allocation and full-employment properties, and while some of these obstructions can be blamed on outside intervention, others need outside intervention to resolve them. But a shift of attention from the market's theoretical maximising capabilities to its practical potential for growth and change produced more definite grounds for belief in its effectiveness. While optimising end-states are the market system's most mathematically impressive feature, it is on ever-improving process that its practical appeal is based.

This chapter summarises the model of rational individual decision that under-lies the view of market processes presented so far. 'Neoclassical' and 'Austrian' approaches are shown as variants on the same essentially individualistic procedure for transaction, their main difference lying in the ways they treat two of the barri-ers to optimal trading identified earlier – inadequate information and inadequate calculating power. Evidence from tests of the theory is reviewed, showing that there remain some conditions under which market-guided choice may not work well for either the individual or the society. Alternative decision styles are consid-ered which aim to resolve the main problems – imperfect and incomplete information, bounded rationality, or lack of communication and co-ordination. This provides a foundation for assessment, in Chapters 6 and 7, of the main alter-natives to market-based transaction.

5.1 The individual decision process

Decisions to transact, and decisions in general, consist of a sequence of events laid out in Figure 5.1. The agent sets an objective (O), identifies the action set (A) of actions that might lead towards the objective, chooses an action (C) from this set, implements it, and observes the results (R). Objectives lead to the action set via a process of search. The action set leads to choice via a process of evaluation. Choice leads to observed results via a process of implementation. If the choice is to be repeated, observation of the results may lead the agent to revise its objectives, action identification, evaluation or implementation method, so the assessment process is seen looping back to previous stages of the decision process.

This model's sympathy with the market-economy perspective is expressed by taking the individual as the unit of decision. Agents think and act for themselves, with other agents' objectives and actions entering only as items of information to take into account during search and evaluation. Implementation and assessment are similarly independent pursuits. But while market transaction (MT) fits most easily into the framework, the three alternatives to be considered can also be interpreted through it. Relational transaction (RT) involves bringing agents together at the search and evaluation phases, so that they may break through interdependencies and, if necessary, overcome co-ordination problems. Informed transaction (IT) provides third-party external input at the search and evaluation stages. Administered transaction (AT) extends third-party input to the objective-setting and results-assessment stages, with the option of simplifying and/or parcelling out decisions whose computational demands are too complex for one agent.

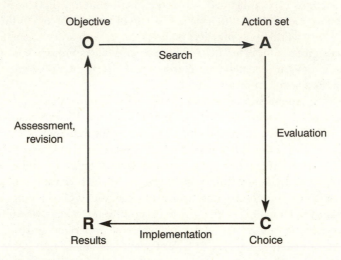

Figure 5.1 The individual decision process

5.2   The market transaction decision: rational choice

Agents who go through the profit- and utility-maximising procedures featured in neoclassical general-equilibrium and growth theories make a systematic one-way journey through the sequence in Figure 5.1. The objective is to close a gap between the agent's present situation and the best that is attainable. To this end, all relevant available actions are identified, and ranked in order of the value of results they are expected to produce. The highest ranked action is then selected for implementation.

5.2.1   'Objective' utility

The ranking of actions is often illustrated as involving the assignment of an actual expected valuation. Conventionally, this involves identifying all the possible outcomes of a particular action and assigning it a magnitude in the same units as the objective (subjective utility or expected profit), along with the likelihood of its occurrence expressed as a numerical probability. Equivalently, an action can be considered as having one outcome under each possible future state-of-the-world, and probabilities are assigned to the occurrence of each of those states. Provided all the possible outcomes of an action have been identified, and each outcome is mutually exclusive, the probabilities are additive (they sum to one). Each action's expected utility is then computed as the sum of the possible outcomes weighted by their probabilities. The rational choice is the action with the highest expected utility.

This 'cardinal' ranking process is most easily illustrated where utility can be measured 'objectively', in money terms. For example, a consumer wants to make the most of her weekend, and identifies three options: applying for a better job (A), going ten-pin bowling (B), and spending the evening at an exclusive club (C). Her objective is, for reasons of model-simplicity masquerading as materialism, purely financial. Successfully applying for the job will win her $5,000 more in (present value) lifetime earnings, but she assesses the chances of getting it as only one in ten. An unsuccessful application wins her nothing. Bowling is worth $1,000 if she finishes on the winning side, which she normally does 70 per cent of the time. If she loses, however, the disappointment has a negative value of $1,200. Going to the club gives her a 30 per cent chance of dancing with a sympathetic partner (worth $500), a 69.9 per cent chance of merely getting enjoyably drunk ($100), and a one-in-one-thousand chance of meeting the famous film actor Derek Chestwigg ($100,000). Her action evaluations are:

A: $0.1 \times \$5,000 = \$500$
B: $0.7 \times \$1,000 - 0.3 \times \$1,200 = \$400$
C: $0.3 \times \$500 + 0.699 \times \$100 + 0.001 \times \$100,000 = \$319.90$

Despite the attractions of rising idols and falling skittles, therefore, the consumer stays at home and applies for the job.

5.2.2 Subjective expected utility

Plausibility is not a strong point in either the contents or the conclusion of the above example. In practice, two important modifications are made to add realism to the rational-choice framework. By introducing an element of subjectivity, these also deflect the charge that 'rational choice' is a prescriptive, deterministic outcome. The framework can still be used to argue that an individual has acted irrationally by taking an inferior choice, but only according to criteria set by their previous behaviour – and which they may always have decided to change.

The first step is to avoid expressing expected utilities as monetary values, for reasons succinctly illustrated by the 'St Petersburg Paradox'. In this game, an agent is offered $2 if they correctly call (heads or tails) for one toss of a coin, $4 if they correctly call two tosses, $8 if they correctly call three tosses, and so on until their financial adviser intervenes. If expected monetary outcomes are equated with rewards, the 'objective' expected utility (probability times outcome) of the game is $0.5.\$2 + 0.25.\$4 + 0.125.\$8 + \ldots (1/2n).2n$ which leads to an infinite sum, each throw adding $1 to the expected value.

Logic suggests that no rational agent will pay an infinite sum to play this game, since further monetary rewards will eventually start to lose their appeal. By making subjective utility diminish at the margin, so that it rises less steeply than the bet's expected value, valuation of the series is made to tail off to a finite sum. 'The St Petersburg Paradox serves to show the absurdity of following the equivalent valuation rule' (Anand 1993: 4). Diminishing marginal utility (as a function of expected monetary value) can in this case be interpreted as risk aversion, expressed through the shape of the utility function linking subjective reward to monetary reward.

Risk-averse agents should, for example, prefer a fairly safe bet (e.g. 90 per cent chance of $100 and 10 per cent chance of $500) to a more adventurous one (e.g. 5 per cent chance of $1,000 or 95 per cent chance of $94.74) even though their certainty equivalents are the same. Risk-attracted agents might, in contrast, value the second bet more highly because of the outside chance of getting a much larger reward.

Having made utilities subjective it is a short step to the second modification, which is to allow the agent to rank their available actions in order of preference without having to place an explicit value on each one. An action's subjective expected utility (SEU) is not directly observable, but must be inferred from the choices an agent actually makes. Under this 'ordinal' system of ranking, an agent's choices are judged rational provided their preferences satisfy the following consistency conditions:

1   Transitivity: preference for action A over B and action B over C implies preference for action A over C.
2   Completeness: the action set can be completely ordered – every action being ranked (above, below or equivalent to) every other action.
3   Independence: the possible outcomes of an action (and the utilities associated with them) are separable, so that the action's value can be expressed as a linear sum of its outcome utilities multiplied by their probabilities.
4   Independence of irrelevant alternatives: the choice among a set of possible actions should not be altered by the introduction of another action, unless this is better than all the actions in the existing set.

Making utility a subjective function of consumption lightens the agent's computational load and relieves them of having to explain why, or by how much, one action is valued above another. The detachment of (average and marginal) utility from money amounts also rescues rational choice from one of the more extreme egalitarian conclusions of utilitarian welfare theory: that diminishing marginal utility of income means that social welfare is maximised when income is equally distributed. Individuals are now allowed to differ in the utility they derive from income as well as in their income, so that it is quite possible for more money to come supplied with a higher capacity to enjoy it. Under SEU, a higher-income earner thus endowed can derive higher average utility from higher consumption (than a lower-income earner) even if their marginal utility is diminishing. The subjective nature of utility rules out its interpersonal comparison, and any attempt to add it up for a social total.

5.2.3   *Two routes to rationality*

Two distinct representations of the market system have been noted in previous chapters: a 'neoclassical' view concentrating on the end-states of market transaction, summarised as optimum allocation and full employment, and an 'Austrian' view concentrating on the process of transaction, resulting in continuous adaptation and growth. These can now be seen to correspond to two distinct interpretations of the rational-choice model, depending on the view taken of agents' powers to gather and process information.

The neoclassical approach involves agents in consciously working through the SEU model, seeking the full range of actions appropriate to a maximising objective and ordering them completely before choosing the highest. The market's strength lies in conveying the necessary information quickly and cheaply. An agent need not gather every marginally relevant scrap of information, but will continue gathering it until the extra utility (in terms of a more accurate decision) ceases to justify the extra cost. If there are time or financial constraints on the depth to which the information can be processed, the agent will once again make a rational decision on when the extra computational cost exceeds the additional decision accuracy it will produce.

Taking the rational decision process literally in this way invokes the same informational difficulties that were encountered with the neoclassical market models in Chapters 2–4. Decision-relevant information may not be available if it depends on future exogenous events, or the future results of agents' current uncoordinated actions. Where those actions depend on mutually dependent expectation, decision calculations may form a loop which overwhelms the agent's computing power. The optimal 'stopping rules' for abbreviating search and evaluation processes do not solve the problem, since the rest of the process would have to be completed before its costs and benefits could be inserted into the calculation on whether the process is worth completing.

The Austrian approach acknowledges that information may be seriously incomplete and imperfect, so that the necessary decision calculations run into bounded rationality. It recognises that rationally choosing agents do not necessarily go through the search, evaluation and selection process consciously, or check their selections to make sure all the axioms have been obeyed, and instead depicts market forces guiding agents to behave 'as if' they were making rational choices. The market system answers, according to Hayek,

> the central question of all social sciences: how can the combination of fragments of knowledge existing in different minds bring about results which, if they were to be brought about deliberately, would require a knowledge on the part of the directing mind which no single person can possess . . . The most significant fact about this system is the economy of knowledge with which it operates, or how little the individual participants need to know in order to be able to take the right action.
>
> (Hayek 1949: 54, 86)

Behind this unintentional direction is a competitive selection mechanism, eliminating agents who make non-optimising choices unless they quickly learn to imitate those who do. (This may itself be a rational choice, but again one which is seen as such only after the event; mistaken imitators will also be squeezed out.)

The market in this view is a device for achieving the effects of rational decision with a far lower informational and computational requirement. The function of market prices, in quickly summarising the collective effects of agents' past actions and the value they place on tradable assets, is accorded special importance in this information- and calculation-economising process.While agents may try to maximise SEU when they can, the assumption is that they do so rarely. Significant choices, where a fully informed and calculated decision would be advantageous, generally offer too little non-contingent information to be consciously maximised; choices for which the relevant information is available and can be fully processed are generally too trivial for the full SEU apparatus to seem worth applying.

As with markets in aggregate, studies of transaction decision have tended to begin 'neoclassical' and then take an 'Austrian' turn. The retreat from SEU began with a consideration of the problems likely to confront its enactment in real economic situations, and has been encouraged by difficulty in confirming the theory's hypotheses even in highly simplified test situations.

5.2.4 Problems in theory: knowing too little, thinking too much

Most actual choice situations supply rather less information than is provided in illustrations of SEU maximisation such as the one used above. The objective may be unquantifiable, or have several different elements which cannot be measured on the same scale or maximised at once. Some available actions may not be known about, or – perhaps because not yet tested exhaustively, if at all – their likely outcomes may not be known. The utility of those outcomes may be hard to judge, if not experienced before. Outcome-utility becomes still harder to judge if it depends on the prevailing state of the world generated either exogenously (will it be raining at the football match?) or endogenously (how many others will decide to drive down this stretch of road?). To get as far as assigning additive probabilities to the possible outcomes requires either extensive observation of past uses of the action under different conditions, or a high degree of faith in more subjective assessments. SEU maximisation may be realistic at equilibrium, where outcomes can be predicted from observed causal links and outcome-probabilities from past frequencies. Its relevance is much less clear to the process of getting into equilibrium, when actions may have tried for the first time with few clues as to their outcomes or probabilities, and where the disequilibrium behaviour of other agents makes their own choice of action and impact on the causal chain much harder to anticipate.

An agent who is missing any of the inputs to the decision process (possible actions, possible outcomes or their probabilities) must deal with imperfect information. It is then not possible to complete the normal process of evaluation and selection, without leaving potentially superior actions out of account. Resultant choices might be intransitive, incomplete, or non-independent. The problem is compounded by incomplete information if the availability, possible outcomes outcome-probabilities or outcome-utilities of one or more actions depend on decisions to be taken independently by other agents, now or in the future. Exogenous future changes, such as a newly discovered preference, new state of the world or new action possibility, add a further complication.

Agents can accommodate the resulting uncertainty by adopting a risk-averse function relating present utility to 'certainty-equivalent' (probability times value) outcomes, and by heavily discounting any future utilities. Overlooking possible outcomes at the lower ends of the probability distribution need not do serious damage to the rationality of the decision, even for risk-averse agents; we might be run over every time we step into the street, but this rarely registers in a decision on whether to go shopping. But risk-aversion can take different forms, each suggesting a different approach to uncertainty, so that fear of being 'wrong for the right reasons' may cause departure from SEU-maximisation even if it would have been adopted were information flows more certain. Among formal alternatives are minimisation of maximum regret (the difference between the chosen action's utility and the best action's utility under a particular state-of-the-world, for which Savage (1954) and Loomes and Sugden (1982) provide possible treatments), and maximisation of the minimum outcome (the choice whose outcome in its worst-case state-of-the-world is relatively highest, an approach popularised by Rawls (1971) in the selection of social welfare distributions).

Even if all decision-relevant information is assembled, the SEU process may fail if evaluation and ranking of actions becomes too complicated or takes too long. *Bounded rationality* may then force the agent to abbreviate the decision process, perhaps by evaluating only a subset of actions, or selecting the first action that surpasses a minimum level of SEU rather than working right through the list to find the one that maximises SEU. Complication may simply arise from the number of actions and states-of-the-world that must be considered, but it intensifies when there is interdependence among decision-makers, whose assessment of actions' outcomes, probabilities and utilities depends not only on the action they themselves take, but also on the actions other agents take concomitantly or in response.

5.2.5 *Problems in practice: systematic axiom violations*

The precision of its forecasts and the ease with which problems could be set up under controlled conditions made rational choice one of the first economic theories to be put to 'laboratory' test. For a theory whose appeal to logical and consistent behaviour gives it a strong prescriptive content, the SEU model's performance under test has, however, been controversial. Even when subjects are chosen from groups relatively well informed about probability, and are offered realistic rewards (or punishments) to ensure that they make an effort to calculate correctly, certain systematic deviations from the predicted behaviour come to light. Among well-known cases, each pointing to a breakdown of one or more of the SEU axioms, are Ellsberg's paradox, Allais's paradox, preference reversal, framing, and Newcomb's paradox.

Ellsberg's paradox

Agents are asked to express a preference between two reward structures for the random selection of a ball from a bag containing 30 red balls, and 60 green and blue balls in unknown proportion. Rewards can be either a sum of money (M) or nothing (O). Figure 5.2 shows the possible reward structures.

	Red	Green	Blue
A	M	O	O
B	O	M	O
C	M	O	M
D	O	M	M

Figure 5.2 Ellsberg's paradox

Over many trials, a majority of subjects prefer A to B, and D to C. Yet the utility function that leads to preference for A over B should lead to preference for C over D, since the introduction of reward M for drawing a blue ball is an 'irrelevant alternative'. Agents seem to be put off by the unknown probabilities attached to Green and Blue, even though this should not affect their subjective valuation. So they initially prefer the choice with known reward probability (A), but switch to the alternative (D) when the reward probability of the other outcomes is made known.

Ellsberg's result drew attention to systematic inconsistencies in individuals' probability judgements, of which others have since come to light. Among these, agents may take small samples to be more representative of their parent populations than is statistically justifiable (Kahneman and Tversky 1972), let their judgement be swayed by specious causal inferences (Tversky and Kahneman 1983), cling to subjective probabilities after subsequent evidence should have modified them (Ross and Anderson 1982), and place excessive confidence in their own probability estimates (Tversky and Kahneman 1974).

Allais's paradox

Here agents know the probabilities of an action's three possible consequences, one of which is highly likely (frequency 89 per cent), one unlikely (frequency 10 per cent) and one highly unlikely (frequency 1 per cent). These possible payoffs are summarised in Figure 5.3. Most agents prefer A over B, implying a readiness to sacrifice the small chance of a high reward (10 per cent × 5) so as to avoid the outside chance of getting no reward (1 per cent × 0). However, the same agents generally prefer D to C, even though the removal of the reward from the highly likely outcome should make no difference. The independence axiom is violated.

Probability	89%	10%	1%
A	1	1	1
B	1	5	0
C	0	1	1
D	0	5	0

Figure 5.3 Allais's paradox

Denied the possibility of receiving anything from the most probable (89 per cent) outcome, agents seem willing to gamble for the smaller probability of the high reward, even though they now have an outside chance of coming away with nothing. The preference for an 89 per cent probability over a 10 per cent probability exceeds the preference for 10 per cent over 1 per cent by more than is implied by the agents' utility function, even allowing for risk-aversion.

Preference reversal

The standard theory assumes that choices among actions with risky outcomes are based on their subjective valuation – agents will choose whichever action they think has most value. However, when asked to choose between a high-probability, low-reward bet (A) and a low-probability, high-reward bet (B), and then put a relative price on them, most subjects select bet A but put a higher value on bet B.

A: 35/36 chance of losing $1 or 1/36 chance of winning $4
B: 25/36 chance of losing $1.50 or 11/36 chance of winning $16

As Lichtenstein and Slovic (1971) argued when introducing the problem, the lack of identity between 'preference' and 'choice' is not unusual in real life, and may not be entirely irrational. Comparison between opinion polls and actual votes suggests that many people prefer one candidate but vote for another (perhaps tactically, perhaps because the better party would put their taxes up). But in these strictly defined experimental terms, preference reversal implies intransitivity in the agents' preference orderings, for which sacrifice of the completeness or independence axioms is not an adequate rescue. 'These ways of "saving" transitivity are implausible and do not account for the details of the data . . . the independence between belief and preference that is fundamental to standard decision theory is cast into doubt' (Hausman 1992: 238, 243).

Framing

Inconsistencies also show up when the same problem is presented in different ways, especially when gain is restated as avoidance of loss. In one of several 'framing' experiments devised by Kahneman and Tversky (1979), agents generally prefer the certainty of receiving a sum of money M to the 50 per cent chance of receiving twice this sum (2M). The certainty equivalents are the same, but agents are risk-averse when the choice is between positive rewards. However, the same agents generally prefer to to run a 50 per cent risk of losing 2M than to accept the certain loss of M. People seem willing to accept sure gains but gamble against sure losses, even though the two choices are equivalent under SEU analysis. (This may have especially serious consequences for the preference evaluations used in cost-benefit analysis – section 2.3.2.)

Newcomb's paradox

Here the choice involves a game situation in which a subject must choose whether to open one or both of two boxes. The first is known to contain a small sum of money. The second will contain a large sum of money, if the owner of the boxes expected the first box to be left untouched. If the owner expected the first box to be opened, the second box will have been left empty. Since the choice over the second box's content has already been made, the rational choice is to open both boxes. In tests, however, a significant proportion opt to open only the second box. They behave as if their reasoning will have been anticipated by the owner, so that their willingness to forgo the certain small reward increases the probability of receiving the risky large reward.

Axiom violations need not dispose of a theory. There may have been systematic errors in setting up the tests that reveal these anomalies, or variations in a background factor which affects individuals' judgement and which should have been 'controlled'. Subjects' behaviour might have been altered by the artificial conditions of the experiment, their failure to understand it or their refusal to take it seriously (especially where choices relate to symbolic rather than actual gambles and rewards). In a tradition dating back at least to Friedman (1953), economists will also conventionally continue to use and defend models based on inaccurate assumptions and axioms provided they explain within-sample (and predict out-of-sample) variations well enough, and generate useful hypotheses. Lack of 'realism' in assumptions can even be taken as a strength, if the purpose of economics is to break through superficial realities to the underlying mechanisms and motives of human action. Again, a model based on fragile or even false premises might be redeemed if it can explain and predict the collective consequences of that action.

But SEU axiom violations remain a serious threat to neoclassical microeconomics, for which self-evident starting-points for deductive reasoning were meant to provide an escape from endless disagreement over which 'stylised facts' should inform inductive reasoning (and which econometric methods were appropriate to test such reasoning). The neoclassical success in recasting macroeconomics on a rational-choice, consistent-expectation microfoundation is also at risk if individuals routinely make non-rational choices or fail to resolve expectational inconsistency. Re-runs of the tests which correct for a large number of possible experimental errors have still revealed systematic violations. Incorporation into the model of possible choice-deflecting background variations can help account for the violations, but at the cost of a more complicated specification, acknowledging a modified form of rationality not always consistent with the choices underlying well-behaved supply-demand schedules, search activity or other neoclassical microfoundations. Non-neoclassical critics liken recent revisions to individual choice models, designed to accommodate the experimental observations without abandoning SEU, to the 'epicycles' that helped bring anomalous planetary movements within an Earth-centred model of the universe. The usual suggested alternative is another seismic shift in deductive starting-point: to a networked, embedded, peer-pressured, advertising-influenced individual whose preferences and choices are shaped by the surrounding social world.

The inconsistency of choices reflecting these paradoxes, with other choices by the same agent or with the outcomes produced in interaction with other agents, deprives the SEU model of the predictive ability that might have provided an 'instrumental' justification for its axioms. These were, in any case, supposed to provide a realistic and uncontroversial starting-point for modelbuilding on the basis of agents who know what they want and pursue it to the best of their financially and informationally constrained ability. As if reacting to John Stuart Mill's century-old contention that 'new knowledge about the economic world must come from inductive reasoning since deductive conclusions are too heavily dependent on what has been input in the starting premises' (Dunn and Maddala 1996: 51), economic agents seem determined not to be bound by the behavioural rules that subjective expected utility sought to inflict on them.

5.3 Alternative decision styles

Exhaustive re-staging of these experiments to eliminate possible misunderstandings or biases has continued to unearth systematic violations. 'If SEU is an empirical, testable theory then it is, in any conventional sense, false' (Anand 1993: 19). The various alternative choice theories devised to accommodate the results require one or more of the SEU axioms to be abandoned, or its optimising properties to be dropped (e.g. through sub-additivity of probabilities or irregularities in the utility function).

Alternative theories also encompass the SEU theory at the expense of adding complication to the agent's decision process, a problematic step given that violations may be due to bounded rationality on the agent's part. The very simple specifications of the tests descibed in section 5.2.5 are designed to eliminate bounded rationality, allowing any subject with basic probability knowledge to work out the expected values and make the best choice. But the violations suggest that agents refuse to work within the very narrow procedural framework set out by SEU theory. In Ellsberg's paradox they attach importance to new knowledge which the theory says is irrelevant to the choice they were considering. In Allais's paradox their utility function appears to shift from risk aversion over the most preferred outcomes to risk-attraction at the least preferred. With framing they put different interpretations on situations which are formally identical, and with preference reversal they appear to distinguish the process of setting relative values from the process of expressing a choice. Perhaps most revealingly, with Newcomb's paradox they break out of the individualistic perspective altogether, and try to infer another agent's motives from the structure of the game, reading more into the evidence than was ever intended by the problem's designer. 'Evidential choosing is widespread, [though] most economists are causal decision theorists' (Anand 1993: 41).

It could be argued that the axioms are too restrictive – especially that of transitivity, which also causes problems for the theory of collective choice (section 2.1.5). But without them, it becomes significantly harder to describe the resulting choices as rational, given the inconsistent actions that can result. Preference or evaluation changes during the test can be invoked to explain the inconsistencies, but the theory's applicability in non-laboratory situations then seems even more remote. The difficulties in operationalising the SEU framework suggest that conditions of uncertainty, interdependency or bounded rationality may call for substantially different decision-making styles.

According to the 'Austrian' view of individual choice, this is what markets actually provide; the neoclassical error is to mistake the formal demonstration of market efficiency with the much more informal process by which markets guide agents' acquisition and use of decision-relevant information. The Austrian defence from within against SEU is examined in the next section, after which three non-market decision styles are identified as alternatives.

5.4 The 'Austrian' alternative to subjective utility maximisation

Experimental violations of 'rational' choice challenge the efficiency of market transaction on the (neoclassical) end-state view, which gives an absolute judgement on the best course of action, which agents are observed not to take. There is no direct challenge to the Austrian process view, since market transaction could still emerge as the most efficient form if it leads to relative improvements in the agent's profit or utility situation, more reliably or rapidly than alternative transaction types. The empirical challenge to SEU prescriptions has encouraged Austrian theorists to stay with their more discursive description of how agents make effective choices with limited information and limited means to process it.

Whereas the neoclassical view abstracts from information gathering and processing limitations in order to show how agents can attain the optimal transaction pattern by trading through markets, their role in the Austrian view is to steer agents towards the optimum by minimising the information gathering and processing requirements. The vulnerability of SEU-maximising decision to information and computation constraints, and the non-maximising nature of alternative decision methods, suggests that most real-life choices involve a trade-off between optimality and tractability. The efficiency argument for market transaction can be recast as a way of making the best of this trade-off.

Five related claims can then be made on the market's behalf:

- It reduces the incidence of imperfect information, by minimising the information needed for a rational choice, and by reducing the cost of acquiring additional information, so dispelling uncertainty about future 'exogenous' outcomes.
- It reduces the incidence of incomplete information, by separating agents' decision processes to reduce interdependency, or by establishing common knowledge, so dispelling uncertainty about future 'endogenous' outcomes.
- By reducing information requirements, it economises on information-processing capacity needs and reduces 'bounded rationality'.

- It promotes co-ordinated or collective action where this is necessary to identify and/or implement the optimum choice, at lower cost than other co-ordination methods and so with the maximum net social benefit.
- It allows remaining, irreducible uncertainties to be commodified and traded, so that risk-averse agents can trade their remaining uncertainties with risk-attached agents, bringing net gains to both.

5.4.1 *The market as uncertainty reducer and information perfector*

'Exogenous' uncertainty can be defined as the blanks in the rational choice procedure arising from lack of knowledge of how the natural environment will develop. It reflects the unpredictability of the present and future availability of actions, of the possible outcomes of these actions and of the relative likelihood of those outcomes (or of states of the world that produce them), caused by changes in supply and demand conditions, preferences and technology that are beyond agents' collective control.

The market reduces exogenous uncertainty, and the information-imperfection arising from it, by quickly and costlessly informing agents of any changes to their decision situation (new actions, new outcomes to existing actions, changed outcome probabilities, etc.). The principal vehicle for this is market price, which – if the market is unencumbered – adjusts instantaneously to changes in supply and demand for existing products, and reveals with minimal delay whether new products have found a market. Retrospectively, the market provides instant feedback on the results of past actions, and allows expectations about outcomes and their probabilities to be rapidly revised. Prospectively, market incentives (the capture of temporary monopoly profits and the discovery of new sources of utility) persuade agents constantly to search for new actions (or knowledge about actions) and to push back the constraints on existing actions. Once new discoveries and innovations take place, information about them is then immediately generalised – by the opening-up of a new market, or changes in relative prices, utility and profitability in existing markets.

Market prices provide a continuously updated, accurate summary of the state of supply and demand, their direction of change, and the most rewarding way of responding to them. The informational input to decision, previously a complex mixture of physical magnitudes, causal processes, and the states of nature and the other agents' expectations that shape them, can thereby be reduced in most cases to the level and movement of relative prices.

> It is more than a metaphysic to describe the price system as a kind of machinery for registering change, or a system of telecommunications which enables individual producers to watch merely the movement of a few pointers, as an engineer might watch the hands of a few dials, in order to adjust their activities to changes of which they may never know more than is reflected in the price movement.
>
> (Hayek 1949: 87)

Stock-markets may play a particularly important role in alerting firms to new profit opportunities, and bond-markets in alerting consumers to changes in the desired balance between present and future consumption.

By implication, there is much external benefit in the production of prices, since they capture information which buyers and sellers may have expended effort to acquire but which are now transmitted free to all other transactors. Agents cannot avoid providing the external benefit in pursuit of their own utility, since their own actions inevitably translate into market price movements outside their control. So while it offers significant 'public good' characteristics, there is no danger of accurate price information being underprovided, or of prices becoming less accurate because of free-riding on those who reveal new information.

5.4.2 The market as interdependence reducer and information completer

Negative overspill can still persist in the form of decision interdependence, where one agent's objective, action set, action outcomes, outcome-utilities or outcome-probabilities depend on the actions chosen independently by other agents. (As examples: the utility of a 'positional' or 'network' good depends in part on how many others plan to buy it; the profitability of a new machine depends in part on how many others plan to install it; the expected utility of a lottery ticket being drawn depends in part on how many others plan to buy one, and the profitability of an investment on how much, and where, others choose to invest.) 'Endogenous' uncertainty can be defined as that which arises from lack of knowledge of how the social environment will develop. It encapsulates the unpredictability in the aims, actions, outcomes and probabilities of decision that arises from agents' own unco-ordinated behaviour, 'the unintended social repercussions of intentional human actions' (Popper 1969: 342).

The market is claimed to minimise the extent of these spillovers and to promote co-ordination to make the best of those that remain, without compromising the individual freedom of action that allows them to develop. As in the case of 'exogenous' uncertainty, the market is claimed to be the quickest and cheapest source of information on others' intentions. These can often be inferred from observation of their previous behaviour – on the assumption that they too are choosing rationally, a condition that competitive markets are assumed to enforce. Even where others' motives and plans cannot be anticipated, or are deliberately misrepresented, they will be quickly revealed by the price system once the action is taken, and this may still give the first agent time to revise their own choice.

The minimisation of decision-makers' interdependence follows from the decentralisation of decision in society. Choices are made by individuals with regard to their own objectives, action-availabilities and evaluations of those actions. Their success is measured with regard to how far the individual's objective is attained, or the gap between their aspiration and actuality narrowed. The individualism and diversity permitted by market specialisation, with everyone 'doing their own thing', minimises the chance of two or more agents pursuing incompatible aims (or, at least, lets the defeated agents switch to alternative actions that are almost as good). The division of labour in production, promoted by the development of markets, has long been depicted as a way to social cohesion through interdependence (Durkheim 1964). More recent (postmodern) analysis tends towards a similar 'division of preference' in consumption (and 'moral relativism' over the accompanying lifestyle standards and beliefs), extending society's ability to accommodate and even celebrate diversity. Where one agent's action still interferes with another's because of scarcity, the market's other promise is to push out the production frontier until all tastes can be catered for.

Expectational interdependence is minimised because each agent follows its own profit or utility motives. While this may give rise to inconsistent expectations, market signals guide transactors into equilibrium without their having to recalculate with a revised view of other agents' intentions, which could lead to an infinite regress. A well-known example is the Cournot duopoly model, in which two suppliers of a homogeneous product must try to choose a profit-maximising output knowing that the other is choosing under the same conditions, and that their own profit will be inversely related to the rival's output decision. Each tries to simplify its profit-maximising decision by assuming that the rival's output decision will be independent of its own ('zero conjectural variation'). The pair then reach an equilibrium at the intersection of their two reaction functions, being the profit-maximising output given the output expected from the rival. While this initial expectation may well be wrong, competitive behaviour and the feedback through price signals move the duopolists into equilibrium. This is, in fact the non-cooperative (Nash) solution to a one-shot prisoners' dilemma-type game where, without collusion, no amount of prior calculation with more sophisticated conjectural variations would have suggested a better alternative. Meanwhile the economy is spared the distortion of a cartel arrangement maximising the duopolists' joint profits, and also the open competition which might leave the sector monopolised or unserved, if increasing returns to scale are the reason for there being only two producers.

5.4.3 *The market as information need reducer and bounded-rationality shield*

Price signals help agents economise on the information needed for rational choice, the speed at which they transmit new information – modifying objectives and making available new choices – making up for any welfare loss from failing to maximise the current objective. Agents do not need to go in for elaborate scenario-building and contingent planning at the pre-decision stage, because information quickly arrives to let them modify their activities post-decision. In common with the view that, collectively, dynamic gains from expanding available resources outweigh static gains from better allocating those resources, the individual does better getting reasonably close to a constantly improving optimum than converging on an unchanging optimum.

The market can be regarded as a device for minimising the incidence of bounded rationality, and so bringing agents as close as possible to rational decision situations. The choice of decision objective is simplified by reducing its many possible dimensions to one of money, so that the optimal choice is the one that brings the highest expected financial reward. The evaluation of possible actions is simplified by the price system, which provides a reliable and immediately available measure of opportunity cost, and one which is known to be common knowledge among all other agents. Evaluation is based solely on the agent's own assessment of their own utility, other agents' assessments having to be considered only to the extent that they might influence their own decision where these are interdependent.

The selection and implementation of action is left to the agent, so there are none of the delays associated with submitting information to or awaiting judgement from other agencies. With the exception of price (which is the product of their interaction across the economy), most decision-relevant information, being based on individual discovery and subjective asessment, arises first at the level of the agent. It is therefore most efficiently processed at that level, any need to refer to higher agency for clearance or guidance resulting in additional calculation and extra delay.

5.4.4   *The market as co-ordinator: 'endogenous' institutions*

There remain two types of decision for which interdependence remains fundamentally destabilising. First, the prisoners' dilemma situation (section 2.2) in which the optimum action for each agent requires them to co-ordinate their actions across space, and so is missing from the action set of non-cooperating individuals. Second, the case where the costs, consequences and/or benefits of an action interdepend with the actions of other agents across time. This tends especially to arise with unprecedented decisions involving large sunk costs, in which actions' outcomes, outcome-utilities and/or outcome-probabilities are so unpredictable without knowledge of others' intentions that everyone waits for others to act first, so that the relevant market signals are never sent.

In these cases, most market theorists acknowledge the need for co-ordinated action, or co-operative sharing of information. 'Institutions are either outside the domain of economic theory or they are explained as bargaining outcomes' (Auerbach 1988: 13). A variety of logical, historical and prescriptive arguments is advanced to show that such co-operative action can arise through private interaction around market process, with no need for the centralising 'visible hand' of corporation or state. Agents are shown as evolving, in the course of their market interactions, certain rules which allow them to learn and anticipate one another's intentionalities, and to devise and enforce the solutions to collective-action problems. As well as leading the economic system towards allocative efficiency and full employment, these rules are also seen as protecting long-run maximising behaviour against any conflicts with short-run efficiency, and so ensuring that innovation and growth are also maximised.

These rules, usually termed institutions, include laws prescribing or proscribing certain forms of behaviour on threat of punishment, informal conventions which are voluntarily obeyed on a tit-for-tat basis, technical standards which avoid wasteful competition where there are network externalities, or rule-setting organisations to which agents voluntarily join up. While they coexist with other institutions which have no economic function (or have lost it over time), it is claimed that a subset of institutions can be identified which arise or survive because they solve one of these co-ordination problems – and so allay the need for external intervention. 'Some social institutions exist because they rationally solve problems of conjectural interdependence that cannot be left to the rational expectations of individual agents' (Leijonhufvud 1986: 212). Institutions achieve this by limiting the action set to those that cause no external conflict, biasing action towards the collectively optimal solution, or improving the evaluation of actions by making others' intentions and behaviour more predictable.

While information-sharing and behaviour-co-ordinating institutions can be imposed on the market from outside, by political or bureaucratic process, 'Austrian' theory maintains that the most important are 'unplanned and unintended regularities of social behaviour (social conventions) that emerge organically' (Schotter 1986: 118). In sympathy with the Axelrod (1984) experimental results, Schotter builds on prisoners'-dilemma supergame theory to depict 'social institutions as sets of rules that evolve or emerge from the repetitive play of an underlying game by a group of rational agents' (1986: 132). Subsequent experiment has confirmed the stability of PD-type supergame co-operation, provided discount rates are low enough and the game long enough for agents to regain through long-term co-operation what they initially lose by co-operating while others do not (and provided the game has no known end-date, to avoid the logical problem of rational non-cooperation on the last round being traced back through all previous rounds). Once co-operative play has become established, agents may become 'socialised' into it and alight on the (C,C) strategy without thinking, so reducing the danger of opportunism dethroning agreement even if threats to punish it cease to be credible. Thus arises the favourable evolution of institutions depicted by 'functionalism' in sociology: 'the persistence of social practices in terms of their latent beneficial consequences for the survival of the equilibrium of the social system' (Baert 1991: 29).

This apparent success at achieving the collective good through decentralised action contrasts with the axiomatic 'impossibility' of deliberately achieving such welfare maximisation through the politically administered pooling of utility information (section 2.1.4). Although many institutions are organisational or political constructions imposed on markets from outside, Austrian theory tends to regard these as the legal formalisation of arrangements which the market had previously self-generated. In the same way, social rule-setting begins with 'common' or 'case' law determined within a particular group, which is later formalised into 'statute' law – by a lawmaking institution which grows out of interactions between groups, in a second-level rerunning of the market institution-generating process.

Even where an institution is clearly imposed without prior market interaction (perhaps in response to its absence), agents will subsequently shape it to their own purposes, whether or not the designers intended this. A frequently observed case is of professional accreditation agencies, initially resisted by the producers on whom they impose extra training and testing costs, who subsequently recognise the entry restriction and pay enhancement these make possible, and use it to solve traditional problems of cut-price 'cowboy' operators whose substandard work damages both the profit and reputation of the industry.

5.4.5   The market as efficient allocator of irreducible risk

Even if the market system generally succeeds in minimising information needs, maximising the perfection and completeness of information and co-ordinating those decisions where individual choice still leads to suboptimal results, some decisions may still be exposed to uncertainty. This can arise where some decision-relevant information is still awaited at the time choice must be made (e.g. because it will arise exogenously in future, or from the collective results of current actions which are still unfolding); where bounded rationality was still encountered in the decision process (so that a non-optimal choice may have been made); where an action taken (by the agent or by other agents with whom there is interdependence) is new, and its outcomes not known in advance; where the agent does not have a clearly defined objective at the time the decision is taken, or where that objective may be subject to (exogenous or endogenous) change at a future date. It can result in objectives changing or being frustrated, and action evaluations and choices being revised. Other agents whose decisions depended on this one may thereby also be forced to change. A serious internal or external 'shock' to expectations could invalidate the whole stock of knowledge on which a set of decisions was based.

The market deals with this problem by developing mechanisms by which, at a suitable price, agents who wish to avoid the potential costs arising from uncertainty can buy protection from agents who are willing to absorb it. This protection may take the form of an insurance policy, which will compensate for losses arising from unpredicted events. Or it may involve direct 'commodification' of the uncertainty through the forward purchase or sale of the product over whose future value or need the uncertainty arises. The sellers of these instruments, those paid to take over the uncertainty, will hope to convert it into risk through its aggregation and probabilistic evaluation, and thereby price the protection sufficiently to return a profit given the actual outturn of uncertain events.

In one of the most detailed 'Austrian' reformulations of individual choice theory, Shackle (1969, 1972) deals explicitly with transactions that are of most interest to the perspective and least comfortably tackled by SEU: those involving one-off, innovative actions about which there is no past utility or probability information. With too many possible outcomes to consider fully, the agent is argued to assign each possible action two 'focus' outcomes, one positive and one negative, with the most interesting balance of likelihood and utility. The chosen action is the one offering the best trade-off of focus gain and loss, assuming risk-averse 'gambler indifference curves' between the two. Where actions are not mutually exclusive, it may be possible to choose a linear combination of two of them to reach a higher gambler indifference curve.

Although they have been dismissed as 'radically subjectivist' and unamenable to testing, individual decision models such as Shackle's differ from the subjectivism of SEU-maximisation only by relaxing some of its more demanding conditions (such as complete listing of available actions and their ranking by full consideration of outcomes and their probabilities). An agent who uses this strategy still acts independently, relying on market-generated information, but escapes informational and computational constraints by constructing just one best and worst case scenario for each action for which these prove interesting. If there is interdependence, however, this style of decision-making is likely to be contagious, since other agents are unlikely successfully to anticipate either the outcomes they choose to focus on or the risk preferences from which these lead to choice. The 'radically subjective' decision-makers of most interest to the Austrian perspective are those identifying and introducing new products, processes or unidentified Pareto-improving trades. Since these will generate supernormal profits if successful, they change the rules of the SEU-maximising game.

5.5   Non-market alternatives

Because of its optimising properties, rational choice was later put forward as a 'normative' theory, one that decision-makers (especially in business) ought consciously to follow. But the problems of doing so in a fully decentralised, competitive market system, implicit in the plight of maximising firms and consumers under general equilibrium (Chapters 2–4), become explicit within the SEU decision framework. Competing, non-communicating agents cannot always adjust by price alone. While market-generated institutions may sometimes solve these problems from within, there remain market failures which can cause agents, by choice or default, to resort to alternative decision styles. Three have drawn particular attention.

5.5.1   *The relational transaction decision: sharing the unknowns*

A *relational transaction* develops when agents get together to discuss intentions and actions that they know are interdependent in terms of outcome probabilities and utilities. By learning one another's motives and sharing information, relational transactors hope to make their expectations consistent, and so choose actions that come closer to the outcomes each wants. Each agent still implements its own decision, and is free (outside the terms of any contract) to alter its terms or move on to other transactions. But relational transactions tend to become stable because of the sunk investments they entail – in getting to know someone, in establishing a reputation to make known to others – and because of the enrichment of search and evaluation that they make possible.

Relational transaction can be viewed as a number of individual decision processes joined at the evaluation stage. Figure 5.4 shows the simplest case, with two transactors. Having seen that their objectives make for interdependence, the two agents share information on the contents of their action sets, agree on how they expect different actions to perform given the other's intentions, and agree a consistent pair of choices. The accuracy of these evaluations is assumed to rise, the more interacting agents can be drawn into the process. However, even if they agree on the outcomes the available actions are likely to have, agents may still give different utility-orderings to those outcomes, so further negotiation is needed to ensure that compatible selections are made. Implementation and assessment are still carried out independently, as is the subsequent restatement or revision of the objective. Once these have been carried out and the transaction completed, agents return to market transaction or re-examine the possibilities for more relational transaction.

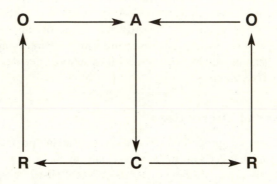

Figure 5.4 Relational transaction decision

The personal contact and personalised negotiation set up by relational transaction makes it a signficant departure from the anonymity and rivalry of the marketplace, but one which is observable in almost every contemporary economy. The special features of relational transaction, and its contrasts with market transaction, are explored in more detail in Chapter 6.

5.5.2　*The informed transaction decision: summoning superior insight*

In *informed transaction*, the agents seek to fill the information gaps in their decision process by appealing not to one another, but to a third-party source of information. This informant, from a vantage point allowing them to gauge the intentions of other agents and the likely collective results of their behaviour, is able to supply extra information on available actions at the search stage, and on actions' likely consequences at the evaluation stage (Figure 5.5). The extra input is purely 'for information', and agents are left free to make and implement their own choice of action in the light of this detail. But the informant intervenes again at the state of assessing results, and so may become indirectly involved in setting or revising objectives for subsequent transactions.

In 'Austrian' theory, markets carry out this informant role, alerting agents to action possibilities and effects through market signals, and guiding them towards actions taken 'as if' exhaustive search and evaluation had been conducted even if time and computing power did not allow for this. The informed-transaction theory argues that markets are not enough: lack of full information still leaves agents unable to devise consistent individual decisions, and lack of co-ordination still prevents them from sustaining socially optimising collective decisions. The informant is thus envisaged as a separate agency outside the market – possibly an arm of government, equally possibly an industry forum or co-operative association set up by agents themselves, or a behavioural convention they find useful to observe. It is an improving rather than an optimising influence, intervening in transaction only when it has already got under way – unlike the Walrasian auctioneer, which must establish complete knowledge of agents' intentions and anticipation of their interactions and enforce the resultant equilibrium prices before market transaction begins. Also unlike the auctioneer, informants have found a very real presence in contemporary economies. They have usually taken the form of government 'indicative planning' agencies set up to improve and co-ordinate firms' decision-taking in key sectors, a concept explored in more detail in Chapter 7.

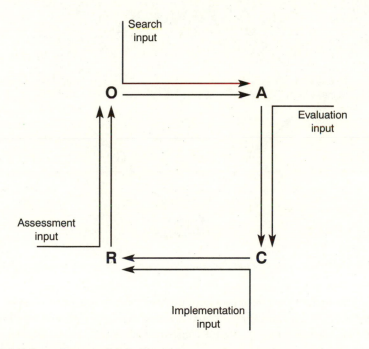

Figure 5.5 Informed transaction decision

5.5.3 *The administered transaction decision: obeying the experts*

Outside agency turns from servant to master on the adoption of *administered transaction*, by which agents submit to central direction in order to overcome their information and co-ordination problems. The usual case involves interdependent agents submitting to the same authority. Bilateral engagement with the central authority replaces agents' multilateral interaction with one another.

Unlike the informant, who tries to enlighten agents so that they can interact to mutual benefit, this authority sets out to minimise the interdependence by guiding each agent down separate, non-crossing paths. This is achieved (as in Figure 5.6a) by imposing an objective chosen for compatibility with other objectives, prescribing an action set designed for minimum overlap with other action sets (or guiding search away from actions which overlap), and simplifying the evaluation process to one in which the chosen action must merely meet certain expected-outcome standards.

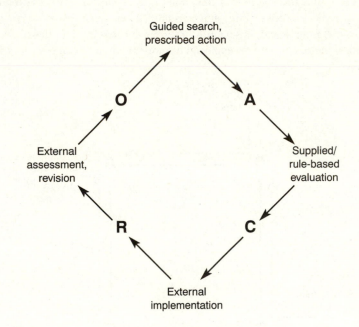

Figure 5.6a Administered transaction: prescribed decision

Agents are sometimes forced into administered transaction, but many submit to it voluntarily. Their motive is often the political one, celebrated by Hobbes (1651/1968), of submitting to the tolerable strictures of a Leviathan to avoid the intolerable conflicts of unmediated human self-interest. It may also be an economic one, based on the (optimising?) belief that the effort saved in following rule-based decision and the outside help with evaluation and implementation, along with the greater assurance that scaled-down objectives will be achieved, compensate for the loss of total freedom to choose. Submitting to instructions may also be a way of defending strategic (long-run maximising) action – the outside agency providing both the compulsion not to take immediate profits, and the support to ensure survival if intermediate actions involve a loss.

Whereas market theorists view institutions as an organic outgrowth of decentralised exchange, the administered transaction approach inclines to the view that they are created not begotten. This is based on the historical difficulty of explaining how agents' market dealings can give rise to a rule-setting convention or agency without some form of political process, and of how agents' behaviour can continue to evolve once such rule-setting has been achieved. The tendency of institutions to enshrine compatible patterns of behaviour – preventing unwanted movement away from equilibrium – conflicts with the historical fact that institutions change over time. It is not clear how such change could be triggered from inside the system, except by mistake. 'Without a change in at least one exogenous variable . . . the long-run neoclassical economy is static, since there is no reason for a change in the endogenous variables (such as institutional constraints) once the optimum values of the institutional constraints have been established' (Boland 1992: 118). Referencing North (1990), Boland cites ideology as one possible exogenous change. The Protestant religious reformation may have served as another (Tawney 1938).

Another rule-changing possibility is the accidental modification of institutional constraints during agents' everyday attempts to reproduce them, analogous to the occasional mutation of cells during the replication of an organic system. The problem with this is that most mutations are harmful (e.g. cancerous), and in a competitive economy market forces could be expected either to correct the change or to select-out the mutated institution. Institutional change might be imposed by powerful agents within the economy, but this implies a departure from competitive conditions in the form of powerful producer (or consumer) conglomerates or coalitions. Without an endogenous process of this sort, however, a role is left for intervention by government, if not as the creator of institutions then as the agency that enshrines them, enforces them and causes them (intentionally or otherwise) to change.

However it arises, an authority can use the decision-shaping power submitted to it by agents to pursue objectives of its own, once it acquires (through further extension of the division of labour specialist leaders who are not wholly aligned to the interests of their member agents). The gains to agents from having their decisions simplified and co-ordinated can be used to compensate them for being hitched to someone else's agenda. For the dominant form of authority in contemporary economies, the firm or organisation, the wider objective is to induce the 'parts' to achieve results which are beneficial to the 'whole', and avoid loss of energy or direction being dissipated internally.

Although most non-routine decisions have to be guided in the way depicted in Figure 5.6a, a certain number of well-rehearsed or well-researched decisions are susceptible to the 'behavioural' simplification of the decision process shown in Figure 5.6b. Here search is replaced by the specification of permitted actions, and the optimising objective by a satisfactory target or pass/fail rule. SEU-style valuation and ranking of actions can then give way to a 'program' (H.A.Simon 1947) through which agents evaluate actions in sequence, adopting the first one that satisfies the decision rule. Although the program may leave out certain actions which would have been available to the agent if it escaped the authority, it may also contain some actions which would not have been available had the authority not been invoked.

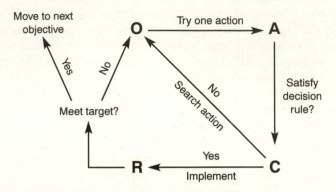

Figure 5.6b Administered transaction: behavioural decision

Judging what these conditions are and selecting the appropriate action from the program is the closest the agent comes to the discretion that is central to market transaction. Programming may allow agents to 'maximise' within certain limits, but these may well be set by the administrator to maximise some larger objective held by the organisation of which the agent is a part.

The other main form of authority, dominant in certain economies until recently, was the central-planning state. With rather more coercion and rather less convincing results, all agents – firms and consumers – submitted to a bureaucratic attempt to generalise programmed decision-making. This goal was never fulfilled, with agents frequently resorting to market transaction through choice when deprived of official supplies through mispricing, and through necessity when trading with partners from a non-planned economy. Arguments that such foreign trade and black-market disturbances undermined the central plan are generally countered by a strong claim that they rescued it, from lack of efficiency and adaptability caused by mis-specifying agents' objectives and forcing them to surrender to central evaluation, implementation and assessment. The differences between firm-level and economy-level administered transaction, and the reasons why the first seemed so emphatically to outperform and outlast the second, are explored in more detail in Chapter 7.

5.6 Mixed decision types: transitory truce or peaceful coexistence?

Each economy contains, and each agent engages in, a combination of market-based, relational, informed and administered transaction decisions. The occurrence of information acquisition and processing problems even in apparently simple decisions suggests that lapses from rational choice will be frequent – occasioned by lack of time, lack of computing power, inadequate knowledge, agents' insistence on considering more information than is (normatively) relevant to the decision, or their (subjective) belief that the benefits from further refining the choice will not justify the extra costs. Before considering the economic significance of non-market transactions in more depth, it is necessary to ask whether they are likely to be a permanent feature, or merely a second-best improvisation destined to yield to market transaction if and when information and co-ordination allow.

The 'permanence' case is that markets can permanently fail to make the best of certain exchanges, so that non-market transaction is adopted as a preferable alternative. In effect, agents take a rational decision to abandon the rational-choice framework where they are sure that markets cannot achieve the information flow necessary for optimum evaluation or the co-ordination necessary for optimum implementation. This implies that other agents who, in the same circumstances, continue to engage in market transaction will get inferior results, and should rationally switch to the alternative.

The 'transience' case is that non-market transaction decisions, although they may for a time perform relatively better than badly informed market transaction, will eventually be overtaken by it as market mechanisms improve (perhaps by formation of the relevant institutions) and agents become better at responding to them. This implies that once some agents have arrived, deliberately or inadvertantly, at the rationally designed market transaction, they will get better results, and those using alternative decision styles should be enticed (or forced) to switch away from them.

In practice, this sharp division between 'optimality' and 'suboptimality' of alternative decision styles betrays a neoclassical presumption that tastes, technologies and initial endowments give the economy one optimal transaction pattern, whose existence and specification are independent of the actions agents take. As seen in the discussion of adjustment to general equilibrium in Chapter 3, unless the restrictive conditions and extensive information needs required by this perspective are met, agents' convergence to them is not assured: 'irrational' action by some agents (e.g. trading at disequilibrium prices) may rewrite the 'rational' action for others. Each agent's optimum transaction pattern depends on what other agents do and plan to do.

5.6.1 *When maximisers meet improvisers*

As soon as information, computation or co-ordination problems lead one or more agents to abandon SEU-maximisation and start to simplify their decision process, the anticipations of their behaviour built into other agents' action sets and evaluations will require further modification. Whether this complicates or simplifies the calculation task for other agents, and raises or lowers their rewards from sticking with SEU-maximisation, depends how many switch to which alternative decision style(s). If the 'simplifiers' start choosing at random, or adopt decision rules which make them seem to do so, the situation for those who continue trying to maximise becomes still more difficult. But if the simplifiers adopt rules which lessen their sensitivity to changes in decision-relevant information, the situation is likely to stabilise.

By insulating their choice from the choices of others, the simplifiers are likely to make themselves more predictable (Heiner 1983), breaking through the potentially infinite loop of interdependent expectations, and allowing other agents to build their moves more reliably into their own action-evaluations. In this case a departure from rational choice, in the sense of ignoring the impact of others' actions on the outcomes and utilities of one's own, may bring the system close to the conditions under which rational choice can be exercised, without running into bounded rationality. There is an obvious affinity with the long-held recognition that a small departure from perfect competition may be needed to let agents adjust into the equilibrium made possible by perfect competition (section 3.14).

The generalisation is incomplete, however, since circumstances can arise where a departure from full rationality imposes a small private loss on the simplifiers who make it, but a much larger loss for the system as a whole (Akerlof and Yellen 1985). For simplifiers to remain small, in numbers and impact on the collective outcome, their actions must be such as to induce the remaining maximisers to adopt different actions (Haltiwanger and Waldman 1990, who call this *strategically substitutability*). Then, since maximisers' persistence with the full decision process gives them higher-utility results, the number of simplifiers will be limited to those (with high information-processing costs) who consider the loss from choosing more rationally to outweigh the gain from acting more rationally. The collective outcome thus stays close to what would have prevailed if all agents had chosen rationally.

The opposite result arises with *strategic complementarity*, under which rational choice leads maximisers to adopt the same action as simplifiers. Since the full decision process no longer has clear utility advantages over the simplified process, agents may now abandon it even if their information-processing costs are low, so that the number of simplifiers steadily arises and the collective outcome is displaced from what would have prevailed if all agents had chosen rationally (Haltiwanger and Waldman 1989). Strategic complementarity is exhibited by, among others, network goods (section 2.2), where utility is highest in joining the network most people have already joined. If simplifiers choose first, and adopt an inferior technology, rational choosers arriving later will be forced to do the same, locking the economy in even when better technologies become available (Haltiwanger and Waldman 1990).

Similarly, if simplifiers seize on past price increases to pile into the stock-market, causing further price increases, rational investors may be forced to follow even after the boom has turned into a bubble. In general, while there will be some circumstances in which departure from 'neoclassical' optimisation is punished, and their followers are required to adapt or die, there may be others in which their departure so alters other agents' expectations that the optimisers are the ones forced to think again. A non-maximising (satisficing) decision style may be driven towards maximisation if, for example, the target is raised whenever it is met or exceeded until the agent has to identify and evaluate all possible actions because only the best will work (Cross 1983). But while an obviously too easy target is likely to be raised, it is not clear that this process will be the continued indefinitely either by the agent (who risks re-encountering bounded rationality as satisfactory actions become harder to find), or any external setter of the target (whose joint-maximising or other-objective-maximising may be undermined if individual maximisation is permitted).

The 'evolutionary' argument that competitive selection will eliminate simplifiers, leaving only those who optimise (consciously or otherwise), is similarly restricted. It depends on the evolutionary selection rule being set independently of the actions currently taken by agents (otherwise, as with strategic complementarity, the sim- plifers will change the rule and survive rather than break the rule and disappear, forcing rational agents to go along with their rationality. It also depends on selec- tion being sufficiently farsighted to avoid eliminating long-run optimisers whose strategy entails short-run suboptimal action (see section 4.1.1). With one-off deci- sions, or changing determinants of actions' outcomes and utilities, there is no guarantee that either Darwinian evolution (inferior performers being filtered out) or Lamarckian evolution (inferior performers imitating superior performers) will lead to the all-round enactment of optimal choice.

Alternative decision styles need not be driven out by rational choice, and may even force divergence from it rather than being drawn into convergence towards it. The close agent-to-agent ties that characterise relational transaction, and the external agencies that intervene in informed and administered transaction, can therefore not be dismissed as impediments to the market without which rational choice procedures would prevail. Such institutions may, instead, survive because they establish a supe- rior trade-off between cost of decision and quality of result. And far from being artefacts of intervention, they can be argued (with a little help from Austrian and repeated-game theory) to be self-generated complements of market transaction to cover those situations where its normal workings are informationally too thin, calcu- latively too complex or implementationally too vulnerable to deceit.

5.6.2 *Alternative styles as rational irrationality*

Where information imperfection or incompleteness leave the agent with more contingent calculations than they are able to deal with, the lapse from rational (maximising) to simplified (satisficing) decision is generally regarded as a switch from 'substantive' to 'procedural' rationality (Simon 1978). The agent abandons any assurance of getting the best decision outcome, recognising the constraint on decision process caused by bounded rationality. However, it is possible to deny the validity of this distinction, and contain the switch within the neoclassical frame- work, by arguing that the simplified decision style can still produce substantively rational results, so that its adoption may itself be a result of rational choice.

Where submission to a market-generated institution or convention produces better results than acting without restraint, it may indeed be plausible to infer a rational choice to forgo rational choice. Co-operating in a repeated prisoners' dilemma, being tied to the mast when the sirens wail and behaving predictably in conditions of interdependence have already been noted as examples of apparent procedural irrationality resulting in substantive rationality. Vickers (1985) provides a complementary example involving shareholders in an oligopoly firm: when man- agers' utility derives from profit and sales volume while shareholders' utility derives solely from profit, shareholders who enforce profit-maximisation achieve less profit than those who tolerate managerial utility-maximisation.

Cases like these allow neoclassical theorists to argue that apparently non-rational choice is actually the result of rational choice, when the agent has calculated that the costs of going through a full maximising process outweight the benefits (Baumol and Quandt 1964). It is not clear that they can do this, however, without working through the full calculation first. The closest approach is probably that taken by chess grandmasters who, unable to think through more than a fraction of the sequences of moves available to them, have arrived at methods of screening-out the less suitable strategies which, in most cases, bring them significantly closer to the best than any less skilled human opponent (and any computer, at least until the arrival of IBM's less selective but faster-processing 'Deep Blue').

Outside the range of clearly specified models, there is no way for an observer to know that an optimising decision not to optimise has been taken, unless able to enter the agent's mind so as to understand their subjective utility function (which can no longer be reliably inferred from their initial choices), and to carry out the full maximising decision so as to compare it with the agent's simplified choice. A more realistic proposition is that agents exercise 'selective rationality', attempting to optimise when the stakes are high or the constraints tough, but settling for more casual methods when under time pressure or less concerned about the results (Leibenstein 1976).

For rational search abbreviation to take place, agents must know the subjective expected value of the actions they leave out of the action set. For rational evaluation abbreviation, agents must know the value of the information they have chosen not to process. 'Rational irrationality' tends to full rationality, because everything must be included in the decision process before the agent knows what it is rational to leave out.

While there are better and worse strategies for sidestepping bounded rationality by filtering possible actions before deciding which are worth evaluating in detail, these do not guarantee that the best action will survive pre-selection. Chess players can still end up choosing from a subset which leaves out the best move, students judging books by their covers can take away an inferior rational choice text, and recruiters who choose to cast out the handwritten résumés may pass over the ideal candidate whose printer was broken when the advert ran.

5.7   Conclusion: getting the best from less

The difficulty of constructing a subjective expected utility (SEU) maximising choice model which individuals conform to, even in well-briefed laboratory situations, suggests the information imperfection, incompleteness and processing problems of operating within markets which can arise in situations much simpler than those an agent in the general equilibrium system is likely to confront. Although modifications to the SEU framework have succeeded in accounting for some of the anomalies, they do so only by dropping assumptions which were previously considered to be criteria for rational behaviour. They also leave room for agents rationally to hold different decision styles which, as observed in section 5.6, can result in non-unique and shifting competitive market outcomes.

The alternative transaction types identified in this chapter represent possible solutions to the information and calculation barriers to SEU decision. The Austrian interpretation of market transaction recasts the market as a device for simplifying calculation and economising on the necessary information. Relational transaction seeks to pool information so that 'common knowledge' is established and contingent calculation simplified. Administered transaction passes on the information gathering and processing task to an outside agent, who either is better equipped to do the full calculation or can simplify the calculation, perhaps by dividing it among several agents. Informed transaction effectively combines the last two approaches, by pooling information via a third party, which can also introduce relevant information from outside the agents concerned. The motivations for these alternative transaction styles, their effectiveness compared with market transaction and their ability to resist market pressures, are the subject of the next two chapters.

6 The negotiated alternative

Relational transaction

When supermarkets hijacked the high street and drove the big spenders out of town, shoppers bemoaned the loss of personal service in the closed-down corner store. Today, the customer who stops to chat is likely to hear the beat of angry baskets behind them in the checkout queue, and the cashier who discounts the aspirins for a neighbour with a sick relative risks disciplinary action. Relational transaction – in which exchange of products involves exchange of other personal information, to which price and delivery terms are adapted – has an archaic ring, as loud as that of the mechanical tills at which unhurried buyers once talked shop. It speaks of villages small enough for everyone to know everyone else, where errands were run in return for a pint and creditworthiness depended on the length of family trees.

Anonymity, cash settlement and credit reference agencies are a welcome step forward for those without friends in high places and unappreciative of the neighbour staring over the fence. Just as economists of the late eighteenth century were the first to see opportunity as well as threat in the shift from mercantilism to free trade, sociologists of the late twentieth century have glimpsed a silver lining on the lonely crowd, as close-knit community disperses into open-minded society 'that is not only egalitarian in several respects . . . but geared towards satisfying the average and common man at the expense of select minorities and distinguished individuals' (Giner 1976: 109).

Where relational transaction is prized for the richness of detail on which it relies, markets draw strength from the paucity of their information needs and interdependencies (section 5.4). They restrict relevant information to the price and quality of the product on offer, pushing personal circumstances out of the picture. Supermarkets' spread, and the penetration of price-directed dealing into other areas of economic life, suggests a social acceptance of the merits, at least in economic exchange, of being judged by what we offer rather than who we are. The rapid rise of internet trading, in which cash changes hands with not even a real name to put to the non-existent face, suggests few limits to the extent to which personality and locality can be squeezed out in pursuit of optimum trade.

But prices do not always capture all that an agent needs to know, and product descriptions do not always paint the full picture. Relational transaction remains alive in trades for which stakes are high and mistakes irreversible. Repeated exchanges are equally open to it, and parts of the middle ground are equally richly relational. This chapter begins with the positive case for transacting relationally, considers the market-based objections, and assesses the extent to which relational transaction can account for systematic differences in national economic structure and performance.

6.1 A rationale for relationalisation

The marketplace is cosmopolitan and crowded. Anyone may enter it and enter into transactions with those already there. Anyone may leave it as soon as their business is done. The transaction ends when a price is agreed, and a product exchanged for a means of payment. 'Under perfect competition there is no room for bargaining, negotiation, remonstration or mutual adjustment and the various operators that contract together need not enter into recurrent or continuing relationships' (Hirschman 1982: 1473). Market transaction (MT) celebrates this interaction as not only non-discriminatory in process, but also superior in outcome compared to other trading systems. It steers trade in existing products towards the most efficient outcome for each agent, and for the system as a whole, while also encouraging the offer of new products which improve potential outcomes from the next set of trades. But the biggest, riskiest and most repercussive trades are rarely conducted through the market. The information needed to set worthwhile terms, and the monitoring needed to ensure compliance with them, are more than an arm's-length transaction can normally provide.

6.1.1 Getting to know the counterparty

Only quickly ended, easily reversed or low-cost transactions are entrusted entirely to the literal marketplace. Almost every non-trivial purchase and sale carries some relational elements, and even a pocket-money trip to the candy stall is rarely wholly free of them. Traders are unlikely to part with a big-ticket item without at least taking name and address in case the cheque bounces. Insurers want to know about our risks before choosing whether to give cover, and on what terms. Cellular phone providers want to study users' budgets and call behaviour before deciding which equipment and charging structure to burden them with. Even suppliers of small items may seek personal details so they can follow up with promotional offers on the range of products where their profit is really made. Similarly, buyers want guarantees and servicing facilities in case the new durable breaks down, insurers with good payout records as well as low premiums, and some indication of the cellphone company's future coverage and charging developments before signing the long contract on which a competitive offer depends. And creditors have not given up tailoring loan amounts, terms and rates to the borrower's personal circumstances and history; they simply gauge these systematically via a credit rating agency rather than more informally by checking local records and opinions.

The larger, rarer, more hazardous and less reversible the transaction, the more buyer and seller will seek to fill in their information gaps by establishing closer relations before they transact. Similarly, the more a transaction's value to buyer or seller depends on what other buyers and sellers do, the deeper the dialogue likely to open up between agents on the same side of the market. Relations are both consequence and cause of high-stakes, low-mobility transactions, their continued success being likely to add to the chance of their continuing because of the trust established between the agents and the power they come to exert over the other. Since it is not in an agent's interest to leave if this means writing-off their investment in transaction-specific knowledge, and not in the other agent's interest to leave if they will carry away non-specific knowledge that could be usefully traded with others, both sides have an incentive to keep the existing transaction going, which may result in considerable flexibility in the terms they agree and comparative insensitivity to the alternative terms on offer from other (unrelated) transactors.

Relational transaction (RT) forsakes the crowded marketplace for calmer committee rooms and café tables, at which a chosen subset of trading partners refine their terms and reveal non-price information relevant to the deal. RT moves the agent from a competitive trading environment into one of small numbers and bilateral negotiation. The locking-in of transactors by privileged information-sharing, sunk investments or contingent decision-making is therefore recognised and made the basis for the trading relationship. Having sacrificed (or recognised the absence of) a costless 'exit' option should things go wrong, relational transactors commit themselves to moving ahead with a deal, pushing for the best terms that will still keep the counterparty on board (Hirschman 1962). Since the effectiveness of such bargaining depends on the relative buying and selling power of the transactors (and any political string-pulling power they can acquire with these), agents must choose their relationships carefully, and maintain a trading reputation that will induce others to choose them.

6.1.2 *Information through informality*

Adding a relational dimension might seem an obvious solution to the information and co-ordination problems outlined in Chapter 7, and one which adds to economic efficiency by extracting and circulating transaction-relevant private information not fully communicated by advertised price. If we don't know whether someone can be trusted, we try to find out more about them and the product they are offering. If we don't know what they plan to do, we ask them; and if their intended action threatens to knock our own on the head or off course, we try to negotiate a mutually more compatible course of action. Among the 'enrichments' to transaction information with which relational trading might overcome recognised market failures are interpersonal utility comparisons to construct a social welfare function (Sen 1982: 18), truthful revelation of product quality to allow mutually beneficial trades under asymmetric information (Akerlof 1970), and truthful revelation of personal demand for public goods so that these can be adequately provided.

Although arguably a product of much earlier, socially unintegrated and relativistic times, RT can claim to be a step forward from market transaction. It moves on from the idealised world of full information, moving competing buyers and sellers and known equilibrium prices into a more familiar world where competition is imperfect, trade involves products of unknown quality, and the consequences of one's own (and others') actions are hard to gauge before the commencement of trade, much of which is therefore likely to be at 'disequilibrium' prices. It is an attempt to overcome the market's information and co-ordination problems by giving both sides of the transaction a chance to discuss and modify its terms. In another respect – more pertinent to MT advocates – RT is a step backwards, from the 'universal' of a large, diversified trading system to the 'particular' of local networks and non-price information. It was a pervasive feature of pre-industrial feudal, patriarchal-family based economies, whose social and economic rigidity the capitalist market system has been widely credited with breaking down.

Economists have often been reluctant to ask people about their beliefs and intentions, believing that the structural relations of macroeconomics and the axiomatic deductions of decision theory will explain their actions in ways they may not even be aware of. People's statements about themselves could be misconceived, or even dishonest: they regularly assure opinion pollsters of their willingness to pay more tax for public services, then vote for parties that reduce both, and a large majority profess to be above-average at tasks ranging from driving to picking horse-race winners. Preference is revealed by action and, having inferred individual preferences from it, a neutral observer can account for an agent's choices and infer what the agent will do under specified future conditions. The 'rationality' of choice allows the model to slide easily from observation and prediction to prescription, leaving the conventional economic approach not far away from psychological behaviourism.

> We can follow the path taken by physics and biology by turning directly to the relation between behaviour and the environment and neglecting supposed mediating states of mind . . . changes in the environment of the individual have quick and dramatic effects. A technology of operant behaviour is, as we shall see, already well advanced.
>
> (Skinner 1972: 20, 24)

The 'self-evident' axioms of rational choice were supposed to set an unarguable standard for the revelation of agents' preferences through their actions, after which their choice in specified future situations could be predicted from the utility information already supplied. Subsequently, the difficulty of matching up agents' real-world information supplies and calculation tasks with those depicted in basic rational choice theory, and of getting agents to obey the rational choice axioms even in highly simplified tests with full information assured, has deflected economists' attention on what agents do when actual decisions cannot follow the prescribed pattern.

Ironically, the extension of markets into previously uncommercialised aspects of social life increases the range of transactions for which agents may feel compelled to swap case notes as well as bank notes. RT can claim not only a longer history than MT, but a wider contemporary relevance, once the range of indivisible, irreversible and uninsurable trades is taken into account, to have been around for much longer, and cover a wide range of economic activity into which the individualistic rigours of MT have only rarely or recently, if ever, extended.

6.2 The economic case for relational transaction

By stepping away from the anonymity of the market, RT moves buyer–seller inter-action beyond the exchange of payment for products at an advertised price. Imperfect information is tackled by sharing knowledge (relating to the product to be exchanged, the future states of the world attending its consumption and further production, etc.). Incomplete information is tackled by sharing beliefs and intentions, and agreeing the strategies to be followed on their basis. Co-ordination problems are tackled by bringing agents close enough together that they can monitor one another's actions, detecting and punishing any departure from the agreed strategy. Unlike the written contracts that characterise market trade, relational contracts are often brief, diffuse or even unwritten. Ambiguity is their special means for achieving agreement across space, and adaptability ensures the durability of that agreement over time.

6.2.1 Relational information-sharing

The preconditions needed for MT to attain its justice and efficiency properties are almost as formidable as the properties themselves, as Chapters 2–5 have tried to show. Information problems arise from uncertainty over future changes resulting from exogenous events or other agents' actions, and the impact these changes will have on future profit and utility. Since information has public-good, external-benefit, joint-product, merit-good and indivisibility characteristics, it is often impossible to trade on the open market; some will become available for free via movements in prices, but this external benefit will deter transactions which without it would be privately beneficial. The uncertainty of entering decision without full information may also be impossible to trade, there being only limited markets for risk and none for genuinely unquantifiable unknowns.

The resultant missing information about the availability, likely outcomes and likely benefits of actions leaves a fully 'rational' choice impossible to specify and/or compute. RT is adopted to increase the chances of reaching a decision which, if not 'rational', will at least be consistent with others and work out according to plan, in situations where utility judgements depend on endogenous future states of the world whose causes lie in other people's actions, and on exogenous future states of the world to which the best response also depends on how others respond to it. Those who lack necessary information may have to work themselves into the confidence of those who have it; and two agents with information they know to be valuable to the other may now have to enter close relations, perhaps with an agreement to exclude other parties, before they can profitably exchange.

Under MT, agents act independently, the market prices they 'take' being their sole way of communicating. Under RT, price becomes one of the variables submitted to negotiation, through which information is transferred by more direct means. The RT takes place between agents who know or have exchanged details about one another, and it usually does not end when the initial exchange has taken place. It tries to solve the information problem by sharing out the knowledge and intentions of the parties, and the co-ordination problem by binding them to certain courses of action and certain responses to contingent future events.

6.2.2 Relational co-ordination

Co-ordination problems arise from uncertainty as to whether other agents will stick to a particular strategy, and whether threats to make them do so are credible, even if all agents know which actions are best for them if taken by all. While a competitive market may be efficient at informing agents of what sort of 'game' they are in, and when co-operation would improve on the payoffs to individual maximisation, it can fail to induce co-operation (e.g. if those who cheat are not detected, or have such high time-preference that future punishment does not annul the one-off gain from cheating). Transactors who know that co-operation would have all-round benefits may therefore seek relational ties with one another to allow it to work.

'Consumption clubs' to finance public goods provision by sharing their costs and internalising their benefits, visited in section 2.2.3, are an example of relational co-ordination on the demand side of a market. Co-operative R&D, by which firms seek to internalise the possible spillovers from innovation which prevent them attempting it individually, are a comparable example on the supply side. As well as enshrining obligations to carry out or refrain from certain actions, and reveal results that are not universally observable, both types of arrangement may extend to a set of side-payments which keep the group together by redistributing gains so that all are better off within it.

Recognising that interdependence is inescapable in many transaction situations, RT tries to turn it into a virtue. By breaking through the anonymity of the market, it offers agents a way of realising the gains from forgoing a 'dominant' self-maximising strategy in prisoners' dilemma-type situations, and of protecting those gains against the opportunism of agents who seek a one-off gain by abandoning the co-operation pact.

6.2.3 Relational risk-sharing

The use of relational transaction to overcome information asymmetry, protect transaction-specific invesments, overcome monopoly-pricing uncertainties and enforce collective-action solutions illustrates the general power of RT to help individuals spread their risks. Firms need no longer risk their future when they undertake to sell an entire product line to one client, or buy a prototype machine from an unknown inventor, or hand the treasury to a brilliant mathematician straight out of college. Consumers can similarly obtain a degree of protection against the computer that won't talk to their printer and the car that breaks down on the way home from the showroom.

Such insurance could conceivably be provided in the market – if not through a separate policy, then through a premium paid by the party with superior information, either to compensate for any deception or to provide assurance that it will not take place. (Warranties and money-back guarantees give the buyer some redress if unknown information turns out to be adverse, but perhaps more importantly gives them more assurance that it will not.) The claim on behalf of RT is that it makes such insurance available more cheaply, by allowing agents to structure their transaction so that relevant information is revealed to the other party, and both sides have a financial interest in continuing to co-operate.

6.2.4 *Relational strategy-protection*

Those who give orders, or place them, have a problem when the other party doesn't immediately do what they are told. Is the R&D department laying the groundwork for a major technical breakthrough, or just messing around with test tubes? Is the consultant pondering the restructuring plan, or merely staring out of the window? Is the driver cutting through backstreets because this is the quickest way to beat the traffic, or because he is hopelessly lost? Under MT, appearance tends to be taken for immediate reality, and those who do not appear to be going straight to the objective are abandoned for those who do. Under RT, information can be gleaned which reveals when today's seemingly inconsequential moves open up better prospects for tomorrow. Strategists can be distinguished from slackers, and left to get on with their ultimately superior job.

By releasing agents from the need to trade under current competitive-market conditions, RT leaves room for agents who wish to make current sacrifices in pursuit of future rewards. Through it, new products can be sold below cost to help establish the market, and to anticipate future cost reductions; suppliers can be supported while they down tools to reinvest in components for the buyer's next model range; employees can be sponsored through an apprenticeship, whose costs will later be repaid out of their higher productivity; savers can be allowed to waive instalments during a spell of unemployment; and shareholders can forgo a dividend while management restructures to revive profitability in a changing market.

There is more to RT than simply coming together, swopping information and agreeing certain modifications to the evaluation and ranking of actions. To ensure that RT terms are believed, when they may involve one side sacrificing immediate self-interest in pursuit of all-round gains (e.g. in a prisoners' dilemma situation) or future gains (in an interdependent strategy), agents must establish a reputation for honesty and dependability – either by displaying it through past actions, or by making investments whose time or money will be unrecoverable if the deal does not go ahead, by investing in arrangements that will punish them if they cheat. To ensure that others (with or without reputation) fulfil their side of the agreement, an agent may invest further time or money to set up a credible punishment threat.

These investments are paid back by the saving of time and cost in calculating the best terms for the transaction, the greater chance of getting the calculations right, and the greater assurance that terms will be enforced. Whereas MT involves minimal start-up costs but can involve substantial follow-up costs (of enforcement, redress when it is broken or write-offs if its terms agreed turn out to be disadvantageous), RT incurs an initial investment cost which subsequently reduces incremental costs.

> People who do not trust one another will end up co-operating only under a system of formal rules and regulations which have to be negotiated, agreed to, litigated, and enforced, sometimes by coercive means. This legal apparatus, serving as a substitute for trust, entails what economists call transaction costs.
>
> (Fukuyama 1995: 27)

Just as large, indivisible, unrecoverable production investments make more economic sense the larger the output over which to spread these overheads is, large, unrecoverable transaction investments are more likely to be made when two agents know they will be making prolonged or repeated transactions, on terms whose breach under the specified circumstances (or non-revision under suddenly changed circumstances) could inflict heavy costs on one or both parties.

In principle, strategists could support themselves in the open market, covering current losses through loans secured against the enhanced future profits that will result. But such hypothetical collateral is rarely accepted on affordable terms. 'Junk bonds' secured on future corporate takeover proceeds found favour only at a time of historically low yields on more traditional assets, and student loan schemes have generally been shunned by private banks despite calculations putting the return to higher education in double figures. Comparing the measurable current losses against the uncertain and immeasurable future gains, and knowing the cost of assessing and monitoring the strategist, the capital market is likely to demand too high a rate of return for many strategies to succeed via MT. Through RT, the strategist can better acquaint a sponsor with the project's risks and rewards, or agree a way of sharing them, and reduce the monitoring cost, sufficiently to be tided over at acceptable cost.

6.2.5 *Relational power-balancing*

Private information confers power, over those from whom it came (and would like it back) and those who would like to acquire it, which may make it a useful counterweight to other agents' buying or selling power. This power gives certain agents the ability to influence or even dictate prices for the whole market, without consulting transactors on the other side or fellow traders on the same side. Whereas MT presumes 'equality before the market', with dispersed agents easily able to switch to what they think are better deals, RT often arises where there are power imbalances between agents (e.g. a small supplier facing a large industrial purchaser) or when power on both sides threatens to stall agreement (e.g. monopolist confronting monopsonist). 'In the matter of contract true freedom postulates substantial equality between the parties' (Hobhouse 1911: 85).

To be able to bargain seriously, agents must try to balance their counterparty's power, by either getting together with or capturing and centralising market power from the other agents with which they line up. They can then drive a harder bargain by increasing the damage they can inflict on the other agent by switching, and reducing the other agent's chances of switching profitably. Relational links between smaller agents on the same side are often a precondition for relational links between two sides of a market, because it is only when power is sufficiently equalised that the stronger party has any incentive to agree, and keep to, mutually non-exploitative terms.

6.3   The relational case against market transaction

The discipline imposed by buyers on sellers in a competitive market is essentially that of 'exit'. By constantly threatening to switch to other sellers, if these offer lower price or a better product, buyers force a seller to meet or exceed the standards set elsewhere, or else to leave the market. Sellers, even if they can hold their own against the current competition, constantly look for a more sheltered existence by differentiating their product or inventing a cheaper process that gives distinct cost or quality advantages. Dissatisfied buyers could choose to bargain with the substandard seller, demanding a better deal and so enforcing higher standards directly. But this is costlier, in terms of money or time, than merely switching to a rival seller. 'Consumer sovereignty' rests on the right to replace a supplier, not to reform them. Reciprocally, sellers must be able to switch easily away from buyers who fail to pay for the product or cause reputational damage by misusing it. From this arises the market system's requirement for a large number of competing producers, and for universally low costs of switching from one counterparty to another.

Where exit costs are high, buyers are left to confront an effective monopolist, who can let prices rise or standards slip without a mass exodus of customers, and so ignore the voices of complaint. Where there is differential exit, 'voice' is muted because it tends to be the richest or best informed consumers – whose complaints would carry most weight – who exit, leaving behind only those who cannot go elsewhere. Their complaints carry progressively less weight because the supplier knows they are an increasingly captive audience. To the extent that they were paying more for the service before they abandoned it (e.g. first class on the railways, higher-margin items in the village shop), the exit of better-off buyers adds a further dimension to the adverse selection, in that cross-subsidies are removed and those remaining will have to pay more. Any escape from this is counterproductive, since if prices are dropped to slow the rate of exit or accommodate the lower ability-to-pay of the survivors, it reduces the supplier's ability to invest to tackle the quality problems.

Hirschman (1962), in originating the concept and the terms, gave the example of railway services, whose performance deteriorated rather than improved as long-distance motoring began to compete for wealthier passengers' custom. To this could now be added public hospitals, social security offices, inner-city housing estates, city-centre supermarkets, launderettes, payphones, and most of the items from which higher-income groups have been able to walk – or drive – away. While these may be instances where private affluence begets public squalor, the private costs of 'exit' may not be as low as those who engage in it initially believe. Buyers who move to a new seller have only basic information about them – the price they charge, the external appearance of their product and premises, the information they choose to hand out. The seller has little incentive to clarify this information, if they know that the buyer will merely exit again if dissatisfied (or if the seller also intends to exit after the transaction). The prospect of serial let-down can therefore loom, as buyers slide between a series of suppliers none of which turns out any better than the one that was abandoned. Often-heard complaints that there are no decent motorway cafés, service stations, minicab operators or plumbers may be the logical consequence of too costless an entry and exit on both sides.

Even where there are enough alternative suppliers to make exit a possibility for all, it may be socially wasteful as an efficiency-enforcement mechanism compared with the alternative of sticking with existing suppliers and improving their performance. 'Costless' exit by buyers can not only impose external costs on less fortunate buyers, as in the railway example, but also impose social costs on the supply side if one supplier now has to close or contract while another opens or expands. Both these operations are likely to incur unrecoverable costs, which may well exceed the costs that would have been incurred in improving the service of the first supplier. (State intervention, normally used to try to internalise such costs, tends in this case to do the reverse: business closures and start-ups both tend to attract financial assistance, so that external costs are effectively being subsidised rather than taxed.)

Competitive markets are often criticised, even by sympathisers, for rendering previously 'human' exchanges impersonal, and extending cold maximising calculation into areas where warmer motivations used to prevail. Unknown, corporately uniformed checkout assistants replace the friendly corner shopkeeper; bank customers become numbers processed by computer at a distant head office; bodies, wombs and kidneys become objects for sale. By breaking through such anonymity, RT may deserve support on social grounds even if it brings no economic efficiency advantages, or represents a sacrifice of efficiency. Concern is also raised that 'equality before the market' conceals power imbalances between buyers and sellers which nullifies the claim that market transactions' outcomes are socially just. By giving both sides a voice in shaping the transaction, and encouraging them to make specific investments in it, RT makes for an exchange between equals – an advantage especially emphasised in the labour market where market transactions may ignore a fundamental power imbalance between labour and capital (section 10.3.3).

Whenever investment involves sunk costs, there is also a social case for RT based on the internalisation of external costs. MT allows private agents to cut their losses by abandoning the investments specific to any transaction that failed to work (closing bankrupt companies, scrapping loss-making assets, sacking redundant workers, etc.). But for society this may be a costlier way of reallocating resources than turning round the company, rearranging the assets or redeploying the workers, which might be possible with the strategy-protection offered by RT. For the private agents involved, turning-away is usually a cheaper option than turnaround, at least in the short term. For society it may well be more expensive, since both the closure of one enterprise and the redeployment of the resources to another generally involve public subsidies (redundancy help, start-up grants and tax breaks), and there is likely to be a longer gap during which displaced labour is unemployed at public expense. Compared with bringing an existing operation back to financial health, closing one operation and replacing it with another relational transaction may reward society with not only a higher gross investment rate because the paybacks are better internalised, but also a higher net investment rate because failing assets are nursed back to health, rather than abandoned with the costs falling on the wider economy.

6.4   Conditions conducive to relational transaction

Buyers and sellers tend to enter extended, relational dealings when their interaction is itself extended (and cannot be reduced to one point in time by a simple contract), or when serious uninsurable losses would follow from the sudden breakdown of a transaction. These losses might arise because its set-up costs are high and unrecoverable, its benefits expected after some date not yet reached, or its enactment a precondition for the success of other irreversibly chosen actions. Once entered into, RT reinforces the conditions that give rise to it by raising the transactors' mutual dependency. Transaction-specific knowledge acquired and investments undertaken make it costlier for them to interrupt the deal; these costs being necessary to deter them from opportunistically breaking the relationship, which would inflict similar costs on the other party.

Critics of RT (to be given more space in section 6.5) continue to cast it as a second-best option when market transaction is made unavailable or unattractive by the absence of necessary information or insurance markets, or of an effective legal framework for enforcing arm's-length contracts. In responding to informational and power imbalances and transaction costs by swapping the handshake for the embrace, RT may merely exacerbate and enshrine the very imperfections it is supposed to overcome. RT advocates view these deficiencies as unavoidable, and identify a more positive economic and social case for knowing who we are dealing with. Most 'market' transaction involves relations of some sort, and the most important can involve considerable investment in the relationship, justified by the even greater cost of transacting without it. A number of common instances conducive to RT can be identified.

6.4.1   Monopoly and monopsony

The locking-in of buyer or seller is one of a more general class of cases in which market transaction breaks down because one or both of the parties has monopoly power. Without an alternative to switch to, dissatisfied buyers or sellers must try to get their grievance rectified by the existing transaction partner. Thus user groups spring up to monitor and take to task natural monopolies (whether or not the state provides a regulator), and producer associations form to counterbalance large purchasers. Even where there is not strictly a monopoly, the same defensive organisations tend to appear where switching costs are high relative to the potential gains from switching. Thus consumer coalitions may form among bank customers, the buyers of certain cars, the listeners to certain radio stations, and others who feel vulnerable to sudden changes in the quality or terms of service because the alternatives are worse, or expensive to move to. Similarly, arms-makers may lobby to get a better deal out of the defence ministry, or food processors out of a large supermarket chain, because it seems cheaper than having to adapt production for a wider range of peacetime industries or small shops.

Being locked into a transaction, like being locked inside a lift, forces people to strike up an acquaintance with others who might normally have remained strangers. In the case of consumers facing a monopoly, the relations sought are usually 'horizontal': joining forces with other consumers with similar concerns to press a collective case. This helps develop a louder and more harmonious voice, and may also, when the monopoly is not complete, pose a more serious threat of exit. In the case of producers facing a monopsony, the relations are more likely to be 'vertical': entering a dialogue with the buyer. By allowing grievances to be aired, and future plans discussed and new ideas exchanged, the producers hope positively to interest their dominant buyer in future trade, and negatively to make it more costly for them to switch away by putting trust and shared information into the present relationship.

Bilateral monopoly, in which a monopolist confronts a monopsonist, might redress the power imbalance that encourages horizontal relations, but it makes vertical relations even more essential. Since both parties have the power to set an 'excessive' price and hold the other to ransom, they have no alternative but to bargain over the terms of the transaction, and establish an enforcement procedure to implement the bargain (or a grievance procedure to deal with cases where it is breached). Given a unilateral monopoly's power to enforce its terms on others through the market, there may be a tendency for monopoly to breed monopsony, and vice versa: workers forming unions to confront strong employers, dissatisfied customers forming a pressure group, a large manufacturer's suppliers forming associations. 'Private economic power is held in check by the countervailing power of those who are subject to it. The first begets the second' (Galbraith 1952: 125).

6.4.2 *Transaction-specific investments*

Locking-in to a repeated or sequential transaction can occur even when monopoly and monopsony are absent if either buyer or seller must make unrecoverable investments to support the exchange. Sellers become trapped if the provision of a product involves costs which are unrecoverable if its buyer subsequently pulls out (because alternative buyers cannot be found, and equipment cannot be costlessly reassigned to making other products). Buyers are trapped if the purchase of a product commits them to follow-up purchases (e.g. spare parts, servicing, software) from the same supplier, or involves them in related expenditures (e.g. training, compatible hardware) whose costs are unrecoverable if the product is subsequently replaced. A firm that installs specialised grinding equipment to fashion aero-engine rotor blades will look for assurance that a certain number of aircraft makers will agree to purchase them. A household that buys an expensive computer-games console will look for assurance that compatible software is available at low marginal cost. Specific investments are unrecoverable if the transaction is not completed, or not repeated a certain number of times.

Production to order, in place of market-oriented production for stock, swops the vagaries of the market for the risk of desertion by specific other agents by turning the product itself into a transaction-specific investment. If the buyer drops out, after specifying the product and before paying for it, the seller is left with goods which may not be saleable to any other buyer at a price which recovers its cost. Buyers can be similarly let down if they place and pay for an order which the seller then abandons, because the seller cannot meet the specification or goes out of business. Either side can be hurt if they agree a price which subsequent market developments make unrealistic. To provide a reassurance against such contingencies, the party more likely to breach the agreement may try to prove its sincerity by attaching extra penalties to doing so. The buyer paying a deposit, the seller providing a guarantee, or both sides submitting to third-party enforcement.

These illustrations highlight the dual role of transaction-specific investment, as a cause of relational transaction which, once it is under way, those involved in it may try to reinforce. Sinking costs into the transaction set-up is a form of 'mutual hostage-taking', giving both sides a disincentive to renege on the deal opportunistically (Itoh 1992). Where information flows easily within conglomerate (*keiretsu*) networks, reputation may be just as effective a sunk cost as any specific physical capital, both being outlays which will deliver future returns only if kept intact and harnessed to the present purpose. Bilateral sunk costs maintain the discipline that is initially achieved by competition for admission into the transaction relationship. Despite their apparent security due to locking-in, both sides have an incentive to keep delivering best performance because of what they would lose if dismissed from the transaction.

6.4.3 Repeated transactions

Even where they do not involve either party in any physical investment, transactions which are repeated under identical or slow-changing conditions tend to set up an informational 'investment' which can be recovered more quickly if the relationship is formalised. Each successful repetition of the transaction reinforces the two sides' assurance about the quality of the product and the reliability of the payment. Both sides will enjoy a saving of cost or time if they make use of this assurance to abbreviate the process – repeating the order without looking round to see if other suppliers have made price cuts or quality improvements, taking delivery of the product without checking its quality, making delivery on credit in the knowledge that the bill will be settled promptly.

In choosing to routinise transaction under stable conditions, agents assume that any payment of too high a price or for too low a quality on one occasion will be balanced over time by similar deviations in the opposite direction, and that the cost of calculating an adjustment to the 'optimum' price and quantity each time will outweigh its benefits. By showing a willingness to make occasional suboptimal trades for the sake of mutual transaction-cost saving, trust is reinforced and the cost of monitoring compliance reduced.

If they keep the transaction in the market, the party which starts to abbreviate its choice in this way may find that the other is taking advantage of it – passing-off products of lower quality, or letting its payments bounce, hoping they will either not be noticed or that the extra profit gained will make up for the subsequent loss of the disgruntled counterparty. Breaking trust in this way is analogous to switching to non-cooperation on the last round of a prisoners' dilemma game (section 2.2), and is characteristic of the one-shot encounters of pure market transaction. The same sort of interdependence arises as with transaction-specific investment, and once again the two sides are likely to try to solve it by forming a relationship. Mutual knowledge of the other's reliability may be enough to cement such a relationship, because such knowledge would take time and costs to acquire if one party went elsewhere, and because both would incur higher costs if they had to go through the full decision process every time they repeat the transaction. But since knowledge is intangible, both parties may try to reinforce the relationship by making specific sunk-cost investments around the transaction, which they would lose if they broke it.

When investments are made whose payback depends on repeating a transaction, or going through a series of related transactions, the party incurring the investment cost will be inclined to strike up a relationship to make sure that these follow-up transactions take place on acceptable terms. Sunk investment by one party effectively makes the other party a monopolist (or monopsonist), creating the same relational incentive as do the more 'natural' monopoly cases discussed above.

6.4.4 *Protracted transactions*

Buyers and sellers avoid specific investments in each other if they buy from, and produce for, stock, especially if stocks are held by retail or wholesale intermediaries who bring greater stability to price. But even producing for consumers in general, or committing to buy from producers in general, can entail risks if production and payment are displaced in time. The generalised demand which a producer sets out to meet may have passed by the time its output comes on stream; the generalised supply for which a consumer puts money aside may have dried up by the time they have saved enough to make their purchase. 'Technology, with its companion commitment of time and capital, means that the needs of the consumer must be anticipated – by months or years. When the distant day arrives the consumer's willingness to buy may well be lacking' (Galbraith 1967: 41). Where the lead-times are long, production for (and consumption from) stock becomes hazardous, and the party taking the risk will prefer to take or place the order at the beginning. Once again, buyer and seller seek a relationship through time so that promises will be kept, and investment in product or purchase repaid.

6.4.5 *Uncertain product characteristics*

One-off transactions, with product and payment exchanged simultaneously, can still run into trouble if the product fails the market 'homogeneity' test. 'Pure' market transactions depend on product characteristics being known to both parties, and standardised across different consignments of the product. This allows traders of the product to arrive at a uniform price, with buyers knowing what they are getting for their money, and sellers possessing a superior product to advertise the fact by setting a higher price. Marketplace techniques apply less easily to products which are newly introduced, whose quality is difficult to assess from outward appearance, or whose exchange requires subsequent renewed contact between buyer and seller (e.g. for replacement parts and servicing, user-training, add-on components, or recovery and recycling at the end of the product's life.

Away from the fruit stall, appearance and casual inspection are rarely sufficient to give an accurate verdict on quality. Machinery, services, employees and most other resources take more time and effort to evaluate, the truth sometimes emerging only after installation and extensive use. The scope for a discrete, one-off transaction is even further narrowed where the product is information, which the seller cannot allow to be viewed before sale, or a service which must be delivered over time and whose precise content must be shaped by interaction with the client during that time.

Where quality is not immediately measurable, those wishing to sell a product through the market must find indirect means to signal their confidence in it. Methods include persuasive advertising and sales literature, free samples, guarantees, independent reliability tests, brand reputation based on experience with previous products, or submission to an industry watchdog with the power to punish poor performance. Suppliers who themselves are unsure of a product's quality may have to extend the reassurance by creating capacity for answering and remedying customers' complaints. These investments are product-specific rather than transaction-specific, and may be recoverable through the product's sale price. With or without them, buyers may also incur certain evaluation costs themselves, gathering opinion from others who already use the product or insuring themselves against the consequences of bad service.

None of these devices can offer complete confidence in a product. Some may even give perverse signals ('the best needn't advertise') and some may push the costs to buyer or seller above those that allow them to agree a mutually beneficial price. The mere fact that someone is trying to sell a product may sometimes generate adverse assumptions about its quality, and so dissuade prospective buyers. Buyers' suspicion that only substandard products are more likely to be sold displaces their estimate of the quality distribution below its true level, so that the maximum they are prepared to pay for a product will often exceed what the seller knows it is worth. The expectation is fulfilled as better products are withdrawn from the market, and transactions are missed which would have been mutually beneficial had quality been known to both sides (Akerlof 1970). The same barrier to mutually beneficial trade can arise if it is sellers who are unsure of a product's quality: they assume that expert buyers will pitch their offers unrealistically low, and so reject even a fairly priced offer.

When quality signalling through the market is too expensive or counterproductive, both parties have an incentive to add a relational aspect to the transaction. Sellers can signal their sincerity by offering a trial period, making the transaction reversible until information gaps are filled in, or a warranty, redressing the costs of any missing information which turns out worse than the buyer had been led to believe. Buyers can hedge their bets, by paying in instalments which they suspend if the product fails to meet its specifications. By imposing a cost on the offending party should they breach the terms of the deal, such relational conditions assure the other party that deliberate deception is unlikely, and accidental deception will be remedied.

The extreme case of unknown characteristics arises when a product is new to the market, with no known benchmark against which to assess performance and no user comments or past record to assess. Suppliers of innovative products, especially those newly arrived with no track record of selling familiar products, may have to go to extreme lengths to get them accepted – offering full money-back guarantees, giving it away or even paying people to be seen using it. Market transaction breaks down for lack of information on the consumer's part about what the product is worth. Producers may be equally uncertain, until they engage directly with prospective buyers, about what demand schedule they face, and hence what profit-maximising price they should set.

Pure market transaction is most likely to survive with low-value, repeat-purchase items, where losses from a single bad purchase are small, and buyers can rely on their own and others' switching threat to ensure that quality is accurately reflected in price. We still feel safe buying bread from the bakery in a village we visit only once, because it looks and feels like bread, and because the bakery is unlikely to have survived if it routinely sells contaminated or imitation supplies. Relational transaction is likely to develop whenever transactions are high-value, single-purchase, or involve agents of unknown reputation. Firms rarely buy their machine tools off the back of a lorry (at least without a heavy discount), and those who travel beyond the realm of convertible currencies often forgo the mutual gains from black-market currency exchange to make sure they are given the right notes, and have a counter to return to if the sums do not add up. Trades in these conditions may involve a 'probationary' relationship, from which the established agent can withdraw if the newcomer (or its product) fails to match expectations. Or if there are sunk costs (e.g. of time lost or inspection costs incurred) in such an arrangement, the established client may demand a 'conditional' relationship under which the newcomer promises to stay in the deal until it has met a certain performance target, or to accept payment conditional on performance.

6.4.6   Positive externalities

Imperfect information blocks privately beneficial transactions by opening a gap between what the product is actually worth to a buyer and what they believe it is worth. A similar gap, blocking socially beneficial transactions, can arise when one transactor gives the other benefits which they cannot capture through the market price. Buyers may be deterred when consumption has external benefits. For example, early buyers of a network product deliver benefits to later buyers (more users, more complementary suppliers, etc.), but will pay the same – possibly more if rising output drives down prices – and so have an incentive to defer the purchase. Sellers may be deterred if production has external benefits. A new product may give rivals a no-cost indication of the existence of a new market and (if not patented) a low-cost demonstration of what they can sell into it, but instead of charging extra for this information content, the innovator may have to sell the product below cost until consumers have been able to assess its value.

Relational transaction allows such externalities to be internalised. The supplier of a network gives discounts to early buyers (perhaps with an incentive to recruit new members). The supplier of an innovation demonstrates its advantages to buyers so that they will willingly pay extra to be first to acquire it. For some network providers, long-term relationships are essential because admission fees never cover the cost of the network, which must be repaid by selling additional services through it. For some innovators, close relations with first users may also be essential for ironing out problems and identifying immediate improvements.

6.4.7   Uncertain transactor characteristics

In the case of network products, a seller may use relational transaction to charge different prices to different buyers who are separated in time, because the later buyer derives more initial utility from joining a larger network (assuming that network externalities are always positive). In other situations, a seller may use RT to charge different prices to different buyers who are separated in space. At its most benign, this can arise with private-sector merit goods provision (section 2.6). The seller collects information about different buyers to assess their needs and ability to pay, and sets individualised prices so as to cross-subsidise the most meritorious and impecunious out of the pockets of those who can afford to pay more or consume less.

In its more malign manifestation, such personalised dealing becomes monopoly price discrimination, through which the seller uses information about consumers to charge each the maximum they are willing to pay. Producers can thereby capture the market's 'consumer surplus', the area between price and the demand curve which previously represented a welfare gain to buyers from paying less than their personal valuation of the product. Price discrimination is possible under market transaction only for a monopolist who supplies two or more markets that are legally or geographically separated, so that other suppliers cannot challenge them when they raise price in one market, and buyers in the lower-priced market cannot re-sell into the higher. The monopolist can then identify a separate demand function for each market, and set the price in each where its marginal revenue intersects with (common) marginal cost. Relational transaction allows the process to be taken much further, effectively isolating each consumer within a single market. Similarly, a discriminating monopsonist can isolate each supplier and pay the minimum that will induce them to sell.

In a normal market, consumers are able to conceal their diverse characteristics, those who value a product most effectively free-riding on the more marginal purchasers who bring down the market-clearing price. RT can be used to prevent the establishment of this price, with its social welfare (consumer-surplus) maximising properties. Unless buyers form horizontal relationships so as to share information and discover the discrepancy in prices, so that they can re-trade, their vertical relations with sellers can – far from allowing trade on more equal terms – become a source of exploitation, by a counterparty who has acquired additional preference information but concealed its own cost information.

6.4.8 *Frequent transaction with slowly changing characteristics*

Where two agents carry out the same transaction repeatedly, RT develops passively because of the knowledge they acquire in the process. The relation may then be formalised to let both sides safely abbreviate the practices surrounding the transaction. In contrast, two agents who transact repeatedly in rapidly changing conditions, or with frequently changing preferences, may enter into RT actively, to avoid the costs of renegotiating or retrospectively modifying a market transaction each time.

Incremental product innovation has already been identified as one example. The producer may be making ongoing improvements which they wish to pass on to the user, and the user may be coming up with discoveries and suggestions which they wish to pass on to the producer. Instead of a straightforward sale, the two enter into a relationship which assists the development of the product. RT delivers benefits to the producer in the form of early debugging and suggestions for improvment, for which the producer repays the consumer by freely upgrading the product, or letting them enjoy privileged use of it before it goes on general sale. This case has clear overlaps with those of protracted transaction and imperfect product information, but an added dimension in the sense that the balancing flows of information go two ways.

Consultancy provides another case: while usually brought in to do a specific job, consultants may sometimes be 'retained' on a general brief which is filled in as the organisation's advice needs become known. This case again overlaps with those of protracted transaction and imperfect product information, but with the difference that the information gaps to be filled in arise from the external environment rather than the two parties or the nature of the product that passes between them. It also points towards labour contracts as a much more general category of relational transaction. Employers want a long contract so as to repay recruitment and training costs and acquire information about the employee, and to fix remuneration across a reasonably long planning horizon. But a fast-changing product market may prevent them from setting out what employees will be asked to do, in the detail required by a market contract. It may also be impossible to know how a worker would best be employed until their strengths and weaknesses have been tested on the job. One solution is a 'relational' contract which fixes the length and broad terms of empoyment, but leaves other details to be filled in through ongoing negotiation, employees being rewarded for this greater flexibility by a higher pay rate or the chance to bargain over what they are asked to do.

6.5 Some special relationships

Relational transactions are costlier to conduct than market transactions, and their departure from competitive conditions can also run them up against regulatory restrictions. But the cost of pre-empting problems, or agreeing a grievance procedure for handling them before they occur, may well be lower than the cost of damage limitation or litigation after. RT's effectiveness in overcoming information and co-ordination problems means that it has come to characterise some of the economy's most important areas, sometimes helped by legislation, which reverse normal pro-competitive presumptions because of the social benefits from closer collaboration.

6.5.1 The labour contract

Probationary and conditional relationships are especially common when labour services are being transacted, because of employers' difficulty in assessing the quality of new employees before they have been observed on the job. Educational and training certificates, interviews and qualifying tests can reveal much about the applicant, but not such qualities as their discipline and motivation, ability to interact with other workers and adaptability to change. Labour law usually allows a probationary window during which new recruits can be rejected if they seriously fall short of expectations. Certain categories of labour, such as consultants and interim managers, can be paid by results or be required to stay until they have delivered them.

Relational transaction with labour does not usually end when information asymmetry has been overcome. Once the probationary period is over, employees tend to be signed up on long duration, or even indefinite, contracts, even though (compared with short-run contracts) these may involve the employer in considerable extra costs in terms of pension contributions, sickness pay, termination benefits, etc. Among the reasons for involving 'core' staff in RT are as follows:

- The firm may wish to make relationship-specific investments in employees, e.g. training them or setting up special project teams around them, whose costs will be irrecoverable if the employee suddenly leaves.
- The firm may wish the employee to make relationship-specific investments,

e.g. learning new techniques, which will not be done unless the employee is sure of being kept on afterwards and rewarded.

- Where the job is expected to continue unchanged for a long period, the firm may find it cheaper to retain the existing employees than continually to return to the market and re-recruit. Any cost from the 'insider' workers getting lazy through the loss of outside competition is judged to be outweighed by the cost of taking replacements through recruitment and probation.

- Conversely, where job demands change frequently, the firm may want a relatively open-ended contract to ensure that employees' terms and conditions can be varied. Long contract duration is a compensation for this. Such adaptability is also likely to require training of the type discussed in the first two points.

- Whereas a standard labour contract – like a standard market transaction – will set one price for all, relational labour contracts can allow remuneration to be varied among employees, through multiple pay schemes or even individual negotiation. An employer may wish to set different pay rates for workers on the same job because one does the work more productively, or because one is still repaying costs previously imposed on the firm (e.g. for training), or because one is known to have greater financial needs (e.g. a family to support), or simply because one was recruited more recently and can only be profitably kept on at a 'marginal' wage rate that is below the average rate.

- Highly skilled or longstanding employees may develop a form of bilateral monopoly relation with the firm. An employer suddenly deserted by the employee would be faced with the expense of seeking out and/or training up employees with the same formal skills, informal knowledge and proven reputation. An employee suddenly dismissed by the employer might find its firm-specific skills hard to sell to rival employers (as well as suffering likely discrimination on age and pay-expectation grounds).

- Where employees are unionised, the employer has an extra incentive to offset the 'horizontal' loyalties among employees with strong 'vertical' ties between individual employees and the firm. A relational contract can go beyond pay and conditions, and any further rights specified in labour law, to enshrine such non-wage benefits as consultation rights, profit shares and private use of company facilities.

- Relational contracts may be needed to build in the necessary productivity incentives, and to assemble the information needed to make them work. For workers, such incentives usually involve supplementing a basic salary with bonus pay based on individual productivity, group productivity or company profitability. For management, the link is more usually made directly to profit, either by linking a proportion of pay to it or by giving part of the remuneration in the form of shares. Under such arrangements, workers must be monitored to ensure that they have not skimped on quality in order to meet a quantitative target, or free-ridden on the rest of their group (or, conversely, fallen below target through circumstances beyond their control). RT makes room for the necessary monitoring. Managers must be monitored to ensure that short-run profit has not been boosted by taking unacceptable risks, or actions which boost current profits at the expense of future profits. RT allows monitoring and may also discipline the manager to take a long-term view of profit performance.

- Relational contracts may allow employees to transfer risk to the firm, on the understanding that the firm can buy insurance against that risk on better terms. Two possible types of 'implicit contract' have been suggested. One treats unemployment as the workers' most serious risk, and suggests that they are willing to accept a wage below the market rate, or one that varies with the firm's fortunes, in return for a guarantee that they will not be dismissed in a downturn. The other treats wage variability as the most serious risk (perhaps because they have contractual payment or loan obligations that demand a steady income), and suggests that workers will be willing to accept unemployment during a downturn (when, presumably, they can collect on previously paid social insurance). A hybrid version is conceivable under which firms try to keep to a fixed wage, using profits made when product markets are strong (and marginal product worth more than the wage) to make up for profits lost when product markets are weak (and marginal product worth less than the wage), laying workers off if the equation overbalances. The RT effectively enshrines an insurance contract, written by the firm with premiums taken from wages, which workers could not buy in the marketplace because insurers have insufficient information on future prospects for the employees and their firm.

6.5.2 Inter-firm collaboration and buyer–supplier links

Firms at the same stage of production may find it useful to collaborate to share the costs and risks of a new product or process development, exchange technical information which cannot easily be traded, achieve R&D scale economies, reduce the lead-times that go with communicating and trading new information, learn about new technologies without sinking large acquisition costs into them, access new markets, set standards, and internalise an innovation's external benefits. Firms at successive stages of production may regard collaboration as the best way to introduce, refine and exploit a new idea to mutual advantage. Collaboration takes the form of joint research projects, joint ventures or more informal sharing of information (and the employees who hold it), and can be especially effective in generating exchange between forms which differ on size, technology area or culture.

> Arm's length transactions can have high costs, but are useful when technology is codified, discrete (non-systemic) and relatively simple. Vertical integration limits transaction costs, but prevents the access of specialisms in other firms. Collaboration allows these specialist skills to be accessed, and can allow complex and tacit knowledge to be transferred, and technology to be 'unbundled'.
> (Dodgson 1993: 49)

Many studies of innovation, especially at the later (incremental) stage when new products are being developed and refined, ascribe an important role to close relations between suppliers and users, the first group making trial alterations and the second group giving suggestions or reporting back on the results. Where dissatisfaction results in early exit, buyers lose the opportunity to get the product improved by giving details of their grievance. This information is similarly lost on those they switch to, who must guess the improvement required and will see the buyer exit again if the guess turns out wrong. Buyers' and sellers' ideas and suggestions are, in effect, an external benefit which cannot be captured by pure market exchange aimed solely at extracting the best price. In the case of US auto makers' market relations with their suppliers,

> securing the cheapest possible price through the mechanism of competitive bidding was given first priority. However, the fact that the relations between the parties could be terminated so easily was not conducive to the building up of mutual trust and the cooperative pursuit of cost reductions through continual technological interaction.
>
> (Asanuma 1992: 105–6)

Like the labour contract, collaborative relations allow agents to establish a mutual interest even though their future contributions and receipts are difficult to specify or quantify. It then becomes safer to commit irrecoverable investments to the project, and easier to monitor the other agent to ensure they are doing the same. Division of results can be negotiated more flexibly, and there is a greater chance of new ideas finding their way to the agent best placed to use them.

Relational transaction often gives way to market transaction once information asymmetries have been overcome and new ideas commodified, or else to full integration once one partner has learnt enough about the other to think it worth acquiring. Much technology-based relational transaction has been promoted by state intervention (Sematech in the USA, Eureka in the European Union, Japan's 'fifth generation' computer project) because of private firms' difficulties in sustaining it. Private collaborative arrangements have often broken down because firms believe benefits, costs and risks have been unequally shared or, in self-fulfilling anticipation of this, withhold information that should have been made common knowledge. However, unassisted collaboration appeared to be on the increase in the early 1990s and

> despite these dangers strategic technology partnering can enhance the flexibility of a company through partnering as a monitoring device and also through incorporating a wider variety of technological sources than its intrinsic ones . . . For a further improvement in particular in global markets an intelligent utilisation of strategic alliances could very well be beneficial.
>
> (Hagedoorn and Schakenraad 1993: 77)

6.5.3 *Industrial finance*

Market-based industrial finance, in which creditors and shareholders 'buy' an essentially short-term holding in a firm which they can sell if performance outlook deteriorates, has often been compared unfavourably with the more relational approach in which providers of finance make a long-term commitment which gives them an incentive to ensure improved performance. Stylising a complicated thesis, it is argued that highly liquid stock-markets and strict bankruptcy laws allow shareholders and creditors in these countries to exit from underperforming companies at extremely low cost. This should, in principle, lessen their risks in supplying finance, and so reduce costs of capital for firms that issue shares which find a liquid secondary market. The development of bonds as a form of tradable credit, and of ways of trading traditional bank credit through bond issue or securitisation, has recently extended this cost advantage into commercial lending. However, 'market' financiers' lack of detailed knowledge about their clients leads them to pursue quick investment paybacks, forcing firms to limit their investment to projects assured of making consistently high profits, and to distribute a high proportion of profits through dividends and interest in order to maintain the loyalty of the highly mobile outside investors.

The result is that capital costs may actually be raised above the socially optimum level, deterring firms from investment projects that could be judged socially worthwhile, from strategic actions (e.g. R&D and labour-skill investment) which incur short-run costs to enhance long-run profitability, and from finding co-operative solutions to collective-action problems. Firms requiring extensive restructuring are deprived of the incentive or financial needs to pursue it, because owners prefer to sell their holding, even at a loss, than to stay around for the short-term costs and uncertain long-term benefits of a turnaround programme. Market-based finance not only allows the ownership of companies to be traded, so deterring or destroying the accumulation of mutual knowledge between owners and management, but also facilitates merger and acquisition which shakes up management and workforce and so impedes the growth of relational transactions within the firm, and between it and other firms. Yet because of their interest in high returns, market financiers may actually be motivated to engineer hostile takeovers, which tend to deliver large capital gains on the losing side and quick asset-sale opportunities on the winning side.

In contrast, the more relational links between finance and industry in the German and Japanese economies are argued to reduce the cost of long-term capital, and allow R&D, investment and marketing strategies which improve long-run company (and macroeconomy) performance. In Germany,

> shares are regarded as tokens of a long-term relationship rather than a trading asset, so that dividend payments can be lower and payback periods lengthened . . . borrowers' loan packages, a mix of public and private loans, are cheaper because the private and public banks themselves need to earn lower financial returns.
>
> (Hutton 1996: 301)

Tied in to their relationship with large companies (of which they are frequently both creditors and shareholders), banks take seats on supervisory boards and take a detailed interest in managements' long-term strategy. Underperformance encourages greater involvement in the company rather than a rush to sell out of it. Similarly, companies in the 'Rhineland' model often take equity stakes in one another to cement long-term trading relationships, under which they often step in to help a struggling partner rather than stepping away in search of replacements.

6.5.4 Insurance

Traditionally, insurance covered contingencies which the buyer regarded as largely unpredictable (accident, illness, unemployment, etc.). The seller, by studying the occurrence of these over the whole population (or the buyer's sub-population) could often, through actuarial risk calculations, get to know the buyers' event risk as well as, or even better than, the buyers themselves. Sellers have continued to refine their knowledge (often amassing information on individual buyers themselves as well as their socio-economic and geographical subgroups). But in some areas of insurance, buyers have also become better informed about their exposure to particular risks (workers with no formal qualifications may know that they are likely to experience unemployment, carriers of particular genes may know they are susceptible to certain medical conditions). In other areas, perhaps equally importantly, buyers have become more confident about their ability to judge their own risk even if these judgements show significant systematic divergences from the actuarial record.

Unless insurance is made compulsory, insurers may become increasingly exposed to adverse selection under which 'good' risks find their policies too expensive and opt out, leaving a diminishing pool of 'bad' risks who stay in because they know they are more likely to need to claim on the insurance. As the premium rises to cover the increased likelihood of paying out to this smaller pool, the adverse selection can become self-reinforcing. The insurer's main safeguard against this is to try to make buyers disclose more information about themselves; good risks can then be kept within the scheme by keeping their premiums down, and the worst risks can if necessary be excluded from coverage. The insurance contract thus becomes increasingly relational – a trend reinforced by the diversification of insurance products to cover non-standard contingencies where individual risks cannot reliably be inferred from population averages.

6.6 Relational economies? Japanese and Rhineland capitalism

Although all economies mix MT and RT, comparative studies suggest they do so in different proportions, and that this may help explain differences in employment and growth performance over time (e.g. Whitley 1992, Fukuyama 1995). Relational transaction appears more prevalent in some countries than others, for reasons partly of historical/social context and partly of legislative/economic choice. Although it is possible that different combinations of MT and RT are optimal for different economic structures and stages of development, the prevailing national transaction style may provide a partial explanation for why some economies outperform others over time.

6.6.1   Grouping for growth

RT considerations have received particular prominence in assessments of the post-war Japanese economy. Here, a significant proportion of the (male) workforce, especially in larger companies, was accepted into 'lifetime' employment – after a tough recruitment and probation process, and subject to exacting requirements for application and adaptation. The firm could then ensure payback on heavy training investments because few want to leave. Workers' deep immersion in one employer's corporate culture meant that few others wanted to poach them, and any worker who voluntarily tried to change jobs would (like a secondhand car offered for sale) be suspected of coming from the lower end of the quality spectrum. Firms' investments in human capital were further rewarded by workers' willingness (in return for stable employment) and ability (through multi-skilling) to move flexibly between tasks and locations as the firm's strategy required.

> The system is not simply altruistic: it is taken as axiomatic that secure and stable employment ensures a cooperative workforce, loyalty to the firm, high-trust industrial relations, higher productivity, flexible production and easy innovation, longevity for the company, and prosperity for all.
>
> (Perkin 1996: 157)

Similar long-term relationships are visible in large Japanese firms' external finance, most of which comes from banks within the *keiretsu* or long-term institutional shareholders, many of which (especially pension and insurance companies) are major customers of the same firms. Insurance companies have tended to retain their holdings, accepting capital growth and group-insurance business as compensation for negligible dividend payouts, and 'when a company adjusts its portfolio by disposing of shares it searches for other stable shareholders and sells the shares to them after consulting with the company whose shares are the subject of the transaction' (McKenzie 1992: 84). Banks exercise more active control over management, but their wider institutional ties to a company mean that underperformance is generally met by corrective rather than evasive measures. 'The main bank system provides a corporate monitoring and takeover function that is intermediate between the internalised control structure of a multidivisional business and the external control structure of a competitive capital market' (Sheard 1992: 20).

To support their efficiency-enhancing techniques of just-in-time production, continuous improvements and concurrent engineering, large Japanese manufacturers were observed to enter into long-term relationships with suppliers, often funding their investment and sharing commercially sensitive information with them in return for meeting tough quality, timeliness and adaptability standards. Banks and insurance companies enter into long-term shareholding relations with large manufacturers, the link being reinforced as reciprocal business is granted and privileged information acquired, raising the mutual costs if either party defects. These financial-industrial *keiretsu* form long-term relationships with distributors, often rewarding their loyalty with investment help and preferential pricing. Through this, producers establish long-term relationships with final customers, discouraging brand-switching and influencing the timing of replacement purchase to even out product-market cycles (Womack *et al.* 1990).

In Germany, a two-tier board system gives employee representatives a voice in shaping larger-company strategy, with 'social partnership' consultation on product, process and employment change.

> The interests of the AG [Aktiengesellschaft, publicly quoted company] are not automatically equated with the short-term interests of its shareholders: the long-term interests of the AG, through its research and development programme, and the long-term interests of its employees through its training programmes are not neglected as they are in Britain.
>
> (P. Hart 1992: 6)

Many large German firms remain privately held, and even the AGs have traditionally minimised their dependence for capital on outside shareholders. Those admitted have been given only limited power to shape policy or extract dividends, often passing their proxy votes to banks because these have greater power and are better informed.

> The modest public availability, close sharing and harbouring of information by firms is at the source of the greater reliance of continental European and Japanese companies on intermediate finance and for the greater use of debt in business financial structures.
>
> (Bisignano 1991: 108–9)

Banks' difficulty in recovering their investment if they abandon the firm gives them a strong incentive to tide it over any difficulties and support it in investment and restructuring programmes to enhance long-run profits, whose design and enactment it can monitor through close relations with management. Shares' concentration among pension and insurance funds, which must invest mainly for growth and steady income, further encourages their holders to support the banks' long-term strategy.

6.6.2 The hybrid proves hard to transplant

For much of the 1970s and 1980s, as Japan recovered from the oil shock to continue its conquest of world markets and Germany returned to the top of Europe's productivity and export league, RT-based economies appeared to be winning over those where MT had the upper hand. Firms' close relations with labour allowed them to invest in productivity-raising training and technical change to compensate for rising wages. Firms' close relations with capital providers allowed them to follow long-term modernisation and restructuring plans, undeterred by early losses. Equally relational ties at the macroeconomic level allowed government to deliver low inflation in return for moderation on long-term real interest rates, and rising social benefits in return for wage restraint.

Critics had tended to argue that relational systems were overly dependent on such background stability, in the macroeconomy and in product and factor markets. They would be successful at improving competitiveness for known technologies whose buyers' price/quality trade-off was relatively unchanging, but would have difficulty adapting to substantial product and process changes necessitates by technical advance, rising labour costs or changes in demand. Introspective, workforce-centred information flows were expected to mean slow apprehension of external forces for change, consensus management and reciprocal obligations an even slower reaction to it. However, relational systems also proved to contain reciprocal rights which enabled management, workforce, customers and financiers to demand rapid adjustments from one another once they agreed on the necessity for change, with high trust and training investments assisting the reallocation of resources and rewriting of implicit contracts. Employer and labour associations also achieved the co-ordination needed to make changes with external effects (such as closure of plants and revision of training procedures) and to take necessary collective actions (such as creation of collaborative R&D facilities and all-round wage restraint when productivity growth slowed).

So when US industrial exporters were hit by domestic recession and an over-strong dollar in 1980–3, it was to Japanese techniques that they turned to cut costs and raise quality. When the UK government decided that deindustrialisation had gone too far, after 20 per cent of its manufacturing capacity disappeared in the 1980–1 recession, it was to Germany's mid-size *Mittelstand* technology-based companies that many of its advisers looked for guidance on how to stay competitive despite rising labour costs by relentlessly upgrading products and productivity. Long craft traditions, closed ownership structures and dispersed R&D programmes did not prevent *Mittelstand* firms from quickly adopting, and in some cases pioneering, new electronic products and computerised processes when the market demanded them. 'They have world market shares in the range of 70 per cent to 90 per cent . . . they began to internationalise as far back as the 1950s and 1960s . . . they concentrate their resources to ensure superiority in the areas customers value most' (Simon 1992: 115–18).

Although highly liquid capital markets were expected to be more proficient at switching capital to new higher-profit uses, it often seemed to be 'long-termist' RT structures which achieved rapid adaptation, while 'short-termist' MT forced firms to maximise current efficiency in ways which impeded incremental improvement and swift adaptation to consumer demands. Emphasis on individual maximising incentives, through productivity- or profit-related pay and intra-firm competition, seemed similarly to have promoted current over future returns. Trade imbalance related to low savings rates and social tension from wide income inequalities seemed to be further obstacles to balanced growth under the 'Anglo-American' system. Without RT between firms and workers, rival firms were free to poach skilled labour, so that training was undersupplied. Without RT between firms and banks, temporary cashflow problems which could have been overcome with more credit, rescuing the asset for future profitability, instead became a cause of bankruptcy through the withdrawal of credit, writing-off the sunk costs both for the firm and for society. Without RT between firms and shareholders, any temporary underperformance – even if in pursuit of long-term gain – was punished by sell-off, with the consequent threat of hostile takeover.

Scepticism of the RT system was strengthened by its frequent difficulty in crossing borders because of the high costs of stretching existing supplier links over long distances and the high cost of establishing new ones on the ground. Large Japanese and German companies did, indeed, often make a comparatively late and slow start on the exportation of production which rising labour costs had made too expensive at home. But while transplantation proved costlier and slower because of the need to replicate relationships at local level, it also succeeded eventually in replicating the same productivity and unit-cost advantages. That these often took several years to achieve, but then set a standard which local rivals were forced to match, is a further tribute to the new multinationals' relational financing arrangements.

The difficulties of exporting RT have been nowhere better demonstrated than by its practitioners' own multinationals, which in Germany's case came late to the cost-cutting transplantation game, and in Japan's case often regretted coming into it at all. Japanese and German attempts to expand overseas through acquisition have been especially prone to problems. Sony's struggles with US entertainment groups and BMW's with the Rover Group (which it plucked from a long-term relationship with Honda) suggesting that those accustomed to relational dealing may have difficulty selecting and handling targets in a more market-based fashion. Their organic expansion, often helped by large firms' domestic relational suppliers following them to new locations, which seems successfully to have combined proprietary capital and knowledge advantages with local cost and market-proximity conditions, has recently shown signs of being copied by a new wave of 'emerging' Asian industrial and service transplants. But this was an expansion based on financial relations which became seriously disrupted in the later part of 1997, setting off a regional crisis from which even the Japanese exemplar has not proved immune.

6.7   Market counterattack: the fear of the known

Since these optimistic judgements were reached, however, most of the world's noted 'relational' systems have sustained further external shocks centred on their capital markets, to which their resilience has yet to be proved. Japan's post-war growth phase ended abruptly with the collapse in share and bond prices after 1992. This destroyed the traditional low payout/high growth compact between main banks and insurers and the firms they finance, and imposed several years of near-stagnation on the previously fast-growing real economy. Five years later, the malaise crossed the South China Sea to the 'new Japans' of South-east Asia, which were plunged into currency crisis – and severe repayment difficulties on foreign debt – as foreign investors suddenly reversed the capital inflow that had been financing their large trade and current-account deficits.

6.7.1 *Information poor once more: the relatives devalue*

While a powerful minority of economists still regard this foreign-investor pullout as a product of irrational (but self-fulfilling) loss of confidence, most have been able to identify a logical reasoning behind it. Returns on capital had disappointed, often because of misallocation and mismanagement of investment through relational 'crony capitalism'. For foreign investors, returns threatened to go negative as governments' adherence to rising real exchange rates, which kept their foreign debts cheaper to service but led to a startling arrest in export growth, introduced an escalating devaluation risk. In their efforts to boost investment performance so that outside investors stayed loyal, banks and corporations turned to real-estate speculation which quickly turned into a bubble – rising property values providing the collateral for new loans which raised them further – whose eventual bursting added to the tide of insolvency and spectacular collapse of real-economy demand.

The sudden reversal of capital inflows to East Asia (in which frightened domestic players joined their fleeing foreign counterparts) may have been triggered by chance events – local stock-market corruption scandals and bank worries, bad trade and foreign-reserves figures, approaching elections, some regional environmental disasters. But (at least in retrospect) sound underlying reasons for the withdrawal can be identified: a buildup of short-term foreign debt which meant either a rash of corporate insolvencies or a run on official foreign-exchange reserves, and low rates of return which meant that 'money centre' investments would regain their attraction once US, Japanese or German interest rates rose again. Once a sizeable number of investors pulled out of the equity, bond and foreign exchange markets, it was individually rational for others to follow them, even if the result was a collectively damaging loss of value and growth prospects. (Some observers even infer a collective rationality on the grounds that governments and multilateral agencies would feel compelled to compensate private investors for any losses due to share-price collapse or loan default. This had occurred with the Mexican rescue operation of 1995 and, over a longer timescale, with the 'Brady plan' for rescheduling and securitising 1980s emerging-economy debt. Ironically, the success of these operations in mitigating foreign investor losses has led to the accusation that they introduced 'moral hazard', by persuading reckless lenders that their high potential returns were not matched by equally daunting risks.)

Market enthusiasts had already taken one successful tilt against the success of the 'Asian model', when a series of mid-1990s studies suggested that the region's impressive growth had been largely due to the mobilisation of labour and accumulation of capital rather than improvement in the productivity of these factors (Krugman 1994, Young 1995). To the extent that labour was mobilised by forced migration, and capital accumulated by channelling captive household saving into state-directed (and subsidised) corporate investment, this factor-augmenting 'extensive' growth caused resource misallocation which helped explain the absence of productivity-raising 'intensive' growth. Although based on a distinction between accumulation and total factor productivity growth (TFPG) which may be statistically hard to sustain without assuming a high degree of capital–labour substitutability (Rodrik 1997), this revisionist analysis of the 'Asian miracle' pointed to problems ahead when capital and labour supplies ceased to be plentiful some time before the crisis actually struck.

When it did so, critics accustomed to ascribing financial crises to excessive public-sector deficits – notably absent in the Asian case – were quick to trace the problem through to senseless and secretive dealing in the private sector, with relational transaction taking a major share of the blame. Condemnation was especially swift from organisations which, under fire for failing to anticipate the crisis, felt they had been deceived by the same inhibited information flow which characterises exclusive, bilateral dealing. According to the deputy managing director of the International Monetary Fund,

> the East Asian crisis will lead to a re-examination of the benefits of the close relationships among government, business and the financial sector that have been practised in several of the East Asian countries. We are likely to conclude that the opacity of financial relations within the corporate sector and among the three sectors that has become so apparent during this crisis should not survive.
>
> (S. Fischer 1998)

The contention that information-enriching relational transaction had degenerated into information-impounding 'crony capitalism' seemed to derive further support from those nations which initially sidestepped the worst of the crisis. Where ethnic Chinese entrepreneurs had the upper hand, a more family-centred brand of 'Confucian values' seems to have prevented the economy from graduating (or in the revisionist assessment succumbing) to the long-range relational dealings that allowed giant networks of relational dealing to develop and then decay.

> The first thing we notice in the industrial structure of Chinese societies like Taiwan, Hong Kong and Singapore is the small scale of enterprises . . . In 1976 the average Taiwanese firm was only half the size of the average Korean firm. Small firm size is, if anything, even more the rule in Hong Kong, which has long been famous as an exemplar of a highly competitive market composed of atomistic firms.
>
> (Fukuyama 1995: 71)

Continued market mediation can now be argued to have helped these economies adapt their sectoral and geographical composition of trade so as to keep external deficits under control – and to avoid the excessive credit dependence and the opaque intercorporate links which tied the other tigers' tails into profitless and pointless prestige projects.

6.72 *The too-quiet life of closely held corporates*

Japan's financial market collapse was itself an indication of breakdown in investor–manager links, many shareholders and firms having engaged in a speculative land- and asset-price bubble to keep capital values growing when the real economy stalled. While this growth slowdown may have been a normal consequence of industrial 'maturity', once resources were fully employed and technological catch-up completed, it undermined a payback system based on capital gains rather than capital income. Shareholders no longer gaining from the markets' anticipation of future profits became impatient to take their profits now, and banks which had been comfortable securing loans against fast-growing asset values suddenly looked overstretched when output growth slowed and land prices collapsed. Higher bank reserve requirements, imposed to meet new international standards, may also have been a factor in reining in credit growth just when the system's liquidity constraints were already turning into more serious corporate solvency problems. The 'bicycle economy' was, as enthusiasts and critics had always feared, unable to stay upright when forced to slow to the rest of the world's more pedestrian pace.

The ramifications of this 'credit crunch' have been equally serious. The damage to financial companies' balance sheets is compelling some to sell out of their 'long-term' participations at short notice, with the concern for maximum price tipping the balance among buyers from patient investors to short-term asset strippers. The weakest firms are having to float new equity or sell strategic stakes to rival (including foreign) companies, with the prospect of radical restructuring and downsizing to repay the acquisition costs and raise the return on equity. Slower growth and unemployment are putting unprecedented strain on 'lifetime' employment arrangements. Recession-induced currency appreciation has renewing the pressure to transfer production abroad, to locations where existing relationships will be hard to replicate, and whose greater competitiveness could force further transparency – and market discipline – on relational dealing back home.

A 'big bang' financial-market deregulation is now under way in Tokyo, and similar removal of restrictions on foreign exchange dealing and foreign ownership is now being inflicted on several other East Asian nations, as a condition of multilateral support for the debt crisis that followed their 1997–8 devaluations. Japan's previous 'bonfires of controls' over product-market entry and operation have not caused radical changes in industry structure or foreign competition, and there is scepticism over how quickly financial deregulation will disturb old stable, interlocking shareholding patterns and traditional, personalised credit assessment methods.

> As in Japan's economy generally, decisions in Japanese financial institutions are based to a large extent on personal relationships with clients (and internally

with one's colleagues) rather than on careful quantitative analysis. These entrenched practices – at the core of what many Japanese believe is the essence of their brand of capitalism – are not easy to change.

(Lincoln 1998: 39)

Given the advantages for investment and growth identified with *keiretsu* co-ordination through main banks and long-term capital supply through captive insurance companies, those whose income and employment depend on the recovery of Japan's real economy – rather than the revival of prices and proceeds on its equity – are indeed likely to regret any substantial weakening of the old boardroom ties.

In the other fallen tigers, greater changes in corporate governance are likely to result from the significant equity-for-debt substitution now being forced on over-borrowed corporates, which has seen – among others – foreign auto companies buying heavily into South Korea's main conglomerates (*chaebol*), and foreign investors forcing their way into bond- and stock-markets long kept on a tight rein for fear of anonymous owners banging the communal corporate table.

Germany's financial-market shock arises from the need to inject more liquidity and transparency into its equity and bond-markets, both to meet European Union harmonisation requirements and to finance rapid reconstruction of the eastern Länder reabsorbed in 1991. Pressure to create a larger, more open secondary share market less dominated by institutional and interfirm shareholding has also been fostered by the larger number of firms seeking to issue equity (as a result of privatisation, rising capital needs or owner-managers' decisions to retire or sell out), and the perceived need to encourage private equity-linked saving for pensions and social insurance. A series of corporate governance lapses in the mid-1990s, including huge oil futures trading losses at Metallgesellschaft, the fraudulent property dealings of Jurgen Schneider and banks' alleged concealment from shareholders of growing losses at Klockner-Humboldt-Deutz, has also cast new doubt on banks' ability to oversee large and complex businesses, and renewed calls for a US-style separation of their credit and equity activities. The Czech Republic, tempted in a similar direction, has seen its growth slowed and industrial restructuring stalled by the tight grip on debt and equity finance obtained by large (state) banks through voucher privatisation, and the illiquidity of non-bank investment funds which scooped much of the rest of the equity.

In a study of linking ownership structures to financial results of quoted German companies including the 110 largest,

We determined that 58 of these corporations were being exposed to 'high potentials of influence' from banks . . . Those companies . . . had consistently lower performance ratios than companies not subject to this influence. Their return on equity, for example, was 1.8% compared with 7.6% . . . The German banking sector is stifling Germany's economic development.

(Perlitz and Seger 1995)

6.7.3   Tired relationships and technological rigidities

While it could be argued that causation runs the other way, banks taking a closer interest in companies that seem to be failing, large lenders' conservatism has been widely blamed for Germany's apparent inability to reach the frontier in new technologies such as semiconductors and biotechnology. Lacking a quick entry and exit route through which equity and venture capitalists can channel funds to start-up innovators in a 'market' fashion, finance and strategy-protection for such technologies has tended to be provided within established large companies, whose size and traditional-product grounding may not provide the best environment for new thinking to develop.

The success of relational transaction in promoting the refinement and diffusion of process technologies contrasts with its problems in embracing new product technology, which may require new players to be brought into the RT network or new information to be passed through the existing network.

> The more open a market, the more likely it is that firms will be able to compete satisfactorily on their own without the need for local partners; the general lowering of fences and the processes of harmonisation and mutual recognition make exporting and unilateral control (through in-house expansion or mergers and acquisitions) increasingly attractive options.
>
> (Kay 1992: 221)

Japanese authorities' efforts in the 1970s to promote collaboration among its mainframe computer makers were undermined by heightened competition, at home and abroad, when the market stopped growing. When firms came together, it was more through merger and acquisition than co-operation. 'Ironically, the objective that MITI had identified of bringing about a greater concentration amongst Japanese mainframe producers was achieved not through government pressure or negotiation, but through the market process' (Fransman 1990).

Japan's collaborative tendency, reinforced by intellectual-property laws which prioritise rapid diffusion over reward for innovation, is widely argued to have helped it acquire and improve on existing product and process ideas but held it back from originating radical new ideas. Once at the technological frontier, a more competitive economy, with improved capital availability to small firms and fewer relational barriers to these and other outsiders, may better incentivise and enable innovation. 'Japan, for example, could not provide the circumstances which led to the development of biotechnology in the USA. It does not have the same tradition of academic spin-offs, a supportive environment for small high-technology firms, and employee mobility to enhance technology transfer' (Dodgson 1993: 137). While the market may fail innovators who cannot sell or license their new idea at a fair price, it can make amends by helping them commercially exploit the new idea themselves. Competition and anti-trust policies, always in tension with public support for technology collaboration, may in some fast-changing circumstances outperform it as a solution to the problem of combining better allocation and faster growth.

6.8 The market case against relational transaction

While distressed for the citizens it reduced from riches back to rags, few economists outside the relational realm zone have decried the derailment of the system. From the market perspective, relational transaction is a retrogressive and repressive solution to the information and co-ordination problems arising from decentralised exchange. It retreats from publicly advertised pricing, offering the same deal to everyone who can afford it, into a myriad of bilateral private deals from which some are excluded and all come away with less than they could otherwise have got. This private sharing of information and transaction strategy leads to limited, localised co-operation, on terms inviting dependency and discouraging adaptation, in place of the globalised co-operation that emerges (in the repeated games of section 2.2) from the public dissemination of information and strategy.

Collective-action problems are 'resolved' through a series of compromise solutions to the co-ordination game, rather than changing the game so that a superior global solution can be found. In place of the market as universal measuring rod and melting pot, capable of involving growing numbers of agents to their own and others' advantage, relational dealing comes across as a formula for inconsistent treatment across time and space, destined to bar its practitioners from potentially beneficial dealings with outsiders, and lock them into suboptimal trades among themselves.

Relying on relations – even if it does not lapse literally into nepotism and cronyism – ties agents into parochial and traditional trade when they have more to gain from novel products and wider horizons.

> Markets are most attractive where individuals have broadly divergent conceptions of the good, where the relations among individuals tend to be one-dimensional, discrete, non-repeating, and where the benefits and burdens of cooperation are spread over persons, time and geography. They are least necessary where interaction is repeated, where relations are multidimensional and direct, and where there are shared conceptions of the good.
>
> (Coleman 1992: 5)

Making price a personal issue between buyers and sellers takes it out of the public domain, raising the spectre of countless personal bargains at non-equilibrium prices, the resultant misallocation being unstoppable because agents lack the information for arbitrage (and would lack the 'relational' authorisation to carry it out, even if they knew how). As well as sabotaging many socially beneficial trades, 'price discrimination' may be the thin end of a prejudicial wedge when transaction is conditioned on personal relations between buyer and seller. Discrimination on the grounds of class, gender, race, age, long hair, wrong school tie and countless other economically irrelevant and socially harmful criteria appear to be invited by a system in which the name on your invoice counts alongside (and helps to determine) the numbers.

All transactions are to some extent relational. But market transaction wherever possible reduces agents' contact to the exchange of price and basic product information, followed by the exchange of the product for the specified price. More complex transactions, whose enactment is stretched over space or time, or whose terms are contingent on new information emerging through time, are governed by agreed rules, or an incomplete contract which authorises one party to insert the missing terms. In contrast, RT eschews rules in favour of bilateral negotiation and bargaining, embedding economic exchange in wider social and cultural exchange. Conferences and corporate hospitality are forms of advertising under MT, but forms of information-sharing and character referencing under RT.

The anonymity of the market also promotes social justice, avoiding discrimination against buyers and sellers on such non-economic grounds as kinship, class, gender or nationality. In the most efficient markets, agents can even refrain from identifying themeslves as buyer or seller until the deal is struck, to ensure symmetry of treatment. As long as they can afford to (and do) make competitive offers and stick to the agreed terms, everyone can buy and sell at the standardised (market-clearing) price. Market transaction is 'money meritocracy', substituting (objective) economic for (subjective) social assessments of an individual's worth.

> If traders encounter complex or difficult relationships, characterised by mistrust or malfeasance, they can simply move on to the legion of other traders willing to do business on market terms . . . In classical and neoclassical economics, therefore, the fact that actors may have social relations with one another has been treated, if at all, as a frictional drag that impeded competitive markets.
>
> (Granovetter 1985: 484)

Under the conventional (western) historical picture, in which the close-knit, locally bounded and personality-referenced relations of 'community' slowly give way to the looser, globally extended and criterion-referenced relations of wider society, RT is an early, defensive and second-best option from which MT is the decisive 'modernising' forward step. Once the market is embraced, earlier retreats from it are revealed as regressive and repressive, the richness of community links preserved only by arbitrary restrictions on wider social life. 'Limitation on the number of potential social relations available to individuals leads to more communal social relations' (C. Fischer *et al.* 1997: 7). With market institutions and disciplines fully established, traders must strike the most mutually beneficial bargain, and stick to it, because otherwise the client will switch to a rival equally keen to capture the business. Separation of and competition between buyers and sellers forces producers to provide what consumers want in the most efficient way, and to switch as soon as possible to better products and better ways of making products. Because of the free flow of information, the system polices itself. Those who break the rules by misrepresenting their products, inflating their prices or reneging on their contracts are punished by loss of future business, even if the law does not intervene.

Relational transaction can be viewed in historical context as a step back from the competitive market to previous, more discriminating and less accountable forms of trade. Under feudalism, landless peasants were tied to a long-term arrangement with their landlords, who offered security of tenure in return for rent payments or crop-shares. Under early mercantilism, similar arrangements prevailed between merchants who supplied machinery and materials and paid for their output, and households which undertook to do the work. The message from these examples is that a step away from impersonal trading relations enriches human relationships in only a very limited sense. Unless the parties to a relational transaction are broadly similar in their resources, economic opportunities and social status, the advantages of the relationship may be highly unbalanced. And the counterpart to better information-sharing and trust within the relational transaction is a growing exclusion of those who are left outside it. The invisible handshake, often with greasy palms, replaces the invisible hand.

The exclusionary potential of relational transacting suggests that the market may be socially preferable – and more efficient in its economic use of talent – for being 'blind' to culture, class, gender, age and other personal features, and less reliant on people's ability to socialise and form networks. The use of internal markets or sub-groups to solve information or trust problems leads to discrimination against agents left outside those coalitions, and possibly to efficiency loss for the economy as a whole. Markets may also be able to capture the trust- and reputation-building properties of RT without entering into its strict one-to-one and networked relationships.

6.9 Relational transaction and regulation

With Anglo-America preparing to celebrate the millennium a year early, while the 'Pacific Century' struggles to stave off recession from day one, current geopolitics show a distinct tinge of MT triumphalism. RT, a hangover from insular history, was kept alive by trade barriers and domestic regulation. Exposed to the rigours of a free world market, its lack of flexibility and transparency – and improved MT technologies – quickly proved which system could trade its way to safety in turbulent times.

The argument that markets need to be supplemented, and in some cases replaced, by more relational forms of transaction rests on two beliefs. First, that problems of deficient information and co-ordination are widespread. Second, that closer buyer–seller relations to improve mutual knowledge are the most efficient way to overcome them. Traditional markets, where homogeneous, divisible, discrete, instantly made products were the norm, are regarded as having been progressively replaced by markets whose products exhibit diverse quality, high value and sunk transaction-related expenses.

Although various information and co-ordination problems have been cited as giving rise to relational transaction, it can be argued that most of these could be rectified within the market transaction framework, retaining the wider benefits of MT. Free entry will dispose of monopoly, free circulation of information will dispose of knowledge asymmetries, and credible tit-for-tat threats will dispose of co-ordination problems. Privileged professions will be expelled from a regulatory shelter which has degenerated from public interest to sectional income protection, unfairly redistributing from consumers to producers. 'If competitive markets are desired, the appropriate policy should be to reduce barriers to free trade' (Thurow 1980: 146).

If RT is indeed a second-best solution, and further development of MT a better alternative, then RT's persistence suggests that something in the trading system is failing to adjust. For those who argue that markets are the 'natural' framework for transaction, and a historic force for breaking down the inefficiencies and injustices of more personal dealing, RT can continue to exist only because of artificial constraints on the system. Either a distortion has been imposed (in the form of regulation, entry restriction, tariffs, taxes, etc.), or public authorities have failed in their duty to prevent monopoly and cartel arrangements from subverting the free market.

The significant relations reviewed in section 6.5 can, indeed, all be seen as products of regulation. Germany's institutionalised, long-term bank shareholding has been promoted by restrictions on competition and liquidity in the equity market. Japan's long-term links between life insurers and business by price-competition limits which leave them needing a negotiated way into group pension business (McKenzie 1992). German co-determination is enforced on large companies by legislation, and some use structural devices to avoid workforce representation/consultation obligations (their longevity suggesting that this is not fatal to long-run competitiveness). By helping relational transactors to restrict entry to the supply-side and 'artificially' raise prices, regulation may also mean a raw deal for those unable or unwilling to enter into RT. Workers not protected by a strong union in Germany or lifetime employment in Japan, and small suppliers on the margins of the *keiretsu* networks, may well become the shock absorbers for the regulated sectors' easy ride, bending to take the strain of an otherwise inflexible system. However, the trust and mutual dependence established by RT can also be a substitute for regulation. Japan's non-poaching ethic and Germany's vocational training system have often been sustained with minimal government involvement, as have industry-wide initiatives to cut costs or close capacity in response to national or global market downturn.

6.10   Some troubled relationships

From a market economy viewpoint, relational transaction appears to give in to monopoly and monopsony where they occur, and to create them in many other situations. Other instances of RT give rise to bilateral bargaining, barriers to entry, discriminatory and rigid pricing, or vertical foreclosure of markets to other suppliers, all of which look like undesirable monopoly features from a MT viewpoint.

6.10.1   Insider–outsider unemployment

Employers generally find information on skills, productivity and reliability much easier to assemble on workers they already employ than on workers who come to them from outside for employment. This gives the 'insider' workforce scope to bargain up its pay and conditions some way above prevailing labour-market norms, without the threat of being replaced by 'outsider' recruits willing to work harder or for less. Insiders are a known quantity, who are likely to have been screened for ability before recruitment, further selected during probationary periods, and subsequently developed on-the-job, and thus represent a selection from the upper end of the quality distribution for this type of labour. Outsiders are an unknown quantity, who must be assumed to be dispersed around the middle of the quality distribution. (If they are unemployed, rather than voluntary departers from education or other employment, they might even be assumed to come from the lower end of the quality distribution.)

Unless they have an effective and costless way of signalling their quality (such as formal qualifications or glowing references), outsider workers who can match the performance of insider workers may nevertheless find it impossible to enter the internal labour market on equal terms. To this localised injustice can be added macroeconomic damage from 'insider' power in the form of higher unemployment and lower productivity, to the extent that higher levels of unemployment are needed (than in a symmetrically informed labour market) to impose wage and work discipline on those already in the workforce (Lindbeck and Snower 1986).

6.10.2 *Disguised protectionism and vertical trade restraints*

Relational transactions between upstream suppliers and downstream clients can exclude new entrants to a market, so restricting competition and reducing social welfare according to the conventional analysis. Retailers which demand close, long-term relationships with manufacturers may bar the way to foreign entry (a feature often blamed for the low level of import penetration into Japan's consumer economy, even after formal tariff reduction). Conversely, manufacturers who develop close relational links with a retailer (perhaps extending to trade credit or subsidised display materials) may be able to debar it from stocking rival manufacturers' products. Suppliers with a large final-market share may even be able to stop the growth of rival retailers by refusing to supply them. Similarly, powerful suppliers of an intermediate product may be able to limit final product-market competition by developing preferential long-term relationships with selected downstream clients.

Where observed, such cases have generally been met by anti-monopoly action. Relational transacting can, in other words, come dangerously close to (or even form a disguise for) restrictive trade practices. Even where it does not, the effect is generally to limit competition in favour of co-operation, whose exclusionary effect is likely to reduce the degree of competition.

6.10.3 *Monopolies and cartels*

Although RT is one way to resolve the power imbalances or indeterminacies of a monopoly situation, it can be a case of capitulating to market imperfections which it might be better to eliminate. And by substituting negotiation for 'exit', RT may also create monopolies where they do not need to exist. In the literal marketplace, those who stand and talk fall under suspicion. They may be planning to rig their prices or differentiate their products to glean monopoly profits, conspire against certain buyers or sellers, or let collective product standards slip.

6.10.4   Price discrimination

Monopoly buyers and sellers may choose to set different prices for different clients, even without any artificial locking-in, if the submarkets are sufficiently separable to prevent those who buy at a lower price re-selling to those not so favoured. By finding out more about its buyers and establishing their willingness to pay, a monopolist can reclaim part or all of the 'consumer's surplus' which arises from charging the same price everywhere under MT. If it is a natural monopolist, with prices continuing to fall as output expands, there may be further gains to be made by bringing in marginal consumers by offering them a lower price than that charged to existing ones. Similarly, a monopsonist may, by acquiring information about its suppliers' costs, identify any cases where 'superprofits' are being made at its expense and bargain them down, thus reappropriating the surplus. Conversely, it can choose to help a marginal supplier (e.g. one which is investing in a better product, or promises to intensify competition among suppliers once it has brought costs down) by offering a more genrous price than its established rivals.

6.10.5   Insider trading

A sharp distinction is drawn in financial market trading between clever speculation, profiting from public information whose substance or significance is grasped in advance of other agents, and insider dealing, profiting from private information before it is made public. The first is legal, and regarded as having social as well as private benefits, speeding up the incorporation of relevant information into price and so keeping the market efficient. The second is illegal, and regarded as bringing private benefit at the expense of society, making private information a temporary monopoly, delaying its arrival in the market, and allowing its privileged holders to make 'unfair' gains by beating the market in what is generally a zero-sum game.

Relational transaction, to which the exchange of private information is central, has greater difficulty in making this distinction. Firms engaged in close relations with their employees, creditors or shareholders may find it quite normal to disclose financial information to them before they announce it in the market. It should be noted that the 'Austrian' approach to market transaction also has some problems defining insider trading, since the battle to be first to identify and use (and profit from) market-relevant information is supposed to be what drives the system towards ever greater efficiency; the sooner inside information is used, the quicker can it become public information by transmission through the price system. However, since unrestricted insider trading could deprive other decision-makers of useful information, leading to some of it never reaching the market, the market perspective assumes that certain levels of disclosure will be ensured by convention or legislation. The relational approach appears to capitulate to the private nature of market-sensitive information, widening it to those who can break into the con-fidential network but keeping out others, who may not even be able to infer it at second hand if subsequent price movements are not observable in an open market.

6.10.6 The fragmentation of trust

There is a tendency to identify MT as 'low-trust' and RT as 'high-trust', on the ground that broken pledges hardly matter for a deal we can walk away from but can cause significant damage if it is something we are tied to. This seems to con-fuse cause and effect, however, and both transaction styles should more properly be viewed as high-trust. Market transactors place little trust in any one counterparty, but a high level of trust in the system as a whole, since they must believe that 'shop-ping around' will eventually identify (and implement) the optimising trade. Relational transactors must often go to substantial lengths to guard against a breach of trust by their chosen counterparty, precisely because the closing-off of alternatives means high sunk costs if the relational deal falls through.

The further the expansion of the market extends the division of labour, the more must agents specialised in one activity be able to rely on the continued co-operation of those specialised in other activities. Complete market-supported specialisation, with everyone doing their own thing, brings with it the spectre that every transaction to obtain other things will be conducted between monopolists, with no certainty that they can efficiently reach the most mutually beneficial deal. But the more the market breaks down into sustained small-numbers and bilateral relations, the more reliant agents become on their network of relations with par-ticular other agents, to avoid being left out in the cold if no one wants to trade or be left holding the baby if someone suddenly suspends co-operation. 'The trust engendered by personal relations presents, by its very existence, enhanced oppor-tunity for malfeasance . . . [a] person's trust in you results in a position far more vulnerable than that of a stranger' (Granovetter 1985: 491).

Both transaction styles could equally be viewed as low-trust, in that both make contingency plans for the other party breaking their word. For MT it is the ability to switch loyalty at little cost, with the implication that gains from trickery will be strictly limited, even though the market's anonymity implies that the trick can be indefinitely repeated. For RT it is the ability to inflict reciprocal damage if the other party reneges on the deal: ensuring, if not that their opportunistic gains will be nul-lified, at least that their reputation for dishonesty will now prevent them sustaining any other relational transactions. In both cases there are also laws – governing general trading behaviour and the enforcement of specific contracts – which pro-vide an outside sanction against opportunism.

The trust problem reaches its height when market or relational dependence are at their maximum, and so ensures that most transactions add a dash of one even if characterised by the other. Market transactors try to build a relational element into their offer by investing in appropriate trust-signals (branding, warranties, codes of practice, payment spread over time, advertisements involving satisfied customers). The cost of these is usually recoverable through a price differential over those who cannot credibly offer such signals, though one powerful trust signal – long trading history – has the advantage of coming free and not being purchasable by newcomers. Relational transactors try to build a market element into their offer by making sure that the counterparty's sudden departure would make things worse on both sides, through loss of future trade if not through the backfiring of trickery on the current trade.

6.11   Will markets drive out relational transaction?

If the choice between MT and RT is a rational one, agents adopting whichever style best serves their private economic interest, then – assuming agents are not systematically wrong in their choice – their continued simultaneous existence suggests that both have advantages in certain situations. MT will prevail over RT in the long run only if the nature of transactions moves in its direction – e.g. through the proliferation of buyers and sellers (increasing opportunities for switching), reduction of sunk-cost elements in transaction-specific investment (reducing costs of switching), and improved information flow about reputations.

If the persistence of RT is dependent on reversible market distortions and regulation, however, then MT can be expected to displace it as those 'imperfections' are removed. This, broadly, has been the history of market-economy development up to now, and there are strong grounds for suggesting that a further wave of MT victory over RT may now be in prospect. Financial market regulation could end the cosy long-term relationships between institutional finance and large corporations, generating competition for retail business which demands a higher return on wholesale investments which, once legal barriers are removed, will mean shorter time horizons and more hostile takeovers to maximise shareholder value. Labour market deregulation could similarly disrupt old industrial relations patterns, with increased mobility and 'poaching' forcing employers to cut their investments in transferable training. Product market deregulation could disrupt long-run buyer–supplier relationships as the stronger party is forced to chase best current-period bargains.

Deregulation of trade and capital flows presents an overall threat to the system, confronting firms with low-cost competition which upsets traditional bargains with the workforce, and allowing investment to flow abroad. Although most 'relational' economies have long exported capital, arguably because of the high savings rate engendered by economic and transactional stability, the flow to higher-yielding foreign instruments of funds previously held captive by domestic regulation may endanger the traditional supply of cheap long-term finance. Greater pressure on firms to distribute profit may, as well as shortening their time-horizons, force governments to reduce the traditionally high corporate taxes that have financed generous infrastructure and public service provision. Labour-cost pressures may similarly force backtracking from the comparatively high payroll charges used to fund state welfare.

Any slowdown in growth or rise in unemployment presents a further general threat to current RT arrangements. A severe downturn in demand forces inevitably puts some 'lifetime' jobs, buyer–supplier links and cost-based pricing under threat, and challenges the basic understanding under which labour has moderated its wage demands in return for security of unemployment and stability of income. Once disrupted by external change, RT can suffer a rapid internal propagation of shocks, as both sides grow disillusioned with it, believing the other has failed in its obligations. Although RT may be efficient in adapting commercial relationships to slow and predictable changes in the environment, faster or less predictable change increases the ongoing cost of renegotiating, and raises the temptation to break the agreement for short-term gain. Uncertainty over present and future developments may encourage one relational partner to breach trust. An agent may judge that the one-off gain from tricking the counterparty outweighs the subsequent loss from ending the relationship (e.g. selling a controlling stake to a hostile bidder now nets a surer financial return than sticking with a company which may have to undertake significant restructuring), or that the opportunism will pass unnoticed (e.g. employers can hold down wages citing a competitive threat which unions do not know they have exaggerated).

Even without external shocks and their internal amplification, RT may be prone to periodic breakdown simply through the way it insulates suppliers from wider constraints. Insider employees may ignore outsiders' rising attainments or push their wage claims too high. Managers may incur unnecessary expenses knowing they can pass it off as 'strategic' action for future profit. Production staff may become too attentive to internally generated technology and marketing ideas, neglecting feedback from customers. By protecting transactors against new entrants, especially from abroad, RT may also blunt the system's competitive edge.

Incomplete and imperfect information appear endemic in the fully competitive market system, causing the disappearance of some markets, and not being solved by the appearance of others. There is a clear case for the effectiveness of relational transaction for transferring information which cannot be commodified or shorn of externalities, for bringing new products and processes to marketability, and for enforcing collectively optimal game solutions where private threats are not credible. But this does not immunise it against the competitive threats posed by deregulation, or public policy action against its monopolistic and exclusionary appearances. Relational transaction occupies a delicate and often shifting middle ground between pure market exchange and the more organised, internalised forms examined in Chapter 7.

6.12   Conclusion: the invisible hand shakes

Extended, information-sharing and trust-building links have been identified as one reaction to the information and co-ordination problems attending certain market transactions. Relational transaction is a reaction to interdependence, but tends also to promote it: agents use transaction-specific investment, bilateral monopoly and other locking-in devices to minimise the chance of being tricked by the party they have come to trust. From a market perspective, transaction relations are retrograde, sacrificing both the efficiency and justice aspects of trade through markets, and held in place only by distortive regulations. But most significant market transactions have been shown to require a relational element, and their prevalence can be a source of economic strength. Market and relational transaction coexist with tension but also some complementarity, and a competitive economy appears to retain important roles for both.

7 Mediated alternatives

Administered and informed transaction

We spend most of our lives taking orders. But those who take them from customers remain an entrepreneurial minority. Most employees remain in organisations which insulate them from direct demand and supply, turning external market forces into internalised managerial orders. Many self-employed or small business operators are almost equally in thrall to corporate command despite being formally outside it. For those excluded from the workforce by retirement or redundancy, the constraints simply come from a more distant and unapproachable (state) agency, or from financial limitations which seem to stem in part from the fragmentation of shared interests when not organised and led as a single group.

There are two main reasons for submitting to authority: because we have to, or because we want to. In economic terms, these shade into one. Accepting the commands of a hostile ruler brings us less pain than defying them, and accepting the commands of a sympathetic ruler brings more benefit than ignoring them. How the second, consensual type of order-taking grows out of the first, coercive type has been a major theme of political study since large-scale societies and politics became observable. Economists have staged much the same debate in confronting one of the most obvious, and problematic, questions arising from market theory. If independent pursuit of self-interest is the best way to collective harmony and prosperity, why do most of us continue to sacrifice much of our economic independence to groups whose collective interest imperfectly matches our own?

7.1 Haggling together to avoid haggling separately

Relational transaction (RT), as depicted in Chapter 6, departs from market transaction (MT) by introducing non-price information about the product being traded and the agent being traded with. But RT retains the individual focus of MT, and still views the path of the economy as beaten by the footing of many individual bills. In contrast, two further types of transactions can be identified in which the exchange of information, and the exchange of products that results, is conducted by clusters of individuals. Trades are entrusted to 'legal' persons, acting in the name of groups of natural persons, and previously autonomous individuals now subordinate their aims and actions to the group.

Relation-building and mutual learning allow agents to overcome many of the information problems that arise from pure market transaction. Conventions and institutions, developed actively as an extension of relationships or passively as an outcome of learning through market transaction, can overcome many of the co-ordination problems that arise when individual maximising actions have contradictory collective consequences. But there remains a large number of transactions which if done, not done or done differently could deliver better results to the economy as a whole, and so potentially to all the agents who comprise it.

Believing that these cannot be reliably attained through acting individually, or under the guidance of purely voluntary institutions, agents turn to external authority for help. Perhaps more accurately, certain agents acquire power over the economic and political activities of the majority, whose exertion is accepted because it can bind or guide the others to better outcomes than they might have expected if continuing to act alone. Two types of third-party intervention in transactions can be identified. Under *administered transaction* (AT), agents agree to let the outside authority rewrite their objectives, alter their action sets and circumscribe their choices, on condition that this results in new actions becoming available, their outcomes being more useful and more predictable, and perhaps their implementation being made easier or better protection being provided should evaluations still prove misguided.

Under *informed transaction* (IT), the organisation's role is to improve individual decisions by making available new information, new actions or new assurances over the likely outcome of those actions. IT tends to preserve the individual's original aims, but gives them better means to attain these. Under AT, the individual accepts altered aims and restricted action possibilities in expectation of greater rewards than if they went their own way in the marketplace. The organisation becomes the decision-maker, turning individual decisions into a co-ordinated means to a collective end. The organisation's task is to study the transactions that occur when agents work individually, identify its inconsistencies and aggregate failures, and modify individuals' choice processes (or at the extreme, impose a choice pattern on them) so as to ensure a better result for the group reflecting improvements for all those within it. Under IT, the outside authority does not alter agents' objective-setting, choice or implementation directly, but uses its overview of the collective transaction pattern to offer help at the search, evaluation and assessment stages. AT aims to achieve better results through instruction, IT through fuller information.

AT takes two significantly different forms, distinguished by the nature of their outside authority. Exercised by central political forces over the whole economy, AT as 'central planning' is generally regarded as an experiment which failed to improve on the market in terms of allocation, employment level or growth, mainly because it involved the planners in information problems every bit as bad as those produced by a pure market economy. But exercised by the management of larger companies, AT as 'corporate planning' is generally recognised as having significantly improved the effectiveness of transaction for creating new resources and moving them to more effective uses. By producing a large increase in action effectiveness for a small sacrifice in the freedom to act, corporate AT may indeed be the closest agents can come to the transaction results they would obtain if allowed to operate in a market with no information availability, information processing or co-ordination failures.

7.2   The imposed alternative: administered transaction

Wartime mobilisation has often shown the power of a common enemy to make competing agents work in harmony. Efforts to establish the same unity or compatibility of purpose in peacetime (and so incidentally reduce the risk of war returning) appeal to a more constructive external authority: experts obeyed because they know more than those they instruct, a boss obeyed because this will bring greater financial rewards than disobedience, or a referee obeyed because this upholds the rules within which personal ambitions can be better fulfilled. Adam Smith's proclamation that decentralised agents could interact to produce order and mutual benefit was an economist's dissent against prevailing political opinion, summarised more than a century before by Thomas Hobbes:

> Being distracted in opinion concerning the best use and application of their strength, they do not help, but hinder one another; and reduce their strength by mutual opposition . . . there be somewhat else required (besides Covenant) to make their Agreement constant and lasting; which is a Common Power, to keep them in awe, and to direct their actions to the Common benefit.
>
> (Hobbes 1651/1968: 224, 226)

Administered transaction dispenses with much of the freedom of choice which market transaction provides through the right of switching to alternative options, and relational transaction provides through the right to negotiate or bargain over contract terms. Under AT agents do what they are told, or select – sometimes mechanically – from a limited range of actions which prescribe what to do in different situations (Simon 1955). Action is largely separated from choice, and agents carry out explicit instructions (orders) or contingent instructions (programmes) on behalf of an external authority. This authority, the principal, has the power to change the agent's orders or programme unilaterally, and to punish them for any breaches of instruction.

At the level of the firm or organisation, AT is regarded as obvious and essential. To put its resources to their optimal use and ensure that all its people pursue the same profit-maximising objective, the firm must limit the decisions its employees have to take and set down guidelines as to how they are to take them. Few firms begin life without a business plan, and few sustain it without strategies and timetables for action. When translated into job descriptions and procedural codes, these take agents well away from the marketplace, usually selling labour services for non-specific lengths of time for variable rewards conditioned on future tasks that are only broadly delimited, and on terms designed for flexibility if the employer's internal or external conditions change. Employees accept such conditions because the resultant transactions are expected to be simpler and more rewarding for themselves, because of the efficiency they bring to the organisation. If widely enough observed, such firm-based AT can also benefit agents in their transactions outside work, by improving performance of the economy as a whole.

Practised at economy level, however, AT has come to be seen as a command structure too far. What works as a solution to information and co-ordination problems among competing firms founders when applied to whole industries, and fails when applied to whole nations. Because of the information and co-ordination problems discussed in Chapters 2 and 3, a completely decentralised market transaction system struggles to attain and maintain allocative efficiency and full employment in the absence of an all-knowing auctioneer. But a completely centralised planned-transaction system recreates these problems at the centre, overloading the planning agency, depriving agents of the means and incentive to use localised information in their own decisions, and failing to supply them with satisfactory substitute instructions (or the means or incentive to carry them out).

7.2.1 Motives for administered transaction

Submission to AT may be a deliberate choice, for any of the following reasons:

- The agent is following a strategy, and needs external discipline to follow the correct intermediate steps (making present sacrifices for future gain), rather than lapsing back into moment-by-moment maximisation.
- The agent is participating in the co-operative solution to a prisoners' dilemma-type collective action problem, and needs external discipline to resist the temptation for myopic maximisation. Submission to such discipline also persuades other agents that this agent will co-operate, so that they do too. This externally imposed avoidance of the 'war of all against all' comes closest to Hobbes's explanation.
- The agent believes that a principal is better informed about the information needed for a successful transaction, or better able to process this information, and so defers to the principal's instruction. The principal's advantage may lie in superior knowledge about the agent's private situation (e.g. a patient consulting a doctor), or about the state of knowledge, belief and intention among a group of agents (e.g. mountaineers deferring to their team leader).
- The agent wishes to enter a transaction for which he or she lacks the necessary resources, or credibility to keep the necessary promises, so the agent looks to external authority to supply these. As a reward for lending additional power in implementation, the principal claims the right to prescribe or circumscribe the transaction.
- The agent wishes to limit or avoid the penalties of a failed transaction, by passing on responsibility for its design. The principal in this case is a specialist risk-taker, whose reward is usually the excess profit from a successful transaction once the agent has been paid a results-invariant retainer.
- The agent wishes to avoid the information-processing costs of transaction, by passing them on to a specialist. The principal is assumed to have natural or

situational 'comparative advantages' in taking transaction decisions, or economies of scale through taking large numbers of this type.

- The agent wishes a transaction to continue, knows that it would normally have to be periodically renegotiated or else made highly contingent on future events to take account of uncertainty, and so gives the counterparty the right (within limits) to set or vary its terms. In this case the principal is usually also the person (legal or natural) with which the agent makes the transaction.

The final case, of letting the other transactor set and vary the terms, may reflect the motivations in the previous cases, but more usually a power imbalance. Typical instances are an employee who gives their employer the right to set their pay and conditions of work, and the small supplier who lets a large manufacturer specify product, price and delivery schedule. Continued employment and continued contracts are so important to the weaker agent that they are willing to accept wide imposed variations in contract terms, which the stronger agent can impose because their market power (of inflicting damage by switching) is greater. Although contract continuity is mainly prized by the agent because alternative income sources are uncertain, one further hope is that the arrangement will help to rebalance the power relations over time (by making the principal more dependent on the agent for its proven reliability, flexibility, etc., or causing them to share sensitive information), thus more willing to accommodate their needs and preferences. Administered transaction may then evolve into something close to relational transaction.

7.2.2   *The efficiency case for administered transaction*

Where applied effectively, AT can allow agents to carry out a transaction they know to be worthwhile, but cannot attain or sustain through either market transaction (MT) or relational transaction (RT). These advantages arise from the 'market failures', and their imperfect resolution by 'relational' alternatives, already examined. Those arising at organisational level apply mainly to allocative and productive efficiency. They form the main 'neoclassical' explanation for the existence of firms, a consideration to which Chapter 8 returns. Those arising at economy level apply mainly to full employment and growth, and formed the once equally respected 'neo-Marxian' argument for the treatment of the economy as one giant firm, through the device of central planning.

7.3   Localised administration: the transaction cost case

The model of optimal resource allocation through competitive general equilibrium assumes that agents pay for what they get and get what they pay for. No cost is incurred in the actual process of transaction. Costs of computing the correct product prices, and the investigation of product qualities, preferences and technologies that underlie this, are absorbed outside the market – by the Walrasian auctioneer, or as an external benefit of agents' private maximising efforts (the 'invisible hand'). Costs of enforcing transactions agreed at the equilibrium price are absorbed outside the market by costlessly developed institutions, or police and judicial systems assumed to be financed by a non-distorting tax. Costs of storing and transporting products, and processing money payments, relate to separate products which, because they are supplied and priced through the market, are assumed to be supplied in optimal quantities.

In practice, computing and enacting transactions is not a costless process, and the existence of transaction costs can obstruct, or scale down, transactions which would promote allocative efficiency. To the extent that it reduces transaction costs, AT can then move the system closer towards allocative efficiency. In some of the following main cases, the terms of the AT may be set out by an actual person in authority. In others, authority is exercised indirectly by a set of instructions. Instructions consist of orders, or of a limited set of actions with strict guidance as to which should be adopted in which set of conditions.

The firm is the principal unit of administered transaction and, at least since Coase (1937), economists have tended to ascribe its very existence to the 'internalisation' of transactions where this reduces their costs. This explanation is examined further in Chapter 8, where the transfer and processing of information and the exercise of power also emerge as possible reasons for the firm's existence. However, the main transaction types open to administration, listed below, show close similarities to those open to relational transaction as described in section 6.3. AT and RT are different ways to approach the operational problems of market transaction, and cast doubt on the firm separation of 'firm' from 'market' that a straight MT–AT dichotomy would suggest.

7.3.1 Repeated transactions

Rather than going through the full transaction process every time, agents who make the same trade regularly can agree to repeat it by invoking a pre-established routine. This avoids the costs of 'reinventing the wheel' by repeating a calculation process which is likely to lead to the same conclusion (e.g. restaurant regulars request 'the usual', shoppers frequent the same store, doctors write repeat prescriptions). It also allows the transactors to invest in arrangements which bring down future transaction costs (e.g. dedicated accounts and specialist handling facilities).

Repeated transactions are most likely to become administered where requisite quantity, quality and market price are relatively stable through time, or fluctuate round a known average. Those who design the transaction then have a high degree of certainty as to the conditions likely to prevail, the actions appropriate to them and the selection rule to set. Agents who submit to this design can fairly safely assume either that the cost saving from abbreviating the decision process will outweigh any losses in not getting the terms exactly right, or that anything lost by the fixed terms being unfavourable at some times will be offset by gains from their being favourable at other times. By demonstrating a willingness to make the occasional suboptimal trade for the sake of mutual transaction cost saving, agents may be able to signal mutual trust, and so reduce the cost of monitoring compliance with the terms.

Where fluctuation around the average widens, AT may give way to MT as agents realise that it would pay to re-run the calculations and change the transaction terms each time. Where fluctuations are small but the average is actually following a trend, the terms of the AT may be subject to periodic step-change revisions as agents realise that benefits from changing to a new fixed formula will outweigh the costs of working it out. But there are occasions when rapidly changing conditions encourage the transition from MT to AT, because of an overriding objective for whose pursuit agents are willing to submit to highly variable demands with few tolerance limits. At national level, war and natural disaster are the most common instances. For the firm, bankruptcy or downsizing pressure are the equivalent survival threats, prompting workers to take wage cuts and managers to take company doctors' orders in ways which might threaten the mutual acceptance of AT under less extreme conditions.

7.3.2 *Spatially or temporally connected transactions*

Where the value of a transaction is time-sensitive, it may have disappeared by the time its terms are calculated or its market exchange carried out. AT is introduced as a way of speeding up the transaction so that some value is extracted, even if it is not the full value that instantaneous market transaction would have achieved. Standard examples are of molten metal, which cools and solidifies while the downstream die-caster is haggling over purchase terms, and computer-systems failure, for which in-house generalist engineers are called in even though an outside specialist might have done a better job if their arrival and terms could have been instantly arranged.

Labour-based services encounter similar externality, since the producer must supply his or her time as well as the service performed during that time. Suppliers of capital-based services can usually separate the two, and so are more likely to trade through the market. For actors, teachers, shop assistants and production workers, for whom such separation is impossible (unless they commodify the service e.g. by recording a past appearance), the more rewarding alternative is often to enter an employment relationship in the hope of being paid for presence as well as performance. (Those in shorter supply, such as consultants, senior lawyers and software engineers, may find their market power sufficient to claim compensation for the inseparability through their fees, while remaining self-employed.)

Integration is not always direct. The first response to spatially or temporally connected transactions is often to locate close together while continuing to trade through the market. However, this tends to set up the repeated transactions and unilateral–monopoly relations which make for relational transaction, and may then make internalisation worthwhile. Similarly, specialist labour may start under an outsourcing (market) contract, which turns to an internal contract once shared information (about the firm's needs and the worker's skills) has locked them into a repeated transaction. This stepwise process, and the possibility of relational transaction as an intemediate stage, is a reminder that 'market' and 'hierarchy' may not be the stark alternatives sometimes suggested.

7.3.3 Transaction-specific investments

While sunk-cost investments to enable or improve a transaction can be protected by relational transaction, this still leaves the investing agent vulnerable to unrecoverable loss if the other party suddenly leaves. Submission to AT can be a means of strengthening the relationship to the point where such defection is impossible, or carries severe penalties, thus creating the security with which to make the investment. The external authority administering the transaction may also be induced to contribute to the investment, since a reward from a share of its returns strengthens their incentive to discipline the transactors.

7.3.4 Joint-product and team-product transactions

Where two or more saleable outputs arise from the same process, it may be impossible accurately to assign marginal costs between them in order to compute optimum prices; or the process of doing so may be judged more expensive than any losses from assigning costs in a more arbitrary fashion. Similarly, when two or more people are responsible for a single output, it may be impossible or too costly to apportion effforts and rewards among them. Agents may then submit to AT as a neutral way to solve disagreements over price and wage setting, either by using simplified rules, or by handing authority to an administrator who tries to judge the maximising transaction terms in return for pocketing any residual excess profits (Alchian and Demsetz 1972).

7.3.5 Resolving bilateral monopoly disputes

Where small numbers of agents confront each other, either as buyers and sellers or as competing sellers, there is generally a range of transaction terms over which profits are maximised for one of the agents, or for all agents jointly. Bargaining can lead to a variety of outcomes, depending on relative power and strategies adopted, and the breakdown of bargaining can lead to inferior results all round. An external authority may then be brought in to impose a solution and, where this is a joint-maximising solution involving a cartel of producers or consumers, to defend it against attemps to profit by breaking the rules.

7.3.6 Collective-action co-ordination

Not knowing what others intend to do in the current period, or what collective results their actions will have in future periods, may complicate competing agents' transaction planning to the point where the costs of computing a maximising decision may well exceed its benefits over a more arbitrary decision. To get closer to optimality, transaction design may then be handed over to an external authority who is regarded either as better able to process the information available to the agent, or in possession of superior information because they have a better insight into the intentions of other agents. This second situation is especially likely where all the most heavily interdependent agents submit to the same external authority, who can then lay down an administratively coherent set of transactions.

Even where full information is available, agents may discover they face a co-ordination problem, under which they will maximise their rewards from taking the collectively optimal action only if everyone else does so. AT may then be established to enforce the arrangement and prevent it breaking down. Either each agent submits to a separate authority who will force them to follow the co-operative strategy; or, perhaps more economically, each submits to the same external authority, whose incentive for enforcing the optimal solution may again be a share of the additional profits that result. Concerned to achieve maximum performance for the wages they provide, a firm's owners can discipline or dismiss employees who try to earn the average pay for less than average effort. Employment within the firm changes agents' payoffs in a prisoners' dilemma-type situation so that they are no longer tempted to be opportunistic, and so transaction-specific investments can be made more safely. It should be noted, however, that whereas such monitoring and sanctions can work both ways under relational transaction, AT tends to make them one way only. The firm in this case could use its knowledge advantage in relation to its own financial accounts, or external market conditions (from which agents have been removed), to blame wage reductions or added work demands on a challenge to profits or competitiveness that does not actually exist.

7.3.7 *Transactions involving sensitive information*

Market transactions can sometimes be blocked because one or other party cannot trade their product without also giving away commercially sensitive information – either contained in the product offered or demand expressed, or necessarily supplied to the other party before they can agree the transaction terms. The information is effectively an unpriced joint product, supplied as external benefit when the original product is traded. By conducting the trade through an external authority, it may be possible to separate the 'public' product from the 'private' information. But in return for performing the service – and as an incentive not to seek profit by divulging the information – the authority must be given the right to set the transaction terms.

7.3.8 *Risk sharing and risk transfer*

He who pays the piper calls the tune, but also has to answer for any noise-pollution complaints. Where a maximising transaction design requires guesswork about future states of the world which leave open the possibility of grave miscalculation, an agent may prefer to give responsibility for it to someone else. In effect, costs are attached to the possibility of miscalculating which detract from the benefits anticipated from correctly calculating, and the agent is willing to reduce the potential benefit in order to escape these costs. An external authority now sets the transaction terms to ensure a fixed reward for the agent and a contingent reward for themselves, taking the bonus for overperformance and any punishment for underperformance.

The firm that internalises its factor supplies, and makes specific (training or machinery) investments in them, adds to its risk of high redundancy costs if it has to sack employees in a downturn and of high sunk costs if its fixed capital becomes obsolete or inoperative. Service providers have effectively locked-in the firm to long contracts so as to avoid the risks of selling their services on an open market. In return, the firm designs these contracts to minimise the risk of having to write-off its specific investments. Employees are given 'fuzzy' job specifications allowing them to be administratively reassigned between tasks and locations in accordance with demand. Reassignment of capital is assisted by the introduction of repro-grammable equipment, or selection of product lines among which equipment is interchangeable (for scope economies). Where more specific capital stick is needed, firms may still step outside the AT framework and enter relational transaction with a specialist provider, who can keep it more fully employed and so pass on scale economies in its charging.

7.4   Centralised administration: the grand plan grounded

Externally devised and enforced solutions to interdependence are effective only if they cover most or all the agents whose individual actions significantly affect the collective outcome. Increasing group size makes for more effective solutions, and solutions for a wider range of problems, provided the appropriate set of adminis-tered transactions can still be devised and enforced. While obstacles to worthwhile trade arising from transaction costs can mostly be eliminated by bringing together just those immediately involved in the transaction, obstacles arising from incom-plete information or lack of co-ordination usually require much wider involvement.

In particular, firms need assurance about aggregate-demand effects across the whole economy if they are to invest enough to ensure full employment, and about the future composition of demand and factor prices if they are to maintain the rate and composition of capital formation that maximises growth. Workers need assur-ance that additional profits will be spent on productivity- and employment-increasing investment if they are to moderate their wage claims, and that additional revenue will go towards the hard- and soft-infrastructure 'social wage' if they are to accept higher income taxes. It was to macroeconomic challenges of this sort, ironing out demand cycles and speeding up supply-side development, that the grander vision of centrally administered transaction was originally addressed.

7.4.1   A rational-control vision

Though its first serious application came with the first Russian five-year plan of 1928–33, central planning as a concept arose from nineteenth-century 'enlightenment' beliefs in the use of scientific knowledge for rational control of social development. Biology had helped control disease through systematic immunisation and public health improvement; physics and chemistry had tamed water and fire for industrial use, and were beginning to do the same with electricity; civil engineering had reshaped the landscape. Social theorists were keen to apply the same scientific principles to political and economic organisation, establishing control over forces previously regarded as naturally immutable or theologically ordained.

Biology provided a popular early template, with 'functionalism' drawing a direct parallel between the division of labour in industrial society and the division of organic function in multicelled organisms. Evolutionary theory provided a second powerful analogy, 'Social Darwinism' identifying a natural way in which free market competition would improve the performance of surviving agents, though one that could be accelerated and improved on by eugenics. These approaches were still inadequate, however, for deriving policy proposals, accounting for what existed but giving little indication of how it would develop. They were also too fatalistic for the growing group of social researchers who regarded present economic and social conditions as materially and spiritually denuded, and believed a political redirection of the system could bring greatly improved results.

Revolutionary socialism made the boldest proposals for central direction of the economic system, summarised in the claim that communism 'overturns the basis of all earlier relations of production and intercourse, and for the first time consciously treats all natural premises as the creatures of men, strips them of their natural character and subjugates them to the power of individuals united' (Marx and Engels 1845/1947: 70). The aim of this subjugation was to overcome the inefficiencies and artificial scarcities of capitalism and so eventually raise productivity to such an extent that the detailed division of labour could be abolished and the state 'wither away' along with the class divisions it was assumed to uphold. But the working class that was to bring about this transformation 'knows that replacing the economic conditions of class labour by the conditions of free and co-operative labour can only be the progressive work of time, that this economic transformation requires not only a change in distribution, but also a new organisation of production' (Marx 1871/1983: 532). So the state, under new management, would initially expand its role to supervise that new organisation.

Marx's followers outside western Europe identified an earlier role for the state, speeding up the processes of accumulation and technology acquisition until it was feasible to refocus from growth onto redistribution, replacing income with need as the basis for allocation. Central planners would be able to fix the rate of capital accumulation at whatever was needed for full employment, given the current productivity of capital and labour. They would raise those productivities by expanding education and systematically applying science to commercial ends, without the uncertainties, financial restraints and monopoly profits on current technologies which held back innovation under capitalist arrangements. Financing for the higher rate of investment would come from recapturing the wealth and luxury-consumption expenditure into which capitalists had diverted industrial workers' surplus, and from transferring agricultural surplus (and labour) to industry far more rapidly than market signals would have done. The state would assist the import of 'best-practice' technology, and upgrade human capital and infrastructure to support the new industrial demands. Dynamic efficiency was stressed, and possible incompatibility with static efficiency was readily accepted, with early Soviet growth theorists (notably Feldman) adding to the range of models showing that 'unbalanced' concentration of investment on heavy industry could contribute more in faster growth and higher resource utilisation than it sacrificed in temporarily inefficient allocation of the resources. This argument allowed early evidence of basic supply–demand mismatches (even the 1930s Soviet and 1960s Chinese famines) to be excused by sympathisers as a necessary sacrifice for future gain.

Central planning also appealed to many who flatly rejected Marx's vision of communism but, for this reason, sought a way to rescue capitalism from its more extreme tendencies towards boom–bust cycles, unemployment, alienation and inequality. Intellectual support for state direction of the economy probably reached its height during and immediately after the Second World War. The Soviet Union, its most complete practitioner, appeared (with a little help from its propagandists) to have transformed an agrarian into a war-winning industrial economy within 30 years, after sidestepping the Great Depression that had afflicted most capitalist economies. The United States and other 'market' economies had adopted extensive forms of central direction for their successful war efforts, which many now hoped to turn with equal effect to the domestic war against poverty and ill-health (their mass unemployment having been largely solved by wartime mobilisation).

The contribution of natural science to winning the war, through such breakthroughs as code-breaking, radar and nuclear weapons, had reinforced confidence in the power of scientific investigation to solve social problems. While few accepted Marxist claims to have produced a 'scientific' socialism, natural scientists were often as drawn to this view as social scientists, especially those who had been part of the state-sponsored efforts that led to radar, code-breaking, the nuclear bomb and other war-winning technologies.

> In general the whole of evolution is concerned with the gradual increase in conscious rational control over ever more complex fields of behaviour. It seems inevitable that at some time the economic forces in society will have to be organised by human thought instead of by the automatic 'laws' of supply and demand.
>
> (Waddington 1948: 113)

Markets were chaotic and wasteful because they left agents battling to outperform and second-guess one another when they could all have done better by co-operation and co-ordination. The prisoners' dilemma-type zero sum game had replaced Adam Smith's equation of private self-interest with public gain, and it was the task of those who had noticed the conflict to give agents a co-ordinated means of escaping it.

7.4.2 *Inherent collapse explanations*

Central planning's appeal was not sustained, and by the end of the century its application had been almost universally abandoned. China hit the 'capitalist road' in 1978, eastern Europe's 'democratic centralism' was swept aside by the revolutions of 1989, Russia had taken its first dose of market 'shock therapy' by 1992, and even those governments still professing loyalty to Marx, Lenin or Mao have allowed large segments of agriculture, trade and natural resource exploitation to move outside the plan. While central planning experiments can claim to have accelerated growth, equalised income distribution and eliminated unemployment in their early stages, their promises to overtake the capitalist economies never materialised. 'Communist' economies were matched by their market-based rivals in the unprecedented northern hemisphere growth surge of the 1950s and 1960s, and joined them in the output- and productivity-growth slowdown after 1973. Thereafter growth was sustained only by heavy foreign borrowing, intensification of employment with corresponding real wage restrictions, and the limited reintroduction of market forces (already tolerated in the form of large 'grey' economies) to overcome rigidities in the plan.

Planners' problems were little different from those of the neoclassical competitive general equilibrium (CGE) and growth models already reviewed. Some CGE theorists, such as Walras and Lange, had readily admitted that what they were describing could just as well be the aim of a socialist system as the outcome of a market system. A centralised transaction plan, designed on the basis of the best technology and a 'fair' initial distribution, could in principle achieve Pareto optimality and overcome the various problems arising from increasing returns, externalities, public goods, monopolies and investment-decision uncertainties. But CGE stopped at an existence proof showing the equilibrium price–quantity matrix as a piece of abstract algebra. Turning this into actual arithmetic gave the central planning agency at least as great an information-processing problem as the Walrasian auctioneer.

To map out a consistent set of transactions that will fully employ resources, optimise their current use and maximise their rate of expansion, central planners must gather together all the relevant supply-capability and demand-intention information held by competing agents. Even if those agents are honest enough to reveal their true knowledge and intentions without coercion, and to follow their instructions faithfully once received, the planners are still left with an intractable calculation problem. A plan set out in advance, even for four or five years, was overwhelmingly large and error-prone, being prey to exogenous disturbances (such as wars, science-based innovations and slowdowns in other economies) even if it correctly forecast endogenous disturbances. A plan continuously adjusted to incorporate new information would forever lag the actual situation, and reproduce the informational uncertainties, time-inconsistencies and destruction of useful strategy it was seeking to escape.

Yet administrative planning, like the market, had to be all-embracing if it were to be effective and sustainable. It was not enough to co-ordinate the investment plans of the larger corporations, if major players in related sectors, smaller players in their own sector, or final demand (consumers) were not given similar guidance. Market forces left to play freely at either end of the production process, or in any of the tributaries feeding into it, would eventually frustrate the plan and 're-infect' the activities that were supposed to have been brought within it. Unless fully empowered to assert the priority of full employment, distribuional fairness and growth, planners would see their grand design dragged down in the pursuit of short-run efficiency.

Much as the 'Austrian' critics had predicted, any inefficiencies from entrusting the economy to markets were overshadowed by the problems of taking them away. Shortages and surpluses became routine as the plan failed to anticipate the pattern of final demand, and as intermediate producers worked to meet quantitative targets without regard to the quality of what they produced, or its consistency with downstream needs. Official (accounting) prices failed to adjust to acknowledge the mismatch, which thus worsened as underpriced supplies were diverted onto illegal private markets. With no direct measurement of capital productivity through the interest on loans or the profits on investment, capital continued to flow into areas of overcapacity. Labour was similarly retained in core industries where political ease of organisation was no longer matched by economic justification, so that even where its physical productivity kept rising, monetary productivity was dragged down by declining demand for the product.

These resource allocation problems might have been worse had planning not switched from accelerator to brake over structural and technical change. Strikingly successful at rapidly adopting the leading technologies at the time of its inception (coal, steel, mass-production machine tools, railways, electricity), central planning was consistently late in recognising the importance of subsequent productivity-raising technologies (microelectronics, telecommunications, microcomputers, auto transport, aerospace, robotics, household electricals, financial and business services, biotechnology, new crop varieties), continuing to concentrate its investment in areas of known strength but (by the early 1970s) global overcapacity resulting from rapid growth in low-wage competition. Planned economies similarly lagged in the adoption of the new organisational forms called into play by new technology (smaller firms, larger retail units, decentralisation, subcontracting) and the development of the new sectors which, where allowed to develop, absorbed a growing proportion of rising income. Ironically, economies dedicated to fairer treatment of industrial labour were led to impose greater discipline, pay restriction and spending curbs (especially those needing foreign exchange) on its workforce to avoid import dependence that would threaten the plan's extension to trade. Workers' efforts to meet their needs by transacting outside the system were similarly curtailed.

Explanations of the command economy's collapse 'from within' ascribe the inability to allocate and slowness to innovate to the removal of market incentives – from individuals by the lack of reward (either from higher pay within the firm to profit from leaving it to set up in business), and from firms by the insulation from demand and customer pressures that generally stimulate product and process change. Origination of new techniques was further slowed by the strong concentration of R&D effort on (usually secret) military applications, the lack of incentives for (or existence of) rival firms to be first to innovate, and political direction of basic scientific research. Adoption of techniques developed elsewhere was impeded by lack of interchange among technologists, and lack of foreign exchange with which to import new technology.

Central planning's effectiveness at organising for a single national aim (supplying the war effort) translated badly to the much more varied production objectives of a peacetime economy, especially as rising income stimulated demand for consumer products and as the flexibility of small production units began to grow in importance relative to the scale economies of the large. Soviet communism's major success had lain in mobilising agricultural savings for investment in a narrow range of complementary heavy industries, whose expansion could be planned through simple quantitative targets and supported by the (often forcible) movement of rural labour and capital into industry. Reallocation, reorganisation and technical change, the main contributors to growth once labour surplus has been absorbed according to most econometric estimates, were less easily handled, resulting in stagnation of older industries and the non-appearance of new ones.

> Between 1948 and 1964, the effectiveness of productive investments in all branches of industry except electroenergy and metalworking fell two to three times . . . the list of goods in short supply was very large and continuing to grow, factories flooded the market with huge quantities of unsaleable goods . . . real earnings were rising very slowly and among some sections of the population were even on the decline.
>
> (Medvedev 1977: 242–3)

In most centrally planned economies unwanted finished products piled up because consumers did not want them, while those that they did were in perpetually short supply (especially non-staple food products, whose growers often found official prices too low to make them worth bringing to market, and preferred to subsist on them instead). Firms, in turn, were unable to signal their need for new raw materials and intermediate products, or to adopt new technologies without planners' consent. Critics argue that collapse would have come much earlier if authorities had not acquiesced in a large and innovative informal (grey) economy. Since the fall of eastern Europe's communism, the most rapid turnaround (Poland's) has been built on the surge of private business activity based on these previously repressed private activities (which in agriculture had been allowed back into the official economy at a very early stage). The slowest (Bulgaria, Russia) have been those where state companies were 'privatised' but allowed to continue operating with the monopoly powers and political relations acquired under the previous AT system.

7.4.3 Contingent collapse explanations

Although communism's demise had long been foretold on the basis of internal information, incentive and democratic deficiencies (e.g. by Hayek 1944 and Popper

1962), there remains an argument that bad implementation and external threats scuppered a design which might have worked in kinder circumstances. With more participation and decentralisation, plans might have been able to adapt adequately to changing demand patterns. Without foreign technology boycotts, and with fewer scientists down saltmines, new technologies might have been adopted earlier – including the information technologies which sparked a late revival of hope for the attainment of efficient central co-ordination. With less military pressure from a hostile (capitalist) outside world, more resources might have flowed into civilian rather than military production and R&D, inward investment might have relieved the need to squeeze domestic incomes so hard for so long, and foreign trade might have established a more appropriate pattern of specialisation. Circulating accurate information, instead of suppressing what was out of line with the plan and incentivising enterprises to invent results in line with it, would have revealed the problems earlier and improved the chances of resolving them. In this more sympathetic view, central planning appears to have failed because it was never properly tried, or applied too early to economies which – as Marx had always acknowledged – needed to advance (and suffer) longer under capitalism before socialist transformation could succeed.

The argument mirrors that used to explain the failure of free market/minimum state experiments, which where declared have always retreated onto the safer ground of mixed economy, selective trade protection and some state welfare. It has the same counterfactual limitations. The central plan's optimal-allocation information needs are probably impossible to fulfil, since some consumer preferences are not communicable in advance of the trading situation arising, and producer preferences are likely to change when the results of their aggregation are known (even if they were reliably reported in the first place). Central collection, processing and dissemination of transaction-relevant information thus seems inherently cumbersome, even with honest and efficient communication channels and the best computing power that industrial spies can reverse-engineer. Workers in receipt of the perfect social-welfare-maximising set of instructions may still hesitate to follow them, if the detachment of personal rewards from personal efforts leaves them too dependent on the comparable efforts of ohers. Stekhanov, Soviet industry's one-man productivity miracle, was more persecuted than impersonated by fellow workers when the publicity drive took off.

Since its most sustained large-scale application was to two economies (Russia and China) which were initially underdeveloped enough for the plan's employment and growth gains to outweigh its allocative disadvantages, and subsequently became large enough to be largely autarkic without meeting scale-economy or natural resource constraints, it could be argued that the choice of testing-grounds prolonged rather than curtailed the system's useful life. Attempts to implement central planning in economies with a more developed industrial (and service) base have in part been frustrated because an enfranchised working population votes heavily against it. 'It is clear that economic planning should go no further than major macroeconomic variables while markets should be allowed to determine detailed output structure and relative prices by the actions of competing firms unencumbered by central controls' (Nuti 1986: 83–4).

7.5   The informed alternative: indicative planning

Dictators perish; their advisers often survive. Even if central authority cannot generally make better decisions than the individuals it surveys, there may well be trends and aggregate oucomes not visible from the ground whose announcement would lead to better decisions being taken there. Even as the planner as commander was beginning to take its first casualties in the 1950s and 1960s, a new vision of the planner as adviser was gaining strength. By sharing information through a neutral central source, it seemed possible for dispersed agents to combine the collective rational control elements of administered transaction with the efficiency and openness of market transaction, and the humanity of relational transaction.

Informed transaction (IT) is based on decisions whose objective-setting, choice and implementation remain with the individual, but whose processes of search, evaluation and assessment are guided from above. External authority is called in to improve the economic background against which transactions are designed, the information flow with which they are designed, the instruments available to carry them out and the statistical documentation of their results. Although their theory (and practice) were closely matched in several non-English-speaking countries, four contributors have won special credit for developing the vision. From Keynes (1936) came the view that governments could stabilise the macroeconomy through aggregate demand management without needing to nationalise major industries or intervene in individual markets. From Beveridge (1942) came the view that, once near-full employment was established, income inequality and associated social deprivation could be tackled through tax-financed social insurance and welfare arrangements, again without undermining private enterprise and thrift as the basis for economic growth. From Crosland (1956) came the view that steady growth, promoted by demand management, could defuse the potentially disruptive demands for redistribution, protectionism and social exclusion by allowing a generalised rise in living standards, with productivity rising fast enough to offset the upward pressure on wages caused by sustained full employment. From Galbraith (1958) came the assurance that, with suitable guidance from the educational and scientific 'technostructure', the private-ownership economy could avoid undermining itself by letting private production outgrow the necessary physical and social infrastructure, overdosing its environment with consumption-related social costs, or inventing enemies that made it overspend on arms.

The state as a democratic and accountable 'facilitator' of better-informed transaction decisions took several guises in the economies that adopted it. Sometimes its intervention was limited to the stabilisation and improvement of investment expectations, encouraging firms to expand on the understanding that real interest rates would stay low, the exchange rate remain competitive and any downturns be offset by cyclical budget deficits. Sometimes the focus was on wage expectations, persuading employees – despite the heightened bargaining power that came with full employment – to tie their demands to moderate their claims on the promise of rewards through lower inflation or higher social spending if all complied. The most detailed application of IT involved enriching decision information on both the demand and supply sides within particular sectors, partly by feeding firms new technological and economic-forecast information from outside, and partly by pooling information on their own intentions to ensure consistent expectation formation.

Indicative planning, variants of which appeared across western Europe and North America from 1950 to 1970, contained some or all of the following elements:

- The submission of natural monopolies, and other strategically important industries, to public ownership or detailed state regulation.
- The use of monetary and fiscal 'demand management' to keep the economy close to full employment, ironing out the previous boom–bust cycles.
- 'Tripartite' consultation among labour organisation, employer association and government representatives to agree sectoral priorities and co-ordinate investment programmes, which formed either a consensus plan setting out (intendedly) harmonious investment and growth targets, or a more prescriptive plan steering resources towards priority projects and sectors.
- The use of labour organisations to impose wage control, to prevent labour-demand pressures at full employment resulting in 'cost push' inflation. Moderation of private wage demands was to be rewarded by the assurance of full employment, and a rising 'social wage' in the form of state-provided social infrastructure, welfare and pensions.
- Promotion of growth through the creation of a stable investment climate, subsidies to 'sunrise' investment, subsidies to R&D for the innovation and rapid diffusion of new technologies (including the formation of clusters for external economies of scale), and promotion of industrial restructuring and merger to achieve internal economies of scale.
- Codetermination, worker-directors, and other forms of workplace democracy, designed to turn an increasingly skilled and educated workforce away from alienation and towards an active input into plant and process management, facilitating productivity growth and adaptation to new technologies.

7.5.1 The mixed-economy vision

Whereas central planning involves top-down imposition of transactions, based on a holistic view of where society should be heading, indicative planning aims to work by persuasion. It assumes that giving agents an informed view of where their present plans will lead, and of what else they could aim for, will lead to a pattern of transactions that is better for the industry and society. Initially, when unemployed labour and spare capacity were widespread, the approach was almost entirely demand-sided, trying to boost consumption and investment to bring these back into productive use. Later, as full employment approached, attention turned to the supply side, and the best ways to raise labour and capital productivity to maintain growth when its 'extensive' phase was over. Often in conjunction with tripartite arrangements for government-business-labour consultation, and usually supported by enhanced efforts to gather sectoral data and forecast the macroeconomy, a central authority seeks to discover private agents' intentions, and help better fulfil them by ensuring more consistency between them.

Individuals' attempts to solve their information and co-ordination problems through relational transaction have been seen to have side-effects, losing other more desirable features of market transaction: the relations become monopolistic, discriminatory and impervious to changes in the external environment. Indicative planning seeks to achieve the same filling-in of information gaps and imposition of co-ordination centrally. Equipped with the information and assurances about others' intentions, and forecasts of future 'exogenous' variables, provided by the plan, agents can more safely go ahead with market transactions – untainted by relational aspects, but with its uncertainties and collective irrationalities removed.

Whereas central planning was a testament to early-century faith in the application of natural science to social problems, indicative planning marked the high point of confidence in 'social science' as a distinct project: particularly over measurement, forecasting, linear programming, project appraisal and the ability to notice and dispose of prisoners' dilemmas. West European and North American economies' wartime success in reviving and mobilising under strict guidance from the centre reinforced the belief that centralised information-sharing was the most effective way to overcome the inefficiencies of uncoordinated markets. The fact that this had been achieved by public purchasing and target-setting without wholesale nationalisation suggested that the necessary co-ordination could be achieved by spreading information rather than imposition, so avoiding the bureaucratic overstretch and democratic deficit that had hampered central planning.

Confidence in the setting and implementation of targets was enhanced by the belief that politicians and administrators would be competent and committed enough to achieve them. Post-war governments were extensively composed of distinguished fighters and administrators, supported by a newly meritocratically selected public service. Increasingly detailed social and economic statistics, new methods of analysis (linear programming, econometrics, input-output analysis, optimal control theory) and the arrival of computers with which to apply them promised an unprecedented wealth of information with which to do so. While social science might not be like natural science, it had already revealed some striking statistical regularities – the 'Phillips Curve' trade-off between unemployment and the rate of wage growth, the lagged covariance of monetary growth and inflation – with which the economy could be guided to a better future, if enough were known about its present state.

By matching demand to supply in the aggregate, government was now seen as improving the conditions in which markets could successfully guide allocation and expansion at the microeconomic level. The essence of planning was not to supplant markets but to make them work better, by improving the information flow to agents making key investment and innovation decisions, and co-ordinating the actions that resulted.

Confirming the conviction that better understanding the present would allow agents to take control of their future, one leading group of protagonists, the 'New Lausanne' school, chose the term 'enlightenment planning' for their approach.

Contrary to Hayek and the Austrians, prices alone were judged inadequate to spread the necessary information and ensure co-ordination. Even if they adjusted immediately in response to demand and supply changes – a questionable assumption when oligopoly and imperfect competition were widespread – prices were insufficiently proactive, capturing the results of past decisions rather than the intentions underlying present and future ones. Nor were they sufficiently uniform, visible or stable to be of much help in predicting what rival agents were going to do, or where the sector would end up as a result. The time needed to bring new capacity on stream meant that today's market conditions were an insecure basis for planning tomorrow's output. Firms had to know what other producers intended to do with their resources, labour representatives with their wage claims and government with their macroeconomic control instruments (taxes, public spending, interest rates, exchange rates), to make sure their future output would stay consistent with demand and with factor and input prices on the supply side. Firms planning to adopt new products or processes also needed some assurance that market demand and new input supplies would make their decision pay off.

7.5.2   *Giving history – and technology – a push*

While the main objective was still faster growth, indicative planning laid simultaneous stress on improving allocation and distribution, and so claimed greater relevance to the high-income economies in which it was mainly devised. Instead of involving government in the cumbersome process of mobilising real resources, under accusations that it was 'crowding-out' private enterprise, it turned bureaucratic paper-pushing into the more laudable information-peddling, with the promise that private enterprise would be drawn into the bigger picture.

> It is only by planning that proper account can be taken of the interplay between the various sectors of an expanding economy and between the component elements of economic policy . . . The basic concept is that business firms, pressure groups or individuals should voluntarily submit to a measure of discipline because, as a result of information issued on the state of the market, they realise that it is in their interest to do so . . . this coordination is not possible unless there is some degree of centralisation of the power to make basic decisions.
>
> (Oules 1966: 29, 38, 44)

Informed transaction appeared to fit especially well with economies where relational transaction was widespread, where recent political and economic upheaval had weakened the (non-government) institutions that had previously assisted information-sharing and co-ordination, and where there was a tradition of close co-operation and interchange between public bureaucracy and private industry. While France became a paradigm for indicative planning within Europe, post-war Japan was following similar techniques, especially emphasising technological forecasting for 'dynamic' comparative advantage.

The Japanese Economic Planning Agency and Ministry of International Trade and Industry make projections of future product and process developments . . . the opportunities forecast in such projections provide guidelines to both the Japan Development Bank and private banks for evaluating an individual firm's proposals for long-term finance. They allow banks to evaluate investment proposals not as discrete projects but as parts of an integrated sector anticipated to become internationally competitive.

(Best 1986: 191)

In the case of electronics, 'The Japanese government (and NTT, an important procurer) have played important roles in economising on the transaction costs involved in establishing research co-operation between competing firms . . . [and] in increasing diffusion beyond what would otherwise have taken place' (Fransman 1990: 257). Even if the government's technological forecast were wrong on the basis of present information, the achievement of consensus among private firms on its importance and the resultant race to attain it may well have helped make misguided expectations self-fulfilling.

Wherever individual agents acting alone risked being forced into abbreviated, non-optimising forms of decision by their information and computation constraints, lack of co-ordination or lack of foresight, centrally informed transaction promised a new route to optimal 'collective' choice. Analysis of trends in the economy and its major sectors, and of plans submitted by main producers, promised the information needed to ensure that investment matched the composition of future supply to that of future demand, and that public investment in physical and social infrastructure kept pace with private investment in capacity. Expertly advised, streamlined government departments, working closely with (and sharing staff with) private industry, promised to make best possible use of the information. As controller of the economy's demand side and overseer of its supply side (part of which it might regulate or own directly, though usually with some private-sector competition retained), the state had both the ability and the right incentives to complete its co-ordinating task at the individual sector level. The apparent consensus around Keynesian techniques promised to insulate indicative plans from any changes of government or shifts of opinion within government.

7.6 The breakdown of indicative planning

Despite its mission to enlighten agents, about the collective consequences of their own plans and new external (market, technological) developments that might affect them, indicative planning involves two sometimes fatal simplifying assumptions. The first is that agents, realising the all-round benefits of the planning exercise, will put aside their usual rivalries and truthfully report their decision-related information and intentions. Though such details could never be divulged directly to a competitor, they can be entrusted to the neutral indicative planner, whose aggregation of the results will avoid disclosing any of their components. The second assumption is that having received the additional information, about what other agents are doing and how technology is progressing, agents will adapt their plans in ways which bring them closer to a harmonious result.

The second assumption, if correct, would justify the first. Agents would honestly reveal their intentions because they know that everyone will gain if all do so – and for this reason, other agents can also be trusted to make a truthful revelation. But the second condition, of 'convergent' revision of informed behaviour, turns out to be deeply problematic. Studying how agents might learn the equilibrium parameters of a transaction system, and so form rational expectations, Frydman (1982) begins by confirming the informed-transaction criticism of market exchange. To adjust to equilibrium, agents must estimate the average expectation of equilibrium price (being the price that is fulfilled by output decisions conditioned on that price, given aggregate demand). But expectations of this 'average opinion' are interdependent, aggregate output being predicated on aggregate price expectation assembled from individual expectations of aggregate output.

Although the case for an indicative planner appears to be established, there is no guarantee that they will help agents break through the interdependence. If the planner collects individual plans and announces the 'average opinion', agents will slot this back into their plans and change their behaviour. The output and price that will occur if they now move ahead with transactions will still not be consistent with those that informed their production and consumption decisions. An iterative process is set up, which Frydman shows will necessarily converge only if agents make 'subjectively rational' forecasts, minimising the error in their price predictions. This might be achieved if everyone adopts the same pricing rule, but such a rule must be invariant to changes in the feedback on average opinion, and cannot be arrived at by an optimising procedure on the part of any one agent. Far from resolving the uncertainty, government may compound it if its macroeconomic policy decisions become a further component of the interdependence, agents trying to guess future levels of interest rates, tax rates and exchange rates which are themselves affected by the actions these guesses lead agents to take. The best the planner can apparently do is to supply an arbitrary rule, for itself and for agents, which will make expectations converge, with no guarantee that convergence will be to an 'optimum' on any allocation, full-employment or growth standard.

The informed transaction perspective had credited agents with the foresight to submit their plans for comparison and analysis, but then demanded a highly simplified response to ensure that consensus was reached.

> Indicative planning was supposed to provide a transparent, consistent and consensual picture of future developments, to which all would conform out of self-interest; but the participants in this exercise often cheated; even when they did not cheat, their views about the future could not be well summarised by single-valued and firm expectations, and even if they all agreed on a possible and desirable scenario they could not agree on their own individual part in it.
>
> (Nuti 1986: 86–7)

Like the pre-Heisenberg science whose method it had borrowed, the approach had ignored the tendency of even a neutral observer to change the magnitude they are trying to measure.

To arrive at consistent expectations and coherent plans might well require more follow-up meetings than chief executives, union leaders and public servants are willing to attend. But in practice, IT procedures rarely progressed far enough to test this theoretical difficulty. Before indicative plans could run up against such 'endogenous' uncertainties, most were blown off course by more 'exogenous' uncertainties, which also disrupted the macroeconomic policies and tripartite 'social contracts' designed to accompany the plan. Economic and technological forecasts can be deflected by exogenous shocks even if the expectations they depict are completely rational, in the sense of using all relevant information available at the time of the decision. Any link between wage moderation and low inflation, higher taxes and better welfare provision or higher investment and higher profit may be stretched so far in a modern economy that causality – hence the credibility of promises built on it – ceases to show.

As a result, indicative plans rarely met any growth target significantly higher than those prevailing before they were introduced, and were equally hardpressed to eliminate old boom–bust cycles around the medium-term rate. During the phase when they performed best, at least in Europe, the 'enlightenment push' may well have been against an open door. Industrial economies, already launched into a phase of historically rapid and stable growth assisted by investment expectations wide enough to be self-fulfilling, were able to subordinate redistribution to growth and to maintain full employment without inflation because wages lagged fast-growing labour productivity. A range of technologies introduced in the 1940s and 1950s were being developed to maturity, along paths which – like that of the economy – could be forecast with reasonable accuracy simply because of the stable trend. The international diffusion of technologies, though speeding up, was still relatively slow, helped by concentration of patent rights in high-income economies. Where technology did move abroad, barriers to trade and international capital movement were generally enough to defer a serious challenge for market share until the originators had moved on to something else.

The door began to close when rising wage expectations clashed with declining productivity growth rates, unemployment undermined the affordability of tax-based welfare arrangements, and the levers of macroeconomic control began to lose their effect. Without the job creation and growth in the social wage for which it had pledged wage moderation, organised labour became increasingly disaffected with tripartite arrangements, and pressures emerged for more prescriptive forms of planning.

'While investment and growth were forthcoming, the increase in [union] power was of little economic consequence because workers were moderate in their claims. But now that growth has slackened the consequences of this increase in power on economic outcomes are profound' (Schott 1982: 180). At the moment when indicative planning was most needed, to avert a downward spiral in expectations, it seemed least able to take effect. What proponents had hailed as a cause of full employment and fast growth showed every sign of being an effect.

7.7   Conclusion: ill-gotten government, well co-ordinated corporations

The disappearance of government-led planning, of both the administered and informed variety, repeats on the supply side the blow to concepts of controlling the macroeconomy already delivered on the demand side by the retreat from 'Keynesian' policy. As recently as the mid-1970s, the apparently comparable aims and effectiveness of public- and private-sector planning was encouraging expectations that the two would converge. 'Capitalism is drifting into planning . . . the political apparatus within capitalism is steadily growing, enhancing its power, and usurping functions formerly dedicated to the economic sphere – not to undo, but to preserve that sphere' (Heilbroner 1976: 17). With this came the confident prediction that 'communist' and 'capitalist' systems would in the end bury their differences rather than each other, as each evolved into mixed economies using markets for their final allocation but a large dose of informed and administered transaction to set their aggregate framework. Pro-marketeers would come to recognise the need for extensive tax-funded social services and public ownership of natural monopolies, but central planners would be forced to return much of their decision-making power to individual enterprises, some of which might even be returned to private ownership.

In contrast to the retreat of centralised administration or informing of transaction, its localised version within the firm appears to have maintained its advance. Firms' success at expanding in size, scope and geographical coverage while retaining co-ordination and responsiveness rests on their success in mixing the four types of transaction viewed in Chapters 6 and 7. Inability to achieve this in the public sector has been one force behind the recent move towards commercial freedom and privatisation for state industry. Chapter 8 looks in more detail at how firms use alternative transaction types both to complement and substitute the market, and how this has influenced the traditional 'theory of the firm'.

8 The firm

Redesigning the market

Until recently, the large company was bad company for the market. Firms were regarded (within economics) as legal devices – for administering a nexus of contracts, assembling technologically linked labour and machinery, packaging fixed assets as security for loans and limiting owners' liability. They engaged in trade as 'legal persons', functionally not dissimilar to the natural persons who traded with them. This characterisation seemed unexceptionable while most firms remained numerous in most markets and under close founder/family control, even when they had substantially outgrown their sole-proprietor origins.

As firms grow relative to their markets, whether by capturing sales from rivals or acquiring those rivals, a stage is reached when the firm's buying and selling decisions have a perceptible effect on prices in the markets on which it trades. One of the requirements of efficient market transaction – many undifferentiated, uncoordinated buyers and sellers – is violated, and the firm attains a degree of price-setting power (often termed market power). Although providing a case for anti-monopoly intervention where it persisted, market theorists have generally remained confident that such power will be self-limiting – undercut by rivals tempted into the market by the monopolist's profits, or superseded by an innovation which drains demand from the industry. This confidence was reinforced by the relatively short lifespan of the early corporate giants. If the pursuit of growth did not leave them financially over-indebted and managerially overstretched, then the product of growth was a complacency that allowed others to win back sales and regain the technical lead. Any cost advantages through economies of scale were seen to be offset by disadvantages as the firm's managerial bureaucracy grew top-heavy, and any first-comer advantages to disappear as proprietory rights to new products and processes expired, and others learnt to adopt or improve on them. The 'creative destruction' of large firms was helped by trade tariff removal which expanded the markets they dominated, and technical progress which made those markets obsolete. Large firms' fall was further ensured by the tendency of owner-proprietors to lose control as rising enterprise size overtook their flagging energies, before handing it down to a second generation which inherited an appetite for the fruits of private enterprise much more readily than a flair for carrying it on.

8.1 Disciplined by the market: the 'old neoclassical' view

Armed with the assurance that enterprise scale was self-limiting, neoclassical allocation and growth theories could simplify the supply side by treating each firm as a single agent. As such, its maximisation of profit on the basis of available technologies and product and factor prices can be treated symmetrically with consumers' maximisation of utility on the basis of preferences and available budgets, or workers' maximisation of utility by balancing the rewards and privations of work. The firm consists of capital and labour employed up to the point where their marginal reward matches the value of their marginal product, with a technologically determined 'production function' deciding what output results from this employment.

This single-agent treatment exempts the competitive general equilibrium model from looking inside the firm, for the source of its objective function or the means of formulating and implementing sales and purchase decisions. The differentiation of functions within large organisations has no bearing on the differentiation of a profit equation to derive the optimum output. The firm as an institution is even less in evidence in the simple neoclassical growth model, where a one-product production function is elevated to the level of the economy, within which capital and labour redeploy themselves in response to price signals without regard to firm or sector boundaries.

The increasing longevity of large firms, and their apparent ability to stay coherent and competitive even when operating from many sites in many countries, challenges the assumption that market power is not sustainable or not important. When large relative size persists, the 'old neoclassical' view of an economy based on competitive optimisation must concede at least two possible alternatives. Firms may be maximising their profit by exploiting monopoly and monopsony advantages (causing allocative inefficiency), or they may be using the luxury of monopoly to incur unnecessary costs (causing productive inefficiency). The wrong way of maximising, and the failure to maximise, both break the link between what is good for the firm and what maximises welfare for the economy as a whole.

These anti-neoclassical perspectives (to be termed 'monopoly capitalist' and 'managerial' in what follows) find strong empirical support, and are examined in more detail in sections 8.3 and 8.4. Before this, however, it is necessary to consider an alternative neoclassical approach which restores the social efficiency properties of the large firm by widening the cost minimisation it is trying to achieve, from the production costs examined in traditional competition theory to the transaction costs which arise from exchange of non-standard products. After examining the counterblasts from critics who continue to see the large firm as a manifestation of market failure, attention is given to the most recent market counterattack: recasting the corporation as a privately generated corrective to market failure. The 'new neoclassical' firm overcomes the problems of uncoordinated markets identified in Chapters 2–4 – and particularly those relating to information-processing outlined in Chapter 5 – by building an improved version of the market within the information and co-ordination structures of the company. The competitive wheel turns full circle, and a unitary, market-disciplined firm reappears inside the multi-national megacorp.

8.2 Complementing the market: the 'enhanced neoclassical' view

From a neoclassical standpoint, what survives in the market has efficiency advantages over what falls by the wayside. If corporate structures are to survive at all, with their overhead costs, motivational problems, rule rigidities and role inflexibilities, they must be delivering something which individual traders cannot achieve. Having identified a range of special trades which would have redeemed some of the common market failures, if they could only be conducted costlessly, economists supplemented the firm as a legal device with a more directly economic role. They are the structures that enforce those market-rescuing deals at an acceptable cost.

8.2.1 *From production cost to transaction cost minimisation*

Firms' growth was initially ascribed to production cost savings. Expansion of output produces scale economies, a growth of output disproportional to the growth in inputs. Greater absolute size reduces unit costs by spreading the 'overheads' of indivisible or scale-invariant investments (such as specialist labour and machinery), thereby encouraging such investments. Higher output also allows the more efficient combination and intensive use of indivisible labour and capital with different work rates and capacities. It makes for cost savings elsewhere in the production chain by facilitating similar fixed investments and scale economies upstream and down-stream.

Diversification of output produces scope economies, the same plant delivering a combination of products more cheaply than if each were made with dedicated equipment in separate plants. A firm diversified along process lines can switch its resources between products in response to relative demand changes more quickly and cheaply than one for which this entails replacing product-dedicated teams and machines. A firm diversified along product lines can switch its managerial, marketing and R&D resources between them depending on which product market displays the best performance and potential. Diversification may also enable scale economies in R&D, by offering more possible applications for new product or process ideas. These technical factors reinforce any advantages to long-term profitability from risk-spreading due to trading in several product or geographical markets.

In some industries, the cost savings across space due to the scale of production are complemented by cost savings across time as 'practice makes perfect' in the execution of production and distribution. Unit costs fall with cumulative output, due to learning economies as capital and labour adapt to the process, identifying and implementing improvements or simply getting more skilled at repeating the task.

Although it implies a sustained cost advangate for the first rather than the biggest producers in a market, larger firms' greater productivity and intensity of working due to scale economies will tend to make this learning-by-doing occur at a faster rate.

Scale economies violate the simple general-equilibrium condition of constant or declining returns to scale with no (or few) indivisibilities. Scope economies undermine the general-equilibrium assumption of single-product firms with no joint production. Learning economies challenge the underlying general-equilibrium assumption that firms must produce at minimum attainable cost to avoid being undercut by new entrants. These sources of intra-firm increasing returns to scale had already posed a threat to partial-equilibrium views of competition, which was mainly countered by denying their sustainability. Scale and scope economies were viewed as limited by the extra cost of managing large and diverse operations. They also traded off against each other, the pursuit of larger scale encouraging sunk investments in product-specific labour and capital which limited the pursuit of wider scope. There was no reason, on these assumptions, for firms consistently to outgrow the market, or continue growing long enough to become large in relation to it.

Increasing returns to scale could be accommodated at the industry level – clusters of firms gaining from shared infrastructure, specialist labour markets and concentration of customers – but not at the plant or company level. The partial-equilibrium approach required diminishing returns to ensure that firms broke even or stayed in profit after repaying their factors according to marginal productivity. The general-equilibrium approach required non-increasing returns so that many competing firms could exist, and aggregate output be computed as the sum of firms' outputs, however small these were (section 2.7).

Scale economies in production could not, in any case, explain the formation of firms. If cost were all that mattered, an entrepreneur – as a single trading agent – would use market transaction to hire separate factors in their optimum combination, without incurring the overheads or incentive difficulties involved in placing them in specialist buildings and on long-term contracts. Even if lower unit production costs accounted for the existence of large firms, and scope advantages for the existence of multiproduct firms, scale economies had to extend to the organisational level to explain why firms in a single market should have more than one plant producing identical products, or should choose to bring successive stages of production under one roof. This implied either that the firm was seeking larger scale for market power (monopoly or vertical foreclosure) rather than efficiency reasons, or that firms' growth brought scale and scope economies rather than diseconomies in management, opening up another source of intra-firm increasing returns to scale. Both possibilities called into question the neoclassical dismissal of profit advantages to large size, even if the relentless pursuit of corporate growth and acquisition in the real economy did not call the small-is-beautiful logic into question.

The 'enhanced' neoclassical solution maintains the assumption of a competitive environment, and looks inside the firm for an extra source of efficiency deployed to deal with that environment. The extra gain, of which organisational size is by-product rather than determinant, arises from minimising the transaction costs and information asymmetries which impede the efficiency of specific types of open market exchanges (section 7.3). The firm provides an arena for a subset of exchanges in which administered transaction (AT) is rationally preferred to market transaction (MT) because it minimises the sum of production and transaction costs. For the economy as a whole it would still be better to eliminate transaction costs, since the firm may well be getting rid of them by incurring additional production costs, either by letting the whole production cost schedule rise or by displacing its output from the lowest point on that schedule. But if transaction costs are irreducible, the firm becomes a market-generated solution for the range of transactions over which giving agents instructions, or a limited set of options, produces better results (for both agent and economy) than letting them search for the 'rational' decision using only market signals. The large firm moves from subverting to complementing the market, a strategic island of AT within the ocean of MT.

8.2.2 *Internalised transaction: where swopping beats shopping*

The enhanced neoclassical view distinguishes three main sources of transaction cost (TC). The first results from uncertainty about the value of the product currently being traded, either now (because of unknown characteristics of the product and/or its supplier) or in the future (because of unknown states of the world to come, extending to uncertainty over what it will want to buy and sell). TC is incurred through obtaining the missing information needed to overcome the uncertainty, ensuring that others take known or predictable actions that dispel the uncertainty, or making the contingency arrangements (insurance, hedging) needed to minimise the effect of uncertainty on long-run profit (section 3.1.1).

The second TC type arises where all the information needed for optimising market trade is in principle available, but its complexity prevents it being assimilated or processed in the time or with the computational power available. Bounded rationality forces the agent to cut short the decision process and settle for a solution which, while satisfying basic requirements, is not known to be optimising. It may arise where (endogenous) uncertainty over current product characteristics or future states of the world results from an infinite regress, because these are dependent on decisions by other agents which interact with the agent's own decision. Or it may simply reflect the fact that contingent contracts or futures-market trades designed to deal with (exogenous) uncertainty become too complicated for an agent to set out in full. TC then arises as the loss incurred by taking a 'satisficing' decision rather than going through the full process to reach a maximising decision. This cost cannot be computed, except by some omniscient observer of the agent's decision. For this reason, bounded-rationality based explanations of administered exchange (originating from Simon 1947 and March and Simon 1958) have tended to be reinterpreted within the missing-information framework (even though they effectively concern a situation where there is too much information to process, rather than too little).

A third category of TC considers the irreversible cost of preparing to engage in a particular transaction, and the implied loss if the transaction does not go ahead at the anticipated volume and price, or is not repeated the anticipated number of times. These sunk costs may arise from investment either in producing for the trade (e.g. buying a machine which needs a certain value of sales to pay back, which only the contracted buyer is likely to furnish) or in positioning to carry out the trade (e.g. setting up supply lines and payment facilities). As well as being unrecoverable if the anticipated custom cannot be found in the market, such transaction-specific investments (if visible to others) pose the 'moral hazard' that such custom is more likely to be withheld, because prospective buyers who realise that the agent is committed to a certain number of transactions will know that they can bargain for better terms. TCs due to transaction-specific investment, which can also be incurred by specialist buyers, are generally a consequence of 'thin' markets, which prevent an agent whose original plans are disappointed from either lining up alternative clients or selling their investment at something close to its purchase price. They may prevent a potentially mutually beneficial trade from taking place through the market, unless similar sunk costs are incurred on both sides so as to create a shared interest in completing the trade.

8.2.3 Why transact outside the market?

Most transaction costs arise from the risk of incurring, or requirement to guard against, the inefficiencies and breakdowns of market transaction identified in sections 6.4 and 7.3. To avoid repetition, and drawing on terminology introduced by pioneers of the TC approach, these can be summarised as follows.

Information inadequacy and asymmetry

- Information impactedness: privileged information held by one party which is costly to acquire, but without which fair transaction terms cannot be gauged.
- Team production: cost of apportioning and valuing individual contributions to a production or transaction process involving several agents, and of monitoring contractually specified contributions.
- Joint production: cost of apportioning the use of resources, and overhead costs, when two or more marketable products result from a single process.
- Risk sharing: variation of the transaction outcome, or its valuation, with future conditions makes the transaction too risky for an agent left to absorb the full risk, but becomes mutually beneficial if agents agree to share the risk. (This is especially common where one transactor's gain is straightforwardly another transactor's loss, as when a long-term supplier is vulnerable to sudden changes in the production cost or market price of what they supply.)

Bounded rationality

- Costs of framing and enforcing a contingent contract capable of specifying profitable transaction terms for any future state of the world.
- Costs of calculating the present value of a transaction whose outcome, or utility and profitability of outcome, depends on decisions to be taken by other agents now and in the future.

Transaction-specific investment

- Costs of writing-off material stocks, equipment or acquired information which have no recoverable value if anticipated transaction does not take place.
- Unrecoverable costs of research needed to put a price on a transaction, and apportion its costs between parties involved.
- Costs of delay, and product decay, while terms of transaction are being researched and negotiated.

These costs to dealing through the market are, in the enhanced neoclassical view, the main reasons why certain transactions are brought within the administrative structure of the firm. The firm 'internalises' transactions in these categories if it believes that the sum of production and transaction costs will be lower when resources are transferred administratively (by AT) than through the market (by MT). Adoption of AT may have its own costs – of monitoring and incentivising to keep the interests of 'agents' aligned with those of 'principals', of trickery when this is not done, of insulation from new developments in the marketplace from which the transaction has been withdrawn – but these are viewed as being outweighed by the transaction-cost savings achieved by abandoning MT. The firm becomes a 'nexus of contracts' through which its members exchange materials and factor services without constant recourse to the market to set terms, and without formal payment between separate accounts (Alchian and Demsetz 1972). These contracts are incomplete, allowing precise design of the transaction (allocation of resources) to be set and modified in response to new information arriving over time. Authority in the firm rests with those with the rights of 'residual control' to fill in the missing detail of the contract (O. Hart 1996). Residual control rights (over contract terms), like residual claimant rights (over the income remaining when employed agents have received their contractually specified reward), usually reside with the holder of user rights to the firm's physical assets: its managers if these have attained the role of principal (see section 1.4.3), or its owners if these have retained the management role (or confined managers to a purely agency function).

Far from a step away from market competition and its efficiency effects, the 'enhanced neoclassical' firm is a response to their intensification. Agents are now required not only to optimise the allocation of their resources between uses and the efficiency of their use, but also to minimise the costs of trading to achieve this optimisation. 'Modern multi-unit business replaced the small traditional enterprise when administrative co-ordination permitted greater productivity, lower costs and higher profits than coordination by the market mechanism' (Chandler 1977). Administrative co-ordination holds out the hope of solving other problems associated with the competitive market framework. In particular, by eliciting further information on agents' preferences, and modifying them where necessary, it may overcome the problem of allocating internal resources in ways which fairly reflect all individual preferences (section 2.1.5). The firm becomes a controlled environment in which improved supply of information – about objectives, the result of actions and the reaction of other agents to them – brings transacting members closer to the conditions for rational choice in an ideal open market.

8.2.4 *From markets to management*

The firm can administer its internal exchange in two ways. A dictatorial approach relegates most employees from transaction (negotiating the transfer of resources) to mere action (carrying out the transfer, or working on resources whose transfer is already mapped out). Those still authorised to transact do so with minimal discretion, being told what to do either through a continuous stream of orders or a menu of actions, to be selected according to clearly specified (market or management) signals. Since continually issuing instructions might well incur as much managerial time cost as is saved in transaction cost, the more usual approach is to 'programme' agents – simplifying their task and stabilising their environment so they can be left to repeat the same action, or to choose from a restricted set of action, without appealing to higher authority. This task simplification has the further advantage of reducing the necessary skill and flexibility (hence cost) of labour and capital employed, and of improving performance through constant practice. 'Programmed' agents can be monitored by periodic inspection of the results of their work rather than continuous observation of its enactment, producing a further saving on management time.

Early 'scientific management', along these lines, envisaged a division of labour within the firm under which each worker performed a set routine, assisted by task-specific, simple-to-use equipment. It also quickly revealed the limitations of this approach: the damage to worker incentives, and additional costs of transferring labour and capital to new tasks which can easily outweigh the cost savings from focusing them on one task. Dictatorship tends to demotivate the agent, and render the organisation vulnerable to changes in internal or external demands to which the appropriate response is not on 'programmed' employees' menus. To the extent that workers are still able and willing to use initiative to adapt to these unforeseen changes, they may merely postpone change and make the required adjustment more difficult, by preventing the already overstretched dictator from picking up signals from outside that point to the need for changed internal routines.

So administered transaction within the firm more usually takes a directional form, in which the agent's decision process is restricted but still contains an element of choice between permitted options. Instructions include guidance on the circumstances in which to select different options, and an 'alarm call' mechanism if unusual circumstances arise, thus allowing the organisation to adapt to local changes in circumstance, while still remaining alert to bigger changes that need a non-routine response. Whereas dictatorship (closely associated with 'Fordist' mass production) extracts information from employees and makes it the firm's property, passing back only what is needed for prescribed action, direction (associated with newer, more modular batch or bespoke production) pools information while leaving employees in ultimate ownership of it, and giving them more discretion to use it within the consistency constraints handed down.

8.2.5 *From roles to rules*

Direction specifies the parameters for the agent's decision, in contrast to dictatorship which takes the decision on their behalf. If the directional instruction-giver is confident of which circumstances are likely to prevail and which actions should attend which circumstances, instructions will take an end-state form, mapping circumstances to actions. More usually, where there is uncertainty about the conditions that will arise and the appropriate response, instructions will take a process form, giving the agent a target and a set of actions and leaving them to select the action which best fulfils the target. This is akin to the 'rational' decision process (Figure 5.1, section 5.2) but with the search and evaluation stages combined. In one influential model based on observation of organisations, the agent is given a minimum-level or 'pass/fail' target and a prescribed action set which they work through in sequence, selecting the first satisfactory action they reach and searching or appealing for more actions only if none seems appropriate (Simon 1955).

Simon's adoption of the term 'behavioural model', and his reference to the choice framework as a 'programme', recognises the intermediate path being trodden between determinism and free will. Successful management achieves within the firm a 'technology of behaviour' which, when confidence in the state as administrator was at its height, some also believe could be achieved within society at large. 'A scientific analysis of behaviour dispossesses autonomous man and turns the control he has been said to exercise over to the environment' (Skinner 1972: 200). To its advocates, such control had always existed, and its new form was a significant advance on the old, guiding individual action through incentive measures (reward) rather than aversive measures (punishment), towards ends which were in the individual's interest (higher productivity, social harmony) rather than self-servingly imposed by autocratic governments or feudal lords.

Directional administered transaction removes individuals from the market while preserving the anonymity attached to market trade. In reducing an operation to simple procedures selected according to specified signals, programming separates the worker from the job. Whereas they may not be replaceable by machine quite as easily as employees under Fordist instruction, those working under a programme are more easily replaced by other workers. Job specifications provide the firm with a memory of past situations and appropriate responses, whose writing-up into formal rule books has been a main feature of the recent trend towards ISO 9000 quality-consistency certification.

As the economic spheres of autonomy and control, 'market' and 'hierarchy' thus came to be viewed as alternative efficiency-generating social institutions, 'understood as sets of abstract rules that constrain the behaviour of economic agents and define for them payoffs that depend on their behaviour (Schotter 1986: 119). Organisational theorists tend to regard these rule systems as conscious creations created by the firm's founders, and imposed with the help of laws equally deliberately framed by government. A more individualistic 'Austrian' view, fortified by recent game theory, treats organisational rules as the products of social experiment and evolutionary selection, for which entrepreneurial imposition and government intervention may not be necessary. Whatever their origins, firms are characterised as voluntary groupings of agents, each of whom contributes to a collective aim and is rewarded with a share of joint profit. Market transaction survives in the transfer of resources between these groupings, with a clear firm/market boundary separating the two.

8.3   Taming the monopoly threat

Transaction cost savings increase the feasible size of the firm, encouraging horizontal integration (the absorption or displacement of rivals) and vertical integration (the absorption of suppliers or downstream buyers) in ways which reduced competition. Multi-divisionalisation allows a firm to ease the problems of co-ordinating plants in different product areas and regions, by giving each relative operational autonomy while keeping strategic decision-making and ultimate financial control at the centre (Chandler 1962). Multinationalisation allows a firm to extend its advantages of proprietary technology, knowledge, capital costs or reputation into new geographical markets (Caves 1982). If separated by trade barriers, foreign markets also increase the scope for raising profits through price discrimination; and if distinguished by tax laws, the scope for preserving repatriated profits through transfer pricing.

The potential for transaction-cost saving is a function of firms' absolute size. However, these organisational devices also give the firm the potential to achieve large relative size (in relation to the national and international market); and the profit advantages claimed for transaction-cost reduction imply that leading firms will achieve that large relative size. By obtaining significant shares of their domestic and some foreign markets, multi-divisional and multinational firms may open up a route to profit-maximisation quite different from that which competitive models had shown to be best for the whole economy. If firms' expansion leads to monopoly power in product and factor markets, or if internal labour and capital markets insulate the suppliers of these factors from external market pressures, relative size may destroy their incentive to minimise costs and maximise allocative efiiciency, even if absolute size has given them the means to do so.

The enhanced neoclassical view offers a variety of responses to the charge that firms' greater profitability (over individual transactors in the same resources) arises from exerting power over the market rather than reducing its imperfections. One is to acknowledge that monopoly power is a danger, and a drawback, and to argue for vigorous anti-trust enforcement to stop it occurring or persisting. An alternative is to point to its socially beneficial short-term effects, and longer-term self-limitation. Temporary monopoly power is the driving force for innovation and improved allocation in the 'Austrian' view, bringing its own end because of rivals' race to imitate and get ahead, and so repaying any temporary costs with long-run social benefits.

More commonly, new neoclassical observers of industrial concentration argue that appearances deceive. Structures which appear monopolistic might actually be devices for transaction-cost minimisation, so also delivering long-term social benefits. In particular, 'price discrimination' might represent repayments for different levels of transaction-specific investment; 'vertical foreclosure' might be a legitimate device for suppliers to recover the costs of investment in downstream distributors (including the maintenance of brand quality), and distributors to maintain leverage over a single supplier; 'supernormal' profits permitted internal finance of projects whose profit-making potential could not be accurately conveyed to the external capital market, or sufficiently freed from moral hazard and adverse selection to win support from them; and bilateral monopoly bargaining may be the most efficient way to balance buyer and seller interests in a specific-asset trade, so ensuring a payback on specialised physical and human capital investment (Williamson 1975). The social costs of monopoly in terms of 'suboptimal' output and 'excessive' profit have to be weighed against the social benefits of encouragement to innovation and strategic action (and are generally judged to be small in comparison).

A firm with no actual competitors in its market may still be unable to exploit its monopoly privileges because of the risk of inviting (and having its profits snatched by) the entry of 'potential' competitors. So as well as keeping firms small relative to their markets by extending the market (through removal of domestic regulations and foreign trade tariffs), governments can keep monopoly in check with measures to promote cross-industry migration of producers and consumers, and the scope economies it permits. Especially important elements of this newer, wider anti-monopoly policy are the breaking-down of artificial market separations (so that, for example, separate electricity, gas and water suppliers are allowed to become multipurpose 'utility' suppliers), the promotion of secondary fixed capital markets (so that entrants forced to exit again because the monopolist they challenged reverts to competitive pricing are not lumbered with a transaction-specific investment they cannot recover), and the integration of their national market with others so that their own giant firms are rendered small again in international context.

Monopolies' abuse of market power might also be restrained by the separation of ownership from control in large corporations, whose dispersion of shareholdings among uncoordinated individual and largely passive institutional owners seemed to give management considerable discretion over pricing, investment and strategic development. If, as variously modelled in the 'managerial' theories examined below, managers' utility lay in the firm's size, rate of growth, number of subordinate employees or freedom from regulatory hassle, then the firm's attainment of monopoly profit becomes self-limiting. Managers use this relief from market pressure to avoid having to maximise profit. Society may lose from firms having higher cost functions than are attainable, but not from their producing at an output dramatically lower than minimum-cost, or charging prices dramatically higher than marginal cost.

8.3.1   *The size limits on hierarchy*

In the old neoclassical perspective, the firm is enabled to expand by its success in making reinvestable profits and acquiring lesser rivals, and is motivated to expand by the prospect of profiting from greater efficiency (further division of labour, plant- and organisational-level scale economies, scope economies, the exploitation of technological or managerial assets in new locations, etc.). While these developments tend to increase the absolute size of the firm, their success is independent of any change in its relative size – which can stay small if governments act efficiently to keep the economy growing, open it to foreign competition and remove any sunk-cost obstacles to entry and exit by potential competitors.

If internalisation could reduce transaction cost without sacrificing any other type of efficiency, the firm's expansion might overstep this, unless stopped at the national border or by antimonopoly intervention. In practice, the prospects of a single diversified firm subjecting the whole economy to administered transaction are limited, for the same reasons that the Walrasian auctioneer and Stalinist central planners were unable to do so. While the switch from MT to AT increases transaction-cost efficiency, it reduces information-processing efficiency, these losses mounting with the extent of internalisation. Transaction-relevant information which under MT is gathered and processed by individual agents must, under AT, be passed upwards to the central administrator. Evaluations and decision rules which agents in MT devise for themselves must likewise be handed down to them under AT. Efficiency is lost as firms expand because of the following factors:

- It takes time to pass information to the centre, and disseminate instructions from the centre.
- During its transfer information can become distorted – deliberately by agents or administrators who try to conceal the true situation to tilt the terms of the transaction to their advantage, or accidentally through misunderstanding and 'noise' in the communication channels.
- The administrator, while perhaps enjoying information-processing scale economies in the early stages of internalisation, eventually runs up against computational limits. There is then either a slowdown in the rate at which transaction terms are adapted to new information, a loss of accuracy as the administrator resorts to abbreviated forms of decision-making, or a loss of coherence as the administrator starts 're-decentralising' the information-processing task to assistants and subordinates.
- The rate at which objective-setting, action-evaluation and implementation in

the decision cycle are improved is slowed down, because information on results is also observed at agent level and must now be passed upwards to the centre. Distortions can again occur, especially as agents who implemented the decision may have an interest in embellishing its results.

As the firm expands by internalising more transactions, communication-channels lengthen and the decision-making burden on central management gets heavier. The quality of information received, and the accuracy with which administered transaction instructions are followed, may also deteriorate, because central monitoring of agents becomes more difficult or costly. Switching from unitary to multi-divisional or 'matrix' organisation delays the onset of this process only by effectively breaking the organisation into several lower-level administrative units, so shortening the channels and dividing the computational workload among several centres. But this begins to reintroduce the information and co-ordination problems which organisation was designed to solve. Those at the top are less able to check that their agents are reporting the situation 'on the ground' accurately, or working as hard as the administered transaction terms assume. Those below them are less well informed of the other decisions being taken on their level, and so less able to co-ordinate their actions to achieve the anticipated effect.

The firm's optimum size is thus determined by the balance between transaction cost economies and information-processing diseconomies. 'While hierarchy centralises information, the price system decentralises it. A decentralised information structure avoids the losses due to information transfer, but experiences the problem of suboptimisation if prices do not provide the "right" information' (Hennart 1993: 164–5). By assuming that these limits set in fairly early, the 'old neoclassical' model can still predict an optimum firm size which will normally be small relative to the total market (especially when foreign trade barriers are lifted), thus keeping monopoly and oligopoly elements out of the system.

'Austrian' theory provides an equally powerful argument for firm-size limitation, based on the dynamic inefficiencies of too large an administrative structure and the competing-out (or forced dismemberment) of firms which run into them. As well as struggling to acquire and efficiently process the information already held by its member-agents, the large firm blunts their incentive to look for new threats and opportunities in the changing external environment, and their ability to signal changes which require rapid redesign (or changes in parameters) of the transactions they enact. While centralised systems can in principle respond quickly to external changes once those at the centre become aware of them, early warning signs often appear some distance from the centre: customers suddenly withdrawing or demanding a product change, a supplier's quality deteriorating, the labour force getting restive.

By turning its employees from negotiators into mere enactors of a transaction, paid a fixed wage rather than by results, the firm risks destroying their incentive to report such changes. Subdividing the firm's actions into relatively self-contained, non-overlapping processes may actually have the reverse effect, speeding up the adaptation to small changes in the environment (containable within an employee's or department's programme) but impeding adaptation that must be co-ordinated across departments.

> Loose coupling lowers the probability that the organisation will have to – or be able to – respond to each little change in the environment that occurs . . . if all the elements in a large system are loosely coupled to one another, then any one element can adjust to and modify a local unique contingency without affecting the whole system.
>
> (Weick 1975: 6–7)

Shock absorption insulates the passengers from the broken road ahead.

The combination of local flexibility and global rigidity can be made worse if the firm has made heavy sunk investments in its current transaction pattern. So, usefully for the neoclassical need to keep markets competitive, hierarchy has its limits. And unlike the division of labour in society, the division of (decision-making) labour within the firm encounters an internal constraint well before it testing the extent of the market.

8.3.2   Make or buy: the firm's clear border

The transaction-cost perspective does not contradict neoclassical theory, but rather extends it by identifying another source of costs which must be jointly minimised (alongside production costs) if the firm is to operate with maximum efficiency. As well as choosing its optimum purchase and sale decisions within the market, the transaction-cost minimising firm makes an optimising choice over which transactions are more efficiently conducted outside the market. The boundary of the firm is thus set by the same sort of maximising calculations

'Enhanced neoclassical' theory tends to regard MT and AT as strict alternatives, glossing over from the intermediate 'relational' transaction (RT) range identified in Chapter 6. This reflects the relatively sharp boundary implied by the maximising calculations over relative costs of markets and administration. The competitive firm takes a series of well-defined 'make or buy' decisions and, though its boundary may shift over time as technical or demand conditions change the cost balance between transaction types, the boundary is clearly defined at any one time.

RT is rejected because, under these well-defined conditions, it may well combine the worst of both worlds. Close relations between two agents, with no market to turn to for substitutes, forces each to choose between taking the other party on trust and risking opportunistic deception, or setting up elaborate monitoring and enforcement mechanisms which reintroduce the transaction costs of the marketplace. Whichever choice is made, the small-numbers (at the extreme, bilateral monopoly) situation makes for costly negotiation on the terms of the transaction. Once settled into a relational transaction, both parties also run the risk that they will fail to notice changes in technical, demand or supply conditions to which market transaction would instantly have alerted them. Going the full way, into administered transaction, gets over the trust problem because the firm can impose a bargaining solution and compel the two sides to stick with co-operative strategies (or credibly punish them for not doing so). It also gets over the slow-adjustment problem if the firm can 'scan' external changes (perhaps by studying price movements) and inform agents when the terms of their transaction need to change.

To shift its border, the old neoclassical firm buys and sells businesses in much the same way as it trades resources. Sections are broken off or stuck onto the administrative core, depending on how the gains of internalised transaction, greater market power and synergy weigh against the losses of greater calls on management and remoteness of market pressure. The takeover threat keeps management on its toes, but takeover is also a means of fending off the threat, by boosting profit through scale and scope economies, lowering of transaction costs or higher mark-ups, or by making the reshaped firm a less desirable property for the bidder. Growth and shrinkage by acquisition come relatively easy to the make-or-buy firm, because there are no internal relational transactions to be upset by the new arrival, and no external relational transactions to be troubled by the shifting boundary. A peppermint is easier to swallow – and to spit out – than a sticky bun. (Extending the analogy, any relational transactions the enhanced-neoclassical firm does enter into may be part of its 'poison pill' defences against hostile takeover.)

8.4 The enhanced neoclassical firm: an American paradigm?

The widespread change from unitary (U-form) to multi-divisional (M-form) structure has been identified as an optimising response to the problems of growth, improving the transaction/information-processing efficiency trade-off so as to push back the upper limits of firm size (Chandler 1962, 1977). By passing down 'operational' decision-making to largely autonomous units, the M-form firm keeps its communication channels short and divides its information-processing among several operations. These may be specialised by product or geographical area, to obtain scale-economies in one line of decision-making while minimising the overspill to other lines. Released from operational concerns, the M-form's central management can concentrate on wider economic and product-market changes and the systematic strategy and structure changes needed to deal with them.

The M-form's central management retains ultimate control by exercising financial control over setting performance targets for each division. Within these constraints, divisional management can take its own decisions, shortening the lines of communication and increasing responsiveness to changes in the local environment. The divisions take responsibility for doing their chosen task as efficiently as possible, and adapting to small changes that impact most heavily on its specific operation. Central management is responsible for allocating the tasks, and adapting the whole organisation to large changes (in the external environment or internal performance) which have an irreversible impact across the divisions.

The M-form also lends itself to multinational extension of the firm, which in the neoclassical perspective is the logical next step in the pursuit of minimum cost and maximum profit once a firm has grown large relative to its home-country market. Firms may go multinational (set up production facilities outside their home country) to access a foreign market closed to exports by trade barriers, transaction costs or product perishability, to make use of lower factor or material costs, or to overcome (by internalisation) the transaction costs of licensing proprietary processor or products to local producers. Letting subsidiaries operate as relatively autonomous 'profit centres' has the advantage not only of relieving information-processing needs at the centre and maintaining information-responsiveness on the ground, but also of reducing home-country hostility to the multinational presence by giving it the appearance of being in local hands.

Perhaps unsurprisingly, a theory developed largely by North American economists corresponds closely with the development path of North American industry. Emerging from the mid-twentieth-century upheavals with a wide technological lead, reflected in the country's large high-technology trade surplus, and with little foreign competition despite the lowering of trade barriers, US firms were mainly concerned to reduce costs in their current operations and generate the long-range innovations that would open up new operations. Domestic rivals were their main competitive reference point, and tacit collusion (price leadership, territorial or product areas differentiation) were common where the pursuit of scale economies had given rise to oligopoly. Strong anti-trust regulation put a barrier against relational transaction between firms, which might be taken as overt collusion. However, knowledge that the USA was at the technological frontier encouraged strong patent protection. The importance of proprietary technology to competitiveness deterred technical collaboration with rivals or suppliers, which firms' large scale and diversity of interests tended also to make unnecessary. When US firms moved abroad, it was mainly to exploit the market power that went with superior technology and organisation, so internalisation again won out over licensing or joint-venturing which would have involved the sharing of technology. 'The American ideal is of the Universal Product, reducible to parts (analysis) and infinitely replicable. We can see this in products as different as microprocessors and M&Ms, Coca-Cola and superconductors' (Hampden-Turner and Trompenaars 1993: 20). Where lower labour costs were the motive, foreign subsidiaries tended to compete directly with domestic subsidiaries to serve the US and third markets, providing management with an additional device to contain labour costs and drive productivity improvement at home.

Corresponding to the clear make-or-buy choice was an equally polar own-or-hire distinction, by which the firm decided which (physical or human) assets to purchase outright (to exercise full ownership) and which to hire on current market terms when required (to exercise user rights). Relatively task-specific capital confronted relatively general-purpose labour, which tended to be further deskilled by the introduction of specialist machines (Braverman 1974, Noble 1979). For this reason, and because workers came to the firm without resources of their own, ownership of most companies rested with the owners of their capital.

Owning its machines, the firm was insulated from inconclusive bargaining over the rewards to separate machine-owners (Leijonhufvud 1986); taking in labour on long contracts, the firm found adaptability by being able to specify its duties in con-siderably less detail than if it had to hire their services in 'spot' labour markets (Williamson 1981). As well as allowing the firm to acquire knowledge about the factor services it is getting (and adjust for any deficiency by either reducing pay or raising demands), internalised contracts allowed the firm to appropriate any ben-efits accruing to the service provider during the transaction process. If it had to service the machine, it gets to enjoy the benefits of the service. If it trained the worker (or if the worker learnt something useful on the job), it gets to enjoy the higher productivity due to the training. The worker's reward for accepting a more open-ended contract was the chance to share in such gains, the greater stability of longer-term employment, and the possibility of acquiring skills which (whether transferable or firm-specific) might improve its future bargaining power.

This stylised account is given in the past tense because, if it were were generally true, it has been extensively superseded by changes in North American business structure and conduct since at least the early 1980s. Among the reasons for this change were the arrival of significant import competition in the USA and its dra-matic slide into trade deficit, the shift of first-mover innovation from large to small/medium firms in some of the areas of fastest growing demand, and the reduced replaceability and raised bargaining power of skilled labour coupled with higher-income households' significant move into share ownership via mutual and insurance funds. The need for this change suggests support for earlier criticisms of US industry as well adapted to static efficiency and radical innovation but stranded on the middle ground of incremental, process-improving innovation. The speed of the change suggests that US companies learnt quickly, if expensively, how they needed to restructure. Possible directions of change are examined in sections 8.5 and 8.6, while one model from which US firms may well have learnt is examined in section 8.7.

8.5 Overpowering the market: the monopoly capital counterattack

To those not convinced by the Adam Smith dictum that pursuit of self-interest pro-motes the collective good, depicting the firm as a device to reduce transaction costs by surmounting information problems, takes too benign a view of human nature. Rational agents will not search for better ways to play by the rules if higher prof-its can more easily be gained by circumventing those rules. The identification of the firm with 'monopoly capital' rests on two observations concerning the growth of the large corporation. First, that cost minimisation cannot be a motive in firm formation, because transaction costs persist within the organisation and new sources of inefficiency (such as agent–principal conflicts) arise within it. Second, that firms continue to expand after any transaction–cost justification for size has been exhausted, exposing their real motive as the maximisation of profit by over-riding markets and exerting price-setting power.

The efficiency losses due to market transaction cost are not automatically over-come by moving to administered transaction. The firm may now avoid the legal costs of chasing up clients who breach their contracts, the search costs of acquiring or replicating a client's privileged information, and the sunk costs of investing in a transaction that is not sustained. But it does so by consciously entering into a bilateral or small-numbers relationship with employees and captive clients which may impose equivalent costs of bargaining, monitoring and internal costing. The contracts that senior managers must draw up to ensure that junior managers and workers are incentivised to fulfil the firm's strategy, despite their temptation to skimp on quality and free-ride on the efforts of team-mates, may be just as complex as the contingent contracts they would need to co-ordinate the operation outside the firm. 'While [transaction cost] theories throw light on the nature of contractual failure, none explains in a convincing or rigorous manner why bringing a transaction within the firm mitigates this failure' (O. Hart 1996: 204).

The switch from market to administered transaction, however, allows the firm to extract higher profits even if its costs are not being minimised and its gains reduce efficiency for the rest of the economy. Oligopolies are well placed to reach implicit understandings which boost industry profits by avoiding price competition, or explicit agreements to carve up the market for joint profit-maximisation. Monopolies can escape the discipline placed on firms by financial markets, since shareholders and creditors are unlikely to object that their higher returns come from price-setting power rather than optimum allocation and cost minimisation. While labour might organise to counteract the wage-setting power of large employers, this too is unlikely to substitute for product-market competition, since wage rises can be passed on as price rises in a monopolised product market, management pacifying the protest by passing on some of the spoils of market power.

As well as the realism of its assumptions (are firms designed, and do they draw their boundaries with such precision?), the enhanced neoclassical theory was quickly challenged over the accuracy of its predictions – particularly the relatively early onset of information-processing limits to firm size. In practice many firms have grown not only beyond the scale suggested by production-cost efficiency (plant-level scale economies, spreading of fixed management costs, R&D economies, etc.), but also beyond the scale suggested by transaction-cost efficiency. They can survive the resultant higher-than-necessary costs of large absolute size because of the 'supernormal' profit afforded by large relative size.

To critics outside the mainstream tradition, this overexpansion represented more than the relatively harmless pursuit of discretionary spending by relatively autonomous managers, and it inflicted losses on society much greater than the underproduction and overpricing of certain products. 'Monopoly capitalism' meant that, at best, managers were destroying through conspicuous consumption a surplus which could have been reinvested in useful production (Cowling 1982); and at worst, that capital was concentrating in ever fewer hands so as to maximise the size of the propertyless workforce, and then to maximise its exploitation of that workforce. On this criterion of corporate success, 'the best single indicator is profits garnered at the expense of employees and the community' (Perrow 1981: 382).

The market system's tendency towards industrial concentration, merger-and-acquisition waves, systematic R&D, scale economies, free trade and free capital movements had been identified by its harshest critic long before most of its supporters became aware of them.

> Self earned private property, that is based, so to say, on the fusing together of the isolated, independent labouring-individual with the conditions of his labour, is supplanted by capitalistic private property . . . hand in hand with this centralisation, or this expropriation of many capitalists by few, develop, on an ever extending scale, the co-operative form of the labour process, the conscious technical application of science, the methodical cultivation of the soil, the transformation of the instruments of labour into instruments of labour usable only in common, the economising of all means of production by their use of as the means of production combined, socialised labour, the entanglement of all peoples in the net of the world market, and with this, the international character of the capitalistic regime.
>
> (Marx 1867/1983: 492)

The process of capital accumulation and industrial concentration would cease only when 'the monopoly of capital becomes a fetter on the mode of production' (Marx 1867/1983: 493), when workers' underpayment causes an overproduction crisis and incites them to seize the means of production, which their centralisation makes easier.

Neoclassical 'exploitation' occurs, if at all, mainly in the setting of prices above marginal cost in a monopolised product market, or the payment of wages below marginal product value in a monopsonised labour market. Both can be restrained by sufficient competition for customers or workers. In contrast, Marx makes exploitation central to the generation of profit, which arises from the 'surplus value' of labour services provided over wage received. Competition actually increases the rate of exploitation, as capitalists struggle to offset a falling rate of profit caused by rising capital–labour ratios and, perhaps, rising real wages. Surplus value created in the production process is 'validated' in the exchange process, but cannot be created there (except where wage differences for the same organic composition of capital give rise to unequal exchange – see section 9.3.6).

As the capital accumulates, its owners can maintain the rate of exploitation only if they prevent it from competing for the services of labour, and prevent labour from acquiring it. 'When capital (whether it was produced in the past or is an appropriated natural resource) becomes private property and is distributed in an inegalitarian manner, differentiation and exploitation arise, through the market process' (Roemer 1988: 24). The firm, by legalising and safeguarding concentrations of capital, becomes an institutional arrangement for the extraction of surplus value. The (administered) employment of labour replaces the (market) hire of labour services not because this saves on transaction costs, but because it allows the extraction of labour services in excess of the 'labour-power' that is paid for. Assembling labour into one workplace may reduce the costs of monitoring and disciplining it (Marglin 1974), but its main purpose is to help increase the rate of exploitation.

8.5.1 'Late' monopoly capitalism: the persistence of profit

Profit rates have not fallen, real wages have not been kept at subsistence, and labour has not seized the concentrated means of production in quite the way Marx seemed to envisage. A sympathetic reinterpretation of his work reintroduces the possibility of firms using monopoly power in the product market to shift exploitation onto consumers, or the transfer of monopoly abroad to shift it onto foreign workers. Both moves allow capitalists to buy the loyalty of their domestic workforce by exploiting them less (or perhaps not at all), at least in production. Monopolies' output restriction and ability to invest in automation also swells unemployment so as to place 'voluntary' restraint on wage demands.

Most 'monopoly capital' accounts assume a direct relation between a firm's market power (proxied by a measure of concentration, such as the Herfindahl index of squared market shares) and its degree of monopoly, given by the mark-up of price over marginal cost $(p-mc)/p$. Higher concentration makes it easier for the firm to raise its price by restricting its own output, and to collude with rival firms to raise industry price by restricting industry output. Relative size may reflect restricted entry to an industry, but absolute size makes for the prolongation of the resultant market power.

> It is the gigantic size of the 'monopolies', in other words the accumulation of certain of its 'many capitals' to astronomic dimensions, which presents formidable barriers to entry into monopolised sectors and thereby extends the duration of surplus-profit appropriation.
>
> (Mandel 1978: 530)

True to Marx's original insight, what is good for monopoly firms and industries may be disastrous for the economy as a whole. Monopoly power causes misallocation as firms battle to obtain and sustain it (e.g. through persuasive advertising, takeover battles, product differentiation), loss of productive efficiency as managers divert retained profit into frivolous expenditures, and possibly stagnation as firms cut back production and investment (Cowling 1982). While damaging for the validation of profits, this development is in principle useful for their generation – the resultant unemployment helping to discipline wage demands, and the excess capacity posing an output-expanding retaliation threat against potential new entrants or existing rivals thinking of breaking a cartel agreement. Government action to expand product markets – by reflating domestic demand or removing trade barriers – may initially lower the degree of monopoly, by reducing concentration and undermining cartels, but 'faced with such mutual adversity we may anticipate that the group will tend to come together . . . if the slump persists we can expect to see a recovery in margins as the degree of collusion within the oligopoly group increases' (Cowling 1992: 152). Monopolisation imposes its own demand-side limits, but has no tendency to retreat from them without external intervenion.

Although its link with industry concentration is not clear-cut and regarded by some as tautologous (Fine and Murfin 1984), mark-up pricing behaviour has been observed in practice (beginning with Hall and Hitch 1939), and also gives a firm's management certain information-processing and co-ordination advantages not available if the same resources were to be deployed through the market. Mark-up pricing simplifies the price-setting procedure by eliminating the need to establish demand or marginal-cost functions. It allows the 'two-handed' use of prices both to clear the market in current production and generate the investment funding needed to plan future production (section 3.15). Where costs are roughly constant, with falling average fixed costs offsetting rising average variable costs, it also introduces a range of output over which a stable mark-up produces stable prices. This may help bring stability to the industry to the extent that it makes similar firms' response to demand changes more predictable, and lets tacit co-operation develop. At home, monopoly power can help defer the fall in profit rates and crisis due to overproduction.

8.5.2 *Monopoly capital abroad: multinational enterprise*

Formal analysis of multinational enterprises (MNEs) can be traced to a Marxist (Hymer 1960/1976), and the early explanations for firms setting up operations abroad rested heavily on market imperfection. 'Horizontal' multinationalisation can occur when a firm with monopoly power in its home market due to technological or managerial superiority chooses to extend its advantage abroad. Where export is blocked by trade barriers, and the sale or licensing of the technology by problems of trading information, direct investment to replicate the home plant may be its only option. Where a rival monopolist already serves the foreign market, the two may find integration (into one MNE) a stabler route to joint profit-maximisation than negotiated market segmentation or cartelisation, which is open to breakdown of trust. 'Complete financial consolidation of the monopolies not only improves the ability to monitor price cutting but practically elminates at source the incentive to cheat. When plants are located in different countries, financial consolidation leads to the creation of an MNE' (Casson 1987: 144).

'Vertical' multinationalisation can occur when a firm wishes to get closer to its upstream input suppliers (to capture profit from them) or its downstream customers (to introduce new products or sales techniques to them). There may be bilateral bargaining problems in the first case, and problems in trading proprietary product and marketing knowledge in the second, both of which press for the administrative integration of local transactors. 'Product-specific information which cannot be traded and which cannot be used to increase direct exports (perhaps because of tariffs, quotas, transport costs or other barriers to trade) will lead to geographical expansion' (Ricketts 1987: 227).

While MNEs usually remit profits to the home country while their initial investment is being recovered, most move on to making foreign units 'profit centres', reinvesting profit and raising additional finance locally, diminishing the element of international exploitation through production.

> Colonial surplus-profits directly produced in the underdeveloped countries, although they remain very substantial in absolute terms in the specific case of British imperialism, have steadily diminished in importance since the end of the Second World War relative to the total profits of the major imperialist companies.
>
> (Mandel 1978: 348)

Exploitation may continue through trade, but MNEs in the Marxian perspective tend to lose their nationality and either recycle surplus-value within its host markets or move it by transfer-pricing to whichever best shields it from taxation and political risk. Large enterprise becomes stateless, and technical transfer which initially impeded economic advance outside the MNEs' countries of origin may begin to speed it up (Emmanuel 1982). Abroad, monopoly power helps spread capitalist relations of production but may also speed the return of profit and overproduction crises.

8.6 Sidestepping the market: the managerial approach

Large firms' separation of ownership from control does not make much difference to monopoly capitalism's managers, who must generally continue to maximise profits even if they do not always spend them the way distant shareholders would like. Closer to the neoclassical approach, however, are several 'managerialist' interpretations under which monopoly profit allows management to stray from the strict interests of capital. As long as profits remain high enough to finance investment needs internally, avoiding a recourse to financial markets that might take a closer look at costs and pricing policies, managers enjoy discretionary power to deviate from the maximisation of present value and shareholder income.

Most models in this vein regard managers as maximising something else – the firm's present output (Baumol 1959), growth rate (Marris 1964), their own security and sales growth (Galbraith 1967: ch. 15) or the size of the managerial bureaucracy they command (Niskanen 1971). In general, they imply the growth of the firm beyond its profit-maximising size, subject to constraints of managerial capacity and span of control (Penrose 1959). Alternatively, management might take monopoly profit as an opportunity not to maximise anything, but simply cut down on its decision-making workload, disregarding upward drifts in costs and downward drifts in prices as long as the mark-up stays above acceptable levels. This pursuit of a 'quiet life' can be transmitted down to the firm's middle management and workforce, through the setting of satisficing targets or the programming of actions according to simple decision rules. After an initial outlay in organisation and programme design such arrangements save on information-processing and co-ordination costs. For relatively large firms, disavowal of overt profit-maximisation may have the further advantage of avoiding competition regulator pressures to control the firm's prices or, at the extreme, break it up.

Although non-maximising in the static sense, quiet-life models may have dynamic advantages which, if not leading to long-run profit maximisation, may eventually allow them to outperform firms that maximise with a shorter time horizon. The processing of new information where it first arises, on the ground, saves the cost of transmitting it to the centre (then awaiting instructions), and so speeds subunits' adaptation to it. The setting of non-maximising goals for interdependent departments reduces the chance of their trying to maximise incompatible goals. By keeping reported profits down and employment up through their discretionary spending, managers may help avoid the attention of competition regulators. By directing resources towards lobbying and 'capturing' the regulator, they may enhance long-run profit-making potential. Similarly, initially 'unproductive' expenditures such as reorganisation, R&D, multi-skilling the workforce or installing expensive new equipment may turn out to be strategic actions, which enhance the long-run profit flow more effectively than period-by-period maximisation. Expanding output beyond the profit-maximising price may secure long-run competitive advantages, by accelerating learning-by-doing that reduces cost or by driving out early competitors who cannot match the resultant lower market price.

By this route, managerialism may arrive via the market power hypothesis at very much the possibility shown by Vickers (1985) using principal–agent theory: that shareholders who give their managers a degree of autonomy can end up better off than shareholders who insist that their managers maximise profits. This supplements the self-correcting possibility offered by monopoly capitalism: that managers' discretionary consumption spending fills the gap in aggregate demand left by firms' production- and investment-expenditure cutbacks as they monopolise. Malthus's (1821) early-industrial defence of aristocrats – that their apparently frivolous conspicuous consumption kept the economy at full employment – makes a post-industrial reappearance. But the possibility remains open that such resources could be put to better use if invested in capacity and infrastructure outside the sphere of private monopoly corporations.

8.6.1 Technocracies, planning and the 'new industrial state'

The benign possibilities of an oligopolised industrial sector are perhaps most completely explored by Galbraith (1967, 1974), who argues that management's primary motive is to stabilise and expand the firm. This means exerting greater control over its environment, to eliminate the surprises that markets can produce. Suppliers of core labour and materials are brought into the firm, or signed up on long contracts, so that their loyalty and flexibility can be 'bought' with greater security. Technical change is mapped out in the laboratories of large firms, supposedly the only ones able to afford the systematic R&D from which high technologies flow. Finance is internalised by funding investment from retained profits, shareholders being kept acquiescent through generous dividends and a dispersion that prevents them from acting in concert.

Final buyers cannot usually be integrated, but 'consumer sovereignty' is dethroned by extensive advertising outlay, and the unspoken agreement among oligopoly firms not to invade one another's territory or compete too strongly on price. Large corporations cannot routinely dupe their customers into buying products they do not need, or could have bought in better, cheaper versions from somewhere else. But oligopoly (and the convergence of firms' offerings within it) helps them restrict the range of genuine choices available, and market power, through the extra profit it affords to firms and the extra hold it gives them over marketing channels, assists the introduction of new products which customers did not know they wanted to buy. The extent to which firms 'reveal' consumers' preferences, rather than respond to them, is disputed by the economists' traditional depiction of the market but fits well with many empirical studies of innovation. The ways in which, in practice, firms construct consumer preference are not always as overt as is suggested by Galbraith: 'If an individual's satisfaction is less from an additional expenditure on automobiles than from one on housing, this can as well be corrected by a change in the selling strategy of General Motors as by an increased expenditure on the house' (1967: 219). Some adopt *ex-ante* procedures such as quizzing focus groups and sample panels to establish what they didn't know they lacked, or observing existing customers for cumbersome practices that could be simplified with a new product or service, and home-made expedients which could be profitably supplied from outside. Others, especially those in industries with a history of 'production-led' innovation, lean towards an *ex-post* 'scattergun' approach: presenting consumers with a stream of finished new products, and seeing how their backroom bright ideas fare under the Darwinian (WalMartian?) selection of shop-shelf competition. Paradoxically, liberal market theorists tend to praise politicians for recognising an unexpressed public need and offering to fulfil it – 'policy entrepreneurship' (Melnyk 1989: 127) – but confine the firm's approved role to answering those public needs (or wants) that have already been expressed.

Government, dependent on large firms for its tax base if not for its re-election expenses, supports the corporate 'planning system' in several ways. To general benefit, it manages aggregate demand to provide firms with a low-inflation, low-unemployment, high-growth external environment (Galbraith was one of the first, and last, prophets of Keynesianism in North America), uses regulation and anti-trust action to balance the interests of scale economies and competition, and provides the public goods to which corporate charity cannot stretch. With a rather more sectional slant it provides a recession-proof, chauvinistic and none too cost-conscious source of demand to specific firms (especially in the defence and infrastructure fields), brings diplomatic and military power to the rescue of those caught up in foreign troublespots, subsidises 'sunrise' start-ups, accords trade protection to those threatened with a premature sunset, and acts as the backstop for large manufacturers and banks 'too big to fail'.

Inverting Marx, who foresaw that 'the lower strata of the middle class – the small tradespeople, shopkeepers, and retired tradesmen generally, the handicraftsmen and peasants – all these sink gradually into the proletariat' (Marx and Engels

1848/1996: 15) as large-scale industry develops, Galbraith argues that the 'market sector' steadily shrinks as corporate planning takes hold, with shopkeepers, small farmers, personal service providers and a few non-standardised manufacturers being the only groups still fully at the mercy of untamed and unmediated demand and supply.

> The scale of the individual corporation has grown enormously. The entrepreneurial corporation has declined. The technostructure has developed, removed itself from control by the stockholders and acquired its own internal sources of capital. There has been a large change in its relations with the workers and a yet larger one in its relations with the state.
>
> (Galbraith 1967: 381)

With firm-administered transaction, long product cycles and systematic innovation can be pursued with less fear of future boom or slump upsetting them. With the government brought onside as co-ordinator and informant, stable shares of an expanding market deliver interdependent firms from the prisoners' dilemma of battling for shares in a stagnant market. Production and investment planning at corporate level becomes the supply-side complement to aggregate demand management through consumption and state expenditure planning by central government. Firms in the Galbraithian perspective can also take over from (and surpass) the capital market as strategy protectors, so adding to dynamic efficiency. 'There would be no flights to the moon and not many to Los Angeles were market incentives relied upon to bring into existence the necessary vehicles' (Galbraith 1967: 349).

The sombre subtext of the 'new industrial state' is that life in the residual market sector – small industrial firms, agriculture, local services, unskilled labourers, the self-employed – is one of low pay, long hours, poor conditions, uncertainty and insecurity. Government's other main task, having stabilised the macroeconomy for the large corporations, is to tax them and their employees so as to offer sufficient economic and social protection to those not so fortunate in fleeing the 'invisible hand'. The more successful is the majority in escaping into the demand-regulated, entry-protected comfort of the industrial planning system, the harder it is to persuade them into civic (and taxpaying) duties on behalf of the unprotected minority (Galbraith 1992). A further danger is that the corporate sector's success (through capital mobility, lobbying and clever accounting) at reducing its own and its employees' tax burden starves the government of funds with which to provide complementary public infrastructure, social services, other public and merit goods, and the economy- or sector-level stabilisation efforts corporations need when their planning calculations go awry.

The wide print (and television) exposure enjoyed by this and other 'institutionalist' analyses ensured their condemnation by mainstream economists, but history has not been kind to the thesis either. Large corporations have not proved immortal, especially where forced to dwell in an international economy largely beyond their planning horizons. Governments have not proved infallible fine-tuners of the macroeconomy. Small firms have reasserted their ability to innovate, often turning giant rivals from dynamos to dinosaurs in the process. Shareholders have hit back against managers who pursue growth or gratification at the expense of profit, while managers have found their own problems keeping underlings' motivation aligned with their own. But this and the other managerial perspectives have established their fundamental point, that large firms with price-setting ability are an irremediable feature of mature economies, with an impact on macro- as well as microeconomic performance. While there may be arguments over what big business does with its power, few still dispute the existence or importance of that power.

8.6.2 Stakeholding: sharing the spoils of imperfection

All the market-power models considered so far are essentially redistributive, benefiting some sections of the economy at the expense of others (compared with the distributinal arrangements a fully conmpetitive economy would produce). The Marxian firm satisfies its owners but exploits its workforce. The market-power firm rewards its owners at the expense of customers and those thrown out of work. The managerial firm is kinder to the workforce (or at least its upper ranks) but short-changes owners, at least those who value current earnings highly. The Galbraithian firm may achieve a satisfactory balance between owners and employees, but manipulates its consumers, and owes part of its stability to the underclass of subcontracted and temporary labour, marginal suppliers, smal distributors and farmers without the privilege of working for (or owning shares in) the corporate planning system.

While hopes that government could redress these imbalances have faded along with the commitments to full employment and redistributive taxation, discretionary profit leaves open the possibility that large firms might themselves take on a wider social mission. Too big to escape its external costs, too dependent on continuous flows and learning-by-doing to afford industrial-relations breakdown or high labour turnover, the 'stakeholder' firm steps beyond an accommodation between owner and employee interests to embrace its customers, suppliers, subcontractors, distributors, the neighbourhoods around its plants and the general social, natural and economic environment in which it operates. 'A company is its history, its structure of relationships, its reputation. These are the things that allow the company to add value, which create shareholder wealth, and to say that shareholders own these things is kind of bizarre. They don't and they couldn't ' (J. Kay 1997). The 'stakeholding' firm combines the information-sharing efficiency of administered transaction with the balance of power and mutual commitment achieved by relational transaction, and hopes to derive mutual empowerment and enrichment gains from both.

As with 'altruism' in the natural world, what is good for stakeholders may be good for shareholders. Making money and doing good are not just the province of charity fundraising: well-treated staff work harder, loyal suppliers turn round the new parts ahead of schedule, happy customers return and impressed local residents don't protest against the site expansion application. Consideration of the firm's wider impact, over space or time, may enable strategies that defend long-term profit (or share value) maximisation at the expense of myopic profit-boosting measures: in particular, loyal shareholders may willingly forgo dividends and protect the firm from hostile takeover threat, reducing its internal cost of capital and making longer-term projects more likely to show positive net present profit, as well as bringing a wider range of projects above the viability threshold. Treating the workforce well can reduce turnover rates and capture the full benefits of training; conserving the environment can avoid an ever more expensive search for vanishing scarce-resource inputs; charitable donations can become a useful source of publicity, and may even be a helpful way to clear old stocks, if given 'in kind'. Growing organically rather than by acquisition can avoid the often deleterious performance consequences indicated by economic analysis of merger (Singh 1971), and corroborated by numerous nightmare tales of culture clashes and balance-sheet bombshells, so possibly rescuing the short-term value maximisers from themselves as much as shielding longer-sighted strategists from their clutches.

A stakeholder firm's 'responsible' image, and its ability to trade off favours with other interest groups, may also win it better political treatment (more lenient planning decisions and regulation, a place on the next trade mission, a helping financial hand if the sacrifice of present profit goes too far). While a case for legislation (to change company statutes or reduce shareholder rights) to enforce stakeholding is sometimes put forward, this is usually to speed the diffusion of better practices, not enforce their creation. Stakeholding pays its own way and brings its own rewards, it is argued, as witnessed by the high profitability of many firms which practise (or at least proclaim) concern for the social and natural environment. This may be reversing cause and effect, with companies being able to featherbed the staff and indulge the clients when profitable but resuming more dictatorial and miserly ways at the onset of crisis (which may itself result from failure to achieve internal cohesion or a co-operative response to external disruption). But some of the most egregious floutings of the value-maximising rule book are also some of the most enduringly successful. Hence the claim that many leading firms already practise stakeholding, and that legislation in ths direction is needed only to generalise their example and prevent a periphery of 'social dumpers' restraining the efforts of the public-spirited core.

However, a consistency between stakeholding and long-run profit-maximisation does not ensure that it will emerge from the existing competitive process. If short-run profit sacrifices are involved, its survival requires a selection process gentle enough to preserve firms which deviate from period-by-period maximisation, or a capital market perfect enough to protect them while they do so. Without these, stakeholding will be confined to those with market power who can afford some short-term profit sacrifice and discretionary spending – power which, as the other theories argue, can equally well be used to take more out of the economy as to put something back in. Any lasting incompatibility between the aims of shareholders and those of other stakeholders implies that stakeholding as currently observed is a privilege of limited monopoly power: only those who take too much can afford to give. So most stakeholding proposals concede that legislative change may be needed to generalise the model. Either existing (limited liability) firms would be obliged to observe a wider range of obligations, or the competitive environment would be modified to ensure stakeholder-enterprise survival. One recurrent proposal (e.g. Hutton 1996, Plender 1997) is to impede the hostile takeovers which at present threaten punishment on any management team which deviates from short-run profit-maximisation.

Where government retreats, corporate governance advances, at least into such areas as training, pensions, local amenity provision and art sponsorship which can directly benefit the firm as well as those around it. But stakeholding's power to substitute for state responsibilities is strictly limited; even as firms in mixed economies are being exhorted to take on a wider role (with tax cuts and a better business environment the main inducement), those in former-communist 'transition' economies are desperately shedding their old obligations of health care, housing, amenity and employment provision to the local community, to survive as subsidies, guaranteed sales and trade barriers disappear. The external benefits of social and physical infrastructure continue to put them beyond the scope of corporate stakeholding. A complementary political stakeholding is needed to rally agents outside the workplace to provide them with sufficient public funds.

8.7   Completing the market: the 'new neoclassical' approach

Neither the old nor the enhanced neoclassical theory of the firm, as outlined in Chapter 7, can easily account for the size, scope and international dimensions taken on by the large corporation. Nor does the focus on transaction cost minimisation through internalisation give adequate attention to the many market-like transactions that take place within large firms, or the restrictions that a firm may place on 'market' transactions outside it. Among the alternatives, however, the monopoly capital approach rests on an uncomfortable balance between the profit motive that drives firms to accumulate and the profit-destroying results of that accumulation, a contradiction whose resultant systemic crisis has been rather long in coming. The managerial approach tends to overstate both the extent to which firms can escape the demands of their shareholders and the incentives they have for doing so.

Out of these perspectives has grown a 'new neoclassical' depiction of the firm, which presents it less as a replacement for the failing market than as a device for restoring the information and co-ordination that cause the market failure.

> Information processing is largely represented in terms of the capacities of different kinds of organisational structure and process to transfer information within an organisation, to move it across the boundaries of an organisation, and to access specific kinds of knowledge and decision making capabilities needed to transform data or information.
>
> (Egelhoff 1993: 188)

From being an island of administered transaction in an ocean of market transaction (Richardson 1960), the firm becomes a more inclusive space within which agents can transact in whichever way best suits their – and the organisation's – purposes: relationally, via the market, using extra information supplied by the firm, or following administrative guidelines set down by the firm.

Where the enhanced neoclassical firm was still an adaptive product of the market, the new neoclassical firm is its progenitor, having some of the external market influence the monopoly capitalism argument alleges, but mainly existing to improve the internal market. Through it, organisations can seek to balance the static efficiency of adapting to present market conditions, which comes of constraining their members' choices, and the dynamic efficiency of anticipating and responding to changes in market conditions, which requires flexibility and innovation on the part of their members. With decision autonomy managed in this way, 'internal differences can widen the spectrum of an organisation's options by generating new points of view. These, in turn, can promote disequilibrium; under the right conditions, self-renewal and adaptation occur' (Pascale 1990: 113). The Walrasian auctioneer has left the market square and entered the corporate boardroom.

8.7.1 The twelve tasks of corporate design

Under this new 'decision-perfecting' characterisation, the firm's main functions are to

- fill in the quality information gaps that may otherwise prevent mutually worthwhile transactions taking place
- allocate tasks so as to minimise interdependence, and so reduce the incidence of arbitrary decisions taken with incomplete information, or computational overload (or avoidance of decision) as complex contingencies are assessed
- reduce interdependence by assigning agents to a role with clearly defined and advertised powers, providing a point of reference if they wish to exceed those powers
- serve as a store of knowledge and past experience which agents can use in seeking, evaluating and assessing actions
- make actions available to selected members which are unavailable to individual agents, and assist with the implementation of chosen actions
- provide the consistency, responsiveness to major external changes and information-processing scale economies that result from remitting certain decisions to the centre
- provide a safeguard against breach of trust in relational transactions, and assisting them to adapt over time through the introduction of new information
- improve the power balance through which relational transaction can be conducted with agents outside the firm
- contribute to informed transaction, and sufficiently delimit agents' responses to new information to ensure that it leads to convergent expectations and consistent action

- design and enforce joint-optimising solutions to collective action problems
- resolve conflicts between short- and long-run optimisation in favour of the long term, and offer strategy protection, in particular by financing intermediate actions which ill-informed external capital markets cannot support
- make possible the co-ordinated price and quantity adjustment which was the missing link between existence and attainment of competitive general equilibrium.

The 'new neoclassical' approach rejects the market-or-plan dichotomy of the old, and thereby the concept of a rationally calculated, precisely bordered firm. It identifies a wider range of transactions over which market transaction suffers cost penalties relative to other types, partly by considering a wider range of types – the relational and informed transactions described in Chapters 6 and 7. It thereby finds a legitimation for market power, as a source of transaction efficiency among individual agents which also reopens the route to socially efficient outcomes. The managerial discretion permitted by market power lets the organisation structure its members' decisions in ways which more closely resemble decisions taken in an open market with perfect and complete information. Structure shapes strategy, reversing the 'enhanced neoclassical' framework in which structure is chosen according to strategy (Chandler 1962).

Since the firm now filters the competitive pressures on its member agents and departments, it is able to protect 'strategic' action which is not continuously maximising, and so achieve a workable compromise between the sometimes contradictory forces between efficient static allocation and the dynamism associated with innovation and growth (section 4.1). Since agents have their action sets specified by, and sometimes take instructions from, the firm, they can also credibly commit themselves to actions which would otherwise be irrational because time-inconsistent. A familiar example is the price war, which two firms in a product-market duopoly may try to avoid by reaching a 'co-operative' game solution where each sets an above-cost price. In a one-shot zero-sum game (section 2.2), each knows that doing this will mean being opportunistically undercut by the rival, who can capture the market by setting a lower price. In an extended game, each can threaten to counter this, and sustain the co-operative solution, by threatening to match any price cut on the next round. But if the payoffs are those of the chicken or reciprocation games (Figures 2.4, 2.5) this threat lacks credibility, because the second player is still better off co-operating on subsequent rounds even if the rival has not co-operated on the first. If marketing strategists can point to the firm's decision rules as a constraint on their action, forcing them to retaliate even if the profit loss is greater as a result, their counterparts may be deterred from making their price cut in the first place – keeping both firms in the higher-profit, co-operative equilibrium.

Workers join the firm so as enjoy the higher pay that goes with working in synergistic teams on increasing-returns processes, the lessened volatility of pay that results from transferring the risks associated with continuous exposure to the external labour market, and access to the capital needed for this, and for other improvements in the power to implement action, unavailable from an imperfect external capital market. The firm invites workers, and other stakeholders, to join it in pursuit of these advantages, in return for the right to set flexible contract terms and take its share of revenues from increased labour productivity. From being viewed as an organism within an environment, the firm itself becomes an environment in which symbiosis as much as synergy is the source of stability. 'Members of different species often have much to offer each other because they can bring different "skills" to the partnership. This kind of fundamental asymmetry can lead to evolutionarily stable strategies of mutual co-operation' (Dawkins 1989: 181).

8.7.2   All alternatives and none: multiple transaction types within the firm

The assumption that all transactions within the firm are administered and all transactions outside the firm market-based, the division resting on whether the efficiency gains of market transaction outweigh its costs, appears to be an oversimplification. Relational and informed transactions also occur, both inside and outside the firm. It is even possible for external transactions to be administered (e.g. by an independent authority recognised by both parties) and for internal transactions to be carried out through a version of the market.

With information enhanced and interdependence reduced by the firm's assignment of powers and responsibilities, agents within it may end up following a transaction decision process which is actually closer to 'rational choice' than that ascribed to agents in open markets. Indeed, internal markets are facilitated by the multi-divisionalisation and multinationalisation identified in the old neoclassical approach. Head offices can avoid the financial and time costs of researching divisions' absolute efficiency by comparing the performance of those working in different product or regional areas. Differences not explained by external conditions become a basis for setting improvement targets for the underperformers, and show the centre where to look for generalisable best practice. Where there is new business to be allocated among divisions (where to produce the next 'world' model, which product area to expand or commission more research in), 'yardstick' competition on past results gives way to genuine internal competition for future resources. This technique has been used especially ruthlessly by multinationals which wish to concentrate nationally dispersed production on fewer sites, and have to choose which plants to close – or wish to use the threat of closure to force all divisions to improve performance. Intra-divisional competition may also be a profit-preserving substitute for competition with rivals, whose entry it can deter (Schwartz and Thompson 1986).

The recent innovative success of small high-technology businesses, especially in electronics and software, has also encouraged large firms to try to replicate small-firm characteristics internally. The first step is often to change remuneration processes to retain the brains which might otherwise leave to start their own firm around their big idea; a $1,000 suggestion-box reward may not be enough for the high-flier whose brainwave could be worth $1 million. The next is to restore other positive aspects of the market which large organisations usually suppress (autonomy, free association, informal budgeting) while continuing to keep out its negative features (financial providers' cold feet, job insecurity, deficiency of the garage as a laboratory). 'Intrapreneuring' does not always succeed, but some corporations have sustained long runs of innovation with it; and the high failure rate of the genuine entrepreneurial article urges caution on the judgement that intra-firm market forces are any more wasteful than those outside. 'Many companies are re-inventing themselves as confederations of entrepreneurs, operating under the main tent of the corporation' (Naisbitt and Aburdene 1985: 63).

By applying market 'tests' to previously administered transactions, many firms have put a price on previously uncosted internal transfers which revises their opinion on the extent of transaction-cost savings. Some transactions have been returned to the market: production units are allowed to buy materials outside if they can be found cheaper, distribution subsidiaries to stock other firms' products, 'non-core' activities from information technology to travel and catering arrangements contracted out. Others have been entrusted to those within the firm who are judged closer to the market.

> The organisation is a dynamic arrangement of functions, services, products, people and physical assets to achieve corporate goals on a continuing basis . . . In tune with the times and the current interest in participation, decision making in many companies has been pushed to lower and lower levels of management and of the entire workforce.
>
> (Rosow 1985: 174, 188–9)

Conversely, the creation of an 'internal market' may also encourage more transactions to be brought inside from the external market, where information is less perfect, less complete and hence less tractable. Internal labour markets have long been used to overcome quality information problems, simplify contingent hiring contracts and internalise the external benefits of training, and internal capital markets to overcome the problems of communicating new-project information to external financiers. Consideration of the price being paid for bought-in materials and equipment has also led to the internalisation of some product markets, if not to replace external suppliers then at least to provide them with additional competition and get a clearer indication of the mark-ups they currently charge.

> The search for universal, uniform recipes on how to manage the transnational or global enterprise would give way to a more complex and variegated view. Not only do parent companies from different home bases display different practices and values, but, within the same corporate group, there may be differences between the parent and each of its overseas subsidiaries, depending on the strength of local institutions, practices and values.
>
> (Hu 1992: 124)

8.7.3 Inside information: the gains from internal labour and capital markets

Gresham's Law of Job Interviews: select the candidate who can't answer any of the questions, because it means they must know something important that they won't divulge until allowed to join the company. Bookham's Law of Recruitment References: select the candidate with the worst references, because that means their past employers wanted to retain them; a good reference is written only if you want someone to jump before they're pushed. These well-tested formulae are not, fortunately, the sole determinant of who gets the job. Friendship with the boss's daughter and freak winds that rearrange the rejected résumé file can also help. Recruitment may have become a profession, but its art still speaks louder than its science. Graphologists and dress consultants will not be seeking other employment any time soon.

The interview invites market failure because neither side can obtain all the information they would like to have about the other, and both sides are motivated to supply the information of their choice. Prospective employers can hear reports, read certificates and study the applicant's own account of their astounding achievements, but cannot know how they will perform on the job until they have been given it. Prospective employees can scan the brochure and hear present staff members wax lyrical about the wonders of the workplace, but they will not find out about the squeaky doors and sixteen-hour days until the contract has been signed. Even learning by mistakes is only 50 per cent effective: recruiters can identify the lowlights they hired much more readily than the high-flyers they left to a rival firm. Perhaps interviews could do worse only if they became a market success, the sale of titles and commissions not having done public services and armies much good in the past.

Wherever possible, companies try to see candidates in action before assigning them a major post. Interviews become day-long assessment courses, tests are set, on-the-job trials are offered, probationary periods are served even after the appointment has been made. But those outside the workforce can still embellish past triumphs and embargo more recent tribulations. The same asymmetry is encountered by the buyer of office equipment, renter of premises and selector of new software: design and specification can be assessed at a glance, but only when put to work and tested at length do the less bright sides come to light. Internal markets in labour and capital equipment allow a company to approach their allocation with a mutual knowledge rarely enjoyed on any foray into the outside factor market. Would-be workers in the wider market can tackle their signalling problem by offering to work for less, or enter at a level below their present status, but only at risk of labelling themselves 'lemons' (section 3.15) whose underpay might cause underperformance (section 2.9.2). Recruitment subsidies may also compensate for the greater risk in taking on an unknown quantity, but can also send an adverse signal because of their usual concentration on the less advantaged and the longer unemployed.

Scope economies build up across time as well as space: a company learns by employing, even as its employees learn by doing. Growth and diversification add to the pool from which the next team can reliably be chosen, and the range of tasks to which it can be confidently put. Only by serendipity or serial retirement to the bar can managers be sure of discovering their receptionist's concealed computer wizardry, or the secretary's Serbian parenthood and burning desire to run the new office in Belgrade. With some specific skills, relational contracts with specialist agencies may provide the screening and certification needed to make a wise choice. But when a recruit is to be invested in, entrusted with proprietary information or written into five-year strategy, the firm that can trade them through its own market has a greater chance of getting what it pays for.

> In Germany's large corporations internal labour markets have become very developed, and employment security has been high by European standards . . . training is not firm-specific, [but] its broad and flexible nature nonetheless makes it a valuable resource which large firms are anxious to retain.
>
> (Lane 1992: 87)

8.7.4   Multiple external transaction types: the firm's fuzzy boundary

Individuals who enter employment with a firm, or sign contracts to trade with it over time, submit themselves to an 'administered' or 'informed' modification of the transaction decision (Chapter 7). The firm may set them a different objective from the one they would follow privately, supply them with a different set of available actions, modify the likely outcome of those actions or their expectation of those outcomes, change the rule for selecting actions, and alter the scope for implementing the chosen action. Or it may leave them to use their own discretion, but supply new information about available actions, their likely effects and the past results of taking them. Each firm continually seeks the balance between the flexibility of dispersed decision-making and the coherence of centralised decision-making that is most appropriate to its particular product area, economic and market conditions, given what it knows of competitors' likely behaviour and what it assumes about future market conditions.

Through this combination of internal transaction types, the firm achieves a coherence with which to approach other (corporate and individual) agents as a single decision-making centre, but can also present itself in different ways to different types of clients. Buyers and suppliers of equivalent size will approach it as a single agent, and may well find themselves dealing relationally or swopping additional information because of their bilateral-monopoly situation and the risk of defection to both sides. Small buyers and suppliers will tend to be referred to the equivalent subunit within the firm, so that what would be a one-sided market transaction if conducted with the head office again becomes a relational or informed exchange with other agents of comparable role and market power. The firm's involvement in a complex project may involve submitting to administration of its final transactions with the project manager, requiring relational co-ordination with its intermediate suppliers and subcontractors, while continuing to buy less important inputs through the market. Similarly, its bid for a large contract will be a purely market-based deal with the agent offering it, but may follow extensive relational exchanges with other potential bidders to avoid a free-for-all and ensure a respectable payoff for whoever wins.

The difficulties of trading information through the market have not, as the enhanced neoclassical view tended to imply, resulted in internalisation of knowledge-intensive transactions. Although many attempts at arm's-length 'technical collaboration' have been abandoned, or given way to full integration between firms, because of their difficulties in sharing commercially sensitive information, more recent patterns of information-technology use suggest that the benefits of internalisation are still being balanced against the savings (in cost, regulatory hassle and monitoring requirements and switching ability) of keeping clients as separate entities. Corporations keep privileged information in their 'intranets' even when these are technically easy to connect with the outside world's extranets and internets, and the interdependency created by electronic data interchange (EDI) with clients may often be more advantageous to a firm than direct administrative power over them. There is a

> need for EDI to be accompanied by closer inter-firm relations, longer-term power-dependent relations whereby customers exert control over suppliers but are themselves dependent on single sources and increasingly on the competitiveness of the supplier . . . EDI requires a scale of effort that is only justifiable for on-going trading relationships.
>
> (Charles 1996: 95)

When the full range of its internal and external transaction types is considered, the large firm appears less an end-state separation of the 'administered' from the 'market' as a process for facilitating and combining different types of transaction. Its boundary is broadened by the wide range of relational transactions between plan and market, and frequently shifts according to market conditions and client type. 'Relational contracting within the diversified multinational corporation and with external partners, customers and suppliers has produced situations where the boundaries of the firm are no longer clear cut' (Doz and Prahalad 1993: 27).

Instead of a clearly distinguished 'organism' reacting to an external 'environment', the firm can be viewed as a zone of self-organisation which tries to interpret, internally reproduce and modify that environment. Previous biological analogies with evolutionary adaptation and homeostasis are replaced by the more recent hypothesis of autopoiesis, under which an organism works to maintain stable internal relations and includes 'the environment' in its system of self-reproduction (Maturana and Varela 1980). Although intended for the study of natural systems, the theory has applications to business organisation because

> the figures and pictures that an organisation produces on market trends, competitive position, sales forecasts, raw-material availability, and so forth are

really projections of the organisation's own interests and concerns . . . it is through this process of self reference that organisational members can intervene in their own functioning.

(Morgan 1986: 241)

The autopoietic firm achieves stability, sometimes mistaken for inertia, through continuous learning and adaptation. This adaptation involves moulding the environment to its needs as much as moulding its needs to the environment, an exercise in market power very much more comprehensive than the standard, static example of monopoly profit-maximisation.

Whereas the previous analogy contrasted 'organic' firms which respond to a changing external environment with 'mechanical' firms that are overtaken by it (Burns and Stalker 1961), autopoiesis suggests that it may be firms that define themselves in relation to their environment that fall victim to rigidity, while those that internalise the environment and try to modify its impact are able to generate the appropriate adaptation. Internalisation corresponds to the use of informed, relational and market transaction inside the firm, and modification to the extension of informed, relational and administered transaction outside the firm. Small disturbances, arising either from (internal) change in decision behaviour or (external) change in the information reaching decision-makers, can be absorbed within the transactions of the immediately affected agents. Larger disturbances have spillover effects on others agents' transactions, and can be propagated to produce wider systemic change.

An understanding of mutual causality in complex systems shows that it is extremely difficult to halt change, to eliminate all positive feedback, or to preserve a given mode of organisation interminably. A more appropriate strategy is to learn to change with change, influencing and shaping the process when possible, but being sensitive to the idea that in changing times new forms of system organisation must be allowed to emerge.

(Morgan 1986: 255)

8.7.5   *From make-or-buy to 'chain integration'*

Management of information, not management of specific human or physical assets, is central to the identity and function of the 'new neoclassical' firm. Since its boundaries can no longer be defined by which transactions are market-based and which administered, there is no necessity for a firm to own (i.e. possess property rights over) the resources it brings together. From being vertically integrated in their early stages (backwards into material and component sourcing, forwards into distribution and retail), and becoming horizontally diversified as they sought to secure scope economies and spread risks, many 'large' firms have been steadily shedding direct control of their operations, making information and co-ordination their sole direct contribution to production. It has been observed for some time that, through relational and informed transaction, many firms occupying one part of a product's supply chain have managed to assert overall control of it. Large grocery retailers displace independent wholesalers, dictate price and quality terms to food-processors, shape the logistics operations of distributors, and even determine the production pattern of farmers, assisted by the dismantling of legal defences such as retail price-fixing by producers and special privileges for small shops. Large automobile makers, from the middle of the chain, set the term for suppliers and control distribution through franchising. Mining groups, from the start of the chain, maintain extensive control over the pricing of precious metals and the use to which they are put – an achievement notably denied to the extractors of petroleum, even though physical forward integration is much more common in this industry.

Attention is now shifting to the possibility of 'chain integrators' taking control of the overall process, without having an ownership interest in any of its stages. Such 'virtual companies' would hold the reins through proprietary product or process designs, information systems to track the product through its stages and marketing techniques reinforced by branding, but with the horsepower coming from licensed manufacturers and distributors held in place by a network of market, relational and administered contracts. Non-ownership of any stage in the chain may even bring competitive advantages – avoiding obvious monopoly elements that might bring hostility from trading partners or investigation by competition authorities, allowing faster adaptation through the reduction of sunk costs, and eliminating the political risk attached to having physical assets in politically unstable countries.

> As competitors increasingly achieve parity in access to resources (including technology) in various parts of the world, sources of competitiveness shift from location-specific factors to firm-specific factors: that is, the overall organizational capability to co-ordinate the use of resources in order to respond to short-lived opportunities that may arise in many different parts of the world.
>
> (Doz and Prahalad 1993: 26)

8.7.6 *From multinational to global enterprise*

If 'chain integration' is an accurate prediction, the multinational enterprise (MNE) may turn out to have been only a transitional stage in the globalisation of production. Direct ownership is needed, as MNE explanations recognise, mainly to overcome the problems of trading information across markets and to achieve the co-ordination by which monopoly advantages can be exercised abroad. Firms acquire their foreign suppliers so as to improve on the terms of a bilateral bargain, and foreclose supplies to rival processors. They take direct ownership of foreign production facilities so as to transfer technological and managerial advantages whose full value cannot be realised through licensing and franchising, and to divide national markets more reliably than collusion or cartelisation could achieve. They buy distributors to communicate new products and brands to an unfamiliar public, and to sidestep vertical foreclosure by rival producers who may control the existing retail chains.

This perspective is closely tied to the view of market and administered transaction as mutually exclusive alternatives, the first occurring outside the firm and the second inside it, with the relative costs of transaction difficulty in the market and incentive and responsiveness loss within the hierarchy causing calculative switches from one to the other. However, through intermediate (relational and informed) transaction types, and the extension of the other types across the firm's boundary, the division becomes more shifting and less sharp. Part of management's task becomes to select the appropriate transaction type for a given situation, or to equip subordinates to do so, as well as to place limits round decisions once their type is chosen. This 'meta-level' of administration further distances management from shareholders, and points towards a new definition of the separation of ownership from control.

The 'global' firms now emerging may well have little or no direct financial involvement in their foreign operations, relying instead on joint ventures, technological and marketing collaborations, or long-term relational contracts reinforced by specific investment on both sides.

> The advent of outsourcing will radically cut the the production role of global producers. They will concentrate their efforts on their core competences as 'what' companies in the areas of product design and market introduction together with chain management . . . The entire supply chain effectively operates as one 'supra' company, that is, on a level of integration above companies.
> (Klapwijk 1996: 65–6)

Information technology, already important in linking the administered component of large organisations' transactions, takes on a crucial role in keeping its new informed, relational and market-based extension under ultimate control.

By maintaining a powerful but respectful distance and letting local operators keep command of local markets, such global firms also escape MNEs' early culture-shock problems: acquiring local knowledge, breaking into local relational networks, overcoming the hostility attending what is seen as overmighty foreign presence. PepsiCo and Coca-Cola, whose cola wars have been extensively fought through franchised bottlers and retailers, and the major parcel-delivery services, may be early examples of global chain integrators whose assets amount to a formula, an information technology system, and a few core staff managing a global network of transactions. The multinational becomes multidomestic, a wordwide presence consisting largely of local transactions, its subdivisions competing as well as co-operating, the size of a planet when the next global product launch is planned and of a local shop when the monopoly regulator calls.

8.8 Keeping the giants competitive

While the firm's role as a transaction-cost minimiser generally allows it to expand beyond the 'optimum' size that would arise from scale and scope economies alone, an upper limit is still placed on its growth by the rising costs of administering and policing transactions outside the market. Once other non-market transaction types are brought within the firm and placed between firm and market, its ability to grow without loss of efficiency is greatly enhanced. Anti-monopoly regulation also appears more difficult, both because of the boundary fuzziness permitted by external relational transactions and internal market transactions, and the spread of activities across national jurisdictions. But in contrast to the 'monopoly capital' prediction, that chain-integrating and globalising forms would enjoy ever-increasing market (and geopolitical) power, the 'new neoclassical' firm is generally regarded as a product – and producer – of escalating global competition as old national, product, labour and capital market divisions are swept away.

The perspective remains neoclassical because managers are constrained to maximise profit (in contrast to the 'satisficing' institutional theories), and because there are still enough market pressures to make them do so through efficiency on the supply side, not exploitation on the demand side. 'Managerial discretion' remains a boardroom daydream; managers who fail to maximise profit will be upbraided by owners who think they should, or replaced by rival-firm bidders who believe they can.

8.8.1 Internal forces for profit maximisation: principal–agent relations

The argument that managers had seized control of large corporations from their shareholders is based on the finding (introduced by Berle and Means 1932 and subsequently replicated for the USA and most other higher-income economies) that most firms' shareholding is highly dispersed and shareholders passive in their exercise of voting rights. Managers' control of company policy through agenda-setting and proxy votes is assumed to lead to departure from profit maximisation (which with a perfect stock-market implies present value maximisation), mainly because of the other managerial motivations (growth, bureau size, perks, etc.) examined in managerial theories. The counterargument against this conflict of interests has four components. First, shareholder power over management remains strong. Second, managers' motivations do not necessarily conflict with those of owners, even if they can be independently indulged. Third, if there is a conflict, owners have ways of realigning managers' motivations with their own. Fourth, even if the capital market cannot constrain managers to maximise profits, there are pressures in the firm's other markets which will force them to do so.

Shareholder dispersion is a two-edged sword: it makes a majority stake more difficult to assemble, but reduces the necessary size of a 'controlling' stake. Professional institutional owners can dominate the voting process at shareholders' meetings with a comparatively small holding, provided other shares are held by inactive individuals. Although pension funds, insurance companies and other institutions tend to intervene rarely, and usually only to change board appointments, this need not indicate surrender to managerial discretion. Where shares are liquid, such holders can use the threat of sale to discipline those directly in charge, forcing them to return at least sufficient profit to pay a regular and rising dividend.

Where owners' commitment is to keeping shares long term, a hands-off attitude to management may still count as maximising if poor short-term performance is consistent with a strategy to enhance profits later. The adverse signals sent by high profit to competition regulators and potential entrants, and the long-run profit advantages of being predictable to other oligopolists (with a credible threat to retaliate if double-crossed), are further reasons why shareholders may stay behind an apparently non-maximising managerial strategy.

This approach need not change if managers have their own agenda, since maximum product may be a necessary condition, if not a joint product, of such alternative aims as maximum security, growth or prestige. If owners know that managers want to follow a contradictory goal, and find monitoring and disciplining threats too expensive a way to stop them doing so, they can attempt a self-enforcing alignment of goals through the design of 'incentive-compatible' contracts. Recognising the cost of monitoring the managerial 'inputs' to profit performance (such as effort and commitment), these generally work by linking the manager's own financial reward to the firm's financial results. Profit-related pay (through managerial share-ownership or profit sharing) is the simplest arrangement. More complicated formulae – to take account of such problems as losses beyond the manager's control, shared responsibility for profit, volatility of profit and avoiding a trade-off between short- and long-run profit maximisation – now form a significant industry for principal–agent theorists and remuneration consultants. Through such measures, shareholding 'principals' may be able to force managing 'agents' to carry out their will even in the absence of close monitoring, with the gain in profits comfortably exceeding the amount that must be passed to managers to keep them on the value-maximising path.

Failure of the present owners to deploy such sticks and carrots does not let managers off the maximising hook, since the firm's share price leaves their performance on continuous display to other potential owners who might believe they can do better. Even if existing shareholders do not threaten to sell, rival firms or financial investors will notice if the firm's market value falls significantly below their assessment of its long-term profit potential, and may launch a takeover bid in which current managers are likely to lose their jobs. Size barriers to hostile takeover have fallen away as the capital market becomes more willing to secure funds against future profit and capital gains, allowing firms or investment vehicles to bid for companies significantly larger than themselves, paying with bank loans, new share issues or high-yield bond flotations.

Similar vehicles may allow the managers of better-performing units to launch buy-out attempts against management they believe is under-resourcing them or using them to cross-subsidise inefficiencies elsewhere. Where shares are floated in the company's operating countries, its subsidiaries' revenue and profit situation has to be put on display, and comes under the scrutiny of investors even better attuned to any gaps between achievement and potential in the local market. The increasing liquidity of markets for the shares against which takeover battles are launched, and of the bonds that finance such bids, may progressively restrict management's scope for a 'quiet life' protected through capital market imperfection.

8.8.2   *External forces for cost minimisation: the persistence of competition*

The pursuit of size, although less effective as a defence against hostile takeover, may give managers an easy route to better profit performance by acquiring and exercising market power. A management's information advantages over the market 'average opinion' may also enable it to play the takeover game to its own advantage, buying assets it can see to be undervalued and selling them off to produce an exceptional profit boost. But the new neoclassical perspective identifies powerful mechanisms by which other markets countervail monopoly, forcing profit maximisation by the socially preferable route of reducing cost schedules and producing at their lowest point. The same forces acting on other firms are argued to reduce the likelihood of asset undervaluation.

'Contestability theory' (sections 2.7, 2.8) has been seen to challenge the traditional structure–conduct–performance link, making firms which look like monopolies still behave like perfect competitors if they fear that pricing for supernormal profit would attract new entrants. This product-market challenge operates directly only if the entrant has higher costs, so that the incumbent can credibly threaten to drop its prices and drive out the newcomer before it can recover the fixed costs of entry. But the removal of trade and foreign investment barriers, the rise of general managers and reprogrammable machinery offering greater scope economies (substitutability in production) and the growing flexibility of consumer tastes for non-essential items (substitutability in consumption) improve the scope for such entry to make a permanent dent in the incumbent's market share and profitability; or, if not, to be followed by relatively costless exit. If it cannot be competed away, a near-monopoly of one product can be sidelined by technical change, as IBM discovered with mainframe computers and Detroit's 'big three' with large gas-guzzling cars.

Rival sellers of a product, actual or potential, can make their presence felt because of consumers' alertness to new offers, and resistance against efforts to lock them into the old. Although rising incomes dampen consumer sensitivity to price differentials – premiums for perceived quality are substantial on clothing, food, automobiles and airline seats – they tend also to raise consumer mobility, within and between product lines. Richer consumers are also generally better equipped to acquire price and quality information, to travel in search of better deals, and to seek to reverse or get redress for transactions they consider unsatisfactory. The greater flexibility and productivity that organisations have won from the public as a workforce is to some extent bought at the expense of greater fickleness and selectivity from the public as clientele.

Rising labour mobility, resulting in part from human-capital investments made in employees by firms and government, also means growing competitive discipline from the skills market. Although the seller's market for labour is currently confined to a small group of highly trained workers in most economies, the coming demographic decline may serve to extend it to lower levels even if rising productivity, slower growth and 'grade inflation' prevent a return to full employment.

Hard-to-replace labour skills present a countervailing monopoly to that tradition-ally enjoyed by recruiters. Upward pressure on market real wages, and on the 'relational' premium that firms must pay to keep workers motivated, flexible and loyal, are a further motive to reduce costs in other areas, once product-market com-petition becomes too intense to pass on pay rises as price rises.

8.9   Keeping the giants awake

As well as shielding the wider economy from monopoly power when at its height, these internal and external sources of discipline shelter the large firm from the often painful legacy of monopoly power. Too long at the top has traditionally been seen as turning the frm into an introspective, inflexible organisation, whose survival is threatened when its market is invaded on the supply side or deserted on the demand side. Firms with the greatest means to adapt and change – sufficient profit to finance R&D spending, long-term restructuring, or the buying-in of new ideas not invented internally, and top management freedom to think strategically – are often those with least incentive, because short-range innovation might snatch profits from the current product range and long-range innovation carries unac-ceptable risks. On the obverse side, crisis-hit firms least well positioned to innovate often have the strongest incentive to do so. Bosses, like the rest of us, tend to settle for sure gains but gamble against sure losses (section 5.2.5).

The new neoclassical firm is argued to be resilient to such a 'winner's curse' for two main reasons. Its shifting transaction structure appears to strike a sustainable balance between absorbing small shocks and responding to larger shocks, so that top management is relieved from 'fighting fires' at the operational level but is alerted to strategic bomb-drops which require a response across the organisation. And as well as being receptive to changes in pressure from without, the relative autonomy of agents brings a steady stream of possible adaptations from within. Some of these arise deliberately, from strategic behaviour promoted by the firm in the areas of research, marketing initiatives, 'intrapreneurship' and collaborations with other firms. Some arise accidentally, like mutations in bio-evolution, from the discovery of new actions, new outcomes or new outcome utilities in the course of taking more routine decisions. This leaves the firm with a store of alternative behaviours which can be tried out in response to exogenous changes in conditions, or even tested proactively to see if they bring better results in existing conditions. The firm continues to generate alternative action possibilities even when its current actions are doing it well. This is assumed to improve its chances of surviving the loss of current advantages, and may even allow the next source of advantage to be pre-emptively launched.

8.9.1   Defending diversification

By diversifying, the firm assuages a longstanding objection to the efficiency of internalisation: that internal factor markets are second-best substitutes for the external version because they trap labour and capital in a narrow range of uses circumscribed by the firm's growth and acquisition heritage, preventing them from flowing to higher-return uses outside the firm. 'Low-profit firms still re-invest in themselves, not rival high-profit firms. Until they diversify . . . internal funds do not have the profit-maximising constraint of external funds' (Thurow 1980: 174). However, diversified firms came under repeated challenge during the 1980s and early 1990s from stock-market raiders who believed (and often proved) that their management had spread itself too thinly to achieve synergies or scope economies, so that a profit could be made from breaking up and re-selling the separate assets. The new neoclassical firm reduces its vulnerability to such attacks initially by dispersing the ownership of its assets among areas of operation, and ultimately – as the chain integration role takes over – by divesting from them, focusing investment on intellectual property and the information systems that transmit its commands. Whereas assemblages of physical assets can sometimes be undervalued in the market because synergies have been overlooked, or different units prevented from maximising because of an imperfect fit between them, the form as a collection of less tangible, organisational assets tends to be worth more than the sum of its parts.

Predators are deterred first by the difficulty of attaining control, and second by the danger of loss if part of the organisation breaks away (or has to be divested to meet competition requirements) as a result of the acquisition. Firms that might previously have tried to gain control of a rival may even settle for entering a closer, more co-operative relationship with it, the hope being to exploit assets without acquiring them or, in the case of skilled teams, entice them to join having established their suitability and without needing to bid for associated physical assets.

8.10 The 'new neoclassical' firm: a Japanese paradigm?

The corporate form described as 'old neoclassical', most thoroughly documented by Chandler (1962, 1977) and Williamson (1975), was suggested (section 8.2) to be heavily influence by North American experience. Contrasting characterisations have been developed of European and North Asian enterprises, which essentially amount to different ways of solving market information problems within a restricted transactional space. The Asian way, of which Japan's has received most attention, appears to lie in bridging the gap between market and administered transaction with a widespread use of relational transaction, both inside and outside the firm. 'Market principles penetrate resource allocation in the organisation and organisational principles creep into resource allocation in the market' (Imai and Hoyuki 1996: 293). Informed transaction is also prevalent in certain industries, with firms acting as informants for their own employees' transactions and the government (especially the Ministry of International Trade and Industry, MITI) as informant for transactions by firms themselves.

Aoki (1988, 1992) identifies the American pattern as a hierarchical 'A-Mode . . . a centralised information-processing mechanism, specialised job demarcation, and a market-oriented incentive mechanism' (Aoki 1992: 42). This is contrasted with the 'J-mode . . . a decentralised, inductive information-processing mechanism, a fuzzy structure of job demarcation, and an organisationally-oriented personnel administration.' In contrast to the clear visions and tight control exercised by A-mode central managers, on the basis of information channelled to the centre, J-mode central management sets only the broad outlines of policy and relies on dispersed employees to fine-tune the company's objectives. Close monitoring and regular reallocation of personnel is used to ensure compatibility between the actions of units acting on decentralised information.

Various explanations have been advanced as to why North American corporations appear geared to channelling resources to radically new technologies and maximising production efficiency in very old technologies – corresponding to the market's static efficiency advantages – while their Japanese rivals seem geared to the incremental improvement of already discovered technologies which is the source of dynamic advantages and high rates of growth. Historically, there is Japan's long struggle to 'catch-up' western technology, and the second-mover advantages of adopting technologies already tried elsewhere. Economically, there is the high savings rate and cheapness of long-term capital, encouraging low discount rates and the pursuit of incremental strategy. Sociologically, there are traditions of 'reciprocal obligation' which make it difficult for managements to sack redundant workers, and lead firms to maintain a flexible internal labour market through which they can instead be shifted to other plants or occupations. The resultant improvement in incentives, skills and labour productivity may yield gains in productive efficiency in the resources' chosen use which outweight the loss of allocative efficiency from removing their use from market discipline. 'It is in the second dimension, in its effect in making "best practice" better and more widely diffused, that the Japanese system of relational contracting has merits which, I suggest, more than compensate for its price-distorting consequences' (Dore 1996: 374).

From a more negative economic angle, there are extensive regulations enshrining labour rights and limiting product- and financial-market competition, reinforcing the entry and exit barriers often created by relational transaction. Limited regional and occupational and inter-firm wage variation, enforced by labour unions with the help of state regulations, defends internal labour markets and firm-sponsored transferable training from the poaching of employees. Culturally, there is the strong emphasis on community and co-operation which makes long-term relationships as customary in transaction as in family or social life, counting against any concept of a 'market' for labour and making it a matter of honour to retain surplus workers even when they cannot be usefully redeployed. A similar cultural value placed on seniority may lead to pay being raised in line with age and job tenure even when productivity is indistinctly or inversely related to these.

The cultural explanation, which also makes for close relationships between big business and its upstream suppliers, downstream buyers and government, has gained ground as similar patterns take shape elsewhere in Asia. 'Chinese companies are family-run networks based on ownership by kinsmen as much as on shareholdings across companies, while the South Korean chaebol incorporates within one organisation a vast cluster of related enterprises . . . Similar variants can be seen in Thailand, Taiwan, Indonesia, Singapore and Malaysia' (Hutton 1996: 275). Probing deeper, Fukuyama (1995) contrasts the Japanese business-building tradition, based on affinity with non-family members which he classifies as 'high trust', with that of China and Korea, whose dependence on kinship ties (reinforced by those of region and educational background) is taken as a symptom of 'low trust'. The first is inclined away from markets and formal contracts because it does not need them (and using them would signal lack of trust), the second because it cannot make them work. Both, with judicious 'administrative guidance' from government, lead to firms which are formally smaller than their US equivalents but whose informal networks spread very much wider, and have allowed them to multi-nationalise with even greater speed.

8.10.1 Rule-governed versus relationally governed structures

Where US companies pursued the division of labour to the point of having separate quality inspectors and line managers, the Japanese tended to keep such tasks as quality-consciousness and discipline within the individual task, with ultimate benefits in terms of combining low cost with high reliability. The US rule-book tendency, clearly specifying employees' and subunits' tasks to avoid any duplicated or cross-purpose activity, and giving them clear financial incentives to perform them efficiently, contrasted with Japanese concern to let employees respond to changed circumstances on their own initiative, and reluctance to link remuneration to individual or even team results. The US structured approach requires a high degree of information-gathering, instruction-giving and financially-based monitoring by the centre, which also tries to use this information to preserve dynamic efficiency through a clear knowledge of when, where and how to make major product, process and organisational changes. In contrast, the Japanese corporation tries to augment the market's learning and adaptation efficiencies while preserving the allocational advantages of decentralised information. When Japanese companies go abroad, they have tended to take relational transacting with them, treating the early forays as a learning as much as a market-capturing experience, and often seeking local partnerships rather than going it alone. Chequered history may have helped: while the war-winning Americans were welcomed into many parts of the world they returned to trade with, Japan's *keiretsu* conglomerates (some still carrying the names and family fortunes of their pre-war *zaibatsu* predecessors) had to maintain a low profile in territories that had suffered under an earlier invasion.

Reflecting the unclear boundary created by plural transaction types, Japanese multinationals initially seemed at once much smaller and much larger than their US counterparts – numbering a much-reduced core staff, but a much-increased totality of employees when considering the long-term suppliers, who were often transplanted along with the main production plant. Similarly, comparisons showed leading Japanese manufacturers with ratios of production to non-production staff whose superiority was much in excess of their productivity differential. This statistical disparity has been reduced, but mainly by the trend towards contracting-out and relational hiring-in by European and US firms. Japanese firms have been reluctant to acquire firms abroad, and their experience when they do so has not been a happy one. However, 'organic' overseas growth has its price, not just through the greater time taken to establish ground-up and grounded operations, but in the risk of beating beaten by more market-based competitors. Honda spent several years building close relational links with the car maker Rover Group in the UK, only to see Germany's BMW acquire it, exposing a vulnerability which may have been one of Fujitsu's motives for vertically integrating after a long supply relationship with UK computer-maker ICL.

Suspicion that the Japanese transaction system is underpinned by regulation has already been noted (section 6.6), and there are other signs that Japan is being forced closer to US patterns – by the removal of trade barriers, shareholder demands for post-crash recompense (reinforced by capital market deregulation), skilled employees' demand for higher differentials and clearer job definition, and the difficulty of retaining labour against a background of slower growth. The stronger yen and the Asian neighbours' invasion of third markets means that, when the domestic economy revives, the *keiretsu* will find themselves conducting at home the battles which previously took place on more neutral foreign territory. Now that catch-up has largely been achieved, such growth must come largely from home-grown innovation and from the replication of leading sectors' productivity gains in the still subsidised, protected and overstaffed transport, service, agricultural and retail sectors. The economy's slowness to respond to an unprecedented combination of monetary and fiscal expansion and exchange depreciation in the mid-1990s casts some doubt on how quickly these new sources of expansion can be achieved.

Despite this, the large Japanese firm begins with a closer approximation to the 'chain integrators' and 'global corporations' now foreseen in management literature, and business-school assessments of Japan's future still tend to be more rosy than economists'.

> In complex manufacturing US companies typically do well in the start-up phase . . . Sheer inventiveness is highly rewarded . . . But soon the market reaches maturity . . . varied products need frequent tool changes, larger inventories of parts, a more skilled, alert, and flexible work force, and better information flows. The Japanese tend to develop massive cost advantages over Americans as industries mature and products multiply.
>
> (Hampden-Turner and Trompenaars 1993: 143–4)

The pathbreakers of Silicon Valley cannot go on doubling microprocessor power for ever, and once it levels off, the system integrators and network builders of Tokyo and Kobe may well be ready to overtake once more.

8.10.2 Credit v equity finance

The dramatic growth slowdown in Japan since the early 1990s, transmitted to its 'high-growth' east Asian partners (notably South Korea, Indonesia and Thailand) by the debt and devaluation crises of 1997–8, has forced a generally negative reassessment of Asian corporate structures and practices as alternatives to the North American model. If the sudden cessation of high growth can be ascribed to external causes – excessive domestic saving no longer offset by sufficient government deficits or current-account surpluses in Japan's case, irrational withdrawal of the capital inflows funding external deficits elsewhere in dynamic Asia – then the woes of the *keiretsu* and *chaebol* are understandable. Borrowing and investment decisions taken on the firm expectation of 5–6 per cent growth will inevitably look foolish when the economy suddenly grinds to a halt. But most (western) explanations for the slowdown assign much of the blame to the large corporations themselves.

By seeking to expand rapidly through outside finance without diluting their trusted-elite or family control, companies are held to have accumulated excessive debt when they should have issued more equity. In Japan's case, debt-financed purchase of real estate entered an upward spiral as inflated assets formed the security for new loans, followed by the inevitable bursting of a bubble which left many banks and enterprises technically insolvent. In the 'tigers' to its south-west, debt-financed overseas investments led to rational panic among foreign creditors over the size of the resultant trade deficits. In both cases, institutionally close – and informationally closed – relationships between locals, corporations and suppliers were seen to have encouraged reckless lending and concealed the extent of balance-sheet overstretch. Cheap credit and insulation from equity market surveillance had allowed lax and often corrupt managerial practices to pass off as long-term strategy, but created the conditions for macroeconomic slump which – extending across the region – caused such strategy to come spectacularly unstuck.

The preference for debt over equity – and for relational debt (bank loans) over market tradable debt – resulted in a highly geared financing structure for many Japanese and East Asian corporates which proved highly vulnerable to the devaluations and bank liquidity squeezes of 1997–8. The result of the 'Asian crises' has been an accelerated move towards greater use of market transaction in capital and labour allocation. Japan in early 1998 announced a 'big bang' deregulation of its equity market which will leave institutional investors much freer to pursue the highest returns, selling out of companies that over-borrow or pay no dividend rather than maintaining traditional loyalties – whose reciprocal benefits are likely to shrink as old anti-poaching rules break down. The severity of domestic and regional recession is similarly forcing Japanese employers to lay off workers, cut training budgets and sever links with long-time suppliers, shrinking their internal labour markets and leaving themselves much more dependent on hiring-in new skills and supplies when expansion resumes. Companies which seemed for many years to be run in the interests of labour, at the expense of return on capital, are now learning from the US bosses they were once invited to lecture. Whether relational or regulatory, strategy protection for the 'Asian growth model' has been seriously eroded. Inability to let long-run advantages survive short-run competitive threats may be one of the failings of the market-trading system (section 4.1); but once future victors are nipped in the bud, it is a failing that may never be known except as bankrupt-corporate counterfactual.

8.11 Conclusion: thinking globally, transacting locally

The information problems surrounding neoclassical competitive general equilibrium, and the attendant constraints on individuals' exercise of 'rational' choice, have given rise to a new theory of the firm as an organisational structure designed (or evolved) to modify agents' decision processes and co-ordinate the transactions that result. It does this by structuring their decisions to minimise their exposure to imperfect and incomplete information, sharing knowledge among them to overcome incomplete information, and simplifying their decision processes to prevent the enriched information set falling prey to any bounded rationality. The result is accepted by agents because it expands their scope for effective action and rewards them for any departure from private motives, but also rewards the firm by allowing it to organise more coherently for transactions beyond its boundaries. True to the neoclassical vision, organisational defusion of information, co-ordination and trust problems can also push the whole economy back towards optimum allocation, full employment and faster growth.

From being an island in the market-transaction ocean, too small to drag it away far into the backwaters of imperfect competition, the firm is now granted a rather larger presence in order to steer it away from the rocks of imperfect information. The 'new neoclassical' corporation is an island of AT surrounded by an archipelago of RT, still in an ocean of MT, but one well plied by the IT fleet spreading news among the landmasses that intersperse the waves of the invisible hand. Although rather wider than those permitted by the previous domain defined by transaction-cost economies, the firm's borders are now also more porous, allowing market transaction to move back inside even if some administered transaction also leaks out. This, and newly sharpened external competitive forces, prevents even apparently dominant firms from exercising monopoly power, except where this yields long-run and external benefits through investment and innovation.

Until tested in a serious world recession, the suspicion must remain that the 'new neoclassical' firm as depicted is a product of sustained upturn since the late 1980s' financial shocks. If and when innovation slows down, trade barriers go back up and the next decisions must include sacking some of the employees currently taking them, older corporate structures could re-emerge.

> During downswings in business cycles, companies may tend to move in the direction of centralisation to conserve and better control resources and to reduce personnel; during upturns, they may go in the opposite direction to encourage innovation and reduce the time required to take advantage of local opportunities that may arise quickly.
>
> (Martel 1988: 237–8)

Something of this kind may already be happening in corporate Japan, now adjusting to possibly permanent slower growth and higher capital costs. But when its physical assets are stripped away, the firm is a system of power to order and reorder its own (and client) agents' transaction patterns. Even a decentralised transaction pattern is the result of central choice and, with administered and informed trade coexisting beside market and relational forms, a simple reweighting of transaction types could re-equip the form for more deprived, dictatorial times.

Through the switch to the new neoclassical view, corporate strength that once threatened to overpower the competitive market model from within is now recast as its rescuer. Seen in this new light, the giant corporation also squares the model's apparently vicious circle, combining the potential for efficient deployment of resources in current best-practice uses and their efficient redeployment to better uses, as well as raising the speed at which therse new uses are found. In the process, the corporation transcends national boundaries and, in defiance of 'institutionalist' arguments, sheds national government as its political and macroeconomic ally. Government's role as anti-trust regulator, public goods and infrastructure provider, income redistributor and industrial promoter is similarly sidelined. It is to the market's latest dethronement of its traditional antagonist, government, that the final chapters turn.

9   The international market

The world's your trust-buster. Opening the national market to external competition offers a short cut to further scale economies and a ready-made source of discipline for domestic monopoly power. But the international dimension throws into sharper relief the tension between the market's allocative, full-employment and growth-maximising missions, and reaping the gains from free trade has proved a serious collective-action problem. While all-round benefits from letting imports flow have been among economists' most enduring claims, their initial 'comparative advantage' demonstration was essentially short-term and static. 'Dynamic' comparative advantage appeared to rely on giving markets a push, if not forcibly changing their direction. A short-run model bringing equilibrium to a world of constant-returns technology on the assumption of full employment sat uneasily alongside a long-run model which based some of the biggest trade gains on increasing returns.

Recasting the gains from specialisation according to factor-supply conditions extended the applicability of the standard model, but still ignored the possibility of protective strategy to anticipate changes in the price of factors, and new technologies that substitute one for another. The case for trade barriers persisted, aimed at changing comparative advantage and promoting industries based on future factor and product market conditions. A new 'competitive advantage' perspective brought static and dynamic considerations together, but reintroduced a role for government in building a supply side better adapted to the international division of labour.

Just as arguments for free markets in a national economy have shifted from their immediate allocation advantages to their long-term encouragement of adaptation, innovation and technical progress, the case for global free trade rests increasingly on the dynamic pull of scale economies and superior techniques. The requirement for an efficient capital market, as a bridge between static and dynamic efficiency, is reinforced, and the cross-border capital flows for which trade was once presented as a substitute now emerge as a vital complement. Multinational enterprise provided an early way round controls on cross-border capital flow, but market-oriented governments are now committed to removing them. Whether footloose capital will carry them or trample them has yet to be discovered.

9.1 Static free trade gains: comparative advantage

Traditional arguments for the gains from trade are best illustrated by returning to the competitive general equilibrium model (section 2.1), and imagining the scatter of consumers and firms to be territorially divided into two or more groups. Each group contains many firms with the same product and technological options, and many consumers with the same preferences and labour capabilities, so that each enjoys perfect competition on both sides of the product and factor markets. However, geographical separation maintains some systematic differences between the groups, in terms of preferences, technologies, and factor and input availabilities.

One way of completing the market, and maximising the allocative gains, would be to let the two groups mix. Preferences could then be harmonised, technologies transferred, factors allowed to migrate and inputs traded from where they are relatively plentiful to where they are relatively scarce. But such mass movements of people and production knowledge may be neither logistically possible nor culturally desirable. Traditional trade theories show that free exchange between the groups will, through appropriate adjustment of prices and of the exchange rate between their two currencies, achieve the same economic optimising effects without losing the political and social advantage of national boundaries. Welfare gains are achieved as if all were part of one national market, and free movement of goods achieves the same distributional results as would the more problematic free movement of people.

Ricardo (1817/1953) is credited with the first formal model of gains from international specialisation, in which national differences arise from different access to technical knowledge. This results in national productivity differences, which may well mean that one nation outperforms another in all industries. They can nevertheless gain by specialising wherever the relative productivity advantage is greatest, provided there is no attempt to block trade between them.

	(Labour) cost per unit of:	
	Cloth	Wine
England	100	120
Portugal	90	80

Figure 9.1 Gains from trade via different technologies

In the basic case (Figure 9.1), Portugal has an absolute advantage in the production of both wine and textiles, requiring less labour than England to produce a unit of either. In neoclassical terms the two countries have different production functions, both of Portugal's lying above England's because it can produce more of either product with the same amount of labour. However, England has a comparative advantage in textile production. To produce another unit of wine it would have to give up $120/100 = 1.20$ units of cloth, whereas Portugal gives up only $80/90 =$

0.89 units. So free trade results in complete specialisation, with England exporting cloth in exchange for Portugal's wine, provided the barter exchange rate is set somewhere between these two internal cost ratios.

Perfect competition and constant returns to scale are assumed in this example, so that average production costs equal prices and are unchanged when production expands or contracts (MC=AC=AR=MR in the shorthand of section 2.1). Full employment is also required, so that expansion of one sector draws labour from the other, the social opportunity cost of employing it in the first being its marginal (= average) productivity in the second. Although mobile between uses within their country, factors are immobile between countries: English capitalists are unable to acquire the superior Portuguese technology, and English labourers cannot secure higher income by emigrating to work alongside the better-equipped Portuguese. At the time this appeared a realistic assumption. Although international labour migration was beginning to take off, especially between Europe and America, international capital movements, even within Europe, did not become significant until the second half of the nineteenth century. In contrast, the significance of international trade was already apparent. 'Between 1780 and 1840 the total international trade of the western world more than trebled; between 1780 and 1850 it multiplied more than fourfold' (Hobsbawm 1962/1977: 211).

Ricardo's main message is that free trade serves all countries' interests, replicating the benefits of international factor movement without its social and political stresses. Protectionism, through blocking trade or setting an inappropriate exchange rate, can raise the incomes of part of a population only at the expense of the whole. Total production (and hence welfare) are raised under free trade because nations can buy more with the surplus from producing only what they are best at than they could make if they continued producing what they are less good at. Certain products can be imported for less than the opportunity cost of of producing them at home, and the resources so released can be transferred to uses where their domestic productivity is maximised.

Technology and technical knowledge have become more internationally mobile since Ricardo wrote, but similar trade gains can be shown to arise when national differences are traced to the availability and relative prices of factors of production. In the still standard model ascribed to Heckscher, Ohlin and Samuelson (HOS), comparative advantage is enjoyed by nations with a relative abundance of one factor in products whose technology intensively uses that factor. Capital and labour, the principal factors, are again assumed mobile between domestic sectors (so that their availability reflects in relative prices) but internationally immobile.

Nations now specialise in products which make intensive use of the factors with which they are best endowed. Specialisation is not complete, because diminishing marginal rates of technical substitution are assumed to give rise to the concave production-possibility frontier shown as FF in Figure 9.2. But from producing a balanced combination of products A and B under autarky, where internal price ratio is Pa, the capital-abundant country's opening to international trade at price ratio Pt allows a shift towards specialisation in product capital-intensive product B

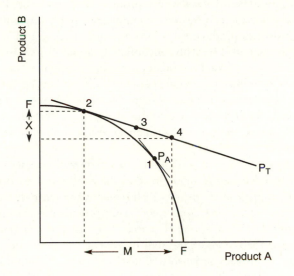

Figure 9.2 Gains from trade via different factor availabilities

at point 2. The country could now, if it wished, consume more of B along with the same amount of A (point 3). However, its higher real income leads to some reallocation of spending, so that more of both goods is now consumed at point 4. By exporting amount X of B, the country can import amount M of B. The reverse case (with a production frontier showing less B for each unit of A) would show its trading partner becoming an importer of B and exporter of A.

Through specialisation, demand for each factor rises in the country where abundance had made it relatively cheap, setting off a competitive equalisation of factor prices first formalised by Samuelson (1948). Trade according to relative factor availability thus replicates the long-run effects of capital and labour migration to the regions where profit and wage rates are initially highest. Free movement of products substitutes free movement of people, a swop most governments – especially those with poorer neighbours across porous frontiers – have been grateful to make. Like Ricardo's, the HOS model assumes full employment, constant returns and perfect competition, the main difference being that technology is now transferable (each country would have the same production frontier if it had the same factor endowment), and that the opportunity cost of one product in terms of another is assumed to increase with its output, reflecting diminishing returns to factors in a particular use.

Both free-trade models were influential in the policy debates of the time, supporting lobbies which knew that trade-barrier removal would be good for themselves but wanted to show that it would also be good for the whole nation, and those who chose to trade with it. Ricardo's British industrial contemporaries were fighting a long (and ultimately successful) campaign to lift agricultural barriers, especially against imported American grain. Protectionism had been prescribed by previous 'mercantilist' theories as a way to promote national wealth by substituting imports, running a trade surplus and accumulating gold. Once they had integrated backwards into production, the merchants recognised that grain tariffs raised landowners' incomes by artificially inflating the staple food price. Industrial profits were thereby depressed (by inflation of the subsistence wage level under Ricardo's theory, by reduced aggregate demand for manufactures under later perspectives). Tariffs were shown to raise the income of certain sectors at the expense of the rest. Commercial pressure led to the scrapping of the British 'corn laws', sparking much political realignment between agrarian- and industrially based parties, in 1846.

HOS modifies the picture of sectional income redistribution, showing (through the related Stolper-Samuelson theorem) that the tariff on a particular product raises the relative income of the factor which is relatively intensively used in making it. Since free trade equalises factor prices, tariffs provide a means to defend the income to factors which are relatively scarce. Thus landowners gained from the corn laws because these boosted the rent to agricultural land; the peasants who worked on it were not necessarily so well favoured. A tariff on relatively labour-intensive products might in support from labour unions in the sector, but still disadvantages the wider economy. Once again, protectionism is shown to enrich a minority at the expense of the majority. Trade liberalisation is associated with political liberalisation, protectionism with the sectional interests wishing to stop the beneficial reassignment of resources.

9.2 Criticising comparative advantage 1: static disadvantages

Global free trade has generally been advocated most enthusiastically in relatively economically advanced countries, and viewed most critically in countries which are seeking to catch them up. The first set of objections relates to the assumptions needed to make the model generate all-round welfare gains. The second relates to the static nature of those gains, and the possibility that they enshrine a specialisation which permanently advantages nations with a head-start in capital accumulation and technology acquisition.

9.2.1 Income redistribution

A move to free trade raises a nation's total income, but not necessarily that of all its citizens. The sectors that had benefited from protectionism lose out under Ricardo's scheme, and the owners of scarce factors under HOS. This presents no social justice problem if the losers had an undue privilege to start with; even if they did not, restoring of their lost income by domestic subsidy may be more economically efficient than maintaining it through protection (Caves 1987). But in conventional welfare-economic terms it is not a Pareto improvement, even if a large majority is enriched at the expense of a small minority, unless the winners compensate the losers so that all are absolutely better off.

9.2.2 Unemployment

The basic models assume full employment before the move to trade specialisation, and a labour market flexible enough to maintain full employment as specialisation occurs. If unemployment were to arise at any stage during the process, a nation might make welfare gains by using trade barriers to divert demand from imports back onto domestic supply, or by devaluing its currency until domestic supply is cheaper than those imports. Whether unemployment is ascribed to the real wage being 'too high' or domestic demand being too low, its existence would invalidate the strong welfare claims for trade theory.

Opening an economy to trade may also cause it to lapse from full employment, although within the theory this can happen only if there is real wage rigidity. Recent studies of unemployment in higher-income economies still tend to ascribe most of it to deficient demand or domestic supply side problems (skills mismatch, capital substitution, poverty traps) but there is some evidence to suggest that a certain amount of low-skilled employment has been displaced by competition from lower-wage economies.

9.2.3 Exchange rate volatility

Economists disagree on what constitutes an 'equilibrium' exchange rate – it might be the rate that balances the current account (flows of goods and services), the overall balance of payments (offsetting a current account surplus/deficit with its opposite on the capital account), or a rate which equalises common-currency price levels for equivalent products in two currency areas (purchasing power parity, whose results depend on which products or product baskets are chosen and which local prices assigned to them). Markets are equally divided, and concern about the volatility of exchange rates has grown as speculative trade in currencies comes to dominate that used for 'underlying' product trade. For governments that have come to regard even a low and predictable rate of domestic price inflation as a source of uncertainty and damage to business confidence, very sudden, wide and unpredictable swings in exchange rates are often seen as one 'free market' too far. Without exchange controls, the inflow of speculative capital in response to a rise in interest rates can expand the monetary base and so defeat attempts to restrain inflation, and foreign financial investors' need to be sure of a currency appreciation to offset falling real interest rates which can cause the exchange rate to overshoot when small corrections are attempted with a view to balancing underlying trade (Dornbusch 1976).

However, fixing (or setting rules for) the exchange rate, as was attempted by most of the world until 1973 (until the US trade deficit forced it to devalue the dollar anchor) and the European Union (whose exchange-rate mechanism has gone through several narrow-band phases and is due to give way to currency unification for qualifying members in 1999), carries equally serious policy costs when capital is mobile. Monetary policy is deflected from domestic to currency-management concerns, external deficit countries being especially vulnerable to having to raise interest rates to defend the currency wherever they are in the business cycle. Fiscal policy must stay consistent with monetary policy, with an expansion that raises real interest rates running the risk of boom as foreign funds flow in, assured against downside currency risk. Surplus nations, meanwhile, may be able to use their exchange rates as a substitute for protection, investing abroad to stop the current-account surplus forcing a revaluation. External-deficit nations' inability to force those in surplus to realign their currencies upwards – being forced instead to devalue – was a principal reason why post-war fixed exchange rates were renounced and not revived.

9.2.4   Optimum tariffs

With constant returns and perfect competition, the expansion of national production that accompanies specialisation does not alter the relative prices that gave rise to it. A nation's terms of trade – the ratio of export to import prices – are assumed not to change when it abandons protection and starts importing the products in which it has comparative disadvantage. However, where one nation buys a significant proportion of a product's export, and its demand is price-elastic on the international market, imposition of a tariff can shift the terms of trade in its favour. The optimum tariff then benefits both government (through tariff revenue) and private buyers (through cheaper imports) in the importing nation, at the expense of the exporting nation, whose income falls as a result of poorer terms of trade.

9.2.5   Capturing foreign monopoly rents

Usually confined to large nations buying demand-inelastic (commodity) imports from small nations, the optimum-tariff argument takes on more general applicability when the import is supplied by an oligopoly industry. Provided it is not too large, the tariff will be absorbed by the exporter's margin, leaving price unchanged but shifting some of the oligopoly rent to the importing country. The importing country gains from the tariff even though there is a net loss of welfare for its trade partner, and for the world.

Even if it causes some loss of consumer surplus through higher prices, the additional domestic profit resulting from application of the tariff raises domestic producer surplus and so produces potential welfare gains for the nation as a whole. A redistributive tax on the newly favoured domestic firm may then help to compensate consumers. This spreading of gains may occur automatically if the higher profit rate for existing domestic producers causes new firms to enter, pushing prices down to offset any rise in the import price (Venables 1985).

9.2.6   Mismatching trade patterns and factor reversals

Specialisation according to internal prices based on comparative factor endowments fitted the pattern of international trade in its initial growth phase, when industrial nations exported capital-intensive manufactures to agricultural nations, which exported labour-intensive natural resource products in return. Its applicability to the more recent period has been less clear, since growth has been fastest in 'intra-industry' trade among (industrial) economies with similar factor proportions, and countries with an apparent labour surplus have increased their exports of capital-intensive products.

Capital-rich countries have also been observed to export labour-intensive products, a tendency first empirically verified by Leontief (1953, 1956), whose input-output study of how US production patterns varied with trade volume suggested that labour-intensive sectors would account for most US export expansion, despite its having the world's highest per capita fixed capital. Once it had been corroborated, several explanations for the Leontief paradox were advanced. The USA may have been exporting products which made intensive use of better educated or more highly skilled labour, with which it was comparatively well endowed. It may have been exporting new products in the early stage of their life-cycle, whose production was labour-intensive during process refinement but would become capital-intensive later (before being transplanted to a lower-wage economy). It may have been exporting products which were relatively intensive in a third production factor (e.g. knowledge, raw materials), not captured in the labour-capital framework. Or assessments of relative labour and capital intensity may have been incorrect.

The final explanation echoes the 'Cambridge' criticism of capital aggregation encountered in section 2.9.3, which attacks the logic of the Stolper-Samuelson theorem and other trade propositions based on intensity of heterogeneous factors. For its explanation of trade patterns to remain consistent, the HOS model must assume a measure of capital that is invariant to changes in income distribution. Without a reliable association between lower interest rates and higher capital intensity of production, it is no longer safe to assume that a factor's price will be relatively lower in economies which use it more intensively, and that countries will specialise in exports of products intensive in the factor that is relatively abundant. Just as the same economy might experience switching back to a previously abandoned 'labour-intensive' technique as profit and interest rates fall, an economy with a lower profit rate – implying capital abundance – might retain labour-intensive industries in its export sector. The dependence of capital valuation on the rate of profit means that the same technique might be capital- or labour-intensive under different distributional arrangements.

9.3   Criticising comparative advantage 2: dynamic disadvantages

The gains from trade exemplify the potential conflict between static and dynamic efficiency identified in section 4.1. Specialisation along HOS lines produces a one-off rise in national income, but subsequent progress – compared with the situation under autarky – depends entirely on how technology, factor proportions and international demands develop subsequently. 'The theory of comparative advantage does not guarantee that because a country has a comparative advantage in a certain line of production at a given time she should grow and expand along these lines' (Sodersten 1980: 164).

9.3.1　*Increasing returns to scale*

Although his own explanation of the pattern of trade, based on absolute cost advantage, soon became a special case of Ricardo's, Adam Smith's more fundamental case for liberalisation was a dynamic one: 'That the division of labour is limited by the extent of the market' (Smith 1776/1979: ch. 3). Division of labour gives rise to economies of scale, but workers can only safely specialise with the assurance of a market for their surplus.

> When the product of any particular branch of industry exceeds what the demand of the country requires, the surplus must be sent abroad and exchanged for something for which there is demand at home. Without such exportation a part of the productive labour of the country must cease, and the value of its annual produce diminish.
>
> (Smith 1776/1979: 472)

Expansion of the market allows a more detailed division of labour, and makes it cost-effective to deploy productivity-enhancing machinery, whose fixed costs can be spread over the higher output (and will anyway fall as rising demand brings the same cost savings to the machine-tool industry). Container ships may have taken over from canal boats, but Smith's historical assessment still rings true.

> By means of water-carriage a more extensive market is opened to every sort of industry . . . it is natural that the first improvements of art or industry should be made where this conveniency opens the whole world for a market to the produce of every sort of labour.
>
> (Smith 1776/1979: 122–3)

Although left out of the Ricardo and HOS models, the association of larger markets with increasing returns to scale (IRS) strengthens the basic case for gains from trade. There is also a damage-limitation aspect: where IRS has given rise to natural monopolies or oligopolies on the domestic market, trade liberalisation can subject these to competition in the much larger world market, provided their product is exportable. By preventing the segmentation of national markets, free trade also puts a stop to monopoly price discrimination: if a firm sets higher prices in one market than another, more than is justified by transport costs, 'arbitragers' will buy low and re-sell high until the differential is closed. Calculations for the gains to be obtained from barrier removal within the European Union market (Emerson 1988) and world agriculture and services markets rely heavily on the driving-down of prices to the lowest initial national-market level, and the achievement of additional scale economies to be gained and the driving-down of world prices towards the lowest national prices now pertaining.

Difficulties arise, however, if competition in IRS industries is sufficient to drive prices down to minimum costs, and if capital markets are imperfect. The first firm or industry to expand into the IRS technology will then have an automatic cost advantage. Increasing returns become a barrier to entry, unless rivals can enter with at least the same scale. Since there need be no link between an IRS industry and any 'natural' condition such as factor endowments, trade patterns may come simply to reflect whoever was first to make a new discovery, realise its commercial potential or offer state assistance to its development. 'Trade need not be a result of international differences in technology or factor endowment. Instead, trade may simply be a way of extending the market and allowing the exploitation of scale economies' (Krugman 1990: 21). The first company to acquire the technology may acquire market power on a world scale, and other countries will be motivated to help their own companies catch up through subsidies and tariff protection (which may also, in the interim, capture some rents from the foreign IRS firm).

The cost-reduction advantages enjoyed by the first firm to embark on IRS production, which can also serve as an entry barrier and so sustain some monopoly profit, makes for the concentration of production on one location and gives regions and nations an incentive to attract the firm to their location. Sometimes this will have been chosen on the basis of supply considerations (resource supplies, skills, comparative costs), or demand considerations (revealed preference, local market size), but often it will merely be the place where the discoverer of the IRS product or process happened to be located. Scale economies thus introduce an element of chance into the pattern of trade in products whose process exhibits them, and of path-dependence into the development of that pattern over time. Whether the first-mover advantage goes to a particular firm or to the industry and location that contains it depends on whether the IRS derive from the particular production process or from the wider range of transactions that surround it.

9.3.2 *Internal scale economies and first-mover advantages*

'Internal' scale economies generally arise from plant-level technological considerations. High fixed costs imply steeply falling average costs as output rises, at least until average variable costs start to increase (e.g. when skilled labour or managerial resources start to run scarce). 'Learning by doing' and organisational refinement can also cause average costs to fall as a plant's cumulative output increases. Even if scale diseconomies eventually set in at plant level, firm-level costs may continue the fall as output grows, through the expansion of newer plants towards their lowest-cost level and organisational learning and falling overhead costs of central administration. Subject to the usual opportunity-cost considerations, internal scale economies may also strengthen the case for subsidising R&D so that domestic firms can be first into the development of a new product or process.

9.3.3   *External scale economies and industrial clusters*

'External' scale economies occur where all firms in a certain location can achieve cost reductions as their output grows, even if existing companies have exhausted their 'internal' plant and firm level economies. Newly arriving or expanding firms derive cost advantages from locating near these incumbents. Such advantages include established final-product markets and distribution systems, specialist intermediate-good supplier networks, appropriate physical infrastructure, ready-trained labour and regional reputation. Among the more often-cited contemporary clusters are of electronics production in California's Silicon Valley and Scotland's Silicon Glen, aerospace in southern France and textile products in central Italy. One Silicon Valley study identifies gains to non-innovators of around one-third those of the innovator (Irwin and Klenow 1994). Innovation continues despite the external benefit partly because the innovators gain more, partly because the process of innovation has performance benefits separable from any of its products (section 4.4.3).

Even if there were a demand- or supply-side reason for the original incumbents to choose this location, the cluster very often takes on a self-sustaining life of its own, growth begetting growth through the continued enjoyment of external economies.

> It seems that the country or region where the industry first happens to be established develops an advantage over other countries or regions. External economies of scale then cause this advantage to become so great that it is very difficult for other areas to catch up.
>
> (Jepma *et al.* 1996: 78)

Anticipation of external economies has sometimes been a motive for government to 'seed' a particular location with interventions such as infrastructure development and technical training, in the hope that it will become the nucleus of a cluster. Where a rival company or region in another country has captured the international market through internal or external economies, there may be a case for infant-industry protection to help domestic firms close the cost gap. The concept of 'growth poles', zones of industrial development whose success draws new enterprises to them, rests on similar foundations.

9.3.4   *Capturing increasing-returns industries*

Traditional trade models recognise a role for temporary subsidies or tariff protection in promoting infant industries, areas of production which promise to attain comparative advantage in future but require initial shelter from competition to attain the technology, skills or customer base needed to survive in a free world market. However, the main source of future advantages, scale economies, are left out of the simple models, and even their inclusion is not a justification for government intervention. An efficient private capital market should be able to recognise the industry's increasing returns, and lend it enough to go straight in at a competitive scale of production. If this is not available, temporary subsidy or, where appropriate, preferential state purchasing appear to be the second-best option. Tariff protection is if anything a third-best option: it imposes costs on the users of the imported product rather than the wider set of taxpayers, is more visible and so likely to invite retaliation, may put upward pressure on the exchange rate, and raises the relative pay of the factor 'intensively' used in the protected industry, with possibly general distortive effects on distribution because of established pay relativities.

In selecting appropriate infant industries, it was still assumed that governments would look to long-term comparative advantage. But increasing returns shift the focus of competitiveness from costs based on relative factor availabilities to costs based on scale of production. They open the possibility that, even if it is not best endowed for it (i.e. does not have the lowest costs for any given level of output), one country's industry can capture a market by entering first, or moving fastest down the cost curve. So temporary assistance may allow an infant industry to grow to maturity even if it is not in line with initial comparative advantage.

The possibility of government intervention promoting one nation by capturing an increasing-returns industry is most graphically illustrated in the case of 'global natural monopoly', where scale economies are so great (or global demand so low) costs are lowest for the producer who can meet the entire world demand. In this case, the battle between two producers can be likened to a prisoners' dilemma (section 2.2). One will make a profit if the other leaves the market, because it can then mark up prices over marginal costs by a sufficient margin. But if both stay in the market (as when both prisoners choose non-operation), both face heavy losses. Provided it can match its opponents in quality, one producer in receipt of a subsidy will be able to capture orders from the rest, which drive its costs down further and so cement its new, 'artificially' created, advantage. The firm can then capture monopoly rents from which the original subsidy is paid back. If these are 'national champion' firms, other governments may retaliate with subsidies of their own. But if the rival is too far down the increasing-returns path the size of the necessary subsidy may now be prohibitive, and the threat non-credible. If it does not charge too high a margin above average costs, the company's scale economies will be a barrier to subsequent entrants, unless these can go straight in at an even higher level of production.

The battle between Europe's Airbus and the USA's Boeing for large civilian airliners may be an extreme case of this capture process, but many other examples (South Korean shipbuilding, French and Polish aerospace) can be seen to have moved on from entry-protected and subsidy-driven initial acquisition of technology and market share to acquire price and technological competitiveness through reaping scale economies. It is through the prospective hope of sparking the growth of a new increasing-returns industry, as well as keeping alive the embers of an old one, that 'nations continue to pursue strategies that attempt to protect and nourish their national champion enterprises and turn the terms of trade in their favour through competition-distorting interventions' (Scherer 1994: 16). As technological knowledge spread and global capital costs converged, these industries might have been expected to move from higher- to lower-wage economies. But precisely which lower-wage countries they moved to seems in many cases to have owed as much to government action as to any inherent supply-side strengths.

9.3.5   *Terms-of-trade pessimism*

To sustain a trade pattern over time, income flows between nations – the balance of payments – must be kept equal through adjustments either in their exchange rate (the relative value of their currencies) or the terms of trade (the relative price in an international currency of one country's exports compared with its imports). In Ricardo's model, nations settle their import bills in gold, and any nation whose imports are initially worth more than its exports must make a net payment of gold to those whose exports are worth more than their imports. Since gold is also the domestic currency (or the monetary base for it), and since full employment means that monetary growth results only in price growth, the net transfer of gold causes prices and wages to rise in the trade-surplus economy and fall in the trade-deficit economy. It is this mechanism that initially establishes trade (allowing, in the example, England to recover from a situation where it imports both cloth and wine from Portugal to one where its cloth is cheap enough to start exporting), and subsequently adjusts the terms of trade to ensure that trade stays in balance.

The HOS model allows two adjustment routes. As before, monetary expansion in the surplus country and contraction in the deficit country cause relative prices to change, making the deficit country's exports internationally cheaper (and imports domestically more expensive) so that its trade returns to balance through a shift from internal to external demand. Alternatively, the same effect can be achieved by allowing the monetary flow to raise the exchange rate of the surplus country against the deficit country. Both approaches imply, however, that the deficit country must accept a deterioration in the terms of trade, and in relative wages, if its trade is to stay in balance.

Over time this can lead to progressive disadvantage for countries whose trade specialisation leads to continuously worsening terms of trade. In various Latin America-based studies influentially conducted for the United Nations, Prebisch (1949) argues that income elasticity of demand for imports (the proportional increase in import demand for a given rise in national income) is greater for exporters of primary commodities than for exporters of manufactured goods. Manufacturing nations are able to economise on the use of imported natural resources, recycle them domestically, replace them with domestically made substitutes, or move on to technologies which require less of them. In contrast, non-industrial nations have a growing appetite for imported manufactured goods once their basic, locally served survival needs have been satisfied. Price elasticity of demand for industrial imports (the proportional volume growth for a particular fall in price) is also higher than that for commodity imports, so that industrial exporters who cut their price will tend to win an increase in the value of sales, whereas commodity exporters who do so will tend to see sales value fall.

The relative imbalance is heightened, in Prebisch's view, by the tendency of manufactured products to be sold internationally in oligopolistic markets, whereas commodities are sold in competitive markets. This results in industrial-exporting nations capturing both the extra profit due to their own productivity increase (because industrial-product prices remain steady while costs fall), and the extra profit due to commodity-exporters' productivity increase (because commodity prices fall in line with costs). Attempts to restrict supply and so prevent the erosion of real commodity prices have rarely succeeded for long, usually because cartel members find it profitable to overstep their quotas, and stabilisation schemes become drained of finance after setting prices at a level which makes for ever-expanding stockpiles.

Although it initially gains from specialisation, a nation with comparative advantage in commodity production thus finds its growth rate constrained and its living standards progressively deteriorating, relative to partners who start with comparative advantage in manufactures. The commodity exporter either suffers a progressive deterioration in the terms of trade so as to keep its payments in balance, or must grow more slowly than industrial exporters (to avoid regular payments crises as imports exceed exports), or incurs an ever larger external debt as it borrows to finance the enduring trade deficit. With hindsight, Ricardo's 'gains from trade' appear in these circumstances to turn an initial absolute advantage into a long-term disadvantage.

> Prebisch would certainly be in agreement with Joan Robinson (1979) when she argues that in Ricardo's classical example Portugal would end up with a low rate of accumulation and having destroyed its promising textile industry, while England ended up with an industrial revolution.
>
> (Palma 1989: 294)

Robinson had earlier spoken for many in arguing that free trade is invariably strongest by counties with a productivity and technological lead which they are beginning to worry about losing. 'In the pre-1914 world Great Britain had everything to gain from other nations' adopting free trade and very little to lose from maintaining it herself' (Robinson 1962: 64). The same may well apply to the post-1914 USA, whose strong support for the Uruguay Round of world agricultural and service trade liberalisation, and accompanying onslaught on alleged Japanese disguised protectionism, reflects exceptional US strength and Japanese weakness in these areas. The situation of commodity exporters – who may now include the makers of low-tech goods and information services – worsens still further if more advanced industrial nations are able to impose optimum tariffs on commodities, or decide to levy environmental taxes on it to deter consumption and speed up the adoption of substitutes.

Increased productivity and welfare for the free-trading system as a whole are clearly a prerequisite for its sustainability, since any nations impoverished by free trade would logically withdraw from it. There no strong institutional mechanism, and little historical precedent, for international compensation payments to share out the gains from trade. The winners might in principle be able to compensate the losers so as to keep them inside the arrangement, but there are no historical instances of such compensation actually being paid for any length of time. (Ironically, the closest approach has probably been with side-payments from one (lightly affected) other (more heavily affected) losers to induce it to continue refraining from trade when a third country has been placed under embargo for political ends.)

9.3.6 Unequal exchange

The empirical evidence that commodity exporters' terms of trade deteriorate over time provides 'neoclassical' support to an argument more normally associated with Marxian price theory, which suggests that the systematic trading of commodities away from their prices-of-production can lead to transfer of surplus value from non-industrial to industrial economies. By taking labour-hours as the unit of production cost and taking this as the domestic price, Ricardo's model ignores the displacement of price from cost that can occur domestically if competition is not perfect, and internationally once money rather than barter exchange rates are admitted. Introducing these considerations raises the possibility that products assembled by equivalent labour units could exchange at different prices.

Although exploitation in exchange within an economy is ruled out by the Marxian scheme, it can occur between countries because of differences in their (subsistence) wage rates and capital endowments. Industrial nations can set their international prices above their prices-of-production by having a wage rate and/or an organic composition of capital (broadly, capital–labour ratio) above the world average (Emmanuel 1972). This allows them to set their export prices above domestically determined prices of production, effectively exploiting their own workforce less than under autarky and making good the loss of profit by exploiting the foreign workforce. Under the Marxian pricing scheme, an above-average organic composition automatically displaces a product's price above its labour content, and it is this which institutionalises exploitation through trade by countries more advanced in their accumulation of capital. 'If one unit of commodity X is exchanged for a certain quantity of commodity Y, but the labour-contents of the two are not equal, it is an instance of unequal exchange' (Sau 1982: 98). For Mandel (1978: ch. 11) international inequality in the price of labour-power is a consequence rather than cause of uneven development, but unequal exchange persists because the forces that equalise profit rates within an economy do not operate between 'core' and 'peripheral' economies: 'The labour of the industrialised countries counts as more intensive (hence more productive of value) on the world market than that of the underdeveloped lands . . . no equalisation of the rates of profit occurs on the world market' (Mandel 1978: 351).

The result still arises if the more general Sraffian conversion from costs to prices-of-production is used in place of traditional Marxian pricing schemes. Significantly it also arises in a framework which assumes global equalisation of profit rates through the international mobility of capital, so that lower-wage countries' ability to fund a chronic trade deficit through long-term borrowing and inward investment from higher-wage countries merely involves recycling through the capital account what they are losing through the current account. The theory has been valuable for Marxists for explaining how advanced capitalist nations can sustain their profit rates despite rising organic composition of capital, without exploiting their own workforces to the the point of revolution. (Working-class unity is also destroyed, since workers in sectors with above-average organic composition gain at the expense of those where it is lower, both in other economies and elsewhere in their own economy.) It reinforces the contention of 'dependency' theorists that nations which take the lead in accumulating capital will move progressively ahead in terms of income, being destined to capture and invest other nations' surplus.

The unequal exchange argument can also be cast in a neoclassical framework, and it moves beyond the elasticity-pessimists' concentration on commodity versus manufactured exports by showing that differences in technical and labour-market conditions could affect the relative export prices if high- and low-wage economies, as well as differences in what they actually export. Singer, who had independently developed the terms-of-trade hypothesis, later noted

> a general shift in the terms of trade discussion away from primary commodities versus manufactures and towards exports of developing countries – whether primary commodities or simpler manufactures – versus the export products of industrial countries – largely sophisticated manufactures and capital goods as well as skill-intensive services inluding technological know-how itself.
>
> (Singer 1989: 326)

He cites post-war time-series data showing that high-income countries enjoyed a relatively stronger rise in their real manufactured-good export prices, and low-income countries a relatively stronger fall in their real commodity export prices.

Although his unequal-exchange theory points to low-wage economies being exploited regardless of what they produce, Emmanuel (1982) concedes that industry's greater price-cost mark-ups and technical dynamism make rapid industrialisation the most effective way to close the global income gap, with multinational companies – often condemned for importing 'inappropriate' technologies and creating islands of high-tech privilege, an effective means for the technical transfer. However, within a decade, it was becoming clear that the first manufactured products to be transferred (such as textiles, cars and basic microchips) had taken on the status of commodities. They were in price- and income-inelastic demand in high-income economies, weak on linkages (often being assembled from imported components in free-trade zones), and tending to convert rising productivity into falling world prices rather than rising wages and profits at home. 'The relative price of manufactured goods will fall with increased competition from developing countries. The current large differences in manufacturing labour costs will be eroded' (Brown and Julius 1993: 15–16).

Table 9.1 Regional trade volumes and terms of trade 1980–97 (annual percentage changes)

	1980–9	1990	1991	1992	1993	1994	1995	1996	1997
Major industrial countries									
Export volume	4.7	7.5	5.6	4.6	2.0	7.9	8.3	5.4	10.3
Import volume	4.8	5.5	2.1	4.2	0.9	9.1	8.3	6.4	9.3
Terms of trade	0.4	–0.7	1.0	0.9	1.1	0.2	0.1	–0.1	–0.6
Developing countries									
Africa									
Export volume	0.1	4.5	1.5	1.8	0.9	11.9	8.4	10.5	5.1
Import volume	1.4	2.9	–2.5	5.1	1.2	6.2	9.9	3.7	8.2
Terms of trade	0.2	2.3	–3.9	–2.8	–2.3	–0.2	–0.2	6.1	0.6
Asia									
Export volume	6.7	10.7	12.1	10.9	11.4	19.4	16.0	7.6	13.5
Import volume	7.5	5.3	8.9	12.6	18.8	14.1	17.4	9.0	6.0
Terms of trade	0.6	–2.2	–1.6	1.7	–0.2	0.8	1.3	1.5	0.4
Western hemisphere									
Export volume	4.5	8.6	5.7	12.4	10.5	10.1	14.0	9.8	10.7
Import volume	–0.5	7.6	17.4	19.0	10.7	16.9	10.6	10.3	17.2
Terms of trade	–1.8	–3.1	–2.9	–6.3	–2.1	3.9	8.3	0.5	–1.4
Middle East/Europe									
Export volume	–1.6	5.4	3.1	13.2	2.4	11.6	3.7	2.9	8.6
Import volume	1.7	8.1	0.6	21.6	1.7	–14.4	7.6	10.0	12.5
Terms of trade	–2.4	9.8	–15.7	6.6	–9.3	–7.2	–0.3	10.1	–0.5

Source: IMF, *World Economic Outlook*, May 1998, Tables A24, A25

Although its causes can be differently ascribed, the differential trade experience shown in Table 9.1 tends to support the fears of the terms-of-trade and unequal-exchange pessimists. Of the world's lower-income regions, only those in Asia and Latin America (western hemisphere) attained consistently faster export volume growth than the major industrial countries in the 1990s, and only in Asia did exports generally expand faster than imports. Only the industrial countries enjoyed a generally positive terms-of-trade trend, with the downturn in world oil and other commodity prices – to the Middle East's particular discomfort – again bringing terms-of-trade relief only to Asia.

9.3.7   Unfair advantages? Social and environmental dumping

Bargainers win praise for setting a competitive wage, but not for suffering low pay. Businesses claim credit for exploiting local carrying-capacity advantages, but not for underpricing the environment. Two of the most important prices determining trade patterns in an international market are those for labour (once adjusted for productivity differences) and those for non-wage production costs. But labour costs can be forced down by killing 'living wage' aspirations, dismantling labour unions, minimising redistributive (income) taxation and eliminating the payroll tax that funds state-run pension and welfare provision. Other production costs can be forced down by failing to put a price on any input that has none in the market-place – including the social costs of work-related health and household breakup, the external costs of pollution and congestion, and any hidden charge that these place on future generations' welfare or present-day quality of life.

Defenders of free trade are automatically suspicious of these arguments because they tend to be voiced by the rich world on behalf of the poor. Left to sell their labour cheap, nations will generate export sales and attract inward investment which can raise their employment and productivity until the same market forces pull up the real wage. As their incomes rise, households will impute a higher cost to the social and environmental damage from exploiting those early advantages, and introduce these into the trade equation either economically (by staking private claim to the 'commons' and pricing them in line with the rising opportunity cost) or politically (using democratic rights, acquired in the growing political market-place, to internalise social and environmental cost). Like any other form of 'dumping', an apparently philanthropic concern that foreign buyers of low-wage exports are raising their own real wage by squeezing others' hides a self-interested fear that those others will capture market share and subsequently push prices upwards. The danger of demanding a 'level playing field' of minimum wages, work conditions, social provision and nature conservation at the outset is that it denies nations with low private incomes to trade on the advantages that follow from it, so ultimately locking them into a low wage and quality of life which market forces would otherwise have allowed them to escape.

The case against social and environmental 'dumping' – selling labour and natural resources at prices which fail to reflect their full (social) cost – persists because of the unclear conversion of 'static' into 'comparative' advantage. Trading on the basis of low comparative wages will not raise living standards if, instead of shifting orders and output to the low-pay location, international firms use the challenge to make matching wage reductions in their higher-cost locations. Where private income stays low, social and natural resources are also kept comparatively cheap according to the 'market' measures usually applied to them. Poisoned air and soil may not concern a family already dying of hunger; trees are worth more as firewood than scenery to those who cannot afford to burn fossil fuel. Attracting industries on the basis of low pay and cheap resources may cause relative disadvantage to be enshrined rather than transcended – local labour and capital being denied the means and incentives to achieve (and charge for) higher productivity, so that foot-loose producers move on when they wish to upgrade. And if scarce natural or social capital is permanently depleted in the process of take-off, no amount of sub-sequent income can buy it back.

Recent negotiation on global social and environmental problems has revealed a convenient contradiction in the attitude of 'affluent' towards 'effluent' societies. The higher social benefit from the unspoilt environment in higher-income countries – because their citizens suffer a larger welfare loss from its destruction and so show a higher willingness to pay for its preservation – is used as a justification for relocating low-wage and high-pollution industries to lower-income locations. But the higher cost of repairing the spoilt environment in higher-income societies – because of the income they would need to forgo – is used as a justification for push-ing pollution-abatement costs onto lower-income locations. In one of the latest twists to the 'polluter pays' principle, the high-income nations which burn most of the world's fossil fuel (and so emit most of its global-warming greenhouse gas) are swinging behind the use of tradable pollution permits, whose initial distribution would recognise their higher starting emission levels, and whose secondary trade would allow them to buy the right to maintain these levels for less than they would pay to reduce them. Low polluters would initially gain from selling their permits for more than the market value of what they could expect to produce with the corresponding emission as a by-product. But if this reflected capacity constraints on present industrial production due to capital shortage, or the (related) use of an excessive discount rate to compare the future value of exercising pollution rights with the present value of selling them, the exchange could prove an unequal one. Higher-income nations will retain that status by cornering the market in a depletable resource, the finite carrying capacity of global pollution 'sinks'; unless the others force the printing of new permits or pollute without permission, in which case the goal of global abatement will be undermined.

9.3.8 Industrial product specialisation: linkages and cumulative causation

Increasing returns, elasticity pessimism and the possibility of unequal exchange have led to a strong emphasis on manufacturing, both in the development policies of lower-income nations and the industrial policies of those with higher incomes. Manufacturing's special significance for employment generation and growth arises in the IRS argument from its potential for raising output and labour productivity simultaneously, in the terms-of-trade argument from the positive demand and supply externalities it generates, and in the unequal-exchange argument from the way it can set prices above costs to produce reinvestible surplus. Special attention is paid to the technical dynamism of manufacturing, and the complementary linkages between its operations.

The argument for prioritising industrial expansion, even if it goes against initial 'comparative advantage', has thus received endorsement from well outside the Marxian and dependency perspectives. In a much-quoted account of Japan's postwar recovery strategy, a Ministry of International Trade and Industry (MITI) official explains that

> MITI decided to establish industries which require intensive employment of capital and technology, such as steel, oil refining, petrochemicals, automobiles, aircraft, industrial machinery . . . From a short-run, static viewpoint, encouragement of such industries would seem to conflict with economic rationalism. But from a long-range point of view, these are precisely the industries where income elasticity of demand is high, technological progress is rapid and labour productivity rises fast. It was clear that without these industries it would be difficult to raise our standard of living to that of Europe and America.
>
> (Best 1986: 190–1 quoting Scott 1984)

A prominent adviser to post-war British governments was equally clear that industry brought a path-dependence which overturned 'comparative advantage' as a policy tool.

> Manufacturing industries are subject to increasing returns to scale – both of a static and dynamic kind – and under these conditions the presumption derived from Ricardo's doctrine of comparative costs – the presumption that free trade secures the best allocation of resources to each and every participant, and that there must be a net gain from trade all round – no longer holds. For under these conditions it may be demonstrated that free trade may lead to stunted growth, or even impoverishment of some regions (or countries) to the greater benefit of others . . . Ricardo's pamphlet . . . was a strong argument against protecting agriculture. The question of protecting manufactures did not arise.
>
> (Kaldor 1978: 237–8)

Kaldor's invocation of Verdoorn's Law, 'the empirical relationship between the growth of productivity and the growth of production' (Kaldor 1966/1978: 106) was keenly disputed on statistical grounds, and later drew something of a retraction. But arguments for the special connection between increasing returns and manufacturing have proved more durable. Manufacturing is variously argued to enjoy greater potential for technical economies of scale and scope, for learning-by-doing to improve the performance of specific tasks, for research and development into capital- and labour-productivity raising machinery, for monitoring and incentive payments to increase employee effort, and for 'creating its own demand' by introducing products for which demand grows ahead of real income. These characteristics also allow manufacturing to raise labour productivity while expanding its employment, whereas agriculture and services can raise it only by shedding jobs.

Beneficial linkages arise on the demand side of an industrial operation through the stimulus to supply of inputs (including commodities), transportation, skilled labour, business services and finance. Investment in 'core' industrial capacity may thus contribute to higher employment (through the multiplier) and induced investment (through the accelerator) and accelerate the growth of efficient labour and capital markets. Linkages arise on the supply side because the outputs from the operation can become a new or cheaper input to the development of wider operations. So prioritising the expansion of a core industry, such as coal-mining, steel-making or railway transport, can help generate a range of smaller industries for which the core is either a reliable high-paying customer or a reliable low-cost supplier.

Comparative advantage lends itself to a balanced approach to growth, under which nations whose capital is scarce in relation to labour should spread it around in labour-intensive technologies 'appropriate' to current conditions (Schumacher 1973). In contrast, the cumulative-causation view provides an argument for concentrating it in capital-intensive sectors chosen for their linkages (Hirschman 1958). The resultant growth will initially be unbalanced but, through their secondary demands and investment inducements, these leading sectors will justify themselves by raising the rate of accumulation, summoning supporting supply-side changes faster than they would appear under balanced growth. Development is market-led, but only after an initial intervention to set the forces in the right direction.

While the Prebisch prescription – import-substituting industrialisation – had mixed success in Latin America, the deliberate overriding of static in favour of dynamic comparative advantage has scored some notable successes elsewhere, notably in Asia. Japan's success did not end with acquiring a range of capital-intensive heavy industries, which in fact were being abandoned by western Europe and North America by the time it had acquired them, and left it uncomfortably dependent on imported oil and raw materials. Through trade barriers, preferential purchasing and state-sponsored collaborative research, Japan clawed back its initial deficit in integrated circuits so successfully that it overtook the USA on world market share in 1986. Innovation (especially early realisation of the importance of dynamic random-access memory chips) helped close the gap, as did the coincidence of small-car product ranges with world oil crisis in Japan's relentless conquest of the global automobile market. But here again, intense domestic rivalry and low-cost, high-quality process innovation were assisted by selective protection, careful entry regulation and state help with technology acquisition. 'Extensive government intervention in oligopolistic industries can alter the relative balance between firms of different nations; even in fragmented industries, it can alter the direction of trade and accelerate/forestall major corporate trade decision' (Yoffie 1993: 16).

9.3.9 Created factor endowments and 'competitive advantage'

Service industries have emerged as sources of export, rising productivity and serial innovation, and with the help of manufacturing's multinationalisation and non-production outsourcing the tertiary sector now accounts for 60–70 per cent of output and employment in most high-income economies. But the dynamic arguments once applied to manufacturing have been generalised rather than abandoned. A reconsideration of 'factor endowments' as sources of specialisation shows most to be at least in part artificially generated, so that intervention can improve a country's long-run trade performance even without increasing returns.

One explanation for the Leontief paradox was that the USA enjoyed a relative abundance of skilled labour, even if in general it was a capital-rich and labour-scarce economy. As industrial production shifts towards less material- and more knowledge-intensive processes, and the structure of demand towards goods and services in which the capital is human rather than physical, the parameters of HOS-type trade theory change even if its conclusions are retained. Comparative advantage now lies in education, training, scientific capability, physical infrastructure, and other factors which are essentially under national industry and government control.

The sources of this more broadly defined competitive advantage have been influentially summarised by Porter (1990), whose 'diamond' identifies three mutually reinforcing determinants in addition to factor supply conditions: local industrial structure (especially the degree of domestic competition and the firms' strategy-pursuing opportunities), local infrastructure (including the efficiency of supplying and servicing firms) and demand conditions. Government departments or agencies are often influential as large, long-term or especially critical buyers, and government can also act to improve local industrial structure and infrastructure. Intervention in each area requires a delicate balance: between driving too hard a purchasing bargain (as a monopsonist) or being too accommodating, between allowing cut-throat competition that keeps operating scale and profits too low and erecting too many entry barriers, and between generous business and social support and low tax and social-insurance rates.

As world industrial production grows more 'footloose' as a result of growing price competition and falling sunk costs (allowing speedier relocation), governments have begun to seek ways not just to promote domestic industries, but to attract and retain inward investment. National governments encounter the additional problem of encouraging regions to promote themselves as industrial locations, without zero-sum competition for investment from abroad or from relocating domestic units. Among the controllable factors expected to shape the future location of export-oriented industries are education and skill levels, R&D capacity and business–higher education links, transport and physical infrastructure, quality-of-life and social infrastructure, transparent and moderate tax systems, efficient bureaucratic and legal systems (Reich 1993). Governments have largely abandoned the protectionist aspects of import-substituting industrialisation, but not its emphasis on diverting investment from areas of present to future competitive strength.

9.3.10   Regional free trade: the European single market

The formal completion of the European Union's single internal market on 1 January 1993, and its extension from twelve to fifteen countries two years later, was far removed from the sudden switch from autarky to free trade depicted in general-equilibrium models of free trade gains. EU members had been dismantling their internal trade barriers for many years before '1992', and had not finished the process by its end. Their market remains a tariff-free space within an external tariff barrier. Whether such customs unions move the world towards or away from free trade depend on 'trade creation' – the discovery of new Pareto-optimal trades as a result of internal tariff removal – outweighing 'trade diversion', the entrapment of trades within the customs union which would have been better conducted with outsiders had the external tariff not been imposed. This has been claimed on behalf of the EU, especially after recent external tariff reductions, but is still disputed over some newer customs unions such as South America's *Mercosur*. Intra-EU trade remains inhibited by currency risk, heightened by the retreat from narrow exchange-rate bands in 1992, and many – including the Commission – believe the single market's full benefits will not be felt until qualifying member states adopt a single currency, timetabled for 1 January 1999.

Despite these cautions, the EU market-unifying experiment has provided an opportunity to assess the gains from free trade among structurally similar economies, and to observe the reaction of firms, governments, finance and labour to the disappearance of formal protection. The EU's own assessment of static (one-off) gains was, perhaps understandably, optimistic, partly because it identified the potential gains from moving to a single market (more strictly, the potential costs of leaving barriers in place), without venturing a judgement on how far or how quickly these would actually be realised. The outlook was still promising when possibly imperfect realisation of the gains was taken into account, 'resulting in estimates which still suggest that growth in Europe may increase by about 0.5 per cent a year to 3 per cent a year' (Mayes 1991: 2).

The longer-run impact, through IRS enabled by market growth and greater competitive discipline instilled by it, might add at least half as much again over a ten-year period. But Mayes's study of key industries' responses to 1992, and others of firms' and public authorities' reactions, suggest that a 'free' internal market may not be attained by tariff removal alone.

The intra-European merger and acquisition wave that attended the 1992 timetable was not unprecedented, and was undoubtedly aimed in part at attaining the additional scale and scope economies foreseen by the programme. But in part it also confirms suspicions that heightened competitive challenges can spur oligopolies to more collusion (or fusion) as well as more competition. 'Slightly increasing the number of oligopolistic firms does not seem to make much difference to market behaviour' (Thurow 1980: 127). Although the Commission had expected and intended the single market to spur collaboration between EU firms over technology and cross-border marketing, the main area of joint-venture growth was between EU and non-EU firms (N. Kay 1992: 222–3).

Harmonisation of product and service standards, while undoubtedly assisting many producers to design for and trade across the single market, has also frequently been attacked as a means for EU incumbents to limit entry and restrict the scope for price competition, a suspicion inevitably heightened by the EU's delegation of much of the task to industry representatives to avoid a bureaucratic overload. National and regional governments, for their part, have greeted the curtailment of traditional industrial-policy instruments (strategic tariffs, subsidies, tax concessions, public ownership and preferential public purchasing) by developing new ones, becoming especially active in infrastructure provision, training, promoting industrial partnerships, and lobbying the Commission for bigger shares of the numerous public handouts that still flow through the EU budget in the form of technical development, social, regional, agricultural and industrial restructuring support. Governments required to ease regulations which they regarded as important to upholding social justice (e.g. minimum wages and conditions of work) and product quality (e.g. financial service standards) have worked especially hard to generalise what is left of these, to avoid seeing bad drive out good through 'social dumping' – notably through the Social Charter of labour rights and a similar package of environmental regulations.

The EU's programme is to unify not only goods and service markets, but also those for labour and capital, eliminating exchange risk and adding the necessary transparency by adoption of a single currency. Main members' efforts to qualify for this by attaining monetary convergence (and other unforeseeable events such as German reunification and the commencement of free trade with parts of eastern Europe) prevent any easy judgement as to whether early *ceteris paribus* projections of the single market's growth effects have been fulfilled. A safe early lesson, however, is that removing tariff and quota barriers to free trade may be only a small step towards the free market, in either form or function. Comparing company reactions in perhaps the EU's most and least regulated large economies, Germany and the UK, 'the institutional, policy and behavioural distinctions between the two countries are . . . striking and do lead to serious questions about the degree to which successful convergence will actually be achieved . . . these differences help explain why the two economies respond differently to the same external pressures' (Mayes and Hart 1994: 215). Five years after 1992, many of those who had done most to promote privatisation, deregulation and *laissez-faire* in the UK were actively opposing the EU's concept of how they should be generalised.

9.4   Market counterattack: capital mobility

On balance, the existence of increasing returns enhances the potential global gains from trade. Any monopolies or oligopolies that they give rise to in the domestic market strengthen the welfare-enhancing argument for opening it to foreign competition. Though it weakens the HOS theory's ability to predict trade patterns and restores a role for state intervention, a wider definition of 'factors' increases the applicability of traditional arguments for comparative advantage. Academic originators of the 'new' trade theory usually strongly object to their arguments being used to support selective protection or 'winner-picking' domestic industrial policy, even if this is less distorting than the trade protection it replaces. 'There is a huge external market for challenges to the orthodoxy of free trade. Any intellectually reputable case for interventionist trade policies . . . will quickly find support for the wrong reasons' (Krugman 1990: 253).

Not for the first time, business-school empirical findings tend to be much less hostile to strategic trade and industrial policies than economists' theoretical models, and any truth probably lies somewhere in between. Intervention to capture increasing-returns production can be shown to improve a nation's capability of benefiting from free trade, and departures from perfect competition in the international market enhance the prospects for one nation to gain from selective protection even if the world as a whole is left worse off. However many multilateral free-trade agreements they sign, nation-state governments find it hard to resist interventions that raise domestic income just because the rest of the world (and global income) can be shown to suffer. With national interests, moral-hazard worries and doubts about the probity of recipient governments limiting the extent of international income transfers, there is also little scope for tariff removal whose redistributive effects require compensation to be paid before the global gains are shared by all.

Whereas criticisms of the closed-economy market model relate primarily to its static allocation claims, and can be redeemed by appeal to the market's facility for growth and change (Chapter 4), criticisms of the world market model hit hardest at its dynamic aspects. The counterattack, in favour of free trade along current comparative-advantage lines, has centred on the abandonment – with empirical support – of another assumption of traditional trade theory. The static and dynamic disadvantages from early market-driven specialisation can both be pushed into the background, if not made to fall away, when international capital mobility is added to the system.

9.4.1 *The growth of capital mobility*

Whereas international labour mobility remains low – and there may be political and social reasons for wishing to keep it so – international mobility of financial and physical capital is now significant. Foreign direct investment flows have risen and fallen since they first took off from Europe in the 1870s, but the first half of the 1990s brought a sustained upward trend from already significant levels, notably in flows to lower-income economies (as shown in Table 9.2).

Table 9.2 Net private capital flows to developing and transition economies 1984–97

(Billion US dollars)

	1984–89	1990–96	1994	1995	1996	(1997)
	(annual averages)					
Asia (total)	13.0	55.9	63.1	91.8	102.2	38.5
Direct	4.5	32.2	43.4	49.7	58.5	55.4
Portfolio	1.5	6.8	11.3	10.8	10.2	−2.2
Western hemisphere (total)	−0.2	45.7	47.4	35.7	80.5	91.1
Direct	5.3	18.7	24.3	25.3	36.9	51.2
Portfolio	−0.9	29.9	60.6	−0.1	25.2	33.5
Transition economies (total)	−1.0	12.8	18.4	29.8	21.3	34.5
Direct	−0.2	6.3	5.4	13.2	13.1	18.2
Portfolio	–	2.0	4.1	2.9	2.2	7.3
Africa (Total)	3.6	4.4	10.6	13.8	4.5	8.9
Direct	1.1	2.9	3.6	4.2	5.3	7.7
Portfolio	−0.8	−0.2	0.5	1.4	−0.3	2.6
Middle East/Europe (total)	1.7	25.2	15.5	14.8	20.7	16.1
Direct	1.1	3.0	4.2	5.1	4.3	5.1
Portfolio	4.4	12.8	12.5	8.4	7.9	6.8
All 'emerging' countries (total)	15.2	148.1	160.5	192.0	240.8	173.7
Direct	12.9	63.1	84.3	96.0	114.9	138.2
Portfolio	4.7	54.1	87.8	23.5	49.7	42.9

Source: IMF, *World Economic Outlook*, May 1998, Table 8

Capital flow from higher- to lower-income economies is predicted by traditional trade theory, since higher incomes result from relative abundance of, and relatively low returns to, capital, whose owners then channel it to regions where it is scarce. That this failed to occur for most of the nineteenth century appears mainly due to the persistence of unequal profit rates within the first industrial economies, which gave safer investment opportunities closer to home, and the fact that labour was the more mobile factor (especially to the Americas) at this time. Its reversal by the middle of the twentieth century reflected political instability and unacceptable investment risks in the economies that might have offered higher returns, followed by new investment opportunities within the industrial economies after their own politics had brought them into conflict. Another reversal, for similar reasons, occurred in 1997, with especially sharp portfolio withdrawals from newly industrialising Asia causing the decade's first drop in net capital inflows to lower-income countries; but with developed-country equity markets already looking strongly valued, a resumption of the upward trend capital flows to emerging markets was widely expected within the next two years.

Efforts at rebuilding international links after the mid-century conflicts centred on the General Agreement on Tariffs and Trade (GATT), whose successive negotiation rounds had by 1967 reduced industrial tariffs 'to an average of 8.6 per cent in the EEC [European Economic Community], 9.9 per cent in the United States, 10.7 per cent in Britain and 11 per cent in Japan' (Luard 1983: 74). Average tariffs were down to 5.0 per cent by the time the most recent Uruguay Round began, but its completion at the end of 1993 saw only modest further progress on industry and limited agreement over services; 90 per cent of the $213 billion boost to world GDP by 2002 calculated by the World Bank and Organisation for Economic Co-operation and Development (OECD) comes from liberalisation of agriculture, but even these gains are uncertain (partly because of likely compliance problems discussed in section 12.2.4). Stronger dynamic effects may well come from the setting of firmer rules on barriers designed to encourage inward investment and protect intellectual property and the environment, and separate agreements subsequently pursued over financial services and telecommunications.

Governments conducted the GATT negotiations, but from a market perspective they were merely correcting their earlier damage. The slow but steady progress of GATT, whose provisions are now actively policed by the supranational World Trade Organisation (WTO), generally had the sympathy of trading enterprises, and could be seen as a success for competing agents in achieving the framework needed for efficient global labour division. Moving to free trade is a collective action problem, those who drop their defences losing unless others follow suit, so that much of the delay can be put down to the difficulties of achieving the necessary trust in what is essentially a worldwide prisoners' dilemma game. Other problems arise from policing the agreement against the opportunistic return of disguised protectionism (the WTO's task), and of agreeing the necessary compensation payments to those industries and nations that lose out from the deal (a matter still not resolved for the main expected loser, Africa).

In recognition of the growth of global capital movements and their apparent benefits both to source and destination, higher income nations had already extensively relaxed their exchange controls and inward investment restrictions through the OECD and European Union, before GATT approached the issue. Many lower-income nations have moved equally fast to remove their barriers to arrival and repatriation of foreign funds, with the International Monetary Fund's Article VIII on convertibility through a freely functioning currency market setting a standard to aim for. History advises against regarding present trends as irreversible, and the historically low interest rates at which emerging economies could raise international finance in 1996 gave way to a sharp return of the risk premium which may interrupt the flow following the series of East Asian devaluations and forced debt restructurings in 1997–8. But the upturn shown in Table 9.1 is notable for surviving a previous major shock to foreign-investor confidence in lower-income economies, the end-1994 Mexican crisis; and it also stops too early to record the surge in direct and portfolio investment to transition (Eastern European and former Soviet Union) economies, which virtually doubled in 1996 and showed signs in 1997 of gaining from a diversion of yield-seeking funds previously destined for dynamic Asia, before a general retrenchment in 1998.

Financial investment enters a country when foreigners (usually institutional investors) buy its financial instruments – company shares and debentures or government bonds. The aim is generally to enjoy a return whose rate at least matches that available in the investors' home country (taking account of political, investment and exchange risks), and whose covariance with the returns on their other assets is low, thus reducing the volatility of their overall portfolio. Portfolio investors do not usually aim to exercise control over the enterprises they buy into, generally seeking income rather than capital gain and responding to any problems by exit, which they ensure by keeping to instruments whose markets are fairly liquid.

Foreign direct investment (FDI) enters a country when foreigners (usually multinational companies) buy fixed assets, either acquiring a controlling ownership interest in an existing enterprise or setting one up via joint venture or greenfield development. The aim is to acquire a productive base which can serve the domestic market, or foreign markets, more economically than exports from the investor's existing production sites. Since the underlying aim is to transfer technology or management techniques rather than capital, direct investors often aim to expand their subidiaries by reinvesting or raising capital locally once the initial FDI transfer has been made.

The nature of capital transfer has also changed significantly. Whereas bank loans were the main vehicle and governments (or state-backed companies) the main recipients during previous expansion phases, multinational enterprises (MNEs) have played an important role in the most recent wave of fixed capital transfers. These tend to finance their initial investment internally (using retained profits from home-country operations), but most (partly for exchange-risk reasons) move quickly to finance expansion from retained profits in the host country, or bonds and shares issued there.

9.4.2 *Rediscovering comparative advantage's advantages*

Completion of the global capital market has strengthened the argument, already encouraged by the mixed experience of 'import-substituting industrialisation', that 'static' comparative advantage can evolve into the dynamic version. Existing export industries can reinvest to take account of changing factor availability (particularly the reduction in capital costs and the disappearance of the labour surplus), while 'infant' and increasing-returns industries can raise privately the finance they need to enter at optimum scale and subsidise their early learning process. Governments' attempts to anticipate future comparative advantage are held to be no better than those of private investors, and probably worse because they are less aware of product market trends and more exposed to sectional political pressures.

Trade intervention for short-term gain can also act against long-term interests. The domestic price-cuts secured through an optimal tariff may well reduce the domestic producers' profitability, nullifying any infant-industry measures. Those infants that do get effective protection may still find themselves undermined, by loss of profit to local rivals if domestic entry to the newly profitable industry is unchecked, or by premature senility if it is too heavily restricted. Most arguments for strategic protection collapse into a negative-sum game if foreign governments retaliate with reciprocal measures. Retaliation is comparatively rare only because so are examples of successful infant-industry promotion. Many state-sponsored industrial projects aimed at pushing comparative advantage in new directions have, far from creating linkages that lift the rest of the economy, been held down by lack of supporting infrastructure, labour skills, transport, marketing channels and imported input supplies, any labour-cost advantage over higher-income-country competitors being offset by inability to match them on quality, productivity or continuity of supply.

Dynamic gains for commodity exporters from keeping with their current comparative-advantage specialisation had been widely expected by classical economists, who expected primary producers' terms of trade to rise over time, mainly because of natural scarcity of minerals and diminishing returns to agriculture as population rose. Global terms of trade did, indeed, move in favour of primary commodities until the mid-nineteenth century. Since then the trend has tended to reverse, for the reasons identified by elasticity-pessimist and unequal-exchange theorists (sections 9.3.4, 9.3.5). But import-substituting industrialisation was an argument for complementing, not abandoning, low-income nations' commodity export base, and subsequent development experience (especially in Latin America) suggests that there are advantages to building on it incrementally.

Deteriorating terms of trade can often be combated by improvements in quality, linked to the development of local processing, and linkages to wider industry can often be created where they do not already exist. For countries, as for companies, long-range diversification is usually the riskiest way to sustain a high-growth target, 'since it involves a simultaneous departure from familiar products and familiar markets . . . many firms have shown in the recent past an unfortunate tendency to plunge rather than probe' (Ansoff 1965: 113–14). Slow-growing but profitable product areas have usually provided the financial and human resources for a push into faster-expanding ones, and firms that nurture the 'cash cows' as support acts to the 'wildcats' have generally done better than those which sacrifice the first to the second.

9.4.3   *Capital import as an alternative to protection*

Terms-of-trade deterioration aroused particular concern because of the belief that sustained trade deficits would leave primary exporters chronically short of foreign exchange, and so condemned to slow growth and continual recessions (adustment through devaluation being useless given the low price elasticity of export demand). Tariff protection and subsidy, or public ownership, of infant industries was supported on the grounds that domestic financial markets possessed neither the capacity to raise the sums needed for industrial diversification nor the foresight to anticipate its long-term profitability.

The prospect of a sustained inflow of foreign capital challenges both these beliefs. It may allow a capital account surplus to offset the current-account deficit for long periods, allowing a country to import investment goods without regularly devaluing or rating its currency. And it may add sufficient depth and liquidity to local financial markets (or give local firms sufficient access to foreign financial markets) to offset any local financial constraints. By increasing the size, liquidity and knowledge base of local capital markets, capital mobility is likely to bring these closer to the 'perfection' assumed in the capital-asset pricing model and efficient markets hypothesis. While markets may also be exposed to more speculative volatility, their main allocative task – supplying realistically priced capital to viable investment projects – is likely to be enhanced.

Many South-east Asian and Latin American economies have experienced faster and stabler growth since opening up to international trade and investment, despite recessionary phases in their main higher-income trading partners. Multiplier effects and linkages from export industries to the wider economy have played a key role in East Asia's success according to the World Bank (1994). This is not always true of the export-processing zones used to attract footloose multinational industry, and other analysis suggests that maintaining a competitive exchange rate (which may require capital inflow to be curbed at times) played at least as important a role (Rodrik 1994). But overvalued exchange rates and low-linkage 'steel-works in the desert' were at least as serious a problem under earlier import-substituting industrialisation strategies, and the opening to capital flows appears to have eased two of the most enduring obstacles to sustained expansion: speeding the introduction of industries with favourable income-elasticities and high export growth potential, and loosening the external financing constraint on keeping domestic demand at high levels without serious inflation or unsustainable current-account deficits.

9.4.4   *Capital mobility as a complement to trade*

In principle, inward investment by multinationals is a substitute for trade. Companies investing abroad to get closer to their market move to producing in the host country what they previously exported to it from the home country. Companies investing abroad to get closer to raw material supplies move to processing in the host country what they previously took home before refining.

In practice, international trade and capital flows have tended to grow together, and there are several ways in which the two are self-reinforcing. The financing effect of fixed capital inflows allows fast-growing and high-investing countries to sustain a long run of current-account deficits, without having to devalue, put up trade barriers or undergo periodic 'corrective' recessions, and without necessarily running up unsustainable external debts. In many ways, the post-1973 regime of floating exchange rates and international capital flows has achieved what the Bretton Woods fixed-rate system lacked: a reliable method of arranging transfers between chronic surplus (net saving) and chronic deficit (net investing) countries, to prevent the first group from becoming a persistent drain on world demand and relieving the second of bearing the full costs of 'adjustment'.

The capacity effect of fixed capital flows has tended to be trade-creating in the long term. After an initial phase when production in the host country replaces exports to it from the home country, the transplanted facility turns into an export base – first to lower-income third markets where low prices are needed to establish the market, and later to higher-income markets, including the home country. Under the 'product life-cycle' model (Vernon 1966), new products are initially produced in a high-income economy, where the initial demand is concentrated and so where the invention and initial refinement is likely to take place. Once product and process are standardised and the market established, concern shifts to raising output and reducing cost, and this leads eventually to the transfer of production to a lower-cost foreign location. From here, exports develop to third countries and eventually to the host, where production is closed down (or, if possible, redeployed to more recently developed products).

Foreign direct investment (FDI) can thus become a means of transplanting export bases, rather than replacing them with domestic production. Where there are plant-level scale economies not impeded by high transport costs or protective walls, FDI can even serve to concentrate production on fewer world sites and so increase the volume of trade at an even faster rate than that of world production. The link between country-of-invention and location of first production may subsequently have weakened, with multinationals able at an early stage to move production wherever it is cheapest, but this serves only to strengthen the link between capital flows and product flows.

The often herd-like movement of multinational enterprises into newly opened host countries gives them protection against being monopolised by one technologically advantaged foreign entrant. With MNEs also crossing onto their rivals' high-income home territory, the danger of competition begetting collusion also seems to be reduced. Even global oligopoly, towards which increasing returns are now driving a number of industries both in manufacturing and services, may not be the competitive dead end (barring some alien 'black ships') it once appeared. Another imported biological perspective points to agents co-operating while there is space enough for all but competing fiercely once the environment's carrying capacity reaches its limits.

In the population ecology literature, convergence is to a hypothetical number of homogeneous firms that can be supported by the environment . . . Whereas some kinds of externality may arise through communication and co-operation and promote group survival, density dependence is usually interpreted as representing competitive pressures forcing a population to some finite number of firms.

(Kogut 1993: 146, 148)

As firms grow big enough in the world to start running short of customers and suppliers, the gloves may again come off the invisible hand.

9.4.5   *Capital mobility as benign macroeconomic policy constraint*

Sustained capital inflows enable a country to run protracted trade and current-account deficits, which would previously have run a country into mounting international debt or forced it into recession and/or devaluation to restore external balance. Whereas the equilibrium exchange rate might earlier have been regarded as that which kept the current account in balance at full employment, it is now possible to identify a fundamental equilibrium exchange rate as that which keeps overall payments in balance, ensuring a capital inflow sufficient to match the current outflow.

International capital flows allow countries with chronic current-account surpluses to finance those with chronic current-account deficits, avoiding the currency realignments that would otherwise be needed to bring the accounts into balance. Sustained current-account surpluses arise when a country is a net saver, regularly producing more than it consumes, and thus running an export surplus. This generally occurs if the country has a high domestic savings rate, or is enjoying a sustained surge in exports (as, for example, when OPEC nations achieved substantial oil price rises in 1973 and 1979). Investing abroad allows them to convert these revenues, which cannot be fully absorbed domestically, into claims on foreign assets, which can be held until some future time at which domestic expenditure moves ahead of current income. Capital export therefore acts as a form of intertemporal, interregional income redistribution, its recipients being countries which are outspending their current income.

This redistribution is co-ordinated by price signals, with the real return on capital (interest rates for financial transfers and profit rates on foreign direct investment) in low-absorption economies exceeding that in high-absorption economies, even when exchange, political and other risks are taken into account. The interest rate itself becomes part of the pricing of foreign-held financial assets, placing further limits on its use as a policy instrument: raising interest rates can create an expectational bubble as short-term capital piles in, adding exchange appreciation gains to the lure of high domestic-currency returns; lowering interest rates too fast can burst the bubble, capital withdrawal sending the exchange rate down until it is sufficiently undervalued for some speculative investment to be drawn back in. The intertemporal transfer is viable provided capital importers observe these new, restricted policy rules, and follow up by fulfilling the longer-term side of the bargain: using their higher absorption capacity to accumulate capital and generate future exports so that repatriation of profit and repayment of loans can eventually be met out of higher national income.

The need to attract sustained capital inflows to fund a current-account deficit disciplines governments to respect private business needs in its macroeconomic and business-environment policies. 'Outward-oriented' strategies tend to focus on low public deficits aimed at low inflation and currency stability, deregulation of capital markets and removal of exchange conrols to encourage capital inflows (with ease of exit used to encourage entry), privatisation of state-run enterprise and removal of restrictions on private business. Tariff, public-ownership and public-purchasing privileges to domestic enterprise give way to non-discrimination between domestic and foreign business, even tipping over into preferential treatment for foreign investors willing to make commitments to long-term investment. Despite their traditionally lower cost of capital, and the 'golden rule' that justifies public borrowing if matched by public asset creation, state agencies and corporations are encouraged to transfer infrastructure financing to the private sector (through build-operate-transfer schemes or outright privatisation) to reduce its impact on official borrowing. Pressure for lower taxation and spending puts the same momentum behind substituting private insurance for state-financed social services and pensions, whatever the merit-good and risk-pooling arguments that have traditionally supported these.

Since governments are now under pressure to curb their deficits and the source of capital import shifts from sovereign borrowing to private-sector borrowing and equity issue, with government's role limited to the provision of loan and investment guarantees, and possibly some emergency safeguards against exchange risk. Where industries were created under, or taken into, public ownership under previous strategies they tend to be privatised, both to improve the public accounts (providing revenue if profitable, reducing subsidy needs if loss-making) and to avoid presenting private-sector entrants with privileged competition. Opening the market to (actual or potential) foreign competition can provide new competitive discipline to state-owned enterprise, and ensure that it does not long remain a monopoly when privatised. Sale of state-owned assets abroad provides additional funds for financing the current-account deficit and repaying national debt (often another legacy of previous inward-looking strategies).

The exchange rate's role as an asset price attenuates the traditional role of monetary policy. Higher domestic real interest rates, previously expected to suppress price inflation at the expense of lower investment activity and aggregate demand, can now have perverse effects: capital inflows' effect in suppressing inflation by appreciating the exchange rate is offset by their effect in expanding money supply, as greater liquidity enters the corporate and banking sectors. Central banks may be forced to sterilise this inflow by issuing bonds, thus accumulating debt at a time when they would hope to be returning it. In the past, less-developed countries' (LDCs) exchange rates tended to seem overvalued because the purchasing-power-parity (PPP) comparisons were made by comparing price indices that mixed traded and non-traded goods. Since LDCs' trade-sector productivity was lower their relative non-trade (service) sector prices were also lower, so that the general price level seemed 'too low' or the exchange rate too high, in comparison with higher-income economies. Now the same tendency to overvaluation is observed because exchange rates tend to remain above levels that would balance the current account, the difference being caused by capital inflows.

Capital mobility also places limits on the tax rates that governments can safely impose on it, placing them in competition with other nations or regions which might use preferential rates to attract capital of certain types. Although the tax burden can be shifted onto less mobile factors, notably labour, the extent to which this is feasible is limited by the ability of labour with high 'human capital' (managers, scientists) to join the exodus, and the tendency of the rest to wreak vengeance at the polls. Capital mobility thus places a general limit on the tax-raising abilities of governments, and leaves them keen to find new revenue sources which will neither migrate from nor militate against higher tax demands. The recent growth of interest in pollution, land and wealth taxes probably owes something to this concern.

These constraints do not end the government's useful role in the economy, but appear to deflect it towards supply-side measures which guide rather than override the market. The government's task is to prepare the ground for arrival of foreign fixed and financial investment, and the complementary development of domestic enterprise linked to it. While this can still involve much Japanese-style intervention in domestic capital allocation and business conduct, emphasis has tended to be placed on promotion of communications infrastructure, power supply, primary education and health, and 'active' labour market policy to move resources quickly between rising and falling sectors. These have the added advantage, from a market perspective, of being amenable to private-sector and foreign investor involvement at an early stage, and thus weighed fully against market interest rates and alternative investment returns to prevent politically inspired 'megaprojects' distorting the resource allocation.

9.4.6 *Capital mobility and the 'freeing' of exchange rates*

The growth of international capital flows has coincided with a general movement away from fixed exchange rates, which prevailed (under the Bretton Woods system) until the early 1970s but were retained by fewer than half the world's single-currency areas in the late 1990s. Fixed rates had initially been regarded as an essential element in rebuilding world trade and containing world inflation. The exchange rate was not treated like any other relative price, or the foreign exchange (forex) market like any other market. Whereas other relative prices (including wage rates and interest rates) can adjust to clear the market in a particular product or factor, the exchange rate compares an index of prices across a diverse range of markets, setting relative prices for the whole of a nation's tradable sector. A rate which prices some products competitively on world markets may underprice those where productivity is higher (leading to accusations of dumping) and overprice those where quality and technique still require upgrading. Similarly, a single rate may prove too strong for industries which rely on exporting domestically sourced products, or on interest and profit flows from foreign operations, and too weak for those which buy foreign inputs for domestically targeted output or have foreign creditors and shareholders to pay.

One solution, often tried by governments with close control over their banking and forex markets, is to sell foreign currency for different uses at different rates, pricing it most cheaply for those whose import needs are greatest (or whose activity ranks highest in official strategy for the economy). Multiple exchange rates have traditionally been favoured by governments which fear unbearable social costs from forcing domestic industries to adjust to a unified rate, or dynamic disadvantages from the pattern of specialisation that this will produce. But to price foreign exchange differently for different industries compromises the role of money as a medium of exchange, since it requires administrative separation of the markets in which each differently priced money is to circulate. Free international trade and capital-market integration require each nation to offer a unified exchange rate, to which domestic industries must adjust through reallocation of resources to more competitive sectors (signalled by higher wage and profit rates). Without regulation of the currency market and segmentation of product markets, those allowed to buy foreign currency cheaply (e.g. for purchase of inputs not available domestically) could profit by re-selling it to those given a weaker official exchange rate, until unofficial exchange rates converge.

Unifying the exchange rate may not end political interference in the forex market, however, since governments may still choose to intervene in the market to alter the price of the currency. Those with large external debts to service or large official import purchases to make may favour an artificially strong currency, and attain it by commandeering foreign reserves from exporters and banks (effectively setting a second, inferior exchange rate for the private sector). Those with differentially high inflation leading to a loss of trade competitiveness may favour an artificially weak currency, keeping the nation's relative price level down through administrative forex operations rather than the more difficult process of raising productivity and restraining price and wage growth in the tradable sector (and possibly using further administrative price controls to stop the resultant higher import prices from feeding through into further inflation that undermines the undervaluation). These dangers of political manipulation of the exchange rate and associated monetary policy led to the Bretton Woods consensus behind fixed exchange rates as the foundation for rebuilding the world trading system, after the Great Depression breakdown and its culmination in world war. Transparency and stability in the global market was held to require a uniformity in the exchange rate across time (internationally fixed rates) as well as across space (intranationally unified rates).

Fixed exchange rates remove political discretion from monetary policy, which now becomes automatically expansionary when a nation's current account is in surplus and automatically deflationary when it moves into deficit. By making national currencies interchangeable, fixed rates end a segmentation of the international market that is often politically rather than economically based. 'Producers from all parts of the country are able to compete more effectively, and uncertainty in transactions is reduced. Hence the arguments for fixed exchange rates are part of a more general case for policies aiming at international economic integration' (Sodersten 1980: 401).

'One market, one money' has underlain the European Union's attempt to follow up its customs union with a system of irrevocably fixed exchange rates leading swiftly to currency union. Under this approach, the national currency market is one (or in the EU case eleven) market too many – putting boundaries round national markets by impeding the flow of price information, introducing exchange risk and assisting the imposition of national tariffs. To the extent that it assists national price adjustment without the difficulty of co-ordinating a national real-wage adjustment or speeding up the reallocation of resources to sectors of greater comparative advantage, price variation in the forex market is dismissed as a second-best solution to price rigidities in other markets – notably those in the capital and labour markets, whose cross-border movement in response to price signals would obviate the need to adjust the exchange rate, if only governments would undertake to keep it fixed.

Ironically, it was the cross-border movement of capital that helped to undermine the fixed exchange rate system in practice, and has subsequently done much to eject it from mainstream theory. Once exchange controls are removed, capital will move abroad if its owners perceive a better combination of risk and reward. Nations with a fixed exchange rate and a current-account deficit offer the best of both worlds, pushing up domestic interest rates to defend the currency and, if the defence is credible, indemnifying foreign speculative investors against devaluation risk. Where the current-account deficit persists, the loss of discretion over monetary policy ceases to be an economically beneficial de-politicisation, and can become an economically harmful disruption for the domestic market. Interest rates may have to be raised to attract capital for financing a current-account deficit when domestic conditions call for monetary relaxation, or lowered to dispel capital and counteract a current-account surplus when internal balance requires a current-account surplus. The consequent rising external indebtedness in the first case, and rising foreign-currency investment returns in the second, will harden political resistance to the market-driven alternatives of (respectively) devaluing and revaluing the currency. Once an economy receives a 'real shock' which realigns its equilibrium exchange rate, the fixed rate becomes as distortive to allocation as any other fixed price: causing excess supply of foreign currency and inflation if the domestic currency is priced too low, or excess demand for foreign currency and rationing if it is priced too high. The misalignment is self-compounding if an appreciating exchange rate encourages the inflow of speculative capital and a depreciating rate encourages its outflow, inflicting 'bubbles' on the asset markets of a country with an overvalued currency and causing the forex market to overcorrect when devaluation is eventually forced on it.

To the further disapproval of pro-marketeers, the power removed from discretionary monetary policy by a regime of fixed exchange rates with free capital movement is bestowed on discretionary fiscal policy, with its attendant temptations of 'Keynesian' demand management to substitute the adjustment of labour, loan and money markets. Whereas monetary expansion fails to resolve a situation of internal imbalance (demand deficiency) and external balance, because the resultant lowering of interest rates causes capital to flow abroad, fiscal expansion can be rendered doubly effective, since any resultant raising of interest rates attracts capital inflows and brings an accompanying monetary expansion. Monetary reflation expends its output and employment stimulus on the rest of the world, while fiscal reflation causes a crowding-in of private investment funds in place of the previously argued crowding-out.

A new pro-market case for floating exchange rates has therefore emerged, based on stopping governments entering, armed with commandeered or borrowed foreign reserves, as (increasingly weak) players on the forex market, and yielding to the market forces which in any case tend ultimately to overpower such interventions. If the nominal exchange rate is not allowed to appreciate when capital movements fail to compensate for a current-account surplus or overcompensate for a current-account deficit, real appreciation will be forced on the economy by a differentially higher inflation rate, as the inflow of foreign exchange reserves expands the monetary base (and hence bank lending) or as the government issues more debt to sterilise this expansion, incurring a higher fiscal deficit because it pays more interest on the new debt than it receives as interest on the deposited foreign reserves.

Floating rates have the further merit of encouraging market-stabilising arbitrage while, in principle, preventing market-destabilising speculation. Fixed rates, once misaligned by differential inflation and productivity growth rates or changes to international demand patterns, invite currency traders to cluster on the selling side of overvalued and the buying side of undervalued currencies, often enriching themselves at the expense of those economies whose governments spend their reserves in their currency's defence. The only 'credible' way to fix the currency in these conditions is for the government to relinquish all control over it, either leaving money supply to be entirely dictated by the level of foreign exchange reserves (the currency board system) or allowing the circulation of another currency over which it has no control (the US dollar for many emerging economies, and the Euro for most European Union countries). Conversely, if left to float, the exchange rate should in theory act like any other asset price, instantly adjusting to capture all new information relevant to a country's present and future monetary conditions and real competitiveness. Buyers and sellers are therefore more likely to stay on both sides and keep the spot rate moving randomly – as those on the more liquid forex markets appear to do, with even the paths recently found to conform to 'chaos theory' being predictable only a few hours ahead (and perhaps losing even this property if and when chaos models are adopted by a majority of speculative traders).

The case for de-politicising the forex market by fixing rates can still be counterposed to that for letting them freely adjust. So it is not inconceivable that a Bretton Woods-type formula will at some stage be resurrected as a formula for completing the global market – much as the EU views the eleven-member Euro as a complement to its single regional market. But the EU experiment can be viewed as a special case of nations which have spent many years harmonising microeconomic conditions and phasing macroeconomic cycles so as to become a single currency area; and one that still draws apocalyptic warnings from those unconvinced that it has achieved the intra-regional price and wage flexibility or factor mobility needed to let all regions prosper without the option of exchange-rate variation. When the world's major economies finished their latest (Uruguay) round of trade barrier removal, their next negotiating project was a multilateral agreement on investment (MAI) to remove remaining barriers to global capital movement, rather than any new initiative to stabilise exchange rates.

This further push for freer capital flow, reinforcing the revived case for floating exchange rates, can also be seen as an extension of the attack on multiple rates. Until now, many nations which have unified their currency and made it freely convertible for current-account transactions have tended to maintain restrictions on their capital account, in effect maintaining an above-market rate for foreign exchange used for investment purposes. The monetary authority can thereby continue to ration foreign currency acquired for the purchase of foreign assets, and to charge a premium price for domestic assets bought with foreign currency. The much greater toleration for multiple exchange rates on capital than on current account reflects the dangers of letting the relative price of stocks (of foreign and domestic capital) affect the relative price of trade flows. In particular, lower-income nations which opt for unified exchange rates and full currency convertibility too early may find their physical and financial assets being bought 'too cheaply' by foreign investors, resulting in capital inflows which strengthen the exchange rate until their tradable products are 'too expensive' on international markets. Market forces will not necessarily resolve this disjuncture, because the unprofitability of current production caused by the overvalued exchange rate will not affect the valuation of capital assets in non-tradable sectors (such as real estate), and may have only a marginal impact on the valuation of capital assets in tradable sectors (if the buyers have low discount rates and expect a more competitive exchange rate in the long run).

In contrast to their strict safeguards against multiple exchange rates, therefore, international commercial arrangements have tended to leave room for price or volume controls on certain types of foreign capital flow, especially that of short-term speculative investment exploiting a combination of high domestic interest rates and a stable exchange rate. Until initially underpriced domestic assets have been revalued, the exchange rate as a relative asset price can thereby distort the exchange rate as a relative product price. From a market perspective, however, this conflict is temporary, and occurs only because of an initial undervaluation – either in product prices (perhaps because a previously administered exchange rate 'overshot' when first released into the market) or in asset prices (perhaps because returns on capital and rents on land and property were deliberately held down under previous non-market price-setting). Full capital-account convertibility remains the long-term goal, and with it comes a unified exchange rate at which capital and entitlements to capital can trade alongside the products that flow from its use.

OECD-brokered talks on the MAI broke down in early 1998 after a series of missed deadlines, and the loss of monetary safeguards through too early a capital-account liberalisation was one of the painful lessons of devaluation crises in South Korea and the Czech Republic (both OECD members) in 1997–8. The national and global welfare-maximising merits of free international capital flow are much more hotly disputed, empirically and theoretically, than those of free international trade (e.g. Rodrik 1998). But restoring the exchange controls or forex turnover taxes needed to re-establish national discipline over capital flows, and then the fixed exchange rate system which once worked under such discipline, implies two highly complex sets of multilateral negotiations. For governments with the millennium in their sights, another round of trade liberalisation in the context of floating exchange rates still seems the more enticing option.

9.5 Getting there: deregulated routes to free trade

Different attitudes towards the symmetry of current and capital transaction have led to something of a paradox in the way free-trade arrangements are pursued. 'Western' trading nations, intent on setting a single exchange rate and applying it to all markets (including a large and integrated capital market), have tended to rely on multiple tariffs and other trade barriers to promote 'infant' industries, and compensate for other disjunctures between static and dynamic comparative advantage. This has led to a large network of two-way trade defences which must be dismantled simultaneously if all parties are to gain. Trade liberalisation has therefore taken the form of complex multilateral negotiations (via GATT and the WTO), with the need for rigid policing once the deal has been signed. The difficulty of co-ordinating and enforcing the necessary collective action has encouraged the formation of regional customs unions (the EU, Nafta, Mercosur, etc.), the barriers between which then require further rounds of complex multilateral bargaining to break down.

In contrast, 'eastern' trading nations, with more recent experience of multiple exchange rates (whose relational-transaction underpinnings are still strong), and smaller and less integrated debt and equity markets, have felt far less restrained in abandoning tariff and non-tariff barriers unilaterally once an industry is considered fit for international competition. Within their region, trade liberalisation has therefore tended to take an 'open' form in which barriers are removed without the need for reciprocal obligation, so avoiding the long negotiation and tight policing entailed by GATT. Under the Asia-Pacific Economic Co-operation (APEC) forum (which, symptomatically of its opennenss, had by 1997 embraced the USA, Canada, Australia, New Zealand, Mexico and Chile as well as eleven East Asian nations), 'There is an ultimate goal – free trade within the region by 2020 – but within this umbrella commitment there is freedom for individual countries to liberalise in their own way and at their own speed' (House *et al.* 1997: 6). So far, the approach has achieved a steady removal of trade barriers without the need for complex negotiations and policing, or for the common external tariffs which lay preferential trading blocs open to the charge of efficiency-destroying 'trade diversion'.

APEC's 'open regionalism' is now under challenge to show that it can maintain momentum – and avoid backsliding – with the region's previously fast growth reduced to near-standstill. The GATT's multilateralism was also slowed by past recessions, and has yet to prove its resilience to a severe international downturn, in which deflationary pressures can be transmitted across trading partners just as readily as those for expansion and structural change. Although predicated on the mutual gains from free trade, and its special advantages for smaller economies with unusual relative cost patterns, it is possible to ascribe the progress (so far) of liberalisation under both arrangements to political expediency rather than economic rationality. The UK, and subsequently the USA, could use their role as major direct investors, creditors, military protectors and aid-givers to extract trade concessions from partner economies to which they wanted fuller access. Japan has recently assumed a similar role in East Asia, while the European Union has emerged as a powerful promoter of its member states' trade interests (in stark contrast to its inability to co-ordinate other aspects of external policy), and the glint of US market access needs has been detected behind the ostensibly theory-driven prescriptions of the IMF and World Bank.

The difficulty of detaching trade liberalisation from geopolitics has been highlighted by recent confrontations between the USA and Japan (incited by Japan's large bilateral trade surplus and alleged institutional import barriers), and the USA and EU (over issues ranging from hormone-treated beef and cheap dollar bananas to trade involving 'expropriated' Cuban-American assets). Such episodes raise the question of whether international trade liberalisation can continue, and avoid recession-induced reversals, when there is no hegemonic power to enforce it in return for capital inflows and other financial and technical assistance. To the extent that trade barriers have continued to fall since the 'cold war' ended, it may be because multinational investors and multilateral creditors have taken the place of hegemonic governments in enforcing market access. Multinational enterprises (MNEs) must sell across the globe so as to recoup the costs of developing new profit-promoting technology, and prospective host nations must welcome them with open arms (and borders) to acquire the technology and capital-market access that they bring (Strange 1998: 106–7).

In this perspective it is neither market-oriented multilateral discussion nor relational open regionalism that gets free trade established, but the hegemony of large-country governments aligned with big business interests. According to the UN Commission on Trade and Development, one-third of world trade in the mid-1990s was conducted within MNEs (as administered transaction), and another one-third between other parties and MNEs (in what may in many cases have been relational transaction). The search for rules to govern the remaining one-third may simply be MNEs' attempt to extend control over the minority of trades still conducted through the global marketplace.

9.6   Staying there: bicycle and limousine economies

Whether or not trade follows the flag, it is apt to be less a bandwagon than a cart that overtakes the horse. Theory presents the removal of barriers as a force for growth and structural change, but slowdown and structural inertia are in practice among the first motives for returning to protectionism. The removal of barriers to capital movement is similarly prone to follow the upturn it was supposed to lead. The volatility of interest and exchange rates induced by the process of capital flow has long been an incentive for maintaining cross-border controls on it. Now that those controls have largely been lifted, or subverted by the market, equally strong protective instincts are provoked by the product of capital flow: the very different commercial and social priorities that can be forced on an economy by foreign ownership, and the equally disruptive effects if it is taken away.

The century that began with Europe colonially controlling much of the world, and preparing to expend its industrial energies fighting for the rest of it, ends with the USA anticipating a ten-year boom as the world standardises on its currency, computers and confectionery, while Japan and its once high-flying Asian satellites must contemplate US-style deregulation and capital-market reform to fend off a ten-year depression. US disadvantage in the global product market – its foreign trade gap widened even as growth was closing its chronic budget deficit – appears more than outweighed by its advantage in the global capital market. Studies have already shown that US trade in the early 1990s would have come close to balance if its multinational subsidiaries' foreign output were included as export (and foreign multinationals' US production included as import). Recent events suggest that US ownership and financing arrangements may be the export that changes the rules by which product exports could not abide.

9.6.1 The East Asian vicious circle?

The two to three decades of rapid, low-inflation growth achieved by 'tiger' economies in East and South-east Asia forced western economists to assess them as a possible alternative growth model to that built on observation of earlier, slower industrialisers. Many found that the Asian success could satisfactorily be explained in conventional terms, as the triumph of decentralised accumulation and allocation of capital in pursuit of private profit, assisted by low rates of taxation, government spending and regulation, free capital markets and unimpeded access to the global product market. But others, including a team at the World Bank (1993), eventually conceded that other, non-market elements in the system might have helped to bring the 'miracle' about. Individual co-operation (expressed through community-like, labour-empowering firms), supported by inter-firm and firm–government co-operation, appeared to have produced not only the spatial co-ordination needed to maintain full employment, but also the temporal co-ordination to sustain high rates of saving, investment and growth.

The Asian 'growth model' rested heavily on relational and administered forms of transaction. Entrepreneurs, concerned to raise capital from sources that would understand their business, and especially its need to sacrifice distributed profit to reinvestment and growth in the early stages of development, looked to creditors who would respect (and further empower) their right to manage rather than share-holders who would reduce them to paid agents for the extraction and payout of profit. Banks, lacking readily available information on business ventures' credit-worthiness or the likely profitability of their new projects, preferred to use long-term relationships to identify good business partners and make them into better ones. The same preference applied to depositors, whose loyalty was made easier to retain by 'non-poaching' conventions among banks (over clients as well as staff) which were reinforced by regulations limiting their ability to differentiate savings products. Households, in turn, were willing to entrust their savings to banks even at low interest rates because even worse returns were expected of cash hold-ings (because of inflation) or equity investment (because of low distributions).

A self-reinforcing cycle developed in which heavy business investment in export-oriented capital- and intermediate-goods production gave households rapidly rising incomes with few consumer goods to spend it on, so encouraging large flows of long-term saving into banks, insurance and pension funds, which maintained the regime of low borrowing costs and high investment.

> Gross domestic savings to GDP ratios in Asia are one third of GDP or more, compared to 15–20 per cent in Western systems. The savings are done in large part by households. Households hold their savings mostly in bank deposits, bank deposits being much less risky than equities. Banks have to lend . . . Such a structure requires co-operation between banks and firms, and considerable government support.
>
> (Wade and Veneroso 1998: 6–7)

The rewards are reflected in Table 9.1, where the significantly higher proportion of direct investment in Asian compared with Latin American capital inflows can be ascribed to higher Asian savings rates and closer-held industrial ownership, which predisposed enterprises to fund investment internally and so placed less political priority on creating stock- and bond-markets and opening them to foreign investors.

Judged by the standards of market transaction-based economies, however, the system looked dangerously unstable. High debt–equity ratios implied that firms were seeking to avoid the external accountability and takeover discipline that went with equity finance, relying instead on captive creditors to roll over short-term loans so that they could fund long-term investment, and (if this went wrong) to write off the debts rather than calling them in. Stock-markets seemed dangerously overvalued in the light of their historically low returns, yet dependent on further increases to give their shareholders any real return. 'Relational' dealing between firms' management, suppliers, creditor banks, the bureaucrats regulating their markets and the politicians shaping industrial strategy seemed uncomfortably close to the nepotism and corruption which had traditionally been seen as retarding eco-nomic growth (and democracy) in the region. Low domestic interest rates, once a tribute to high household and corporate saving, were an encouragement to waste-ful corporate and government investment projects.

When monetary authorities tried to address this (and quell inflation) by raising domestic interest rates, fixed or informally targeted exchange rates allowed private companies to go abroad for cheaper loans. By implicitly indemnifying corporate borrowers against exchange risk (and, in the case of banks and conglomerates 'too big to fail', implicitly guaranteeing their debts), governments had thereby made it economically as well as politically costly to consider devaluing the currency, even when export growth slowed sharply. It was equally costly to permit the burst of price inflation which would traditionally have rescued borrowers from a rising domestic debt burden, since such inflation would only make the currency more overvalued and choke off exports, which were needed to service hard-currency debt and to ward off the demand deficiency that threatens a high-savings economy when domestic investment wanes.

> When exchange rates are fixed and capital movements restricted, as under the post-war Bretton Woods system, excess savings at first slows growth in the surplus savings country . . . The only system which will tolerate large and persistent trade surpluses is one where capital is free to move from one country to another. Falling interest rates in the surplus savings country leads to capital outflows, which lower the value of its currency.
>
> (Reading 1992: 38–9)

In East Asia excluding Japan, devaluation pressure intensified because large corporations' scramble to invest abroad (to evade foreign trade barriers and escape rising domestic labour costs) maintained a heavy export of capital even after stagnant exports had pushed the current account back into deficit. The easiest alternative to devaluation was to invite more inflows of capital, which western financial institutions were initially keen to subscribe to the 'miracle', leading them to press for liberalisation of Asia's banking, bond, equity and foreign exchange markets. But in deregulating financial services and removing capital-account restrictions, East Asian governments enabled their own long-term capital to flow abroad in search of higher returns, leaving domestic banks borrowing short and lending long to satisfy corporate clients' low-cost capital needs. 'They removed or loosened controls on companies' foreign borrowings, abandoned co-ordination of borrowings and investments, and failed to strengthen bank supervision. By doing so, they violated one of the stability conditions of the Asian high debt model' (Wade and Veneroso 1998: 9). Flagging growth fed back into a diminishing flow of new saving, and monetary relaxation to stabilise the banks encouraged the remainder to flow into equities or foreign bonds, bypassing the banks.

By early 1997 the prospect of currency weakness, slower growth and overhanging debt in the 'tiger' economies was causing enough concern for a growing number of domestic and foreign investors to liquidate their equity exposure and cease lending to them. The ensuing currency collapse and bad-debt explosion was exacerbated by the economies' extensive trade and capital-market integration, and by lack of co-ordination among the countries' creditors and investors which made rapid exit the privately most profitable (or least loss-making) strategy even if staying in for an 'orderly' debt workout would have been collectively less damaging. Deteriorating expectations of East Asia's ability to maintain the export and currency strength that underwrote its large foreign debt exposure and the growth rates that justified its high stock-market valuations were to a large extent self-fulfilling. Sudden reversal of capital inflow forced a series of devaluations which left many firms unable to keep up payments on their foreign debt. Currencies' overshoot pushed domestic interest rates to levels at which local-currency debts were similarly underserviceable, thereby inflicting cashflow and liquidity difficulties even on companies and banks which had avoided heavy foreign exposure.

With growth dramatically slowed by the collapse of investment, stock- and bond-markets felled by the high interest rate, and the loans collateralised against these vanished assets destined anyway to be non-performing at the growth and interest rates now prevailing, the previous high debt–equity ratios and appreciating real exchange rates now gave ample retrospective reason for fleeing the 'tigers' – even if, as some economists argued, it had been an irrational panic at the time. The 'panic' explanation is supported by the observations that few foreign investors anticipated the crisis, few had reason to believe that governments or multilateral lenders would bail them out of it, most engaged in a wholesale withdrawal which included the abandonment of viable enterprises, most as a result stand to lose more on bad debts than would have been lost through an orderly workout that let illiquid but solvent enterprises continue trading, and most took flight before it was clear that stock and land prices were collapsing rather than merely correcting (Radelet and Sachs 1998: 8).

Critics of these critics argue that market players were rational in withdrawing once they realised that shrinking foreign reserves and slowing growth rates made devaluation and debt deflation inevitable (and would point out that the 'panic' proponents, Sachs in particular, had previously endorsed the East Asia's 'very fast growing economies' (VFGEs) for their macroeconomic virtues of high private saving and low government borrowing, and the use of fixed exchange rates to combat inflation).

> The overall image of VFGEs as open economies, with small government sectors, and with a light degree of government regulation, may surprise some readers . . . [but] on an international comparative standard, the East Asian economies stand out as highly market oriented, with a long period of relatively free trade, low levels of government spending relative to GDP, and limited distortions from government regulations.
>
> (Sachs and Warner 1996: 14–15)

This macroeconomic perspective may have overlooked the relational nature of much of the transaction taking place against this market-friendly background, but the social solidarity which provided a stable background for such relations will have been severely, perhaps irreparably, damaged by the VFGEs' sudden change of fortunes and the bouncing of long-term commercial links into the bankruptcy courts.

The 'bicycle' economies, which needed to keep moving forward in order to stay upright, had been exposed as 'bubble' economies. As the only suppliers of credit capable of tiding them over the crisis, western economies (and the multilateral agencies in which they have a majority shareholding) are now free to set the terms on which to push-start them. Their remedy appears to be a rapid conversion of the Asian 'relational' model to a western alternative based on market transaction in goods, labour and capital. Governments (including that of Japan) are being pressed to deregulate their equity and bond-markets and open them to foreign competition. 'Excess' debt is being converted into equity, through the acquisition by western multinationals of large stakes in those Asian conglomerates which cannot service their debts. Those firms, under western creditor pressure, are also abandoning their commitment to 'lifetime' employment, sacking workers made surplus to requirements by the unanticipated standstill in the real economy and inflicting more flexible contracts on the rest. When they can afford to raise external finance again, it will be via equity and bond-markets which monitor financial performance much more closely, and treat poor results as a signal to sack managers or sell out, rather than a symptom of long-term market-building strategy.

Relational economies have undergone previous external shocks, notably when forced to adopt western-designed international trade rules so as to find outlets for their export-driven growth. This required the loosening of close supplier–manufacturer–retailer links which were viewed from outside as market entry barriers and vertical foreclosures, and the abandonment of multiple exchange rates. Sectoral exchange-rate variation had proved durable in economies where agents were accustomed to striking bilateral deals with foreign clients or the central-bank intermediary, and lacked either the information or incentive to undermine the system by re-trading foreign currency with those who valued it differently. In the aftermath of war, Japanese manufacturers found that

> to be able to sell abroad, prices for export goods had to be at whatever level in terms of dollars such goods could be sold in foreign markets, which meant that the actual dollar price for each good had a controlling effect on the specific yen–dollar ratio for each good . . . Such specific ratios ranged, in 1948, from 180 yen to 800 yen a dollar.
>
> (Tsuru 1993: 49)

Forced by a large trade deficit (caused in part by converting export revenues at higher yen rates than import prices) and US occupiers' pressure to unify the exchange rate, the government did so – on Tsuru's advice – at the relatively low rate of 360 yen/dollar, putting the long-term competitiveness needs of manufactured exporters above the short-term cashflow needs of commodity importers. Japan's subsequent boom appeared to justify the decision, and the rate did not need to be changed until 1971 (when it was strengthened, to 308 yen/dollar). But the adjustment of Japan – and the 'new Japans' to free international trade was conducted on their own terms, in a way which preserved relational and administered transaction on the home market (of a kind which frustrated trade partners often condemned as concealed continuation of protectionism and price discrimination). The adjustment to free international capital movement is being conducted on terms drawn from a very different economic environment. To the extent that it imposes a move to generalised market transaction in labour and capital markets which have traditionally used it sparingly, this new shock may make it very much harder for formerly dynamic Asia to go on growing its own way.

9.6.2   The North American virtuous circle?

Those who stand over the sedated Asian tigers, administering their painful market medicines, have found what were previously regarded as structural weaknesses turned to international strengths. In comparison with the eastern debt-based model, the western financial market-based model was long viewed as incapable of sustaining full employment or high growth. North America appeared locked into a cycle of low savings rates, low investment, slow growth, wage inflation controllable only by periodic doses of mass unemployment, high labour turnover which limited human capital accumulation, and chronic trade and current-account deficits which made it the world's largest importer of capital, culminating in President Reagan's infamous doubling of the US national debt. Western Europe managed a higher private savings ratio, but was seen as squandering it on large public-sector deficits as governments took over industries, social provisions and income distribution for which markets were deemed a more efficient vehicle.

Reinterpreted to reflect the late 1990s' economic power balance, the North American 'market' approach emerges as the winner, beating the 'relational' approach at what had threatened to turn into a zero-sum game. The low US savings rate keeps aggregate demand at (or above) full-employment level without Asian-style dependence on an export surplus which would eventually impoverish the foreign buyers on which it depends. Low savings mean a positive interest rate which forces investors to send capital where its returns are highest. Improved allocation of capital compensates for the lower volume of capital and so enables faster long-run growth: high interest rates turn from a symptom of profligate short-termism to a symbol of how productive (and profitable) investment becomes when market forces tell it where to go. With higher returns on claims to physically invested capital (equity) than on deposited financial capital (debt), households channel their savings to industry via mutual funds, whose strong capital appreciation substitutes for saving (or even collateralises further borrowing) and so lets the economy run at even higher levels of aggregate demand.

> The result is that many Americans have had the luxury of feeling wealthier (and, on paper, being wealthier) even as they save less than ever before. They achieve this by investing in stocks rather than less lucrative alternatives, such as bank deposits, money-market funds and savings certificates.
>
> (R. Samuelson 1998: 35)

While asset prices climb, consumer and producer price inflation stays low because the higher demand is matched by rising productivity of capital and labour – and, if not, can be expended on higher imports because high interest rates and equity returns attract a steady foreign capital inflow. The corresponding current-account deficit is not a concern because high-performing mutual and pension funds substitute for state welfare provision, and (together with sustained rapid growth) eliminate the public-sector deficit.

The 'limousine economy' stays upright even when moving slowly, or occasionally forced to a halt, as well as giving its occupants a more comfortable ride when external conditions get turbulent. With the toppling bicycles cleared from their path, the equity-driven vehicles may be able to run even faster, relieved of inflationary pressures by cheap East Asian imports and subdued commodity prices, and enriched by equally cheap East Asian assets snapped up in debt–equity swaps. Critics continue to view it as a bubble car which will eventually drive off a cliff. In their gloomier next chapter, rising external debt will force the government to close the current-account deficit through fiscal and monetary contraction, depressing corporate profit and revealing the equity markets as overvalued. At this point households will reduce spending sharply, debts secured against inflated assets will prove unrepayable, and banks will suffer for the risks they took with exotic derivative instruments when ordinary lending was made unprofitable by falling interest-rate spreads and disintermediation via equities. International financial leverage will then return to those nations whose high savings have turned them into global creditors – notably Japan, whose present deflationary plight arouses US sympathy less through altruism than because it invites a further flood of cheap Japanese exports at the expense of American industry and a calling-in of the debts which financed the US 'twin deficits' for most of the 1990s.

If, indeed, the US is a paradigmatic market model (something that observers of its large market-share concentrations, corporate structures and government-business links may contest), it may owe its success to special factors: possession of the world's largest domestic market, too big for foreign creditors to allow to fail, and the world's reserve currency, which uniquely allows it to run up external debts in its own currency and, if necessary, bringing them down by repaying them with printed money which exports inflation to the rest of the world. But western Europe, through its single market and single currency, now aspires to similar privileges. And even if the US–EU advantage proves temporary, it is being used to rewrite the laws of the jungle in ways which may make it very hard for Asia's tigers to bite back. Western economic philosophy, unable to replicate relational 'Confucian' structures, has inverted an equally venerable folk wisdom: if you can't join them, beat them. Market-based trade and capital movements may not have been the only, or the best, full employers and growth promoters. But their hold over allocation seems – in the absence of international rules to preserve co-ordination across space and time – to have made them the one that wins, when rival systems' protective barriers are prematurely taken down.

9.7 Conclusion: throwing caution to the trade winds

Long regarded as desirable by economists but unenforceable by governments, free trade's steady advance may owe as much to nations' seeking to keep their own market imperfections under control as to open up new Pareto-improving trade abroad. But where 'comparative advantages' are unequal across time and space, and open to improvement by government intervention, the dismantling of trade protection is more than a co-ordination problem. Whole nations, not just sectional interests within them, may be adversely affected by low elasticities and unequal exchange. Greater foreign competition may also bring collaboration rather than competition among market-powerful companies. On their own, the economic arguments for free trade are unlikely to have brought the world so far towards it.

In contrast, capital movement has been actively sought by growth-seeking nations for its promise of technology transfer and the opportunity to invest while continuing to consume. Fixed inward investment often means importing the home country's productivity requirements long before its wage rates, and inward portfolio investment can be attracted only by leaving open the door for sudden departure, but the jilted host feels the need for it more acutely only when it is gone. With Japan already showing what disasters can happen when a country grows too rich and saves too much, most forecasts of global recovery are founded on high-income nations rediscovering the need to fund their retirement from work by investing for faster growth where incomes are still low. Since the rich world's retirement from work is as much due to shifting industrial geography as rising gerontocracy, they will still expect to buy what comes out of the transplanted factories. Far from substituting trade, by taking production inside the borders to which products were once sent, cross-border investment has tended to increase it, reflecting the growing role of multinational and global companies as its carriers. The need to accommodate capital imposes a discipline on government policy discretion which market economists under autarky rarely managed. But if they do not complete the global market voluntarily, the transplants in their midst may force them to do so, encouraged by countries of origin no longer sorry to see them go.

10 Market rewards

The distribution of income

To nutritionists, we are what we eat. To geneticists, what our chromosomes dictate to us. To psychologists, the euphorias and phobias the world has put into our minds. Economists have borrowed from – and can claim to have contributed to – all these disciplines, but can offer an even narrower reductionism: we are what we are paid. The parallel is an unfair one because few nutritionists, geneticists and psychologists contend that the phenomena they study are the only ones that shape us. In contrast, when it comes to valuing people, many economists view the market as the fairest – and perhaps the only – judge of what we are worth.

The suspicion that markets are the worst form of social organisation, except for all the others, is nowhere more evident than in attitudes to income distribution. Concepts of a 'fair' or 'living' wage, assigned according to preparation, effort or the moral worth of output, have tended to last far longer than that of a 'just price' for inanimate products. The labour theory of value may have been discarded, but a value theory of labour is still appealed to when employees expect their better skills or longer experience to generate higher pay, regardless of the price put on the results. Objections to supply and demand being the only determinant of personal worth are strengthened by some of the obvious anomalies thrown up by the 'labour market'. A celebrity may 'earn' as much for a minute spent advertising lager as a surgeon receives for a day spent saving lives. (Worse, 'tournament theory' suggests that professions whose earnings depend extensively on luck, as might be argued for the music, sport and film worlds, should raise rather than lower their stars' differential over others – the 'best' winning huge premiums over the merely very good, and needing incentives to assure their audience they made their millions on merit.) Injustice seems just as strong when the inconsistency is temporal rather than spatial. Poverty may sometimes inspire artists, but more often brings forward their expiry, any rarity value this adds to their work sharpening the spectacle of its being rejected on first appearance and orbitally priced on posthumous resale.

10.1 Value and and distribution: inconveniently inseparable

An earlier strand of economic thought, unhappy that free-market agents should carry a price on their heads, attempted to maintain a distinction between the allocation of resources (a task for the market) and the distribution of income (a precondition of market trade which was open to social engineering through wage-setting and tax arrangements). The view received probably its clearest English-language expression from John Stuart Mill (1806–73), who endorsed the 'classical' view of production as determined by natural resource availability and technology, but rejected his predecessors' picture of a naturally determined (subsistence) wage. 'The laws governing the distribution of the social product, however, fell into a different category. In this case the outcome was socially determined and subject to human control' (Barber 1967: 100). But the 'marginalist' distribution theory that emerged shortly afterwards (section 10.2.3) insisted that workers could raise their real wage (and preserve full employment in their labour market) only by raising productivity, or demand for their product. The general equilibrium models that followed could accommodate a variable – and possibly socially determined – initial resource endowment (section 2.1.3), but was otherwise loyal to the new view that real wages were a relative price for which only one value would clear each labour market. Among more recent theories, only that of 'efficiency wages' – reversing marginalist causation so that the wage rate affects productivity – offers significant scope for distribution to be independent of, or a determinant of, the level and composition of production.

By turning the real wage into a price, which workers (the sellers of labour services) trade off against the 'opportunity cost' of the substitute product, leisure, economists have rejected Mill's separation of production from (initial) income distribution. Although a general competitive equilibrium can emerge from any initial distribution of property, its income flows will depend on relative supply of productive factors and their marginal productivity. The source of the market's legitimacy shifts from the social justice of its starting-point to the economic efficiency of its outcomes. Indeed, to the extent that unemployment is traced to the overpricing of labour, any attempt to fix rewards independently of the market is seen as undermining the fairness it set out to promote.

10.2   Pricing the pay: market income determination

Mill's attempt to divide the price of people from the price of their products was the last of many distinguished triumphs of social hope over economic inference. Most previous macroeconomic models, including those of Smith and Ricardo, drew a similar distinction between value (relative prices) and distribution (the rates of wages, interest and profit). Markets for 'factors of production' were not an unfamiliar concept (Smith drew a salary, Ricardo was a stockbroker), but their relevance to distribution was limited because long-term returns to land, labour and capital had a more fundamental explanation. Their cost-based explanation of reward rates is now sidelined from conventional economics, as one of the 'institutional' theories considered in section 10.4.

In one of the few 'revolutions' they acknowledge from within, economists in the late nineteenth century dropped the distinction between value and distribution. By treating labour and capital as 'factors of production' traded like the products they create, income levels could be shown to emerge from the same market process that determined prices. Wages and profits adjusted to clear the labour and capital markets, with employment and capacity utilisation the associated equilibrium quantities. The relative wage (money wage deflated by a *numeraire*, or 'real wage' if this were an index of product prices) would rise in times of labour shortage and fall in times of unemployment. If unemployment persisted, it was because labour had been overpriced. To the extent that capital and labour were substitutes, machines would replace workers who asked for too much. To the extent that they were complements, over-rewarding one factor might lead to the other sharing in its unemployment at the margin.

Marginal productivity tends to be as empirically elusive as it is theoretically restrictive (see sections 4.5 and 4.6), but general equilibrium theory sidesteps the aggregation problem to reinforce the message that agents get as good as they give. Since the only exogenous elements in the general-equilibrium income flow are technologies, preferences and initial endowments, the resultant distribution has an aura of inevitability. Any other attempt to change the income distribution, without a change in these conditions, dislodges the system from its optimum allocation and causes a lapse from full employment. Against egalitarians' exploitation of apparent leeway over the initial distribution, incentive arguments for inequality offer the twin defence of higher productivity made open to all by rising social mobility.

10.2.1 Income as factor price: marginal productivity theory

Demand for labour in this 'neoclassical' model derives from the value of its marginal product, the market value of what an extra employee can produce. Under perfect competition this is the marginal physical product – the output added by an extra worker – multiplied by the product's market price. Labour's marginal productivity is assumed to be declining over the relevant employment range (the best workers are recruited first, or there is a fixed amount of capital for them to work with), so that employing the last unit of labour for exactly the value of its marginal product means making a profit on all the intra-marginal units.

Supply of labour reflects the amount of work a person will do at different wage rates, a higher rate being assumed to elicit longer or more intensive effort. The positive substitution effect of a wage rise, leading to more work being offered because the opportunity cost of non-work is higher, is assumed to outweigh any negative income effect, of less work being necessary to obtain the same total payment as before. This is one of the few points at which social considerations are allowed to intrude on an essentially technologically determined theory. In some pre-industrial societies it is observed that higher wages cause workers to knock off earlier, but this is assumed to be 'cured' once diversified production has given them a more enticing range of products on which extra income could be spent.

Firms' demand for labour derives directly from households' demand for their products, while the supply of labour to firms depends on the aggregate of households' offers to work at different wages. Labour is employed up to the point where its rising marginal cost (more having to be offered to attract more supply) meets the value of its declining marginal product (each extra unit adding less to production than the one before it, at least while capital stock is fixed). This break-even point sets equilibrium employment, and the wage to be paid to all employees.

The neoclassical model admits the possibility of labour being 'exploited' where it encounters monopolised or cartelised demand, which allows a profit-maximising employer to pay a wage that is less than the marginal product value. Exploitation can also arise from imperfection in the product market, which pushes the value of marginal product below the marginal revenue product. But where competition prevails, wage rates and differentials are explained entirely by preferences (of workers supplying labour) and technology (determining labour productivity). 'In the absence of market imperfections, income is determined by how much one's labour and owned resources add to market-valued goods and services. Competitive pressures push wages towards levels that reflect the marginal (last-hired) labourer's additional contribution to output' (Rhoads 1985: 86).

Unemployment is a principal source of income inequality, since it tends to befall individuals with few sources of non-work income and so reduces them to what the state or private charity will provide. Long spells of unemployment tend also to dislodge their victims from the career 'ladder' which might have assured them steadily rising income through accumulating skill or seniority. Marginal distribution theory provides the assurance, if sufficient competition is applied, that all those wanting work will find it if they are willing to adjust their pay demands to their productivity. Those out of work are reaping the punishment for producing too little or demanding too much, unless they prefer to live on handouts. In its simplest version, the logic of 'mainstream' theory is indeed remorseless.

10.2.2   *Income as investment return: human capital theory*

Certain types of genius may be born not made, but a worker's productivity usually comes at least partly within the person's control. Labour can improve its wage-earning prospects by raising its productivity, assuming that the usual comparison of marginal costs and benefits shows this to be worthwhile. The first step is to find the occupation where present skills are valued most highly. The second is to acquire additional skills. In a valuable extension of the neoclassical symmetry between the two main factors of production, workers can accumulate 'human capital' in just the way that owners accumulate physical capital, and earn higher rewards because of their greater contribution to production value in any given time.

Education, training and learning-by-doing are all investments in labour quality which, if correctly chosen, will be paid back by the higher earnings they make possible. Studies of the return on human capital investment have mostly concerned university education, where costs (course fees and forgone earnings) and benefits (graduate/non-graduate salary differentials) are fairly easy to separate and measure. They traditionally show a return well into double figures, although as everywhere else, the growth of first degree supply relative to the demand for 'graduate' work tends at times to depress the differential and send students scrambling for second degrees to protect the value of their investment.

10.2.3   *Income from factor ownership*

Human capital theory introduces the idea that employees own an asset, their ability to generate marketable labour services, and that their pay is a return on investments made to maintain and improve that asset. But people may also own capital and real estate, which give them additional income streams in the form of interest, profit or rent. The pejorative term 'unearned income' reflects the common suspicion that these holdings of non-labour assets, which can generate so much more income than a full-time job as to make it unnecessary, are socially difficult to justify. The same argument is sometimes used regarding 'natural' talents which can attract rewards without apparent effort, ranging from looks and knockout punches to perfect pitch and a perfect pitching action.

In practice, titles to property income may be acquired through saving out of labour income, making them socially legitimate to the extent that this income was legitimate. If assigned arbitrarily, property ownership may still have an economic justification in rescuing all agents from externality or common-pool resource problems (sections 2.3, 2.5). If inherited, they may represent the necessary enactment of the process which incentivised a previous agent to accumulate them for social benefit. A case can usually be made for even the most 'natural' of gifts to have been self-improved. The one objection a market perspective might raise to large payments for exceptional (or exceptionally marketable) talent relates to the differential of the income received over what the holder could earn in their next most lucrative employment. If, as some have been known to admit, the megastar's choice was between movie-making and pasta-making, they may be earning a large 'rent' above the minimum that could keep them in their current profession. A maximising employer might be able to capture some of that rent by paying less, or a knowledgeable tax authority by charging more. The problem then reduces to one of monopoly – many employers or tax jurisdictions competing for the services of one star – whose cure might be the extension of the market, but might also involve breaking the monopoly by subsidising rival supply expansion, or countervailing it by letting the buyers co-ordinate their bids.

The market judgement is more scathing against high returns which relate to artificial scarcity, because owners of human or physical capital have succeeded in limiting its acquisition or expansion. Industries whose incumbents secure supply restriction through licensing (e.g. banking permits, taxi badges), and professions which bar entry on anything other than quality grounds, are accused of stopping the market process halfway. Pay differentials are supposed to encourage more people to invest in meeting the entry conditions. If such entry is not allowed, pay in these sectors remains inflated to the detriment of the wider economy, and a room for nepotism, prejudice and other less economically and socially desirable selection methods is introduced as employers choose from the lengthening queue. Entry restriction has limited justification from a possible time-inconsistency problem: an income differential may close too quickly to repay human capital investment if it induces many simultaneous, uncoordinated decisions to invest (a labour-market analogy to the problem of the expanding firm under perfect competition, identified by Richardson 1960).

10.2.4   *Alertness, opportunism and luck*

Stock-market killings and lottery wins may be comparatively rare, but for those on the receiving end they tend to make regular income flows seem rather insignificant. Over time, such windfalls and people's freedom to transfer them significantly shapes the distribution of an economy's wealth-generated income, which tends to widen the inequality in work-generated incomes, especially at the upper tail. Successfully laying claim to disputed or unsuspected sources of income is a principal means by which people can transform their personal income situation. 'Instant wealth arises in the process of capitalisation . . . to become very rich one must generate or select a situation where an above-average rate of return is about to be capitalised' (Thurow 1980: 173).

The social justice aspects of such claims are debatable. The randomness of lottery wins, and – despite the best efforts of professional stock-pickers – of their stock-market equivalent, the sudden capital gain, might seem to justify big wins in that potentially anyone could make them (if ticket prices and dealing costs are not too high). But randomly distributed gains and losses will, for purely statistical reasons, progressively widen income inequality. Given the element of luck involved, the limited downside risk compared with virtually unlimited upside opportunities, and the excess of these gains over any that can be ascribed to individual effort or merit, this might seem to be intrinsically unfair.

Capitalisation gains which require some effort to identify and capture need not appear any more just. 'Demutualisation', the distribution to customers of financial surpluses accumulated by mutually owned financial and insurance institutions which seemed to sweep English-speaking economies in the late 1990s, appeared to consist of the present generation of members choosing to spend a store of wealth which had been built up by previous generations and would otherwise have passed on to future generations. Supporters of the process argued that members' freedom to save (or spend) the money held in their name as they wished, and demutualised companies' access to cheaper funds and financial discipline on the stock-market, was a market-driven improvement in allocation. Similarly, pension funds which accumulate large surpluses of income over payout obligations, the ownership of which is not always spelt out in their statutes, have tended after setting aside appropriate contingency reserves to pay over the extra money to either the employees or the employers who contribute to the scheme, arguing that these can put it to better use.

Windfall gains can also result from more directly productive (as distinct from redistributive) activities, and it is to the effects of these – particularly in rewarding and incentivising entrepreneurial risk-taking and innovations – that market advocates in 'Austrian' mode prefer to draw attention. Those who invest directly in a company that suddenly takes off can be seen as being rewarded for their foresight and willingness to take risks, and for the external benefits they bring to society from speeding the development of an industry which (through its profit taxes if not through its product) enriches the rest of society. Those who secure temporary monopoly profits through patent protection or entry barriers around a new invention are similarly taking a reward for ingenuity and risk, which then encourages others to push the state of technical knowledge forward. To the extent that they divert such productive risk-taking of the primary capital market into the redistributive risk-taking of the secondary market, windfall gains in the financial sector of the economy have sometimes been condemned as parasitic on those in the real sector. The ratio of speculative to underlying share, bond and currency transactions has risen almost as dramatically as that of stock-exchange floor to shopfloor salaries since one famous player of the markets observed that 'Speculators may do no harm as bubbles on a steady stream of enterprise. But the position is serious when enterprise becomes the bubble on a whirlpool of speculation' (Keynes 1936: 159).

Faith in the survival of incentives to 'productive' opportunism is based, paradoxically, on the hope that redistributive (arbitrage) trades will kill themselves off by adjusting prices ever more rapidly, reducing the number of places on the bandwagon (another case of the capital market losing function as it approaches perfection). Failing this, there is the more cynical hope that speculative trades intertwined and uncoordinated through ever more complex 'derivative' contracts will eventually bring returns on the main financial markets crashing down.

10.3 The origins and uses of inequality

In contrast to their disbelief in free lunches, the popularisers of market economics have a strong appetite for cake. It is assumed that economies begin with a small one which leaves everyone dissatisfied by the absolute size of their share. A bigger cake is needed. But if the small one is shared out equally no one will have the energy to bake it. And if the bigger one is also to be shared out equally, anyone who did have the energy would still not find it worth their while, since their reward will be no bigger than if others had been left to do the work. The secret of long-term success for this exercise in home economics is an unequal division of the initial cake, giving the better-fed agents the ability to serve up a bigger one, and of the subsequent cake, so that they have the incentive to do so. Those who go hungry at the beginning will soon find themselves better off because their slices become larger in absolute terms, even if small fractions of the total.

In more scholarly and less culinary terms, the basic economic argument for inequality is that (static) relative disadvantage promotes (dynamic) absolute advantage. How much inequality this 'inequality surplus' justifies depends on precisely whose standpoint within society is taken. At one extreme is the Pareto principle, which only allows that some agents' income can rise more rapidly in a situation where every agent's income stays stable or rises from the initial situation. At the other is the 'difference principle' (Rawls 1971), under which any increase in inequality is permissible provided it raises the absolute value (compared with the initial situation) of the income that is relatively lowest. (The initial situation is here assumed to be one of equality, from which departures are permitted only if they satisfy the difference principle, because agents do not know where they will stand in the resultant unequal distribution.) Between these come various 'utilitarian' prescriptions under which more inequality is allowed if it leaves a majority with higher absolute income.

More accurately, these approaches relate to the distribution of utility, assumed to be derived from the absolute level of income. The possibility of 'relative depriva-tion', in which people's ultimate happiness depends on how they stand relative to others as well as in absolute terms, has obvious difficulties for 'inequality surplus' arguments and maintains a shadowy presence in standard welfare theory.

From this standpoint, the differences in inividual income observed within com-petive market-based economies can be justified according to five principles.

1   *Proportional reward:*   Wage differences reflect differences in agents' quantity and quality of labour services supplied, assuming they are able to raise their pro-ductivity or move to occupations where it is higher. Non-wage income differences reflect the extent to which agents have saved rather than spent, and their skill in choosing the best-yielding savings instruments.

2   *Allocative efficiency:*   Wage differences show agents which types of work are most highly valued by society, and encourage them to go there. Non-wage income differences show which investments yield (or are expected to yield) the highest return, and encourage savings to be assigned there.

3   *Investment and growth:*   As returns on human capital, wage differences encour-age agents to invest in improving their productivity, and show them where it is likely to be maximised. Non-wage income differences provide the incentive to invest in physical capital in pursuit of the higher returns, to innovate, and to take other actions which drive the economy towards faster growth.

4   *Social mobility:*   Even if wage and non-wage income differences contain an arbitrary element, or reflect innate productivities and initial property distrib-utions which are beyond an individual's control, they are justified provided access to the roles to which they attach are open to all, and assigned accord-ing to economically or socially justified principles.

5   *Inferiority of alternatives:*   Even if wage and non-wage income inequality are found not to conform to any of these justifications, external (state) intervention in the distribution of income or property may still do more harm than good (to individual and collective welfare).

The first four of these cases are examined in this section. Alternative modes of income distribution are considered in section 10.4, and the neoclassical case against them in section 10.5.

10.3.1   *The reward justification*

Under competitive conditions, workers are paid their marginal products as valued at the market-clearing (and socially optimum) product price. If an employer can observe individual output (quantity and quality) and set the wage accordingly, individuals can attain a higher wage rate by working harder, longer or more effec-tively. If observation is not possible, makes too big a 'deadweight' subtraction from the wage-bill, there is a case for paying everyone the value of the marginal worker's product this is because the marginal worker could be any member of the workforce, not just the most recently arrived. While it may be true that intra-marginal workers deliver a higher physical product, and could claim a higher wage if employment were scaled back, the decline in marginal labour productivity as a firm's employment expands is mostly due to the falling capital–labour ratio, not any necessary inferiority in the last-recruited workers. So equal pay seems fair, and wages being the highest level that a competitive profit-maximising employer can set at its (and society's) optimum production and employment level.

10.3.2 *The allocation justification*

As well as working more productively in their present job, workers can migrate to other jobs or regions, where market signals indicate that they can earn more through having their effort better motivated or their talents more effectively employed. The excess of an alternative job's reward over that of the present job provides the incentive for any moving or retraining costs that must be incurred before making the move. Similarly, the increased reward for exercising more skill and responsibility by being promoted in the present job is an incentive for further training or other workplace self-improvement. These optimising adjustments to the human capital stock are possible only if all agents can finance the necessary initial cost, out of past savings or through loans collateralised against future income at a realistic interest rate. Outside the occasional MBA course, lenders are rarely so accommodating, being unsure of the returns on a non-physical investment; the borrower might not get the new qualification, or it might not bring them a better job. But other market incentives can still correct for any failures in the capital market. For employers, hiring a worker means, as with hiring a machine, buying the right to a series of returns from future activity whose present discounted value is assumed to exceed that of the wages to be paid. Since firms also gain from higher labour productivity, they have an incentive to substitute for the capital market if (as appears usual) it fails to offer such training support or charges 'too high' an interest rate for doing so. A firm can fund the employee's investment explicitly by funding skills improvement itself (reclaiming the expenses by keeping wage below marginal product for some time after this has risen as a result of the training) or offering traineeships with lower than usual wages to account for the investment whose returns the trainees can then keep to themselves.

10.3.3 *The growth justification*

Over time, the dispersion of wage income is held to raise productivity and promote growth by encouraging workers to move up the distribution, working more efficiently in their current job or moving to work where equivalent efforts are better rewarded. The dispersion of non-wage income gives a matching incentive to identify and close all allocation-distorting price misalignments and be the first to introduce new technology. What the propertyless lose in their initial disadvantage compared with those favoured by the initial distribution, they soon make up by a rising productive tide lifting all incomes. Acquisition of physical property rights is an incentive to produce more, and acquisition of intellectual property rights an incentive to introduce new processes and products.

Profit bonuses and share options, a major cause of the recent rise in relative pay of top executives, may be a necessary device for tying their interests to the maximisation of the firm's value. Firms' willingness to compensate executives for recent efforts (especially in the USA) to tax additional payments suggests that their incentive role is taken seriously, and that intervention can be counterproductive by raising pre-tax income dispersion (quite possibly with the costs passed on to lower-income earners). Employers' defence has been just as strong for 'golden handshake' compensation when leaving the firm (possibly a retrospective inducement to those now joining it) as for 'golden hellos' for recruitment and performance-linked bonuses for retention.

Even the private assignment of property rights in assets previously unowned or communally owned can produce social benefits, by ensuring the optimal output of products with externalities and ensuring the optimal use of scarce resources. Inequality may further stave off the natural and social limits to growth if it restricts (to the richest) products whose inputs are exhaustible or whose outputs yield utility only when few consume them; those deprived can be consoled that they simply cannot obtain the product, or wouldn't enjoy it if they did. To the extent that property inequality has always existed, the market system harnesses it to the general good by inducing its holders to invest rather than consume their income from it. Feudal landlords' frivolous expenditure might, as Malthus suggested, have helped reduce unemployment and depression after major shocks such as the Napoleonic Wars, but it was capitalists' accumulation which raised productive potential so that today's poor can get to consume like yesteryear's rich.

10.3.4 The mobility justification

Even if it produced no static or dynamic advantages, inequality among the different 'roles' within an economy would be of no concern if agents could freely move between them. Someone must always fill the lower-paid jobs and hold the smaller property shares. But if meritocratic selection rewards effort (which is under agents' control) rather than intrinsic ability (which lies beyond it), and if growth ensures a constant upgrading of all roles' wage and non-wage income, equal access appears to justify unequal distribution. Objections to hierarchy drop if all can aspire to reach the top. The openness of roles to meritocratic selection is consistent with efficiency maximisation – putting the best person in the job, and defusing social tension over the exercise of privilege. It has been widely credited with maintaining social peace even when the faster-growth justification of inequalities has seemed weak.

There is little firm evidence that upward mobility is significant, increases over time, or is higher in market-based than other types of economy.

Even if those processes seen by liberal theorists as making for increased social fluidity do indeed operate, they are none the less regularly opposed and offset by other processes . . . while the functional requirements of industrialism may best be served through the development of more universalistic, achievement-oriented processes of social selection, the members of more advantaged and powerful classes can be expected still to try to maintain ascriptive elements in such processes.

(Erikson and Goldthorpe 1993: 368)

This conclusion relates to inter-generational mobility, offspring receiving a significantly different relative income from their parents. Movement between occupational levels within an agent's lifetime are generally even more restricted, at least for the majority who still begin in lower-grade roles. But it is the subjective belief in moving up that the mountain that defuses people's inclination to flatten it, and the existence of even a few rags-to-riches cases may be enough to maintain the mobility incentive.

The high transmissibility of relative social position across generations, and difficulty of making long-range upward moves, suggests imperfections in the market for 'cultural capital' (status, social networking, self-esteem) as well as physical and human capital. As well as handing down their concentrations of property, those currently high up the income distribution can buy educational and presentational advantages for their close relatives which increase their chances of entering the distribution high up. But these advantage-preserving mechanisms seem at least as strong in economies which have yet to embrace the market as an organising principle, or have tried to replace it. To the extent that markets ignore cultural characteristics in favour of ability to pay, and relate this at least in part to personal enterprise and effort, they can be seen as offering at least the possibility for high rates of mobility, even if there are many imperfections in other capital markets still to overcome.

10.3.5 Attacking the alternatives 1: the 'inequality surplus'

The belief that income inequality promotes innovation and growth, so that even the relatively worst off find their absolute incomes growing faster than if relative incomes were kept more equal, appears deeply ingrained in societies which view themselves as structured around market transaction. Even the 'radical' distributive justice theory of Rawls (1971), who takes the welfare of the (absolutely) worst-off as the key meaure of social justice, assumes an 'inequality surplus' that will justify departures from income equality, even if income (or the ability to earn it) is arbitrarily assigned. Historical analyses of industrialisation in western Europe and North America have tended to conclude that inequality had to rise before wider material-goods availability could 'trickle down' to raise the majority living standard. The 'supply-sider' prescription for another burst of post-industrial growth tended to argue, without apparent irony, that the rich needed to get higher rewards (through a cut in redistributive income tax) before they would apply their skills and innovate to enrich the economy, whereas the same incentives for the poor required their redistributive benefits and minimum wages to be cut.

Substantially different evidence on, and attitudes to, income inequality and growth arise from the more recent development of societies where relational transaction is more common. In particular, the spectacular growth of a number of East and South-east Asian countries between the mid-1960s and mid-1990s was associated with little departure from, and in some cases a further narrowing of, income differentials which were already relatively low at the start of the 'take-off'.

> Some of the fastest-growing East Asian economies – such as Japan, Hong Kong and Singapore – are the most equal. As a result of the rapid, shared growth, human welfare has improved dramatically . . . In the HPAEs [high-performing Asian economies], the proportion of people living in absolute poverty, lacking such basic necessities as clean water, food and shelter, dropped – from 58% in 1960 to 17% in 1990 in Indonesia, for example, and from 37% to less than 5% in Malaysia during the same period . . . A host of other social and economic indicators, from education to appliance ownership, have also improved rapidly in the HPAEs and are now at levels that sometimes surpass those in industrial economies.
>
> (World Bank 1993)

How much of this progress will survive the 1998 credit crunch in the HPAE region, and whether the World Bank's 'East Asian Miracle' will avoid the slide from showpiece to museum piece, is an uneasily open question as this book goes to press.

Although its causes are hard to generalise, the preservation of income equality during rapid growth tends to arise from early land reform which gives most people some user rights over the rural means of production, and is sustained by extending those same rights to the urban means of production as industrialisation proceeds. There are several reasons why such widening of income-generation opportunities – to include residual claims and capital gains – is more likely to occur where relational transaction (RT) is widespread than where market transaction (MT) generally rules. RT makes it easier for agents controlling small units (of land) or interdependent units (of capital equipment) to make the bilateral and multilateral agreements needed to co-ordinate their activities and jointly invest in indivisible capital stock (which is then collectively shared). RT encourages investment in human capital, by workers and their employers, by providing firmer guarantees that future wages and prices will provide a worthwhile return on it, so that initially widespread access to the 'social primary good' of education generates widespread access to the higher-earning job opportunities that a better education provides. The tendency of companies in extended networks to share profits with their employees and split residual-claim gains and losses with their long-term suppliers has led some commentators to characterise them as labour-managed organisations, giving workers far more direct access to the return on capital and collective labour (as well as on their individual labour) than in MT-rich societies, where this would require them to purchase shares or set up their own business. If reciprocal obligation also extends to people's dealings with the state, RT is more supportive of redistributive tax and social provision to assuage what inequality remains.

To the extent that faster growth results from higher rates of private, social and human capital, RT also enables a faster rise of absolute incomes and greater mobility between income bands, so accelerating the conversion of rising average income to rising income for the absolutely worst-off. (Where RT is concentrated among families or other closely knit social groups, it may create barriers to inter-occupational and inter-generational mobility; but the award of RT on merit rather than kinship has been a feature of some of the most successful HPAEs, notably Japan.)

From an RT perspective, income inequality inverts the supposed advantages claimed for it under MT (section 10.1). Inequality makes it harder for the poorer side in a transaction to carry out the specific investments that would make it sustainable. It reduces the work incentives of the relatively worst-off (and may sap the work capability of the absolutely worst-off) as well as eroding faith in the overall relationally managed system. To the extent that it causes underconsumption (relative to a more equal system in which the rich have less to save and the poor have more to spend on basic items), inequality will impede growth and so slow the trickle-down which was supposed to make up for it.

The survival of growth-with-equality in East Asia and elsewhere now appears under threat, as the recent growth slowdown forces them to deregulate in ways that undermine traditional relational dealing. It is already clear that the abandonment in eastern Europe and China of administered transaction (AT), which could keep (formal) income differentials low by using non-price allocation, has led to sharp increases in income inequality. As well as legitimising the free-market dealing which had already widened the informal income gap in most 'communist' societies, the move to MT from AT – with many product prices starting well below market-clearing level and many asset prices well below the present value of prospective earnings – presents short-run opportunities for massive capital gains for those who are first to stake residual claims. The move to MT from RT, which enshrines similar price 'distortions' due to bilateral monopoly and the private withholding of price information – also raises the prospect of small numbers getting rich very quickly, as well as much larger numbers finding their income differentials widened as more attempts are made to 'price' labour by its individual productivity, and incentivise work through financial rewards (rather than those of status or long-term employment stability).

10.3.6   Attacking the alternatives 2: the minimum wage

The market case against legislated minimum wages is as straightforward as the basic supply-demand representation sketched in Figure 1.1. Set below the equilibrium point, the imposed price of labour will mean workers getting paid less than they get now, delivering employers an undeserved extra profit. Set (more realistically) above it, some will gain, but others will be overpriced and forced out of a job. Worse, by sparking matching rises among workers accustomed to a differential over the lowest paid, wages may be forced above the equilibrium – and jobs lost – even in markets which are not directly affected because their pay was already above the new statutory floor.

This unashamedly microeconomic attack can be rejected on at least six grounds. First, a national minimum wage, or one affecting a large section of the workforce, will have macroeconomic effects, stimulating demand in ways which may well create new jobs (and probably raising aggregate demand if, as seems likely, low-paid recipients save less of the extra income than would the employer if allowed to retain it). Second, where labour faces a monopsonistic employer (who initially pays below the value of marginal product), an imposed wage rise can cause the employer both to pay more and to employ more. Third, in flat organisations – and flat economies – floors become ceilings, and as well as workers whose low pay is levelled up to the new minimum, there may be at least as many whose slightly higher pay is levelled down to it. Fourth, to the extent that it forces low-paying employers to fill an income gap previously restored by state benefits to the low-paid, the minimum wage merely privatises a public (corporate) welfare cost, releasing budgetary resources to be spent in other areas or passed back as tax cuts. Fifth, employers for whom the minimum wage is above the current 'equilibrium' may respond not by sacking them, but by training or investing to raise their productivity to that which can justify the new pay scale (accepting the neoclassical marginal-productivity distribution model, but gently realigning cause and effect). Sixth, the efficiency wage theory – and a number of other alternative models – deny that labour supply and demand take the traditional shape depicted in Figure 1.1

However, it is still to the microeconomic labour-market model with 'well-behaved' schedules that the minimum wage debate tends to refer – rather than the numerous empirical studies which fail to show that setting or raising such minima can be linked to loss of jobs. The objection seems sometimes as much philosophical as economic: to legislate for a higher living standard seems akin to legislating for Pi to equal 4, or the sun to rise early. (President Aleksandr Lukashenko of Belarus did decree a 10 per cent rise in real national income for 1998, but at mid-year it seemed his economy might well need to be indicted for non-compliance.) Opponents know that the further the ceiling's height is reduced, the less of a difference it can make to the poorest, and the more its coverage is narrowed, the smaller will be any macroeconomic demand boost to offset the loss in micro-market demand. Supporters know that no onslaught on the low wage will tackle the greatest cause of poverty, which comes of having no wage. So the search for a statutory minimum work income leads inevitably to the search for new ways into work. The privatisation of corporate welfare goes hand in (invisible) hand with the marketisation of social welfare (section 11.5.2).

10.4 'Institutional' income determination

The explanation of income differences presented so far differs significantly from that of earlier market economists, who maintained a sharp distinction between the processes determining value and distribution. The setting of relative prices was logically distinct from the determination of aggregate income and its division among production factors, even if the two seemed to take place at the same time. One version of the sequence, taken up by Marx and formalised in 'neo-Ricardian' versions of his economic model, shows distribution as being decided first, and going in to determine both value (because wage and profit rates determine price) and output (because profit rates determine investment, which is the aggregate component of aggregate demand). Another, which resembles the 'neoclassical synthesis' of Keynes with his partial-equilibrium predecessors, depicts distribution determining value (prices being a mark-up on prime costs) and value determining output (the aggregate price level determining the aggregate real wage, which determines aggregate employment, which determines output through the aggregate production function).

10.4.1 *Market model indeterminacy: initial distribution*

The fleeting egalitarian promise of market general-equilibrium theory – that optimal competitive outcomes can emerge from any initial resource allocation – is quickly dispelled by the determination of incomes by supply and demand within that system. Everyone begins, in the Arrow-Debreu (AD) model, with an endowment that includes some tradable resources and some entitlement to company profit through shares. Both can be retained, so as to generate a stream of income additional to that gained from trading labour services, or sold, raising (at equilibrium price) the present-value equivalent of those future income flows. Income from these non-work sources might conceivably be reinvested, either in the accumulation of more non-human resources and shares or in skill enhancement that will raise the future working wage. However, initial endowments will have to be very large, or reinvestment of their proceeds remarkably successful, to overcome the income inequalities brought about by market determination of the real wage.

Empirical assessment of property distribution in mature market-based economies denies that this is practically possible and there are grounds for denying its theoretical possibility, based on the limited nature of non-work income claims represented by an initial endowment of shares. As noted in consideration of property rights (section 1.4), the residual claim to profit tends to devolve to the holder of user rights over capital stock rather than staying with the holder of ownership rights. 'Capitalists' who rent out their property, or even those who entrust it to specialist management, tend to be relegated to the status of another fixed cost. The user-rights holders get to retain all revenue not spent on wages, inputs, rental costs of land and capital, and paying capitalists their accustomed dividend and interest. They also exercise 'residual control' over the day-to-day specification of labour tasks left incomplete in original contracts (O. Hart 1996). Endowing workers with an initial stock of resources or shares does not therefore give them a residual income, independent of that from labour, unless they retain user rights as well as ownership rights, i.e. become entrepreneurs. Most lack the skills to do this, or hold an endowment too small to make it worth the risk, and so end up either selling the endowment or letting user rights devolve to company management. Their income then becomes dependent on selling labour services to that same management, for a wage devoid of any residual claim.

> Prior to any market activity, ownership of corporate shares is only an indirect form of ownership of resources . . . The Arrow-Debreu model mistakes the whole logic of appropriation. The question of who appropriates the whole product of a production opportunity is not settled by the initial endowment of property rights. It is only settled in the markets for inputs by who hires what or whom.
>
> (Ellerman 1992: 194–5)

Earlier general-equilibrium models avoided the problem only by abstracting from the problem of profit and its distribution, by assuming constant (not diminishing) returns to scale. These and other difficulties with the general-equilibrium model of market systems (see Chapter 2) have enabled a theoretical revival of earlier characterisations, which reconciled a market system of resource allocation with a non-market (social) system of initial income and resource distribution.

10.4.2 Making initial distribution matter: the Sraffian alternative

The identification of a circularity in the standard 'capital market' model, in which demand for capital depends on a rate of return which it must also determine, revived the search for an alternative general-equilibrium pricing system in which demand does not appear. In the 'neo-Ricardian' version, prior-determined wage and profit rates replace demands in closing the system, producing a set of relative prices whose determinants are technical and factor-price conditions on the supply side (section 3.16.1). Except in the special cases of capital–labour ratios being the same in all sectors (and preserved during growth by Hicks-neutral technical change), or of the numeraire being a commodity whose price is invariant to income distribution, relative prices will depend on the initial setting of wage and profit rates.

Those who devised this alternative system, whose definitive statement came from Sraffa (1960), were renewing a search for the 'centres of gravity' around which day-to-day market prices fluctuated. The main purpose is to show the values towards which market prices must tend if aggregate output is to be replicated or steadily expanded – and to expose the way in which 'neoclassical ' price-setting must assume what it sets out to explain.

> A structure of market demands can only be derived from consumers' desires, preferences or behaviour-reactions on the assumption of consumers being equipped with a given money income. Hence an initial distribution of income between individuals is implicit in the general pricing-process, in the sense that it must be included as one of the determinants of the structure of demand

from which all prices (including prices of productive factors) are derived; the whole pricing process being relative to this postulated distribution.

(Dobb 1973: 34)

In neoclassical general equilibrium, changing the initial distribution leads to a different set of budget constraints, and an entirely new, Pareto non-comparable, price vector.

The actual determination of relative wage and profit rates has been variously ascribed to subsistence needs (if employers are powerful enough to resist paying workers anything more than this), class struggle (if employees have enough power to bargain over their rewards), the degree of monopoly, the rate of growth, the distribution of property and non-wage income, or customary ideas about the fair wage for different types of work, which may relate to their perceived social value or the extent of skill and preparation needed to do them. Once the resultant wage and profit rates are entered into the price-setting system of transactions, agents may still emerge with an income which appears to match their marginal productivity. But causation has been reversed: wage determines marginal product, which provides nothing more than a technical explanation for it. 'The view that the marginal product of labour, the *sine qua non* of the [neo]classical tradition for determining who gets what, has some ethical significance, has not been held by any major economist since John Bates Clark in the early twentieth century' (Hirsch 1976: 153).

The initial distribution of private property plays an inescapable part in setting the underlying (and self-justifying) income distribution pattern, since it determines both the technical conditions that limit labour productivity and the balance of power between labour and capital in their struggle over reward rates. Although agents can accumulate property by saving out of their incomes once market trade is under way, the property held at the start of trading is generally a legacy of previous economic formations. Thus capitalism in western Europe began with a distribution of property closely related to feudal land ownership, and the user rights acquired by some of those who farmed it. In North America its property-holding was shaped by the land claimed for cultivation or construction by early settlers as they spread westwards. More recently in former state-socialist eastern Europe, capitalism has been reintroduced with a property distribution closely related to the control patterns of bureaucrats and managers over state-sector industry (which they have often acquired through the privatisation process). East Asia's success, in recovering faster from a substantially lower industrial base, owes much to its initial rural labour surplus (agricultural resources being easier to reassign to new industries than resources already tied up in old industries), and to a better initial climate for trade and capital flows; but much has also been ascribed to the balanced income distribution (e.g. Rodrik 1994), often consequent on post-war land reform, and sustained by egalitarian wage-setting policies associated with relational transaction and teamwork.

In western economies, the power enjoyed by those with early concentrations of property appears to have been important in imposing the division of labour, and forming the company structures with which the 'take-off' into sustained economic growth got under way. Although the early 'horizontal' division of labour, between broad occupational categories, may accord with natural differentiations in ability and interest, the further rise in productivity depends on an increasing 'vertical' division of labour in which tasks are divided within the workplace. Those assigned a specific, repetitive operation can quickly become exceptionally good at it, and may even come to like it, but this is consequence rather than cause of a work pattern which is essentially imposed. Even Adam Smith, after giving a largely voluntaristic account of how division of labour arises through the exercise of natural abilities and interests, admits that the structure can quickly become an imposed one:

> The difference of natural talents in men is, in reality, much less than we are aware of; and the very different genius which appears to distinguish men of different professions, when grown up to maturity, is not upon many occasions so much the cause as the effect of the division of labour.
>
> (Smith 1766/1979: 120)

Important though they may have been for getting industrialisation started, the forced differences of detailed labour division seem less appropriate in a world where 'flexible specialisation' is taking over from mass production, necessitating greater employee involvement in designing their operations and ability to adapt them or switch between them.

Although the market system internalises price determination, it does so within limits set by the initial income distribution, rather as an individual may take actions which appear to be spontaneous but are actually governed by knowledge and values imposed by formative experience. Once they begin to trade, agents can add to or subtract from their stocks of physical and human capital, and the income they derive from them, but these adjustments occur only at the margin, and any ability of under-endowed agents to close the gap is offset by others' ability to capitalise on their initial advantage. 'While within the market inequalities in rewards appear to be largely determined by supply and demand, supply is itself importantly determined by inequalities operating before the market' (Erikson and Goldthorpe 1993: 394, supporting Phelps Brown 1977).

Searching for what would comprise a 'just' distribution, Rawls (1971) argues that, where agents are not fully detachable from roles (because at least some earning power derives from innate personal characteristics) and where agents do not know beforehand what abilities and roles they will occupy, the socially just distribution is whichever gives the best absolute situation for the relatively worst-off agent. A more traditional utilitarian argument would support any departure from equality which makes a majority better off so that the economy's total utility rises. This would remain compatible with Rawls's account provided income were then redistributed to ensure that absolute improvement reaches all the way down the distribution. But even with roles allocated entirely according to characteristics that are under an agent's control, there may be strict limits to the extent of 'inequality surplus' a society will be willing to buy. M. Young (1958) speculates that removing all innate or non-discretionary elements in assigning merit will ultimately undermine meritocracy, because agents who end up in lower-paid roles, who could previously have cited circumstances beyond their control, now have no one to blame but themselves.

10.4.3 *Market model indeterminacy: information problems*

Even if relative wages are accepted as strictly determined by agents' preferences, productivities and technical opportunities, rather than a validation of conditions imposed by initial income and property distribution, there are familiar problems with the use of wages as a price for improving allocation, clearing labour markets and accelerating growth. For employers to recruit until the market wage matches the marginal product, they must know (or have reliable expectations of) the future prices of what workers will produce and the efficiency with which they will produce it. Future product value may be fairly accurately predicted from current product-market prices, especially if these are generally stable over time or if the employment is on a short contract. But a worker's productivity can be difficult to gauge, without first giving them an employment or relational contract to see how they perform.

Inferring an unknown worker's productivity from their qualifications and past work record gives only an imprecise picture of their practical skills, motivation to use them, and ability to fuse them with those of current employees. Inferring quality from the wage demanded, on the grounds that better applicants make bolder demands, gives rise to the same indeterminacy as the 'efficiency wage' (section 2.9.2). Supply and demand are no longer independent because productivity is affected by the wage offered, whose equilibrium level is therefore indeterminate. Inferring quality from superficial signals, such as presentation or performance at interview, may be efficient to the extent that these proxies' loss of accuracy is compensated by their cost saving over more 'objective' investigation methods. But it reintroduces the danger of efficiency and ethical damage due to discrimination, which fully informed market transaction is supposed to dispel.

The use of wages as a quality signal can prevent unemployed workers pricing their way into jobs, by making perceived marginal productivity a moving target. Imperfect information thereby adds a microeconomic dimension to the macroeconomic price-adjustment problem encountered earlier, under which labour in general cannot adjust its real wage to the 'equilibrium' level because changes in its money wage are matched by changes in the aggregate price level, which lies beyond its control. Early forms of employment arrangement avoided these problems by tying the worker's rewards to output, so that quality differences would automatically be matched by payment differences. Piece rates offer a fixed monetary reward per item produced (perhaps with a payment-free minimum quota to cover overhead costs) and are especially effective where employees work on their own on products whose quality can be easily assessed. Share-cropping, under which the reward is an agreed proportion of physical output, has the further advantage of insulating the employer from any unanticipated fall in product price, effectively fixing the output-determined wage in real rather than money terms. Both schemes allow an employer to take on labour without knowing its quality beforehand, letting its performance determine remuneration.

Modern labour contracts tend to relate pay to the time worked rather than the service performed, which is captured (if at all) by generalised bonus systems often related to group performance. Output quality may be too variable to ensure efficiency under piece rates or share-cropping, which in their crude form reward only quantity and ignore any non-physical aspects of the job. By tying rewards to performance of a specific task, these payment methods also reduce flexibility, making labour more difficult to reassign between tasks without losing time to negotiation or additional money for compensation. Any element of teamworking, or of working with capital supplied by someone else, will introduce either additional measurement costs or demotivation and disputes involving workers (and capital suppliers) unconvinced that their input has been fairly acknowledged.

The response is often to move to linking pay to time spent on the job, with variations only under special and clearly measurable circumstances (e.g. overtime or weekend working). Time-linked pay is often generalised across a department or group, because variations in individual contribution are impossible or too costly to identify. Many of labour's products are bundles of physical outputs and services which resist separate quantification and valuation. Many depend as much on the capital with which labour works as the skills it exercises; even wholly separable, physical products can be the result of joint or team efforts whose individual members' contributions cannot be accurately apportioned.

Although these difficulties of relating reward to individual contribution are among those that underlie 'relational' transaction (section 6.3), they do not automatically cause a move away from market-type transaction. Intervention by labour unions or regulators violates the condition that market transactors should be independent and competing, but upholds the condition that the market 'price' of a particular labour type be openly publicised across the market. By establishing rates and conditions for the job and maintaining firm- or industry-level pay bargaining, labour unions' 'monopoly' on supply raises the likelihood of those supplying equal quantities of a particular labour surplus being paid the same. 'Relational' labour contracts (section 6.4.1) may be concluded by employers either with individual agents (workers) or general agents (unions, professional institutions, etc.). Individualised contracts preserve competition but may lose transparency. While pay variations may reflect relevant relational aspects (e.g. the profitability of the particular firm, any training the worker has recently received at the firm's expense), they may also signal that employers (and sometimes employees) are exploiting the other side's imperfect knowledge of occupation or industry 'going rates'. Negotiating and monitoring costs are usually higher. Generalised contracts preserve transparency but introduce a bilateral monopoly element into negotiation. Transaction costs are saved by setting standard rates of pay, but the chance of adjusting rewards to individual circumstance and performance is reduced. There is no guarantee that rates will standardise around the level that a competitive market would have set. Indeed, the original reason for forming labour unions was to countervail an employer monopsony so as not only to narrow the dispersion of ages around the average (a transparency gain from the market viewpoint), but to raise the average (a monopoly loss).

Where output is multidimensional or not possible to measure directly, the setting of a single measure as an index or proxy can also cause efficiency loss by distorting an agent's incentives. Hospitals funded according to levels of treatment may 'rotate' their patients to record more admissions, and educational institutions whose grants are linked to measured internally assigned attainments may be tempted to drop standards and award higher grades. Once again, a wage-setting model which may have rung true when artisans worked individually in low-capital operations making standardised products can adapt only as vague analogy to the world of multiple, service-based products, high technology and teamworking. Another perverse incentive can arise with profit-linked executive pay, which can bias action towards short-term profit enhancement and, where higher profits are rewarded without equivalent sanctions for incurring losses, towards high-risk, high-reward gambles whose benefits are kept by the individual and external costs imposed on the firm.

Once human capital considerations are introduced, the price of labour takes on two functions: clearing the market for this type of labour in the current period, and determining the reward differential for this type over lesser-skilled types. The second function both validates human-capital investment decisions made in the past and motivates human-capital investments made in the present. As with fixed capital, however, both functions are certain to be fulfilled only in very special conditions of full information leading to perfect foresight. Otherwise, the relative value of different skills signalled by today's prices may fail to fulfil the expectations that led to skills being acquired in the past, and may lead people to acquire skills in the present whose future rewards will not fulfil the expectations that led to them. Like the fixed investor, the investor in skills does not know the state of future supply (how many others are simultaneously acquiring the skill, and how successfully they will do so) or of future demand (whether the skill will be in greater or lesser demand at a given price, in the light of developments in the product market from which demand derives).

10.4.4 *Institutional wage-setting and social justice: factor asymmetry*

The determination of wages and profits through the marginal productivity of labour and capital achieves a symmetry between these 'factors of production', which in practice have very different characteristics.

First, capital owners can detach themselves from their (financial or fixed) investment and the services it provides, whereas workers are inseparable from their skills and knowledge and must be present in the workplace to provide their labour services. In the terms of Chapter 1, labour's ownership rights and user rights are necessarily bound together, whereas those of capital are detachable.

Second, capital owners can specify the service to be provided, and charge appropriately for it, being helped by the limited range of tasks most equipment can perform and the limited range of speeds at which it can operate. Workers generally enter contracts which set only broad parameters around the tasks they are expected to perform, so are open to 'exploitation'; in the sense of working at different tasks or at greater intensity than those they expected when they agreed the rate of payment.

Third, the firm's product-market risks are differentially shared between capital and labour. Traditionally, labour is assumed to reduce its risks by signing up for contractual employment at a fixed wage, rather than continually re-entering the market for work of uncertain wage and duration. Owners of capital take over this risk, by accepting an uncertain payback (reflected in fluctuating profits and/or dividends), and incurring sunk costs which mean their fixed capital cannot be costlessly transferred to other equally profitable uses or re-sold with full recovery of cost. This asymmetry, which leads to capital receiving an unpredictable residual component of firms' profits, has often been put forward as the reason why ownership of firms is assigned to the owners of its capital, not its customers or workforce. However, the increasing stability of dividend payouts and variability of labour incomes (through cyclical real-wage variation and/or spells of unemployment) has led some to argue that labour is now the main bearer of residual risk, and should have a greater voice in managing the firm for this reason (Plender 1997). Even if their profit stream from one particular firm is highly variable, capitalists can spread their own risk by pooling entitlement to other firms' capital through a portfolio of shares. The inseparability of work from workers prevents labour from achieving the same diversification, with multi-skilling being the closest they can get to spreading risks across a number of firms.

Fourth, capital whose income falls to zero is written off or scrapped, its owners emerging possibly broke but still alive. Labour whose income falls to zero starves unless it can find a source of non-labour income. Whereas a society can tolerate almost any payback on its machines, it tends to require that workers get at least a 'living wage'.

These differences provide an argument that labour income should be detached from the productivity and allocation criteria that determine capital income, even if there is some economic efficiency loss from doing so. The symmetry between factors is seen at best as a simplifying assumption to make economic models of distribution more tractable and elegant, at worst as an ideological disguise for pay-setting arrangements institutionally biased in capital's favour.

10.4.5   *The desirability, and difficulty, of redistribution*

The dependence of relative prices on an initial income distribution set outside the model appears to make the case for *ex-ante* redistribution. By changing the initial pattern of payment and property holding, it may be possible to achieve a distributional outcome from market transactions which more closely matches one of the criteria for justice, such as higher overall utility or higher utility for the least well off. A shift in the division of income between wages and prices can alter the pattern of relative prices, the nature of technologies adopted and the level of output and employment. The 'neoclassical' market model rules this out by treating labour and capital as products, commensurable with themselves and all other products, whose income is uniquely determined by its own preferences, productivity and technical conditions.

Even if the initial distribution is regarded as just, or held to be irrelevant by keeping to the neoclassical general-equilibrium model in which value and distribution are determined simultaneously, a case for *ex-post* redistribution can be made if the pattern of rewards is seen to have departed from that set by marginal productivity alone. This can happen if 'unearned' non-labour income has risen to match or exceed 'earned' labour income for a large section of society, and if the property-holding that gives rise to non-labour income owes too much to inheritance and windfall gains and not enough to purposeful accumulation. Both these aspects of non-labour income tend to make for ever widening inquality. Wealth breeds more wealth ('it takes a million to make a million'), and windfall gains will widen income dispersion over time even if they occur randomly.

Ongoing income redistribution, via progressive taxes on income (the rich paying more) and progressive social provision and benefit payouts (the poor receiving more), was originally introduced to try to narrow the dispersion of income. In practice, it generally served only to offset the gradual rise in inequality, with the division of national income among households (measured by the shares going to different percentile groups) staying roughly constant while growth drove up the level of income. This stability of relative income shares may have been important for social cohesion, since the interest of middle-income earners in preventing the poor from getting absolutely poorer is matched by their interest in preventing them getting relatively richer.

> Most people's concern with their income is at least as much with how it compares with the income of others as with how big it is in itself . . . rising productivity entails an increase in individual income to secure certain satisfactions earlier attainable with lower income.
>
> (Hirsch 1976: 111, 113)

The greater emphasis placed on market allocation of capital and labour and distribution of income since the early 1980s has been accompanied by rising income inequality in most economies that have adopted it, especially those reverting from systems of central planning. Although plausibly an effect of the freer play of market forces, greater inequality may also have been – or become – one of its causes. Rising unemployment, the shift to less progressive tax systems (lower income-tax gradations and more use of indirect taxes), the reduction of social subsidies and widening skill differentials are among the causes of a recent widening of income dispersion in the UK (Atkinson 1997), where after many years of similar growth rates the top 10 per cent of income earners enjoyed a gross pay rise of more than 50 per cent between 1979 and 1992 while incomes of the lowest 10 per cent stagnated. In the still more dramatically re-marketising former Soviet and eastern European economies, even allowing for misleading income figures before the fall of communism and greater difficulty in measuring it afterwards,

> available figures strongly suggest that both distributional inequalities and the incidence of poverty have increased sharply in many countries in the region during the 1990s . . . in principle, the movement towards a market system, based on reward-oriented incentives and private ownership, must inevitably involve an increase in inequalities, at least when compared to a system where a commitment to equality is put into practice.
>
> (EBRD 1996: 29)

Even where it survives, that commitment to equality – or to no more inequality than is required to maintain socially beneficial incentives – may be getting harder to uphold. The proximate causes of rising inequality may reflect the breakdown of an underlying process by which lower incomes were supplemented with transfers and public services financed by tax on middle incomes. While there was full employment, middle-income earners could restore the loss by taking up second-earner opportunities opened up by the growth of middle-management and government employment. As rising productivity and slower economic growth reduce employment availability and security, middle-income earners revolt against their tax obligations, thereby reducing the possibilities for redistributive transfer payments. The net payers' protests become self-compounding as reduced revenue forces governments to target welfare payments, leading to punitive marginal tax rates on the lowest incomes when they first start to rise (as income tax cuts in and means-tested benefits cut out), which gives many of the poorest a disincentive to self-improvement or renewed employment, which reinforces the middle-income view that such indolence should not be given state support.

With uneven incidence of unemployment leading to a growing polarisation between two-earner and no-earner households, and more break-up into non-standard (single-person, single-parent) households, rising participation rates begin to widen rather than lessen inequalities.

> One of the two sources of constant family income shares is about to reverse itself and become a source of greater inequality. We are entering a period of rising inequality where conventional income transfer programs will be incapable of preserving the current degree of inequality.
>
> (Thurow 1980: 161)

Recent moves to raise the minimum wage in the USA and to introduce one in the UK may reflect less the altruism of middle-income earners (who have consistently voted for tax cuts) than their concern to stop state income supplements becoming a subsidy to low-paying employers, and to lessen the poverty traps that block the take-up of low-paid work.

Such a breakdown in the effectiveness of redistribution and willingness to finance it may be self-compounding. Government's attempts to lower the tax burden on middle-income earners leads to closer targeting of public services and income transfers which further excludes them, and to restraint on the public employment and expenditure on which many of them depend. The initial reaction to widening post-tax inequality is to try to strengthen the redistribution mechanism, but this becomes counterproductive as middle-income earners find new ways to avoid tax or take second jobs which could have gone to those without work income. The origins of income inequality present a strong case for reducing it. But redistribution proceeds along a knife-edge between ineffectiveness which leads its recipients towards more radical responses, and over-effectiveness which sends its net contributors into revolt.

10.5 Market counterattack: the importance of being earners

'Revolt' may be too strong a word as yet for the situation in most market-based economies, and it is unclear whether their recent retreat from redistributive arrangements is a cause of their widening inequalities or a consequence of previous transfers' inability to contain them – or the product of a third force such as technical change or low-wage competition forcing up unemployment. However, a common pattern of retreat now seems evident. Taxes are shifted from higher onto lower incomes through the reduction of marginal tax rates and increase in sales and value-added taxes. Social subsidies to those on low or no incomes are reduced, with unemployment benefits turned into inducements to move into lower-paid work. Direct interventions in market wage-setting are reduced as labour unions' powers are curbed, minimum wages are reduced in coverage and real value, and jobs are switched from public to private sectors through privatisation or contracting-out.

The trend is politically driven, but with some enthusiastic economic arguments in a supporting role. With a tactical retreat from strict marginal-productivity assumptions, market-based income determination has re-emerged – if not as necessarily a force for social good, then as a better alternative than those in which the 'visible hand' reaches into private sector pockets.

10.5.1 Rejecting the equality presumption

Many who oppose the pursuit of equality in the final income distribution, for its destruction of incentives and failure to reward different effort levels, remain sympathetic to equality in the 'initial' income distribution. Equality of opportunity is likely to narrow the inequality of result, and certain to provide it with greater legitimacy. Earlier interpretations of market welfare economics appeared to offer three reasons for preferring greater income equality to less, and the first task of the revitalised approach is to dispose of these.

The growth-promoting view of property inequality disposes of any egalitarian interpretation of the second 'fundamental welfare theorem' (section 2.1.3), which shows that any initial allocation of property (initial endowments) can lead to a

Pareto optimal market trading outcome. From a purely static viewpoint, evenly distributing initial endowments before trading begins would not affect the welfare-maximising outcome. But over time, all agents would be made worse off by the damage such equality would do to incentives. Reversing etymology, society is judged better served by a common weal than common wealth.

Further incentive damage could arise from the methods used to redistribute property and income, if they involve taxes which affect marginal rates of substitution or technical substitution between products or factors. On these neoclassical terms, all common taxes except lump-sum transfers cause such allocative distortion. A proportional tax on any product displaces its price above marginal cost, reducing its output (unless demand is completely price-inelastic) and inflicting a deadweight loss similar to that under monopoly. A proportional or progressive tax on factor incomes raises its marginal cost relative to its marginal product, reducing employment (as employers hire less and households swop work for leisure at the margin) and inflicting a similar loss. By reducing only the income from work, compared with indirect taxes which devalue all forms of income, the 'wedge' between gross and net wages inserted by payroll tax may have a serious effect in raising real wages to employers, deterring work effort by employees, and so raising the 'natural rate' of unemployment (Phelps 1994). The only redistributive tax that is 'efficient' in the sense of leaving marginal equivalences alone is a system of lump-sum taxes. But tailoring these to agents' ability to pay, given the initial inequality, may well cost more to administer than it raises in revenue, while charging the same (poll) tax on everyone violates the common perception that social justice requires tax burdens to vary with ability to pay.

While the use of initial endowments as one determinant of general equilibrium might seem to allow initial property and income distribution to be modified (in the direction of greater equality) before trading begins, incentives can be preserved only by allowing inequality to widen again. Agents can generate income by selling property or plough income into buying more of it, their additional income coming from sale of labour services (for varying amounts reflecting differing marginal productivities) and, in the short-run model, receiving profit shares which are also likely (as with profit rates) to vary between industries. However equal the distribution is at the start of trading, it is likely to change once the transaction pattern is mapped out. And if the distribution were 'just' to start with, the resultant prices (including wage and interest rates) can be seen as a fair consequence of free choices by profit- and utility-maximising agents, even if it results in high and rising inequality.

Since the market system allows agents to buy and sell existing property, as well as to accumulate more of it through saving, property allocation will change over time. This 'process' argument for the social injustice of state intervention in property distribution has been taken furthest by Nozick (1974), who argues that existing property-holding should be regarded as fair unless one or more of the exchanges leading up to it can be shown to have been unjust. A wide definition of justice in acquisition and transfer (acceptable so long as no one is made worse off than they would have been without private property appropriation), and the mists of time surrounding how private property appropriation first occurred, implies approval for most current possession that does not follow from obvious theft or fraud. On this basis no involuntary transfer of property can be socially justified, and any forced change will produce adverse economic results.

While property-holding changes as a result of market transaction, the link between property-holding and income may also change, for reasons far beyond the arrival of property and capital-income taxation. By the 1940s it was evident that one market efficiency requirement – appointing technocrats to run large companies – had passed *de facto* control of the income from commercial assets to managers who did not own them (Burnham 1945). Since the 1970s another market efficiency requirement, takeover discipline, seems to have passed much *de jure* control to equally unsung pension and insurance policy holders, allowing some more ambitious market theorists – and Marxists – to argue that ownership of capital and its income has finally been handed back to the working class.

Dynamic considerations are equally effective in denying a 'utilitarian' argument for income equality, based on the diminishing marginal utility of money. While spreading incomes more equally might initially raise total utility, the millionaire's last dollar yielding more satisfaction if handed to the mendicant, such transfers (as well as violating the Pareto principle) will set back the society in the long term through a dual destruction of incentives. For higher earners, the inducement to efficiency improvement is weakened because some of their financial reward for doing so is taken away. For lower earners, the inducement to attain any level of efficiency is weakened because extra rewards are received for which they have done no work.

The paradox that the rich work harder if given more, and the poor work harder if given less, depends on particular assumptions about the relative power of income and substitution effects at different income levels, and has become a favourite target for objectors to solely market-determined pay. But this argument is a step forward from the earlier static argument against utilitarian egalitarianism, which was simply that utility is subjective and cannot be compared or summed across individuals – so that the millionaire may well get at least as much pleasure as the mendicant from that marginal dollar. The Smithian supply-side assumption of social gain if all are allowed to keep their private gains offers rescue from the more sybaritic demand-side assumption, that the ability to enjoy rises in step with the ability to spend.

A macroeconomic case for income equalisation based on the higher savings rate of the rich, and hence the ability of lower earners to spend the economy out of recession if income is redistributed to them, is rejected (along with Keynes's General Theory and, possibly, macroeconomics in general) by reassertion of the market claims to full employment and faster growth. To the extent that their savings are invested, the rich – whether or not their income was earned – do society the dual service of keeping it currently employed and enhancing its future wealth. A case for equality based on the existence of 'merit goods', which can be more safely assigned through the market if all people have the same buying-power there, is rejected on two alternative default grounds. Either there are no merit goods (for reasons considered in section 2.6.1), or what they really call for is a distribution of income based on need, which Marx envisaged for the later stages of the proletarian revolution, but whose achievement in any market economy would entail such expensive bureaucratic assessment and such extensive incentive destruction that the loss of capacity to produce the goods would far outweigh the (private and social) gain from what was left of the market allocating them more fairly.

10.5.2 The negative case for market pay

Intervention in pay-setting is permitted, even in neoclassical models, where perfect competition and perfect information do not exist and cannot be easily resurrected. But even then, there are 'market' methods of determining rates of pay, in ways which promote justice to the extent that this provides incentives for efficiency. A standard example is team production, under which several workers contribute to output in unknown proportion, and a pay-setter must either try to separate their marginal productivities or pay each of them the average. One solution, which has even been advanced as a reason for the formation of firms (Alchian and Demsetz 1972), is to make the pay-setter the owner of the firm. By calculation, imitation or competitive selection, the owners who survive will be those who have structured pay to maximise incentives, productivity, and hence profit.

In general, intervention to correct labour market imperfections runs into the same problem as intervention in imperfect product markets. No external authority seems likely to be better at acquiring or processing the relevant information, so informed or administered transaction will be no more efficient than market transaction. It may even be less so, since the mechanism for its arrangement insulates it from competitive pressures which may force unintentional maximisation on both sides of the employment relation. Labour markets might not be especially good at setting wages, on either an economic efficiency or social justice criterion, but other ways seem destined to be worse.

Alternative schemes based on contribution to the work process require measures of effort, reliability and contributions to group morale or team spirit, which are distinctly harder to measure than time spent on the job. Even if such input-based measures are possible, they ignore the market value of what is done, implying that the hard-working dancer who draws no audience should still be paid more than the lazy singer who happens to enjoy a cult following. Schemes based on qualification for work are even more detached from market value. Much time and money may have been spent taking training, doing tests and winning certificates, but these guarantee that dedicated and high-quality work will be performed not that the market will place a high value on what results. The more an economy's output and employment structure shifts from industrial production (where workers tend to have an individual, physically measurable product) to service production (where teamwork is more prevalent and outputs are measurable only by subjective assessment or indirect material consequences), the more its wage-setting is likely to be left to the market by default.

10.5.3   *The positive case for market pay*

Even if it improves on an imperfect market situation, intervention in the wage-setting process may be a second-best solution. The preferred alternative from a neoclassical perspective is to perfect the market, by removing competition imperfections or filling in information imperfections. The Alchian-Demsetz view of the entrepreneur as team co-ordinator raises the possibility that pay setting is a separate area of utility-creating, value-adding activity. To the extent that this was a missing market in earlier stages of the economy's development, it is now commercially available via the services of remuneration consultants and committees. Their task involves identifying the work inputs and product outputs that can be personally assigned to the employee, deriving a measure of their 'value-added', and then adjusting this for extraneous elements such as good or bad fortune (the variation of output for any given input), varying external conditions (any trend in general output which their input can be seen as affecting), comparability (what others are receiving for similar work), and varying internal conditions (in capital equipment, resources, colleague support, etc.) that might explain some of the variation in that comparison.

Though subjectively arrived at, these assessments will generally be tested in the market. The use of comparability ensures a direct link with market conditions, subject to the usual free-rider caveat that a certain number of employers must be making productivity calculations and not merely free-riding on knowledge of what others pay. If it is wrongly applied, workers who feel themselves undervalued may try to move to where pay is higher, and those that have been overpriced will eventually learn that a pay cut is needed to ensure the survival of the firm, or at least of their job.

10.6   Conclusion: pay on display

As with previous instances in which relational, firm- or state-administered transaction replaces market transaction, institutional pay determination is shown up in the revitalised market perspective to be less a consequence of market imperfection than its cause. Individual citizens' increasing willingness to 'sell' themselves directly on the market – from electricians and carpenters going self-employed to rock stars breaking out of their captive contracts – exposes the degree to which their previous administered pay was both economically disincentivising and socially unjust. Minimum wages, and any other limitation on private-sector setting of work conditions, are turned from a socially improving measure to one that ties employers' hands and denies employees the right to low-paid or ultra-flexible work, to the presumed detriment both of these agents and society. Professional regulation, designed to preserve quality of service and ensure an incentivising payback on the cost of training to provide it, is reduced to a device by privileged dections of the workforce to boost their pay by artificial entry restriction. This suspicion is apparently confirmed when those professions lobby against their own deregulation: what ought to set them free actually forces them to sell their services for less.

The difficulty of identifying neoclassical 'equilibrium' wages, or proving the alignment of actual wages to them, has strengthened rather than weakened the case for letting the market decide. There may be difficulty in getting priced into a job when (lower) wage demands are taken as (inferior) quality signals, or when 'insider' labour can command a premium because it is better known, but firms which go too far with such non-maximising recruitment rules will perish in the product marketplace. There may be a time-consistency problem in inducing everyone to study for an MBA because it comands a high salary, only to see MBA salaries reduced because of the oversupply of new graduates (with the lone engineering graduate hitting the jackpot instead). But this is simply the market doing its normal efficiency-promoting work, correcting a relative shortage signalled by temporarily higher prices. Inter-occupational mobility may not be perfect or perfectibility, individuals differing in their aptitude for different tasks even if capital markets will finance them to train for anything, but rates are generally high enough to make inequality tolerable. The way to keep mobility rates high is to maximise the growth rate, which requires incentives to work harder, invest and innovate, which are maximised by relating pay to the market value of performance. And if labour income turns out to be a lottery, there is always a lottery we do not have to work for, whose rewards are far greater and whose equality of opportunity is (except to the roulette wheel psychics) not in doubt.

11 Disinventing government
The state goes on sale

Dwellers in dream houses demolished by planning curbs and business venturers strangled in red tape used to grumble that you can't fight city hall. Today's complaint is more likely to be that you can't find it. The once proud agencies of national local government complain of lacking resources to promote the public good, and of selling out to private interests in their effort to secure them. In formerly communist Russia, a government that cannot collect its taxes is forced to auction prized state assets and delay employees' pay in order to make ends meet. Its counterpart in proudly capitalist USA, once willing to spend whatever it took to fend off the red, regulatory menace, now tells its poorest to work for their welfare, and follows up its military adventures by passing round the gunboat-diplomatic hat.

Outside the superpower sphere, Lebanon is ruled by a president whose company is also rebuilding the capital city. London's seat of local government is converted to a block of luxury flats. Afghanistan and Albania struggle to establish any form of central government, while Angola and Bosnia-Herzegovina are just as hard-pressed to squeeze two into one. Almost everywhere, the governments that once built infrastructures for their businesses, and bailed out the biggest when they failed, now turn to the private sector to plug holes in their own budgets. The levers that bureaucrats used to pull, convinced they could steer the economy, now lie out of their reach in corporate control rooms – or must be tied down to stop them rebounding in statism's suddenly unacceptable face.

In principle, the state ends the twentieth century as strong as it has ever been. The grim foundations of its growth – waging war and imposing civil order – have not gone away, but a succession of rosier responsibilities have been added. Governments try to grow the national income by keeping demand at full-employment level and channelling it to physical and human investment. They try to spread that income fairly, through redistributive taxation and welfare benefits for the worst-off. They try to resolve market failures by supplying information and co-ordination unavailable to dispersed private agents, and products they want to consume but not produce. They try to identify, and promote, new products and practices that will enhance collective welfare, and to curtail those perceived to harm the social whole. To support these efforts, governments typically make first call on 25–35 per cent of national income, spending up to half of this share directly and redistributing the rest between private pockets through the public purse. They fund this expenditure by taxing, borrowing and taking over commercial activities from the private sector, in ways which significantly alter the opportunities and constraints of private agents, many of whom now look directly to the state for employment, orders and supplies. Even this may understate states' impact on private-sector activity, which extends to the unaccounted financial demands of personal profit-seeking bureaucrats, and the publicly costless (but often privately expensive) legislation of obligations, restrictions and guidelines on firms' and individuals' behaviour.

In practice, this looming presence has turned from a sign of strength into a source of serious weakness. Governments are seen to have tried and failed in most of these areas, throwing good public money after bad when initial expectations were not fulfilled. Even where their stabilising, growth-promoting and income-spreading efforts have met with success, they are often seen as having counterproductive side-effects so costing too much in terms of the overall social benefits they bring. Taxes (especially on income) are reassessed as distorting and demotivating, and state borrowing rejected as deferred tax which also 'crowds out' private-sector credit. The public rediscovers an appetite for spending its own money, as public servants come to be viewed as buying less wisely when the cash is not their own. With legitimacy and liquidity constrained, governments of all political colours have resorted to selling state-sector companies into private ownership, contracting-out public services to commercial operators, simplifying and scrapping rules which no longer (if they ever did) serve private business interests, and turning remaining taxes from a general charge to a specifically targeted subscription, enabling payers to judge how effectively their money is being spent (and to vote out those held responsible for personal contributions moving above personal rewards).

The breach of the 'social contract' could not in itself undermine the state's role. Like the nail in a tyre that has so far stayed inflated, a malign presence may do even more damage if abruptly removed. For government's role in the economy to be substantially wound down, the public had to be convinced that the alternatives were better. Fading memories of mass unemployment, poverty and exploitation in the days before government were one step towards this, an implicit reward to interventionist government's success. But, as previous chapters have tried to show, many minds were also changed by the perception of government failure, and new insights into how markets could do better if given a second chance. This chapter considers the accusations levelled against the state's involvement in the economy. It goes on to assess the main tactics now being adopted to disengage it. It ends by considering the various explanations as to why the ideal of the minimum state, apparently in retreat for so much of this century, has come closer to political reality as the – privately sponsored – new millennium celebrations approach.

11.1   The rise and fall of government

Economists' list of government's essential economic duties was always short. But the first free market thinkers considered them primary, and were prepared to pay a lot for them, since they include several preconditions for making markets work.

The state must devise and defend the legal requirements for market transaction, including money (legal tender), property rights, limited liability, enforcement of contract, ways of giving and recovering credit, internal and external security. It must prevent the market from being subverted from within, by acting to prevent monopoly and collusion. It must provide the unavoidably collective (public) goods that would go unsupplied or undersupplied in the market. And it must stop market forces engulfing the small range of products which society chooses to allocate on grounds other than willingness and ability to pay. This list, its core determined by democratic choice but lengthened by special pleas from ethics, religion and commercial interest, includes basic education and health care, national parks and forests, child labour, sports and arts prizes, transplanted organs, transfused blood, top jobs, public honours, prescription drugs and sex.

For liberals in the classic (philosophical) sense, this is where the socially useful role of government ended. 'Maintain external order, suppress violence, assure men in the possession of their property, and enforce the fulfilment of contracts, the rest will go of itself . . . Government must keep the ring, and leave it for individuals to play the game' (Hobhouse 1911: 58, 60). Liberals more exposed to the practicalities of politics have come to acknowledge extra duties, such as steering the economy between the cyclical excesses of inflation and unemployment, and ensuring that all citizens have enough purchasing power to play by the market rules (or are compensated when they do not, if only to stop them violating those rules). Democratic socialists argue that achieving these aims, and extending fairness from market opportunities to market outcomes, requires intervention in specific markets – notably those for labour and capital – in which transactions are distorted by monopoly and information asymmetry. Revolutionary socialists retain a vision of government, swept to power by class resentment against these imbalances, seizing the new digital means of production first to perfect a system of allocation by merit rather than market, and then to eliminate the profit system's 'artificial' scarcity so there is no longer a need to allocate at all.

Although few approved of the trend, many mid-century observers viewed a slide down this list, from classic *laissez-faire* to ever more detailed types of state intervention, as almost unavoidable in maturing economies with parliamentary democracies. The promise of a short-cut to such industrial strength through state-led accumulation and innovation suggested that younger states, in newly independent 'developing' countries, would grow even faster. In practice the state's macroeconomic role – measured by the proportion of national income spent or redistributed by the government, and the tax rates required to let it do so – developed somewhat erratically, rising and falling with the stop-go cycle (failure to resolve which only increased its quest for monetary and fiscal leverage) and ratcheting upwards at all-too-frequent times of war.

The state's microeconomic role – measured by the weight of regulation and the height of compliance officers' paperwork – grew more gradually but more ineradicably. Sporadic attempts to disengage government from the macroeconomy seemed only to lengthen its shadow over the microeconomy. Privatised 'commanding height' industries had to be regulated, contracted-out services required monitoring, employers' freedom to hire and fire was viewed more apprehensively once public servants despaired of their demand-side power to preserve full employment. Attempts to cut bureaucratic wastage seemed only to swell the bureaucracy, and periodic bonfires of controls only seemed to clear the ground for more to grow.

Despite launching itself with the argument that markets would generate order and serve the public good without external guidance, economics spent much of its early history legitimating an expanded role for the state. Legislative needs grew with the increasing sophistication of products, the complexity of market transactions, the new structural and financing needs of larger enterprises, the geographical extension of markets, and the growing ingenuity with which crime or breach of trust could disrupt market relations. Monopoly elements became more prevalent as technical change created new 'natural' monopolies, as other firms grew relative to their markets or adopted co-operative behaviours, and as innovators demanded defence against immediate imitation. New public goods came to light, external costs were identified which property-rights assignment could not easily correct, labour demanded rights defined by what natural justice and a living wage demanded rather than what employers said they could afford. More markets appeared to fail, including those for scarce resources, capital and information. Concepts of the 'non-market' sphere expanded to cover a wider range of merit goods, and 'natural monopolies' were widened to include network products which, although suppliable in the private sector, were thought more fairly or cheaply provided by the state.

To these microeconomic duties was added, through the general acceptance of Keynes (1936), the macroeconomic task of enabling (or at least speeding up) the return to full employment after phases of depression, and of managing demand to eliminate the business cycle. For lower-income economies whose future seemed to be mapped out by the industrial expansion of northern Europe and North America, the state was a vehicle for growth through faster and more directional accumulation. In higher-income economies, for reasons of macroeconomic health and social peace as well as fairness, it became a suitable vehicle for redistribution. The observation of 'planning' by large corporations prompted the view that state-co-ordinated indicative planning could well be complementary, and with the apparent separation of ownership from control came the possibility that large sections of the economy might be taken into public ownership with no adverse impact on the way they were run.

Except where suppressed in defence of communism's dictatorially administered and fascism's poisoned-relational transaction, counter-beliefs in the bad state and the more benign market never went away. But those who bemoaned the extension of public authority into private boardrooms, budgets and pay bargains stood accused of looking into the past for a golden age that was actually all around them. Between the end of wartime goods rationing and oil exporters' 1973 imposition of petroleum rationing, more of the world's economies grew more consistently and strongly than ever before. Even when the 'middle way' between free markets' depression-prone invisible hand and central planning's iron fist ran into renewed inflation and unemployment problems, a return to pre-Keynesian minimal-statism seemed unlikely. Predictions of capitalist–communist convergence in the mixed economy of 'industrial society' were commonly heard until the early 1980s. Their inversion, to a vision of small and shrinking spheres of useful government action, seems to have come as a surprise to all political sides.

11.2 Government failure: the charges

The case against government taking on more than its inescapable minimal role can be summarised in three contentions. First, that state intervention is unnecessary to achieving society's economic priorities: full and efficient deployment of resources, and the widest distribution of their income that is compatible with their maximum growth. Second, that even where, in principle, the state can make some useful contributions, its restricted information and distorted motivation make it incompetent to perform them. Third, that even where there are useful tasks which the state is able to perform competently, the long-run efficiency and equity losses from doing so outweigh the generally short-run gains.

11.2.1 Irrelevant to full employment

General equilibrium, the adjustment of prices to establish an optimal allocation of resources automatically brings the economy to full employment. Any persistent unemployment is due to price rigidity, in the labour market or possibly in the capital and product markets. These rigidities will be eliminated over time and, if government has any role, it is to speed up their elimination. To the extent that such rigidities are caused by government action (e.g. setting minimum wages or giving legal immunities to labour unions), its primary task is to stop interfering in the price system.

If accepted, this version of the market model disposes of the Keynesian argument that government has a role to play in keeping the economy at full employment. In the neoclassical interpretation, Keynesian 'involuntary' unemployment results from the setting of too high a real wage. Since labour can bargain only over its money wage, which it may have difficulty in adjusting relative to the aggregate price level, government may have a transitory role to play in expanding the money supply and driving down interest rates so that investment demand rises, prices stabilise, and the return to full employment is hastened by a fall in real wages and rise in aggregate demand. But the market can achieve this just as efficiently through a rise in the real money supply as prices fall, provided there is a stock of 'outside' money (Patinkin 1965).

In any other situation, the government's apparent success in reducing unemployment by raising aggregate demand will be the result of temporary tricks played on wage and price setters. Monetary expansion causes price and wage increases which may induce firms to produce more, and households to supply more labour, but only until they realise that the price movements are general so that relative prices are unchanged. After that, output and employment will be scaled down again. A faster inflation rate is all that remains.

11.2.2   *Harmful to spatial resource allocation*

Although the competitive general equilibrium (CGE) model depicts an optimal outcome to market processes without any explicit role for the state, it does not rule out
a role for government as a desirable means to this end. Intervention might help in

- eliminating conditions that can lead to the non-existence of CGE (e.g. by dismantling or regulating monopolies, controlling access to common-pool
  resources)
- eliminating conditions that can lead to the non-attainment of CGE (e.g. by
  spreading information among interdependent agents and eliminating price
  rigidities)
- speeding up the attainment of CGE (e.g. by expanding nominal money supply
  when price rigidities prevent the attainment of full employment)
- altering income distribution to attain a CGE which, without violating efficiency conditions, also satisfies certain social fairness criteria.

The 'Austrian' perspective on market processes provides a powerful corrective to
these ideas. Far from being best placed to solve information and co-ordination
problems, governments are likely to be their biggest victims, since the preference,
technological knowledge and price expectations which shape demand and supply
decisions – and drive them towards consistency at full employment – are all held by
individual agents in the first instance. The process of collecting, processing and disseminating information to achieve expectational and transactional consistency is
judged to be more efficiently done through the price system than through admin-
strative intervention. Where a degree of administrative co-ordination proves useful,
because of transaction costs, intermediate forms such as firms and consumption
clubs are judged more efficient than full-blown state intervention.

The advantages of leaving resouce allocation to private action – by individuals
or voluntary associations of individuals – are accentuated by the distortions
imposed on the economy by state intervention. The government's exposure to
conflicting internal interest and unrepresentative external pressure groups delay
and distort its allocation decisions relative to those reached in the market. Price signals are disregarded, resulting in overproduction of products and overinvestment
in low-return projects on unclear 'external benefit' grounds. Even where resources
are correctly allocated, inadequate monitoring of resultant production and distribution – often related to the state being both purchaser and supplier – lets
production costs creep up unnecessarily. Favoured companies and industries are
promoted by subsidies and tariff protection at the expense of the wider economy.
Regulators are 'captured', and become reinforcements for monopoly, by restricting
entry or guaranteeing rates of return.

Whole government departments, especially in social services, can be captured by
consumers who vote for an overproduction of 'public' goods because net recipients
outnumber net taxpayer contributors. Governments' desire for re-election makes
them condone this distortion, and also encourages stop-go macroeconomic

management in place for the stable, predictable monetary and fiscal rules which would allow private agents to form consistent expectations.

The possibility of the state's role choosing the 'best' among possible optimal resource allocations, by identifying and maximising a 'social welfare function' subject to the economy's production possibilities, is rejected by the impossibility of generating conistent and non-dictatorial social preferences over the possible allocations (section 2.1.3). The possibility of the state intervening to create the 'best' distribution of property and income before market trading starts is dismissed as both historically impossible and economically unjustfiable (section 10.5.1). But in the more cynical 'public choice' view, government would not carry out such public-spirited actions even if it could. Politicians and public servants are individual and collusive maximisers like the rest, intent on the non-productive expansion of bureaucratic power and prestige, thereby drawing private agents the equally non-productive pursuit of politically protected monopoly power and regulation-shielded rents. Even where beneficial, government activity must still be financed by taxation (which upsets marginal equivalences and distorts resource allocation) or borrowing (which crowds out private investment and slows the growth rate), leaving it unclear whether any net social benefit has been delivered.

11.2.3 Harmful to intertemporal resource allocation

Governments' ability to avoid the 'myopia' of markets and take a long-term view of resource allocation, by accumulating assets, controlling the run-down of scarce resources and internalising external costs, has rarely been confirmed in practice. Oil reserves have been exhausted, oceans polluted, public infrastructure neglected and accumulated assets sold off to fund current consumption under a wide variety of political arrangements, while some of the most far-sighted investments (from roads and railways to cloacae and cathedrals) have been carried out largely in the private sector.

Public-choice theory has been quick to supply reasons as to why intertemporal allocation is not safe in state hands. Governments' time horizons are shortened by the electoral timetable. They can be lobbied (if not bribed) to ignore long-run external costs. While their ability to set a low discount rate, because of privileged access to credit, should improve the chances of projects with early costs and deferred benefits passing a CBA test, it implies a bias of current investment towards public-sector projects which could cause misallocation of resources (and slower growth) through time. To the extent that board members' tenure exceeds that of most cabinet members and that private assets will be devalued now if investors suspect a drop in value later, companies might even turn out to be more trustworthy intertemporal allocators with lower discount rates.

11.2.4 Harmful to growth

To the extent that these temporary upsets to the price level confuse private-sector expectations and undermine confidence, government may actually deter savings and investment decisions and reduce the economy's rate of growth. Investment is further damaged if the use of government borrowing to finance 'demand management' crowds out private borrowing, which is generally assumed to go towards projects with higher rates of return.

Although demand management was expected to raise the rate of growth by making it more even – flattening out the booms so as to avoid the slumps – firm evidence of a long-run trade-off between cyclicity and growth has been hard to identify. This is possibly just as well, since, after a run of success for 'Keynesian' interventions in the 1950s and 1960s, government's efforts at 'fine-tuning' have increasingly appeared mistimed, often heightening the boom and deepening the slump. Sympathisers ascribe this to lags in the detection of private-sector slowdown and delays in corrective measures taking effect, the government's own information problems which might be solved by better understanding of leading indicators and earlier implementation of appropriate actions. But again there is an opposing story which makes the state-supervised stop-go all too deliberate: a political business cycle under which politicians on fixed terms squeeze inflation at the beginning and dash for growth and full employment at the end, relying on feel-good votes being cast in their favour before the inevitable prices rises, devaluations and tax hikes start the down-cycle again.

11.2.5   Irrelevant in a globalised market

Government functions remain predominantly attached to nation-states, with very little in the way of shared international institutions, regulation and law, or shared or co-ordinated policymaking. The pursuit of self-determination and democratisation has led to an expansion in the number of nation-states and devolution of power within nation-states, even as the 'global reach' of multinational companies, financial markets, environmental problems and potential military confrontations has been expanding. So even if the state can intervene beneficially in the areas of economy and society under its control, those areas appear to be a diminishing part of the total. Government's omnipotence, as well as its omniscience, is steadily eroded.

An external trade sector reduces the 'multiplier effect' of increased aggregate demand on national output, while cross-border capital mobility weakens the power of monetary policy to effect such a demand increase by reducing interest rates. The growth and integration of capital markets has also eroded the state's microeconomic powers, especially in its role of filling the gap left by 'capital market failure' in the financing of large infrastructure projects. The sheer size of these, and the long-term, non-appropriable or non-financial nature of their returns, has traditionally been taken to mean that their finance will be too costly to raise privately. Governments were the appropriate financing vehicles because of their higher credit ratings, greater capacity to borrow from cheaper foreign sources (including other governments), and unique ability to charge for the project's external benefits through taxation.

Capital-market integration has increased the scope for private investors to raise long-term loans and equity at competitive rates, at a time when governments are finding their capital budgets one of the easiest targets for cuts in pursuit of a lower fiscal deficit. Privatisation has made the private sector primarily responsible for investment in a range of key sectors, including energy and transport, and private capital is taking a growing role in public investment projects, notably through build-operate-transfer projects and profit- or production-sharing joint ventures. Although governments often make private participation possible by guaranteeing an investment's rate of return or eventual saleability, many private investors which do not enjoy explicit state backing have nevertheless achieved equivalent (or even higher) credit ratings than their national governments. This in part reflects evidence that, as well as running current operations more effectively, private operators achieve better allocation, more productive use and greater accountability over their use of capital, pointing to higher long-term returns and greater receptiveness to outside creditor and shareholder demands.

In contrast, many governments have seen their credit ratings stagnate or deteriorate as lenders start to question their past investments' ability to pay back (either directly as profit or indirectly through strengthening the economy and tax base), and so become more concerned about the weight of their existing debt. Past confidence that governments could always stay solvent because of their ability to tax has been undermined by the limit on capital tax receipts placed by cross-border mobility of capital, and on labour tax receipts by workers' declining tolerance for higher tax rates, linked to declining confidence in government's ability to spend their money wisely. By entering 'partnerships' which transfer large-project profits to the private sector while keeping the investment-risk public (through revenue guarantees or buy-back arrangements), governments risk adding to these solvency fears by storing up unknown future liabilities. But as they run out of businesses to privatise for funds to reduce their debt, cash-strapped governments seem destined to privatise more infrastructure projects, relying on private partners' better reputation for keeping capital and operating costs down.

11.2.6 Harmful to income distribution

While the model of factor rewards based on marginal productivity is rarely taken as literal truth and sometimes rejected as tautology, pricing of capital and labour in an open market like any other resource appears to offer allocation and incentive advantages above those of more 'institutional' wage-setting methods such as customary rates, committee votes or power struggles between unions and management. Governments' efforts to equalise the dispersion of income has, at best, prevented inequality from widening, through a 'social contract' between taxpayers and benefit recipients which may be breaking down. In achieving this limited success, they may seriously have eroded the incentives to indulge in growth-generating behaviour such as invention, investment and self-improvement.

Rather than narrowing income differentials, government might be better employed in raising opportunities for social mobility so that anyone can achieve a higher income with suitable effort. This means expanding educational opportunities, which, given state budget limits and the private payback on skills investment may require more market-based provision of education. It also means abandoning the various regulations which, though possibly imposed for quality, safety or environmental reasons, have become industry and profession entry barriers which keep some people's incomes artifically high. Luck or innate ability will always allow some to achieve higher-earning status than others, but this is the market's judgement on their worth: Bill Gates would not earn his million a day if people thought nothing of his software or marketing skills. Since brilliant business brains and perfect golf swings cannot be separated from the people who own them at least without destroying their function, the market's inducement to get them used in the public interest may do more social good than state intervention to stop their owners using them for private reward.

11.2.7 Undemocratic and unaccountable

The claim that market-based choices are more democratic than political choices seems counterintuitive in a world of (generally) universal suffrage. One-person-one-vote gives equal weight to each opinion (at least under proportional representation), in contrast to 'consumer sovereignty' exercised in proportion to personal income and wealth whose distribution is highly unequal. Indeed, for most of the twentieth century there have been influential calls for democratic control to be extended into areas of commercial life, ranging from voting workers onto boards (where German codetermination has been inspirational) to putting a representative shopper onto the commission vetting comanies' price increases (a short-lived British anti-inflation experiment in the mid-1970s).

State intervention in resource allocation has often been justified, notably in the 'merit goods' case (section 2.6), on the basis that the state is a better allocator of certain scarce resources than the market, because of its ability to assess need without regard to ability or willingness to pay. The market system is a plutocracy, shaping the production structure and allocating its output according to who has the purchasing power. As well as social injustice, this can lead to economic inefficiency by allocating resources suboptimally (e.g. education to the inbred aristocrat while brighter students miss out, or food to the idle rich while productive workers starve).

But the market may also be a form of direct democracy, to which the state is at best an inefficient and at worst a counterproductive alternative. In the economic marketplace, assuming that the income distribution is within tolerable limits, consumers can express their wishes directly, and producers must compete to satisfy those wishes in the most efficient way possible. Provided there is not too much interdependence in the decision process and not too much externality in consumption, consumers get what they want with minimal interference from other consumers. Prices keep consumption within the limits of production, ensuring neither a resource-depleting free-for-all nor persistent unemployment and undercapacity operation.

In the political marketplace, by contrast, agents have to express their wishes indirectly, electing representatives who must then bargain among themselves as to how resources will be allocated. Their choice is a diffuse one, because politicians generally stand for election on multi-point manifestos which leave many future questions about their conduct unanswered – in economic terms, most of the policies they want are in joint supply with other policies with which they may have little agreement. Even if politicians' wishes exactly coincide with electors' and they have no hidden agenda to maximise their own utility, government has the fundamental problem of being central, and therefore detached from the decision-relevant preferences and information held by individual agents.

Whenever it tackles allocational questions, therefore, government is condemned to choose more slowly and less efficiently than if the public was left to pursue its own interest through self-interested decisions in a competitive market.

> Any form of group decisionmaking necessarily involves the prevention of some members from realising their preferences. Political decisionmaking, even in its most efficient democratic form, is an inferior mechanism, and should be resorted to only in cases where a market decision system cannot operate for some reason.
>
> (Plaut 1985: 44)

Because market competition encourages producers to differentiate existing products, and introduce new ones, markets can be argued to expand the range of choice. This increases the consumer's opportunity to switch from one product to another if the first does not match expectations – or to use the threat of such a switch to force improvement in the first product.

In contrast, political competition can encourage parties to move their programmes closer together, in pursuit of the 'median voter' whose support is decisive under a universal franchise with equally weighted votes. This convergence reduces voters' options for switching, thereby also reducing their power to press for policy change. Even if a variety of political programmes is preserved, elections tend to be a winner-takes-all affair in which the party elected by a majority governs on behalf of all. Those who voted for the losing side must thus conform to the winners' choices, with no chance (short of emigration) of having their own preferences directly taken into account. Whereas the market caters for all (or most) tastes, politics forces everyone to conform to the majority choice. Corrupting Newton's laws in support of probity in public life, transaction and reaction are equal and opposite. A democratic 'tyranny of the majority' appears inescapable since, whereas market choice is limited to Pareto-optimising actions permitting only change from which no one loses, political choice extends into areas where (majority) gains are traded off against (minority) losses – with or without any payment of compensation.

Even such basic institutions as progressive income tax, free primary schooling and health care and subsidised public transport are unlikely to be achieved if the net losers are able to opt out of arrangements for their provision. The combination of multi-dimensional party programmes and majority voting requirements leads inevitably to 'log-rolling', under which elected politicians and their supporters express their intensity of preferences indirectly by agreeing to vote with opponents against a policy with which they weakly agree in return for support for a policy with which they strongly agree. Markets allow everyone with money to say what they wish. If lack of money constrains some to silence, the solution may lie not in letting them vote for an income transfer, but from helping them back into work that will generate new income – provided the tax system lets them keep it.

11.2.8 *Disincentivising and dissipating*

Once state-owned industries have been written off as less productive than their private-sector equivalents, and state-provided services as a similarly wasteful replacement of what private profit-making or voluntary co-operation could provide, government becomes essentially unproductive. At best it costlessly redistributes income generated in the private sector, to no overall advantage. At worst, redistribution causes a loss of efficiency which impedes private-sector activity, so that it benefits a minority at the expense of the majority and causes a self-compounding scramble for the political assignment of diminishing resources. State redistributive action is argued to disincentivise productive profit-seeking (Bhagwati 1982), through the discouragement of efforts by high (marginal) tax rates and the encouragement of dependency by high levels of social support, and at the same time to incentivise unproductive profit (rent) seeking by winning tax or subsidy favours from government. 'The state legislates almost exclusively to distribute unearned income and has formed us into a democracy of pressure groups' (de Soto 1989: 191). Rising regulation heightens the incentive to seek rents.

Although intended to reflect the balance of public opinion (or at least of the majority who voted for the government), political tax and spending decisions may become overly influenced by small but vociferous pressure groups which capture the ear of politicians. They will tend to ignore price signals, thus laying claim to more of a resource than is currently available (resulting in inflation and the crowding-out of private expenditure), and ignoring the opportunity cost of other (public or private) uses that could have been made of the same resources. Because state expenditures benefit particular groups whereas the state financing burden falls on the whole population, governments will tend to expand both their tax and borrowing activities in order to finance higher state expenditure over time. This is exacerbated by the tendency of state bureaucrats to pursue their own utility, which may well reside in the size of their departmental budget and staff as in any useful services that they eventually give back to the public.

Once government becomes a source of discretionary expenditure based on its powers to borrow and tax, market theorists identify a slippery slope from private-sector profit-seeking into public-sector rent seeking. Entrepreneurs come to realise that, compared with the inherent (because competitively disciplined) vagaries of the market, the state sector provides a relatively sheltered, steady-growing and uncritical source of demand. Their energy is thus diverted towards securing subsidies, tax concessions, public contracts, and regulations that will boost demand to their industry, restrict competition within it or prevent new rivals from entering it.

11.3   Revitalising the market: deregulation

Although the largest items in its budget usually relate to interpersonal income transfers – directly through tax and subsidy, or indirectly through tax-based social services – government may have an even heavier impact on allocation and incentives through the rules it sets for private-sector income generation. Regulation implies and generally starts out as, an intervention to prevent the distortion of allocation through abuse of the market – exercise of monopoly power, imposition of external costs, inadequate or deceitfully presented product quality. But it can quickly introduce new distortions, some of which come to be seen as worse than what it was intended to correct, and some even as reinforcing the original distortion. Market economists have long preferred rules which change the way a failing market operates to rules which override it, putting administered or relational transaction in its place. They have also long deplored rules introduced to deal with market failures that might not have existed. To their surprise, and occasional anguish, many once highly regulated economies have since the late 1970s been steered towards this more economically liberal stance.

11.3.1   'Natural' monopoly deregulation

The 'pure' natural monopoly, whose costs fall continuously with scale (section 2.7.1, Figure 2.7), presents the government that takes it over with a no-win nationalisation. Pricing at the socially optimum level, where average revenue (AR) equals marginal cost (MC), or even at the loss-minimising price where marginal revenue (MR) equals MC, will require a continuous subsidy at taxpayers' expense. Pricing to break even, with AR equalling average cost (AC), still punishes the taxpayers by setting an output that is higher than socially optimal (assuming full employment of resources). Pricing for profit, with AR above AC, commits the even greater federal felony of using statutory monopoly to shift from a transparent to an undeclared tax. If the monopoly is providing a basic product (such as telephone connections), covering its costs through price may be socially regressive compared with subsidising its losses from MC=AR pricing through direct taxes, especially when the price contains a large fixed (standing charge) element.

Because, by definition, competitors could not match the incumbent's costs even if permitted to enter, many state-owned natural monopolies have for long periods achieved the outwardly desirable combination of high and rising efficiency with healthy treasury profits (notably in post, telecommunications and aerospace). But party politics tends over time to spoil the microeconomic party spirit. Forced to hold down public-sector prices and increase public-sector costs as part of its anti-inflation and job-creation strategies, governments incur the twin charge of producing at the wrong point on an unnecessarily high cost schedule (simultaneous allocative and productive inefficiency), and covering the sin with an excessive break-even price. Adding to this the evidence of lethargic service, lagging technical change and politicised management among state-held monopolies (extended to product content in the case of government-owned broadcasting media), and the

fading memory of how previous private monopolies performed, the case for disengaging the state from natural monopoly provision has tended to strengthen over
time.

Economic growth which stretches the industry's output towards the point where
costs turn upwards, and technical change which reduces the scale at which new
entrants can match the monopolist on cost, reduce the number of genuine 'natural
monopoly' cases. Even where an industry's costs continue to decline across all feasible outputs, competition can be instilled across space (by opening up the market
to foreign rivals, or other sectors offering partial substitutes) or across time (by franchising the monopoly periodically to the company promising the lowest price
structure). Spatial competition's assumed benefits of higher productive efficiency
(forcing cost schedules down) compensates for its loss of allocative efficiency
through sacrificing scale economies (leaving competitors producing smaller outputs
at higher points on the schedule). This raises the hope that a private monopoly will
offer better service to the public, while still paying enough for the monopoly privilege to compensate the government for its loss of future state-monopoly revenue.

In general, privatised natural monopolies have been subjected to continued regulation. Governments come under pressure, especially where they have sold assets
to the highest bidder, to ensure that any public subsidy the new owners receive goes
into reducing losses and holding down prices rather than lining shareholders'
pockets, and that any unsubsidised profit they generate is achieved by driving
down average costs rather than raising prices above them. The regulators' main
role is to promote sustainable price reductions, while preventing 'predatory' cuts
designed by the privatised incumbent to keep out new entrants, or by new entrants
to drive out the incumbent and re-establish its monopoly. Intervention may also be
needed to force the former monopolist to open up its publicly financed infrastructures and proprietary technologies to new entrants, to protect service standards
from erosion by price competition, and to maintain any social obligations (such as
universal basic coverage) previously imposed on the state-owned provider, at least
until an alternative social subsidy scheme is in place.

Despite this initially crowded agenda, industry-specific regulators are usually
presented as a temporary measure. If they do the job properly, they will put themselves out of a job by reintroducing product-market competition to the sector.
Where rival firms cannot be nurtured, the former state monopoly may have to be
broken up, or the sector opened to foreign competition so that other nations' natural monopolies can take it on. The incentive to make regulators aim for
self-liquidation is strengthened by fears that they will never be fully effective in forcing competitive pricing and adequate investment on the natural monopolies
(because of the firm's power to withhold information on its market and financial
conditions), and that they will be 'captured' by the firm's own interests if left to deal
with it too closely for too long. Privatisation and deregulation, always together in
the pro-market programme, are intended to move from being substitutes to complements once the initial task of creating a competitive market is complete.

Once under way, deregulation tends to be contagious, spreading and self-fuelling
after the fashion of the regulation it seeks to reverse. The removal of price or entry

controls from one area forces their removal in others, as demand threatens to desert those whose prices are still artifically high. Even so, many regulations still serve their original, social-utility promoting outcome, notably those which prevent product quality and wage levels being competitively driven down to dangerously low levels, those that protect common-pool resources from free-for-all depletion, and those that internalise measurable and remediable external costs. Nor has deregulation marked an entirely clean break with previous controls. Competition regulators continue to take a keen interest in former monopolies' market shares and pricing behaviour, and governments periodically resort to windfall taxes to reclaim 'excess' profits let through by insufficiently strict competition or past regulation. But many regulators are working to abolish themselves, tweaking the rules so as to allow new entrants the preparation time and strategy-protection needed to build themselves into viable rivals for the current incumbent. And many expect to be swept aside when ready-made competition arrives, in the form of international free-trade arrangements already common between adjacent electricity grids, being finalised in airlines and telecoms, and on their way in several other network product areas.

11.3.2 *Industry deregulation*

Earlier regulatory agencies, set up as an alternative to nationalisation in sectors where competition was limited or considered harmful, are also being pushed to make more use of market (or quasi-market) discipline, or being pushed aside in favour of such discipline. Regulation, generally of price or rate of return, was originally imposed for a variety of reasons:

- Where monopoly profits would otherwise prevail, or where the product was held to have 'merit' characteristics from which the poor should not be excluded (e.g. electricity, gas). In general price regulation was chosen if the regulator had a clear idea of the industry's cost conditions, and wanted to give incentive to reduce costs, rate-of-return regulation if cost conditions were less familiar.
- Where one product was held to compete against others unfairly because of external production costs, or was felt to be undesirable because of external consumption costs. The less desirable product could be given a high relative price (e.g. road freight transport priced high to prevent it capturing trade from railways, private mail delivery priced high to preserve the state post office's letter monopoly), or the more desirable product could be given a low relative price, supported by general or investment subsidy.
- Where producers are liable to cut quality in order to cut costs, in ways which buyers may not be aware of and are not in their best interests. The approach has generally been to set minimum prices in conjunction with statutory product specifications (e.g. in insurance), or to regulate entry according to producer quality, perhaps with maximum prices to prevent the resultant capacity shortage being exploited (e.g. doctors' and lawyers' services).

- Where producers are liable to underpay their workforce in pursuit of price advantage (e.g. agriculture, textiles and other sectors where statutory minimum wages have sometimes been set).

Like regulation, deregulation is a decision taken by governments, and various motivations are evident. A powerful motive has been the lack of any system of regulation that can balance the interests of producers and consumers in the industry without placing unrealistic demands on the regulator's information and computational powers. Price controls steer the regulated firm's profit-making energies into cost reduction, and encourage innovation of new products which escape the curbs. But they can deter new entry into the industry (the market solution to monopoly profit), and restrict the internal funding for investment. Rate-of-return limits ensure that the firm does not profit excessively from its monopoly power and from too lax a price curb, but they may encourage the firm to undertake socially wasteful investment, and again discourage entry. Compared with price, rate of return tends also to be harder to measure (even if firms supply accurate financial data), and is a more volatile measure which may need to be varied with cyclical-demand and main input-price fluctuations.

To the extent that they form trade barriers, and thus geographically restrict the market, national regulations may actually create or sustain the monopoly whose effects they are set up to deal with. Even if such regulations are true to their ostensible purpose – protecting the environment, consumer safety, workers' rights, intellectual property rights, etc. – they end up protecting trade, with a net loss of social welfare both to the regulating country and those trying to export to it. In the market perspective, exporting countries should have the right to select their own production conditions and product characteristics, and home-country buyers should be left to choose whether to accept the offer that results.

Producers' privileged information about the state of their own costs (and frequently about market conditions) has led to widespread suspicion that they can 'capture' regulators, turning a public-interest intervention into one which actually serves their own profit and growth (or quiet-life) interests. Quality (of output) or qualification (of input) standards serve as an implicit barrier to entry. This can be made explicit if the firm can persuade the regulator that it needs supernormal profits to maintain socially useful cross-subsidies (e.g. telecoms' universal service obligation, railways' rural branchlines), whose existence can also justify an easing of price curbs.

For government, releasing a regulator from captivity is a more obvious response than scrapping it. But with the danger of capture added to the difficulties of making regulation both workable and effective, governments appear to have become unusually open to external advice urging the abandonment of regulation altogether. 'Probably not since the rise of free trade in the nineteenth century has so broad a professional consensus been so well reflected in policy. The reason for this consensus is economists' belief that deregulation enhances efficiency' (Peltzman 1989: 18). Ironically, where regulation has been too effective in driving down an industry's rates of return, or where it prevents the industry from fully passing on an upward shock to costs, firms' willingness to lobby for continued regulation will be weakened by the smaller supernormal profits at stake.

Deregulation enhances efficiency if it makes way for other forms of price and quality competition – as the regulation of newly privatised utilities is intended to do over time. In one of the earliest and most celebrated instances, US airline deregulation in 1979, passenger growth projections suggested that competition could replace regulated monopoly on most internal routes, because of the development of smaller aircraft and the potential entry threat of operators who could enter (and exit again) at low cost by switching planes from other routes. (Low sunk costs of entry has made this a favourite example of 'contestable markets', where competitive pricing prevails even if there is only one supplier.) Telecoms deregulation has generally followed the break-up of the former monopoly into separate providers with equal access to the network, or a long-enough phase of regulated oligopoly for new entrants to complete their investment in rival (e.g. cable and cellular) networks. The traditional subsidisation of local out of long-distance services, a remnant of earlier cost structures, was thus allowed to lapse.

Telecoms also illustrates the power of technical change to introduce competition to what was once a natural monopoly: linked computers (the inexorable internet and intranet) now offer an alternative system of communication, combining old and new physical networks, from outside the traditional telecoms industry. (For their part, phone companies now handle computer data traffic, and are acquiring the technical capability to enter the entertainment business through music and video transmission – if deregulation permits.) Rail regulation, once designed to protect customers against monopoly, turned into a device for protecting providers against the new competitive threat from long-distance road transport, which became regulated partly to the same end – until governments moved to deregulate both activities, again beginning in the USA in the late 1970s.

11.3.3 Financial deregulation

The 'wholesale' financial markets have traditionally attracted heavy regulation because of their apparent instability, and tendency to transmit it to the real macroeconomy. Stock- and bond-markets rally improbably and then crash, destroying wealth and loan collateral and causing a deflationary spiral of expenditure reduction. Banks become overextended, by lending to fast-expanding industries or stock-market 'bulls' whose self-fulfilling expectations set off a speculative bubble. When this bursts, the banks cut off new loans and call in old ones, forcing the government to relax monetary policy regardless of its other economic priorities, and sometimes to bail out the worst-hit institutions to avert a systemic collapse.

Retail financial markets have also been held to a tight set of rules because of the need to attract household savings into them, and the political sensitivity should any misjudgement or mismanagement inflict large losses on small investors. Thus retail banks have frequently been set both maximum and minimum interest rates, insurance companies made to stick close to statutorily defined policy wordings, and private share investments steered into heavily regulated mutual funds or government stock.

After many years of closely watched and nationally segregated capital markets, fortunes (personal and corporate) have again been thrown to the winds in recent years. Governments in both industrial and industrialising economies have progressively removed the exchange controls that once restricted capital movements between them, along with the domestic restrictions on who could trade that capital and how. This is in part a reflection of the growing unenforceability of the rules as traders successfully sidestepped them, and the allocative distortions when they did not. Thus in the USA, retail banks' deposit-rate ceilings were undermined by rising interest rates and the regulation-avoiding switch to bonds and mutual funds (Peltzman 1989: 33–5). Domestic wholesale banks (and foreign entrants) found ways round the legal separation of commercial from investment banking. More recently, investors in heavily indebted countries where exchange controls persist have been able to sidestep them by buying dollar-denominated bearer bonds in the domestic market and selling them abroad.

A competitive element to deregulation also became evident, once the initial relaxation of rules broke down the barriers between countries or sectors. Thus among the major stock exchanges, New York's deregulation (scrapping of fixed commissions and relaxation of entry restrictions) in 1975 precipitated that of London in 1986 and Japan in the late 1980s, all investing heavily in information technology to speed up dealing times and reduce costs, with London later switching from a marketmaking to order-driven system in a further effort to keep down commissions and avoid loss of trade to other European exchanges. Additional motivation came from the movement of trade-off exchanges to escape regulation, and (at least in the UK case) the government wanting to cut its own funding and dealing costs after ending up on the sharp end of regulation-protected commissions and co-operative dealing practices.

Restriction-dodging innovation – perhaps the most famous being the 1963 take-off of the Eurodollar market as dollar holdings fled the USA to escape its interest-rate ceilings – also alerted governments both to the dangers of regulation to their domestic financial makets and the potential for further financial engineering progress if regulations were dropped. Systematic deregulation has duly given companies new instruments for finance-raising (eurobonds, convertible bonds, leveraged buyouts, etc.), financial restructuring (debt securitisation and rescheduling), hedging risk (futures and options contracts, derivatives) and speculation (especially with derivatives). It has also given governments a new way to borrow, via the international bond-market, and let those who borrowed too much in the traditional form of bank-loans to reduce and restructure their debt via Brady bond issues and debt-for-privatisation-equity swaps.

The old regulations did not disappear without leaving some powerful reminders of why they had existed. The USA, UK and Japan ended the 1980s with varying degrees of 'debt deflation' as newly liberalised credit markets fuelled stock, bond and real-estate booms, whose eventual collapse led to recessions with which Japan was still grappling as late as 1996. Consumers also felt the loss of regulatory protection in a more direct way – among US savings-and-loan investors, the Barings Bank subordinated debtholders, and the half-million UK occupational pension payers who were wrongly advised to opt into private schemes. The financial world has yet to see what happens when highly leveraged and interlinked derivatives markets are crash-tested against a severe loss of confidence or liquidity. But the tide of financial deregulation, probably made unstoppable by the mobility of capital and the speed of new communication technology, has generally been welcomed by governments, for the same economic reasons that have propelled deregulation in other areas.

> At the forefont of the liberalization process has been the effort to let the market decide on the allocation and pricing of economic resources . . . liberal markets and systems tend to be open, providing greater ease of access, greater transparency of pricing and information.
>
> (O'Brien 1992: 17, 19)

As already noted, a high level of capital market efficiency and capacity is now seen as important to the health of free markets generally – especially in protecting long-term strategy and averting aggregate demand failures. National deregulation was a necessary step towards the completion of the global capital market, whose role in reducing investment funding costs and channelling capital to the higher-returning lower-income countries has led to increasing optimism that a long period of historically high global growth is now in prospect – and that the system, released from national borders, has finally achieved the size and stability that can avoid the inflationary expansion, asset price collapse, demand downturn and protectionist backlash that has brought previous 'golden ages' to a painful end.

11.3.4 *Professional deregulation*

Perhaps the strongest evidence of governments' confidence in the virtues of the market overpowering the lobbying efforts of those who gain from regulation is given by the increasingly critical official attitude towards 'the professions'. Traditionally, occupations requiring high skill or long training have enjoyed a legally backed accreditation system which limits the number of entrants, and often sets standard service terms and fees to avoid quality-jeopardising price competition. The main justification offered by the professions concerned (among them law, medicine, accountancy, financial advice) lies in the need to maintain standards and ethics by keeping out 'cowboy' operators – untrained intruders who would capture business by charging lower fees for a worse service, exploiting the customer's difficulty in judging quality before purchase. Professional accreditation, backed by sanctions against those who abuse or fail to live up to it, is also held to be an efficient signal of service quality, reducing clients' transaction costs by saving them having to gather information on the supplier or enter a relational transaction with them. From heating engineers and psychiatrists to nightclub bouncers and dog groomers, other occupational groups have sought similar institutional-membership or certification schemes, and sanctions against those who practise without holding them.

Scepticism has developed because regulations, ostensibly designed to protect standards and ensure an adequate incentive to train for the profession, has the additional useful effect of restricting entry and so keeping up rates of pay. Sympathy for the professions endured while their demand was expanding (so that pay could be kept high even with fairly low entry barriers) and their standards clearly superior to those of non-accredited operators. It may also have helped that their services were bought mainly by relatively uncritical institutional or rich-individual clients, and by a code of ethics which restrained some professional groups from fully exploiting the market power that their entry-restriction provided. High representation of professionals within national legislatures was a further source of help.

Professions have been among the groups most successful, so far, in resisting deregulation. But even here the tide has recently appeared to turn, with (among other instances) non-lawyers being allowed to conduct some real-estate transactions, nurses being permitted to take over some routine tasks from surgeons, and minicab drivers being allowed to compete for taxicab business. Some professions may have invited this loss of privilege by overreaching themselves, raising fees until the incentive to find cheaper alternatives became overwhelming. Where government has expanded its role as a buyer (e.g. in health care, legally aided prosecution services, investment bank advice over privatisation) its budget constraints have made it more aware of costs, and alerted it to reducing professional fees as one way to cut them. Some professions have also suffered from an expansion of general educational and training attainments, eroding that their accreditation genuinely sets them apart. Driving instructors and carpenters lose business to the do-it-yourself version, and even doctorate-laden economists struggle to stop the more ambitious journalists, historians and bar-room orators claiming ascent to their ranks.

11.3.5 Labour market deregulation

Employees not blessed with entry-regulated skills, or the means to attain them, have fared less well in protecting their own interests. The quest for labour market 'flexibility', now a priority in most OECD economies, has meant a sustained attack on regulations related to pay, hours of work, health and safety, unfair dismissal and union rights often built up over several decades of political and workplace campaigning. Unemployment, fragmented workplaces, multinationals' power to relocate production, and legal curbs on union activity have weakened the power to redress these through collective action.

Several long-run developments have strengthened belief in the necessity for labour-market flexibility. Removal of trade barriers and accelerated acquisition of best-practice technology in lower-income regions, often under multinational supervision, has left certain tradable-sector employees (especially those with fewer skills) competing more directly with lower-wage, less regulated foreign counterparts.

New technologies make greater demand for non-standard work patterns (e.g. week-end working, shift labour), as do improved staff deployment techniques designed to maximise productivity or responsiveness to demand (leading to more part-time, temporary and seasonal labour). The pursuit of fixed exchange rates, as an anti-inflation device or (in the European Union case) an attempted step towards currency union) deprives nations of devaluation as an instrument for correcting rel-ative price- and wage-competitiveness disadvantages, displacing the adjustment burden more directly onto wage moderation or productivity improvement in the labour market.

As ever, some labour regulations are abandoned after proving unenforceable (employers adopting non-standard contracts to avoid the obligations attached to full-time employees, fragmenting their enterprises to avoid the obligation to estab-lish works councils, etc.), or counterproductive (costlier dismissal procedures deterring recruitment and, on a strict neoclassical microeconomic view of the competitive labour market, minimum wages merely swapping the poverty of low pay for the poverty of unemployment).

The deregulated labour market is only one approach to labour flexibility. Some economies appear to attain it through high levels of training (and a vigorous rented-property market) which make for high rates of inter-occupational and inter-regional mobility, and well-developed internal labour markets sustained by labour turnover which make for high rates of intra-firm mobility. These features may well be underpinned by regulation, especially of training standards and employment rights. But adjusting an employee's wage rate to the value of their product will tend always to be quicker and easier than adjusting productivity to the wage rate, where regulations do not obstruct it. The quest for speed in preserving employment against growth and trade shocks and in redeploying resources to new-technology areas seems likely to continue promoting market-based approaches to flexibility, with efforts to unify labour markets across borders (as now under way in the European Union) providing a further incentive to round employee regulations down to the lowest national level, if not out altogether.

11.4 Remarketising 'public' industry: privatisation

Choosing what to nationalise was never an exact science. Most nations' public sec-tors have contained, in varying proportions, natural monopolies for which outright state ownership was viewed as more efficient than regulation as a means to avoid client exploitation; natural and other monopolies regarded as a useful non-tax source of government revenue; increasing-returns companies whose need for state subsidy was seen as meriting state control; increasing-returns industries whose firms the government chose to merge and restructure itself because private banks and shareholders seemed incapable of doing this; infant industries considered incapable of genesis or growth in the private sector; 'strategic' industries considered too important to leave to the private sector (e.g. because they might underinvest, trade with an enemy or go bankrupt), and other firms with significant linkages or employment whose private management seemed incompetent or ineffective.

The choice of what to privatise has similarly reflected a variety of motives. Greater efficiency and accountability (to customers and shareholders) is ostensibly the main goal. But the one-off revenue gain from selling profitable state firms, the chance to clear the current budget of recurrent subsidies to unprofitable ones (at the expense of a one-off capital charge), the possible votes to be gained from offering cheap equity to households, the boost to stock-market development when that equity started trading, and the chance to discipline labour forces whose militancy the state as employer found politically hard to tackle, also ranked high as reasons to sell. Even where governments have been unable or unwilling to transfer operations fully to the private sector, they have moved to make public provision more market-like, by inviting private tenders for state-financed services which the state also used to provide, or introducing user charges to deter excessive use of 'free' goods and services (and cut their subsidy requirement).

11.4.1 Motives and methods

A certain amount of denationalisation has always gone on, as governments swung from left to right, infant industries reach adulthood or enterprises rescued from bankruptcy 'in the national interest' (notably banks) are allowed to regain their independence after appropriate reorganisations and capital injections. But by the early 1980s state enterprise sales had acquired the status of policy within certain industrial and industrialising-country governments, and acquired the positive name 'privatisation'. By the 1990s it had become a standard prescription – for low-income economies seeking faster development, and high-income economies looking to stay competitive against their encroachment. Indeed, for the former state-socialist economies of the 'second' world and the heavily indebted former colonies of the 'third', wide-ranging privatisation was now regarded as the only way to restore budgetary balance, close the productivity gap and get the debts repaid.

Narrowly defined, as a change of ownership from public to private, the arguments for privatisation are mainly macroeconomic. Sale of profit-making enterprises, if at a price close to their present value, releases funds with which the government can repay debt or reinvest in public infrastructure. The first is desirable because it cuts public debt-servicing outlays and reduces the 'crowding-out' of private borrowing, the second because hard infrastructure (public goods) and soft infrastructure (merit goods) are assumed to be more appropriate tasks for government than running firms that could exist in the private sector. 'Sale' of loss-making enterprises, even if it nets no revenue after acquirers have received the necessary incentives and debt write-offs, removes a persistent drain from the national accounts.

More broadly, as a change in the firm's objectives and external constraints, privatisation provides several spurs to microeconomic efficiency. It relieves management from (often inconsistent and shifting) political motives to concentrate on the profit motive, to which its pay can be more closely linked as an additional incentive. It opens up greater product-market competition, once removal of regulatory restrictions and the special advantages of state financial backing has allowed others to enter the market. It exposes the firm to a competitive capital market, as both a cheaper source of funds (now that it can issue shares and escape treasury rules designed to limit public borowing) and another enforcer of profit-maximisation. It allows the firm to restructure in pursuit of greater internal efficiency, and to internationalise. Six years into the UK's recent privatisation wave, with telecoms, steel, gas, airways and airports already sold, 'performance pay had become commonplace amongst senior and middle managers; and multi-divisional structures has also increased in importance' (Bishop and Thompson 1994: 353). In bringing large firms to the capital market, and encouraging citizens to buy and trade shares (often for the first time), it promotes the development of mutual and pension funds and other savings vehicles, with the promise of a higher savings rate and increased scope to re-privatise pension and welfare provision.

11.4.2 Predictions and results

Showing in advance that privatisation increases efficiency is not easy, since there were few cases of directly comparable private and public firms within one industry, and generally too many accompanying changes for comparison of pre- and post-nationalisation performance to be much of a guide. Pryke (1981) drew some unfavourable assessments of UK nationalised industries, but Millward (1982) found no clear evidence for public-sector underperformance. Studies of early UK privatisation suggested that ownership transfer was not a sufficient condition for improved productive efficiency; more competition also needed to be introduced if additional profit were to be achieved by greater efficiency and not merely the less restricted exercise of monopoly power (Vickers and Yarrow 1988). But a late 1980s review of the literature caught the consensus of the time in concluding that:

> Market systems tend to be more efficient in the use of resources at a given point in time, and more innovative, dynamic and expansive over time . . . From the standpoint of effective economic performance, the record strongly suggests that the shortcomings of nonmarket failure overwhelm those associated with market failure.
>
> (Wolf 1988: 153, 171)

Even a privatised monopoly was widely expected to hold costs lower and innovate faster than its state-sector predecessor, if only because the lack of a deep public pocket meant a limit to its excesses. 'Of course, private firms can make expensive mistakes; but the fact that they are dependent on markets sets a limit to the amounts they can lose. In the public sector the limits are less well drawn, and often ineffective' (Henderson 1986: 86).

Whereas the government's generally lower cost of capital and (hence) longer time horizons had been an argument for its taking responsibility for strategic industrial and infrastructure investment, whether or not external benefits were involved, the perception of government as an inherently less efficient producer switched the priority to improving the long-term capital supply to private enterprise. The first step that governments could take, it seemed, was to stop 'crowding out' private investment through its own calls on the capital market. The second was to end the subsidy, cheap capital and political privileges of public enterprise, so that private firms could compete with it on more equal terms. Much the easiest way, where the size of capital markets and potential acquirers allowed, was to let the private sector take over the state firm.

Natural monopoly presented more of a problem. Where domestic competitors need time to develop, or are kept out by the former state monopoly's scale-economies and sunk investments acting as entry barrier, competition has generally needed to be substituted by regulation, exchanging one intervention in the market fo another. Over time, therefore, enthusiasm has grown for following privatisation with moves to generate additional product-market competition – internally by break-up of the former state monopoly (horizontally into rival suppliers and distributors interconnected to the natural-monopoly network, and/or vertically into competing integrated producers), or externally by opening the market to international competition (including that from other countries' national champions and natural monopolies).

Privatisation has achieved some spectacular successes – notably in telecommunications, where technical change has significantly reduced natural-monopoly elements – and some notable failures, with the UK still struggling with higher charges, substandard quality and frequent shortages of water seven years after floating the industry. But aside from the faith that greater efficiency will eventually win through, another more immediate advantage of privatisation has become apparent: the large sums of money that can be raised from selling assets into a rising stock-market, which can be used either to reinvest in the industry, to repay public debt, to invest in other more appropriate public assets (infrastructure, education) or – with rather less respect for 'golden-rule' preservation of public-sector net worth, but a possibly beneficial effect on private investment – to finance tax reduction.

Financial as much as efficiency-generating motives seem to be behind the willingness to expand privatisation into uncharted territory, such as the electricity grid (pioneered by the UK, quickly taken up by Hungary in the struggle to contain its foreign debts) and railway network. A cynic might argue that, in this respect, Britain produced a privatisation pioneer rather earlier than Margaret Thatcher: King Henry VIII, who seized and sold the assets of England's monasteries in 1536. But governments with debts to liquidate, demographic overhangs to fund and new capital projects to finance are inevitably led to review their present stock of assets as a possible alternative way to raise revenue from the private sector than imposing another tax.

11.5 Remarketising social welfare provision

Even if they have become less concerned about the relative dispersion of private incomes, governments continue to worry about the causes of poverty – sickness, unemployment, old age and other misfortunes for which individuals left to themselves may be unwilling or unable to afford contingency cover. In many countries the welfare state has literally replaced the warfare state, redistributive social payments (to individuals in adversity or retirement) overtaking the defence budget. In those with the highest income, transfer payments exceed all 'final' state consumption and investment expenditures. 'When we talk about the growth of government expenditures since World War II, we are talking about the growth of direct income transfers' (Thurow 1980: 159). The growth is even more dramatic when transfers in kind – the free provision of merit goods – are considered alongside transfers are either in cash.

11.5.1 *From social to private insurance*

Provision for future personal contingencies is a matter of social concern because of the external costs that arise when individuals cannot support themselves in adversity. We suffer psychologically when hungry hands plead for money from shop doorways; we also suffer economically when the unemployed cannot find work, and physically when the sick infect us or the poor decide that the short cut to wealth is through the money in our pockets.

Private insurance for life's crueller contingencies runs into the familiar problems of adverse selection and moral hazard. Those most likely to become unemployed, sick, poor or forced into early retirement are those on the lowest incomes, who are least likely to be able to afford the premiums commensurate with such risks. Since those who could most afford to pay for the insurance are those most likely to decide they don't need it – or to buy it from an 'elite' insurer which keeps premiums low by screening out the bad risks – competitive private insurance provision quickly loses any scope for maintaining universal coverage. Unless the insurance is privatised as a monopoly – introducing another set of failures – privatisation invites low-risk applicants to opt out of their previous obligation to cross-subsidise high-risk applicants. They will be helped by private insurers anxious to 'cream' the lowest risks. 'If purchasers can choose for whom they will purchase, and providers can choose for whom they will provide, that is, if they can skim off the cream, then welfare services may not reach those who need them most and equity will not be achieved' (Bartlett and Le Grand 1993: 32, whose study shows the problem extending to quasi-markets within state-funded health and social housing services).

Even if they can convince an insurer that they have not been adversely selected, those least able to afford insurance premiums may still be faced with the highest ones because of greater moral hazard. The smaller gap between their regular (in-work/in good health) income and the payout on the insurance (if paid at a flat rate) implies a smaller incentive to avoid needing the payout. People on lower incomes thus risk being seen as more likely to risk incurring the contingency, for example by abusing their health or getting themselves dismissed from work.

Those who set up social insurance schemes for these reasons tended to believe (like those who founded state-funded health-care services) that demand would diminish over time because of the rise in absolute incomes achieved by economic growth. By implication, the need to draw on social insurance would diminish through time, and the ability to pay for it would increase. Declining moral hazard and adverse selection risks might therefore make privatisation a socially safe option once national income has surpassed a certain level. Diseases of affluence, white-collar unemployment, relative deprivation and the tendency for the rich to replace old risks with new have made it hard to sustain this optimism. The recent slow-down in global growth, followed by a recovery characterised by higher rates of unemployment, income inequality and structural change, has meant that any improvement in the distribution of risks caused by generally rising incomes has been offset by greater difficulty in establishing the distribution. Many high (average) incomes are now accompanied by – and perhaps explained by – substantial vari-ability of those earnings and discontinuity of employment. Some of the potentially largest and least calculable risks – notably that of long and medically expensive old age – may in fact attach to affluent people previously considered to be in the lowest-risk groups. In its broader sense, of personal welfare depending on institu-tions, machines, political changes and confluences of events over which individuals have no control, privately non-insurable risk may have grown more prevalent as societies grow more prosperous.

Rather than the piecemeal remedies of providing direct support to those who cannot afford private insurance, or topping-up the payouts (when needed) of those with inadequate private cover, governments have tended to impose compulsory social insurance, collecting contributions alongside taxes (with some variation according to income) and paying out from a central state-administered fund. This keeps premiums low by forcing all risks into a common pool (becoming doubly redistributive if contributions are graded by income) and also captures for the state the profits which would otherwise accrue to private insurers. The sharing of contributions between employees, employers and government (general taxpayers) has often been a centrepiece of wider corporatist efforts to build co-operation in the workplace and national pay bargaining. As a single purchaser of in-kind ben-efits such as health care, the government is better placed to monitor and minimise its costs of provision. State-run insurance can also reduce the moral hazard prob-lem. To the extent that government can affect the insured contingencies, it now has an extra incentive to keep unemployment down, prevent inflation that can put fixed-income earners into poverty, and take preventive health and public health ini-tiatives. And rather than merely supporting people in their suffering, it has a long-term financial interest in getting the unemployed back into work (e.g. through retraining), the sick back into health and the low-paid out of poverty. (And, per-haps, the rejuvenation of old-age pensioners when medical science allows.)

Compulsory insurance still encounters equity and efficiency problems, espe-cially in the inclusion of those whose social disadvantage prevents them ever paying in, and the maintenance of separate social funds whose off-budget status often reduces fiscal transparency. Noting that compulsory insurance contributions are a tax in all but name, some governments have gone further and made most social benefits a general expenditure item, funded by taxation and made available to all who need them. This motive is reinforced by the argument that health, housing and education provision are merit goods with external benefits, that unemployment is an economic and social cost which state support (if linked to training or job-creation) can help to alleviate, and that pensions and child support are costs which most people will incur at some stage in life, with a presumption that a decency threshold (if not equality of provision) should be observed. (Although birth rates in some high-income economies have fallen so low that childless households are beginning to outnumber those with children, there is still an argument that child-rearing brings external benefits, if only to pay the pension and national debt obligations that past and present generations have already run up.)

11.5.2   *From welfare to workfare*

Unless the distribution of income, life chances and private risks is unusually even, an element of welfare is inherent in social insurance schemes. The poorest need their premiums topped up, and the chronically disadvantaged need the state to step in when their premium-based entitlement runs out. The need for public subsidy to insurance is usually made explicit by a range of basic benefits presented as merit goods, and so available even to those who rarely or never pay into the social insurance system.

Despite its equity and efficiency claims, state welfare provision has been linked with serious moral hazards. Social critics identify a 'dependency culture' under which some (especially low-paid) households get themselves dismissed, turn down job opportunities, fall ill and beget children, knowing that the state will defray the costs. Economic critics argue that governments will be more inclined to bring down unemployment (which brings an automatic saving in compulsory payouts) at the expense of higher inflation (which, by advantaging fixed-term borrowers at the expense of lenders, and dragging unchanged real incomes into higher tax brackets, carries out a complementary redistribution while also adding directly to government revenues).

As well as creating its own demand, state-subsidised welfare and merit-goods provision stands accused of choking off the alternative (and pre-existing) market supply. Voluntary schools and hospitals, mutual and co-operative societies, credit unions and charities provided contingent social help to the poorest long before the state systematically intervened. These private-sector solutions disappeared, or were driven to seek more profitable (and exclusionary) business, once welfare 'nationalisation' took place, so that from being a foundation whose holes the state filled in, private insurance is now in many cases an optional podium on a foundation laid by the state. Left to itself, goes the pro-market counterfactual, a growing economy would simultaneously have reduced the need for welfare provision – by generating jobs, improving health and lifting people out of poverty – and developed its own equally equitable and more efficient systems for compensating social disadvantage.

Rising state-sector employment, far from revealing a natural redirection of demand towards public or merit goods as incomes grew, is accused of slowing that income by distorting the supply side. The workers involved would have been better employed in the private sector, and the tax required to pay their state salaries was destroying incentives to save and invest. 'The increase in employment to provide more public services continued through boom and recession, and until 1975, each increase was permanent; so the workers taken on in recession were not available to industry in subsequent booms' (Bacon and Eltis 1978: 15). Because of work involved redistributing existing income, public service employment was even less productive than that in public industry, which (if sometimes at subsidy) at least sold its output, and even exported a proportion of it. Bacon and Eltis acknowledged that the state could try to correct its own faults by sponsoring a programme of fixed investment, but the option more enthusiastically taken up in the UK (which they analysed) was that 'the market sector of the economy can be made larger compared to the non-market sector by cutting public spending and nationalised industry losses and subsidies' (1978: 32).

.The most recent extension of the pro-market case is that state provision has actually slowed the economic growth which ultimately underwrites rising welfare and that the damage is set to worsen as rising costs lead to an ever heavier tax burden. Technical change and structural mismatch appear to mean prolonged if not permanent mass unemployment, to which the dependency culture (and associated forcing-up of wage rates for those still in work) is accused of contributing. Earlier and longer retirement, combined with lesser and later entry to the workforce, mean an ever-rising pension bill to be met by ever fewer taxpayers. The same demographic 'overhang' combines with rising medical costs and expectations to produce an equally inexorable rise in health-care costs. To meet these needs out of social insurance universal state provision will, the critics argue, require an unsustainable rise in contributions or taxation.

The critics' solution – turning the clock back to where they believe it should always have been – is to restrict state-funded provision to those who genuinely cannot meet the costs. In recommending that those who can afford private insurance must be allowed to take it, the assumption that these genuine 'can't pay' cases are few in number, so that the state can get by with a substantially smaller welfare budget, concentrated on the small minority to whom private insurers cannot offer affordable cover. Today's large welfare rolls are seen as having been swelled by people drawn away from paid work by over-generous welfare benefits, lulled by past welfare dependency that they no longer realise they are capable of work and would gain financially from it, or rejected by employers because of their past lapse into welfare dependency. One solution – turning payments to the unemployed into a subsidy to business to employ them – has won special attention because its appeal overrides the economic cycle. Continental European and Japanese governments, stuck in recession or slow growth, recognise the potential for reducing unemployment at no extra cost to the welfare budget (which will actually fall if, as the evidence suggests, the return to work increases employability and so allows the subsidy-benefit to be phased out without the job being lost again). US and UK governments, near the top of a cycle which has already reduced unemployment substantially, recognise the strength of the argument that all but the most seriously disadvantaged could find useful work if they wanted to – needing only to be rescued from dependency by being made to work for their benefit.

'Workfare' does not return to the pre-industrial system of simply withdrawing welfare benefits to the 'able-bodied' poor, sending them into the workhouse or out to beg if they could not find a regular job. By continuing the payout (as an employment subsidy) after the welfare recipient returns to work, it tackles the 'poverty trap' that may have previously deterred them (because they stood to lose more in resumed tax and relinquished benefit than they would have gained from the unsubsidised wage). The benefit is generally tapered according to the wage, and may be withdrawn after a certain period. But by allowing employers to try an applicant 'for free', it overcomes the information asymmetry that may previously have prevented their recruitment, allowing those previously kept out of employment by illness, injury or sheer unavailability of work that they are capable of doing the job in hand.

Thus redirected, a welfare benefit accused of distorting resource allocation can now be viewed as correcting a market failure, arising from employers' taking long-term unemployment as a signal of unemployability in the absence of genuine information about a candidate's skills and circumstances. The correction of this information deficiency reduces the danger of subsidising an employer who would have recruited the applicant anyway. It leaves open the danger that the employer will recruit them in place of a more deserving candidate who does not receive the subsidy; but in a comprehensive workfare scheme this could apply only to those already in work (and seeking to switch jobs) or those becoming available for work for the first time (so not previously eligible for benefit). Targeted at those too severely disadvantaged to offer themselves as cheaper substitues for existing employees, workfare also promises that the fall in unemployment that it achieves will not unleash any intensified wage-inflation pressure.

The effectiveness of 'workfare' substantially depends on the extent to which present benefit recipients are prevented from taking up available jobs, by the disincentive of poverty traps, inability to persuade employers of their suitability, lack of knowledge about job opportunities or lack of belief in their capacity to take them up. Lack of suitable skills is often added to this list, and many schemes include an element of training provided by the state or (with further subsidy) by the employer. Lone parenting duties are another cause for which welfare conversion, this time into childcare subsidies, is being considered (see section 12.2.2). But lack of available jobs is no longer considered the principal obstacle. Whereas past recruitment-subsidy and job-guarantee schemes were generally proposed in conjunction with a 'Keynesian' macroeconomic programme for correcting a perceived deficiency in aggregate demand, recent programmes have tended to take a much more exclusively microeconomic focus. Their success will be determined by the extent to which economies can go on creating jobs whose wage exceeds present welfare benefit levels by enough to compensate for the cost of getting to work (and the opportunity cost of leisure forgone while doing it).

If output does not grow fast enough for both employment and labour productivity to rise, this will be possible only if the government is willing to reduce workfare benefits in line with falling real employment incomes, or to concede that welfare without work must continue to be paid to those for whom there is no job available that pays a living wage.

11.5.3 Pension privatisation

Pensions differ from most other types of social insurance in that people hope to draw the benefit at a specified future time, and to go on drawing it as long as possible. This greatly raises their incentive to contribute to a pension scheme. But with effective retirement ages falling and life expectancies rising, and with every contributor aiming to become an eventual beneficiary, it also requires substantially larger premiums. Because payouts cannot usually be claimed until the specified retirement age, even if retirement happens earlier, pension funds have the advantage of being able to seek higher returns by investing their contributions over longer time horizons.

Many employees have, however, traditionally depended on state pensions paid out of general taxation, having lacked the steady employment and income needed to subscribe to a private fund. The danger of those who do well in the labour market maintaining their advantage in retirement through a private scheme, while disadvantage at work leads on to disadvantaged senescence on a basic state pension, provides a social justice argument for including everyone in a tax-funded retirement scheme. There are also strong arguments for a state scheme's economic advantage over, or equivalence to, private pension arrangements. But these arguments are currently in worldwide retreat against the efficiency claims being made for a shift to private pension funding.

The economic superiority of privately funded over tax-funded pensions and insurance rests on two premises. First, private funds will secure a higher return on the existing contributions, with better management channelling them into portfolios of faster-growing private securities rather than the infrastructure projects on which government's capital budgets tend to be spent. Second, contributions will increase because people's incentive to save is raised when their savings are on their own account, targeted at their own future benefits. The higher national savings rate contributes to faster economic growth, which feeds back into the better performance of private share portfolios. Growth is further improved if lower rates of taxation, enabled by the switch to private contributions, increase work incentives and improve the allocation of resources.

Without faster growth and stronger savings incentives, universal private pensions and insurance would be functionally little different from present 'pay-as-you-go' tax-funded schemes. Contributions would still be compulsory, and the social benefits still paid out of currently generated national income, this merely being deducted from corporate and personal income through dividend payments and equity sales rather than through tax. Since government must still undertake to pay the pensions of those who have saved nothing or not enough, a residual role for tax-finance pensions must remain, This role will be substantial if volatile stock-markets leave many with equity-linked pensions which have grown too slowly, or force pension funds for safety to invest a high proportion in government stock (on which repayments come from the treasury).

Occupational pension funds forced to sell assets to meet the increasing demand for income from retiring members may actually contribute to making stock-markets more depressed and more volatile.

The pension funds must, with an ageing population, become net sellers of securities . . . this would worsen the investment performance of pension funds of all kinds, because capital gains comprise the greater part of their returns on assets . . . higher company contributions (to meet their pension funds' solvency requirements) will hold back the growth of dividends, and thereby reduce consumption. This is one way in which the burden of an ageing population will be borne by non-pensioners, even with funded pensions.

(Crawford 1997: 40–1)

The existence of a serious 'demographic overhang', whose threat to the solvency of pay-as-you-go state funding underlies the pressure for self-financed pensions, is not beyond dispute, despite coming close to received wisdom. In some 'ageing' countries fertility decline has followed the fall in death rates quickly enough for relative pensioner numbers to be approaching a plateau. In others, rapid productivity growth of those still in work and relatively frugal provision to those due to leave it (who often work beyond retirement age in response) could keep a higher proportion of pensioners supportable under existing arrangements, provided sharp reductions in the tax base are avoided. A study of pensions in Poland in advance of that country's planned switch to partial private finance in January 1999, although sympathetic to the reform, noted that the state-financed system could continue to operate within reasonable budget targets through a combination of narrower eligibility, means-adjusted payouts, higher participation encouraged by the rise in wage rates relative to pension rates, a wider tax base and higher labour productivity (Perraudin and Pujol 1994). Reallocating the tax burden from employers to employees emerged as a more immediate priority than reducing it.

Similarly, an early simulation of Kazakhstan's funded pension scheme (launched in January 1998) suggests that the saving on tax-funded pension payouts will not match the loss of payroll-tax revenue for at least the first twenty-eight years of the scheme, resulting in substantially higher state pension fund deficits up to 2026 than if associated reforms (higher retirement ages, tighter eligibility, more employee contributions) were applied to the previous state-funded arrangement. These findings cast doubt on the prospects for phasing-out of the state pension (as planned) within sixty years, without a serious fall in average payouts compared with what could have been expected from the modified state system (especially for women, with shorter average working lives and longer retirement lifespans).

Even in the long run, the system of funded pensions is clearly inferior to the reformed pay-as-you-go approach with regard to the financial burden imposed on the Republican Budget. The apparent superiority of funded pensions . . . is nothing but an effect of the decision to raise the retirement age and to abolish early retirement and favourable pensions.

(Spiecker and Zweiner 1998: 40)

Ironically the UK, with one of the highest proportions of funded pensions among

OECD economies, is among those facing the least serious rise in 'dependency ratios' of non-working to work-eligible citizens.

Given the general rise in relative pensioner numbers through longer retirement spans and lower workforce entry rates, private pensions also rely on high rates of employment and of income growth and a rising equity market, to ensure that most of the current workforce can amass a sufficient pension without needing tax-funded supplements when retirement comes. Social security privatisation tends thus to be embedded in a wider process of privatisation and deregulation, to whose attainment it also contributes. Private insurance and pension funds are a principal constitutent of the institutional investor base supporting the flotations, with occu-pational pension funds alone now owning almost one-third of UK listed shares. The UK and USA's lead in maintaining or restoring the private ownership of major utilities is closely connected with their early development of private savings vehicles; they held around 75 per cent of the world's private pension fund invest-ment in 1996 (Minns 1996: 48). Other nations embarking on large-scale privatisation programmes have had to rely on local banks and/or foreign investors to support share flotations, sold directly to (usually multinational) corporate buyers, or treated the enterprise as a past collective purchase and issued equity to citizens for vouchers at a nominal price.

The rapid growth of compulsory savings schemes in Chile and Singapore (for pensions and general welfare respectively) suggests that a compelled private sector may at least match a more politically distracted public sector in building up a stock of wealth from which to fund future social transfers. It is less clear that pen-sion privatisation has contributed to faster economic growth in the countries that pioneered it, since some were already growing rapidly and others' acceleration has been accompanied by rising public debt, an implicit charge on future retirees. An analysis of Chile's experience suggests that private pension funds' virtuous circle of higher household saving, lower capital costs, higher investment, faster growth and stronger savings incentives may be broken by the 'wealth effect' of rising asset values on consumption.

> Contrary to the common belief about the effects of the pension reform, the empirical findings suggest that the direct effect of financial market develop-ments on the private saving rate was negative . . . These results also temper the optimism reigning in countries in Latin America and Eastern Europe, where pension reform is seen as an easy vehicle to boost national saving, and thus capital accumulation and growth.
>
> (Holzmann 1997: 175)

The public appeal of pension reform in these countries has come as much from the fear of a steady run-down in the real state pension as from any great hope that private pensions will earn a better return. It also owes much to governments' will-ingness to fund the transitional deficit on the state pension fund, caused by continuing to pay today's pensioners while allowing today's workers to divert their payroll tax contributions, through extra borrowing rather than extra tax –

postponing a payment burden which may catch up with tomorrow's private pensioners if they achieve the long and prosperous retirement they hope for. (Some governments have plugged part of the gap by privatising state assets, but the effect is equivalent to extra borrowing, in that spending capital receipts on current transfers reduces the net worth of the public sector and requires higher future taxation to substitute for the lost property income.) If Latin American research is correct in concluding that pension privatisation does not directly raise an economy's growth rate, it would appear that recent growth would equally well have improved the viability of previous 'pay-as-you-go' pension arrangements, since they promise the next generation significantly higher real incomes than the present one. The reasons for public enthusiasm for private pensions are then deflected uncomfortably from positive economic hopes to more negative human fears, regarding future generations' willingness to finance transfers of income across either time or space. The lesson of recent tax revolts is that ability to pay for others' welfare is often inversely related to ability to pay. Resultant fear of relative deprivation in retirement, if dependent on tax alone, may explain the real appeal of private arrangements ensuring that what is saved from work income will really be paid back, with interest, when work comes to an end.

Whether higher-income nations that go down the private pension route can grow their retirement funds at the same rate remains a still more open question, given the slower growth of their economies (and therefore of stock-market capitalisation), and their intention – partly through welfare privatisation – to reduce the size and cost of government debt. If they do not, so that pension funds have to take higher risks in search of higher rewards, the world's new spatial division of labour may come to acquire a time dimension. The intriguing prospect arises of western industrial workers relying for retirement income on the profits generated by emerging-economy workers who captured their jobs. In terms of global equity, and sending capital to where it is most needed, the vision has much to recommend it. The abrupt interruption of such capital flows in late 1997, and the instability across the world's stock-markets that followed it, was a reminder that safe retirement may not be assured when state retirement can no longer be afforded.

11.6 Remarketising merit goods

However far insurance extends, certain goods and services will still need to be provided to people who cannot pay for them, either on social grounds (that all have a basic entitlement to them) or on the economic grounds that they should go to those best able to use them, and/or their consumption brings external benefits. But while such 'merit goods' require non-market distribution, they do not necessitate non-market production. Merit goods are characterised by administered transaction only, it is argued, because government in its role of providing the money has also taken power over deciding the merit. Greater efficiency in the production and allocation of merit goods could be achieved by separating supply and demand within the subsidised system of provision.

Stronger internal financial controls and accounting can go some way towards this, but only with the risk of introducing new transaction costs which negate any gains from more efficient resource allocation and use. The more ambitious approach is to break up the monolithic structure of public provision. State subsidy is switched from 'providers', the (generally state-owned) producers of the merit good who until now have also been in charge of assigning it, to 'purchasers', those shown to merit the good, who can now choose their supplier, and change it if not satisfied. Having established the purchaser–provider split, the government retires to the sidelines as fundraiser and referee for the system, leaving delivery to a con-structive battle between autonomous agents on either side of the market.

Purchasers establish their clients' needs, and seek out the providers who can best meet them. Public funds are then summoned, either to let the purchaser pay the provider, or the provider service the purchaser free of charge. Although purchasers and providers may still be public-sector agencies, spending and receiving public money, splitting them apart is assumed to rule out 'government failure' by dropping the requirement that they be selfless servants of the public interest. Instead, their self-interest is acknowledged and given free rein, the quasi-market's task being to ensure that it gives rise to behaviour which best serves the public. This is done by linking providers' profits to the quantity and quality of health care delivered, the size of schools' rolls and the height of their attainments, the number of homeless people housed and jobless people found work, and so on. Purchasers, similarly, have their funds linked to the quantity and quality of service procured, so that the best see their budgets rise. The freedom of purchasers to shop around for better deals also encourages new, private providers to open for business, putting further pressure on the existing ones to improve.

As well as going with the (assumed) grain of agents' motivation, the use of profit as a performance criterion also overcomes a longstanding difficulty over the mea-surement of merit goods output and efficiency of production.

> The more effective is the structure of positive incentives for the contractor to perform, the less need there will be for monitoring and maintenance . . . Contracts will more easily be self-enforcing the more visible the output, and the clearer the relationship between inputs and outputs, and in such cases it will be easier to have a performance based approach to payment.
>
> (Walsh 1995: 49)

The quasi-market is designed to ensure that scarce resources are still allocated on merit, but with a clear supply–demand split which avoids the inefficiencies, unac-countabilities and bilateral monopolies that can arise when one agency both assesses and administers to a need at public expense. Patients are still treated in accordance with the severity of their illness, pupils assigned to school and college places on the basis of their academic interests and strengths, the homeless rehoused and the jobless retrained on the basis of relative disadvantage and assessed need. But once their merit has been established, and funds put towards it by the pur-chasing agency, providers must compete for their custom. As long as the purchasers remain sufficiently well informed about clients' needs and providers' capabilities, competition within both groups will be on combinations of cost and quality, so that standards of service and cost-efficiency both rise.

Providers will, the theory goes, be encouraged to pool their facilities where this creates scale or scope economies, avoiding excessive competition which would add to costs. Any resultant monopoly power can be countered by purchasers, who can likewise co-ordinate their demand when there are economies in treating like-needed clients in strict sequences or groups. Far from fragmenting previous centrally controlled provision in the quest to make supply more sensitive to demand, price-setting in an internal market is intended to bring lower overhead costs (as well as better allocation) than the bureaucratic form-filling of administered transaction.

Quasi-market solutions have been especially keenly sought in two of the largest public expenditure items: health care, because of the efficiency gains needed to accommodate seemingly ever-rising demand, and education, because of the perceived need for competitive pressure to raise standards and spread best practice from good schools to bad. In both, attempts to make state provision work more like the market have also been provoked by growing private provision, which threatens to allow richer citizens to opt out into better and faster provision, worsening the service deficiencies for the rest even if their needs and merits are greater. Hospitals and schools become the providers. To redress their monopoly power over product and product knowledge, doctors and parents become purchasers on behalf of the ultimate consumers, patients and pupils.

11.6.1 Quasi-markets come to health care

Arguably the largest market-based merit good system is that which has been grafted onto US health care, which began the twentieth century as an insurance-based system. Aware that many were failing to receive merited care because they lacked adequate insurance cover, the government in the 1960s extended federal funds (Medicare and Medicaid) to subsidise the insurance premiums of those unable to afford them, and from the 1970s required most employers to contribute to their employees' cover. Entering on the demand side, the government found common cause with private insurers in seeking the best deal from hospitals, most of which remained privately run. Blue Cross insurance providers, assessing care whose design they had tended to leave to the hospitals, had already found that these were giving longer and more frequent treatment so as to maximise the payout.

> They began, in cooperation with the hospitals in their communities, to build mild control mechanisms into their plan-provider contracts to deal with individual cases and unnecessary days of hospital care . . . It has become entirely commonplace for most Americans to get their medical care in schemes where the plan that pays for the care also has a significant voice in care delivery. That voice is expressed through stable, non-adversarial, long-term contracts between the plans and the doctors and hospitals.
>
> (Henning Sieverts 1996: 12–13)

More than half US citizens now subscribe their health insurance through 'managed care organisations' (MCOs) which act as expert purchasers for large groups of clients. These seek efficiency gains by, where possible, aggregating individual plans and block-booking their contracts. Providers have accused them of also trying to cut costs by exerting monopsony power, but supporters of the system regard MCOs as bringing consumer sovereignty to a market doctors and hospitals previously monopolised by exploiting their expertise.

> Healthcare is run by a management team which decides the appropriate mix of factors needed to create a product – in this case, the healthcare of a defined population. In ways not previously possible, such management also negotiates prices of raw materials – drugs, doctors, nurses and hospitals . . . Managed care stands as one of the only healthcare systems capable of systematically containing and even reducing costs. It also promotes community care and preventive medicine.
>
> (Woods 1997: 5, 12)

Although competition between MCOs encourages them to pass cost savings on to subscribers, and government tries to fund those who still cannot afford the premiums (or get their employers to do so), many US citizens have inadequate health insurance, or resort to cut-price schemes providing limited cover. Profit-motivated MCOs have also tended to grow at the expense of those set up as non-profit, without systematic evidence that they are more cost-efficient, suggesting a tendency to raise profit through market power which may reduce care quality and squeeze the margin through which hospitals could fund new facilities and research.

These shortcomings are intended to be overcome in the health care quasi-market now being developed in the UK, which began at the opposite end with a state-funded National Health Service (NHS) charged with both diagnosis and delivery. NHS hospitals have now been converted into independently managed trusts, which sell services to state-funded regional health authorities or general practitioner (GP) practices. Over time, fundholding GPs are intended to take over as the main source of health-care demand, using their expert knowledge to overcome the information asymmetry from which patients would suffer if given the money and told to purchase their treatment direct. (Previously, hospital doctors on the 'provider' side could, as in the USA, dazzle them with science to dictate unnecessary and expensive treatment.) By organising GP fundholders into local purchasing groups, it is also hoped to offset any monopoly power held by local providers, and ensure a pooling of purchasing resources to avoid patients having treatment unduly delayed because their GP runs short of funds.

The separation of demand from supply is argued to offer gains both in fairness and efficiency. Hospitals will compete for doctors' custom by adapting to expressed demand and raising their quality of service. Doctors will compete for patients' custom through the skill with which they can diagnose health needs and match them to the best available treatments. Hospitals will be deterred from over-treating and doctors from over-prescribing to improve their own revenues at state expense, and there will be safeguards against doctors biasing demand towards facilities in which they have a supply-side interest. Savings could also arise from improved targeting of essential treatment on state-funded patients, with some non-essential cases choosing to pay for private treatment to avoid long waits. (Since most private treatment takes place in National Health trust hospitals, such private expenditure becomes an extra source of funding for the public service, partly compensating for its longstanding supply of trained doctors, surgeons and nurses to the private health sector.)

The UK system has been criticised for incurring higher transaction costs (through the need to itemize and administer separate payments), sacrificing scale and learning economies as hospitals invest competitively in new competences and facilities, involving GP fundholders in guesswork over what treatments to pre-purchase, and not always matching purchasing power to the most acute needs. The government's concern to contain the NHS budget despite rising health-care needs has prevented it from furnishing demand at levels that would encourage new private provision; although new hospitals are being built (with part-private finance), health-care 'supply' continues to be rationed, and attempts to stop the growth of waiting lists have been criticised for placing waiting time ahead of urgency of need in patients' order of merit. Some areas of research risk being underfunded because budgets are allocated on the basis of treatment, and because further aggregation of GP fundholders could tighten the squeeze on hospitals' cashflow. (Even more than with industrial research, the rapid dissemination of medical research results makes it unlikely that one provider can profit from an innovative treatment for any length of time, even if it wishes to. The most likely means is to acquire experience with the technique which draws purchasers towards it, but even this will be something rivals – and the system's regulators – will be keen to curtail, others acquiring experience by poaching the innovator's staff if they cannot easily train their own.)

Over time, a more equal power balance between purchasers and providers may, along with switching costs (reflecting patients' reluctance to travel) and difficulties in exchanging information at a distance, lead purchasers and providers back from the market towards informed or relational transaction. For the present UK government, which created the NHS in 1948 as an administered transaction system, this may prove an acceptable halfway house.

11.6.2 Commerce hits the campus

While Europe lags behind the USA in marketising health care, some of its countries can claim a lead in bringing market forces to bear on higher education. After centuries of trying to turn it from a private purchase into a merit good, cost pressures now threaten to move it the other way, as governments attempt to increase student numbers without picking up the extra bill for fees and maintenance. Taking the view that post-compulsory education and training are actually human capital investments with a privately appropriable return, attention has shifted to overcoming the capital market imperfections which prevent students from paying their own way through college on loans secured against future higher income.

One option is to extend the credit market. The state supports banks to providing long low-interest loans to students, or assigns them 'learning accounts' which they can spend on training at public expense, but are encouraged to augment through further saving so as to support study towards a higher qualification. Another option, the 'graduate tax', effectively extends the equity market: government effectively treating the student as a human capital investment. The government funds them through the course, but recovers its fees through tax (either relying on the extra qualification to push them into a higher tax bracket, or imposing a special surcharge once a minimum income is reached). Evidence in western Europe is ambiguous as to whether steps towards these arrangements have reversed the rise in numbers seeking or attaining university places, though some countries have experienced an above-trend rise in applications in the year before such changes are expected to start.

In eastern Europe, numbers at university have tended to fall since state funding dried up, despite a sharp rise in unemployment, from which college might provide temporary shelter if not permanent escape through better qualification. But while many potential students cannot afford to attend, there are also signs that some could no longer consider it worthwhile. The collapse of the state has brought deterioration on the supply side as faculties are drained of funds and staff, and a steep decline in relative public-sector pay, removing the differential through which professionals employed there might once have expected to repay their training fees. The fall of communism led many students, fresh from felling the old order with their protests, to turn their minds from studying to capturing the large profits to be made from start-up business ventures – a case of the market impinging on student choices rather more directly than higher education reformers had foreseen.

11.7   Missing in (trans)action: the red tape rewinds

For more than a century, neoclassical allocation, employment, distribution, growth and trade theories have offered an intellectual case for letting unfettered markets guide transaction. More recently, public-choice theory has given equally forthright reasons as to why even 'market-correcting' state interventions may follow private and sectional rather than social agendas. But these theories also gave persuasive reasons as to why intervention and regulation will slowly suffocate the free market, and prove impossible to dislodge (at least democratically) once in place. Instead of resisting the erosion of their freedom, companies would vie (or even collude) with labour unions to tighten their hold over the microeconomy, prompting politicians to extend a similar rein over the macroeconomy. The state would steadily expand as producer, employer and collective consumer as rising income shifted consumption onto public goods, merit goods, natural monopoly products and scarce resources. The 'rent-seeking' carrot would reinforce tax and regulatory sticks as inducements into state-sector employment.

11.7.1 The accidental revolutionaries

The gains from competing to win within the market are limited in scope, uncertain in occurrence and quick to disappear again as rivals imitate and improve on the winning strategy. In contrast, the gains from combining to win over the market – by co-ordinating action on the demand or supply side, or persuading government to fix prices and limit entry – are large, certain and potentially permanent. The distributional coalitions that campaign for these market distortions can share out the benefits among everyone who joins them, while spreading the (greater) social costs over everyone left outside them (Olson 1982). Since narrow special interests are easier to organise than unfocused general interests, the lobby groups that gain from forestalling the market are always more powerful and cohesive than the general interests that lose (Olson 1965).

Among the 'silent majorities' too dispersed in location, or too diverse in opinion, to form stable coalitions against the noisy minorities' special pleading, consumers and taxpayers tended to feature prominently. Nader's Raiders and the Californians who rallied to Proposition 14 were taken as encouraging but eccentric exceptions. In general, companies seemed as likely to deal with a poor product by stepping up its advertising than by raising its quality, and governments seemed destined to claw back through hidden charges or inflation any cuts in headline tax rates. Full employment and rising participation made it almost possible to detect a regulation-spawning consensus under which people accepted a raw deal when they spent their income as the price of improved conditions in which to earn it. The prospect of an army of shoppers turning to fight, and the top-rate taxband flexing its muscles by taking flight, was not one in which pro-marketeers were wont to place much hope.

Governments were seen as giving in to producers' rent-seeking pressure because their own employees take their share of the reward, through the formal pay packet as well as the informal payoff. Politicians are unlikely (viewed from the neoclassical rationality perspective) to give up the right to manage an economy whose resources fund their own discretionary expenditures. Bureaucrats will not put effort into strategies for dismantling controls whose exercise justifies their job, and the power and prestige that go with it. Likewise, large firms, self-selecting professions and less enlightened self-interests will not turn against political protection from, and regulation of, the markets in which they would otherwise have to compete. Liberal belief in the chances of reviving non-interventionism and reversing the descent waned as business leaders and professional employees, ostensibly those with most to gain by rolling back the state, found advantages in log-rolling with it or even curling up to it.

Many who were convinced of the market's merits found themselves joining with its detractors in claiming the inevitability of the mixed economy. Some even lost the morosity of tone that might have kept the two voices distinct. When they contemplated the growth of production scale, technical indivisibility and transaction complexity in the modern economy, some prominent liberals found themselves inclining to the interventionist case. There were growing doubts about the scope for internalising external costs and benefits at the individual level, for maintaining the necessary power balance in transaction (between small and large businesses, labour and capital, high- and low-income nations), and for scattered self-interested actions sum to a coherent whole.

> Just as government first secured the elements of freedom for all when it pre-vented the physically stronger man from slaying, beating, despoiling his neighbours, so it secures a larger measure of freedom for all by every restric-tion which it imposes with a view to preventing one man from making use of any of his advantages to the disadvantage of others . . . As experience of the social effects of action ripens, and as the social conscience is awakened, the conception of injury is widened and insight into its causes is deepened. The area of restraint is therefore increased . . . Thus individualism, when it grap-ples with the facts, is driven no small distance along Socialist lines.
>
> (Hobhouse 1911: 91, 92, 100)

Mirroring Marx, who in the nineteenth century had lauded the organisational and technological achievements of capitalism, marketeers raised a half-full glass to the stabilising force of aggregate demand management, corporate and social wel-fare, prudent regulation and central standard-setting. The state was needed to save the market from its own excesses: breaking up monopolies, enforcing mini-mum product and labour standards, supplying the infrastructure that businesses needed but could not bury their rivalries enough to pay for, keeping inequality within safe limits, and pulling the economy out of slump.

Just as Marx had struck his praises on the backhand, glimpsing in capitalist overproduction and falling profit rates the forces that might bring socialism to power, liberal fans of planning within free markets could see potential seeds of its own demise. Full employment would fuel inflation. Rising expectations of state benificence would be crushed by the hospital queue, wage freeze and marbled pres-idential palace. Workers would recognise that legislative and labour-union privilege in the workplace had its obverse in worsening treatment in the marketplace, and fewer jobs. With social contracts dishonoured and social solidarity lost, taxpayers would revolt against charges they saw as subsidising sloth or enriching the bureau-cracy that was meant to pass them on.

But the market counterattack looked like being a long and low-key campaign, weakened by opponents' power to buy off its supporters. Like freedom fighters wrong-footed when the hated dictator suddenly steps down, pro-market economists were largely unprepared for the sudden chance to practise what they preached. Contemplating the contemporary scene, in which new 'left' governments embrace privatisation, deregulation and balanced budgeting with a converts' enthusiasm that even surpasses that of the radical right, the followers of Adam Smith could be forgiven for echoing the words of his Orwellian namesake Winston: 'I understand how. I do not understand why' (Orwell 1949).

11.8 Reasons for retreat

Before discussing why governments have changed their approach, it is necessary to decide who determines that approach. Most economists assume that the government's mission is to preside over a high, sustainably growing and equitably distributed national income. Most go on to depict the mission as best fulfilled if government presides as spectator, rather than playing an active part. However, this interpretation is questioned by other perspectives, which regard the state as serving only one section of society, even if apparently under the democratic control of all. Marxists have, with varying degrees of sophistication, traditionally identified the state as co-ordinator and legislator on behalf of business interests. More recently, disillusioned pro-marketeers have regarded it as captured by labour to promote its interests against capital (even though labour's jobs and incomes ultimately depend on this), by state employees to improve their condition at the expense of private employees, or by welfare beneficiaries to improve their deal at the expense of all those in work.

As well as a variety of motives for reducing its economic involvement, there is thus a variety of possible sources for each motive. Politicians may have judged that disengagement was in the wider public interest. They may have been pushed to do it because the dominant lobby no longer wanted it. They may have come under the influence of a new public pressure group with different, less dirigiste interests. Or they may simply have found themselves unable to do what their supporters wanted them to do.

11.8.1 *Mission accomplished: the creator-state retires*

Push-starters know that their job is done when the wheels start turning without their help. A similar role can be argued for government in relation to the market. Central political authority is needed to solve the initial co-ordination problems involved in its creation. So government must initially intervene to create reliable systems of money and credit, build the first transport and communication infrastructures, set common standards for network technologies, negotiate the removal of local trade barriers, and create the institutions through which prisoners' dilemma-type problems can be resolved. But once this is done, the visible hand can withdraw and let the invisible hand take over. Virtuous circles become self-sustaining and, just as gods need no longer intervene from day to day by throwing lightning bolts or briefing prophets, governments have no further role in telling economic agents what to do next.

Societies are thus seen as (literally) growing out of administered, informed and relational transaction and into a market system, whose possible failings are overcome as people get wealthier and wiser. (The market, once it takes hold, is assumed to increase the rate of wealth and knowledge growth, so preparing its own pitch.) Rising income expands the market, reducing the danger that any supplier can hold power over it, and reduces the number of cases where need or desert cannot be backed by ability to pay, so making possible the market provision of merit goods.

Rising knowledge, achieved both by better general education and greater practice at dealing through markets, reduces producers' power to distort consumer choice through incomplete or imperfect information. Consumers' greater awareness and articulacy allows them to form their own coalitions, countering the producers' lobby groups and squeezing greater information from them about products' quality, cost and suitability. Like supply-side arguments regarding infant industries and incontestabilities, demand-side reasons for transacting outside the market are presented as applying – if they ever did – with decreasing force over time.

Under this perspective, the transition from a state-mediated mixed economy to a world of unfettered markets resembles the Christian switch from Old to New Testaments. In the first, rules are still being set and roles defined with the help of an outside agency. In the second, the aims and means of righteous life have been clearly established, and people are now trusted to pursue them with only occasional guidance from above. For God read Government (though the latter was always at a disadvantage in the omniscience and omnipotence stakes); and for Crucifixion read Communism, as the dire warning of what lies ahead if superseded rules continue to be followed. For the forces of choice, chance and natural selection to take their rightful place among spurs to social development, the object of worship must turn from site manager into architect. The designer steps aside after creating the initial conditions, leaving the occupants to decide what happens next.

In the 'post-political' economy, the market system is depicted as having finally achieved its basic requirements for static and dynamic equilibrium. There is a unified world market within which increasing returns are achieved but even the biggest firms stay relatively small, free flow of information to keep competitive markets operational, a capital market perfect enough to achieve consistency between short- and long-run efficiency by supporting strategic action, and legal and policy frameworks which keep private decisions time-consistent. The state played a part in setting these up, but has now served its purpose. Private enterprise can now achieve the co-ordination and strategy-protection they need, and deliver the results society wants, without public help. The time has come to link the last discretionary elements of policy – monetary and fiscal instruments and public ownership – into the long-term, non-political framework, and retire from the stage.

Many neoclassical observers would argue that the creator-state outstayed its welcome, and some argue for a spontaneous generation in which market institutions can arise without any political help. The concept of a state which oversees and overrides the market at certain critical times, and subsequently retires into the background, is more sympathetically viewed by some alternative perspectives, notably Marxism. Here, because the market process is viewed as inherently unstable rather than self-sustaining, government is expected to step in periodically to resolve the profits crisis and defuse the social discontent that might turn it into a political crisis. Political authority is more watch-maker than world-maker, having to return on occasions to wind the mechanism up, replace worn components or resynchronise the hands.

Previous downturns in North America and western Europe have certainly been accompanied by increased state intervention, often with the explicit aim of restoring private-sector profitability by helping firms restructure (nationalising them if the turnaround task is severe), imposing trade protection, offering capital subsidies to maintain investment and social subsidies to subdue labour unrest. Similar tactics have been deployed in 'latecomer' economies (including Germany in Europe and Mexico in central America) to speed up technology acquisition and get industrialisation started. Cynics might even argue that international war, beginning with a rearmament boom and ending with the wholesale destruction of 'surplus' capital, was governments' ultimate contribution to ending an underconsumption crisis and relaunching the accumulation process.

But the recent pattern of state activity has tended to reverse this. Governments remained deeply engaged in the economy after the slump came to an end, apparently establishing a permanent role as regulators of aggregate demand, owners of natural monopolies and major industries, providers of long-term capital and organisers of permanent income redistribution through progressive tax and extensive welfare provision. When growth and profitability next turned downwards – possibly as a by-product of the full employment and high investment thus generated – governments responded by denationalising, deregulating, scaling-down welfare provision and cutting taxation. They also persisted with international integration, through removal of barriers to trade and capital movement, rather than putting up barriers and preparing for war. It was left to private capital markets to finance restructuring (through merger, acquisition, divestment and downsizing), and private labour markets to quell wage growth so that profitability could revive. To many, notably Marxist, observers of this trend, the state is merely respecting capital's wishes at a time of restructuring in which full employment and welfare supports must be sacrificed to the revival of profit margins, by a less intermediated confrontation with labour and with other capitals.

> An over-accumulation of capital leads capitalist organisations to invade one another's spheres of operation; the division of labour that previously defined the terms of their mutual co-operation breaks down; cut-throat competition among capitalist agencies – including hostile take-overs – consolidates what we may call the 'supply' conditions of sustained financial expansion.
>
> (Arrighi 1997: 156)

By implication, bureaucrats may make a comeback when material accumulation re-starts and revived profit-makers call on their creator again.

11.8.2 *Mission recanted: politicians discover the* *'silent majority'*

The interpretation mainstream economists would prefer is that governments have recognised what the textbooks could long ago have told them. Their mission to better the condition of society is best achieved by leaving most parts of its economy alone. Realisation may have been delayed until the alternatives had been tried, and found universally wanting. A more realistic explanation is that politicians once under the sway of powerful minorities have finally awoken to the *laissez-faire* tastes of the hitherto silent majority. In the battle to identify unorganised interest groups and bid for their votes, 'policy entrepreneurs' finally alighted on the scattered but substantial number who lost more through higher prices, higher taxes and slower growth than they gained from any of the individual interventions which collectively led to these. 'At some point, the political pressure from the losers builds up, and the regulator must provide protection for consumer interests to avoid being voted out of office' (Baily 1989: xii). Electorates may wonder retrospectively why they did so, but the pro-market rhetoric of Reagan and Thatcher was swept to power by electorates for whom featherbedded state-sector workers and state-supported non-workers were living a little too well at other people's expense.

Why did the 'silent majority' take so long to realise that it was being short-changed by sectionally motivated intervention, or to reward politicians willing to proclaim a stand against it? A 'neoclassical' explanation emphasises technical and social change which increases the number of people excluded from the regulated/relational transaction sphere, and exploited by those within it. New-technology businesses confronting old oligopolies (and their captive banks), new occupations ignored by the old professional associations, and newly arrived citizens marginalised by the established social circles reinforce the rallying cry of individual against institution. Institutional explanations are more inclined to claim these as the penalties of success – demand management and supply regulation having accelerated the rates of technical and social change – and to stress internal sources of pressure for change. Higher average incomes offer more scope for individuals to absorb risk, and so seek individual gain where they were previously content to go along with smaller but safer collective-action payoffs. Greater concern for higher relative income (exacerbated by the growing number of socially and materially scarce products, available or valuable only to a few) also erodes loyalty to collective schemes for demand-side redistribution and supply-side standardisation.

Along with reduced concern for income and opportunity differences across space comes greater concern for present over future income, turning people against institutional arrangements to conserve materially scarce resources, invest in long-lasting 'social' capital, or legislate to defer gratification. Rates of time preference rise, assisted by the higher interest rates necessitated by an ageing population or the shorter time horizons inflicted by growing ecological and geopolitical uncertainty (compounded in the Christian world by the Millennium, and the computer world by the Millennium Bug). Greater prioritisation of present over future rewards promotes efforts to unlock the collective benefits stored up in state-owned industry, occupational pension schemes and mutual savings institutions – sharing them out among members, to invest in their own way or consume if they prefer. Production-era politics, as opinion-formation, might have been inclined to counter such spatial and temporal myopia. The new consumer politics, preoccupied with reflecting rather than revealing preferences, plays along with it, as macroeconomic sovereignty passes to financial market traders and microeconomic sovereignty to shopping-mall crusaders.

Advocates of a slimmed-down state do not necessarily share the neoclassical view that constructive government intervention is inherently impossible. They merely regard it as ruled out by a political process that favours vociferous minorities over the silent majority. Deep commercial or campaign-group pockets buy legislator loyalty, with North American and European lobbyists and old college ties proving just as corrupting as the more open graft and venality of which these regions accuse African, Asian and Latin American politics. 'Our legislative system is largely the captive of special interests. Generally – whether the government is dealing with issues such as gun control, textile import quotas, energy taxes, air bags, immigration policies, or health care costs – the nation cannot face a problem and expect that it will be met with a reasonable, workable public policy that is in the public interest' (Etzioni 1995: 215–16).

The silent majority cannot counter-organise against the special pleaders, because a coalition of diverse public interests will never match the cohesion and single-mindedness of a closely organised, narrowly defined private interest (Olson 1965). In this view, the general public votes for deregulation and bureaucratic disengagement once it realises how systematically specific private interests have subverted the legislative process – if there is anyone left to vote for with sufficient rectitude or independent riches to resist the pull of preference-warping dollars.

11.8.3 Mission cancelled: intervention's benefits outweigh its costs

For 'left' critics of intervention, which was seen as patching up a flawed free-enterprise system rather than dragging down a perfect one, the state had never been dominated by a worker or welfare lobby. It was in service to the owners and deployers of capital and changed its tune because its paymasters had changed their priority. In one interpretation, such centralised devices as demand management, nationalisation, regulation, income redistribution and 'indicative' planning had all proved ineffective, been made counterproductive by their side-effects (such as growing organised labour power and rising taxes), or served a temporary stabilising purpose which was now at an end.

A closely related possibility is that state action was still working in the capitalists' interests, but their own rivalries undermined the conspiracy that allowed them to support it. Too many firms free-rode on the government's training initiatives, took its subsidies without paying its taxes, and used its infrastructures without investing in the plant they were supposed to support. The government chose to take its revenge by turning state subsidy back into commercial cross-subsidy, withdrawing benefits so that employers had to offer higher wages, and leaving the private sector to build its own hospitals, phone networks and roads.

Alternatively, interventionist devices had worked, but entrepreneurs' changing needs had given them a different set of policies to browbeat the bureaucrats for. The old special interest groups are still in control, but they have found new ways to pursue their interests which need not involve the state. Firms are big enough to handle their own disputes with organised labour (playing one workplace off against another, or invoking the unemployment threat), to solve their own capital market problems (through internal finance and self-insurance), to limit entry and preserve income and profit without recourse to government regulation (scale economies and collusive arrangements can be adequate). Opposing pressure groups are cynical enough about the political process or confident enough in the power of direct action to pursue environmental, consumer rights, civil rights and even radical political campaigns outside the established political process.

This change comes about partly because of actions the state has taken, but partly because politics was always a 'second best' way of defending (and attacking) business interests. State apparatuses cost money to run, and tend to get into trade- and capital-flow-disrupting conflicts with other states. Sectional business interests regard them as vulnerable to discovering a wider 'public purpose', or being taken over by popular forces who believe in one. 'The effective functioning of market systems can be seriously jeopardised by pluralistic, democratic processes' (Wolf 1988: 173). Sectional pressure groups on other issues are equally convinced that government is financially and politically dependent on big business and a high-growth, high-profit economy, so are equally willing to take the battle from parliament back into the workplace and onto the streets.

Marxists, once willing to brand the state as the bourgeousie's executive committee, adding the conquest of colonies, the suppression of labour organisation and the redistribution of profit among firms to its functions, had come to see that it could serve other interests. Under Napoleon III

> the power of the government, with its standing army, its all-directing bureaucracy, its brutalizing clergy and its servile judicial hierarchy, had grown so independent of society itself, that a grotesquely mediocre adventurer with a greedy band of desperadoes behind him sufficed to manipulate it.
>
> (Marx 1870/1983: 524–5)

What a grotesquely mediocre adventurer could do, a socialist party could do as well, suggesting that the capitalist state could be hijacked rather than ransacked, but the large and expanding economic role for that state was not in question. Only in the later stages of communism, with class divisions dissolved and abundance secured, was it expected to wither away.

These predictions may have been right. As observed in the introduction to this survey, the 'market revolution' remains only a suggestion, and it is possible to argue that today's state is as (or more) powerful as it has ever been. In no states, except those reverting from central planning to the mixed economy, has government's claim on national income or final expenditure dropped significantly. Nowhere, even after privatisation and deregulation, has government detached itself from political involvement with big business, still less from financial dependence on the profit it generates. And some of the biggest macroeconomic shocks (expansionary in Reagan's USA, contractionary in Mulroney's Canada and Pinochet's Chile, both extremes in Thatcher's UK) have been administered by governments which formally denied that fiscal and monetary levers could have any lasting effect.

11.8.4 Mission impossible: policy trains hit the buffer solution

If pro-market rhetoric did not win politicians over, their government-failure liturgy may still have done the trick. Socialists can still protest that their good idea has never actually been tried; but by now it is tempting to conclude that this is because it cannot be. If governments cannot tax capital without it fleeing to another jurisdiction, or labour without its withdrawing its vote; if monetary relaxation raises prices without affecting real output, and fiscal expansion reduces private demand as fast as it raises public demand; if central banks must anyway be made independent for their actions to produce the desired effect; if trade defences are ruled out by international treaty, and regulations retuned to the needs of inward investors; then there may be nothing useful for governments to do. In corporate strategy terms, the state is relegated from a profit centre to a cost centre, its once independent management reduced to taking its instructions from outside. The instructions tend to say discipline your workforce, but otherwise let the show run itself. Good governance was not tried and found wanting, it simply proved impossible to try.

11.8.5 Mission usurped: other non-market forces take over

Although the state's role is perceived as having shrunk, markets of the traditional type have not always replaced it. Quasi-markets and internal markets are much in evidence, especially where the embers of administered state-transaction are still warm. A final possibility thus presents itself: interventionism is as extensive – and effective – as it ever was, but simply being carried out by a different non-market agency. Large multiproduct and multinational corporations have become the new instruments for economic and social administration, which were once the reponsibility of a politial executive. They have also become the main arena for battling and bargaining between the 'stakeholder' interests of workers, consumers, financiers, suppliers and communities, which used to take place in the political legislature. Corporations have clear advantages over governments in these roles. They are increasingly international where most governments remain predominantly national (some even dispersing or fragmenting their power, something firms can also do but within a framework that keeps strong central control when it matters). They have first command over economic resources, whereas governments have to acquire these at secondhand through an unpopular process of taxation. Their discretion and speed of response is not circumscribed by having parliaments and electorates to account to. Yet they can also be genuinely popular, because they offer people practical advantages – products, jobs – whereas governments deal in the less tangible commodities of freedom, justice and sustainability. The benefits of the first are appreciated when we have them, of the second only when they are gone.

11.9   Remarketising politics

As more of the state's former instruments – and employees – are displaced by or reconsigned to the market, the survivors are rushing to copy its battleplan. Politics itself is becoming a more market-like process.

The market system is in part a political construct, requiring at least the legislatively protected mechanisms decribed in Chapter 1. While (barter) trade in particular items may arise spontaneously, a sophisticated market system requires rules of exchange (contract, legal tender, redress procedures, etc.) which will be hard to draw up and enforce except with a political system of legislature, executive, judiciary and police. Markets provide the vehicle for an efficient co-ordination of human action and distribution of its rewards, but the state still has a continuing role in providing the infrastructure down which the vehicle travels.

Politics, in turn, is in part an extension of the market, in which policies take the place of products and votes are the currency for which they trade. But it is not an extension of which either pro- or anti-marketeers approve. The sale of policies by self-interested office-seekers and bureaucrats in return for the votes of self-interested agents, analysed by Downs (1957), became a formative text in the 'public choice' attack on the justice and efficiency of government intervention. Companies that give people what they want are rewarded with profits and product awards. Politicians who give people what they want are branded as populists. Leadership in a product market is considered bad for the economy, because it implies a step towards collusion, firms accommodating the price and output choices of their biggest or most efficient competitor instead of competing directly against it. Leadership in the political market is considered essential to democracy. Division of labour applies in the debating chamber as much as in the workplace. People are sent into government because they are regarded as having comparative advantage in political decisions and, just as a surgeon is not expected to ask patients how they want their hips done, a politician is not expected to ask voters how to handle the next economic summit or arms reduction talks.

Yet the revival of market economics has brought a resurgence of market politics, in some cases stopping only slightly short of the direct overlap (bribes replacing votes and handouts replacing policies) which prevailed before independent scrutineering.

Instead of deciding a programme according to externally derived principles or ideology which it then tries to 'sell' to the electorate, parties are learning to consult the people and formulate the programme most closely in line with what a majority wants. Opinion sampling, focus groups, citizens' juries and statistical behavioural information provide an ever more detailed and more up-to-date gauge of expressed public opinion. Majorities can stay silent, or not say what they mean, or follow the twentieth-century Marx in not wishing to vote for any policy which takes their views into account. But while not necessarily gaining in accuracy, these consultative efforts appear to exercise an increasing influence over what electorates are offered. Like modern art, modern politics turns from viewers studying what was in the painter's mind to painters giving the viewer a blurred canvas onto which to reflect their own thoughts.

Although apparently a move towards fuller democracy, this populism has been deeply resented in the past. Profiting by giving people what they want, the essence of the marketplace, attracts accusations of opportunism, weak leadership and lack of principle when practised in the political arena. Whereas economic consumers are regarded as the best judges of their own and the collective interest, political consumers are still regarded as in need of guidance, education, and restraint from certain choices they ought not to make. What people want may be spatially inconsistent – more public spending with no increase in taxes or state borrowing, more throwaway consumer goods with a greener environment, increased consumption and increased investment. It may be time inconsistent – upsetting the next element in a strategy laid down earlier, and/or deterring beneficial current action by threatening its future payoff. It may be based on impossible aggregation – an elite education for everyone, the universal right to drive down a clear road. Or it may simply be misguided because 'correct' judgement requires expert knowledge not available to the general public.

Aware of these dangers, most political systems give their politicians a triple double insulation against public opinion. Options are presented to the electorate as broad party programmes, so that they must vote on a whole package of policies, giving the opportunity to slip in a few 'necessary but unpopular' policies among those that prove attractive. (Once inside the parliament or congress, parties can similarly 'log-roll' unpopular measures past their opponents by tying them to favoured ones.) The chance to vote is given only at intervals of several years, between which parties can follow strategies whose early actions may be highly unpopular (e.g. deflating the economy to stabilise prices so that growth can resume). And certain issues are placed outside or above politics, on the assumption that they are a part of the democratic framework, and so not something that can safely be debated within that framework.

The acclamation of consumer sovereignty in the economic sphere makes 'voter sovereignty' hard to keep out of the political sphere. But just as the economic market has been seen to hit problems when it 'endogenises' the property distribution, information, technologies and preferences that compromise its framework, the market economy runs a similar risk when it endogenises the political process that designs that framework. If global market realities have, indeed, narrowed the range of discretion over economic policy, which in turn constrains the options for social, foreign, educational and environmental policy, politicians may need to be lecturing voters more strongly on the limited scope for action, rather than inviting suggestions whose reconciliation into consistent and achievable policy is difficult (even, according to the Arrow theorem, impossible).

Populism triumphs because, for those in politics, the alternatives are worse. Without it, power might pass outside the political market, to the administered organisational world within the corporation or the relational world with which business tackles an increasingly uncoordinated and internationalised economy. In trying to retain a role in allocation, distribution and growth which is separate from that of the market, politicians who are unwilling or unable to override the market are likely to find it rising over them.

11.10   Conclusion: minimising the state

To establish – as market-economy and public-choice theorists believe they have done – that the government's role in the economy has been overextended does not automatically mean that it should now be reduced. Like the nail through a tyre which causes a puncture only when removed, government may be so firmly embedded that its sudden disengagement would do more harm than good. Economic expectations are now founded on the state as a significant consumer, investor and redistributor, and social expectations on the state as a provider of certain services and transfer incomes, so that rapid dismantling of the public sector might lose more in the disruptive transition than it could hope to gain from the eventually superior end-state.

Despite this, the coincidence of declining confidence in the efficacy of state intervention and growing confidence in the viability of market alternatives has led, at least since the late 1960s, to an increasingly ambitious strategy for reducing the role of the state in the economy. This works at four complementary levels:

- in the macroeconomy, reducing government expenditure (exhaustive and redistributive), taxation and borrowing, and ensuring the least welfare losses from the taxes and expenditures that remain
- in the tradable sector, disengaging the state from direct production (through privatisation) and scaling down its indirect interventions (through deregulation, and subsidy withdrawal)
- in the non-tradable sector, privatising 'public' service provision where possible, and making the provision of the rest more market-like within the public sector
- in the household sector, promoting self-help and profit-making initiative, through the carrot of lower taxation and the stick of less automatic taxation-based social protection.

Explanation of why the strategy came to be implemented must take place outside the models most often used by economists, who for many years seemed as convinced of the political infeasibility of disengaging the state as they were of its economic desirability. This chapter has identified possible reasons for 'remarketisation' in the main areas of state activity, deriving partly from the changing external pressures on the state and partly from the changing needs of those it exists to serve. It is intended to make some economic sense. It has not been tested against a detailed knowledge of the politics that have actually shaped this process. Since political motives are rarely fully revealed at the time, and so well adapted to revision as events unfold, explaining why the market project returned to favour at this time remains a considerably more speculative task than merely describing how.

12 Conclusion

Its limits

How far can markets go? This book has argued that as the information limitations on market transaction have come to be recognised, the case in its favour has shifted from the efficiency of its outcome to the efficiency of the process of arriving at that outcome. A superlative, the best available allocation and production, is replaced by a comparative, better results than any alternative. Markets' strength moves from one of achieving the best end for a transaction to one of offering the best means of transaction – with the unknown, hence undicted, outcome being one of its strengths.

Retrospectively, some form of relational or administrative intervention might be argued to have offered better results, by letting individuals co-ordinate their efforts across space (employing resources more fully) or time (reallocating and accumulating resources more quickly). The Great Depression and the East Asian crises may have wasted nations' accumulation and diversification efforts, and Qwerty keyboards may have wasted typists' time. But alternative transaction forms need not have made things better. Had they, market theorists argue, it would probably have been by delaying the invention of typewriters and wordprocessors and stopping the American, European and Asian economies reaching a height from which they could convincingly collapse.

This book has tried to summarise the theories put forward for regarding markets as routes to economic efficiency and social justice, and suggest some reasons as to why – despite economists' fears of rationally deaf ears – these theories have come to be applied to many areas once considered beyond the price system's reach. Along the way, it is hoped, due coverage has been given to the extant limitations of markets, the way in which organisational attempts to improve the market can also create the power to subvert it, and the ways in which politically engineered 'quasi-markets' fall short of the real thing. The first section of this concluding chapter considers the way in which economists' shift from an outcome to a process characterisation of markets, which for a time seemed threatened by experimental psychologists' discovery of 'irrational' behaviour even in simple rational choice tests and has recently been reinforced by arguments for the 'naturalness' of market dealing from evolutionary biology, computer science and neuroscience. Just as misgivings have earlier been raised about economists' attempt to rewrite other social sciences, these intrusions from natural science into economics are argued to have serious limitations.

The second section considers the limits that societies still place on markets, and the extent to which these limits are 'internal' or 'external'. Internal limits arise from the difficulty of trading a product through the market, of ensuring that market trade produces the economically efficient and socially justifiable outcome, and of ensuring that this outcome reproduces the conditions in which the transaction can be repeated with similarly beneficial results. External limits arise from agents' tendency (expressed democratically or more directly) to support the allocation of certain products on grounds other than the ability and willingness to pay, even when market trade is feasible and sustainable. A sample of the more common 'market-protected' products is used to show how internal and external obstacles commonly intertwine.

The final section considers the possibility of the internal limits being overcome, and the external limits being withdrawn, as market processes are improved by new information, transaction and organisational technologies. It examines arguments that new electronic 'networks' are overcoming the information and co-ordination limitations that underlie most market failure – and concludes that what passes down networks, as well as network infrastructures themselves, are just as likely to exacerbate those failures as to resolve them.

12.1   Markets as 'natural order'

Economists are accustomed to assessing markets that already exist, or are known to have existed until monopoly or bureaucracy suppressed them. When asked where markets came from, their inclination – unless eyeing employment opportunities as architect or regulator of a new quasi-market – is to favour evolution over creation. Markets come into existence because individual agents find them a satisfactory way to redistribute their resources to mutual benefit. They remain in existence only if enough people agree to trade through them for the medium of exchange to attain its external (network) benefits, for transaction-specific investments to pay back – and for those who renege on contracts and free-ride on reputations to be a cost small enough for honest traders to write off.

12.1.1   Dealing by default

Left to themselves, agents who want to change their material situation seem only too willing to develop market mechanisms through which to do so. They agree a form of money, invent trading conventions and devise credible forms of punishment to ensure these are observed. Confirmation of the 'naturalness' of market transaction appears prevalent. Prisoners swop their rations according to taste using cigarettes as currency (in today's jails the illegal tender may be a somewhat harder drug). Eastern Europe's mass-privatisation voucher holders trade them in the street months before the first shares are issued, using bargaining skills honed on the private market trade that flourished in the days when it did not officially exist. Even computers, supposedly so quick that they can afford to waste some calculation power, adopt a decentralised price-setting method when pressed to maximise their speed and optimise their capacity use.

> The command and control solution became hopelessly bogged down by the costs of coordination . . . [with an internal market] less than 10% of each machine's time is wasted on the bidding process . . . computers have demonstrated the profound similarities of ecology and economics . . . profit-seeking is a self-organising system, impossible to eradicate.
>
> (Rothschild 1992: 265, 266, 269)

Natural urges are not necessarily self-justifying. The defeat of childhood impulses to lie, demand immediate gratification, wake the neighbours and ingest at will is counted as one of the minor triumphs of civilised living. But in conventional economics, self-interest is turned to public good if there are adequate markets to channel it. Adam Smith's pioneering contribution was to synthesise two previously opposing views about the workings of a market system. One, optimistically, assumed that the personal gains from mutually beneficial market exchange would allow it to continue indefinitely, with minimal need to set formal rules or coercively enforce them. The other, pessimistically, feared that the even greater gains from distorting markets through domination and regulation would mean their continual descent into zero-sum opportunism, unless subjected to cumbersome rules and coercive enforcement which subtracted from their efficiency and added to the dangers of abuse. The inequalities of personal wealth and enterprise size needed to incentivise and operationalise efficient market operation threatened to subvert that operation – unless regulated by governments, which would then be drawn by their own self-interest into other interventions which were not so market-friendly.

Smith synthesised the two views by showing how markets could survive and grow by playing off their would-be subverters: governments preventing private enterprise from rigging the market by ensuring that buyers and sellers stayed numerous and separate, and private enterprise preventing governments from rigging the market by trading around (or in defiance of) every transaction-restricting regulation. The trading 'instinct' establishes the market by tying consumer rights to proportional producer obligations, giving everyone an interest in continuing to transact. With a secure and self-sustaining market in place, individuals can move away from personal self-sufficiency and concentrate on what they do best. By exchanging their surplus product for the products they no longer make, they raise not only their own productivity and income but also that of their society as a whole.

12.1.2 Born to barter?

Smith was not particularly concerned whether 'the propensity to truck, barter and exchange one thing for another' (1776/1979: 117) arises naturally, or is a social product of private property already existing and scarcity already being imposed. People are entitled to indulge it because it brings collectively beneficial results. The prevalence and persistence of markets, even where organisations or governments try to stifle them, is taken to confirm that, for once, public experience is fully in accord with economic pronouncement. Where information is incomplete and imperfect, market signals are claimed to require less of it, and enable faster and fuller use of it, than other transaction methods. Where wealth and power are unevenly spread, markets are claimed to offer the have-nots a fairer and faster way to amass their own – or rise the position that bestowed it on others.

The process reason for preferring markets beat a temporary retreat when experimental subjects were found not always to display the consistent judgement or calculation hypothesised by rational choice theory (section 5.2). But while some advocates found ways to modify the axioms to fit observed decisions, and others went off to run courses teaching decision-makers to obey the axioms, alternative justifications for the process view were being assembled. Perhaps the most powerful is that market trade is what comes naturally – as a psychological trait, embedded in genetic inheritance, arising from the superior economic performance (and hence survival chances) of societies which organise themselves through market transaction.

It may take a highly skilled evolutionary biologist to explain why grey squirrels supplanted red squirrels, or why birds with curved beaks were selected over rival birds with straight ones. In contrast, the most casual television viewer can understand why a nation with grain surpluses and universal health care offers its citizens lower perinatal mortality and longer life expectancy than one which cannot afford to feed itself or fund its hospitals. Once contraception extends rational choice to family size, wealthier nations measure their competitive success by the quality rather than quantity of lives within them. But the market impulse – be it biologically inherited gene or socially constructed 'meme' – may still come to populate the world, through the international transmission of successful economic systems contemplated in section 9.6. The drive to seek better material conditions through trade appears evident from the rampant black markets of the planned economy and prison camp. For confirmation of the urge to rank options by a single, simple value measure and to honour the one that comes top, it seems we need look no further than school league tables, classical music charts and the European professional golfers' money list.

The search for biological roots to market transaction has grown more sophisticated as evolutionary biology shifts the unit of analysis for evolutionary selection from the organism to the genes that are now known to shape it. Organisms may be able to rationalise the mutual benefits of trade to establish and sustain a market system, adding further conventions to break through the incompleteness of information and so protect themselves from bounded rationality. The humble double helix has no such awareness.

> In some chapters of this book we have indeed thought of the individual organism as an agent, striving to maximise its success in passing on all its genes. We imagined individual animals making complicated economic 'as if' calculations about the genetic benefits of various courses of action. Yet in other chapters the fundamental rationale was presented from the point of view of genes.
>
> (Dawkins 1989: 234)

Economists, analysing the agent, saw market behaviour being generalised across a society through choice. Biologists, focusing on the gene, can now offer an alternative generalisation through chance. Individuals with a stronger propensity to trade, or greater skill in doing so, will tend to finish ahead in the competitive struggle. If the propensity for decentralised, competitive trade did not bring the best results for self and society, it would have been outcompeted by beings whose instinct is to submit to a central allocator, adapt their preference to circumstance, or fulfil all their needs themselves. In practice, both choice and chance seem to be needed, because of the uneasy flitting between agent (gene) and system (organism) level identified by Dawkins. If an agent's survival chances improve even more if the agent subverts the market – cheating or free-riding on those who play by its rules – then the mutually beneficial system will break down, in the manner of a parasite killing its host.

To succeed, the evolutionary explanation must ensure that the market system's rationality is recognised and endorsed at the level of the agent. The economist's task turns out to be simpler than the biologist's, because agents (unlike genes) have the power to think, and to appeal to past experience. By choice, agents can decide to follow market rules provided others do so, and thus deliver the mutually beneficial outcome – the tit-for-tat 'evolution of co-operation' confirmed by the experiments of Axelrod (1984). By chance, natural variation makes some agents better able than others to anticipate when others will fail to play by the rules, or to detect when they have done so. Competitive selection favours such awareness at agent level, and so reinforces the competitive selection of market mechanisms at system level. The co-ordination problem of getting all (or most) to play by the market, which appears to rely on reciprocal altruism, now has a selfish, Darwinian-selectable rationalisation.

> Our lifestyles and our minds are particularly adapted to the demands of reciprocal altruism. People have food, tools, help and information to trade. With language, information is an ideal trade good because its cost to the giver – a few seconds of breath – is minuscule compared with the benefit to the recipient . . . The minimal equipment [for sustaining mutually beneficial exchange] is a cheater detector and a tit-for-tat strategy that begrudges a gross cheater further help.
>
> (Pinker 1997: 402–3)

In this modified evolutionary perspective, markets survive because they improve a community's material living standards and resolve tensions within it, so that members (and their genes) have a better chance of surviving to reproduce. The market must be a superior social organising principle, because other means of acting were long ago selected out. 'Markets, exchanges and rule scan develop before government or any other monopolist has defined their rules. They define their own rules, because they have been part of human nature for millions of years' (Ridley 1996: 204). The market is nature's way of mixing high productivity and harmony without collective control. This does not mean that human societies cannot be organised in other ways. If civilisation means anything, it is humanity's ability to rescue its more vulnerable members, and ultimately itself, from a struggle in which only the fittest survive. But there is, in this version of the evolutionary perspective, a clear biological advantage to species that trade, based on their ability to maintain and develop genetic diversity.

For the economy, genetic differences ensure a variety of skills and interests, setting up the comparative advantages that allow for division of labour and superiority of trade over autarky. For ecology, they protect the species against the vulnerability of monoculture and the poverty of undivided labour, as well as allowing the improvement of the species through genetic recombination. The naked ape must have traded its way to the top.

> Even if I am wrong, even if trade between groups came much later, at the brink of recorded history, its invention represents one of the very few moments in evolution when Homo sapiens stumbled on some comparative ecological advantage over other species that was truly unique.
>
> (Ridley 1996: 210)

Without the market to channel acquisitive instincts into mutually benefical transactions, such natural instincts in the face of diversity might well have led to the less evolutionarily stable tendencies of war, crime and the suppression of difference. The biological basis for trust enables Ridley and others to deny the necessity of any outside agency to establish relational or legal foundations for the market.

> Government, law, justice and politics are not only far more recently developed than trade, but they follow where trade leads . . . Only later did government try to take it over, and with mostly disastrous results.
>
> (Ridley 1996: 202)

12.1.3 Economy with the truth

Ants, bees and various other animals carry out exchanges which might be described as trade, but only within homogeneous groups. Human trade, uniquely, has most to offer when conducted between heterogeneous groups (where it promotes the division of labour) and between them (where system-level specialisation brings 'comparative advantage'). Durkheim (1964) anticipates much of the recent biological argument in his identification of markets as a means of social progression from mechanical solidarity (cohesion arising from pursuit of a common task, usually a fairly basic one like hunting an animal or battling the next tribe) and organic solidarity (cohesion arising from pursuit of diverse tasks, creating an interdependence which is sustained because its mutual gains are recognised).

Like its biological counterpart, the organic society once formed has every incentive to stay together. Division of labour delivers higher productivity at the cost of greater insecurity, to the extent that the individual now relies on other people's production (and willingness to trade their surplus product) for a large proportion of their own needs. Those who enter it must be assured both that their own surplus product will continue to be accepted by others as an adequate exchange for theirs, and that the relevant supplies will continue to be available at prices that can be paid. Since all must now trade in order to have enough to live on (and all are richer than when they were individually self-sufficient), it is in no one's interest to cease to trade, or to destroy the mechanisms through which trade takes place. Trust is built into the system; communities whose members routinely cheated on their trading obligations would simply not survive.

But Durkheim's sociological depiction takes up the theme of a market society a long way further forward than the biological depiction leaves it off. The 'spontaneous' trades that predate government, law and literacy are of a highly simplified kind, generally lacking money and detailed division of labour, and exchanging easily recognised material products through largely relational transaction. It is open to question (though, perhaps fortunately, not easy to test) whether Yir Yoront Aboriginals could trade cars or financial futures quite as easily as they trade polished stone axes, without first developing such institutional supports as contracts, credits, a legal system and a motoring press. The transition from simple material to complex information and service products is a revolutionary rather than an evolutionary step, requiring a move to complex labour division and impersonal transaction which neither biologists' reciprocal altruism nor the closely related repeated game solutions (section 2.2) can easily account for. Rather than appealing to a leap of faith, agents tend to look for externally enforceable obligations and restraints before submitting to being cogs in a larger economic machine.

Without such central safeguards, situations may arise where a trade cannot be completed. Exchange can break down because the required product is not available, or because the product on offer is not judged valuable enough to exchange for it, or because the other party finds it more personally profitable to renege on the transaction. Individuals who trust in the market by adopting a specialism which commits them to trade on it thus require assurance against two types of transactional breakdowns: the loss or invalidation of the tradable product which they bring to the market, and the refusal of others to complete the trade that they intended to make. To these spatial dangers of unregulated evolutionary competition must be added two temporal dangers: that behaviour involving short-term sacrifice for long-term gain will be dumped in favour of immediate gratification, and that behaviour which brings best results when only a minority adopts it will be made dysfunctional by its own generalisation. The system needs outside help to stop competitive selection undermining its multi-stage strategies, and eliminating the variation on which new strategies arise.

It is possible to envisage the market providing its own solution to these problems. An individual could buy insurance against the failure of a transaction, or its profitability, due to the instability of the market or the iniquity of other market participants. Those who trade with today's riskier companies or countries can, indeed, buy political and credit risk insurance against their possible losses, and those unsure of the future value of their own products or purchases can trade them through a forward market. In both cases, by further division of labour, another specialised agent to take over the risk. Alternatively, the agent could engage the services of private security staff and debt collectors to make sure that counterparties remain willing to carry out the desired trade at an affordable price. But solving market failure by creating additional markets is hazardous. On a microeconomic level, new markets of this kind risk being costly to organise, thinly traded and prone to distorted or deficient information. Macroeconomically, this raises the danger of co-ordination failure leading to inadequate aggregate demand and destabilised growth.

As with the derivation of income distribution from general equilibrium or consumer choice from revealed preference, however, the belief in market 'instinct' may be guilty of assuming what it sets out to explain. The differences that give rise to voluntary trade are only in a limited sense biological. It may be natural for (on average) stronger men to wield the spear while subtler women cook the carcase, and for the fleet of foot to carry messages for the eloquent of pen. But today's detailed division of labour reflects (and perpetuates) differences in capability which are largely artificially imposed by geographical and social location, training opportunities and recruitment vagaries. Differences in preference may well have been shaped by differences in capability, as coats are cut according to cloth.

Material self-advancement may be a motive for a meritocratic assault on such artificial (and often inefficient) differentiation; but it could equally be another artificially imposed external constraint. The urge to own private property may not arise until private property has been created, by legally sanctioned appropriation. We might have been happy owning everything in common, grabbing a piece for ourselves only when other people grabbed theirs. Without such commandeering of resources, and resultant exclusion of others from their use, there might not even have been an economic problem to be tackled by rational-maximising solutions. 'How can it be assumed that partial scarcity is the universal plight of humanity when it can be argued that scarcity is the result of needs engendered by private property?' (Carter 1989: 121).

Long-held beliefs in free will and the malleability of human nature are clearly circumscribed by recent evolutionary theory and genetic research. Although their origins can be disputed, every society experiences market forces in some measure. Although not always welcomed, the shared experience holds out the hope that markets can guarantee cohesion within and between societies through a common set of values, preserving diversity while promoting the specialist production and networked delivery that global efficiency requires. Counterarguments, that different traditions and social psychologies in different societies cause different transaction arrangements to flourish there, have received a double setback from economic developments outside the western hemisphere. First, various traditions deemed inimical to industrial development (notably Chinese Confucianism and communism) began to nurture it at unprecedented rates. Then a number of the growth miracles wrought by more progressive 'Asian values' abruptly unravelled, revealing their vulnerability to much more Anglo-American imperatives of profit and loss.

From the wreckage of such relativistic views comes the ultimately more optimistic prospect that anyone can succeed in the market, given the right basic set of legal defences, shared initial resources and shared interests, while preserving other positive aspects of difference. But the optimism does not rely on there being anything natural, primordial, or (hence) universal about the human urge to trade. From not eating between meals ('deferred gratification') to not claiming an offside goal ('the referee is always right'), there are many personally beneficial traits that do not come naturally. Instead, individuals arrange to have these traits imposed on themselves, knowing the results will be better than if immediate self-interest is pursued at all times. Some behaviour patterns are acquired so rapidly, and so independently of the social environment, as to be plausibly considered to arise from an inner template. Grammatical language learning (Chomsky 1975) is one of the best documented, and one for which genetic analogues are now being sought. But while language learning begins in infancy for the vast majority, non-relational transaction takes longer to acquire – and only an entrepreneurial minority ever seeks it on an open-ended, continuous basis. In the absence of an identifiable 'market instinct', we are unlikely to isolate the trading gene. If good business brains were hereditary, many more family firms would survive the transfer to the next generation. Those seeking better ways to do business would be advised to stick with the MBA; the gene therapy course may take rather longer to pay back its fees.

12.2 Where traders fear to tread

Even if evolution can account for certain tendencies towards trade, it was never biologists' intention to make them universal. Indeed, most genetic research points to human preference for family members over strangers, and small groups over large, which are far more in tune with relational than market transaction. If economists have sought to generalise the message of the selfish gene, it is because they have already sought to generalise the market motivations that might arise from it. In the evolutionary struggle between competing social sciences, the neoclassical model has left a trail of alternative grand theories in its wake.

Far from narrowing the range of transactions to which market reasoning is held applicable, the subsequent shift from an 'outcome' to a 'process' case has greatly widened its application. Time and space (perhaps because short-supplied in their own markets) have not permitted a full exploration of applications of market thinking outside economics. Rational-choice explanations have been offered for, among other activities, marrying, divorcing, staging extra-marital affairs, stealing, migrating, voting, bribing (and being bribed), launching nuclear war, engaging in dangerous sports, having another drink, dropping out of college, even for behaving non-rationally. (And, with a bit more mathematical complication, for almost any combination of these things.)

The near-universal applicability of private cost-benefit reasoning is taken by critics as a sign of its essential tautology – a presumption of rationality, according to economists' favoured axioms, ensures that everything an agent does can thereafter be 'rationalised'. But to supporters, the economy of those axioms recommends the economics built upon them. Psychology may shape the preference function, social circumstances limit the available actions and politics constrain the maximisation, but microeconomics provides the deeper explanation for an individual's actions. Macroeconomics, similarly, can offer underlying explanations for apparently social or cultural phenomena, ranging from schooling as capitalism's device for attaining scale economies and internalising external benefits in human capital production to marriage as working men's chance to do to a spouse at night what is done to them by employers during the day.

There is, however, a substantial gulf between rationalising observed activities through market theory and recommending that they become market practice. Despite attempts to extend the sphere of market discipline, as reviewed in Chapters 6–11, it is not the only form of transaction in any society, and transaction is not the only form of human activity. A number of allocations and activities continue to be kept outside the market – sometimes because economists have found no way to marketise them, sometimes because governments and electorates have no wish to let them do so. The market may, indeed, have established its global reach by knowing how not to over-reach itself. But for a device whose general-equilibrium properties depend on the avoidance of missing markets', the range of exceptions is troublingly long.

12.2.1 *The environment*

A supermarket slogan rings through the rainforest: lowest ever price, buy now while stocks last. Hailed as humanity's device for harnessing the natural world, to enrich its legacy for future generations, the market is now widely accused of doing such damage as to leave them no future at all. The litany of environment-related market failures is formidable: unpaid external costs (pollution, gene-pool depletion, drug-resistant pests), unrewarded external benefits (oceans and forests providing carbon sinks, trees giving scenery and anchoring topsoil), common-pool resources (reservoirs, fishing grounds, oil wells), other exhaustible resources, public goods (the atmosphere, seas, public parks), exhaustible resources (fossil fuels, mineral deposits), merit goods (clean water and air, ancestral lands), and positional goods (sunbathing space on the undiscovered, unspoilt beach). Fundamentally, a transaction method designed to deal with continuous product flows is not well suited to depletable or finite stocks, and a method which envisages private owners pricing and assigning user rights has difficulty dealing with resources whose life-supporting character suggests that they should belong to all.

The earliest, and still most common, reaction to these problems was to take environmental resources out of the market. Optimum output of products and processes with environmental externalities, and optimum depletion of scarce resources, required administered transaction under a public authority concerned to preserve consumption opportunities across time and space, or relational transaction between those with a shared interest in conservation. The limits were usually direct: discharge limits or clean-up requirements for polluters, consumption ceilings for users of exhaustible or common-pool resources, public rights of access to (if not nationalisation of) privately appropriated commons. Where the problem was judged to be one of (non-depletable) public goods, or (inappropriable) external benefits, intervention aimed at raising rather than lowering the volume of transaction. Governments are now under pressure to legislate for a 'right to roam' over tracts of rural land, royalty-free access to patented genetic material, and subsidies to farmers for their 'stewardship' of the landscape to supplement any income they gain from selling its products (or compensate them for conserving those products).

More recently, intervention has moved from the replacement to the rehabilitation of markets, by adding the elements that are missing from them or adjusting the incentives they produce. External costs and benefits can be internalised through tax and subsidy, the resources still being traded through markets but at a modified price. This has the important allocative advantage of leaving agents to decide whether their private interest is better served by paying the higher price (e.g. a pollution tax) or paying to avoid the higher price (e.g. by cleaning up emissions), having ensured that either outcome fulfils the public interest. However, since most external environmental costs cross national boundaries, internalising measures such as a 'carbon tax' must be applied internationally if first adopters are not simply to disadvantage themselves economically.

> The setting and changing of international taxes may prove too difficult to implement and is not amenable to the kinds of adjustments that are required . . . where taxes have been employed as environmental control instruments in other contexts, the level of charges has consistently tended to be too low.
>
> (Markandya 1991: 56)

An alternative solution is to assign property rights in externality-producing resources to a self-interested private owner whose interests coincide with the public interest, who then charges for the benefits they give others or the costs that others inflict on them. This may allow government intervention to be reduced from a continuous tax-benefit redistribution to a one-off property rights assignment. But aligning private with public interests often means giving the new private owner a monopoly intermediary role, requiring regulation to stop them passing on more than the internalised cost or less of the internalised benefit. As well as raising a social-justice question as to why one private agent should be empowered to own (and act) on behalf of society, the assignment of all-encompassing property rights invites a relational rather than a market transaction outcome, and so poses economic efficiency risks – of indeterminate bilateral-monopoly bargaining or exploitative unilateral-monopoly pricing. While these may be 'solved' by making government the monopoly trader in externality-producing resources, public-choice analysis warns that governments may be as keen as individuals to inflict social costs, and reluctant to charge for social benefits with what is in effect an extra tax.

Whether property rights are private or public, natural-resource externalities present an additional social-justice problem to the extent that they reward inaction and penalise action. Urban taxpayers in Europe were not amused when farmers, long subsidised for their production, which they had therefore intensified at considerable external cost to scenic beauty and soil and river quality, started to receive additional subsidies for non-production, under the set-aside scheme designed to reduce output surpluses and let the land recover. The appearance of being paid for doing nothing, under the blackmail threat of doing something negative, has also been one reason for opposition (from the external beneficiaries) to proposals for nations which deliver environmental benefits to the world to be rewarded with international financial transfers. Costa Rica recently pioneered a 'debt-for-nature' swap under which the World Bank agreed to relieve it of debt in return for its undertaking not to relieve the rest of the world of its rainforest. But several further rounds of world environmental talks have failed to extend this implicit (and retrospective) subsidy to an explicit, proactive payment of 'rent' from rich inflictors of global pollution to poor preservers of global carbon sinks – however credible is developing nations' threat to strike back in the pollution race by burning off their trees.

A market remedy for these internalisation problems is to turn the externalities themselves into products, so that consumers pay directly for the unpriced benefits they receive, and producers for the unpriced costs they impose. Since external costs are usually easier to put a price on, efforts so far have focused on commoditising pollution, forcing producers to buy licences for their discharge into land, sea and air. Quotas for drawing on to common-pool and exhaustible resources can be similarly opened to trade. By commoditising rather than internalising externalities, public authorities can retreat to the sidelines after setting the individual size and aggregate total of licences and quotas – letting markets decide how they should be priced, and so redirecting externalities to the places where (when forced to put a price on them) society values them most.

United Nations 'Earth Summits' in the 1990s have resulted in agreement on a reduction of greenhouse gas emissions through the international trading of pollution licences, but the setting of 1990 levels as the baseline has proved problematic. By enabling the former Soviet union countries, whose energy-intensive industrial production collapsed in the eight years after 1990, to sell pollution quota they can no longer fill, and major hydrocarbon burners like the USA to buy it, the system may result in unchanged or even higher global pollution levels.

All proposals for pricing the environment can be faulted for using market-based calculation to tackle the deficiencies of market transaction. True to their standpoint that individuals are the best judges of their own welfare, economists have worked hard to find ways of pricing the environment that are grounded in revealed individual preference. The benefits of scenery and costs of noise are proxied by price differentials between a normal town house and its equivalent next door to a park or an airfield. The market price of pollution licences shows what polluters are willing to pay to go on damaging the environment, and the subscription to appeals for buying forest stands before they fall to developers shows what recipients of clean air and greenery are willing to pay to preserve it. Yet these methods of pricing externalities make use of market prices which may be too low because of the treatment of stocks as flows, market discount rates which myopically value present over future consumption (because the next generation isn't in the market), and willingness-to-pay measures which reflect the prevailing, very unequal distribution of income within and between nations.

Market-based economies' national accounting methods have long been criticised for understating social and environmental impacts, by misrepresenting externalities and confusing stock changes with income flows. The draining of an exhaustible resource counts as income, whereas it is really a balance-sheet change which actually reduces future income-generation potential unless the proceeds are invested in alternative capital projects. Conversely, the income earned from conserved environmental resources is understated, since their sustainably generated income (e.g. felled timber limited to natural growth, power from a dam small enough not to damage the river) is only a fraction of the total benefit delivered, most of which goes unpriced. Expenditures to avert or correct environmental damage count as additions to national income, when they do little more than quantify a negative externality which should more correctly have been subtracted from the previous income total. While nations take pride in building up a physical capital stock which will yield financial benefits to future generations, they neglect (through failing to put a price on it) the corresponding run-down of the 'natural capital' stock whose depletion denies its benefits to future generations.

> Careful inspection of the value of natural capital (i.e. looking at what environmental assets do for us) will show that the trade-off has been biased in favour of eliminating or degrading those assets in favour of either 'consuming' the proceeds (i.e. not reinvesting at all) or investing too readily in man-made assets. Very simply, if the 'true' value of the environment were known, we would not degrade it as much.
>
> (Pearce *et al.* 1991: 2)

One particularly controversial outcome of the market valuation of externalities is that measures of external cost, if based on people's willingness to pay for environmental improvement, or on the loss of welfare due to environmental degradation, link the external costs of pollution to the level of national income. This creates an economic case for concentrating environmentally damaging processes in lower-income countries, reinforced if these are currently less polluted (and so have a higher absorption potential before damage starts to be felt). If only market values are placed on the environment, and if local incomes enter the calculation of those values, toxic dumping becomes cheap where life is cheap. Because higher-income nations value a clean environment more and are deemed to suffer more from a dirty one, 'the logic behind dumping a load of toxic waste in the lowest-wage country is impeccable', as one leading World Bank economist infamously put it (Lawrence Summers, quoted in Cairncross (1995: 28), thereby showing that public-servant reputation is another scarce resource whose stocks are hard to replenish through the market).

Trading in toxic waste remains the market's preferred solution to environmental externalities, since it is by attaching a price to a by-product's disposal that polluters may be induced to cease or reduce its production. But the protestors digging up the track in front of nuclear fuel train movements and the processors who fly-tip commercial waste suggest a difficult job (and another market) policing pollutant movements. Where backyards are not for sale at any price, the full life-cycle of many toxic products will continue to be incompletely priced and thus excessively pursued.

12.2.2 The family

If this book runs to a second edition, the 'marketisation of the family' might well be its unlucky Chapter 13. Economics began in the home (the term deriving from a Greek word for housekeeping), and shows every sign of wanting to get back inside it. Like firms, households – here assumed to be family-based – in the interim come to be treated as islands of administered transaction within the general market stream. Families buy products from, and sell labour services to, the wider economy. They may even value time spent in the home by its 'opportunity cost' of income forgone in not working outside it. But their internal exchanges are done without prices being set or money changing hands. Even more than in most firms, because of their smaller size and the closer ties of their members, families' internal transaction design and administration are carried out on the basis of co-operative discussion, not competitive dealing of a market or even a relational kind.

Non-market transaction within families was vital to the early development of most market economies. Much early production took the form of outwork, the processing in the home of materials delivered and collected by merchants. It was at this stage that work preferences began the shift from a backward-sloping to the conventional ascending supply curve, the substitution effect of a higher wage extracting more effort despite the income-effect inducement to settle for the same from less work. Later, production was moved out of the home, to specialist factories, where management could raise productivity through improved division of labour, and profitability through better supervision and benchmarking of employees. At the same time consumption moved into the home, which began to assume the roles previously contracted-out to public entertainment centres, canteens, telecommunication facilities, libraries and (treating private transport as an extension of the home) commercial rail and coach. As transactions were taken out of the marketplace, they were taken out of the market. Family members lent money to one another through love or trust, without regard to the short-term return (a form of venture capital still unmatched in modern financial markets, and often central to the heroic investment and innovation efforts with which nations embarked on industrialisation). Income was shared without regard to who earned it, personal property pooled, and most parts of the home deemed common-pool resources. Social services and merit goods were also widely provided through the extended family, before state welfare funding and compulsory schooling pushed it aside.

Many sociologists ascribe recent signs of family fragmentation in market economies to the side-effects of economic pressure. Economists, never quite the dismal scientists of legend, seem more inclined to look on the bright side, where they see evidence of underlying economic logic. Going without children may be inevitable if the forgone earnings and extra expenditures entailed are compared with the utility of spending such money on adult pursuits. Divorce – its costs reduced by the absence of offspring – may be the mutually loss-minimising solution to a misjudged marital investment (especially if one or both partners is in receipt of a generous takeover bid). From a global viewpoint, the tendency of 'child costs' to rise with national income (they cost more in terms of expenditure and lost income, give a smaller support payback in old age, and are even opting-out of paying their parents' pensions) may make for a fair and efficient coincidence of the highest incomes and the lowest birth rates – children being least numerous in those parts of the world where their claim on natural and social resources is the heaviest.

But as with their problems with the 'enhanced' neoclassical theory of the firm (section 8.2), economists have long been aware of the potential distortions caused by non-market transaction within the home. The source of the problem, as with most other market failures, is the 'missing market' caused by failure to price intra-household trade. Almost a century ago, the pioneering economist Alfred Marshall reflected ruefully on the damage he would do to national income if he married his housekeeper, inducing her to do for love what she previously did for money. By the late 1980s, those less willing to subjugate emotion to economic aggregates were having a dramatic statistical effect. In one of the most detailed recent studies, valuing domestic unpaid labour at its opportunity cost in terms of net average wages, housework performed in Canada in 1986 was equivalent to 33 per cent of its GDP (Chadeau 1992: Table 4).

Since household members, too, can perform such evaluations, the 'problem' of unpaid domestic work is in some ways self-liquidating. The larger the income that can be earned by going out into the labour market, the fewer will be willing to stay indoors and work for nothing. In the USA in 1996, in the midst of a sustained boom which had lifted real wages even for all but the least skilled and most casu-alised paid workers, 84 per cent of married couples involved both members working outside the home. Dual earning patterns override the business cycle, a rise in relative wages increasing the opportunity cost of unpaid work in the home (pos-itive substitution effect), while a reduction making it more likely that a partner must return to work to supplement household income (positive income effect). (Statistically, an adult's chance of finding paid work also rises if the partner already has it.)

The tendency for families to be smaller and start later as adults' income rises makes such dual-earner households easier to manage. But even when children arrive, the income effect of working for cash tends to override the substitution effect of quality parental time in the formative childhood stages. Women start their maternity leave later and return to work earlier, and some of their partners are by legend too wedded to the workplace even to sit out the unpaid labour (let alone do more around the house when the new member takes up residence).

The arrival of little ones drives a large wedge between economic and social concepts of welfare. Psychological observation can now draw on persuasive evo-lutionary argument for its contention that child-rearing is best left to one or both natural parents (or failing that, a close relative).

> The love of kin comes naturally; the love of non-kin does not . . . Relatives share genes to a greater extent than nonrelatives, so if a gene makes an organ-ism benefit a relative (say, by feeding or protecting it), it has a good chance of benefiting a copy of itself.
>
> (Pinker 1997: 429–30)

Given that legislation against child labour and for compulsory school education have turned children from a benefit into a cost from the purely financial viewpoint, it must be assumed that the decision to have them reflects anticipation of psycho-logical benefit, most of which is gained from observation of and interaction with the infant in question.

But in neoclassical economics, the social injustice of a rarely equal division of labour in the home is matched by the economic efficiency of bringing childcare into the workplace division of labour. Specialist child-minders can develop the spe-cialist skills to achieve best-practice, and achieve economies of scale by caring for several children at once. (They can also reap scope economies through the inter-change of learning materials and playthings, and minimise sunk costs by ensuring that child-specific investments can be handed down to the next arrival, if the pre-vious owner left them intact.) Jobs are created and national incomes rise if parents pay child-minders out of the paid work they return to, rather than giving up the paid work and minding the child themselves without pay. The recent rebranding of relational transaction as 'crony capitalism' signals economists' general scepticism over letting kinship ties shape resource allocation. On their own (national) accounts, prosperity lies in sending children outside the home, not bringing parents back within it.

Economic pressures are pushing governments towards the commercialisation of childcare. At present the state tends to incur a double cost from intra-household child-rearing. It forgoes tax revenue on the income given up by the home-working parent, and instead pays the parent a welfare benefit for the child (as well as any subsidy paid to the ex-employer for maternity and paternity leave). The rationale for child benefits – that those who have children confer external benefits on those who do not – is increasingly open to challenge when many of the services con-sumed by children (notably health and education) are also socially subsidised, many of the reverse inter-generational transfers (notably pay-as-you-go pensions) are likely to be withdrawn by the time they reach adulthood, and family planning has made more pregnancies a matter of choice presumably motivated by private rather than social gain. The prospect of capitalising some of that uncounted 33 per cent of GDP into national income is also tempting in a world where growth by more orthodox means is getting harder to sustain. Recent changes in government–household relations, such as separate taxation, have therefore leaned towards the reciprocal double employment gain: of parents returning to paid work and other professionals taking over their tasks of kid, kitchen and carpet-cleaning management.

UK family policy has taken an especially intriguing turn, with the government significantly raising its support payments for single parents who return to work (or vocational training) and employ professional childcare. The economic rationale is one of lone parents wanting to work, and frequently having skills which are a social sunk cost unless employed outside the home. Any damage to children's welfare from being detached from the natural parent (which is anyway a fate shared by many children of workaholic dual parents) is argued to be compensated by the better material provision their parents' paid job can provide. However, neoclassical economists opposed to any form of labour subsidy point out that the resultant rise in employment and income will come at government's expense, if the paid work that lone parents now take involves minding the children of other lone parents. Neighbours who previously raised their own children for free can now potentially swap their children (or houses) during the daytime and draw the state subsidy. Avoiding the spread of such 'childcare entrepreneurship', especially when output and employment growth turn down again, may require additional interventions to raise the differential of private-sector wages over childcare allowances. One, a recruitment subsidy for those taking on long-term jobless youth, was already in place in the UK in 1998; another, a national minimum wage, was about to be introduced.

But other aspects of UK experience cast doubt on how far the political market will permit marketised household relations to be taken. An earlier venture, the Child Support Agency, sought to reduce the state's subsidy bill to lone parents by extracting due maintenance payments from their absent other half. It has attracted criticism from all sides for failing to trace the most egregious non-payers, over-charging those it finds, inflicting poverty on men's second families by forcing them to fund the (often more affluent) first, and re-awakening the animosities which led to the original split. To Canadian premier Pierre Trudeau's observation that 'The state has no place in the nation's bedrooms', many would add that the market has no place anywhere in the house.

Biology stops short of making parenting a market transaction. Society still frowns on sex being made so, and heaps uneasy ridicule on legally minded (or separation-wary) couples who include an asset division in their marriage contracts. One of modern literature's most marketable anti-heroes can still win sympathy from his childhood brush with the profit-and-loss account. 'My father hit trouble on the tables and the track and . . . He submitted a bill for all the money he had spent on my upbringing . . . Inflation had been taken into account. I'd cost him nineteen thousand pounds' (Amis 1985: 178). Reproductive functions, once an administered transaction within the family, are increasingly offered for sale outside it as technology permits. But public unease at such developments has meant a heavy regulatory role for government, and a backlash in favour of the traditional (if mythical) 'internalised' family has long threatened to resurface.

> Many societies can be seen to swing gently between two extremes . . . The one extreme is characterised by spontaneity, taking no thought for the morrow,

'doing one's own thing'. The other extreme is characterised by inhibition, self-control, conformity to custom . . . Who knows, therefore, whether within a generation or so, the Western world will not be herded back into a new Victorianism?

(G. Taylor 1974: 45, 47)

12.2.3 Food

Food appears to be the merit good that economics forgot. Other obviously essential survival needs – water, health care, shelter – are either provided entirely outside the market, or subsidised for those who cannot pay the market rate. Yet with agricultural production, market failures are recognised predominantly on the supply side, leading to support for producers which can actually worsen the situation on the demand side. Because the strict ceiling on nutritional needs makes demand for food insensitive to price, farmers can be ruined by a good crop, with staple products yielding lower revenue and perhaps even lower volume sales when higher output reduces prices. The eponymous Giffen gave the potato as his prime case of the poor man's product with the overwhelmingly negative income effect (section 2.9.1). 'The fertile earth, the straight tree rows, the sturdy trunks, and the ripe fruit. And children dying of pellagra must die because a profit cannot be taken from an orange' (Steinbeck 1939/1951: 320).

Disaster can follow disaster if one poor harvest leaves farmers without the money or seeds to sow the next. But where last year's finance is not a constraint, endless slump can give way to endless instability, as excessive output leads to a price slump which causes capacity to be closed or transferred to other crops, which causes declining output and a price rise, which encourages capacity to be switched back, resulting in boom and bust in alternating seasons. Just as farms' ability to switch land between uses is of little help in achieving stable prices and viable income, nor is the prevalence of joint production: too many live cattle will generally mean too much beef, leather, tallow and bonemeal, as a slaughter to stabilise prices in the main market deflects the oversupply into subsidiary markets.

Most industrial nations regard it as anomalous – and dangerous – that farmers should prosper when their harvests fail, and offer price or income support to re-establish a positive relation between agricultural production and income. The external benefits of food production – 'stewarding' the countryside, keeping villages alive – receive attention over the external benefits of food consumption, whose quality and diversity are increasingly linked with physical (and even mental) health. Urban households are assumed rich enough to find an adequate diet affordable through the market – and rural households to get enough outside the market, leaving genuine hunger limited enough for charitable soup kitchens to deal with. Labelling and ingredients lists are assumed adequate to redress any information asymmetry between the farmer who knew the pork chop as a piglet, and the shopper who first comes across it as a shrink-wrapped packet on the supermarket shelf.

This delicate balance may be upset, however, by the greater subjection of food to market transaction, especially the agricultural component added to the General

Agreement on Tariffs and Trade (GATT) in 1994. As within nations, unequal distribution of income between nations can swing the allocation of low-income communities into conformity with the preferences of high-income communities. This is nowhere truer than of food, where land that once grew staple food for local peasants may be turned over to cash crops for foreign tables (or worse, needles), the income from which rarely returns to the local economy. Even with the income redistribution necessary to bring a static welfare gain, cash crops may introduce unfavourable income dynamics, displacing labour through technical and land-management changes, and raising local prices. Once sown to luxury or cash crops, land cannot quickly be turned back to the production of staples, and may have been drained of the nutrients to support them. As well as a merit-good case against rationing food by the purse in low-income societies, it is possible to argue that the fundamental premises of market allocation break down when food becomes scarce. The market wage may be below the 'efficiency' wage if it cannot buy enough food energy to sustain the work, and people confined to a subsistence diet will not be willing to move away from it in search of a 'higher-welfare' combination with other goods. 'Poverty even when thus defined does not pick up the underlying non-convexity associated with undernourishment' (Dasgupta 1992: 25).

Higher-income nations have already seriously distorted world food trade through an intervention in their own markets – the subsidisation of their own farmers, mainly through inflated consumer prices preserved with high import barriers, and the regular dumping of resultant surpluses on international markets. This dumping drives down prices for lower-income producers, especially those who switched to cash crops. Although 'first-world' grain surpluses have in the past helped avert famine in the aftermath of 'third-world' crop failures, their market-distorting effect cannot always be detached from the cause of those failures – and late delivery of relief supplies can result in their flooding the market and forcing down prices just as local farms are trying to revive their production after the famine. Industrial nations' agricultural supports are being scaled down, and until they go, world trading rules allow lower-income countries to maintain protective tariffs for their own farmers. But even if, as is intended, trade helps raise their agricultural productivity, this may lead only to greater rural unemployment and inequality, unless there is an equivalent growth in the industrial and service sectors for the displaced labour to move to.

Agricultural trade may even have adverse outcomes for the wealthier parties, who have already seen virulent animal and human diseases cross national borders in a carcase, and appear to have assembed a truly cosmopolitan set of ingredients at just the moment that country, farm or factory of origin become a health and hygiene concern. Yet without a variety of sources, food security is at risk, from the diplomatic isolation of a particular supplying country or the disease devastation of a particular supplying crop.

Seeding and breeding are also two early battlegrounds in the growing global battle over patenting and marketising genetic material. Already, some improved seed varieties – whose free circulation drove the first post-war 'green revolution' – are unavailable to lower-income farmers because royalties are due to those who engineered them. If, as some national legislatures may decide, a patent can be taken on genes isolated from plants or animals already under cultivation, there is an outside chance of some farmers having to pay extra for what they already grow – a grim echo of colonisation in an earlier phase of global market development, when local growers were forced to pay rent on land they thought they always owned.

12.2.4   Charity and trust

Gift and theft are the good and bad of one-sided transaction. Money or property rights pass one way, but no product or service is provided in return. Many charitable acts may be reinterpreted as economic transactions: an investment in reputation, a purchase of approval, of the joys of feeling generous, or of the future entitlement to a good deed in return. Biologically, an altruistic act by an individual, promoting partner or group survival, may be a selfish act by their genes. But genuine acts of charity do appear to happen; or at least, obvious opportunities to make gains for oneself rather than for a total stranger are sometimes forgone. Single people with no descendants or dependants routinely fail to spend through their savings before death, even when they profess no belief in immortality and have made no will that will pass their estate to a favourite charity rather than the state.

The granting of 'trust' is a similar unidirectional act. For this reason, the centrality of trust to workable market systems remains controversial. Belief that a counterparty will act honestly, or reciprocate, is essential to any purely market transaction: if the seller pockets the money and refuses the service, the buyer has little defence. Trust can be established in cases of repeated market transaction, and cemented in the relational transaction into which this usually turns. If getting to know the counterparty fails to make them act honestly and return favours, it can at least allow those they deceive to seek legal redress, or mete out reputational damage that will prevent others from suffering at the same unreliable hands. But attaining trust on the one and only encounter, as pure market transaction requires, is a hazardous undertaking. In the original prisoners' dilemma game, played only once, both suspects incurred maximum sentences.

12.2.5   Cultural products

The European Union's misgivings about US film imports, and desire to maintain major televised sports events as a public rather than private network offering, is symptomatic of more general misgivings over subjecting art and culture to the market. With political populism, so with popular culture, there is a fear (at least among the powerful minority of opera-goers and gallery visitors) that what most people want to buy is not what is best for them, and that certain other artforms should be preserved whether or not they find a viable market. The experience of various posthumously recognised great artists suggests there may also be a delay in the matching of reward to merit which not only does an injustice to the producer, but also may be economically damaging for society by prematurely ending or warping their output.

In general, public support for the arts might be justified on the grounds of its being a public good, a bringer of positive externalities, a merit good, a common-pool resource (in the case of non-reproducible work which would otherwise be stashed in private collections), or even a producer of cohesion and common values which is part of the market framework and cannot be successfully brought within it. For some defenders of state support, its difference from other products lies on the supply side.

> The greatest industrial achievement, myth to the contrary, emerges from committees. But not the greatest painting, sculpture or music . . . [the artist] cannot work on or with a team. We have here a principal explanation of why the high technical and productive achievements of the industrial system are so regularly combined with banal or even offensive design.
>
> (Galbraith 1967: 344–5)

Once the competitive pressures and wealth taxes have depleted the ranks of disinterested patrons, only public subsidy can rescue the artist from sacrificing creativity to committee. (Perhaps understandably Galbraith exempts literature from the list of endangered arts, his own books having proved eminently successful in the marketplace.) Others weather the charges of elitism to maintain a demand-side defence, that people should consume art which informed critics find pleasing as well as that which they instinctively prefer.

The distributional implications of such arguments are often uncomfortable (opera tickets being subsidised from rock fans' income tax), as are many of the products produced by artists insulated by subsidy from public taste. Fine arts can also survive in the marketplace, if not by combining public with critical acclaim, then by attracting commercial sponsorship, or by its practitioners taking a day-job. But the concept of all cultural products being subjected to market tests is generally resisted, and the 'commercialisation' of traditional artforms a concern for anthropologists as much as aesthetes. Even network television, once condemned as destroying the art of conversation, is now being hailed as a focus for shared interest and experience under threat from the individualising tendencies of cable, satellite and internet transmission. The persistent desire to protect culture, as common heritage if not as collective consumption product, suggests continued sympathy among users for the fear of its more idealistic producers, that societies grow poorer when their only values are market values.

12.2.6 'Recreational' drugs

Global agricultural trade already includes a large 'cash crop' of narcotic substances, grown in Latin America and Asia and mainly consumed in North America and western Europe, with unhealthy intermediary profits in the Middle East, and central America and eastern Europe on the way. The war against drugs has been most intensive on the supply side, with seizure during the movement across borders or destruction at source. But until the demand side is tackled, prices in western markets seem likely to remain far higher than for the soft fruits or cereals that might grow in their place.

These high prices result from the ban on dangerous or addictive drugs in high-income markets, which limits supply to smuggling and underground processing and distribution. The ban reflects an official perception that, for once, consumers do not know best, either because they are already addicted to the substance or because they do not know the full damage that will result from becoming addicted. A 'market' solution, tentatively tried for the most common and least immediately harmful recreational drugs in some countries, would be to legalise the supply: the profits to distributors would then fall, greater visibility of the traffic would allow better monitoring of quality and addiction and the imposition of taxes, and legality might remove some of the attraction to users. But lower prices are likely to encourage general consumption (even if lost illegality reduces the glamour to some current users), unless taxes are set very high, in which case there will have been an unbalancing redistribution from poor-country growers to rich-country governments. For now, political and public opinion generally seems to favour keeping the market at bay, even if it is a bay into which mysterious speedboats come and go at dead of night.

12.2.7 *Personal data*

Marketers want to know more about their public, so that they can match people's preferences to their products, and perhaps eventually match their products to people's preferences. Much can be learnt from publicly available information such as name, address, type of house, age, marital and family status. More can be gleaned from transaction records, responses to surveys, credit applications, and other information submitted to companies which then enters list or database trade with other companies. National treatment of the trade in personal information varies widely. Some governments have set strict data protection laws, allowing individuals to inspect the information held on them and authorise its transfer. Others have allowed the trade to develop without restraint, some even making publicly available their own official data collections. Public opinion, perhaps unexcited by the prospect of a better selection of junk mail, has generally shown misgivings about a free trade in data, confirmed by the continued reluctance – despite promises of safe encryption – to engage in the transfer of personal details needed to get 'internet' trade off the ground.

While marketers bemoan the useful detail that they know exists but cannot rent or buy, pro-marketeers may have some cause for relief. Effective insurance markets depend on the pooling of risks whose characteristics are known only in aggregate. Too much personal risk information, such as discovery of a person's genetic test results, penchant for hang-gliding or holiday in Chernobyl in 1986, might lead to large numbers being unable to obtain insurance cover, a socially questionable development even if an even larger number would enjoy lower premiums. In some industries, the logical culmination of unrestricted personal data gathering is the effective end of the market, as manufacturers switch from producing for stock to producing to (customised) order. But information-gathering can work two ways. The system that tells a seller all about the buyer might also tell the buyer all about other sellers, including their prices, eroding the price advantage that makes customisation profitable. A little bit of knowledge is a dangerous thing, but at least it has scarcity value. Data trade has already destroyed much arbitrage trade by speeding the closure of financial-instrument price differences, and may yet do the same for the real economy if ignorance is too effectively dispelled.

12.2.8 Road space

Even if the gaseous by-products of their movement can be filtered away, the solidity of their non-movement is of increasing concern to those for whom private motor cars are a triumph of private markets. While it may seem irrational to spend longer sitting in an inner-city traffic jam than would be needed to complete the trip by bicycle, leaving the car at home under these circumstances would be equally irrational. The owner not only would sacrifice quadraphonic stereo, car-phone conversation and numerous other tailback entertainments, but also would make it easier for others to beat the jam by staying in it, while giving up their own chance of a clear run if everyone else decided to leave the car at home.

The gridlocked city may seem a classic collective action problem, in which everyone ends up suffering from a non-cooperative zero-sum game 'solution' when they would do better to submit to a central authority limiting traffic to what the carriageway can bear. But from a neoclassical perspective, traffic congestion is less a case of market failure than of markets not being permitted to succeed. Roads are overused because they are unpriced – a common-pool resource with no property-rights holder who can restrict entry to sustainable capacity. Road pricing would impose such restriction, and – if introduced through a tax spent on further road construction – also respond to the unmet demand which is expressed in non-financial form (queues and fumes) while road space continues to be rationed by non-financial means.

Road pricing is alread a reality on toll motorways and bridges, and is set to reach the inner city as electronic tagging and billing brings down the cost and time lost in imposing the charge. But the movement is meeting tremendous resistance from those who believe that access should stay free because city roads were built with public money; and from those who believe that if it is to be rationed at all, road access should be allocated by merit rather than money. Among proxies for merit are the nature of the vehicle (business over pleasure), the number of occupants (sharers over sole drivers), journey length (distant over local licence plates) and occupants' age (pensioners having earned a rest from their pedals). Auto culture will slide into autocracy if the round-tripping rich can buy their way onto the byways while the delivering poor are forced into the bike lane. So far, citing administration cost, most city governments have banned all traffic when the smog gets too intoxicating. Equality before the traffic light (and in the endless wait at crowded junctions) survives where equality before other markets has long been eroded by premium services and preferential deals. Until allowed to buy the roads – at which point a regulator might be able to enforce concessional access fees for the the highways' lower means – those who like to drive as if they own the road will not, it seems, be allowed to put their money where their motors are.

12.2.9   *Knowledge*

Markets depend on the free flow of knowledge, yet market production of knowledge requires that its flow be restricted. Economists have long accepted that the creation and dissemination of non-commercial knowledge should be left to publicly provided education, and that commercial discovery should either be made privately appropriable (through temporary patent rights or monopoly) or be subsidised to compensate for the external benefits bestowed on imitators. New information technologies may have reduced the transaction costs that stand in the way of physical property rights being tradable, but only by increasing the pre-production costs, which may be unrecoverable given the ease with which software can be copied and codes reverse-engineered. Rising innovation cost and falling imitation cost threaten to arrest an innovation process based on continuous profit maximisation.

> Today it has become absurd to have rival groups of scientists and engineers developing the same products in secrecy from each other, to have massive teams of scientists and programmers designing rival – and almost identical – micro-computers, word-processors, telephone exchanges and cloned drugs . . . To have the key industries of the future under private ownership will result in an increasing proportion of society's resources going into ever more ingenious means of retaining the benefits of research within the individual company.
>
> (Costello *et al.* 1989: 99)

Where such appropriation strategies are successful, as when with Microsoft and Intel's 'Wintel' turned a duel into a duet, governments have tended to force open the codes to let others compete.

The enhanced scope for private appropriation has had the opposite effect on higher education, however, giving many governments the exchequer-driven excuse they needed for reducing public funding to universities and their students. Researchers are now expected to recover more of their own costs by licensing or selling their new discoveries, or by charging for tuition. Students are expected to meet more of their tuition fee because of the private return they will make on an additional qualification. To the extent that university degrees have become a 'positional' good, valued for their relative scarcity rather than their intrinsic merit, charges will reduce the student intake to those who actually expect to learn something useful; the fact that such reduction will yield them a 'positional' bonus merely adding to the private gains which merit the scaling-down of public funding.

But marketised higher education – with its corollary of a marketised student life swopping lecture halls for bars and burger stands – poses two threats to the market system it seeks to complement. Conducting research solely in areas believed to have commercial application will miss the seemingly irrelevant 'basic' discoveries which later make (and lose) millions, past examples of which range from the nuclear fission to neural nets. Allocating places on ability to pay rather than ability to learn will, without generous scholarship provision, risk reducing ivory-tower output by leaving some of the brightest out of the class. Employers may, of course, find tomorrow's graduates insufficiently more productive than their school-leaver peers to merit the extra pay needed to redeem their student loans or return their extra taxes. If so, it could be an unflattering reflection of tuition standards when lectures become loss-leaders for laboratory work, and of final results when the opportunity costs of another hour's study is suddenly turned into the very real cost of waitress tips forgone.

12.2.10 Politics

As observed in section 11.9, responsive producers are popular and responsive politicians are populist. The public expects commercial marketplaces to serve them, but political marketplaces to take decisions for them and occasionally (for strategy or time-consistency reasons) make them do something they would rather not. Marketising politics may not produce the sort of government which will best handle the limits of the market in other areas. And few enjoy dealing with the best bureaucrats money can buy.

Whereas the typical economic decision is decentralised, so that harmony can be achieved even if each does their own thing, the typical political decision is centralised. A single action must be taken in the name of the whole group (e.g. signing a treaty), or else group members' actions must be co-ordinated to achieve a target outcome for the whole group (e.g. restricting car use to cut air pollution). Whereas the information relevant to an economic decision usually arises at the decentralised level, with individual agents, information relevant to political decisions usually first arises at the centralised level. Through their intelligence services, governments usually know before most individual citizens that a foreign power is about to attack them. Through their statistical and economic divisions, they usually know before individual companies that the downturn in demand signals the onset of a recession affecting all businesses, not just a miscalculation by one that has made customers switch to another.

Market-based politics featured heavily in recent elections in the USA, Russia and the UK. But bad political products still seem generally harder to sell than bad tomato tins, if only because of the indivisibility involved (winning just 20 per cent of the vote does not make you one-fifth of a president) and the relational aspect of the transaction which allows the electorate to find the quality defects at the second election if they did not spot them at the first. And with political programmes invariably bundled and not infrequently bungled, voters can never be sure of what they are voting for. Since they may at times need policies they do not like, this may be another case of optimal ignorance which representative democracy dispels at its peril.

12.2.11   *The problem with exceptions*

The belief that a rational plan, scientifically advised and democratically chosen, could bring superior results to the unpredictable march of uncoordinated markets, came easily to a society which had seen science recently triumph over disease and deprivation, and democracy beat dictatorship in war. Fifty years on, the acceptance of market trade as an efficient forum for decisions, using scattered, subjective and hard-to-process information, comes much more easily to a world whose complexity and interdependence make even human-made machines unpredictable, which has seen its natural sciences retreat from solid proof to sets of ideas still awaiting refutation, and whose democratic masters are not above jailing those who violate the plan. With utopian end-states disposed of, the market gains a newly legitimated appeal as a a rational procedure with no predictable outcome. The American dream speaks with an Austrian accent.

But when economists try to formalise that dream, it is still with models that depict the market system as an all-or-nothing process. Assigning the wrong price, or no price, to any one product may unbalance the pricing and allocation of all other products. Economically, for reasons reviewed in Chapters 2–4, markets may not be able to establish their static and dynamic superiority unless they are allowed to get everywhere – competitive markets being created for what are currently externalities, monopoly products, merit goods, risk and uncertainty, and all transaction-relevant information. Socially, for reasons reviewed selectively in this section, there may be reasons why a majority do not want markets to intrude into these areas. Revolutions rarely overturn all elements of the old order at once. The recent attack on non-market allocations has, if anything, added logic and legitimacy to those that survive.

Alternative transactional forms, as described in Chapters 6 and 7, may still be socially acceptable. They may succeed in preserving the general health of markets by replacing them in the small number of cases where they fail. But the importance of those cases, and the tendency of markets to subvert other transaction types, makes this a far from stable solution. Second-best solutions beckon, and the social boundary rope around markets' acceptable application can easily be pulled into an economic noose.

12.3   Next step: networks?

Networks appeared in Chapter 2 as one of the stumbling-blocks to market transaction. The wires, waves, pipes and channels that link them are a natural monopoly, wasteful to replicate but under no pressure to price its access competitively – unless placed under a regulator, who even then may be kept in the dark about the network operator's costs and captured by its special pleading. Networks reappeared in Chapter 6 as the foundation for relational transaction, a first-name-terms alternative to the market which can overcome problems of information and trust, but swaps the transparency of competitive markets for the captivity of bilateral bargaining. With a shift of technology from the handshake to the handheld computer, networks return in this final chapter as a possible escape from the so-far irreducible limits to the market. The new network enthusiasts identify, in particular, an end to the market's information and co-ordination difficulties over space and (by collapsing the future into the 'nanosecond' present) over time.

12.3.1 *Hayek goes digital*

The integration of computer and communication technologies promises to solve the information problem, by giving decentralised agents both the information they need for transaction and the instant means to process that information. Some of the relevant information will be missing, because it consists of other people's unknown or unformed intentions; and some of the information used in its place will still defy processing, because it consists of endless contingent conjectures on decisions which interdepend on the agent's own. But instant communication can now enable interdependent agents to co-ordinate their decisions, transacting with firm knowledge of what others intend to do, backed up by continuously updated information to confirm that they are doing it. Internets, intranets and extranets combine with electronic data interchange, cellular phones and round-the-clock news media to give transactors the complete picture for the first time.

> When Adam Smith described the concept of markets in *The Wealth of Nations* in 1776, he theorised that if every buyer knew every seller's price, and every seller would know what every buyer was willing to pay, everyone in the 'market' would be able to make fully informed decisions and society's resources would be distributed efficiently. To date we haven't achieved Smith's ideal because would-be buyers and would-be sellers seldom have complete information about one another.
>
> (Gates 1995: 157)

Hayek interpreted Smith as praising the market for reducing agents' uncertainty, interdependency, information needs and co-ordination tasks (section 5.4). Now the bringer of encyclopedias on disk interprets him as prematurely celebrating its capacity to help surfing shoppers ride the information flood.

Linked via networks, individuals can combine their unique local knowledge with just enough shared and co-ordinated 'system' knowledge to pursue their own goals while avoiding zero-sum clashes with other networked individuals. The network uses 'distributed processing' to maximise the speed of information use, and 'multiple routing' to raise the speed and security of its transmission. It can thus easily extend to new members, and works better the more that interconnections deepen and widen between existing members. New members are thus welcome to join, on equal terms, and are judged by what they bring to the network rather than who they are; the use of coded log-on names emphasising the cultural, locational, age and gender impartiality of the virtual community. No single, central observer can hope to understand all that is happening in the network – hence the futility of trying to guide or control it using primitive 'linear' planning techniques – but we can be certain that this is the best way of combining the opportunities and constraints of the whole with the wishes and wisdom of the autonomous parts.

Contemplating the frequent failure of econometric models to predict the outcome of market processes adequately, even after the 'endogenisation' of previously independent variables (such as interest-rate and commodity-price changes) and the incorporation of model-consistent expectations, some economists now argue that applied mathematics has yet to catch up with the complexity of market processes. Whereas, a century ago, best linear unbiased estimation appeared capable of capturing the time paths of main macroeconomic variables, recent reassessment of today's richer data runs suggests that reality is more complex. Feedbacks, and the changes in agents' behaviour they give rise to, may mean that market outcomes are shaped by non-linear processes (those that depart from straight line when the dependent is graphed against independent variables), whose higher-order parameters make them highly sensitive to initial conditions. 'A policymaker receiving advice based on a linear model of the world – where such sensitivities to initial conditions never occur – would misinterpret the consequences of his or her policy, believing in the short-run that it had failed . . . [For example] conventional economics pays too little attention to this interplay between profits and unemployment as the key determinant of business cycles – an interplay which is obscured in the empirical data' (Ormerod 1995: 186, 188).

Stripped of their digital jargon, modern American descriptions of the virtues of networking closely parallel the enthusiasm and evangelism of earlier 'Austrian' depictions of the market. After Adam Smith, Hayek's is the name and imagery most commonly evoked.

> A single variable – the price – is used to regulate all the other variables of resource allotment. That way, one doesn't care how many bars of soap are needed per person, or whether trees should be cut for homes or for books. These calculations are done in parallel, on the fly, from the bottom up, out of human control, by the interconnected network itself. Spontaneous order.
>
> (Kelly 1994: 157)

The whole is more than the sum of the parts, because it utilises the sums of the parts. Bounded rationality is confounded as silicon rolls back constitutional constraints, and transaction costs fall towards zero – rendering unnecessary the market-modifying structures designed to economise on them.

> Research shows that the transactional costs needed to maintain the quality of a task as it stretches across several companies are higher than those if the job stayed within one company. However: (1) these costs are being lowered every day with network technology such as electronic data transfers and video-conferencing, and (2) these costs are already lower in terms of the immense gains in adaptability.
>
> (Kelly 1994: 246)

The generic network replaces the market-segmenting brands of market-insulated companies, letting disintermediated buyers and sellers deal directly for the first time.

12.3.2   The sole-provider spectre

The network fits the modern, 'emergent' conception of markets in being purely a process, with no identifiable end. This feature also shields it from any administrative or relational attempts to co-ordinate the network or steer its outcome towards particular goals. It does not need such guidance in order to fulfil individuals' wishes, and any regulation attempts are likely to act against those wishes. For large and technologically complex economies, the network sums individual choices into compatible collective results without the logical contradictions of a centrally calculated 'social welfare function', and harnesses global action to local thought without the inefficiencies and iniquities of central planning.

Prospects for improving the collective outcome by empowering individuals' incentives and information use are equally strong for organisations within the digital economy. The 'networked firm' promises to combine the top-down directional strength of unitary structures with the base-up flexibility of decentralised divisions, without running into the overloaded reporting channels and constantly shifting responsibilities that befell earlier attempts at 'matrix' or 'lattice' organisation.

> Networks, in one form or another, offer an answer which encourages and develops the strength inherent in interdependence without encumbering the organisation with layers of coordinating management and procedures. The promise is for a means of rationalising the inherent contradictions of big companies trying to perform as nimbly as small companies while using their resources effectively.
>
> (Business International 1992: 20)

As with markets, explaining the virtues of networks tends to be easier than tracing their origins. General equilibrium has unrivalled outcome-efficiency properties, but lives beneath the shadow of perhaps needing an omniscient dictator or mythical auctioneer to bring it about. Similarly, networks may have unrivalled process-efficiency properties, but seem to need more than an invisible hand to set them in motion. Companies generally network themselves under central direction, as top management realises the error of its overarching ways and parcels out its mandate (wrapped in a microcomputer) to those closer to the ground. Agents in an economy have no such central agency to solve the initial co-ordination problems of entering the network (not worth doing unless others also enter), and ensuring the compatibility of channels feeding into it.

> The network must allow a wide range of different kinds of equipment to communicate with one another. This requires the definition and imposition of

common rules . . . this standard must be the same, even internationally, if smooth and efficient communications are to be possible in the future.

(Costello *et al*. 1989: 154–5)

Such interconnection does not have an immaculate conception. It has generally had to be imposed, either by governments or by early network builders who establish monopoly power. Our coaxial phone systems interconnect because governments built them, our cablephones and railways because governments franchised regional monopolies to build them, our cellphones because governments licensed them to a common standard, and our software because a single private firm has risen to dominate the market for operating systems.

Pro-marketeers point out that the communications revolution gained momentum after national telecoms networks had been privatised and deregulated. But the incentive to extend those networks has come from their continued monopoly power. The UK's former monopoly still held 90 per cent of the call market ten years after privatisation. Merger and acquisition among the US 'baby bells' had by 1998 created higher market concentration than before the old AT&T monopoly was broken up. The incentive to build rival networks has similarly been created by exclusive franchises and regulation – which, ironically, has meant restricting main providers' ability to cut prices and expand services, while their incipient rivals gain scale economies and capture market share.

The 1998 anti-trust challenges to Microsoft by the US Justice Department and rival software companies centred on the question of whether users gained more from the private imposition of standards on the network than they lost through the denial of choice in interconnection to, and information flows through, that network. Personal computers based on Microsoft operating systems by this time accounted for more than 80 per cent of the world's installed base of networked computers, and the company's share of new system sales had moved even higher. With America Online building on this standard to capture more than 60 per cent of the world's online services market, the world's long-distance telecoms operators forming 'strategic alliances' abroad as fast as their markets are deregulated at home, and large companies linking their 'intranets' into globe-spanning 'extranets' that internalise deals they currently make on the internet, it is not clear that today's 'public' networks will remain forever free of monopoly pricing and proprietary sequestration. Far from dissolving the role of the large corporation by reducing transaction costs, as the 'enhanced neoclassical' theory of the firm implies (section 8.2), new network technologies are vastly extending large firms' extra-corporate knowledge and leverage, a concession to the alternative theory stressing price-setting power (section 8.5).

Microsoft answered its monopoly charges by arguing that competition between hardware and software designers, their products directly substitutable because built to a common ('Wintel') standard, had dramatically cut the price of personal computing and extended its users' choice of program. Its opponents saw a potentially dangerous monopoly over the 'start-up' screen which Microsoft was using to extend its market power over other parts of the network. In particular, by making its search engine the default option on the operating system, and coding into it a specially adapted version of the supposedly universal 'Java' language, the company was suspected of seeking a monopoly on internet access. The relentless acquisition by Microsoft (and its billionaire co-founder William Gates III) of archives, artwork and copyright material that could form the network's future traffic added to the spectre of a single firm subverting the dream of an unowned, uncharged and undirected 'net'.

12.3.3 Flies in the worldwide web

Once in motion, the network arouses other fears which echo those surrounding the untrammelled market. Because it transcends individual control or understanding, we cannot be sure where the network is taking us, or whether the way it channels the flow of information and distributes its processing is in fact the most efficient. Digital gurus acknowledge a trade-off between optimality of process and optimality of product. 'We gladly trade the wasteful inefficiencies of multiple routing in order to keep the Internet's remarkable flexibility' (Kelly 1994: 31). Because agents and their messages are accorded equal worth, 'spam' fills the emailbox and urgent business calls must queue behind frivolous chat-lines. Although the ambition is to link everyone to everyone else, network efficiency may actually be slowed if too many lines are drawn. And because even the cheapest 'net' can reach only where computers exist and phone lines function, the cyber-world remains a subset of society which may leave the modem-less stranded on an information-superhighway sliproad, to the detriment of wired and non-wired alike.

Instant information brings temptation for instant gratification, and the danger that agents' efforts to optimise at every point in time will prevent adoption of strategies which improve the flow of benefits over time. To this lack of temporal co-ordination can be added a potential loss of spatial co-ordination, despite the network's apparent power to get everyone working in harmony. By dealing directly, agents avoid the transaction costs of dealing through an intermediary, but also give up the added benefits those intermediaries may have provided – such as risk absorption by marketmakers, order-aggregation and bulk-breaking by wholesalers, and the checking and interpretation of raw information by editors. By getting exactly what they want (even down to the pages of newspaper that interest them, and the video on demand) people lose the serendipitous discovery that may reveal new preferences, and the common cultural ground that holds societies together. Because network users are encouraged to inform their actions through the network, but not to worry about the effects of their actions on the network, there is no guarantee that interdepencies across space and time will be adequately taken into account. 'Within a virtual market the real world truly is irrelevant, and the invisible hand becomes a blind hand, with no reason to take account of how it affects other people, or future generations' (Mulgan 1997: 238).

Mulgan expresses a widely held misgiving about the impersonality of network transaction, through which agents can log on from anywhere in the world, send unsolicited messages to thousands of addresses simultaneously, or join in online 'chats' with pseudonymous others whose names and locations they will never know. But when network use turns from pleasure to business, and banknotes as well as bytes must be committed to a transaction, the network's weakness is in the opposite direction. Since it is so hard to be sure who we are dealing with, or whether anyone else is tapping in to the deal, considerable resources must be invested to ensure that commercial information transmitted is going to the right person, and only that person. As with low trust in the marketplace, low trust on the network is met by seeking strong relational ties before making value-added informational exchange.

The extensibility and interconnectability of networks fuzz the boundaries between firms, and tinge their market competition with elements of relational co-operation. The diagnosticians of this 'Co-opetition' place companies at the centre of a Value Net, within which counterpart firms may be 'complementors' who help expand the market as well as competitors who try to capture it, and customers and suppliers are served through specially strengthened channels. 'A player is your complementor if customers value your product more when they have the other party's product than when they have your product alone' (Nalebuff and Brandenburger 1996: 16).

To the extent that they override traditional industry boundaries, networks (as process and product) promote the kind of competition that makes market transactions efficient.

> As Microsoft and Citibank each work to solve the problem of how people will transact in the future – whether it be E-money, smart cards, on-line transfers or something else – they might end up being competitors . . . Phone companies and cable televison companies are both working to solve the problem of how people will communicate with each other and access information in the future. Again, different industries – telecommunications and cable television – but increasingly one market.
>
> (Nalebuff and Brandenburger 1996: 17)

Yet that one market will grow faster, and its pioneers will grow fatter, if they co-operate in setting standards and ensuring the recovery of early research and set-up costs.

> Between development costs and building a new fabrication plant, Intel will spend well over a billion dollars to develop the next-generation chip. Intel will be able to spread that cost among Compaq, Dell, and all the other hardware makers . . . As we continue moving into the information economy, supply-side complementarities will become increasingly the norm.
>
> (Nalebuff and Brandenburger 1996: 18–19)

The need to ensure that customers will buy the costly innovation – and that creditors will fund production for a market not yet established – makes for priority, two-way traffic between the most interdependent nodes of the network, before they can begin the wider, one-way selling process that ultimately generates their profit.

For some enthusiasts, this relational dimension is one of the network's strengths. Again a biological metaphor is popular, this time of the symbiotic relationship between organisms of very different size, power and interest, which even keeps free-riding under control by making parasites aware of their dependence on the host.

> Business consultants commonly warn their clients against becoming a sym-biont company dependent upon a single-customer-company, or single supplier. But many do, and as far as I can tell, live profitable lives . . . the surge of alliance-making in the 1990s among large corporations – particularly among those in the information and network industries – is another facet of an increasingly evolutionary economic world . . . Even though one side gains at the expense of the other, both sides gain over all.
>
> (Kelly 1994: 96–7)

But where both sides gain over all, it may be because they are driving through a mutually lucrative deal at others' expense. The trouble is, we may never know. Encrypted signals down dedicated lines can lead to a multiplicity of private prices, precisely the opposite of the open, transparent dealing the wired market was sup-posed to promote.

As friends cling together to avoid being swept away in a crowd, so netizens (i.e. members of the internet community) learn to shun 'spam' and treasure their online address books. Networks' vastness, interconnectedness, local-level anonymity and system-level unpredictability place a premium on special relations. Prioritised in this way, the network is just as powerful in promoting focused bilateral dealing as it is in letting lone cyber-voices address the worldwide audience. With elec-tronic data interchange, final transactions can switch from market to relational, as retailers take orders from clients before they place orders with suppliers, providing products made to specification instead of drawn from generalised stock. Intermediate transactions can switch from market to administered, as those in charge of the bespoke order-book co-ordinate the upstream production activity and grow with its flow. Far from completing the market, the network may well be about to usurp it, in favour of bilateral monopoly and price discrimination more widespread, and less open to anti-trust redress, than any experienced before the marketplace entered cyberspace.

It is undeniably tempting to believe that the invisible hand has binary digits, and revisualise Walras's auctioneer with Intel inside. But this is not the first time that computer and communication technology have been hailed as the saviours of a troubled transaction type. In the 1950s they were supposed to rescue administered transaction from the bureaucratic quagmire of the central plan. In the 1960s they were supposed to draw the warring communist and capitalist worlds into a 'global village' of relational transaction. The guru of the time, Marshall McLuhan, saw Technicolor, jetplanes and the other new media of the time as a fast track away from the household, national and cultural boundaries that groomed and grew from private self-interest. 'The aspiration of our time for wholeness, empathy and depth of awareness is a natural adjunct of electric technology. The age of mechanical industry that preceded us found vehement assertion of private outlook the natural mode of expression' (McLuhan 1962: 13).

McLuhan also famously observed that the form a new medium took could not be separated from the messages sent down it, and the way they were perceived. Economists' efforts to distinguish the 'natural monopoly' of the network from the competitiveness of its transactional traffic appear similarly doomed. Perfect information may be the ruin, not the rescue, of perfect competition. Agents empowered to compete via the network may equally well collude through it, and agents which manufacture the network may end up managing and monopolising it. Market failure cannot be easily turned into the market's successor. Net profits will be handsome, but there is no guarantee they will be earned the way the market model recommends.

12.4   Conclusion: a market's place is in the marketplace

This volume's title was more provocation than proof. Undeniably, central planning is no more. International trade and capital flows are rising. A semiconductor plant strike in South Korea can dent the share price of an assembler in South Dakota, and South Korea's financial crisis may sink a small bank half a world away. Governments from social-democratic and even communist traditions are now renouncing public ownership, surrendering monetary policy to central banks (having already lost exchange-rate policy to currency markets) and abandoning stabilisation through fiscal fine-tuning, in favour of cutting both expenditure and tax in the hope of private investment filling the gap. Ministers who once promised to do a better job than the market now claim credit for creating a market that can do them out of a job.

Yet governments still spend a large proportion of their national incomes directly, redistribute another large proportion, and regulate much of the private production and consumption that remain.

Even the market's triumphs to date must be regarded as provisional. The world has known equally free product and capital mobility before, and even freer labour movement – only to see protectionism and intervention return under the strains of production and employment collapse, inflation and unbalanced trade which the free play of market forces was, at best, powerless to avoid. Phases of rapid technical innovation, bringing sharp changes in domestic industrial structures and international labour division, have also come and gone. It takes only a few changes of head or heart at the ballot box to set present pro-market political adventures on a very different course.

As well as its many still unresolved failures, there are five ways in which markets can be undermined by their own success. The winning firms can become monopolies and upset efficient allocation. Growth can push savings ahead of investment and upset full employment. Faster growth in material output can bring forward the moment of society's reckoning with resources that are naturally or socially scarce. Full employment can push wages up ahead of productivity and squeeze the profits needed to fund the growth. Prolonged prosperity, as much as poverty and instability, can induce electorates to vote to regulate the market, even if its freedom can be credited with conjuring the comfort from which to do so. And where prosperity hurts the farms and firms that bring it about, there need be no shortage of lobbying pressure to stop the competition before more winners and losers emerge.

The 'Market Revolution' is an observation, not a recommendation. Although it set out to identify an economic basis for the current re-emergence of free markets as an organising principle, it has largely failed to produce a coherent account. This may reflect poor authorship, but a deeper problem arises from there being a number of competing interpretations of the market, often intermixed yet drawn from very different premises. The revolutionaries often expound North American theories in an Austrian accent with heavy appeal to a particular reading of Asian experience. This book has tried to show that, in identifying 'market' and 'government' as binary and mutually exclusive alternatives, what is presented as an extension of the market is often merely a change in the location of administered transaction (from state to firm), or an incursion against both administration and market of the intermediate flows of informed and relational transaction. These are frequently regarded, especially in economies now making the 'transition' from plan back to market, as inferior alternatives, established when trust is lacking, information deficient, or old-order privilege still a barrier to equality before the market. The account of non-market transaction types given here is more benign. In government or monolithic industry hands they may dictate or dissipate, but within modern commercial organisations they may combine the incentive to efficiency provided by the market with the means to efficiency which only co-ordination and consultation bring.

Concepts of globalisation and universal competition have given the superstate's retreat and the supermarket's advance an aura of inevitability. Macroeconomic policy options are certainly constrained in a world of mobile (and increasingly untaxable) capital, expectationally set exchange rates and an urge to keep incomes private which puts governments under equal pressure to turn production private. International economic integration adds to the pressures on wage setting and competitiveness already set in motion by rapid technical change, itself partly a consequence of rising market pressures. But before a previous favourite scenario of economic visionaries, the inevitability of planning and the convergence of economies on a social-democratic pattern, is dismissed as fundamentally misguided, it is worth asking who, even now, is – and wants to be – entirely at the disposal of supply and demand. Most employment is still with government institutions, or large organisations engaged in similar exercise of control over their internal and external environment. Most pay, even for the self-employed, is set by bargaining within a legal framework rather than open trading in a purely market framework. Much production takes place under similar regulatory restrictions, often strengthened rather than weakened by the privatisation of enterprises which were once nationalised for sound economic reasons, and by the growth of large private enterprise which has always been the market's path to destruction through its own success.

The signatures on global trade agreements are also on social, environmental and human rights charters which fit uncomfortably alongside them, and could easily provide the pretext for renewed disengagement. Trade theory has never denied that global gains can be unevenly spread, and the $500 billion boost to world production projected by GATT for the first ten years of its latest agreement is still small beside the dynamic consequences – positive and negative – it promises to set in train for different regions, nations and occupational groups within them. Where government power to shape the outcome remains, the power of lobbyists is never far behind, that of entrenched potential losers often overwhelming that of potential gainers still struggling for life against a less-than-perfect capital market. The perfect competition and information on which markets formally depend have never existed, and there is evidence that they would frustrate the operation of markets if they did exist. As with any trend whose practitioners get ahead of its theorists, perceptions of the market, the agents within it and the authorities that set its rules are all changing at least as rapidly as the economies and individuals affected by its return.

This book is presented in the hope that economics is also changing, in its view of the world and its relationship to other social sciences. At the high point of its model-building phase, the neoclassical method appeared to be all-conquering. Rational weighing of costs and benefits appeared a template for choice on any social situation – the general planning a small war as much as the shopper mulling milkshake flavours on the supermarket shelf. With enough repeats, game theory resolved the small number of small-numbers cases in which equilibrium required consistent guesses of what other players would do. Economists did indeed, like the cynics decried by Oscar Wilde's Lord Darlington, appear to know 'the price of everything, and the value of nothing' (Wilde 1892/1997: 375). Cecil Graham's rejoinder, that 'a sentimentalist . . . is a man who sees an absurd value in everything, and doesn't know the market price of any single thing', was of little consolation when rational choice theory sidestepped its distributional dilemmas (section 10.4.1) and empirical disconfirmations (section 5.2.5) by invoking precisely the interpersonally non-comparable values that sentimentality implies.

Now the magnitudes seem less measurable, their connections look less linear, and even in stylised tests people often fail to act as rational axioms say they should. Newer social research disciplines, struggling to match economists on the height of their received-theory constructions and the breadth of their consensus, have often proved more receptive to ideas from outside and better able to link them constructively. In looking beyond constrained optimisation to the context in which people receive information, the methods they bring to assessing it and the power of government and corporate structures to affect it, economics would be relinquishing a powerful monopoly. A richer understanding of the market process might, with luck, result.

References

Akerlof, G. (1970) 'The market for lemons: qualitative uncertainty and the price mechanism', *Quarterly Journal of Economics* 84: 488–500.

—— (1982) 'Labor contracts as partial gift exchange', *Quarterly Journal of Economics* 97: 543–70.

Akerlof, G. and Yellen, J. (1985) 'Can small deviations from rationality make significant differences to economic equilibrium?' *American Economic Review* 75: 708–20.

Alchian, A. and Demsetz, H. (1972) 'Production, information costs, and economic organisation', *American Economic Review* 62: 777–95.

Amis, M. (1985) *Money*, Harmondsworth: Penguin.

Anand, P. (1993) *Foundations of Rational Choice under Risk*, Oxford: Clarendon Press.

Ansoff, H. (1965) *Corporate Strategy*, New York: McGraw-Hill.

Aoki, M. (1988) *Information, Incentives and Bargaining in the Japanese Economy*, Cambridge: Cambridge University Press.

—— (1992) 'A bargaining game theoretic approach to the Japanese firm', in P. Sheard (ed.) (1992a).

Arrighi, G. (1994) *The Long Twentieth Century*, London: Verso.

—— (1997) 'Financial expansions in world historical perspective', *New Left Review* 224: 154–9.

Arrow, K. (1951) *Social Choice and Individual Values*, New Haven, CT: Yale University Press.

—— (1959) 'Towards a theory of price adjustment', in M. Abramovitz (ed.) (1959) *The Allocation of Economic Resources*, Stanford, CA: Stanford University Press.

Arrow, K. and Debreu, G. (1954) 'Existence of an equilibrium for a competitive economy', *Econometrica* 22: 265–90.

Arrow, K. and Hahn, F. (1971) *General Competitive Analysis*, San Francisco, CA: Holden-Day.

Asanuma, B. (1992) 'Japanese manufacturer–supplier relationships in international perspective: the automobile case', in P. Sheard (ed.) (1992a).

Atkinson, A. (1997) 'Bringing income distribution in from the cold', Royal Economic Society presidential address, *Economic Journal* 107(441): 297–321.

Auerbach, P. (1988) *Competition: The Economics of Industrial Change*, Oxford: Blackwell.

Averch, H. and Johnson, L. (1962) 'Behaviour of the firm under regulatory constraint', *American Economic Review* 52: 1052–69.

Axelrod, R. (1984) *The Origin of Co-operation*, New York: Basic Books.

Bacon, R. and Eltis, W. (1978) *Britain's Economic Problem: Too Few Producers*, London: Macmillan.

Baert, P. (1991) *Time, Self and Social Being*, Aldershot: Avebury.

Baily, M. (1989) 'Summary of the papers', *Brookings Papers on Economic Activity*, Microeconomics 1989: ix–xlix.

Baldwin, R. (1989) 'The growth effects of 1992', *Economic Policy: A European Forum* 9: 247–70.

Barber, W. (1967) *A History of Economic Thought*, Harmondsworth: Penguin.

Barro, R. (1974) 'Are government bonds net wealth?', *Journal of Political Economy* 82(6): 1095–118.

—— (1996) 'Determinants of economic growth: a cross-country empirical study', NBER Working Paper 5698, August.

Barry, N. (1989) 'Ideas and interests: the problem reconsidered', in Institute of Economic Affairs (1989).

Bartlett, W. and Le Grand, J. (1993) 'The theory of quasi-markets', in J. Le Grand and W. Bartlett (eds) (1993).

Barzel, Y. (1989) *Economic Analysis of Property Rights*, Cambridge: Cambridge University Press.

Batchelor, R. (1994) *Henry Ford – Mass Production, Modernism and Design*, Manchester: Manchester University Press.

Baumol, W. (1959) *Business Behaviour, Value and Growth*, New York: Macmillan.

Baumol, W. and Quandt, R. (1964) 'Rules of thumb and optimally imperfect decision', *American Economic Review* 54: 23–46.

Baumol, W., Panzar, J. and Willig, R. (1982) *Contestable Markets and the Theory of Industrial Structure*, New York: Harcourt Brace Jovanovich.

Baxter, J. (1988) *Social and Psychological Foundations of Economic Analysis*, Hemel Hempstead: Harvester-Wheatsheaf.

Benassy, J.-P. (1989) 'Disequilibrium analysis', in J. Eatwell *et al.* (eds) (1989a).

Berle, A. and Means, G. (1932) *The Modern Corporation and Private Property*, New York: Commerce Clearing House.

Best, M. (1986) 'Strategic planning, the new competition and industrial policy', in P. Nolan and S. Paine (eds) (1986).

Beveridge, W. (1942) *Social Insurance and Allied Services*, The Beveridge Report, Cmd 6404, London: HMSO, reprinted (1944) *Full Employment in a Free Society*, London: Allen & Unwin.

Bhagwati, J. (1982) 'Directly unproductive, profit-seeking activities', *Journal of Political Economy* 90(5): 988–1002.

Bishop, M. and Thompson, D. (1994) 'Privatization in the UK: international organization and productive efficiency', in M. Bishop *et al.* (eds) (1994).

Bishop, M., Kay, J. and Mayer, C. (eds) (1994) *Privatization and Economic Performance*, Oxford: Oxford University Press.

Bisignano, J. (1991) 'Corporate control and financial information', in R. O'Brien (ed.) (1991).

Blanchard, O. (1985) 'Monopolistic competition, small menu costs and real effects of nominal money', mimeo.

Boland, L. (1992) *The Principles of Economics*, London: Routledge.

Bowles, S. (1985) 'The production process in a competitive economy', *American Economic Review* 75(1): 16.

Braverman, H. (1974) *Labour and Monopoly Capital*, New York: Monthly Review Press.

Britton, A. (1986) *The Trade Cycle in Britain 1958–1982*, Cambridge: Cambridge University Press.

Brown, R. and Julius, D. (1993) 'Is manufacturing still special in the New World Order?' in R. O'Brien (ed.) (1993).

Buckley, P. and Michie, J. (eds) (1996) *Firms, Organisations and Contracts*, Oxford: Oxford University Press.

Burnham, J. (1945) *The Managerial Revolution*, Harmondsworth: Penguin.

Burns, T. and Stalker, G. (1961) *The Management of Innovation*, London: Tavistock.

Business International (1992) *The Management Network Revolution*, Research Report M147, with Boston Consulting Group. London: Business International.

Cairncross, F. (1995) *Green, Inc*, London: Earthscan.

Caporaso, J. and Levine, D. (1992) *Theories of Political Economy*, Cambridge: Cambridge University Press.

Carter, A. (1989) *The Philosophical Foundations of Property Rights*, Hemel Hempstead: Wheatsheaf.

Casson, M. (1987) 'Multinational firms', in R. Clarke and T. McGuinness (eds) *The Economics of the Firm*, Oxford: Blackwell.

Caves, R. (1982) *Multinational Enterprise and Economic Analysis*, Cambridge: Cambridge University Press.

—— (1987) *American Industry: Structure, Conduct, Performance*, Englewood Cliffs, NJ: Prentice-Hall.

Cecchini, P. (1988) *The European Challenge of 1992*, Aldershot: Wildwood House.

Chadeau, A. (1992) 'What is households' non-market production worth?', *OECD Economic Studies* 18: 85–104.

Chakravorti, C. (1998) 'Demi-monde of progress in IT', *Financial Times* 28 May.

Chandler, A. (1962) *Strategy and Structure: Chapters in the History of Industrial Enterprise*, Cambridge, MA: MIT Press.

—— (1977) *The Visible Hand*, extract in L. Putterman (ed.) (1986).

Charles, D. (1996) 'Information technology and production systems', in P. Daniels and W. Lever (eds) (1996).

Chomsky, N. (1975) *Reflections on Language*, New York: Pantheon.

Clower, R. (1965) 'The Keynesian counter-revolution: a theoretical appraisal', in F. Hahn and F. Brechling (eds) (1965) *The Theory of Interest Rates*, New York: Macmillan.

Coase, R. (1937) 'The nature of the firm', *Economica* 4: 386–405, in L. Putterman (ed.) (1986).

—— (1960) 'The problem of social cost', *Journal of Law and Economics* 3: 1–30.

Cohen, M. and Axelrod, R. (1984) 'Coping with complexity', *American Economic Review* 74(1): 30–42.

Coleman, J. (1992) *Risks and Wrongs*, Cambridge: Cambridge University Press.

Coombes, R., Saviotti, P. and Walsh, V. (1987) *Economics and Technological Change*, London: Macmillan.

Costello, N., Michie, J. and Milne, S. (1989) *Beyond the Casino Economy*, London: Verso.

Cowling, K. (1982) *Monopoly Capitalism*, London: Macmillan.

—— (1992) 'Monopoly capitalism revisited', in A. del Monte (ed.) (1992).

Crawford, M. (1997) 'The big pensions lie', *New Economy* 4(1): 38–44.

Crosland, A. (1956) *The Future of Socialism*, London: Jonathan Cape.

Cross, J. (1983) *A Theory of Adaptive Economic Behaviour*, Cambridge: Cambridge University Press.

Cyert, R. and March, J. (1963) *A Behavioural Theory of the Firm*, Englewood Cliffs, NJ: Prentice-Hall.

Daniels, P. and Lever, W. (eds) (1996) *The Global Economy in Transition*, Harlow: Addison Wesley Longman.

Dasgupta, P. (1992) 'Nutrition, non-convexities and redistributive policies', in J. Hey (ed.) (1992).

Dasgupta, P. and Heal, G. (1979) *The Economics of Exhaustible Resources*, Cambridge: Cambridge University Press.

Dawkins, R. (1989) *The Selfish Gene*, 2nd edn, Oxford: Oxford University Press.

Del Monte, A. (ed.) (1992) *Recent Developments in the Theory of Industrial Organisation*, London: Macmillan.

Denison, E. and Chung, W. (1976) 'Economic growth and its sources', in H. Patrick and H. Rosovsky (eds) (1976) *Asia's New Giant*. Washington, DC: Brookings Institute.

Dobb, M. (1973) *Theories of Value and Distribution since Adam Smith*, Cambridge: Cambridge University Press.

Dodgson, M. (1993) *Technological Collaboration in Industry*, London: Routledge.

Domar, E. (1947) 'Expansion and employment', *American Economic Review* 37: 34–55.

Domberger, S. and Piggott, S. (1994) Chapter in M. Bishop, J. Kay and C. Mayer (eds) (1994) *Privatisation: An Economic Analysis*, Oxford: Oxford University Press.

Dore, R. (1996) 'Goodwill and market capitalism', in P. Buckley and J. Michie (eds) (1996).

Dornbusch, R. (1976) 'Expectations and exchange rate dynamics', *Journal of Political Economy* 84(6): 1161–76.

Downs, A. (1957) *An Economic Theory of Democracy*, New York: Harper & Row.

Doz, Y. and Prahalad, C. (1993) 'Managing DMNCs: a search for a new paradigm', in S. Ghoshal and D. Westney (eds) (1993).

Dunn, L. and Maddala, G. (1996) 'Extracting economic information from data: methodology in an empirical discipline,' in S. Medema and W. Samuels (eds) (1996) *Foundations of Research in Economics*, Cheltenham: Edward Elgar.

Durkheim, E. (1964) *The Division of Labour in Society*, New York: Free Press.

Eatwell, J. and Milgate, M. (eds) (1983a) *Keynes's Economics and the Theory of Value and Distribution*, London: Duckworth.

—— (1983b) 'Introduction', in J. Eatwell, and M. Milgate (eds) (1983).

Eatwell, J., Milgate, M. and Newman, P. (eds) (1989a) *The New Palgrave: General Equilibrium*, London: Macmillan.

Eatwell, J., Milgate, M. and Newman, P. (eds) (1989b) *The New Palgrave: Economic Development*, London: Macmillan.

Edgeworth, F. (1881) *Mathematical Psychics: An Essay on the Application of Mathematics to the Moral Sciences*, London: Routledge & Kegan Paul.

Egelhoff, W. (1993) 'Information processing theory and the multinational corporation', in S. Ghoshal and D. Westney (eds) (1993).

Ellerman, D. (1992) *Property and Contract in Economics*, Oxford: Blackwell.

Elster, J. (1980) *Ulysses and the Sirens*, Cambridge: Cambridge University Press.

Emerson, M. (1988) *The Economics of 1992*, Cambridge: Cambridge University Press.

Emmanuel, A. (1972) *Unequal Exchange: A Study of the Imperialism of Trade*, New York: Monthly Review Press.

—— (1982) *Appropriate or Underdeveloped Technology?*, Paris: Wiley.

Erikson, R. and Goldthorpe, J. (1993) *The Constant Flux*, Oxford: Blackwell.

Etzioni, A. (1995) *The Spirit of Community*, London: Fontana.

European Bank for Reconstruction and Development (EBRD) (1996) *Transition Report 1996*, London: EBRD.

Feldman, G. (1964) 'On the theory of growth rates of national income', in N. Spulber (ed.) *Foundations of Soviet Strategy for Economic Growth*, Bloomington, IN: Indiana University Press.

Feldstein, M. (1997) *Privatising Social Security: The $10bn Opportunity*, Washington, DC: Cato Institute.

Fine, B. and Murfin, A. (1984) *Macroeconomics and Monopoly Capitalism*, Brighton: Wheatsheaf.

Fischer, C., Jackson, R., Stueve, C., Gerson, K. and Jones, L. (1977) *Networks and Places: Social Relations in the Urban Setting*, New York: Free Press.

Fischer, S. (1998) Speech to World Bank Annual Board Conference on Developing Economies, 20 April, http://www.worldbank.org.

Fransman, M. (1990) *Cooperation and Competition in Information Technology in the Japanese System*, Cambridge: Cambridge University Press.

Friedman, M. (1953) *Essays in Positive Economics*. Chicago, IL: Chicago University Press.

—— (1957) *A Theory of the Consumption Function*, Princeton, NJ: Princeton University Press.

Frydman, R. (1982) 'Towards an understanding of market processes', *American Economic Review* 72(4): 652–68.

Fukuyama, F. (1995) *Trust: The Social Virtues and the Creation of Prosperity*, New York: Free Press.

Galbraith, J. (1952) *American Capitalism: The Concept of Countervailing Power*, Boston, MA: Houghton Mifflin.

—— (1958) *The Affluent Society*, Boston, MA: Houghton Mifflin.

—— (1967) *The New Industrial State*, London: Hamish Hamilton.

—— (1974) *Economics and the Public Purpose*, London: Andre Deutsch.

—— (1992) *The Culture of Contentment*, London: Sinclair-Stevenson.

Garegnani, P. (1983) 'Notes on consumption, investment and effective demand', in J. Eatwell and M. Milgate (eds) (1983).

Gates, W. (1995) *The Road Ahead*, London & New York: Viking.

Geanakoplos, J. (1989) 'Arrow-Debreu model of general equilibrium', in J. Eatwell *et al.* (eds) (1989a).

Geroski, P. and Machin, S. (1992) 'Do innovating forms outperform non-innovators?' *Business Strategy Review* summer: 79–90.

Ghoshal, S. and Westney, D. (eds) (1993) *Organization Theory and the Multinational Corporation*, New York: St Martin's Press.

Giner, S. (1976) *Mass Society*, London: Martin Robertson.

Godley, W. and Cripps, F. (1983) *Macroeconomics*, London: Fontana.

Goldthorpe, J. and Hirsch, F. (eds) (1978) *The Political Economy of Inflation*, London: Martin Robertson.

Gould, S. (1996) *Life's Grandeur*, London: Jonathan Cape (published in the USA as *Full House*).

Grandmont, J. (1985) 'Endogenius competitive business cycles', *Econometrica* 53(5): 995–1046.

Granovetter, M. (1985) 'Economic action and social structure: the problem of embeddedness', *American Journal of Sociology* 91(3): 487–510.

Griffin, K. (1987) *World Hunger and the World Economy*, London: Macmillan.

Habermas, J. (1976) *Legitimation Crisis*, trans. Thomas McCarthy, London: Heinemann.

—— (1982) *Legitimation Crisis*, Baltimore, MD: Beacon Press.

Hagedoorn, J. and Schakenraad, J. (1993) 'Strategic technology partnering and international cooperation strategies', in K. Hughes (ed.) *European Competitiveness*, Cambridge: Cambridge University Press.

Hahn, F. (1989) 'Conjectural equilibria', in J. Eatwell *et al.* (eds) (1989a).

Hall, R. and Hitch, C. (1939) 'Price theory and business behaviour', *Oxford Economic Papers* 28: 240–57.

Haltiwanger, J. and Waldman, M. (1989) 'Limited rationality and strategic complementarity: the implications for macroeconomics', *Quarterly Journal of Economics* 104: 463–83.

—— (1990) 'Responders and nonresponders: a new perspective on heterogeneity', mimeo.

Hampden-Turner, C. and Trompenaars, F. (1993) *The Seven Cultures of Capitalism*, New York: Doubleday.

Harcourt, G. (1972) *Some Cambridge Controversies in the Theory of Capital*, Cambridge: Cambridge University Press.

Harcourt, G. and Kenyon, P. (1976) 'Pricing and the investment decision', *Kyklos* 29: 449–77.

Hardin, G. (1968) 'The tragedy of the commons', *Science* 162 December: 1243–8.

Harrod, R. (1939) 'An essay in dynamic theory', *Economic Journal* 49(193): 14–33.

Hart, O. (1996) 'An economist's perspective on the theory of the firm', in P. Buckley and J. Michie (eds) (1996).

Hart, P. (1992) *Corporate Governance in Britain and Germany*, Discussion Paper 31, London: National Institute of Economic and Social Research.

Hausman, D. (1992) *The Inexact and Separate Science of Economics*, Cambridge: Cambridge University Press.

Hayek, F. (1944) *The Road to Serfdom*, London: Routledge & Kegan Paul.

—— (1949) *Individualism and Economic Order*, London: Routledge & Kegan Paul.

Heilbroner, R. (1976) *Business Civilisation in Decline*, London: Marion Boyars.

Heiner, R. (1983) 'The origins of predictable behaviour', *American Economic Review* 73: 560–95.

Henderson, D. (1986) *Innocence and Design*, Oxford: Blackwell.

Hennart, F. (1993) 'Control in multinational firms: the role of price and hierarchy', in S. Ghoshal and D. Westney (eds) (1993).

Henning Sieverts, S. (1996) *No Pain, No Gain: Lessons from US Healthcare*. Briefing no. 5, London: Fabian Society.

Hey, J. (ed.) (1992) *The Future of Economics*, Oxford: Blackwell.

Hicks, J. (1937) 'Mr Keynes and the classics: a suggested interpretation', *Econometrica* 5: 147–59.

—— (1939) *Value and Capital*, Oxford: Oxford University Press.

Hirsch, F. (1976) *Social Limits to Growth*, London: Routledge & Kegan Paul.

Hirschman, A. (1958) *The Strategy of Economic Development*, New Haven, CT: Yale University Press.

—— (1962) *Exit, Voice and Loyalty*, Cambridge, MA: Harvard University Press.

—— (1982) 'Rival interpretations of market society: civilizing, destructive or feeble?' *Journal of Economic Literature* 20: 1463–84.

—— (1989) 'Linkages', in Eatwell *et al.* (1989b).

Hobbes, T. (1651/1968) *Leviathan*, ed. C. MacPherson, Harmondsworth: Penguin.

Hobhouse, L. (1911) *Liberalism*, London: Williams & Norgate.

Hobsbawm, E. (1962/1977) *The Age of Revolution*, London: Abacus.

Holzmann, R. (1997) 'Pension reform, financial market development and economic growth: preliminary evidence from Chile', *IMF Staff Papers* 44(2) June.

House, B., Drysdale, P. and Vines, D. (1997) *Europe and East Asia: A Shared Trade Agenda?*, Global Economic Institutions Newsletter 5, Oxford: Institute of Economics and Statistics.

Hu, Y.-S. (1992) 'Global or stateless corporations are national firms with international operations', *California Management Review* 34(2): 107–26.

Hutton, W. (1996) *The State We're In*, London: Vintage.

Hymer, S. (1960/1976) *The International Operations of National Firms*, Cambridge, MA: MIT Press.

Imai, K. and Hoyuki, I. (1996) 'Interpenetration of organisation and market: Japan's firm and market in comparison with the US', in P. Buckley and J. Michie (eds) (1996).

Institute of Economic Affairs (IEA) (1989) *Ideas, Interests and Consequences*, London: IEA.

Irwin, D. and Klenow, P. (1994) 'Learning-by-doing spillovers in the semiconductor industry', *Journal of Political Economy* 102(6): 1200–27.

Ito, T. (1997) 'What can developing countries learn from East Asia's economic growth?', in B. Pleskovic and J. Stiglitz (eds) (1997) *Annual Bank Conference on Development Economics*, Washington, DC: World Bank, 183–200.

Itoh, M. (1992) 'Organisational transactions and access to the Japanese import market', in P. Sheard (ed.) (1992a).

Jepma, C., Jager, H. and Kamphuis, E. (1996) *Introduction to International Economics*, London: Longman/Netherlands Open University.

Jevons, S. (1871) *The Theory of Political Economy*, Harmondsworth: Penguin.

Johansen, L. (1991) *An Introduction to Modern Welfare Economics*, Cambridge: Cambridge University Press.

Jones, H. (1975) *An Introduction to Modern Theories of Economic Growth*, London: Nelson.

Kahneman, D. and Tversky, A. (1972) 'Subjective probability: a judgment of representative', *Cognitive Psychology* 3, 430–54.

—— (1974) 'Judgment under uncertainty', *Science* 185: 1124–31.

—— (1979) 'Prospect theory: an analysis of decisionmaking under risk', *Econometrica* 47: 263–91.

Kaldor, N. (1958) 'Capital accumulation and economic growth', paper prepared for International Economic Association meeting, reprinted in F. Lutz (ed.) (1961) *The Theory of Capital*, London: Macmillan, and in N. Kaldor (1978).

—— (1962) 'A new model of economic growth', *Review of Economic Studies* 29(3), reprinted in N. Kaldor (1978).

—— (1966) 'Marginal productivity and the macroeconomic theories of distribution', *Review of Economic Studies* 33(4), reprinted in N. Kaldor (1978).

—— (1972) 'The irrelevance of equilibrium economics', *Economic Journal* 82, reprinted in N. Kaldor (1978).

—— (1978) *Further Essays on Economic Theory*, London: Duckworth.

Kalecki, M. (1966) *Studies in the Theory of the Business Cycle, 1933–39*, Oxford: Blackwell.

Kamenka, E. (ed.) (1983) *The Portable Karl Marx*, Harmondsworth: Penguin.

Kay, J. (1997) 'Shareholders aren't everything', interview in *Fortune*, 17 February.

Kay, N. (1992) 'Collaborative strategies of firms: theory and evidence', in A. del Monte (ed.) (1992).

Kekic, L. (1988) 'Policy and long-term growth', *Global Outlook* 3rd Quarter 1998, London: Economist Intelligence Unit.

Kelly, K. (1994) *Out of Control: The New Biology of Machines*, New York: Addison-Wesley.

Keynes, J. (1936) *The General Theory of Employment, Interest and Money*, London: Macmillan.

Kirzner, I. (1979) *Perception, Opportunity and Profit*, Chicago, IL: University of Chicago Press.

Klapwijk, P. (1996) *Global Economic Networks*, Amsterdam: Klapwijk Holding.

Klein, B. (1988) 'Luck, necessity and dynamic flexibility', in H. Hanusch (ed.) *Evolutionary Economics*, Cambridge: Cambridge University Press.

Kogut, B. (1993) 'Learning, or the importance of being inert: country imprinting and international competition', in S. Ghoshal and D. Westney (eds) (1993).

Krugman, P. (1990) *Rethinking International Trade*, Cambridge, MA: MIT Press.

—— (1994) 'The myth of Asia's miracle', *Foreign Affairs* 73(6): 62–78.

Kydland, F. and Prescott, E. (1977) 'Rules rather than discretion: the inconsistency of optimal plans', *Journal of Political Economy* 85(3): 473–92.

Lane, C. (1992) 'European business systems: Britain and Germany compared', in R. Whitley (ed.) (1992).

Lange, O. (1936) 'On the economic theory of socialism', *Review of Economics and Statistics* 4: 53–71 and 123–42.

Langlois, R. (ed.) (1986) *Economics as a Process*, Cambridge: Cambridge University Press.

Lawson, T. (1985) 'Uncertainty and economic analysis', *Economic Journal* 95(386): 909–17.

Layard, R. and Nickell, S. (1985) 'The causes of British unemployment', *National Institute Economic Review* 111: 62–85.

Le Grand, J. (1982) *The Strategy of Inequality*, London: Allen & Unwin.

Le Grand, J. and Bartlett, W. (eds) (1993a) *Quasi-Markets and Social Policy*, London: Macmillan.

—— (1993b) 'The theory of quasi-markets', in J. le Grand and W. Bartlett (eds) (1993a).

Leibenstein, H. (1976) *Beyond Economic Man*, Cambridge, MA: Harvard University Press.

Leijonhufvud, A. (1986) 'Capitalism and the factory system' in Langlois, R. (ed.) (1986).

Leontief, W. (1953) 'Domestic production and foreign trade: the American capital position re-examined', *Proceedings of the American Philosophical Society* 97: 332.

—— (1956) 'Factor proportions and the structure of American trade: further theoretica and empirical analysis', *Review of Economics and Statistics* 38(4): 386–407.

Leyshon, A. (1996) 'Dissolving difference? Money, disembedding and the creation of "global financial space"', in P. Daniels and W. Lever (eds) (1996).

Lichtenstein, S. and Slovic, P. (1971) 'Reversals of preference between bids and choices in gambling decision', *Journal of Experimental Psychology* 89: 46–55.

Lincoln, E. (1998) 'The "big bang"? An ambivalent Japan deregulates its financial markets', *Brookings Review* winter.

Lindbeck, A. and Snower, D. (1985) *The Insider–Outsider Theory of Unemployment*.

—— (1986) 'Wage setting, unemployment and insider–outsider relationships', *American Economic Review* 76: 23–50.

Lipsey, R. and Lancaster, K. (1957) 'The general theory of second best', *Review of Economic Studies* 24: 11–32.

Little, I. and Mirrlees, J. (1968) *Manual of Industrial Project Analysis in Developing Economies*, vol. 2, Paris: OECD.

Loomes, G. and Sugden, G. (1982) 'Regret theory: an alternative theory of rational choice under uncertainty', *Economic Journal* 92: 805–24.

Luard, E. (1983) *The Management of the World Economy*, London: Macmillan.

McKenzie, C. (1992) 'Stable shareholders and the role of Japanese insurance companies', in P. Sheard (ed.) (1992a).

McKenzie, L. (1954) 'On equilibrium in Graham's model of world trade and other competitive systems', *Econometrica* 22: 147–61.

McLuhan, M. (1962) *Understanding Media*, London: Sphere.

Madden, P. (1989) 'General equilibrium and disequilibrium and the microeconomic foundations of macroeconomics', in J. Hey (1989) *Current Issues in Microeconomics*, London: Macmillan.

Mahalanobis, P. (1953) 'Some obervations on the process of growth of national income', *Sankhya* 12: 307–12.

Malthus, T. (1821) *Principles of Political Economy*, Boston, MA: Wells & Lilly.

Mandel, E. (1978) *Late Capitalism*, London: Verso.

Mankiw, G. (1995) 'The growth of nations', *Brookings Papers on Economic Activity* 1: 275–310.

March, J. and Simon, H. (1958) *Organisations*, New York: Wiley.

Marglin, S. (1974) 'What do bosses do? Origins and functions of hierarchy in capitalist production', *Review of Radical Political Economics* 6: 60–112.

—— (1984) 'Growth, distribution and inflation: a centennial analysis', *Cambridge Journal of Economics* 8(2): 115–44.

Markandya, A. (1991) 'Global warming: the economics of tradable permits', in D. Pearce *et al.* (1991).

Marris, R. (1964) *The Economic Theory of Managerial Capitalism*, London: Macmillan.

Marsden, D. (1995) *Management Practices and Unemployment, Centre for Economic Performance* Discussion Paper 241, London School of Economics.

Marshall, A. (1961) *The Principles of Economics*, vol. 1, 9th edn, London: Macmillan.

Martel, L. (1988) *Mastering Change*, London: Grafton.

Marx, K. (1867/1983) *Capital*, vol. 1, reprinted in E. Kamenka (ed.) (1983).

—— (1871/1983) *The Civil War in France*, first draft, reprinted in E. Kamenka (ed.) (1983).

Marx, K. and Engels, F. (1845/1947) *The German Ideology*, vol. 1, New York: International Publishers.

—— (1848/1996) *The Communist Manifesto*, London: Pheonix.

Masson, R. and Shaanan, J. (1982) 'Stochastic-dynamic limiting pricing: an empirical test', *Review of Economics and Statistics* 64: 413–22.

Maturana, H. and Varela, F. (1980) *Autopoiesis and Cognition*, London: Reidl.

Mayes, D. (ed.) (1991) *The European Challenge*, London: Harvester-Wheatsheaf.

Mayes, D. and Hart, P. (1994) *The Single Market as a Stimulus to Change*, Cambridge: Cambridge University Press.

Medvedev, R. (1977) *On Socialist Democracy*, Nottingham: Spokesman.

Melnyk, A. (1989) 'On ideas and interests', in Institute of Economic Affairs (1989).

Millward, N. (1982) 'The comparative performance of public and private ownership', in E. Roll (ed.) *The Mixed Economy*, London: Macmillan.

Minns, R. (1996) 'The ownership of capital', *New Left Review* 219: 42–61.

Minsky, H. (1986) *Stabilizing an Unstable Economy*, New Haven, CT: Yale University Press.

von Mises, L. (1949) *Human Action*, New Haven, CT: Yale University Press.

Mishan, E. (1982) *Introduction to Political Economy*, London: Hutchinson.

Monk, P. (1989) *Technological Change in the Information Economy*, London: Frances Pinter.

Morgan, G. (1986) *Images of Organization*, New York: Sage.

Morishima, M. (1992) 'General equilibrium theory in the 21st century', in J. Hey (ed.) (1992).

Moss, S. (1982) *An Economic Theory of Business Enterprise*, Oxford: Martin Robertson.

Mulgan, G. (1997) *Connexity: How to Live in an Interconnected World*, London: Chatto & Windus.

Murphy, K., Shleifer, A. and Vishny, R. (1989) 'Industrialisation and the Big Push', *Journal of Political Economy* 97(5), 1003–26.

Naisbitt, J. and Aburdene, P. (1985) *Reinventing the Corporation*, London: Futura.

Nalebuff, B. and Brandenburger, A. (1996) *Co-opetition*, London: HarperCollins.

Nelson, R. and Winter, S. (1974) 'Neoclassical v evolutionary theory of economic growth: critique and prospectus', *Economic Journal* 84: 886–905.

—— (1977) 'Simulation of Schumpeterian competition', *American Economic Review, Papers and Proceedings* 67(1): 271–6.

—— (1982) *An Evolutionary Theory of Economic Change*, Cambridge, MA: Harvard University Press.

Niskanen, W. (1971) *Bureaucracy and Representative Government*, Chicago, IL: Aldine Press.

Noble, D. (1979) 'Social choice in machine design: the case of automatically controlled machine tools', in A. Zimbalist (1979) *Case Studies in the Labour Process*, New York: Monthly Review Press.

Nolan, P. and Paine, S. (eds) (1986) *Rethinking Socialist Economics: A New Agenda for Britain*, Cambridge: Polity Press.

North, D. (1990) *Institutions, Institutional Change and Economic Peformance*, Cambridge: Cambridge University Press.

Norton, R. (1997) 'George Soros: billionaire, genius, fool', *Fortune* 17 March.

Nozick, R. (1974) *Anarchy, State and Utopia*, New York: Basic Books.

Nuti, M. (1986) 'Economic planning in market economies', in P. Nolan and S. Paine (eds) (1986).

O'Brien, R. (ed.) (1991) *Finance and the International Economy 5*, Oxford: Oxford University Press/Amex Bank.

—— (1992) *Global Financial Integration: The End of Geography*, London: Pinter/Royal Institute for International Affairs.

—— (ed.) (1993) *Finance and the International Economy 7*, Oxford: Oxford University Press/Amex Bank.

Olson, M. (1965) *The Logic of Collecctive Action*, Cambridge, MA: Harvard University Press.

—— (1982) *The Rise and Decline of Nations*, New Haven, CT: Yale University Press.

Ormerod, P. (1995) *The Death of Economics*, London: Faber.

Orwell, G. (1949) *Nineteen Eighty-Four*, London: Secker & Warburg.

Ostrom, E. (1982) *Governing the Commons*, Cambridge: Cambridge University Press.

Ostroy, J. (1989) 'Money in general equilibrium theory', in J. Eatwell *et al.* (eds) (1989a).

Oules, F. (1966) *Economic Planning and Democracy*, Harmondsworth: Penguin.

Palma, J. (1989) 'Prebisch, Raul', in J. Eatwell *et al.* (eds) (1989b).

Pareto, V. (1909/1971) *Manual of Political Economy*, New York: A. M. Kelley.

Parfit, D. (1987) *Reasons and Persons*, Oxford: Oxford University Press.

Pascale, R. (1990) *Managing on the Edge*, New York: Simon & Schuster.

Pasinetti, L. (1962) 'Rate of profit and income distribution in relation to the rate of economic growth', *Review of Economic Studies* 29: 267–79.

Patinkin, D. (1965) *Money, Interest and Prices*, 2nd edn, New York: Harper & Row.

Peacock, A. (1979) *The Economic Analysis of Government*. Oxford: Martin Robertson.

Pearce, D. (1991) 'The global commons', in D. Pearce *et al.* (1991).

Pearce, D., Barbier, E., Makandya, A., Barrett, S., Turner, R. and Swanson, T. (1991) *Blueprint 2: Greening the World Economy*, London: Earthscan.

Peltzman, S. (1989) 'The economic theory of regulation after a decade of deregulation', *Brookings Papers on Economic Activity, Microeconomics* 1–41.

Penrose, E. (1959) *The Theory of the Growth of the Firm*, Oxford: Blackwell.

Perkin, H. (1996) *The Third Revolution: Professional Elites in the Modern World*, London: Routledge.

Perlitz, M. and Seger, F. (1995) 'When banks and business make bad bedfellows', *Wall Street Journal Europe* 4 April.

Perraudin, W. and Pujol, T. (1994) 'A framework for analysis of pension and unemployment benefit reform in Poland', *IMF Staff Papers* 41(4): 634–74.

Perrow, C. (1981) 'Markets, hierarchies and hegemony', in A. van de Ven and W. Joyce (eds) *Perspectives on Organisation Design and Behaviour*, New York: Wiley.

Phelps, E. (1994) *Structural Slumps*, Cambridge, MA: Harvard University Press.

Phelps Brown, H. (1977) *The Inequality of Pay* Oxford: Clarendon Press.

Pinker, S. (1997) *How the Mind Works*, New York: Norton.

Plaut, S. (1985) *The Joy of Capitalism*, London: Longman.

Plender, J. (1997) *A Stake in the Future*, London: Nicholas Brealey.

Pool, R. (1997) *Beyond Engineering: How Society Shapes Technology*, Oxford: Oxford University Press.

Popper, K. (1962) *The Open Society and Its Enemies*, 4th edn, London: Routledge & Kegan Paul.

—— (1969) *Conjectures and Refutations*, 3rd edn, London: Routledge & Kegan Paul.

Porter, M. (1990) *The Competitive Advantage of Nations*, London: Macmillan.

Prebisch, R. (1949) *The Economic Development of Latin America and its Principal Problems*, Economic Commission for Latin America, New York: United Nations.

Propper, C. (1993) 'Quasi-markets, contracts and quality in health and social care: the US experience', in J. le Grand and W. Bartlett (eds) (1993).

Pryke, R. (1981) *The Nationalised Industries: Policies and Performance since 1968*, Oxford: Martin Robertson.

Przeworski, A. (1985) *Capitalism and Social Democracy*, Cambridge: Cambridge University Press.

Putterman, L. (ed.) (1986) *The Economic Nature of the Firm*, Cambridge: Cambridge University Press.

Radelet, S. and Sachs, J. (1998) 'The onset of the East Asian financial crisis', mimeo, Harvard Institute for International Development, Cambridge, MA.

Radner, R. (1968) 'Competitive equilibrium under uncertainty', *Econometrica* 36: 31–58.

—— (1989) 'Uncertainty and general equilibrium', in J. Eatwell *et al.* (eds) (1989a).

Rawls, J. (1971) *A Theory of Justice*, Cambridge, MA: Harvard University Press.

Reading, B. (1992) *Japan: The Coming Collapse*, London: Orion.

Reich, R. (1993) *The Work of Nations*, New York: Basic Books.

Rhoads, S. (1985) *The Economist's View of the World*, Cambridge: Cambridge University Press.

Ricardo, D. (1817/1953) *Principles of Political Economy and Taxation*, ed. P. Sraffa, Cambridge: Cambridge University Press.

Richardson, G. (1960) *Information and Investment*, Oxford: Oxford University Press.

Ricketts, M. (1987) *The Economics of Business Enterprise*, Brighton: Wheatsheaf.

Ridley, M.M. (1996) *The Origins of Virtue*, London: Viking.

Robinson, J. (1962) *Economic Philosophy*, London: D.C. Watts.

—— (1971) *Economic Heresies*, New York: Basic Books.

—— (1979) *Aspects of Development and Underdevelopment*, Cambridge: Cambridge University Press.

Rodrik, D. (1994) 'King Kong meets Godzilla: the World Bank and "The East Asian Miracle"', Centre for Economic Policy Research (CEPR) Discussion Paper 944, April, London: CEPR.

—— (1997) 'Total factor productivity growth controversies, institutions and economic performance in East Asia', National Bureau of Economic Research (NBER) Working Paper 5914, Cambridge, MA: NBER.

—— (1998) 'Who needs capital account convertibility?', Princeton Essays in International Finance 207, Princeton, NJ: Princeton University.

Roemer, J. (1988) *Free to Lose*, London: Radius.

Rosenberg, N. (1976) 'On technological expectations', *Economic Journal* 86: 523–35.

Rosenstein-Rodan, P. (1934) 'The role of time in economic theory', *Economica* (new series) 1: 77–97.

Rosow, J. (ed.) (1985) *Views from the Top*, London: Facts on File.

Ross, L. and Anderson, C. (1982) 'Belief perseverance in the face of empirical challenges', in D. Kahneman *et al.* (eds) *Judgement Under Uncertainty: Heuristics and Biases*, Cambridge, Cambridge University Press.

Rothschild, M. (1992) *Bionomics: The Inevitability of Capitalism*, London: Futura.

Rowthorn, R. (1980) *Capitalism, Conflict and Inflation*, London: Lawrence & Wishart.

Samuelson, P. (1948) 'International trade and the equalization of factor prices', *Economic Journal* 58: 163–84.

—— (1958) 'An exact consumption-loan model of interest with or without the social contrivance of money', *Journal of Political Economy* 66: 467–82.

—— (1962) 'Parable and realism in capital theory: the surrogate production function', *Review of Economic Studies* 29: 193–206.

Samuelson, P. and Modigliani, F. (1966) 'The Pasinetti paradox in neoclassical and more general models', *Review of Economic Studies* 33: 269–301.

Samuelson, R. (1998) 'Why we're all married to the market', *Newsweek* 27 April: 33–6.

Sargent, T. and Wallace, N. (1975) 'Rational expectations, the optimal monetary instrument and the optimal money supply rule', *Journal of Political Economy* 83(2): 241–54.

Sau, R. (1982) *Trade, Capital and Underdevelopment: Towards a Marxist Theory*, Calcutta: Oxford University Press.

Savage, L. (1954) *The Foundations of Statistics*, 2nd edn, New York: Dove.

Sawyer, M. (1992) 'On imperfect competition and macroeconomic analysis', in A. del Monte (ed.) (1992).

Scherer, F. (1994) *Competition Policies for an Integrated World Economy*, Washington, DC: Brookings Institution.

Schmookler, J. (1966) *Invention and Economic Growth*, Cambridge, MA: Harvard University Press.

Schott, K. (1982) *Policy, Power and Order*, New Haven, CT: Yale University Press.

Schotter, A. (1986) 'The evolution of rules', in R. Langlois (ed.) (1986).

Schumacher, E. (1973) *Small is Beautiful*, London: Blond & Briggs.

Schumpeter, J. (1942) *Capitalism, Socialism and Democracy*, Cambridge, MA: Harvard University Press.

Schwartz, M. and Thompson, E. (1986) 'Divisionalisation and entry deference', *Quarterly Journal of Economics* 101: 307–21.

Scott, B. (1984) 'National strategy for stronger US competitiveness', *Harvard Business Review* March/April: 77–91.

Seldon, A. (1990) *Capitalism*, Oxford: Blackwell.

Semler, R. (1992) *Maverick*, London: Century.

Sen, A. (1982) *Choice, Welfare and Measurement*, Oxford: Blackwell.

Shackle, G. (1969) *Decision, Order and Time*, Cambridge: Cambridge University Press.

—— (1972) *Epistemics and Economics*, Cambridge: Cambridge University Press.

Shapley, L. and Shubik, M. (1977) 'Trade using one commodity as a means of payment', *Journal of Political Economy* 85(5): 937–68.

Sheard, P. (ed.) (1992a) *International Adjustment and the Japanese Firm*, St Leonards: Allen & Unwin.

—— (1992b) 'Introduction', in P. Sheard (ed.) (1992a).

Simon, H. (1992) 'Lessons from Germany's midsize giants', *Harvard Business Review* March/April: 115–23.

Simon, H. A. (1947) *Administrative Behaviour*, New York: Wiley.

—— (1955) A behavioral model of rational choice', *Quarterly Journal of Economics* 69: 99–119.

—— (1978) 'Rationality as process and as product of thought', *American Economic Review*, Papers and Proceedings, 68: 1–16.

Singer, H. (1989) 'Terms of trade and economic development', in J. Eatwell *et al.* (eds) (1989b).

Singh, A. (1971) *Takeovers*, Cambridge: Cambridge University Press.

Skinner, B. (1972) *Beyond Freedom and Dignity*, London: Jonathan Cape.

Smith, A. (1776/1979) *The Wealth of Nations*, Books I–III, Harmondsworth: Penguin.

Sodersten, B. (1980) *International Economics*, 2nd edn, London: Macmillan.

Solow, R. (1956) 'A contribution to the theory of economic growth', *Quarterly Journal of Economics* 70(1): 65–94.

—— (1957) 'Technical change and the aggregate production function', *Review of Economics and Statistics*, 39(3): 312–20.

Soros, G. (1997) 'The capitalist threat', *Atlantic Monthly* February.

de Soto, H. (1989) *The Other Path*, London: I.B. Tauris.

Spiecker, F. and Zweiner, R. (1998) 'Are funded pensions better than a pay-as-you-go system? A critical view on Kazakstan's pension reform', *Kazakstan Economic Trends* February: 30–52.

Sraffa, P. (1960) *Production of Commodities by Means of Commodities*, Cambridge: Cambridge University Press.

Steinbeck, J. (1939/1951) *The Grapes of Wrath*, Harmondsworth: Penguin.

Stewart, T. (1997) *Intellectual Capital*, New York: Doubleday.

Strange, S. (1998) 'Who are EU? Ambiguities in the concept of competitiveness', *Journal of Common Market Studies* 36(1): 101–14.

Swan, T. (1956) 'Economic growth and capital accumulation', *Economic Record* 32(63): 334–61.

Tawney, R. (1938) *Religion and the Rise of Capitalism*, Harmondsworth: Penguin.

Taylor, G. (1974) *Rethink*, Harmondsworth: Penguin.

Taylor, M. (1976) *Anarchy and Cooperation*, London: Wiley.

—— (1987) *The Possibility of Cooperation*, Cambridge: Cambridge University Press.

Tellis, G. and Golder, P. (1996) 'First to market, first to fail? Real cases of enduring market leadership', *Sloan Management Review* 37(2).

Thurow, L. (1980) *The Zero Sum Society*, New York: Basic Books.

Tsuru, S. (1993) *Japan's Capitalism: Creative Defeat and Beyond*, Cambridge: Cambridge University Press.

Tversky, A. and Kahneman, D. (1974) 'Judgement under uncertainty: heuristics and biases', *Science* 185: 1124–31.

—— (1983) Extensional versus intuitive reasoning: the conjunction fallacy in probability judgment, *Psychological Review* 90: 293–315.

Venables, A. (1985) 'Trade and trade policy with imperfect competition', *Journal of International Economics* 19: 1–19.

Vernon, R. (1966) 'International investment and international trade in the product cycle', *Quarterly Journal of Economics* 80(2): 190–207.

Vickers, J. (1985) 'Delegation and the theory of the firm', *Economic Journal* 95 (supp.): 138–47.

Vickers, J. and Yarrow, G. (1988) *Privatisation: An Economic Analysis*, Cambridge, MA: MIT Press.

Waddington, C. (1948) *The Scientific Attitude*, Harmondsworth: Penguin.

Wade, R. and Veneroso, F. (1998) 'The Asian Crisis: the high debt model versus the Wall Street–Treasury–IMF complex', *New Left Review* 228: 3–23.

Wald, A. (1936/1951) 'On some systems of equations of mathematical economics', trans. O. Eckstein, *Econometrica* 19(4) (1951): 368–403.

Walras, L. (1874/1954) *Elements of Pure Economics*, Homewood, IL: Irwin.

Walsh, K. (1995) *Public Services and Market Mechanisms*, London: Macmillan.

Weick, K. (1975) 'Educational organisations as loosely coupled systems', *Administrative Science Quarterly* 21: 1–19.

Weiss, A. and Stiglitz, J. (1981) 'Credit rationing in markets with imperfect information', *American Economic Review* 71: 393–410.

Whitley R. (ed.) (1992a) *European Business Systems*, London: Sage.

—— (1992b) 'Societies, firms and markets: the social structuring of business systems', in R. Whitley (ed.) (1992a).

Wilde, O. (1892) *Lady Windermere's Fan*, reprinted in T. Gaynor (ed.) (1997) *The Works of Oscar Wilde*, London: Senate.

Williamson, O. (1975) *Markets and Hierarchies: Evidence and Antitrust Implications*, New York: Free Press.

—— (1981) 'The modern corporation: origins, evolution, attributes', *Journal of Economic Literature* 19: 1537–68.

Wolf, C. (1988) *Markets or Governments*, Cambridge, MA: MIT Press.

Womack, J., Jones, D. and Roos, D. (1990) *The Machine that Changed the World*, New York: Rawson Associates.

Woods, D. (1997) *The Future of Managed Care and its International Implications*, Research Report N147, London: Economist Intelligence Unit.

World Bank (1993) 'The making of the East Asian miracle', *World Bank Research Bulletin* 4(4), August–October.

—— (1994) *The East Asian Miracle: Economic Growth and Public Policy*, Washington, DC: International Bank for Reconstruction and Development.

Yoffie, D. (1993) 'Introduction: from comparative advantage to regulated competition', in D. Yoffie (ed.) *Beyond Free Trade*, Boston, MA: Harvard Business School Press.

Young, A. (1995) 'The tyranny of numbers: confronting the statistical realities of the East Asian growth experience', *Quarterly Journal of Economics* 110(3): 641–80.

Young, M. (1958) *The Rise of the Meritocracy*, Harmondsworth: Penguin.

Index